FIFTH EDITION

BEHAVIOR MODIFICATION IN APPLIED SETTINGS

FIFTH EDITION

BEHAVIOR MODIFICATION IN APPLIED SETTINGS

ALAN E. KAZDIN
YALE UNIVERSITY

BROOKS/COLE PUBLISHING COMPANY
PACIFIC GROVE, CALIFORNIA

I(T)P ™ The trademark ITP is used under license.

A CLAIREMONT BOOK

Brooks/Cole Publishing Company
A Division of Wadsworth, Inc.

Printed in the United States of America

10   9   8   7   6   5   4   3

Library of Congress Cataloging-in-Publication Data
Kazdin, Alan E.
    Behavior modification in applied settings / Alan E. Kazdin. — 5th
ed.
        p.   cm.
    Includes bibliographical references and index.
    ISBN 0-534-21786-9
    1. Behavior modification.   2. Psychology, Applied.   I. Title.
BF637.B4K4   1993
153.8′5—dc20   93-27397
                                                 CIP

Sponsoring Editor: *Claire Verduin*
Editorial Associate: *Gay C. Bond*
Production Editor: *Nancy L. Shammas*
Manuscript Editor: *Betty Seaver*
Permissions Editor: *May Clark*
Interior Design: *Vernon T. Boes*
Cover Art: *Laura Militzer Bryant*
Cover Design: *Laurie Albrecht*
Art Coordinator: *Lisa Torri*
Interior Illustration: *Gloria Langer*
Typesetting: *TCSystems, Inc.*
Cover Printing: *Phoenix Color Corporation*
Printing and Binding: *The Maple Press, Inc.*

Credits continue on page 505.

To Leon and Harry
and their enduring presence

Contents

CHAPTER FOUR
How to Evaluate
a Behavior Modification Program   97

CHAPTER FIVE
Positive and Negative Reinforcement   129

CHAPTER SIX
Punishment   172

CHAPTER SEVEN
Extinction   211

PREFACE

The purpose of this book is to provide an introduction to behavior modification techniques in applied settings. The major focus is on the application of operant conditioning principles, implementation of behavior modification techniques, and assessment and evaluation of program effectiveness. The applications include a variety of settings, such as hospitals, institutions, schools, the home, day-care centers, businesses and industry, and communities, as well as outpatient applications for clients who come for treatment. By emphasizing the application of operant procedures, details are provided that would ordinarily be sacrificed in a cursory review of the entire domain of behavior modification. Yet, the focus is one of emphasis rather than one of exclusion. Because of their increased use in applied settings, procedures that rely on other conceptual views, such as social learning theory and cognitively based interpretations of behavior, are also discussed.

An enormous number of books on behavior modification have appeared. These books include introductory manuals designed for specific audiences, such as parents, teachers, or mental health workers, and scholarly texts that present theoretical issues and review the field generally. There is an obvious hiatus between "how-to-do-it" manuals and extensive scholarly reviews that de-emphasize applied research in behavior modification. Behavioral techniques in clinical and applied settings have been well studied, and recommendations for treatment can often be derived from research findings. A need exists for a text that integrates research and practice for audiences of diverse disciplines who wish to learn about behavior modification. In this book, I attempt to emphasize applied research and clinical intervention techniques to achieve a balance not usually found in other texts.

Like the previous editions, the fifth edition discusses and illustrates major techniques for altering behavior and the conditions that influence their effectiveness. This edition reflects several developments within the field. First, and perhaps foremost, there has been increased interest in behavioral research on the factors that maintain behavior, and on documenting the role of these factors, and using the information to develop effective treatments. The analysis of the functions that behavior serves and the conversion of this into treatment techniques have accelerated within the past few years. The process and advances this focus has generated are included in the present edition.

Second, applications of behavioral interventions have continued to extend to many areas of life such as to the prevention, treatment, and management of physical disease such as AIDS, cancer, and diabetes; to the diverse facets of parenting and child rearing over the course of child development; to the treatment and care of elderly persons; to child abuse and neglect; to personal safety and productivity in business and industry; and to community issues. Several of this vast range of applications are sampled in the book.

Third, many issues *within* the field have received increased attention and are reflected in the book. The use of aversive events, including how, when, and whether to use these events, has been widely discussed and investigated and are elaborated in this revision. Other issues, such as the extent to which behavioral programs can produce long-term changes in behavior, are also discussed. Large-scale applications and programs with long-term changes in behavior are readily available in the field. Several of these, such as extensions to entire school systems and the workplace, are illustrated. Current issues and advances are also discussed not only to continue to chart the progress of the field but also to identify new ways of designing effective programs and evaluating their impact.

Apart from reflecting new developments of the field and expanded areas of application, this edition provides updated information regarding the techniques and their effects and limitations. This revision has encompassed many different substantive areas. For example, progress has been made in identifying techniques to promote maintenance of behavior change and transfer of change to new settings once behavioral programs have been terminated; in developing self-control and cognitively based techniques for use in applied settings; and in extending interventions to many areas of everyday life. This edition not only provides contemporary examples but presents new techniques, procedural variations, and research findings as well. Advances with many reinforcement and punishment techniques reflect creative practices that were not available, widely used, or carefully evaluated only a few years ago.

The overall organization of the book is similar to that of the previous editions. Chapters 1 and 2 place the behavioral approach, broadly conceived, in historical context and detail assumptions, characteristics, and principles that underlie applications of behavioral techniques. One of the most distinct characteristics of behavior modification is the careful assessment of behavior and evaluation of treatment techniques. The methods of assessment and evaluation are discussed (Chapters 3 and 4) because of their importance for designing effective interventions. A major part of the text elaborates positive and negative reinforcement, punishment, and extinction (Chapters 5, 6, and 7). Different technique options, factors that dictate program effectiveness, issues, and limitations, are discussed in each chapter. Special technique variations to enhance program effectiveness, self-control techniques, and cognitively based techniques are detailed in separate chapters (8, 9, and 10). Chapter 11 covers response maintenance and transfer of training, areas where considerable progress has been made. Chapter 12 focuses on current applications of behavioral techniques and expands upon the range of foci highlighted in previous chapters. Behavioral techniques are illustrated in several areas, including the prevention and treatment of medical and psychological dysfunctions, development of personal safety at home and in business and industry, aiding parents and children in many of the challenges that emerge over the course of development, and fostering behaviors of widespread social concern, such as energy conservation, traffic safety, obtaining employment, and many others. Complex multifaceted behavioral programs, large-scale applications, and evaluation of long-term effects of interventions are discussed as well. The final chapter (13) examines key characteristics that account for the widespread applicability and effectiveness of behavioral techniques. The chapter also evaluates the social, ethical, and legal issues raised by applying intervention techniques, limitations of the behavioral approach, and future directions.

Several teaching aids have been included with the text. Outlines at the beginning of each chapter convey the content, direction, and key points that are to be covered. Suggested readings are provided at the end of each chapter to foster further discussion of conceptual, procedural, and practical issues for the development of behavioral programs. As in previous editions, a glossary is included at the end of the book to help review concepts introduced in the text.

Many people have contributed significantly to completion of the book. In particular, I am grateful to Professors E. Scott Geller, Robert H. Horner, and Nirbhay R. Singh, who shared their reflections on important advances in the field and provided suggestions that guided the revision. Other reviewers I would like to acknowledge and thank include Emmanuel Enekwechi, University of Iowa; Michael Wolf, Southwestern Oklahoma State University; and Sherman Yen, Essex Community College. Special appreciation is extended to both my daughters, Nicole and Michelle; they have enhanced my comprehension of behavior change techniques, how the techniques work, and their beneficial and adverse side effects by unwittingly (but effectively) applying the techniques to their parents on a daily basis. In particular, over many years now they have greatly helped me realize how much of human behavior I cherish but do not understand. Michelle Kazdin, also, was very helpful in checking my work in several ways during preparation of the manuscript and this improved both the process and outcome of the product. I am quite grateful for the support of a Research Scientist Award (MH00353) and a grant (MH35408) from the National Institute of Mental Health during the period in which this book was written.

ALAN E. KAZDIN

Fifth Edition

Behavior Modification in Applied Settings

Introduction

Behavior modification is an approach to the assessment, evaluation, and alteration of behavior. The approach focuses on the development of adaptive, prosocial behavior and the reduction of maladaptive behavior in everyday life. Although many people associate behavior modification with a specific form of treatment, in fact the approach embraces a large number of quite different intervention techniques. Many of the techniques are applied to *treat* various clinical problems such as anxiety, depression, aggression, substance abuse, child and spouse abuse, sexual deviance and dysfunction, pain, and hypertension. Interventions also are applied to *prevent* a variety of medical and behavioral problems, such as injury from unsafe practices at home or at work, birth complications, aggression among children and adolescents, and untoward reactions to stressful events. In general, behavior modification is more than a set of interventions to treat or to prevent problems. As we shall see in subsequent chapters, behavior modification is often used to improve a variety of behaviors in everyday life. Developing healthy lifestyles (such as eating a well-balanced diet, exercising), altering child behavior in nonpunitive ways, and interacting more positively with one's spouse and children are examples of such applications.

The techniques of behavior modification have been applied to a broad range of persons and populations, including children, adolescents, and adults in such everyday settings as the home, school, and workplace as well as special populations such as psychiatric patients, prisoners, nursing home residents, and autistic children. Behavior modification includes many different theories about how clinical problems emerge and are maintained. These theories vary in their explanation of behavior and in the role they accord to the influence of processes within the individual (for example, thoughts, beliefs, and perceptions) or processes resulting from events in the environment (such as cues, feedback, and consequences that behavior produces). In short, behavior modification encompasses many treatments, clinical problems, populations, and conceptual views.

MAJOR CHARACTERISTICS

Because of the diversity of treatments and applications, a simple definition of behavior modification is difficult to provide. Yet several characteristics distinguish behavior modification as a unique approach to treatment.

Primacy of Behavior

Within behavior modification, overt behavior plays a major part in the assessment and treatment of clinical dysfunction. Whenever possible, clinical problems are operationalized in terms of overt behavioral referents. Indeed, symptoms or groups of symptoms that go together (syndromes or disorders), such as fear and avoidance, autism, depression, hyperactivity, substance abuse, and sexual deviance, are conceptualized primarily as problems of behavior.

Although emphasis is placed on behavior, or what people do, this does not mean that problems are viewed solely in terms of overt actions. How people feel (affect) and think (cognition) are often central to the specific problems brought to treatment. For example, depressed persons often feel sad (affect), believe they cannot do anything right (cognition), and engage in few activities (behaviors) in their everyday lives. Although affect and cognition are important, behavioral treatments give primary attention to behavior as a means of dealing with the clinical problem. In the treatment process, a depressed patient may be encouraged to engage in specific activities involving interactions with others and in setting goals for accomplishing specific tasks at home or at work. Increases in activity and completion of tasks are behaviors that have been found to alter depressive symptoms, including feelings and thoughts. Consequently, behavior modification often focuses on behavior both as an end in itself and as a means of changing affect and cognition.

Importance of Learning

An assumption of behavior modification is that behaviors of interest in the context of therapeutic, educational, social, and other settings can be altered by providing new learning experiences. Understandably, the approach has drawn heavily on learning theories and research in psychology. Using learning as a point of departure, behavioral treatments essentially provide special learning experiences to alter deviant or clinically maladaptive behavior and to increase adaptive behavior in everyday life.

It is important not to overstate the claim that new learning experiences can change behavior. Proponents of behavior modification do *not* necessarily adhere to the view that all behaviors are learned and can be changed through learning. Diverse biological, behavioral, social, cultural, and other factors influence behavior. The influences that control behavior are not fully understood. Thus, behaviors are often difficult to alter. In any given case, a particular behavior or client may not change at all. The key feature of the behavioral approach is recognition of the plasticity of behavior or the amenability of behavior to change when systematic learning experiences are provided. Whether providing new learning experiences will effectively alter behavior can be determined only by testing what changes occur. The assumption that learning experiences can alter behavior has proven to be extremely helpful in developing effective treatments.

Directive and Active Treatments

Behavior modification techniques usually rely on directive and active treatments. This means that clients who come for treatment are given specific directions for the procedures that they are to perform. This does not mean that clients are simply told what to do. Indeed, in most cases involving children, adolescents, and adults, the client plays an important role in developing the plan of action to change behavior. Behavioral techniques do not rely heavily on the therapeutic relationship or such therapeutic processes as talking about one's problems to relieve emotional distress or to develop insight. To be sure, these processes may have beneficial effects during the course of treatment. However, talking about one's problems is not viewed as the most effective way of producing behavior change. Rather, explicit training experiences are prescribed in treatment.

Actions or activities to help achieve desired changes are often carried out during treatment sessions. Often such actions or activities are also assigned to persons as "homework." Therapeutic change in behavior modification is conceptualized as *learning new behaviors* that are to be performed in everyday life. Specific and direct activities serve as the basis for developing these new behaviors.

Importance of Assessment and Evaluation

A central characteristic of behavior modification is a commitment to the assessment and evaluation of alternative treatments. The effects of treatment are evaluated empirically, by measuring the impact on the client or patient seen in treatment.[1] The evaluation of treatment involves several components.

First, the behaviors to be altered are carefully assessed. The assessment may consist of several ways of measuring the problem or desired behavior, including direct observation of how the person performs at school or at work, evaluations by significant others (parents, spouses, peers), and, of course, evaluations by the clients themselves. The assessment is central to identifying the extent and nature of the problem.

Second, the goals and the means for reaching them are usually well specified. Before treatment, the therapist conducts a careful evaluation to identify what the problem is, how the client and others are affected by it, and the circumstances under which it emerges. Once the problem has been carefully identified and assessed, the procedures and the goals toward which they will be directed can be specified. Explicit formulation of the procedures and goals is an important characteristic of behavior modification.

Third, the effects of treatment are assessed to determine whether the desired outcomes have been obtained. In research, behavior modification places major emphasis on measuring outcome and evaluating treatment in controlled studies to decide whether alternative treatments are effective and which treatments are more effective than others. The emphasis on research to investigate treatment has been a hallmark of the approach. Evaluation is also very important in clinical work with individual clients. In this context, evaluation refers to measuring the specific behaviors of interest and thus to monitoring the progress that the client makes during the course of treatment. Such evaluation may be accomplished by having the patient complete various questionnaires about the severity of specific symptoms or by having the patient keep a record or diary of activities. For example, a patient who abuses alcohol may rate, on a daily or weekly basis, the extent to which drinking or the urge to drink is a problem. Also, a relative (for example, spouse) who lives with the client may keep records of the number of drinks that the client actually consumes.

Ideally, of course, the information (data) obtained during treatment reveals that the client is improving and that treatment is working. However, one of the most useful features of the evaluation is that one can identify when treatment is not working. The therapist can use this information to alter treatment and, if necessary, to try different techniques. In general, evaluation of progress in treatment is facilitated by having clearly specified goals and procedures.

Use of Persons in Everyday Life

Behavioral techniques are often carried out outside the therapist's office. Applications are often conducted at home, at school, in various institutional settings (psychiatric hospitals, prisons), in business and industry, and in the community. Persons responsible for the care, management, and education of the clients, such as parents, teachers, relatives, spouses, roommates, peers, supervisors, and colleagues, are often utilized to help with the behavior change program. These persons are occasionally referred to as *paraprofessionals* because they work along with professionals in achieving therapeutic change.

Paraprofessionals who are in frequent contact with the client can observe the client's behaviors in the actual situations in which they are performed, so they are in the best position to focus on behavior as it is actually occurring. In applications with children, for example, parents, teachers, and peers are often trained in behavior change techniques and can work on changing behaviors of interest (for example, tantrums, oppositional behavior, completion of homework). Paraprofessionals can often identify these behaviors when they occur and can then immediately provide consequences intended to develop more adaptive behaviors.

Case Illustration

The above characteristics of the behavioral approach are quite broad. Breadth and perhaps ambiguity are required to encompass the many techniques that behavior modification embraces and the many behaviors and clinical problems toward which those techniques are directed. An illustration will convey more concretely how some of the behavioral approach characteristics are manifested in actual practice.

Consider the case of Arlene, a 35-year-old woman who suffered from agoraphobia (fear of open spaces). Persons with agoraphobia often remain at home as much as possible. When they leave home, they experience high levels of anxiety, which is reflected in agitation, worry, arousal, sweating, and in general, great discomfort. Anticipation of leaving home and going to public places may increase their anxiety and their belief that they will lose control, faint, and even become insane in the presence of others. It is not clear how agoraphobia develops, though many theories have been advanced. Even though the causes of the problem are not known, effective behavioral treatments have been developed. For the behavior therapist, the task of treatment is to provide new learning experiences that will eliminate anxiety and help the patient function adequately in a variety of everyday situations.

Before treatment began, the therapist interviewed Arlene for approximately two hours to discuss exactly what she considered to be the problem. The therapist asked about the times she felt anxious, about the range of the circumstances in which anxiety emerged, and about how this anxiety interfered with her everyday life. In addition, Arlene completed a questionnaire that asked about a number of problems, including anxiety, depression, sleep disturbance, and uncontrollable thoughts and urges. The purpose of the questionnaire was to assess the full range of problems that she may have experienced. Arlene's problems focused on anxiety when she left her house or thought about doing so. She rigidly structured her daily activities to accommodate her anxiety. For example, to avoid going to a store on her own, she ordered the delivery of groceries or paid a neighbor's teenage boy to pick them up.

After the evaluation, the therapist explained what the treatment was and how it would be used to overcome anxiety. For Arlene, the techniques of graduated exposure and relaxation training were used. She was introduced (exposed) to a variety of situations outside her home. The situations were introduced on a graduated basis. At first, situations were introduced that were not too demanding or threatening while the therapist was present. As Arlene progressed, more difficult situations were introduced and the therapist was absent.

Before Arlene began specific tasks, she was trained to engage in deep muscle relaxation. The purpose was to provide her with a technique for remaining relaxed when she felt that anxiety might develop. Developing the ability to relax deeply usually requires only a few sessions. Relaxation was developed by having Arlene first close her eyes and remain quiet. The therapist then instructed her to focus attention on various groups of muscles (for example, lower arm, upper arm, neck and shoulders). She alternately tensed and relaxed muscle groups encompassing the major skeletal muscles in response to the therapist's instructions. In this way, Arlene learned how to use the release from tensing the muscles as a way of achieving a relaxed state in those muscle groups. As she completed the tensing and relaxing cycle for each of several muscle groups, she became deeply relaxed. After a few sessions, she became relaxed relatively quickly with little or no assistance from the therapist.

After Arlene learned how to relax, treatment continued with a series of behavioral tasks. At first, she was required to take a short walk with the therapist near her home, so that the location would be familiar and probably not very anxiety provoking. If she became anxious, the therapist helped her to relax. The brevity of the walks, the presence of the therapist, and the use of relaxation decreased the likelihood that high levels of anxiety would emerge. Within two sessions, a significant reduction of anxiety was evident on these brief walks.

In further sessions with the therapist, Arlene was exposed to additional situations, including walking to various stores, driving in a car to a restaurant and a shopping mall, riding a bus, and other tasks related to situations that she found anxiety provoking. She was also given "homework" assignments—activities to carry out on her own. The first assignment was to visit a friend who lived a few houses away from her. Arlene and her friend spoke on the phone for extended periods each day. The assignment was to visit the friend and talk to her for at least 30 minutes on at least two separate days during the week. The friend, who was well aware of the problem, was eager to help and did so by having Arlene over for coffee. After three visits, Arlene felt better about leaving her home. She was then assigned to go to a store with her friend and to walk to a mailbox (two blocks away from her home) by herself. After further practice trials with the therapist and further homework assignments, Arlene reported very little anxiety about being out of the house, going out on errands alone, or being in crowds.

Throughout the course of treatment, Arlene kept a daily diary regarding her behavior and anxiety. In it, she recorded each trip she took, how long she was out of the house for the trip, and how much anxiety she felt, as rated on a scale from 1 (perfectly relaxed) to 10 (extremely uncomfortable and anxious). At the beginning of treatment, Arlene made few entries in the diary. At that time, she left home only when absolutely necessary— about twice a week. On these occasions, her trips were brief (usually less than 30 minutes) and were rated with very high levels of anxiety (9 or 10 on the rating scale). After many sessions and after homework assignments had been in effect for some time, she left home 15–20 times per week (going out to visit a neighbor, walking to a store, driving to a shopping mall). Most of the trips lasted well over an hour. Arlene's anxiety decreased, as reflected in ratings of 3 and 4 on the scale. Eventually, her anxiety for all the outings decreased to 2, 3, or 4 and she stated that being out of the house and in public places did not bother her. Over the course of treatment, the information provided by the diary was useful in deciding when to proceed to more difficult tasks and whether the treatment was achieving its goals.

In Arlene's case, treatment progressed relatively quickly. Within 10 weeks, her ratings indicated that she was not bothered at all by being out of the house. She engaged in more social activities, including going out evenings with her friend and a group of new friends. In addition, within four months after treatment ended, she obtained a full-time job in a department store. Thus, by her own report and information about her activities, therapy apparently achieved its goals.

General Comments

Several features of the behavioral approach can be seen in the case of Arlene and her treatment. The focus on behavior, the use of active treatments to reduce anxiety, applications in everyday situations, and involvement of others in treatment are primary examples. Perhaps less dramatically illustrated but even more important was the effort to evaluate Arlene's progress. The central question is whether the treatment is achieving the desired ends. The data gathered about Arlene's progress were obtained to address this question.

Although the general characteristics of behavior modification have been conveyed by key points noted previously and by the case illustration, the story is incomplete. Behavior modification includes different views and techniques of treatment. To convey these different traditions within the field, it is useful to highlight the historical foundations of behavior modification and the emergence of behavior modification as a contemporary approach to treatment.

FOUNDATIONS OF BEHAVIOR MODIFICATION

Many paths led to the emergence of contemporary behavior modification (see Kazdin, 1978). Although these paths cannot be examined in detail here, a few are especially noteworthy.

Experimental Animal Research

Classical Conditioning
Behavior modification can be traced to laboratory research in physiology in the 1800s and 1900s. Among the many influences, the work of the Russian physiologist Ivan P. Pavlov (1849–1936) is particularly significant.

Pavlov studied digestion, especially how reflex responses were influenced by substances placed in the digestive system. He stimulated various portions of an animal's digestive system with food or food powder and observed the physiological reactions. As part of his studies, he found that gastric secretions were stimulated when animals—in this case dogs—merely saw the food or heard the preparation of the food. This was significant because it suggested that digestive processes could be stimulated even without direct physical stimulation. Pavlov thought that this resulted from the animal's experience in the laboratory (that is, learning). He shifted his research to study how connections were made between various environmental stimuli (sights and sounds) and reflex reactions such as salivation in response to food.

The type of learning that Pavlov studied has been referred to as *classical* or *respondent conditioning.* Classical conditioning is concerned with stimuli that evoke responses. Certain stimuli in one's environment (such as noise, shock, light, and the taste of food) *elicit* reflex responses. These responses are referred to as *respondents* or unconditioned responses. Respondents are frequently viewed as involuntary or automatic responses that are not under control of the individual. Examples of respondents include a startle reaction in response to loud noise, salivation in response to the presence of food in one's mouth, pupil constriction in response to bright light, or flexion of a muscle in response to pain. The connection between the unconditioned stimulus and the response is automatic (that is, not learned). However, reflex behavior sometimes occurs in response to a stimulus that does not automatically elicit the response.

Through classical conditioning, a neutral stimulus (that is, a stimulus that does not elicit a particular reflex) can be made to elicit a reflex response. In a simple arrangement to achieve this, the neutral stimulus (referred to as a conditioned stimulus) is paired with a stimulus that elicits a reflex response (an unconditioned stimulus). If the conditioned stimulus is consistently paired with an unconditioned stimulus, the conditioned stimulus alone can elicit the response (referred to as a conditioned response). The process whereby new stimuli gain the power to elicit respondent behavior is called classical or respondent conditioning. This is not a mechanical process in which merely pairing stimuli automatically leads to their connection. Learning the relation between stimuli depends on a variety of factors that help or hinder the association and determine whether the neutral stimuli elicit the unconditioned response (see Rescorla, 1988).

Pavlov's work was significant because of both his specific findings and his methods of investigation. His findings suggested one way in which behaviors could be learned. The concepts of conditioning from his laboratory work were extended to explain virtually all learning, including such broad areas as the learning of language, the acquisition of knowledge, and the development of deviant and maladaptive behavior (for example, alcoholism). It is clear today that the concepts were overextended because they did not give accurate or complete accounts of these areas. Also, more recent research has shown that conditioning itself is more complex than originally thought (for example, certain kinds of connections are more easily learned than others, and pairing stimuli does not automatically lead to learning). Pavlov's significant contribution was his scientifically and learning-based explanation of behavior. His clear demonstration of the process of learning under well-controlled conditions helped foster more elaborate studies of different kinds of learning.

Another significant feature of Pavlov's work was the method of his experiments. Pavlov used precise methods that permitted careful observation and quantification of what he was studying. For example, in some of his studies, drops of saliva were counted to measure the conditioned reflex. His meticulous laboratory notes and his rigorous methods helped greatly to advance a scientific approach toward the study of behavior. Because his methods were described so clearly, they could be used by others. Also, the *zeitgeist* fostered application of the scientific approach to diverse areas of inquiry. Pavlov seemed to exemplify scientific values and hence served as a model to others. His receipt of the Nobel Prize (1904) in physiology for his research on digestion increased the visibility of his work and adoption of his methods.

Operant Conditioning

While Pavlov was conducting his experiments, a type of learning that did not involve reflex responses was under investigation. Investigators were evaluating the impact of different consequences on the development of new behaviors (see Kazdin, 1978). Along these lines, the work of Edward L. Thorndike (1874–1949) is noteworthy. Thorndike was concerned with the learning of new behaviors, rather than with establishing new connections of reflex behavior. Among his many animal experiments, the most well known are his puzzle-box experiments with cats.

Thorndike placed a hungry cat in a box and recorded how long it took the cat to escape by moving a barrier. A small piece of food placed outside the box provided the cat with an incentive for learning to escape. The cat immediately attempted to escape by exploring diverse solutions in a trial-and-error fashion. Eventually, the cat removed the barrier and consumed the food. The cat was then placed in the box again. With repeated trials, Thorndike found that it took less and less time for the cat to escape. Eventually, as soon as the cat was placed in the box, it removed the barrier, escaped, and ate the food. Thorndike plotted the time it took the cat to escape over repeated trials and reported a learning curve. This curve reflected the fact that the animal took less and less time to perform the behavior.

From many similar experiments and observations, Thorndike formulated laws or principles of behavior. The most significant of these was the Law of Effect, which states that consequences that follow behavior help learning. The rewards (for example, food for the cat after escape) provided consequences that increased learning of the behavior. Thorndike's emphasis on the consequences of behavior was a significant preview of subsequent developments in laboratory and applied research.

B. F. Skinner (1904–1990) was influenced by Pavlov and Thorndike and also conducted a number of animal laboratory studies. Like Thorndike, Skinner explored the impact of various consequences on behavior. He helped clarify learning that resulted from consequences and its differences from the respondent conditioning studied by Pavlov. He noted that many behaviors are *emitted* spontaneously and are controlled primarily by their consequences. He referred to such behaviors as *operants* because they were responses that operated (had some influence) on the environment. Operant behaviors are strengthened (increased) or weakened (decreased) as a function of the events that follow them. Most of the behaviors performed in everyday life are operants. They are not reflex responses (respondents) controlled by eliciting stimuli. Operant behaviors include reading, walking, working, talking, nodding one's head, smiling, and other freely emitted responses. Operants are distinguished by virtue of being controlled (influenced) by their consequences. The process of learning operant behaviors is referred to as *operant conditioning.*

Several types of consequences and principles were developed to explain how operant behaviors could be developed and altered. The major relations that were investigated can be seen in Table 1–1, which summarizes the basic principles of operant conditioning. These principles provide general statements about the relations between behaviors and environmental events. Investigations of these principles began with laboratory animals (for example, rats, and pigeons) engaging in simple responses (for

TABLE 1–1
Summary of Basic Principles of Operant Conditioning

Principle	Characteristic procedure and its effect on behavior
Reinforcement	Presentation or removal of an event after a response that increases the frequency of the response.
Punishment	Presentation or removal of an event after a response that decreases the frequency of the response.
Extinction	No longer presenting a reinforcing event after a response that decreases the frequency of the previously reinforced response.
Stimulus control and discrimination training	Reinforcing the response in the presence of one stimulus but not in the presence of another. This procedure increases the frequency of the response in the presence of the former stimulus and decreases the frequency of the response in the presence of the latter stimulus.

example, pressing a lever) under highly controlled conditions. Current applications of the general principles bear very little resemblance to these experimental beginnings.

As with Pavlov's work, the significance of Skinner's work stemmed from the approach toward the study of behavior. Skinner's method included a focus on overt behavior, assessment of the frequency of behavior over extended periods, and the study of one or a few organisms at a time. His goal was to identify the variables that influenced behavior by careful and intensive study of one or two subjects. Because of their contemporary influence on behavior modification, we shall return to the principles of operant conditioning and the method of study developed by Skinner.

Development of Behaviorism

The late 1800s and early 1900s reflected a broader orientation of which significant contributors such as Pavlov and Thorndike, and later Skinner, were a part. Increased interest in the scientific method was evident in diverse areas of work that extended beyond a single discipline such as psychology. Sciences in general were emerging with an empirical and experimental focus. The broader context can be seen by noting the work of Charles Darwin (1809–1882), the English naturalist, whose contribution to the understanding of evolution is well known. Darwin's writings on evolution, such as *Origin of Species by Means of Natural Selection* (1859) and *The Descent of Man* (1871) suggested there was a continuity of species and that humans and infrahumans were part of an ongoing process and subject to similar influences and principles such as natural selection and survival of the fittest. The impact of Darwin's writings was enormous. One aspect of this influence germane to the present discussion is the relevance of research on infrahuman species. Given the continuity of species, the study of animal behavior assumed increased importance. Obviously, studying infrahuman species could not tell us all there is to know about humans. Yet, processes such as learning and principles identified in the laboratory and naturalistic research with infrahumans, apart from interest in their own right, might also shed light on human functioning and adaptation as well. Research on animal learning became an important line of work that greatly influenced the emergence of behavior modification. Again, animal research was part of a larger context of a more scientific approach to the study of behavior. This was a movement that was evident in Pavlov's work, as an example, but extended beyond a single investigator or country.

Psychological research was greatly influenced not only by the specific contributions of Pavlov and his contemporaries but also by the larger movement toward more objective methods of studying behavior. In the United States, for example, John B. Watson (1878–1958) crystallized a movement in psychology that is referred to as behaviorism. Watson was interested in animal psychology and in applying methods from animal research to the study of human behavior. He criticized psychology because of its use of subjective methods such as introspection (for example, asking people to report on their private experience) to study mental phenomena (such as thoughts and feelings). This method of study, Watson contended, was neither objective nor scientific.

There were several converging influences leading to the more scientific study of behavior. Indeed, Vladimir Bechterev (1857–1927), a contemporary of Pavlov, was also conducting animal research on conditioning. In the early 1900s, Bechterev had written about the scientific study of human behavior, a field called objective psychology and later reflexology (Kazdin, 1978). The approach greatly influenced Watson, who brought together the concepts and methods of conditioning research developed in Russia. Watson argued for a new "behaviorist" approach in psychology. His position, as reflected, for example, in *Psychology from the Standpoint of a Behaviorist* (1919), greatly influenced the shape of psychology. He accorded learning a critical role in many areas. In fact, he suggested that learning could entirely shape human behavior. In addition, he used conditioning as the basis for explaining virtually all behavior that was acquired as part of development. Watson's purpose was to win support for the view that the concepts of conditioning and scientific methods could be applied to the study of behavior. Many of his specific statements about human behavior and its development were extreme and went well beyond what was known at the time. Behavior modification had not yet emerged formally. Watson's major contribution was that of moving psychology toward the scientific study of behavior.

EMERGENCE OF BEHAVIOR MODIFICATION

The emergence of behavior modification as an approach to treatment and clinical work can be considered from at least two interrelated perspectives. One of these perspectives concerns the extension of the concepts of conditioning and scientific methods to clinical work. The second perspective concerns the prevalent theoretical orientation toward abnormal behavior and its treatment at the time that behavior modification was developing. Considerable dissatisfaction with the prevalent approaches to clinical problems and with alternative psychotherapy techniques helped spawn behavior modification.

Clinical Extensions

Respondent and operant conditioning were used increasingly as a basis for conceptualizing personality, psychotherapy, and behavior change. Also, concepts of respondent and operant conditioning were used to develop new techniques for treating adults and children for a host of psychological and behavioral problems. A few illustrations will convey important steps that led to contemporary work.

Respondent Conditioning

A historically significant attempt to show the importance of respondent conditioning was provided by Watson and Rayner (1920), who conditioned a fear reaction in an 11-month-old boy named Albert. Prior to the study, the investigators noted that a loud noise (unconditioned stimulus) produced a startle and fear reaction (unconditioned response) in Albert. In contrast, Albert freely played with a white rat without any adverse reaction. The investigators wished to determine whether the startle reaction could be conditioned to the presence of the white rat. To condition the startle reaction, the presence of the white rat (neutral or conditioned stimulus) was immediately followed by the noise. Whenever Albert reached out and touched the rat, the noise sounded and Albert was startled. Over a period of one week, the presence of the rat and the noise were paired only seven times. Finally, when the rat was presented without the noise, Albert fell over and cried. The conditioned stimulus elicited the fear response (conditioned response). Moreover, the fear generalized to other objects that Albert had not been afraid of previously (for example, a rabbit, a dog, a Santa Claus mask, a sealskin coat, and cotton wool). This suggested that fears could be acquired through respondent conditioning.[2] Of course, it is difficult to say whether fears evident in everyday experience are in fact acquired through respondent conditioning because one rarely has access to an individual at the time that fears develop. Other evidence suggests that fears may be acquired for objects with which the individual has had no direct personal contact (Marks, 1987). Independent of how fears are actually learned, respondent conditioning may be useful in ameliorating fears because the power of conditioned stimuli to elicit fear reactions can be altered.

Another early extension of respondent conditioning was in the treatment of enuresis (bed-wetting). Enuresis can be conceptualized as a failure of certain stimuli (bladder cues) to elicit a response (waking) so that the individual can get up and urinate appropriately. To condition waking to the bladder cues (distension), a stimulus that elicits waking is required. O. H. Mowrer and W. M. Mowrer (1938) devised an apparatus to classically condition waking to the cues that precede urination while the child is asleep. The apparatus includes a liquid-sensitive pad that is placed in the child's bed. As soon as the child urinates, a circuit is closed and an alarm is activated. The alarm serves as an unconditioned stimulus that eventually elicits waking prior to urination and the sounding of the alarm. The procedure results in control of urination and permits the individual to sleep through the night without urination. This procedure, an effective technique for dealing with enuresis, was actually available prior to the 1930s. Historically, its reemergence was significant because the procedure was couched in terms of respondent conditioning.

A more contemporary extension of respondent conditioning to clinical work was made by Joseph Wolpe (1958), who developed a procedure for the treatment of anxiety. Wolpe, a physician working in South Africa, conducted experiments investigating anxiety and avoidance reactions in laboratory animals (cats). He investigated a phenomenon referred to as experimental neurosis—an experimentally induced state in which animals show agitation, disruption of behavior, and other signs that resemble anxiety in humans. Experimental neuroses had been studied for some time, beginning in Pavlov's laboratory. Wolpe's special contribution was to develop a procedure for overcoming anxiety in the cats he studied and then to extend the method to the treatment of humans with anxiety disorders.

After anxiety had been developed, Wolpe gradually exposed the cats to situations that elicited anxiety. When the cats were exposed to the situation (room) in which anxiety had been developed, they showed severe signs of anxiety and would not engage in any other behaviors. Wolpe then exposed the cats to cues (other rooms) that only resembled the original situation. With less avoidance and agitation due to a reduced dose of anxiety-provoking stimuli, he encouraged them to engage in other responses such as eating. He reasoned that exposure to a series of anxiety-provoking situations while engaging in competing responses would gradually overcome the anxiety. Continuation of this procedure eventually eliminated the anxiety of the cats.

An especially significant step was Wolpe's use of the information he derived from experiments with cats to develop a technique for treating human anxiety. Wolpe developed *systematic desensitization,* a treatment in which humans were exposed in real life or in imagination to situations that provoked anxiety. They were exposed in a graduated series of stimuli. To overcome anxiety, Wolpe trained clients to become deeply relaxed so that exposure to mild representations of the anxiety-provoking situation would cause very little anxiety. Over time, the clients were exposed to or imagined situations that provoked greater anxiety and relaxation would overcome that anxiety. Eventually, the clients responded without anxiety to the situations that originally provoked anxiety.

The procedure was conceptualized from the standpoint of classical conditioning. Certain cues or stimuli in the environment elicit anxiety or fear. The fear can be altered by conditioning an alternative response (relaxation) that is incompatible with fear. As relaxation becomes associated with the imagined scenes, the capacity of the stimuli to elicit fear is eliminated. Altering the valence of the capacity of stimuli to elicit reactions adheres closely to the respondent conditioning paradigm.

Wolpe (1958) reported the use of this technique in various forms with more than 200 patients. He claimed the treatment had been effective. Case studies are not acceptable scientifically because the basis for the change cannot be determined. Yet Wolpe's technique and claims eventually stimulated a great deal of research on the effects of systematic desensitization. From a broader perspective, Wolpe's work was quickly assimilated because of other influences, such as his reliance on animal laboratory methods, his use of learning concepts, and his concerns over objective bases of developing treatments.

The above illustrations are among the well-known extensions of respondent conditioning to clinical problems. Many other behavioral techniques derived from classical conditioning have been used to alter a variety of behaviors, including excessive eating, the drinking of alcohol, cigarette smoking, and deviant sexual behavior (Kazdin, 1978; O'Leary & Wilson, 1987). Such procedures alter the valence of events by pairing them with real or imagined stimuli.

Operant Conditioning

The control that rewarding consequences exerted over behavior was not a new insight identified by laboratory research on operant conditioning. However, laboratory research on the lawful effects of rewarding consequences on behavior was eventually extended from infrahuman species to humans (Lindsley, 1956, 1960). Some of the early laboratory work seemed to have clinical relevance. For example, laboratory studies were conducted with hospitalized psychotic patients who performed on various apparatus daily to earn small rewards (for example, money, pictures). The purpose was to examine response patterns under various arrangements of rewarding consequences. The results showed that the response patterns of psychiatric patients differed from the patterns that had been evident in "normal" adults. Also, performance on the laboratory apparatus was often interrupted by pauses in which psychotic symptoms (such as vocal hallucinatory behaviors) could be observed. These observations suggested that the operant conditioning paradigm might be an objective way to study psychotic behavior. Perhaps of even greater significance was the finding that responding to laboratory tasks appeared to result in a reduction of symptoms (for example, staring into space) both in the laboratory and on the hospital ward (King, Armitage, & Tilton, 1960; Lindsley, 1960). This clearly suggested that symptoms might be altered in important ways by increases in operant responding.

Laboratory extensions of operant conditioning were made to study the behavior of many populations, such as mentally retarded children and autistic children. In most of the studies, the goals were merely to use operant conditioning laboratory methods to investigate how special populations responded. Operant conditioning methods were soon extended to human behavior outside the laboratory. Quite simple demonstrations suggested that important behaviors might be greatly influenced by environmental consequences.

Several demonstrations were completed in the 1960s to examine the extent to which consequence could influence the behavior of hospitalized psychiatric patients. One of these demonstrations involved a depressed patient who complained of sleeping difficulties and reported pains in her back, chest, head, and shoulders (Ayllon & Haughton, 1964). Medical evaluation revealed no physical problems to account for these difficulties. It appeared that these bodily (somatic) complaints might be influenced by their consequences, namely the reactions of staff to her complaints. Observations were made to record the daily frequency of the patient's complaints for several days. After these observations (referred to as *baseline*), staff

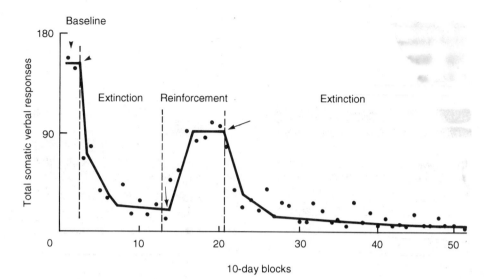

FIGURE   1–1

Frequency of complaints during the baseline, extinction, reinforcement, and extinction phases. During baseline, staff behaved as usual. During the reinforcement phase, they provided attention when the patient complained. During the extinction phases, staff ignored the patient's complaints.

SOURCE: Ayllon & Haughton, 1964.

were told to change the way they reacted to the patient. Specifically, staff were instructed to ignore complaints rather than to provide the usual consolation, sympathy, and attention that they had given. Perhaps attention had served as a reward (reinforcer) for the behavior, leading to its high levels; if so, cessation of the attention would reduce the behavior. Observations of complaints continued. After several days, staff were told to revert to their previous ways of responding to the patient's complaints. If staff attention was really influencing the complaints, one would expect the complaints to increase again. After several days of this, staff were finally told to withdraw their attention.

The effects of altering consequences for somatic complaints can be seen in Figure 1–1. The frequency of complaints is evident during baseline (staff behaving as usual), extinction (staff ignoring complaints), reinforcement (staff attention for complaints), and extinction (ignoring as before). The frequency of complaints changed dramatically as staff behavior changed. These results suggested that attention and consequences from others can greatly influence patient behavior.

These demonstrations and many others like them indicated that human behavior in applied settings could be altered by changing the consequences. The idea of using consequences to change behavior was not new: numerous examples of rewarding and punishing consequences for behavior could be found throughout civilization. What was new was the application of such consequences under a variety of special conditions and with careful assessment of behavior. The early extensions of operant conditioning principles to human behavior merely began an area of research. The present book illustrates the breadth and range of applications resulting from the extension of operant conditioning principles and approaches.

In passing, a unique extension of operant conditioning is worth noting. Skinner's work (1938) was primarily restricted to animal laboratory demonstrations, the significance of which was acknowledged. Soon after that work was well under way and had made important progress, he began extending the principles of operant conditioning well beyond the laboratory. Skinner (1953) made major conceptual leaps by discussing the relevance of operant conditioning to everyday life, including education, government, business, religion, psychotherapy, and social interaction in general. He wrote a well-known novel about a utopian society (*Walden Two*) in which the principles of operant conditioning served as the basis for structuring the community (Skinner, 1948). These extrapolations went way beyond what was known from laboratory research. It was not really clear that operant conditioning principles could be readily applied to complex human behavior and could alter socially significant behaviors. However, these extrapolations drew attention to Skinner's findings and methods and posed important challenges to those interested in applying operant conditioning principles to clinical ends.

Traditional Approaches Toward Maladaptive Behavior

The development of laboratory research and the scientific study of behavior were significant ingredients underlying the development of behavior modification. No less significant was the emerging dissatisfaction with traditional approaches to clinical problems. Behavior modification represents a significant departure from traditional conceptualizations of personality and behavior that dominated mental health—related fields, such as clinical psychology, psychiatry, social work, counseling, education, and rehabilitation.

Intrapsychic Approaches

Traditionally, personality had been viewed by many theorists as an assortment of psychological forces inside the individual. Although these forces vary depending on specific theories of personality, they generally consist of such psychological factors as drives, impulses, needs, motives, conflicts, and traits. The traditional approach to understanding behavior, both abnormal and normal, can be referred to as *intrapsychic* because psychological forces within the individual are accorded the crucial role. "Normal" behavior generally represents a socially acceptable expression of intrapsychic forces. On the other hand, "abnormal" behavior reflects disordered personality development or psychological processes.

Many intrapsychic theories have been proposed to account for personality. Certainly, the most influential intrapsychic theory of personality is psychoanalysis, proposed by Sigmund Freud (1856–1939). Freud explained virtually all behaviors by referring to manifestations of unconscious personality processes. In his view, understanding behavior required a careful scrutiny of personality to determine the meaning of behavior—that is, what motives behavior represents. He regarded the psychological processes and motives behind behavior as existing in the individual. The Freudian view is frequently referred to as a *psychodynamic* view. *Dynamic* refers to a branch of mechanics (in physics) in which phenomena are explained by referring to energy forces and their relation to motion and change in physical matter. Freud's dynamic view of personality describes behavior in terms of psychological energies, or motivating forces, drives, and impulses, and their interrelations. It traces growth and psychological development to psychological impulses and their expression at various stages early in the child's development. It holds that diverse behaviors can be traced to the expression of a few psychological forces.

According to the psychoanalytic view, normal behavior develops from the expression of impulses, wishes, and desires in socially appropriate ways and abnormal behavior develops from the disruption of the normal unfolding, expression, and gratification of drives and needs. Psychological drives can become blocked or can fail to find expression in socially appropriate ways. Drives and unresolved conflicts may, however, find expression in psychological symptoms or aberrant behaviors.

Psychoanalytic theory provided several important contributions to the understanding of behavior. First, it advanced the notion that behavior is determined. This means that behavior, whether deviant or normal, is not random but can be traced to specific causes. For example, Freud suggested that abnormal behaviors, habits, dreams, slips of the tongue, and indeed all facets of behavior could be traced to intrapsychic processes formed early in child development. Second, psychoanalytic theory stimulated other theories on the psychological bases of behavior. Many of Freud's disciples began to develop their own intrapsychic theories; others developed theories that completely challenged the basic tenets of psychoanalysis. Third, psychoanalytic theory stimulated the development of psychological forms of treatment. If psychological forces caused emotional disturbance, treatments were needed to alter those forces. Psychoanalytic treatment began as a method of uncovering and resolving intrapsychic processes that were assumed to underlie behavior. The primary method of treatment was talking with a therapist and working through various impulses, conflicts, defenses, and unresolved childhood experiences. Many variations of psychotherapy also emerged that relied on talk as the primary medium of change.

Intrapsychic approaches to clinical problems generated a number of psychotherapy techniques. Various forms of psychotherapy have been applied to help people resolve the underlying causes presumed to account for their distress and abnormal behavior. Treatments based on intrapsychic views tend to focus on bringing to light underlying feelings, motives, and thoughts that are considered responsible for behavior. The primary agents for change are talk, expression of feelings, and the development of a close relationship with the therapist. Clients are encouraged to understand their own motives and to express thwarted feelings. Psychotherapy based on the intrapsychic approaches has been applied to many clinical disorders, including psychoses, depression, anxiety, obsessions and compulsions, alcohol and drug abuse, and antisocial behavior.

Dissatisfaction

As noted previously, the emergence of behavior modification was facilitated by expressions of dissatisfaction with traditional notions related to assessment, diagnosis, and treatment of deviant behavior. The intrapsychic approach to personality and behavior grew from the disease approach of medicine in the late 1800s and early 1900s. Successes in identifying causes of many diseases furthered a more general approach of looking for underlying causes of symptoms. Freud, himself a physician, advanced a disease-type view in his model of psychoanalysis. An intrapsychic view suggests that psychological symptoms (deviant behavior) owe their origin to underlying dysfunction (personality conflicts). The dominance of the disease orientation in clinical work is reflected in such terms as mental *illness,* mental *health,* and mental *patients* and in references to persons who receive treatment as having *symptoms* or being *cured.*

Criticisms of intrapsychic approaches, especially psychoanalysis, increased in the 1950s and 1960s. The criticisms focused on difficulties in empirically verifying many of the claims of psychoanalysis, inconsistencies within psychoanalytic theory and in the therapeutic procedures derived from psychoanalytic theory, the neglect of social and cultural influences on behavior, and the lack of empirical support (see Salter, 1952; Stuart, 1970). Perhaps most significant was the fact that psychoanalytic views did not seem to be based on research or easily subjected to scientific inquiry. With behaviorism on the increase, there was a need for and strong interest in approaches that were more amenable to scientific research.

It was not merely the intrapsychic view or the general approach of psychoanalysis that was subjected to criticism. Considerable dissatisfaction was also voiced over the focus on intrapsychic processes that characterized the traditional forms of psychotherapy. In the early 1900s, psychoanalysis and psychoanalytically oriented psychotherapy dominated clinical practice. In the 1940s and 1950s, many researchers began to question and criticize the effects of these techniques. In 1952, Hans Eysenck published a paper that expressed dissatisfaction with traditional treatments. He reviewed contemporary research and claimed that the evidence did not support the efficacy of psychotherapy. He noted that providing psychotherapy seemed to be no more effective than simply leaving people alone (no treatment). Eysenck's paper and subsequent revisions in the 1960s yielded a simple conclusion, namely that traditional forms of treatment had not been shown to work. His evaluation of the available research and his overall conclusion were very actively debated.

Eysenck had also suggested that learning-based treatments were more effective than traditional forms of treatment. At that time, there was no clear evidence that provided a strong basis for this claim. Yet the claim helped polarize the field of psychotherapy in different ways. To those interested in traditional psychotherapy, Eysenck's papers served as a challenge to conduct the research needed to determine whether, or to show that, the treatments were really effective. To those dissatisfied with the traditional approaches, Eysenck's work helped point the way to learning-based approaches.

Over the past 30 years, a tremendous amount of research has emerged on the effects of psychotherapy (Bergin & Garfield, 1994). The findings cannot be easily summarized since they vary among the different types of treatment and among the different clinical problems to which those types of treatment are applied. Generally, large-scale evaluations have suggested that psychotherapy often leads to positive changes in behavior (Brown, 1987). In contrast to Eysenck's claim, it has been found that treatment is usually significantly better than no treatment. But over 400 different current forms of psychotherapy have been identified for adults (Karasu, 1985) and well over 200 have been identified for children and adolescents (Kazdin, 1988), and the fact remains that very few of these forms have been studied. Consequently, the effectiveness of most types of treatment remains unknown.

Current Perspectives

The emergence of behavioral approaches to treatment and dissatisfaction with intrapsychic approaches, especially psychoanalysis, are important to consider in historical context. The broad movement toward scientific research, beginning in the middle and late 1880s, ultimately was extended to the development of behaviorism and extensions of research to clinical work. At the inception of behavior modification in the 1950s and 1960s, there was a tendency to polarize different views about human behavior. As in the beginning of many movements, sharp distinctions were drawn. Behavior modification was compared to psychoanalysis and firm claims were made, noting, for example, that deviant behavior was learned, that psychoanalytic views could not be tested empirically, that traditional (intrapsychic) methods of psychotherapy did not work, and so on (see Kazdin, 1978). Such claims were important to help the movement toward behavior modification achieve autonomy and independence as a new paradigm. At the same time, extreme views were proposed (Eysenck, 1959) that have been tempered by the perspective of time, by a deeper understanding of human behavior, and by research findings from diverse perspectives. As an example, psychoanalytic theory has evolved considerably over the years. Major additions and reformulations have since given greater attention to the influence of external events and social experiences on behavior. Similarly, behavioral views have evolved as well. Many influences that are not external to the individual (for example, cognitions) play a central role within various views of behavior modification. Yet, important differences remain between intrapsychic and behavioral conceptualizations of behavior and in the treatment techniques on which they rely. The major characteristics, outlined earlier, largely define the field of behavior modification and do not characterize most other views.

CONTEMPORARY BEHAVIOR MODIFICATION

Contemporary behavior modification represents a convergence of different theories and influences into a heterogeneous movement. The central characteristics that unite the movement pertain primarily to an orientation toward treatment, a focus on behavior, an emphasis on learning, and assessment and evaluation. Two central themes evident in the animal research and early extensions of concepts from the laboratory to clinical populations pertain to the importance of learning and the careful assessment of behavior.

Current Theory in Behavior Modification

Learning continues to occupy a central role in contemporary behavior modification. Three types of learning are considered important in developing and altering behavior. Classical (or respondent) conditioning and operant conditioning have been discussed previously. A third type of learning that has been important is referred to as *observational (vicarious) learning* or *modeling*. Observational learning occurs when an individual observes another person (referred to as a *model*) engage in a particular behavior. The observer sees the model perform the behavior but does not engage in overt responses or receive any consequences. The observer learns the behavior merely by watching a model.

To clarify modeling effects, it is important to distinguish *learning* from *performance*. The requirement for learning through modeling is observation of a model. The modeled response is assumed to be acquired by the observer through cognitive or covert coding of the events observed (Bandura, 1977). However, whether a learned response is actually performed may depend on the consequences of the response or on the incentives associated with the response.

The importance of response consequences in dictating performance was demonstrated several years ago (Bandura, 1965). Children observed a film in which an adult modeled aggressive responses (hitting and kicking a large doll). For some children, the model's aggression was rewarded; for others, it was punished; and for still others, it met with no consequences. When the children were given the opportunity to perform the aggressive responses, those who had observed the aggression punished displayed less aggression than did those who had observed the aggression rewarded or ignored. To determine whether all of the children had learned the aggressive responses, an incentive was given to them for performing those responses. There were then no differences in aggressive responses among the three groups. Apparently, all of the groups had learned the aggressive responses, but the consequences to the model and the observer determined whether those responses would be performed. The extent to which modeling stimuli influence performance also depends on other factors, such as the similarity of the model to the observer; the prestige, status, and expertise of the model; and the number of models observed. As a general rule, imitation of a model by an observer is greater when the model is similar to the observer, more prestigious, and higher in status and expertise than the observer and when several models perform the same behavior.

A frequently cited example of modeling in the history of behavior modification was reported by Jones (1924). In this example, a young boy named Peter, who was afraid of a rabbit and several other furry objects (for example, a fur coat, a feather, cotton wool), was placed in a play situation in which three other children and a rabbit were present. The other children, selected because they were unafraid of rabbits, interacted with the rabbit in a nonanxious fashion. Peter touched the rabbit immediately after observing others touch it. Other procedures were employed to overcome Peter's fear, such as associating the rabbit with the presence of food, so that the precise contribution of modeling in reducing the fear is uncertain.

Modeling has been used in behavior modification to alter a variety of behaviors. In many therapeutic applications, problems such as fear or lack of social skills have been treated effectively with both children and adults. In most applications modeling is utilized along with other behavioral procedures. For example, in applications of operant conditioning techniques, modeling often plays a major role in conveying to the client exactly what the desired responses are. Yet it is supplemented with other techniques such as feedback and positive reinforcement.

Social Learning Theory: An Integration of Learning Concepts

Each type of learning has been developed largely on its own by means of extensive laboratory research, often with infrahuman subjects. Obviously, however, clinical problems that are evident in human behavior represent much more complex phenomena than the behaviors studied in animal research in laboratory settings. Animal research often does not reflect the complexity of processes that appear to be involved in human behavior such as language and thought.

Several authors have provided theories of behavior that attempt to integrate aspects of different learning paradigms and to take cognitive processes into account (Fishman, Rotgers, & Franks, 1988; Reiss, 1991). For example, Bandura (1977, 1986) proposed a social learning theory that encompasses various types of learning and the wide range of influences that each type entails. Thus, social learning approaches utilize elements of classical, operant, and observational learning to explain behavior. They integrate events in the environment and, to a much greater extent, cognitions (thoughts, beliefs, perceptions) about environmental events into a general framework that depends on different learning experiences. Social learning approaches emphasize the multiple types of influences on behavior that occur in the context of social development and provide a framework from which behavior in general can be explained. The advantage of social learning approaches is that they can account for a broad range of behaviors to a greater extent than accounts based on simplistic applications of one type of learning rather than another.

In behavioral treatment, knowledge of the different types of learning is essential. In understanding how behavior develops and how it can be altered, the concepts from various types of learning need to be integrated. Social learning provides an integrated conceptual approach to understanding clinical problems and their treatment.

Even when concepts from one area of learning are relied on for a particular purpose, other types of learning are relevant as well. For example, behavior modification programs in applied settings such as the home, school, hospital, and institution rely heavily on operant conditioning techniques. Nonetheless, knowledge of other types of learning is important in implementing operant techniques. For example, an operant program in a classroom setting may increase a student's desirable behavior, such as working on assignments, by following such behavior with a favorable consequence or event, such as praise from the teacher. Yet modeling and respondent conditioning as well as operant conditioning may be operative in the situation. Students other than the one who is praised may increase in desirable behavior because of modeling influences (that is, observing their peers). Classical conditioning may also be involved in the control of classroom behavior. For example, if a teacher shouts at a student (unconditioned stimulus), a startle reaction (unconditioned response) may occur. The teacher's close proximity to the child (conditioned stimulus) may, through repeated association with shouting, eventually elicit anxiety and arousal (conditioned response). Of course, if the teacher's proximity to the child elicits anxiety, this may detract from the teacher's reinforcing properties. As is obvious by now, a behavioral approach draws heavily on the psychology of learning to explain how behavior develops, is maintained, and is altered.

Applied Behavior Analysis

Most of the behaviors of concern in applied settings and everyday life can be conceptualized as operants. That is, the behaviors operate on the environment and have consequences that affect the likelihood that they are performed in the future. The range of behaviors that operate on the environment is virtually unlimited. Examples that are often the focus of behavioral research include problematic behaviors among persons who seek psychological treatment, academic performance of children, exercise and dieting among children and adults, and others. Such behaviors can be altered by applying techniques derived from operant conditioning.

The extension of operant conditioning principles and methods of studying human behavior to clinically and socially important human behaviors has become an area of research within behavior modification. The principles of operant conditioning, previously noted in Table 1–1, refer to the relations between events in the environment and changes in behavior. The principles, such as positive reinforcement and extinction, are simple, and indeed, many consider it simplistic to extend them to explain the complexities of human behavior. Yet, the issue is the extent to which those principles can be used to develop effective interventions for significant clinical and social problems. That issue can be decided only by examining the research itself, as covered in subsequent chapters.

The current approach to behavior change in applied settings is more than an extension of specific principles. Behavior analysis is an experimental approach for studying behavior in the laboratory in which the behavior of one or a few individuals is assessed over time to monitor the changes due to various interventions. The extension of experimental methods to applied settings generated a new area of research referred to as applied behavior analysis (Baer, Wolf, & Risley, 1968). Various characteristics of applied behavior analysis are highlighted in Table 1–2. The special focus of applied behavior analysis is on clinically or socially relevant behaviors in such areas as psychological and psychiatric disorders, education, rehabilitation, medicine, business, and industry.[3]

Applied behavior analysis, unlike other areas within behavior modification, is often referred to as *radical* behaviorism. It is considered radical because its focus is exclusively on overt behavior rather than on subjective states (affect) and thoughts (cognition). The focus of applied behavior analysis can be clarified by noting other conceptual views within behavior modification.

Current conceptual views within behavior modification can generally be cast as mediational or nonmediational. Nonmediational views focus on direct connections between environmental and situational events and behaviors. The consequences that follow behavior serve as one major category of environmental events. For example, praise for a job well done can increase performance at home, at school, or at work through the principle of positive reinforcement. The consequences in nonmediational views refer

T A B L E   1–2
Characteristics of Applied Behavior Analysis

Characteristics
• Focus on overt behaviors.
• Focus on behaviors of applied (social or clinical) significance.
• Search for marked intervention effects that make a clear difference to the everyday functioning of the individual.
• Focus on the behaviors of one or a small number of individuals over time.
• Assessment of behavior through direct observation, as in counting the frequency of responses.
• Assessment continuously over time for extended periods (hours, days, weeks).
• Use of environmental (and observable) events to influence the frequency of behavior.
• Evaluation and demonstration of the factors (for example, events) that are responsible for behavior change.

primarily to events in the environment, such as praise from others. Operant conditioning and its extensions to behavior reflect a nonmediational view.

In contrast, mediational views emphasize the cognitive underpinnings of behavior. These underpinnings, such as perceptions, plans, attributions, expectations, and beliefs, are considered in mediational views to play a central role in behavior. According to mediational views, environmental events can influence behavior, but the person processes these events through his or her beliefs and attributions. Thus, cognitive processes imbue an event with meaning and help determine its impact. The influence of perceptions and beliefs on behavior is obvious in everyday life. For example, the way in which we behave in response to a glance from another person on the street or on a bus depends on whether we *perceive* the glance as threatening or friendly.

The dominant view within behavior modification is *social learning theory*, which recognizes the importance of both cognitive and environmental influences and their interaction. A broad social learning view is a useful way of considering multiple influences on behavior and of incorporating research from many areas. Applied behavior analysis has been criticized for not addressing the full range of the influences that may account for behavior. However, the goal of applied behavior analysis has not been to develop a broad theory of behavior. The overall questions of applied behavior analysis concern the extent to which principles developed in laboratory research can be useful in developing effective treatment, education, and rehabilitation programs and the extent to which human behavior can be altered in significant ways to improve functioning in everday life. Those questions can be answered empirically, that is, by seeing what can be accomplished by applying the principles. The present book elaborates the principles and the techniques that derive from them and illustrates applications that address the overall questions of applied behavior analysis.

Notes

1. The term *client* will be used throughout the text to refer to the person for whom the intervention is provided. The reference is a convenient way to encompass different persons (for example, psychiatric patients, children and adults in therapy, students, employees in a factory). Historically, the term has also been important as a substitute for the term *psychiatric patient.* This has been an issue because the term *patient* reflects the medical orientation toward deviant behavior to which proponents of behavior modification have objected.
2. The Watson and Rayner demonstration had remarkable influence in suggesting the role of classical (respondent) conditioning in the development of maladaptive behavior. As a technicality noteworthy in passing, the original demonstration with Albert may be more appropriately conceived of as operant rather than classical conditioning. In operant conditioning, consequences follow responses—that is, the individual *does something,* after which some event follows. In the Watson and Rayner demonstration, Albert reached for or began to touch the rat (Albert's response), at which point the loud noise sounded (aversive event). This sequence of events more closely follows a punishment paradigm of operant conditioning (see Kazdin, 1978). The main point of the demonstration can be taken to be more general, namely that learning can play a role in the development of maladaptive behavior.
3. Research in applied behavior analysis is published in many journals in psychology, education, rehabilitation, community work, and other areas. The *Journal of Applied Behavior Analysis* is devoted exclusively to this type of research.

For Further Reading

Baer, D. M., Wolf, M. M., & Risley, T. R. (1968). Some current dimensions of applied behavior analysis. *Journal of Applied Behavior Analysis, 1,* 91–97.

Baer, D. M., Wolf, M. M., & Risley, T. R. (1987). Some still-current dimensions of applied behavior analysis. *Journal of Applied Behavior Analysis, 20,* 313–328.

Catania, A. C. (1992). *Learning* (3rd ed.). Englewood Cliffs, NJ: Prentice-Hall.

Kazdin, A. E. (1978). *History of behavior modification: Experimental foundations of contemporary research.* Baltimore: University Park Press.

Lattal, K. A. (Guest Ed.) (1992). Special issue: Reflections on B. F. Skinner and psychology. *American Psychologist, 47,* 1269–1533.

Skinner, B. F. (1953). *Science and human behavior.* New York: Free Press.

CHAPTER TWO

PRINCIPLES OF OPERANT CONDITIONING

In the previous chapter, three kinds of learning—classical conditioning, operant conditioning, and observational learning—were discussed. Although all three types of learning are evident in behavior modification, programs in applied settings, such as the classroom, hospitals, institutions, and the home—and even in society at large—rely heavily on the principles of operant conditioning. The present chapter briefly explains the basic principles.[1] Later chapters elaborate on the major principles and on the various procedures that have been developed from them.

CONTINGENCIES: THE ABCS OF BEHAVIOR

The principles of operant conditioning describe the relationship between behavior and the environmental events (antecedents and consequences) that influence behavior. This relationship, referred to as a *contingency*, includes three components: antecedent events (A), behaviors (B), and consequent events (C). The notion of a contingency is important not only for understanding behavior but also for developing programs to change behavior. Antecedent events refer to stimuli before the behavior, such as instructions, gestures, or looks from others. Behaviors refer to the acts themselves (that is, some response that the individual performs). Consequences refer to events that follow behavior. Table 2–1 illustrates the three components of a contingency with simple examples from everyday life.

Developing effective programs depends on understanding the types of antecedent events and consequences that influence behavior and how they operate. In consideration of the ABCs or contingencies, it seems that antecedent events should be discussed first. Apart from the fact that they come before behavior, on *a priori* grounds, the first line of attack in changing behavior might be to alter antecedent events. Presumably, if antecedent events that control behavior were understood and altered, there may be

TABLE 2–1
Three Components of a Contingency and Illustrations from Everyday Life

Component		
Antecedent	Behavior	Consequences
Telephone rings	Answer phone	Voice of person at the other end
Wave from a friend	Approach friend	Visiting and chatting
Parent instruction for the child to clean his or her room	Child picks up toys	Praise and allowance
Warning not to eat spoiled food	Eating the food	Nausea and vomiting

little or no need to alter the consequences for behavior. For example, if a parent's nagging (antecedent event) of a child is creating a problem, elimination of the nagging might alter the problem behavior. Generally, antecedents include the contexts in which behaviors and consequences occur and hence are important as an initial basis for understanding behavior. Notwithstanding the logically prior nature of antecedent events, we shall first begin with a discussion of consequences. We begin with consequences for three reasons. First, in most programs, emphasis is placed on the consequences that follow behavior. The use of rewarding and punishing consequences is familiar in everyday life and hence represents a useful transition from commonsense applications to a more technical presentation of the principles. Second, antecedent and contextual influences are often more subtle and thus more difficult to detect and to alter. Antecedent influences can occur at distant and current points in time and can include multiple influences, all of which affect current behavior. These influences are less well understood, even though they are subject to a great deal of attention in current research. Third, and perhaps most important for present purposes, many antecedent events acquire their influence because of their association with certain consequences. For example, facial expressions, verbal gestures, comments from others, traffic signals, ambulance sirens, and other stimuli in the environment often acquire their influence as antecedents because of the consequences or anticipated consequences with which they are associated. Thus, understanding antecedent events is facilitated by outlining different consequences that are used to atler behavior.

For a consequence to alter a particular behavior, it must be dependent or *contingent upon* the occurrence of that behavior. Stated another way, *behavior change occurs when certain consequences are contingent upon performance.* A consequence is contingent when it is delivered only after the target behavior has been performed and is otherwise not available. When a consequence is not contingent upon behavior, this means that it is delivered independently of what the person is doing. The noncontingent delivery of consequences ordinarily does not result in systematic changes in a preselected target behavior because the consequences do not consistently follow that behavior.

For example, if a psychiatric patient receives attention (the consequence) from an attendant on the ward each time he or she speaks, the attention is considered to be contingent upon speech. On the other hand, the patient may receive attention every so often from an attendant independently of what he or she is doing. In that case, attention is delivered noncontingently. To increase speaking, attention should be contingent upon instances of speaking. In everyday life, many consequences are contingent upon our behavior. Wages are contingent upon working, grades are contingent upon studying for exams, and health is contingent to some extent upon the care with which we treat ourselves.

The notion of contingency is important because behavioral techniques alter behavior by modifying the contingencies that influence behavior. The principles of operant conditioning refer to different kinds of contingent relationships between behavior and the events that follow behavior. The major principles are reinforcement, punishment, and extinction.

REINFORCEMENT

The principle of *reinforcement* refers to an increase in the frequency of a response when that response is immediately followed by certain consequences. The consequence that follows behavior must be contingent upon behavior. A contingent event that increases the frequency of behavior is referred to as a *reinforcer*. Positive and negative reinforcers constitute the two kinds of events that can be used to increase the frequency of a response (Skinner, 1953). *Positive reinforcers* are events presented after a response has been performed that increase the frequency of the behavior they follow. *Negative reinforcers* (which will also be referred to as *aversive events* or *aversive stimuli*) are events removed after a response has been performed that increase the behavior preceding their removal.

Positive Reinforcement

Positive reinforcement refers to the increase in the frequency of a response that is followed by a favorable event (positive reinforcer). In everyday language, such positive or favorable events are frequently referred to as rewards. However, it is desirable to distinguish the term *positive reinforcement* from the term *reward.* A positive reinforcer is defined by its effect on behavior. If an event follows a behavior and the frequency of that behavior increases, the event is a positive reinforcer. Conversely, any event that does not increase the behavior it follows is not a positive reinforcer. An increase in the frequency or probability of the preceding behavior is the defining characteristic of a positive reinforcer. In contrast, rewards are defined merely as something that is given or received in return for doing something. Rewards such as prizes, sums of money, and vacations are usually highly valued, but they do not necessarily increase the probability of the behaviors they follow. The distinction between rewards and reinforcers may seem subtle, but it plays an exceedingly important part in the development of an effective treatment program.

Many rewards or events that a person evaluates favorably when queried may serve as reinforcers. Yet, the reinforcing value of an event cannot be known on the basis of a person's verbal statements alone. A person may be unaware of or not consider as rewards many events that are reinforcers. For example, verbal reprimands (such as, "Stop that!") and physical restraint have occasionally served as positive reinforcers (for example, Favell, McGimsey, & Jones, 1978). Yet it is unlikely that anyone would ever refer to these consequences as rewards. Hence, a reward is not synonymous with a positive reinforcer. Whether an event is a positive reinforcer has to be determined empirically. Does the frequency of a particular behavior increase when the event immediately follows the behavior? Only if the behavior increases is the event a positive reinforcer.

Examples of positive reinforcement in everyday life would seem to be abundant. However, rarely does anyone actually measure whether a favorable event that followed a behavior increases the frequency of that behavior. Nevertheless, it is useful to mention some everyday situations that probably exemplify positive reinforcement. Studying for an exam is probably reinforced if a student receives an A. Studying reinforced by an excellent grade is likely to increase in the future. Alternatively, if a child whines or complains before going to bed and is then allowed by his or her parents to stay up longer, the frequency of whining before bedtime may increase. Letting the child stay up is likely to be a positive reinforcer. Winning money at a slot machine usually increases the frequency of putting money into the machine and pulling the lever. Money is a powerful reinforcer that increases performance of a variety of behaviors.

Types of Positive Reinforcers

Positive reinforcers include any events that, when presented, increase the frequency of the behavior they follow. There are two categories of positive reinforcers, namely *primary,* or *unconditioned,* and *secondary,* or *conditioned,* reinforcers. Events that serve as primary reinforcers acquire their reinforcing value without special training. Food and water are examples of primary reinforcers. Primary reinforcers may not be reinforcing all of the time. Food will not serve as a reinforcer to someone who has just finished a large meal. When food does serve as a reinforcer, however, its value is automatic (unlearned) and does not depend on a previous association with any other reinforcers.

Many events that control behavior are secondary, or conditioned, reinforcers. Conditioned reinforcers, which include events such as praise, grades, money, and completion of a goal, have acquired reinforcing value through learning. Conditioned reinforcers are not automatically reinforcing. Stimuli or events that were once neutral in value may acquire reinforcing properties by being paired with events that are already reinforcing (either primary reinforcers or other conditioned reinforcers). If a neutral stimulus is repeatedly presented prior to or along with a reinforcing stimulus, the neutral stimulus becomes a reinforcer. For example, praise may not be reinforcing for some individuals. To establish praise as a reinforcer, it must be paired with an event that is reinforcing, such as food or money. When a behavior is performed, the individual's behavior is praised and reinforced with food. After several pairings of the food with praise, the praise alone serves as a reinforcer and can be used to increase the frequency of other responses (Lancioni, 1982).

Some conditioned reinforcers are paired with more than one primary or conditioned reinforcer. When a conditioned reinforcer is paired with *many* other reinforcers, it is referred to as a *generalized conditioned reinforcer.* Generalized conditioned reinforcers are extremely effective in altering behaviors because they have been paired with a variety of events. Money is an example of a generalized conditioned reinforcer. It is a *conditioned* reinforcer because its reinforcing value is acquired through learning. It is a *generalized* reinforcer because a variety of reinforcing events contribute to its value. Additional examples of generalized conditioned reinforcers include attention, approval, and affection from others (Skinner, 1953). These are generalized reinforcers because their occurrence is often associated with a variety of other events that are themselves reinforcing. For example, attention from someone may be followed by physical contact, praise, smiles, affection, or delivery of tangible rewards (such as food) and other events.

In behavior modification programs, generalized reinforcers in the form of tokens are used frequently (Kazdin, 1977a). The tokens may consist of poker chips, coins, tickets, stars, points, or check marks. Tokens serve as generalized reinforcers because, like money, they can be exchanged for many other events that are reinforcing. For example, in an elementary school classroom, tokens may be delivered to students for raising their hands to speak, for completing assignments in class, for attaining correct answers and other behaviors. The tokens may be exchanged for special in-class activities such as educational games or movies, extra recess, or free time in class at the end of the day. The potency of tokens derives from the reinforcers that back up their value. The events that tokens can purchase are referred to as *back-up reinforcers.* Generalized conditioned reinforcers, such as money or tokens, are usually more powerful than any single reinforcer because they can purchase many different back-up reinforcers.

In identifying positive reinforcers, it is important to keep two considerations in mind. First, an event (for example, praise, candy, or a pat on the back) may be a positive reinforcer for one person but not for another. Although some events have wide generality in serving as reinforcers, such as food or money, others may not (for example, sour candy). Second, an event may be a reinforcer for one person under some circumstances or at some times but not under other circumstances or at other times. These considerations require careful evaluation of what is reinforcing for a given individual. Because of cultural norms and the common experiences of many people, some suggestions may be given as to events that probably serve as reinforcers. However, there is no guarantee that a particular event will be reinforcing.

The Premack Principle

The reinforcing events referred to above include *stimuli* or specific events such as praise, smiles, food, or money that are presented after a response. Yet, reinforcers are not limited to the stimuli presented to a client. Allowing an individual to engage in certain *responses* can be used as a reinforcer. Premack (1965) noted that when an individual is given the opportunity to select among various responses, behaviors performed with a relatively high frequency can reinforce behaviors performed with a relatively low frequency. If the opportunity to perform a more probable response is made contingent upon performance of a less probable response, the frequency of the latter should increase. On the basis of laboratory research, the *Premack principle* has been formulated to reflect this relation: *Of any pair of responses or activities in which an individual engages, the more frequent one will reinforce the less frequent one.* Stated more simply, a higher-probability behavior can reinforce a lower-probability behavior.

To determine what behaviors are high or low in frequency requires observing the behaviors that a person performs when given the opportunity to engage in behavior without restraints—such as what someone does when given free time at home, at school, or on the weekends. A behavior observed to occur more frequently can be used to follow and reinforce a lower-frequency behavior (for example, studying, engaging in chores). For example, for many children, playing with friends is performed at a higher frequency than is practicing a musical instrument. If the higher-frequency behavior (playing with friends) is made contingent upon the lower-frequency behavior (playing the instrument), the lower-probability behavior will increase.

Although the Premack principle is effective as a basis for identifying reinforcers, it is not entirely clear why it works. One explanation, referred to as the *response deprivation hypothesis,* suggests that the effectiveness of making one response contingent upon another has to do with setting up a deprivation condition (Timberlake & Allison, 1974). Stated simply, the individual is deprived of opportunities to perform the desired (high-probability) behavior when that behavior is contingent upon completing some other response (low-probability behavior). Performance of the target response increases to overcome the decreased rate (deprivation) of the preferred response. The importance of response deprivation has been corroborated in laboratory and applied work (Konarski, Johnson, Crowell, & Whitman, 1981).

For applied purposes, the Premack principle is useful for expanding the range of reinforcers that can be used to alter behavior. Behaviors or activities that individuals appear to engage in during opportunities for free time, or self-reported preferences about what clients like to do, have been used to reinforce behavior in many applications. Of course, frequently performed behaviors or highly preferred activities may not serve as reinforcers. Yet a number of demonstrations attest to the utility of various activities as reinforcers.

An example of the use of the Premack principle to increase the activity of schizophrenic patients was reported by Mitchell and Stoffelmayr (1973). The patients frequently sat or paced in the ward. To increase their activity, the investigators wished to develop work at a task (stripping coil from wires). The two behaviors of interest were inactivity or sitting (higher-probability behavior) and work (lower-probability behavior). To increase work, sitting was made contingent upon doing some work. The investigators set a criterion for completing work before the clients earned the opportunity to sit down. Gradually, they increased the amount of work required to earn the opportunity to sit. The results showed a marked increase in work behavior when it was followed by sitting.

Numerous relatively frequent behaviors that an individual performs—for example, going on trips, being with friends, engaging in certain activities, hobbies, or privileges—can serve as reinforcers for other behaviors. The Premack principle requires that the target response be of a lower probability than the behavior that will reinforce it. Of course, in everyday life, high-probability behaviors often *precede* rather than follow low-probability behaviors. For example, students may study (low-probability behavior for many students) after going out with their friends (high-probability behavior). Spouses may complete yard work (low-probability behavior) after watching a football game (high-probability behavior). In such cases, the low-probability behavior is not likely to increase in frequency unless the sequence of the behaviors is reversed. Performing the high-probability behavior before performing the low-probability behavior amounts to the noncontingent delivery of reinforcers.

Negative Reinforcement

Negative reinforcement refers to the increase in the frequency of a response by removing an aversive event immediately after the response has been performed. Removal of an aversive event or a negative reinforcer is contingent upon a response. An event is a *negative reinforcer* only if its removal after a response increases performance of that response (Skinner, 1953). Events that appear to be annoying, undesirable, or unpleasant are not necessarily negatively reinforcing. The qualifications made in the discussion of positive reinforcers hold for negative reinforcers as well. An undesirable event may serve as an aversive event for one individual but not for another. Also, an event may be a negative reinforcer for an individual at one time but not at another time. A negative reinforcer, like a positive reinforcer, is defined solely by its effect on behavior.

It is important to note that reinforcement (positive or negative) always refers to an increase in behavior. Negative reinforcement requires an ongoing aversive event that can be removed or terminated after a specific response has been performed. The aversive event is "just there" or present in the environment. Once this event is present, then some behavior may stop or end it. That behavior is negatively reinforced. For example, if a young neighbor constantly turns on very loud music, this music is likely to be an aversive event to another neighbor who is not of the same generation (over 40 years old). The bothered neighbor has an ongoing aversive event, so a critical condition for negative reinforcement is present. To terminate the event, the neighbor screams, "Stop that _____ music, or I will call the _____ police." Assume for a moment that this behavior (screaming, swearing, and making a threat) stops the noise. The behavior has been negatively reinforced because it was followed by elimination of the aversive event. Thus, the likelihood of future screaming, swearing, and threatening has been increased.

Other examples of negative reinforcement abound in everyday life. Taking medicine to relieve a headache may be negatively reinforced by the termination of pain. Similarly, nagging by a parent may increase room cleaning by a child. The aversive event (parental nagging) is terminated by performing the behavior. Strictly speaking, negative reinforcement occurs in the above examples only if the behavior that terminates the undesirable state increases.

Interesting combinations of positive and negative reinforcement that may foster socially undesirable behavior occur in social interaction (see Patterson, Reid, & Dishion, 1992). In social interaction, the response of one individual is sometimes negatively reinforced because it terminates an aversive behavior initiated by another individual. At the same time, the aversive behavior of the other individual may be positively reinforced. For example, if parents pick up a young child who is whining, whining is, for the parents, an aversive event that is terminated after they respond. Picking up the child is negatively reinforced by a cessation of whining. Yet, the child's whining may be positively reinforced because he or she receives parental attention contingent upon this behavior. Positive and negative reinforcement in social interaction also occur when the victim of an aggressive act (such as physical assault) complies with the wishes of the aggressor (for example, giving up his wallet) in order to terminate an aversive situation. Unfortunately, the act of compliance positively reinforces the aggressor, increasing the probability of future aggression by the aggressor.

Negative reinforcement requires presentation to the individual of some aversive event, such as shock, noise, or isolation, that can be removed or reduced immediately after he or she responds. Because of the undesirability of using aversive stimuli, negative reinforcement is used infrequently in programs designed to alter behavior. Also, several less objectionable and more positive procedures are readily available.

As with positive reinforcers there are two types of negative reinforcers, primary and secondary. Intense stimuli, such as shock or loud noise, that impinge on the sensory receptors of an organism serve as primary negative reinforcers. Their aversive properties are not learned. In contrast, secondary, or conditioned, aversive events become aversive by being paired with events that are already aversive. For example, disapproving facial expressions or saying the word *no* can serve as aversive events after being paired with events that are already aversive (for example, Dorsey, Iwata, Ong, & McSween, 1980).

Escape and Avoidance

Negative reinforcement occurs whenever an individual escapes from an aversive event. Escape from aversive events is negatively reinforcing. Avoidance of aversive events is negatively reinforcing too. For example, one avoids eating rancid food, walking through an intersection with oncoming cars, and leaving the house without an umbrella on a rainy day. Avoidance occurs *before* the aversive event takes place (for example, becoming sick from rancid food, being injured by a car, getting wet from rain). The avoidance response prevents the aversive event from occurring. Since no aversive events seem to have occurred, how are avoidance behaviors maintained?

Avoidance learning is an area in which classical and operant conditioning are operative. Avoidance behavior is sometimes learned by pairing a neutral stimulus (conditioned stimulus) with an unconditioned aversive event (unconditioned stimulus). For example, a frown (conditioned stimulus) from a parent may precede corporal punishment (unconditioned stimulus) of a child. Corporal punishment may elicit crying and escape from the situation (unconditioned response). The child learns to *escape* from the situation when the adult frowns and thereby *avoids* corporal punishment. The sight of the frowning parent elicits crying and escape. Avoidance of unconditioned aversive events is actually escape from conditioned aversive events. Thus, classical conditioning may initiate avoidance behavior. Operant conditioning is also involved in avoidance behavior. Behaviors that reduce or terminate an aversive event are negatively reinforced. The escape from the conditioned aversive event (for example, the frown) is negatively reinforced because it terminates the event. To reiterate, the conditioned aversive event elicits an escape response (classical conditioning) that is negatively reinforced (operant conditioning).

Operant conditioning is involved in yet another way in avoidance learning. A conditioned aversive event serves as a cue signaling that particular consequences will follow. The presence of the conditioned aversive stimulus signals that a certain response (escape) will be reinforced. A variety of cues control avoidance behavior in everyday life. Indeed, most avoidance behavior appears to be learned from verbal cues (warnings) by others, rather than from direct experience with unconditioned aversive stimuli. For example, a sign saying "Danger" or "Beware of Dog" signals that certain consequences (physical harm) are likely to occur if a particular response (trespassing) is performed. The escape response made after reading the sign is not *elicited,* as are reflex responses. The sign merely acts as a cue that consequences of a particular sort are likely to follow alternative courses of action. An individual does not have to experience physical harm to learn to avoid particular situations. In examples from everyday experience, avoidance behavior is under the control of antecedent stimuli (for example, screeching car brakes, threats, and traffic signals) signaling that a

particular event is likely to follow. Traditionally, both respondent and operant conditioning have been considered to influence avoidance learning. Yet
the processes by which avoidance behavior is developed, maintained, and
eliminated are not completely understood.

PUNISHMENT

*Punishment is the presentation of an aversive event or the removal of a
positive event following a response, which decreases the frequency of that
response.* This definition is somewhat different from the everyday use of
the term. As ordinarily defined, punishment refers to a penalty imposed for
performing a particular act. The technical definition includes an additional
requirement, namely, that the frequency of the response is decreased.
Because of the negative connotations frequently associated with punishment, it is important to dispel some stereotypical notions that do not apply
to the technical definition of punishment. Punishment does not necessarily
entail pain or physical coercion.[2] In addition, it is not a means of retribution
or payment for misbehaving. Punishment is sometimes employed in everyday life independently of its effects on subsequent behavior. For example,
misbehaving children are "taught a lesson" by undergoing a sacrifice of
some kind. Similarly, criminals may receive penalties that do not necessarily decrease the frequency of their criminal acts. *Punishment in the technical sense is defined solely by the effect on behavior.* In this sense, punishment is operative only if the frequency of a response is reduced. Similarly, a
punishing event is defined by its suppressive effect on the behavior that it
follows. As will become evident in later chapters, a variety of events that
suppress behavior depart from ordinary practices that are termed punishment in everyday life.

There are two types of punishment. In the first type, an aversive event is
presented after a response. The numerous everyday examples of this type
of punishment include being reprimanded or slapped after engaging in
some behavior. Similarly, being burned after touching a hot stove involves
the presentation of an aversive stimulus after a response. The second type
of punishment is the *removal* of a positive event after a response. Examples
include losing privileges after staying out late, losing money for misbehaving, being isolated from others, and having one's driver's license re-
voked. In this type of punishment, some positive event is taken away after a
response has been performed.

Punishment and negative reinforcement are often confused even
though they are very different. *The key difference is that reinforcement,
whether negative or positive, always refers to procedures that increase a
response, whereas punishment always refers to procedures that decrease
a response.* In negative reinforcement, an aversive event is *removed*

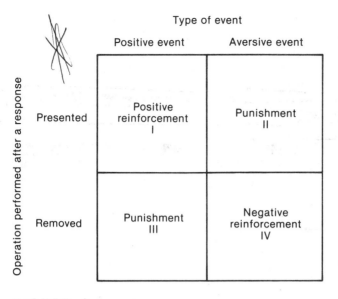

Type of event

	Positive event	Aversive event
Presented	Positive reinforcement I	Punishment II
Removed	Punishment III	Negative reinforcement IV

Operation performed after a response (left axis label)

FIGURE   2–1

Illustration of principles of operant conditioning based on whether positive or aversive events are presented or removed after a response has been performed. The figure provides a simple way to convey the major principles of operant conditioning, but the simplicity of the figure has a price. In fact, a more technical discussion of the principles would quickly reveal inaccuracies in the figure. For example, the figure implies that a particular event that can negatively reinforce behavior can also be used to suppress (punish) some other response that it follows. Although this is usually true, many exceptions exist. It is not necessarily the case that the same event whose removal negatively reinforces a behavior will suppress a behavior when it is presented, or vice versa. Hence, in the present text, the term *aversive stimulus*, or *aversive event*, will be used to refer to any event that may be negatively reinforcing and/or punishing. In general, the principles of operant conditioning refer to more complex relationships than are depicted here. Interestingly, behavior modification programs tend to rely on the simple versions of the principles discussed here.

after a response; in punishment, an aversive consequence *follows* a response.

Figure 2–1 provides a simple way of distinguishing the operations involved in reinforcement and punishment, depicting two operations that can occur after a response has been performed. An event can be presented to, or removed from, the client after a response (left side of the figure). The figure also shows two types of events that may be presented or removed, namely, positive and aversive events. The four combinations forming the different cells depict the principles of positive reinforcement (cell I), negative reinforcement (cell IV), and the two types of punishment (cells II and III).

EXTINCTION

An important principle of operant conditioning is not represented in Figure 2–1. This principle does not involve presenting or withdrawing events in the usual sense. Rather, it refers to no longer following behavior with an event that was previously delivered. *Extinction refers to the cessation of reinforcement of a response.* Nonreinforcement of a response results in its eventual reduction or elimination. It is important to keep this procedure distinct from punishment. In extinction, *no consequence* follows the response; an event is neither taken away nor presented. In punishment, some aversive event follows a response or some positive event is taken away. In everyday life, extinction usually takes the form of ignoring a behavior that was previously reinforced with attention. A mother may ignore her child when the child whines. A teacher may ignore children who talk without raising their hands. A therapist or counselor may ignore certain self-defeating statements made by the client. In each of these examples, the reinforcer (for example, attention, approval, or sympathy) previously given for the response is no longer presented.

As an example, extinction was used as part of a program to change several feminine sex-typed behaviors of a 5-year-old boy named Kraig (Rekers & Lovaas, 1974). Kraig continually engaged in traditionally female-typed behaviors, such as dressing in women's clothes, playing with dolls and cosmetics, and mimicking feminine gestures and mannerisms. He avoided all male-typed activities. Treatment was implemented because of the social difficulties that cross-gender activities may create for a child and also because such behaviors are often precursors to later sexual deviance, such as transvestism (cross dressing) and transsexualism (role identity with the opposite sex). At the clinic, the mother and child were placed in a room where the child had the opportunity to play with what were traditionally regarded as female-typed objects (such as dolls, cosmetics, and women's clothes) or male-typed objects (such as cars, boats, and guns). The mother was instructed to ignore any play with female-typed objects by simply reading a book that she brought into the room. The purpose was to extinguish play with female-typed objects by withholding attention. The mother was also instructed to reinforce play with male-typed objects. The mother was instructed to provide attention, smiles, and praise whenever Kraig played with these objects. Thus, extinction was combined with positive reinforcement. The program was also carried out at home, where Kraig received token reinforcement for many gender-appropriate behaviors. Interestingly, the program led to a dramatic increase in masculine behaviors and a dramatic decrease in feminine behaviors. These treatment effects were maintained when Kraig was checked 26 months after treatment.[3]

In everyday life, extinction may contribute to behavioral problems as well as ameliorate them. Often, desirable behavior is accidentally extinguished. For example, parents sometimes ignore their children when the children are playing quietly and provide abundant attention when the children are noisy. This may extinguish quiet play while positively reinforcing noisy play. Merely altering parental attention so that it follows appropriate play is often sufficient to develop appropriate behavior and to extinguish inappropriate behavior.

Cessation of attention is not the only example of extinction. For example, putting money into vending machines (a response) will cease if the reinforcer (for example, cigarettes, food, or drink) is not forthcoming; turning on a radio will cease if the radio no longer provides sound; and attempting to start a car will cease if the car does not start. In each of these examples, the consequences that maintain the behavior are no longer forthcoming. The absence of reinforcing consequences reduces the behavior. Extinction can be used as a technique to reduce or eliminate behavior. First, though, the events that reinforce behavior must be identified so that they can be prevented from occurring after the response.

Developing Behavior

An outline of major principles that can be used to alter behavior has now been presented. Detailed elaboration of each of these principles follows in subsequent chapters and includes discussion of ways to apply procedures to maximize their impact. Several procedures have broad applications for developing behavior and are discussed next.

Shaping and Chaining

Reinforcing a response to increase its frequency is not always possible. In many cases, the response may never occur. The desired behavior may be so complex that the elements making up the response are not in the repertoire of the individual. For example, developing the use of words requires, among other things, the use of sounds, syllables, and their combinations. *In shaping, the terminal or goal behavior is achieved by reinforcing small steps or approximations toward the final response rather than reinforcing the final response itself.* Responses are reinforced that either resemble the final response or include components of that response. By reinforcing *successive approximations* of the final response, it is gradually achieved. Responses increasingly similar to the final goal are reinforced, and they increase; responses dissimilar to the final goal are not reinforced, and they extinguish.

Shaping, along with other procedures, is used to develop the use of language in children. Responses that approach the final goal are reinforced. Responses that do not approach that goal are extinguished. For example, when parents are trying to develop use of the words *mommy* or *daddy* in an infant, they usually reinforce any approximation (for example, *ma* or *da-da*) by smiling, hugging, and praising effusively. At the same time, but usually without thinking about it, they do not attend to (extinguish) sounds that are not close to the words they wish (for example, *goo, milk*). Over time, the parents reinforce sounds and syllables that come closer to the words *mommy* and *daddy*.

An obvious example of shaping is training animals to perform various tricks. If the animal trainer waited until the tricks were performed (for example, jumping through a burning hoop) to administer a reinforcer, it is unlikely that reinforcement would ever occur. Animals normally do not perform such behavior. By shaping the response the trainer can readily achieve the terminal goal. First, food (positive reinforcement) might be delivered for running toward the trainer. As that response becomes consistent, the trainer might reinforce running up to him when he is holding a hoop. Other steps closer to the final goal would be reinforced in sequence, including walking through the hoop on the ground, jumping through it when it is partially on fire, and finally, jumping through it when the hoop is completely on fire. Eventually, the terminal response will be performed with a high frequency, whereas the responses or steps developed along the way will have been extinguished.

As an example, shaping was used to develop appropriate speech in Alice, a 15-year-old mentally retarded girl who was severely withdrawn (Jackson & Wallace, 1974). At first, her speech was almost completely inaudible. A reinforcement program was used to shape progressively louder speech while she read various words in experimental sessions with a trainer. A microphone that she wore was used to detect the volume of her speech. At the beginning of training, only slight increases in voice volume were required. When the desired volume was registered through the microphone, a token was automatically delivered. The tokens could be used for various items that Alice desired, such as a photo album and beauty aids. When Alice's voice consistently met the volume required to earn tokens, the requirement was increased slightly. She gradually developed louder and louder speech until her voice volume was equal to that of her peers.

Shaping requires reinforcing behaviors already in the repertoire of the individual that resemble or approximate the final goal. As the initial approximation is performed consistently, the criterion for reinforcement is altered slightly so that the response to be reinforced resembles the final goal more closely than does the previous response. Through reinforcement of responses that approach the final goal and extinction of responses that do not, the terminal response is developed. In the above example, shaping was used to increase voice volume. Training began with the existing response and gradually increased volume over time. Reinforcing successive approximations is used in an identical fashion to develop new behaviors that have never been performed by the client, such as feeding, walking, and dressing.

Most behaviors consist of a sequence of several responses. A sequence of responses is referred to as a *chain*. The component parts of a chain usually represent individual responses already in the repertoire of the individual. Yet the chain represents a combination of the individual responses ordered in a particular sequence. For example, one behavioral chain that illustrates the ordering of component responses is "getting dressed." Getting dressed is a set of behaviors often trained among severely mentally retarded children. A sequence of behaviors can be identified, though this may vary depending on the specific skills of the individual. For example, the sequence may include such behaviors as taking clothes out of the drawer, placing them on a bed, putting on a shirt, and so on for other articles of clothing. Putting on individual articles of clothing also consists of a chain of behaviors. Putting on a turtleneck shirt can be divided into several constituent behaviors such as pulling the shirt over one's head, putting one's arms through the sleeves, pulling the shirt down, tucking the shirt in, and so on. These examples reflect chains of behavior because they comprise many individual responses that are linked together in a specific order.

There are many sequences or behavioral chains in everyday life. It is often the case that long sequences of behavior are performed, even though the reinforcer comes only at the very end of the chain. For example, dieting, mastering a musical instrument, preparing for athletic competition, studying for an advanced degree, and writing a book all require a series of intermediate responses before the final reinforcing event is achieved. The major question is, What maintains all of the intermediate responses that precede attaining the final goal? The answer requires explaining the factors that link the response components of a chain.

To begin with, it is important to note that an event immediately preceding reinforcement becomes a signal for reinforcement. An event that signals that behavior will be reinforced is referred to as a *discriminative stimulus* (S^D). An S^D *sets the occasion for behavior: it increases the probability that a previously reinforced behavior will occur.* An S^D not only signals reinforcement but also eventually becomes a reinforcer itself. The frequent pairing of an S^D and the reinforcer gives the S^D reinforcing properties of its own. This procedure was mentioned earlier in the discussion of conditioned reinforcement. The discriminative stimulus properties of events that precede reinforcement and the reinforcing properties of these events when they are frequently paired with reinforcers are important in explaining how chains of responses are maintained.

Consider the chain of responses involved in completing a painting. The sequence may include an indefinite number of components, beginning perhaps with purchasing paints and canvases, sketching drafts of the painting on scratch paper, drawing an outline on the canvas itself, actually painting the canvas, and finally seeing the finished product. The first response (purchasing the materials) is quite far removed from completion of the painting. Assume for a moment that seeing the final product (or for those more materially oriented, selling the painting) is the final reinforcer. Only the final response near the reinforcer—placing the final strokes of paint—are followed by the reinforcing consequences (seeing the finished product). This final response is directly reinforced with seeing the finished product. Recall that any event that precedes reinforcement becomes an S^D for reinforcement. In this chain of responses, the last response performed (painting the final strokes) becomes an S^D for reinforcement, since the response signals that reinforcement will follow. Yet the pairing of an S^D with the reinforcer (seeing the product) eventually results in the S^D's becoming a reinforcer as well as a discriminative stimulus. Hence, the response preceding direct reinforcement has become an S^D for subsequent reinforcement and a reinforcer in its own right. It serves as a reinforcer for the previous link in the chain of responses. The response (putting strokes on the canvas) becomes a reinforcer for the previous behavior (sketching the canvas). Since sketching the canvas now precedes reinforcement, it too becomes an S^D. As with other responses, the pairing of the S^D with reinforcement results in the S^D's becoming a reinforcer. The process continues in a backward direction so that each response in the chain becomes an S^D for the next response in the chain and serves as a reinforcer for the prior response in the chain.

Although the sequence appears to be maintained by a single reinforcer at the end of the chain of responses (seeing the finished product), the links in the chain are assumed to take on conditioned reinforcement value. To accomplish this, building response chains requires training from the last response in the sequence that precedes direct reinforcement back to the first response. Because the last response in the sequence is paired immediately and directly with the reinforcer, it is most easily established as a conditioned reinforcer that can maintain other responses. Also, the shorter the delay between a response and reinforcement, the greater the effect of reinforcement. The last response in the chain is immediately reinforced and is more likely to be performed frequently.

In principle, shaping and chaining are both suitable for developing new behaviors. With each technique, discriminative stimuli (such as instructions or gestures) and direct reinforcement (such as praise) may be provided for the desired behavior. The differences between shaping and chaining as well as the conditions that dictate their use may be unclear. The major difference is that *shaping* proceeds in a forward direction by developing a behavior and increasing the complexity, frequency, duration, or sequence in a progressive fashion. *Chaining* usually proceeds in a backward direction by training the final response in a sequence and building prior behaviors to develop larger units of behavior. Moreover, in shaping the goal is to develop a terminal response. The behaviors developed along the way toward the goal usually are not evident when shaping is completed. In chaining, individual behaviors developed early in training are still evident when training is completed.

In practice, shaping is the procedure used much more frequently to develop behavior. Sequences of behaviors (chains) can be developed by shaping and using cues and reinforcement for the performance of behaviors in a particular sequence. Thus, in many situations either chaining or shaping may be used. For example, toilet training of children consists of a series of responses that follow in sequence: walking to a bathroom, lowering pants, positioning oneself in front of or on the toilet, and so on. Following completion of the entire chain, praise for proper elimination can serve as reinforcement. Both shaping and chaining have been effective in developing this sequence of responses (Azrin & Foxx, 1971; Mahoney, Van Wagenen, & Meyerson, 1971).

In applied settings, shaping usually is more easily understood by those who oversee and implement behavior modification programs. Intuitively, building behavioral units or sequences that are increasingly more complex and that move toward some final goal is consistent with everyday experiences in, for example, child development or mastering a skill, such as music training, where simple responses and smaller units *precede* more complex responses and larger units of behavior. Even so, the notion of chains of behaviors is very important in its own right. The concept alerts us to the fact that our interest is not merely in increasing this or that behavior but rather in building sequences of behaviors. For example, to increase a child's completion of homework, the sequence of behaviors may include bringing home an assignment book and the books needed to do the homework, working on the homework, completing that homework, reviewing or showing this work to a parent, and taking it to school the next day or due date, and so on. In developing this sequence, it is important to be mindful of the constitutent behaviors as well as the sequence of behaviors. At the inception of the reinforcement program, we may reinforce individual acts; eventually, we wish to provide reinforcement at the end of the entire sequence of behaviors.

Prompting and Fading

Developing a behavior is facilitated by using cues, instructions, gestures, directions, examples, and models to initiate a response. *Prompts are events that help initiate a response.* They come before a response has been performed and are designed to facilitate its performance. When a prompt results in the response, the response can be reinforced. Without the prompt, the response might occur infrequently or not at all. Prompts serve as antecedent events (e.g., instructions, gestures) that help generate the desired response.

Behavior can be prompted in different ways, such as *guiding* the behavior of a person physically (for example, holding a child's arm to assist him in placing a spoon in his mouth), *instructing* a person to do something, *pointing* to a person to do something (for example, to come inside the house), and *having a person observe* another person (a model) perform a behavior (such as, having a person watch someone else play a game). Prompts play a major role in shaping. Developing a terminal response using reinforcement alone may be tedious and time consuming. Assisting a person in beginning the response can enable the person to make more rapid approximations to the final response. For example, several different types of prompts were used to teach a job skill to profoundly retarded adult women (Schepis, Reid, & Fitzgerald, 1987). The women could comply only with simple requests and engaged in aggressive and self-injurious behavior. The goal was to train a job skill that consisted of preparing envelopes for mailing, including stamping a return address on the envelopes. To train the task, different kinds of prompts were used. Verbal instructions (verbal prompt) were provided to explain the sequence of behaviors; modeling (visual prompt) was provided if the individual did not show the requisite behaviors; finally, the individual was aided by guiding her through the task with physical assistance (physical prompt). These prompts were designed to increase the likelihood of correct performance of the behaviors, so that reinforcement (in this case praise) could be provided. While a response is being shaped, prompts may be used frequently to facilitate performance of the terminal response.

Although prompts are cues that initiate behavior, they often take on the value of events (consequences) that follow them. Thus, if the prompted behavior is consistently reinforced, the prompt may become an S^D for reinforcement. For example, if a parent tells a child to return home from school early and the child is praised when he or she does this, the instruction (prompt) becomes an S^D. Instructions signal that reinforcement is likely when certain behaviors are performed. Eventually, instructions alone are likely to be followed by the behavior. In general, when a prompt consistently precedes reinforcement of a response, the prompt becomes an S^D and can effectively control behavior.

Prompts can become aversive if they are associated with punishing consequences. For example, parents may constantly remind (prompt) their teenage son or daughter to clean his or her room, to practice playing a musical instrument, or to do homework. These prompts become aversive because they are cues for other aversive events (for example, threats, loss of privileges and reprimands at home; poor grades at school). It takes little time for such prompts to become aversive in their own right. A child may try to terminate the aversive prompts by completing the prompted behavior, leaving the room, or shouting at the parent. In behavior modification programs, prompts typically are used to initiate behavior, so that it can be positively reinforced. Once reinforcement can be provided, the behavior can be maintained by the reinforcing consequences.

Usually, the ultimate goal is to obtain the terminal response in the absence of prompts. Although prompts may be required early in training, they can be withdrawn gradually or faded as training progresses. *Fading refers to the gradual removal of a prompt.* If a prompt is removed abruptly early in training, the response may no longer be performed. But if the response is performed consistently with a prompt, the prompt can be progressively reduced and finally omitted. For example, teaching a person how to serve in tennis or how to play the piano may include reminders (prompts) regarding how to hold the racket or how to place his or her fingers on the keys. As the person begins to perform these behaviors, the prompt can be provided less frequently. The correct behaviors are reinforced without reminders and soon do not need to be prompted at all or only very rarely.

For example, in the study mentioned previously, prompts were used to train a specific set of behaviors with mentally retarded women (Schepis, Reid, and Fitzgerald, 1987). Over the course of training and as the behaviors were performed correctly, trainers began to fade the prompts. The number of prompts was decreased over time, and more intrusive (physical) prompts were decreased or eliminated. The terminal goal of the project was to develop the behavior so that it could be performed independently (that is, without prompts). This goal was facilitated by introducing prompts to develop the behavior and by gradually fading and eliminating the prompts and reinforcing independent performance.

The achievement of behavior without prompts requires fading and reinforcing the responses in the absence of prompts. It is not always necessary to remove all prompts. For example, it is important to train individuals to respond in the presence of certain prompts, such as instructions, that exert control over a variety of behaviors in everyday life.

ANTECEDENTS OF BEHAVIOR

Consequences *are* very important, but theory, research, and common sense tell us that they are insufficient in understanding or, in many instances, changing behavior. Different types of antecedents are used in behavior modification and in programs designed to change behavior. Prompts have already been discussed as one type of antecedent event. It is useful to consider antecedents more generally.

Setting Events

Setting events refer to contextual factors or conditions that influence behavior. They are broad in scope and include conditions that influence what type of stimuli and responses may follow. Such events set the stage for the behaviors and contingencies that follow. Setting events include features of the situation, features of the task presented to the individual, conditions within the individual (for example, exhaustion, hunger), or behaviors of others that may influence what the individual is likely to do and what consequences will follow. For example, a child may hear a heated argument or perhaps witness violence between his or her parents before going to school. That day at school, the child may be more irritable, more reactive, and less attentive to schoolwork. These events in turn may lead to a sequence of contingencies with teachers and peers. As another example, an elementary school teacher may have learned of an unexpected salary increase in the morning before his or her first class. After the good news, the teacher may respond slightly differently than usual by infrequently invoking classroom rules or providing aversive consequences. In each of these examples, the setting events refer to factors that influence subsequent sequences of behavior.

Setting events are important, which is not the same thing as saying they are completely understood. They are often difficult to identify because they do not necessarily occur immediately before behavior. Loss of a parent, for example, is a setting event that may, over time, influence many domains of behavior in different ways and with varying degrees of influence. To propose a simple relation between a setting event and a sequence of behaviors that follows would be oversimplistic. Yet, the general class of setting events is important to acknowledge and distinguish because they influence complex sequences that follow, including antecedent-behavior consequences that are likely to occur (Wahler & Fox, 1981).

Setting events are less well studied in applied research than are consequences. Even so, their influence has been amply demonstrated to convey the importance of their consideration. For example, how parents interact with their oppositional children appears to be influenced by parent social interaction outside the home (Wahler, 1980). When mothers experience positive social contacts outside the home with friends, they show more aversive interchanges and promote deviant child behavior at home. As assessed on a daily basis, mothers' social interactions seem to provide a setting event that influenced subsequent contingencies in the repertoire of the mothers and then their children. Similarly, in a classroom situation, disruptive behavior during a storytelling period varied as a functioning of the antecedent activities before storytelling (Krantz & Risley, 1977). Disruptive behavior was greater when the prior period included physical activity than when it was a quiet (rest) period. In lay language, one might say that the children "had to calm down" before the story. The formulation in terms of setting events is more helpful because calming down is not necessarily the issue. Rather, it is useful to consider the more general principle, namely, that the contexts, situations, and settings alter the probability of subsequent sequences of behaviors. In some cases, systematic assessment of setting events can suggest interventions that are likely to be helpful, a topic to which we shall later return.

Stimulus Events

Stimulus events are more specific and discrete types of antecedents that influence behavior. The specific stimuli increase the likelihood that specific behaviors will follow. It is important to note that stimuli that precede behavior do not *cause* behavior to occur. Rather, the presence of some stimuli increase the likelihood of a particular behavior; the absence of the stimuli or presence of different stimuli have no influence or decrease the likelihood that same behavior will occur.

More is known about stimulus events and how they acquire their value and influence than about the more global, contextual setting events mentioned earlier. Stimulus events appear to acquire their ability to exert control over behavior by their associated consequences. In some situations (or in the presence of certain stimuli), a response may be reinforced; in other situations (in the presence of other stimuli), the same response is not reinforced.

The concept of differential reinforcement is central to understanding stimulus events and their influence. *Differential reinforcement refers to reinforcing a response in the presence of one stimulus and not reinforcing the same response in the presence of another stimulus.* When a response is consistently reinforced in the presence of a particular stimulus and consistently not reinforced in the presence of another stimulus, each stimulus signals the consequences that are likely to follow. As mentioned earlier, a stimulus whose presence has been associated with reinforcement is referred to as an S^D. A stimulus whose presence has been associated with nonreinforcement is referred to as an S^Δ (S delta). The effect of differential reinforcement is that eventually the reinforced response is likely to occur in the presence of the S^D but unlikely to occur in the presence of the S^Δ. When responses are differentially controlled by antecedent stimuli, behavior is said to be under *stimulus control.*

Instances of stimulus control pervade everyday life. For example, the sound of a doorbell signals that a certain behavior (opening the door) is likely to be reinforced (by seeing someone). Specifically, the sound of the bell frequently has been associated with the presence of visitors at the door (the reinforcer). The ring of the bell (S^D) increases the likelihood that the door will be opened. In the absence of the bell (S^Δ), the probability of opening the door for a visitor is very low. The ring of a doorbell, telephone, alarm, and kitchen timer all serve as discriminative stimuli (S^D) and signal that certain responses are likely to be reinforced. Hence, the probability of the responses is increased.

Stimulus control is also evident in the selection and consumption of food. For example, the color and smell of foods (such as an orange that has turned blue or milk that smells sour) influence the likelihood of eating them. Characteristics of the foods are cues for particular consequences (such as flavor or nausea) and exert stimulus control over our eating. In recognition of this point, natural foods (for example, fruit) or products (for example, leather) often have artificial colors and fragrances added to increase the likelihood of their purchase. In social interaction, stimulus control also is important. For example, a smile or wink from someone is likely to occasion a social response on our part, such as the initiation of conversation. Whereas a smile serves as an S^D (signals that reinforcement is likely to follow our social response), a frown serves as an S^Δ (signals that reinforcement is not likely to follow a social response).

People in everyday life are quite familiar with the concepts of differential reinforcement and stimulus control, although these terms, of course, are not used. For example, children behave differently in the presence of their mothers and fathers in part because of the different reinforcement contingencies that operate. Children often know whom to ask (mother or father) in making specific requests because the likelihood of reinforcement (affirmative answer) differs between parents on various issues. Similarly, at home children often behave quite differently than at school. The different performances may lead to perplexed parents and teachers who argue that the child is not "really" like that. Yet, the child's behavior may vary considerably as a function of different reinforcement contingencies at home and at school.

The significance of differential reinforcement and stimulus control is difficult to convey in everyday examples because many events are operative that obscure the factors that control behavior. The impact of differential reinforcement and its role in leading to differences in behavior are illustrated clearly in a study completed several years ago (Redd & Birnbrauer, 1969). In this study, two adults working at different times provided mentally retarded children with food (candy, ice cream, or sips of cola) and praise for performing a specified response (for example, playing cooperatively with another child). When the first adult was with one child, reinforcement was administered for the cooperative response (contingent delivery of praise). When the second adult was present, reinforcement was delivered to the same child independently of actual behavior (noncontingent delivery of praise). Overall, each adult administered the same amount of the available reinforcers. In a short period, the adults exerted stimulus control over the behavior of the children. The presence of the adult who was associated with the contingent delivery of praise led to cooperative play, whereas the presence of the adult who was associated with the noncontingent delivery of praise did not. The children discriminated the different contingencies associated with the adults. Thus, adults can serve as discriminative stimuli for reinforcement. Children respond differentially to adults, depending upon the behaviors that are reinforced in each adult's presence.

The notion of stimulus control is exceedingly important in behavior modification. In many programs, the goal is to alter the relation between behavior and the stimulus conditions in which the behavior occurs. Some behavior problems stem from a failure of certain stimuli to control behavior when such control would be desirable. For example, children who do not follow instructions given by their parents illustrate a lack of stimulus control. The instructions do not exert influence over the children's behavior. The goal of a behavior modification program is to increase responsiveness to instructions.

DISCRIMINATION AND STIMULUS CONTROL

There are additional ways to refer to the influence of antecedent events that are directly related to the preceding discussion. When the presence of the stimulus events leads to an increase or decrease in the behavior, the individual is said to have made a *discrimination* and behavior is said to be under *stimulus control*. Discrimination refers to the fact that the individual *responds differently under different stimulus conditions.* Discrimination and stimulus control are always operative in behavior modification programs. Programs are conducted in particular settings (for example, the home) and are administered by particular individuals (for example, parents). Insofar as certain behaviors are reinforced or punished in the presence of particular individuals or certain environmental cues and not in the presence of other stimuli, the behaviors will be under stimulus control. In the presence of cues associated with the behavior modification program, the client will behave in a particular fashion. In the absence of those cues, behavior is likely to change because the contingencies in new situations are altered.

A familiar example of discrimination and stimulus control that may arise in a behavior modification program pertains to the behavior of students when the teacher is in, rather than out of, the classroom. As most of us recall from elementary school years, the amount of disruptive behavior often varied depending upon whether the teacher was in the room enforcing the rules of the classroom. Once the stimulus (teacher) associated with the reinforcing or punishing consequences was no longer present, behavior often deteriorated. Indeed, the stimulus control that individuals such as parents and teachers exert over behavior often creates a problem in behavior modification. The children may perform the responses in the presence of parents or teachers but not in their absence. Special contingency arrangements are often needed to ensure that the desired behaviors transfer to new people, situations, and places.

The control that different stimuli exert over behavior explains why behavior often is situation specific. Individuals may behave one way in a given situation or in the presence of a particular person and behave differently in another situation or in the presence of another person. Because different reinforcement contingencies operate in different circumstances, individuals can discriminate among the stimuli that are likely to be followed by reinforcement.

People make discriminations across a variety of situations for most behaviors. For example, eating habits probably vary depending upon whether one is at home or in a restaurant. At home it is more likely that people will place bunched napkins, books, elbows, and feet on the table when they eat meals; these behaviors are much less likely in a restaurant. Discriminations are made that are even more subtle. Eating behavior may differ depending upon whether one is in an expensive or a fast-food restaurant. Also, people behave differently in the presence of fellow workers than with their boss. Numerous other variations in behavior are evident because of differences in situations and the contingencies associated with them.

GENERALIZATION

The effect of reinforcement on behavior may either extend beyond the conditions in which training has taken place or extend to behaviors other than those included in the program. The ways in which effects of the program may extend beyond the contingency are referred to as *general-ization.*

Stimulus Generalization

Behavior occurs in specific situations. A response repeatedly reinforced in the presence of a particular situation is likely to be repeated in that situation. However, situations and stimuli often share common properties. The control exerted by a given stimulus is shared by other stimuli that are similar or share common properties (Skinner, 1953). A behavior may be performed in new situations similar to the situation in which reinforcement occurred. Stimulus generalization occurs if a response reinforced in one situation or setting also increases in other settings (even though it is not reinforced in the other settings). *Stimulus generalization refers to the generalization or transfer of a response to situations other than those in which training takes place.*

Generalization is the opposite of discrimination. When an individual discriminates in the performance of a response, this means that the response fails to generalize across situations. Alternatively, when a response generalizes across situations, the individual fails to discriminate in his or her performance of that response.

Figure 2–2 illustrates stimulus generalization. S_1 refers to the *stimulus condition,* or the situation in which the response is reinforced. R_1 refers to the *response,* or the behavior that is reinforced. The figure shows that the trained response (R_1) is performed across a variety of stimuli or situations (S_2, S_3, S_4, S_5). The degree of stimulus generalization is a function of the similarity of new stimuli (or situations) to the stimulus under which the response was trained. Of course, over a long period of time, a response may not generalize across situations because the individual discriminates that the response is reinforced in one situation but not in others.

Examples of stimulus generalization are frequent in everyday experience. For example, a child may talk about certain topics in the presence of his family because talking about those topics is reinforced (for example, discussed freely, attended to) among family members. The child may also discuss the same topics in the presence of company. In that case, the child's behavior (talking about certain topics) has generalized across situations. Parents may show considerable embarrassment when children freely discuss family secrets or embarrassing personal topics (for example, how one's father puts on his toupee or how a parent looks in the shower). Generalization is also readily apparent when a child responds to a teacher in a fashion similar to the fashion in which he or she responds to a parent (for example, in the expression of affection). To the extent that a child sees parents and teachers as similar, the stimulus control exerted by parents will be shared by the teacher. Because the antecedent events (approaches by the adult, expressions of affection) and the consequent events (hugs,

Stimulus conditions
(situations)

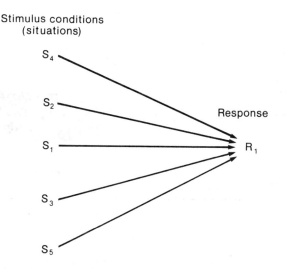

FIGURE 2–2
Stimulus generalization: A response (R_1) reinforced in one situation (S_1) generalizes to other, similar situations (S_2, S_3, S_4, S_5).

kisses) are different for the child in relation to teachers and parents, the child quickly learns a discrimination. Consequently, expressions of affection are more likely in the presence of parents (S^D) than of teachers (S^Δ).

An example of generalization across situations and stimulus conditions was reported in a program for a 21-year-old hospitalized schizophrenic patient (Fichter, Wallace, Liberman, & Davis, 1976). The patient was very withdrawn and spoke inaudibly when he did speak. Also, he spoke very briefly and engaged in inappropriate hand gestures, such as tapping his face with his fingers, biting his fingers, and rocking with his hands between his thighs. Treatment consisted of prompting louder and longer speech and appropriate use of hands and arms (for example, placing them on the armrests of a chair) while he interacted socially with a staff member. The prompting procedure was conducted in the hospital. After the patient was discharged, observations were also conducted in the residential care home where he lived and in the day-treatment center where he spent his days. The observations revealed that the improvements achieved in the hospital extended to these other settings, even though the prompts were never used there. Thus, behavior *generalized* to new staff members, new settings, and across new topics of conversation that were not included in training.

Stimulus generalization represents an exceedingly important issue in behavior modification. Invariably, training takes place in a restricted setting such as a classroom, a home, a hospital ward, and/or an institution. It is desirable that behaviors developed in these settings generalize or transfer to other settings.

Response Generalization

Another type of generalization involves responses rather than stimulus conditions. Altering one response can inadvertently influence other responses. For example, if a person is praised for smiling, the frequency not only of smiling but also of laughing and talking might increase. *The reinforcement of a response increases the probability of other responses that are similar* (Skinner, 1953). This is referred to as *response generalization.* To the extent that a nonreinforced response is similar to one that is reinforced, the probability of the nonreinforced response increases. Response generalization is depicted in Figure 2–3, where S_1 refers to the stimulus condition in which training of a response takes place and R_1 refers to the response that is reinforced. Although only one response is trained in the situation, a variety of similar responses (R_2, R_3, R_4, R_5) may also be performed.

Altering one behavior is often associated with changes in other behaviors as well. For example, according to one report, altering noncompliance (not completing the requests of adults) in four children also decreased such inappropriate behaviors as aggression (pushing, hitting, biting), disruption (whining, crying, screaming), property destruction (pushing, kicking furniture, pounding on or throwing objects), and the placing of inedible objects in their mouths (Parrish, Cataldo, Kolko, Neef, & Egel, 1986). Alternative procedures, based primarily on variations of positive reinforcement, effectively increased compliance among these children. Interestingly, when their compliance increased, their aggression, disruption, and other inappropriate behaviors decreased, even though there had been no specific focus on these other behaviors.

The notion of response generalization is often used to explain changes in responses other than the target response. Technically, the term *response generalization* may not be accurate for two reasons. First, responses that are not supposed to be focused on may inadvertently receive reinforcing consequences. For example, a child praised for studying in class may improve in reading even though reading may not have been the response to which the reinforcing consequences were directed. Although this may be spoken of as generalization, it may reflect the direct operation of reinforcement and not be generalization at all. When a child is praised for paying attention, he or she may be reading on some of the occasions that reinforcement is delivered. Thus, it is difficult to speak of response generalization, because the behavior was directly reinforced.

There is a second, slightly more complex reason that response generalization may not accurately account for the many changes that occur with treatment. Response generalization refers to changes in behaviors that are similar to the target behavior. Yet research has shown many examples in which change in one behavior has consistent effects on other behaviors that appear to have no direct relation or resemblance to the target behavior. For example, in one study, the excessive talking of a 7-year-old boy was altered

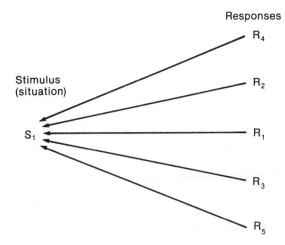

Responses

FIGURE 2–3

Response generalization: Reinforcement of one response (R_1) in a given situation (S_1) may result in an increase of other, similar responses (R_2, R_3, R_4, R_5).

by withdrawing teacher attention (Sajwaj, Twardosz, & Burke, 1972). Other behaviors changed as well; for example, the boy's conversation and cooperative play with his peers increased and his use of "girls'" toys during free play decreased. These behaviors had no clear relation to the target focus and could not be accounted for by changes in teacher attention to them. It is unclear why the other behaviors changed because only excessive verbalizations with the teacher were altered. Similarly, other studies have shown that changing one behavior may result in changes in behaviors bearing no obvious relation to that behavior (see Kazdin, 1982a).

The reasons that various responses change when treatment focuses on a particular behavior are unclear. Wahler (1975) has carefully observed children over extended periods in the home and at school and has found that individuals often have clusters of behavior (that is, groups of specific behaviors that consistently go together). For example, for one child, engaging in self-stimulation, socially interacting with adults, complying with adult instructions, and other behaviors tended to go together. Treatment that focused on one behavior that was part of the cluster altered other behaviors as well. The spread of treatment effects to those behaviors could not be explained by the similarity of the behaviors.

The tendency of responses to change together or as a cluster has been referred to as *response covariation.* The responses co-vary (are correlated and change together). A number of studies have demonstrated that behaviors cluster and that altering one of the behaviors in a cluster alters other behaviors as well. The spread of the effects of altering a behavior in a cluster can be predicted by knowing what other behaviors are in the cluster.

That behaviors cluster and often come in "packages" with other behaviors is fairly well established (Elliott, Huizinga, & Menard, 1988). How the clusters of behaviors are formed and why particular patterns are found is less well understood.

In behavior modification, the concepts of stimulus and response generalization are ordinarily used to denote that changes occur across various stimulus conditions (situations or settings) or across responses. In fact, however, there is rarely any evidence that the spread of treatment effects across stimulus or response dimensions is actually based on the *similarity* of the stimuli or responses to those used in training. Technically, therefore, the terms *stimulus* and *response generalization* are often used incorrectly. Even so, the technical difficulties in using these terms do not detract from the importance of the spread of treatment effects across stimulus conditions or behaviors during the course of treatment.

CONCLUSION

The principles outlined in this chapter provide the basis for most of the operant conditioning programs in applied settings. The principles may seem overwhelming at first because of the many different terms that were introduced. Yet these principles describe basic relationships between events and behavior and account for diverse treatment interventions. The complexity of the programs used in behavior modification cannot be conveyed by a mere statement of the principles. Each principle requires elaboration because a number of factors determine its effective application. In later chapters, principles that have been widely employed in a variety of settings will receive detailed attention.

Notes

1. Discussion of the principles introduces several new terms. To aid the reader, major terms and their definitions are italicized when they are first introduced. Also, a glossary at the end of the book provides a summary definition of the major terms that arise in this chapter and throughout the text.
2. As Skinner (1974) has noted, the word *pain* traces to Latin and Greek. The Latin word from which it was derived refers to punishment, which explains in part why the two notions are inextricably bound in language and thought.
3. Altering the sex-role behaviors of children has raised many controversial issues about whether the definition of appropriate behaviors should be based on traditional values, whether treatment of the children was warranted, and whether the long-term goals of heterosexual adjustment were appropriate or necessarily facilitated by treatment (see Nordyke, Baer, Etzel, & LeBlanc, 1977; Winkler, 1977). Issues raised in the selection of behaviors for intervention will be discussed further in Chapter 13.

For Further Reading

Catania, A. C. (1992). *Learning* (3rd ed.). Englewood Cliffs, NJ: Prentice-Hall.

Cooper, J. O., Heron, T. E., & Heward, W. L. (1987). *Applied behavior analysis.* Columbus, OH: Merrill.

Sulzer-Azaroff, B., & Mayer, G. R. (1991). *Behavior analysis for lasting change.* Fort Worth, TX: Holt, Rinehart & Winston.

Wahler, R. G., & Fox, J. J. (1981). Setting events in applied behavior analysis: Toward a conceptual and methodological expansion. *Journal of Applied Behavior Analysis, 14,* 327–338.

C H A P T E R T H R E E

How to Identify, Define, and Assess Behavior

A behavior modification program is not begun merely by choosing a particular technique and trying it out on a client. The success of behavior modification has resulted not only from the specific techniques that are used but also from the ways in which behaviors are measured and intervention programs are evaluated. Successful treatment depends on carefully identifying, defining, and measuring behaviors. If behaviors are carefully identified and defined, then consequences contingent upon their performance can be applied. If behaviors can be consistently observed, one can evaluate whether the behavior modification program is leading to change. If the program is not working, the intervention can be modified until behavioral change is obtained.

Apart from observing the behavior of interest, observations can be made of situational and environmental events that may contribute to behavior. As mentioned in the previous chapter, setting and stimulus events are important because they provide clues about features of the situation that lead to the behavior of interest. When such events can be identified, developing behavior change programs can be greatly facilitated.

This chapter and the next consider requirements for measuring behavior, evaluating whether behavior change has occurred, and determining whether the behavior modification program was responsible for the change. These topics are important for understanding how to implement various behavioral techniques, for selecting which interventions are likely to be effective, and for deciding whether treatment has or has not produced the desired change.

IDENTIFYING THE GOAL OF THE PROGRAM

Implementation of a behavior modification program requires clearly stating the goal of the program and carefully describing the behaviors that are to be developed. The main goal of a program is to alter or develop a particular behavior referred to as the *target behavior*. If the target behavior is performed too infrequently or not at all, it should be increased; if the target behavior is performed too frequently, it should be decreased. The goal of changing behavior applies to a particular stimulus condition (such as the home, the classroom, certain times of the day, the presence of particular individuals). Thus, both the behavior and the situation in which it is or is not to be performed must be identified.

Guidelines

Identifying the goal of the program is often obvious and straightforward because the importance, adaptiveness, and need for the behavior is widely accepted and the consequences for not engaging in the behavior are undesired. Many target behaviors in behavior modification are of this ilk, and examples would include encouraging individuals to eat healthy foods or reducing fighting among children repeatedly expelled for aggressive behavior. These behaviors generally are well accepted as important insofar as health and adaptive interpersonal interaction are viewed as important.

It is useful to go beyond examples and to consider some of the salient criteria invoked for selecting goals of behavioral and other programs (see Hawkins, 1986; Nelson & Hayes, 1986). These criteria are better conceived of as guidelines derived from an examination of what is, in fact, the focus of many intervention programs. Table 3–1 lists some of the criteria/guidelines that determine the goal of a program and target behaviors that are examples of each criterion. Obviously, a given behavior may meet more than one criterion.

An issue raised by the criteria in the table is the direction of change desired. In many cases the goal is to increase positive, prosocial behavior (for example, increase interactions with peers); in other cases the goal is to decrease undesirable or inappropriate behavior. In behavioral approaches to treatment, this distinction is often blurred because there is an effort to develop positive, prosocial behaviors in virtually all programs. Even when the goal seems to be to decrease, suppress, or eliminate behaviors, the conceptualization of the problem and the interventions used to change the problem are often based on developing positive, adaptive behaviors. The importance of developing positive behaviors is discussed further in later chapters.

The criteria regarding the selection of goals and target behaviors listed in Table 3–1 are helpful only in a general way. Firm and fast criteria are difficult to identify because the focus of intervention research often de-

T A B L E   3–1

Selected Criteria for Identifying Goals of Intervention Programs

Criterion/guideline	Target behavior examples
Behaviors that bring clients to normative levels of functioning in relation to their peers	Interaction with peers; exercise and activity of elderly persons
Behaviors that are dangerous to oneself or to others	Self-injurious behaviors; fighting at school; spouse abuse
Behaviors that decrease risk for injury, illness, or physical or psychological dysfunctions	Safe sex practices; not smoking cigarettes; wearing seat belts
Behaviors that affect adaptive functioning	Deficits in social interaction; not attending school or work
Behaviors that can lead to other positive changes	Increasing prosocial speech; taking medicines as prescribed
Behaviors that reduce felt problems of individuals (parents, teachers, colleagues) with whom client is in contact	Tantrums of child; poor marital communication

pends on definitions of abnormality, deviance, dysfunction, inappropriate behaviors, and desirable and undesirable lifestyles. In extreme cases, there is agreement on a given focus. Yet, appropriate goals for intervention research are debated within and well beyond behavior modification. We shall look at controversial issues regarding target behaviors in the final chapter of the book. For now, rudimentary information about selecting and assessing target behaviors is more critical.

Although the goal of the program may be to change some behavior, the situation or context in which the behavior occurs is likely to be very important. Thus, it is also important to specify the conditions under which the behavior is to be performed (antecedents, consequences). For many behaviors, the definition of the problem includes contextual and stimulus conditions. For example, many behavioral problems stem from a failure to perform behaviors in the presence of particular antecedent events. Such failures are considered to reflect a lack of appropriate stimulus control. For example, a child may complete schoolwork when he or she should be looking at the board, reciting, or playing at recess. The teacher may constantly remind the child to put his or her materials away or to pay attention. Yet the child's behavior is not controlled by these instructions (antecedent events). Training may focus on instructing the child to engage in some behavior and on reinforcing compliance.

Similarly, parents may wish to train their children not to talk to strangers who offer them candy or ask them to enter their cars. Parents do not want children to act suspiciously toward some of the new adults they meet (for example, new teachers at school, distant relatives they have not seen previously, parents of their friends). The goal requires training children to act cautiously only in special circumstances that may be dangerous. Thus, the antecedent events and situational cues become essential for deciding what behaviors are to be performed. For all behavioral programs, one can ask a basic question: Under what circumstances or in the presence of what cues should the target behavior be performed? Ultimately, the program will focus on developing specific behaviors in the presence of certain cues and not in the absence of those cues.

In some cases, the initial goal of the program may be to develop the responsiveness of individuals to certain consequent events. These individuals usually do not respond to events that play a major role in social interaction, such as attention, physical contact, praise, or mild disapproval. For example, autistic children, who show pervasive deficits in language and social behavior, are often unresponsive to events that are reinforcing for most children (Schreibman, 1988). Similarly, delinquents and conduct problem children in the home are often unresponsive to praise (Herbert, Pinkston, Hayden, Sajwaj, Pinkston, Cordua, & Jackson, 1973). In such cases, contingencies are devised to alter the value of such stimuli as physical contact or praise from an adult. In these programs, neutral stimuli (for example, statements of approval) are paired with reinforcing events (for example, food and termination of an aversive event). Eventually, the previously neutral stimuli serve as positive reinforcers. Once the events have been established as reinforcers, they can be used to develop specific behaviors.

Task Analysis

It is often the case that *a* target behavior is identified and the goal, for example, is to increase the frequency of a single or simple behavior (such as correctly completing assignments). In many cases, the goal of the program is to develop a complex set of behaviors. Altering more complex sets of behaviors is facilitated by a process referred to as *task analysis*. Task analysis is a way of proceeding from the general goal of the program to a number of small, trainable, and highly concrete behaviors. The purpose of task analysis is to identify specific behaviors required and to break down or divide a complex sequence of behaviors into component parts.

A task analysis is deceptively simple because the behaviors that eventually are selected may seem obvious and straightforward. The initial component of task analysis is to identify the desired behaviors. This component may follow from an evaluation of appropriate or competent behavior among persons who are performing well. Thus, if one wishes to develop social skills in a withdrawn or rejected child, an initial task is to examine the competent social behavior of children who are functioning well (that is, those who are accepted or popular). Competent social behavior helps to identify the terminal behaviors that are required. In some cases, the desired behaviors are identified by soliciting the input of persons with expertise in specific areas. Such persons are consulted to identify the behaviors to be performed or how they are to be performed. For example, developing a program of behaviors to prevent or to detect a disease early may require soliciting the views of health experts. The behaviors they identify (for example, how to check oneself for early signs of the disease) are translated into concrete behaviors that form the goals of the program.

However the behaviors are identified, a critical feature of task analysis is to specify the requisite behaviors in small, trainable units. This component may be difficult, because there are no firm rules for dividing behaviors or for establishing the units that constitute trainable components. Training may require smaller or larger units of behavior, depending on the initial level of client skill or ability. Along with the identification of specific trainable components, the order or sequence of the behaviors needs to be specified. Training then proceeds to develop each individual component into the larger sequence until the entire set of behaviors is trained.

Task analysis is nicely illustrated in a behavioral program for brain-injured adolescents and adults who suffered injuries from vehicle accidents (O'Reilly, Green, & Braunling-McMorrow, 1990). Each individual experienced severe cognitive and behavioral dysfunction due to his or her injury. The purpose of the program was to train individuals to prevent hazards in daily living. Common preventable home hazards that most frequently lead to injury were identified from materials available from the National Safety Council. Task analysis for each hazardous situation was developed by observing how nonhandicapped adults remedied unsafe situations. Hazards were identified in separate rooms of an apartment used for training. Behaviors for rectifying hazards in relation to the kitchen, one of four rooms studied, are listed in Table 3–2. As the table shows, very concrete behaviors were identified. Completion of these behaviors would constitute appropriate behaviors to prevent common accidents in the kitchen.

The careful specification of behavior in the previous example illustrates the behavioral approach toward identifying goals of the program, translating these goals to concrete behaviors, and previewing the task of treatment, namely, training the specific behaviors. In the case of this example, safe behaviors were trained by practice, prompts, and reinforcement to develop each of the constituent behaviors in each of the rooms. Task analysis was useful in breaking down the behaviors so the correct number

TABLE 3–2
Task Analysis for Remediating Hazards in the Kitchen

Kitchen
A. Grease on stove top.
   1. Get paper towels and appropriate cleaner from materials box under sink.
   2. With towels and cleaner, wipe grease from stove until no grease can be seen.
   3. Throw paper towels in trash and return cleaner to materials box.
B. Paper napkins on stove top.
   1. Remove paper from stove top.
   2. Place paper in trash.
C. Smoke detector beside stove.
   1. Remove smoke detector from cooking area.
   2. Get paper towel from materials box under sink.
   3. Wipe dust from smoke detector until no dust is visible.
   4. Press test button to make sure smoke detector is working.
   5. Place smoke detector near ceiling at least 15 feet from stove.
D. Trash can beside stove.
   1. Place trash can at least 5 feet away from stove.
E. Drinking glasses at edge of kitchen counter.
   1. Place glasses at least 1 foot from edge of counter.
F. Broken glass on floor.
   1. Get broom and dustpan from broom closet.
   2. Sweep glass into dustpan until dustpan is full.
   3. Empty dustpan into trash.
   4. Repeat until no glass can be seen on floor.
G. Cleaner (poison) beside food in cabinet.
   1. Place cleaners at least 5 feet away from food.
   2. Place cleaners that are not in their proper containers in the trash.

SOURCE: O'Reilly, M. F., Green, G., & Braunling-McMorrow, D. (1990).

of trials could be assessed and for shaping behavior—that is, developing successive approximations of the behavior.

In a quite different focus, adult males (ages 25 to 35) were trained to examine themselves for signs of testicular cancer (Friman, Finney, Glasscock, Weigel, & Christophersen, 1986). Such self-examination is important because testicular cancer is one of the leading causes of death of men ages 15 to 40. To train correct self-examination, it was first critical to identify precisely what behaviors were required. The list of required behaviors was obtained by discussing the task with urologists and by consulting written and film materials about testicular cancer. The specific behaviors that constitute appropriate self-examination are listed in Table 3–3. Again, careful identification of the requisite behaviors greatly facilitated evaluation of the program and effective training. Individuals were successfully trained in self-examination and reported continuing performance of the behaviors up to several months later.

In many behavioral applications, task analysis has been crucial in breaking down complex behaviors so that they can be assessed and trained. Task analyses have been extremely helpful in training persons in cardiopulmonary resuscitation (CPR) techniques to help revive individuals who have suffered a heart attack (Seaman, Greene, & Watson-Perczel, 1986), in teaching adults with a diagnosis of autism to purchase items in stores (Haring, Kennedy, Adams, & Pitts-Conway, 1987), and in training persons with mental retardation to engage in first-aid skills (Marchand-Martella, Martella, Agran, Salzberg, Young, & Morgan, 1992) and food preparation for themselves (Griffen, Wolery, & Schuster, 1992).

The persons who design behavioral interventions often do not have the expertise needed to identify the desired behaviors for a task analysis. To identify such behaviors, they may have to consult experts or other persons with special knowledge in specific areas. In the above examples, this was done to determine what behaviors were required for apartment upkeep and for correct self-examination for signs of testicular cancer. The task of the

TABLE 3–3
Tasks Required for Testicular Self-Examination

1. Gently pulls scrotum so that it hangs freely.
2. Uses fingers and thumbs of both hands to isolate and examine one testicle.
3. Locates the soft tender mass (the epididymis and spermatic cord) on top of and extending behind the testicle.
4. Rotates the entire surface area of the testicle between fingers and thumbs.
5. Uses fingers and thumbs to isolate and examine the other testicle.
6. Locates the soft tender mass on top of and extending behind the testicle.
7. Rotates the entire surface area of the testicle between fingers and thumbs.

SOURCE: Friman, P. C., Finney, J. W., Glasscock, S. G., Weigel, J. W., & Christophersen, E. R. (1986).

person designing the behavioral program is to translate into concrete steps and small units of behavior the larger goals or practices that have been identified.

A complexity of task analysis has to do with the degree of specificity of the individual behaviors and with the unit or amount of behavior that any one step should include. For some behaviors or clients, many small units of behavior may be grouped into one step in the task analysis; for other behaviors or clients, many more steps may have to be delineated and trained separately. As an example, training dressing skills might require different steps in a task analysis for severely retarded children than for nonretarded children. Division of the behavior into smaller units might facilitate training with the children functioning at a lower level. There are no firm guidelines for delineating the number of steps, but it is likely that the decision will be based on the complexity of the goal, the initial behaviors (baseline level) of the persons who are to be trained, and the speed with which the behaviors are acquired during training.

The effectiveness of behavioral interventions very much depends on identifying specific behaviors so that they can be assessed and trained. Once specific behaviors have been identified, they can often be changed. Many behavioral techniques (for example, shaping, feedback, positive reinforcement) can readily alter the specific behaviors of interest and ensure performance of the desired sequence of responses. However, the initial task is careful identification and specification of the behaviors to be changed. The significance of this task is easily overlooked because it is much less dramatic than the techniques actually used to alter behavior.

DEFINING THE TARGET BEHAVIOR

Task analysis identifies the steps when there are multiple behaviors that constitute the overall goal. Each behavior must be carefully defined. Usually, a behavioral program begins with a statement from someone that there is a problem or a need to intervene to address a particular end. Global or general statements of behavioral problems are usually inadequate for actually beginning a behavior modification program. For example, it is insufficient to select as the goal alteration of aggressiveness, learning deficits, speech, social skills, depression, psychotic symptoms, self-esteem, or similar concepts. Traits, summary labels, and personality characteristics are too general to be of much use. Moreover, definitions of the behaviors that make up such general labels may be idiosyncratic among different behavior change agents (parents, teachers, or hospital staff). The target behaviors have to be defined explicitly so that they can actually be observed, measured, and agreed upon by individuals administering the program.

Operational Definitions

An initial task of scientific research in general is to identify the construct, domain, or focus of interest and to translate it into measurable operations. For example, we may be interested in changing anxiety in an adult referred for outpatient therapy or in eliminating temper tantrums in a child. Anxiety and tantrums are important initial designations to help direct the focus. Yet, the concepts included in the initial abstract notions must be operationalized, that is, made into operational definitions. *Operational definitions* refer to defining a concept on the basis of the specific operations used for assessment. Paper-and-pencil measures (questionnaires to assess the domain), interviews, reports of others (for example, parents, spouses) in contact with the client, and direct observation are the most frequently used measures to operationalize psychological constructs. For example, an operational definition of anxiety refers to the procedures or methods used to measure anxiety in a particular behavioral program. Several measures might be selected (self-reports of anxiety, physiological measures of arousal, nonverbal facial expressions that suggest the experience of stress, direct signs of avoidance or turning away from the anxiety-provoking stimuli, and so on). Obviously, there are many ways to operationalize a response domain of interest.

In behavior modification, emphasis is placed on direct observation of overt behavior because overt behavior is viewed as the most direct measure of the treatment focus. For example, one could assess the frequency and severity of tantrums by having parents and teachers complete paper-and-pencil measures of a child's disruptive behavior. However, if possible, it would be useful to observe the tantrums directly and to see when they occur, under what circumstances, and whether they change in response to intervention.

Operational definitions are essential to begin to assess, change, and evaluate interventions. At the same time, it is important to recognize that operational definitions are limited. In defining an abstract construct (for example, anxiety or tantrums), an operational definition does not capture all of the domain of interest. Overt behavioral signs of anxiety—or tantrums for that matter—are also not all of the domain. There may be associated feeling states, thoughts, and correlated behaviors that are part of the package associated with anxiety. An operational definition is a working definition. Ideally, the definition reflects central features of the abstract notion. In addition, when change is achieved on the measure that is used to define the concept, other features of the domain may change as well.

Different types of measures (self-report, reports of others, questionnaires, interviews, psychophysiological measures) of a given abstract notion assess different but overlapping facets of a concept. One measure does not necessarily replace or obviate another type of measure. For this reason, many studies designed to evaluate treatment or other intervention programs usually use several different types of measures to see the breadth of change. In most behavioral programs, whether or not multiple measures are used, overt behavior is the salient assessment procedure and hence constitutes the focus of this chapter.

Criteria for Defining Behavior

We begin by specifying the general domain (for example, tantrums) and then by identifying a specific definition that permits assessment. This operational definition notes how the behavior will be assessed for purposes of observation and intervention. As a general rule, a definition should meet three criteria: objectivity, clarity, and completeness (Hawkins & Dobes, 1975). To be *objective,* the definition should refer to observable characteristics of behavior or environmental events. Definitions should not refer to inner states of the individual, such as aggressiveness or emotional disturbance. To be *clear,* the definition should be so unambiguous that it can be read, repeated, and paraphrased by observers. Reading the definition should provide a sufficient basis for beginning actual observations. To be *complete,* the definition must delineate the boundary conditions so that the responses to be included and excluded can be enumerated.

Developing a complete definition often creates the greatest difficulty because decision rules are needed to specify how behavior should be scored. If the range of responses included in the definition is not described carefully, observers have to infer whether such a response has occurred. For example, a simple greeting response such as waving one's hand to greet someone may serve as the target behavior. In most instances, when a person's hand is fully extended and moving back and forth, there would be no difficulty in agreeing that the person was waving. However, ambiguous instances may require judgments on the part of observers. A child might move his or her hand once (rather than back and forth) while the arm is not extended, or a child may not move his or her arm at all but simply move all of the fingers on one hand up and down (in the way that infants often learn to say good-bye). These responses are instances of waving in everyday life, because we can often see others reciprocate with similar greetings. For assessment purposes, the response definition must specify how these and related variations of waving should be scored.

Behavior modification programs have reported clear behavioral definitions that were developed from global and imprecise terms. For example, in one program conducted in the home, the focus was on bickering among the children (Christophersen, Arnold, Hill, & Quilitch, 1972). Bickering was defined as verbal arguments louder than the normal speaking voice between any two children or among all three children. In another program, the focus was on reducing the frequency of talking to oneself for a hospitalized schizophrenic patient (Wong, Terranova, Bowen, Zarate, Massel, & Liberman, 1987). Self-talk was defined as any vocalization not directed at another person but excluding sounds associated with physiological functions, such as coughing. These examples illustrate how clear behavioral definitions can be derived from general terms that may have diverse meanings to different individuals.

Before developing a definition that is objective, clear, and complete, it is useful to observe the client informally. Descriptive notes of what behaviors occur and which events are associated with their occurrence may be useful in generating specific response definitions. For example, if a psychiatric patient is labeled as being withdrawn, it is essential to observe the patient's behavior on the ward and to identify the specific behaviors that have led to the use of the label. The specific behaviors rather than the global concept become the object of change. A useful preliminary exercise, before embarking on a behavior modification program, is to select various concepts and trait labels used in everyday language and to provide alternative behavioral definitions for each of them. Although the definition of the target response may differ across behavior modification programs—even for two individuals who are referred to as aggressive—practice in specifying target behaviors is valuable.

ASSESSMENT

When behavior has been defined in precise terms, assessment can begin. Assessment of behavior is essential for at least two reasons. First, assessment determines the extent to which the target behavior is performed. Assessment reflects the frequency of occurrence of the target behavior prior to the program. The rate of preprogram behavior is referred to as the *baseline* or *operant rate*. Second, assessment is required to reflect behavior change after the program is begun. Because the major purpose of the program is to alter behavior, behavior during the program must be compared with behavior during baseline. Careful assessment throughout the program is essential.

It may be tempting to rely on human judgment or general impressions, rather than on objective assessment, to evaluate the extent to which behavior is performed or whether change has occurred with treatment. Yet human judgment may greatly distort the actual rate of behavior. For example, such behaviors as tantrums may be so intense that parents or teachers may recall them as occurring very often even when they are relatively infrequent. In contrast, some children have so many tantrums that their parents have become accustomed to a high rate and perceive tantrums as being less frequent than they really are. Judgment may also be inadequate to evaluate whether behavior change has occurred. Human judgment sometimes does not correspond to the actual records of overt behavior. Indeed, parents, teachers, and institutional staff may judge behavior as improving when there is no change or even when the behavior has become worse (Kazdin, 1973a; Schnelle, 1974). Judgments about behavior can be influenced by many factors other than the behavior itself. For example, in clinic settings, parents (usually mothers) are asked to evaluate the behavior of their children. Parent evaluations are influenced not only by the child's level of deviant behavior but also by such factors as the psychological state of the parent. Parents who are more depressed or anxious or who are experiencing marital discord and stress in the home tend to rate their children as more deviant (see Kazdin, in press).

Direct observations are designed to reveal more directly than global impressions or ratings the level or amount of the target behavior and the degree of behavior change. Observing behavior has its own obstacles, sources of bias, and pitfalls. For example, direct observation of behavior is not entirely free from human judgment. Typically, observers or persons within the environment must record (judge) the occurrence of behavior, and many extraneous factors can influence the results. However, overt behavior is a direct measure of how well or poorly a behavior change program is working and provides a very useful basis for making decisions about the intervention and about whether changes in the program are needed.

Functional Assessment

Recording the occurrence of the target behavior excludes a great deal of important information that may be useful in designing a behavior modification program. Various antecedent and consequent events are likely to be associated with the performance of the target behavior. In most applied settings, social stimuli or interactions with others constitute a major category of events that influence client behavior. For example, parents and teachers may provide verbal statements (instructions, praise), gestures (physical contact, motions, nonverbal directives), and expressions (smiles, frowns) that exert control over behavior. These stimuli may precede (as do instructions) or follow (as does praise) a particular target behavior.

Informally, one may have several ideas about events that may relate to, precede, or follow behavior. These antecedent and consequent events associated with the target behavior may generate hypotheses about which events control behavior and thereby can be used to alter behavior. These hypotheses can be tested directly by altering the events to determine their influence on behavior. For example, informal observation may indicate that the target behavior is performed at a particular time during the day, before a specific event, or in the presence of some other person. These clues, if borne out by careful assessment, may provide insights about stimulus conditions that exert control over the target behavior.

The assessment as well as conceptualization of the relations among setting events, stimuli, consequences, and the target behavior represent an important part of evaluation and intervention. The assessment approach that examines the target behavior in relation to other conditions is referred to as a *functional analysis*. A functional analysis is the systematic effort to *identify the relations between behaviors and the antecedents and consequences with which they may be associated.* Behavior is a function of some conditions; that is, it does not occur randomly or without some relation to ongoing events in the individual's environment, life, and so on. A functional analysis is designed to identify the conditions that relate to behavior. Informal observation, description, and conjecture about events associated with behavior are often helpful by themselves. A functional analysis examines more precisely what contributes to behavior so that the information can be used to identify effective interventions.

A functional analysis can be accomplished in many different ways. Direct observation is the usual method of conducting functional analyses. One method is to observe the behavior in it's natural situation to detect systematic patterns between setting, stimulus, and consequence events and the target behavior. Occasionally, researchers have gone beyond naturalistic observation and have altered the setting and stimulus events for a functional analysis. This procedure consists of arranging different conditions in which a stimulus or setting variable of interest is present and another during which it is absent. Behavior is observed under these different circumstances. The goal here is not to intervene to achieve a therapeutic change yet but rather to assess whether behavior is influenced by a specific environmental event or set of events. Methods of functional analyses and the yield from such analyses is discussed later in the chapter because they depend first on various methods of assessing behavior, which are discussed next.

STRATEGIES OF ASSESSMENT

Assessment of the target behavior is critical to the behavioral program. Understanding conditions related to performance of the behavior, application of the intervention for occurrences of the behavior, and evaluation of the program's impact depend on defining and assessing behavior carefully. In most behavior modification programs, behaviors are assessed on the basis of discrete occurrences of the response or on the amount of time that the response occurs. However, several variations and different types of measures are available.

Frequency Measures

Frequency counts simply require tallying the number of times the target behavior occurs in a given period of time. A frequency measure is particularly useful when the target response is discrete and when it takes a *relatively constant amount of time* each time it is performed. A discrete response has a clearly delineated beginning and end, so that separate instances of the response can be counted. The performance of the behavior should take a relatively constant amount of time, so that the units counted are approximately equal. Ongoing behaviors such as smiling, sitting in one's seat, lying down, and talking are difficult to record simply by counting because each response may occur for a different amount of time. For example, if a person talks to a peer for 15 seconds and to another peer for 30 minutes, these might be counted as two instances of talking. However, a great deal of information is lost by simply counting instances of talking because they differ in duration.

Frequency measures have been used for a variety of discrete behaviors. For example, in a program for an autistic child, frequency measures were used to assess the number of times that the child engaged in social responses such as saying hello or sharing a toy or object with someone and the number of times that she engaged in self-stimulatory behaviors such as rocking or repetitive pulling of her clothing (Russo & Koegel, 1977). With hospitalized psychiatric patients, one program assessed the frequency with which patients engaged in intolerable acts (such as assaulting someone or setting fires) and social behaviors (such as initiating conversation or responding to someone else) (Frederiksen, Jenkins, Foy, & Eisler, 1976). Additional discrete behaviors can be readily assessed with frequency counts, including the number of cigarettes smoked, the number of times a person attends an activity or hits another person, the number of objects thrown, the number of times homework is turned in, the number of times medication was taken, and so on.

Frequency measures require merely noting the instances in which behavior occurs. Usually, there is an additional requirement that behavior be observed for a constant amount of time. Of course, if behavior is observed for 20 minutes on one day and 30 minutes on another day, the frequencies are not directly comparable. However, the *rate of response* each day can be determined by dividing the frequency of the responses by the number of minutes observed each day. This measure will yield frequency per minute, or rate of response, which is comparable for different durations of observations.

A frequency measure has several desirable features for use in applied settings. First, frequency is relatively simple to score. Keeping a tally of behavior is usually all that is required. Moreover, counting devices are available, such as a golf counter worn as a wristwatch to facilitate recording. Second, frequency measures readily reflect changes over time. The number of times that a response occurs is sensitive to change resulting from alterations in contingencies. Since the principles of operant conditioning refer to changes in the frequency of a response, it is desirable to observe the response frequency or rate directly. Third, and related to the above, frequency expresses the *amount* of behavior performed, which is usually of concern to individuals in applied settings. The goal of most programs is to increase or decrease the number of times that a certain behavior occurs. Frequency provides a direct measure of the amount of behavior.

Discrete Categorization

Often it is very useful to classify responses into discrete categories such as correct/incorrect, performed/not performed, or appropriate-inappropriate. In many ways, *discrete categorization* is like a frequency measure because it is used for behaviors that have a clear beginning and end and a constant duration. But there are at least two important differences. With a frequency measure, performances of a particular behavior are tallied. The focus is on a single response. Also, the number of times that the behavior may occur is theoretically unlimited. For example, one child hitting another may be measured by frequency counts. How many times the behavior (hitting) may occur has no real limit. Discrete categorization is used to measure whether several different behaviors have occurred. There are only a limited number of opportunities to perform the response.

For example, discrete categorization might be used to measure how messy a college student's roommate is. A checklist can be devised that lists several behaviors, such as putting one's shoes in the closet, removing underwear from the kitchen table, putting dishes in the sink, and putting food in the refrigerator. Each morning, each behavior on the checklist could be categorized as performed or not performed. The total number of behaviors or steps that have been performed correctly constitutes the measure.

Discrete categories have been used in many behavior modification programs. For example, in one project personal appearance was altered among autistic children and adolescents living in community-based group homes (McClannahan, McGee, MacDuff, & Krantz, 1990). Twenty behaviors related to personal appearance (for example, having a clean face, unstained clothing, shoelaces tied, matching socks, and so on) were included in a checklist and classified as appropriate or not. Improvements in the number of discrete behaviors performed was used to evaluate training. As another example, in a camp setting, cabin-cleaning behaviors of emotionally disturbed boys were evaluated using discrete categorization (Peacock, Lyman, & Rickard, 1978). To evaluate the effects of the program, such tasks as placing coats on hooks, making beds, having no objects on the bed, and putting toothbrushing materials away were categorized as completed or not.

Discrete categorization is very easy to use because it requires listing a number of behaviors and checking off whether they were performed. The behaviors may consist of several steps that all relate to the completion of a task, such as dressing or grooming behaviors in children. Behavior can be evaluated by noting whether or how many steps are performed (for example, removing a shirt from the drawer, putting one arm through, then the other arm, and pulling it over one's head). On the other hand, the behaviors need not be related to one another, so that performance of one behavior may not have anything to do with performance of another one. For example, room-cleaning behaviors are not necessarily related; performing one behavior correctly (making one's bed) may be unrelated to performing another behavior (cleaning up dishes). Discrete categorization can yield convenient summary scores as reflected in the total number of the desired behaviors performed or the percentage of correct responses (calculated by forming a ratio of occurred or performed responses to total possible responses and multiplying by 100). A familiar example is correct responses on an examination, which can be expressed as either a total number or a percentage. Overall, discrete categorization is a very flexible method of observation that allows assessment of all sorts of behaviors independently of whether they are necessarily related to one another.

Number of Persons

Occasionally, the effectiveness of behavioral programs is evaluated on the basis of the number of persons who perform a response. The measure is used in group situations such as a classroom or a psychiatric hospital or in society at large. In such cases, the purpose is to increase the overall performance of a particular behavior, such as completing homework, coming to an activity on time, or driving a car safely. Once the desired behavior has been defined, the observations record how many participants in the group have performed the response. As with frequency and categorization measures, the observations require classifying the response as having occurred or not having occurred. But here the number of *individuals* are counted rather than the number of times that an individual performs the response.

Several programs have evaluated the impact of treatment on the number of people who are affected. For example, in one program the investigators were interested in reducing speeding among highway drivers (Van Houten, Nau, & Marini, 1980). To record speeding, a radar unit was placed unobtrusively along the highway. A feedback system visible to drivers was evaluated by measuring the percentage of drivers who exceeded the speed limit. Another program was designed to improve seat belt use among elementary school children (Sowers-Hoag, Thyer, & Bailey, 1987). The effects were evaluated by recording the percentage of the children who used their seat belts when picked up by their parents at the end of the day.

Knowing the number of people who perform a response is very useful when the explicit goal of the program is to increase performance in a large group of subjects. Consistent with this overall goal is developing behaviors in an institution and even in society at large. Increasing the number of people who exercise, give to charity, or seek treatment when early stages of serious diseases are apparent and decreasing the number of people who smoke, overeat, and commit crimes are important goals of this kind that behavioral interventions have addressed.

Many programs do not provide information about the performance of particular individuals. The number of people who perform a response may be increased in an institution or in society at large. However, the performance of any particular individual may be sporadic or very low. One really does not know whether a particular individual has been affected. This information may or may not be important, depending on the goals of the program.

Interval Recording

A frequent strategy for measuring behavior in applied settings is based on units of time rather than discrete response units. Behavior is recorded during short periods of time falling within the entire time that it is performed. The two most frequently used methods of time-based measurement are interval recording and response duration.

With *interval recording*, behavior is observed for a *single block of time*, such as 30 or 60 minutes once per day. A block of time is divided into a series of short intervals (for example, each interval may equal 10 or 15 seconds). During each interval, the target behavior is scored as having occurred or not having occurred. If a discrete behavior, such as hitting someone, occurs one or more times in a single interval, the response is scored as having occurred. Several response occurrences within an interval are not counted separately. If the behavior is ongoing with an unclear beginning or end (such as talking, playing, and sitting) or occurs for a long period of time, it is scored during each of the intervals in which it is occurring.

Behavior modification programs in classroom settings frequently use interval recording to score whether students are paying attention, sitting in their seats, and working quietly. The behavior of an individual student may be observed for 10-second intervals over a 20-minute observational period. For each interval, an observer records whether the child was working quietly in his or her seat. If the child remains seated and works for a long period of time, many intervals will be scored for attentive behavior. If the child leaves his or her seat (without permission) or stops working, inattentive behavior will be scored. During some intervals, a child may be seated for half of the time and out of the seat for the remaining time. Because the interval has to be scored for *either* attentive or inattentive behavior, a rule for scoring behavior in such instances has to be devised. Often, getting out of the seat will be counted as inattentive behavior and will nullify the portion of attentive behavior within the interval.

Interval recording for a single block of time has been used in many programs beyond the classroom setting. For example, one program focused on several inappropriate behaviors, such as roughhousing, touching objects, or playing with merchandise, that children performed while they accompanied their parents shopping (Clark, Greene, Macrae, McNees, Davis, & Risley, 1977, Exp. 3). Observers followed the family in the store to record whether the inappropriate behaviors occurred during consecutive 15-second intervals. Interval assessment was also used in a program de-

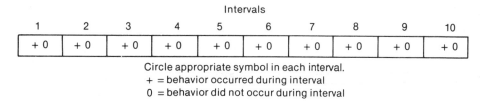

FIGURE 3-1
Example of interval scoring sheet for one individual.

signed to reduce self-injurious behavior (biting one's own hand, arm, or shoulder and scratching oneself) in a way that caused bodily damage to two profoundly retarded adolescents (Pace, Iwata, Edwards, & McCosh, 1986). Observations in the hospital were conducted daily in an individual therapy room and a group therapy room. In each setting, an observer recorded whether any self-injurious behavior occurred during each of several 10-second intervals.

Interval scoring of behavior is facilitated by a scoring sheet on which intervals are represented across time. In Figure 3-1, each number across the top denotes a time interval. During each interval, a + or 0 is circled or checked to denote whether the behavior has occurred for the subject. The basic sheet can be expanded to include many subjects and intervals, as shown in Figure 3-2. For example, each student in a classroom or each patient on a ward can be observed for a large number of intervals. The first person would be observed for the first interval (for example, 15 seconds). After that person's behavior has been recorded, the second person would be observed. This would be continued until each person has been observed for one interval (down the left column in Figure 3-2). The order would then be repeated until each person had been observed for another interval, and so on for the remaining intervals. Often more than one behavior is scored during an interval, so that the presence of several behaviors will be judged during each interval. To accomplish this, a data sheet may include many symbols in each interval block so that various behaviors can be coded. A letter or symbol is checked or circled for the different categories of behavior that occur during the interval.

In using an interval scoring method, an observer looks at the client during the interval. When one interval is over, the observer records whether the behavior occurred. If an observer is recording several behaviors during an interval, a few seconds may be needed to record all of the behaviors that were observed during that interval. If the observer records a behavior as soon as it occurs (before the interval is over), he or she might miss other behaviors that occurred while the first behavior was being scored. Hence, many investigators use interval scoring procedures that allow time for recording after each interval of observation.

Intervals

	1	2	3	4	5	6	7	8	9	10
1	+ 0	+ 0	+ 0	+ 0	+ 0	+ 0	+ 0	+ 0	+ 0	+ 0
2	+ 0	+ 0	+ 0	+ 0	+ 0	+ 0	+ 0	+ 0	+ 0	+ 0
3	+ 0	+ 0	+ 0	+ 0	+ 0	+ 0	+ 0	+ 0	+ 0	+ 0
4	+ 0	+ 0	+ 0	+ 0	+ 0	+ 0	+ 0	+ 0	+ 0	+ 0
5	+ 0	+ 0	+ 0	+ 0	+ 0	+ 0	+ 0	+ 0	+ 0	+ 0
6	+ 0	+ 0	+ 0	+ 0	+ 0	+ 0	+ 0	+ 0	+ 0	+ 0
7	+ 0	+ 0	+ 0	+ 0	+ 0	+ 0	+ 0	+ 0	+ 0	+ 0

Individuals

FIGURE 3–2
Example of interval scoring sheet for many individuals.

A variation of interval recording is referred to as *time sampling*. This variation uses the interval method, but the observations are conducted for brief periods *at different times* rather than in a single block of time. For example, with the time-sampling method, a child might be observed for 10-second intervals, but these intervals might be spread out over a full day.

As an illustration, psychiatric patients participating in a hospital reinforcement program were evaluated with time-sampling procedures (Paul & Lentz, 1977). Each hour, an observer looked at a patient for a 2-second interval. At the end of the interval, the observer recorded the presence or absence of several behaviors related to social interaction, activities, selfcare, and other responses. The procedure was continued throughout the day, sampling one interval at a time. The advantage of time sampling is that the observations represent performance over the entire day. Of course, in many settings, such as the home or the classroom, it is more convenient to complete observations in a single observation session.

There are significant features of interval recording that make it one of the most widely adopted strategies in applied settings. First, interval assessment can record virtually any behavior. Whether a response is discrete and does not vary in duration or is continuous or sporadic, it can be classified as occurring or not occurring during any time period. Second, the observations resulting from interval recording can be easily converted into a percentage. The number of intervals during which the response is scored as having occurred can be divided by the total number of intervals observed. This ratio multiplied by 100 yields the percentage of the intervals in which the response has been performed. For example, if social responses are scored as having occurred in 20 of the 40 intervals that were observed, the percentage of the intervals of social behavior is 50 percent (20/40 × 100). A percentage is easily communicated to others by noting that a certain behavior occurs a specific percentage of time (intervals). Whenever there is doubt as to what assessment strategy should be adopted, an interval approach is always applicable and can be readily employed.

Duration

Another time-based method of observation is *duration,* or the amount of time that the response is performed. This method is particularly useful for ongoing responses that are continuous, rather than for discrete acts or responses of extremely short duration. Programs that attempt to increase or decrease the length of time that a response is performed might profit from a duration method.

Duration has been used in fewer studies than have interval observations. As an example, one investigation trained two severely withdrawn children to engage in social interaction with other children (Whitman, Mercurio, & Caponigri, 1970). Interaction was measured by simply recording the amount of time that children were in contact with each other. Duration was also used to measure the suspicious and accusing statements that an elderly male stroke victim directed toward his wife (Green, Linsk, & Pinkston, 1986). His wife's use of praise for appropriate verbalizations was effective in decreasing the amount of time each day in which her husband engaged in such statements.

Another measure based on duration is not how long the response is performed but rather how long it takes for the client to begin the response. The amount of time that elapses between a cue and the response is referred to as *latency.* Many programs have used response latency to evaluate treatment. For example, in one report, adults (ages 60 or over) who suffered insomnia received treatment based on stimulus control procedures (Puder, Lacks, Bertelson, & Storandt, 1983). Treatment consisted of having clients associate drowsiness with going to bed. Sleep-incompatible behaviors (such as worrying, eating, or watching TV) were to be performed in a room other than the bedroom. Gradually, the consistent association of the bedroom with sleeping helped clients get to sleep better. The effectiveness of treatment was reflected in the reduced latency in going to sleep after going to bed.

Assessment of response duration or latency is a fairly simple matter: one starts and stops a stopwatch or notes the time when the response begins and ends. However, the onset and termination of the response must be carefully defined. If these conditions have not been met, duration and latency are extremely difficult to employ. For example, a child in a tantrum may cry continuously for several minutes, whimper for short periods, stop all noise for a few seconds, and begin intense crying again. In recording the duration of the tantrum, a decision is required to handle changes in the intensity of the behavior (for example, from crying to whimpering) and pauses (such as periods of silence) so that these are consistently recorded as part of the response or as a different (for example, nontantrum) re-sponse.

Response duration generally is used in situations in which the length of the time that a behavior is performed is a major concern. In most behavior modification programs, the goal is to increase or decrease the frequency of a response rather than its duration. There are notable exceptions, of course. For example, it is desirable to increase the length of the time that students study or that persons practice a skill they wish to learn, such as playing an instrument or speaking a foreign language. However, because interval measures are widely used and readily adaptable to virtually all responses, they are often selected as a measure over duration. The number or proportion of the intervals in which study behavior occurs reflects changes in study time, since interval recording is based on time.

Other Strategies

One of the above methods of assessment is generally used in behavioral programs. Occasionally, other measures are used because they provide direct measures of behavior that are of obvious importance. For example, behavior modification programs for obesity or cigarette smoking have evaluated intervention effects by simply recording client weight in pounds or the number of cigarettes smoked. In other programs, the specific behavior may lend itself to a measure unique to the investigation. For example, interventions designed to conserve energy can monitor gas or electric meters at home or look at a car's odometer to record whether home or car use of energy has changed. In applications to medical problems such as hypertension or diabetes, specific measures such as blood pressure or the glucose concentration in the patient's urine have been used to evaluate behavioral treatment programs.

Selection of an Assessment Strategy

In most situations, the investigators use an assessment procedure based on frequency, interval, or one of the other methods mentioned above. Some behaviors, such as the number of profane words used or the number of toileting or eating responses, lend themselves well to frequency counts or categorization because they are discrete; others, such as reading, work-ing, or sitting, lend themselves well to interval recording; and still others, such as time spent in studying, crying, or exercising, lend themselves well to duration. Target behaviors can usually be assessed in more than one way, so there is no single strategy that must be adopted. For example, an investigator working in an institution for delinquents may wish to record the aggressive behavior of a particular adolescent. Hitting others (for example, making physical contact with another individual with a closed fist) may be the response of interest. What assessment strategy should be used?

Aggressive behavior might be measured with a *frequency* count by having an observer record how many times the youth hit others during a certain period each day. Each hit would count as one response. The behavior might also be observed using interval recording. A block of time such as 30 minutes could be set aside for observation. The 30 minutes could be divided into 10-second intervals. For each of these intervals, the observer would record whether any hitting had occurred. Perhaps time sampling might be used. Each hour during the day, the youth could be observed for a 15-minute period, for which the presence or absence of aggressive behavior would be recorded. This interval method has the advantage of sampling behavior over the entire day.

A duration measure might be used. It may be difficult to time the duration of hitting because instances of hitting are too brief to clock unless there is a series of hits (as in a fight). Recording the amount of time from the beginning of each day until the first aggressive response might be easier. This *latency* measure records the time of no hitting. Presumably, if a program decreased aggressive behavior, the amount of time from the beginning of the day until the first aggressive response would increase.

Although many different measures can be used in a given program, the measure finally selected may be dictated by the purpose of the program. Different measures sometimes reflect slightly different goals. For example, consider two behavioral programs that focused on increasing toothbrushing, a seemingly simple response that could be assessed in many different ways. One of the programs observed the *number of individuals* in a boys' summer camp who brushed their teeth (Lattal, 1969). The boys knew how to brush their teeth, and an incentive system increased their performance of the response. In the other program, the clients were mentally retarded residents at a state hospital (Horner & Keilitz, 1975). The residents were unable to brush their teeth at the beginning of the program, so the many behaviors involved in toothbrushing were developed. Discrete categorization was used to assess toothbrushing; each component step of the behavior (wetting the brush, removing the cap, applying the toothpaste, and so on) was scored as performed or not performed. The percentage of steps correctly completed measured the effects of training. Although both of these investigations assessed toothbrushing, the different methods reflect different goals, namely, getting children who can brush to do so or training the response in mentally retarded residents who did not know how to perform it.

FUNCTIONAL ANALYSIS: ASSESSMENT AND INTERVENTION

In behavior modification, assessment is not an end in itself. Rather, the goal is to use the assessment information to design and to evaluate interventions. The interrelation between assessment and intervention is conveyed especially well by functional analysis (see Iwata, Vollmer, & Zarcone,

1990). Functional analysis is designed to identify the *functions* that the behavior serves for the individual—that is, the outcomes that result from the behavior. The purpose of functional analysis is threefold: to describe behavior and events with which it is associated; to make predictions (hypotheses) about factors controlling behavior based on the observed relations of behavior and events; and to test these predictions by altering the presumed factors to see whether behavior varies as predicted.

A functional analysis depends on showing that a given target behavior is controlled by specific events. Control is demonstrated by showing that the occurrence of the behavior is systematically influenced by variations in the specific antecedent or consequent conditions. This control is often demonstrated by actually altering the conditions briefly during baseline assessment to see whether systematic changes occur by altering the conditions. This baseline assessment amounts to a preview of what might be used as an effective intervention. The intervention would be selected on the basis of the information that reveals one or more conditions that seem to control behavior. For example, a maladaptive behavior may serve a particular function such as obtaining attention or escape from some demand. Once this is identified, the functions served by the target behavior can be shifted to support adaptive behavior.[1]

Methods of Assessment

As mentioned earlier, the goal of functional assessment is to identify the relations among antecedents, behaviors, and consequences. There are different strategies for obtaining the information and for identifying the functions that the behavior serves (O'Neill, Horner, Albin, Storey, & Sprague, 1990). The methods vary in the degree to which they systematically examine functional relations.

Interviews
One way to conduct a functional analysis is to interview individuals in contact with the client. The interview is designed to describe behavior, setting events in which the behavior appears, and possible functions the behavior may serve. Description of the behavior refers to defining the behavior in concrete, operational terms, as discussed earlier. During the interview individuals would discuss precisely what the target behavior is. The setting events are the full context in which behavior appears. This would include the routine of the individual, activities immediately before and after the behavior, who is present in the situation, and any other events before, during, and after the behavior. The function of behavior concerns the consequences or results that occur when the behavior is performed. Perhaps reinforcers (attention from others) or opportunities for escape (for example, the person is allowed to leave the situation or escape from some demand) are some of the consequences that follow the behavior. The point

here is to seek information about the functions that the behavior might serve.

The interview is useful insofar as it seeks information about the behavior, stimulus events, and consequences. Developing a behavior change program at the very least begins with this information obtained from the reports of the clients or those with whom the client interacts. The interview is less preferred because the information constitutes verbal reports of events rather than observations of the events themselves. Such descriptions, whether obtained from clients, persons in the clients' everyday lives, or professionals, are limited by biases of human judgment that affect one's ability to describe details accurately and identify relations between events (see Nezu & Nezu, 1989). Nevertheless, the interview is worthwhile as a basis for identifying leads for treatment and because more direct assessment may not be feasible.

Direct Observation

Direct observation of the target behavior in the situation along with the consequences associated with it is another way to obtain the information required for a functional analysis. Functional analysis usually is based on direct observations. There are many different observational systems. One method is to ask persons in applied settings to record detailed information and consequences throughout the day. Consider the example of a 10-year-old boy who teases others and precipitates fights at school. Behavior might be observed at school across different classrooms. Each day the teachers might complete a report that focuses on events surrounding teasing and that might be helpful in designing a behavior change program. The form in Figure 3-3 allows teachers to record antecedents and setting events, behaviors, and consequences. Each teacher assesses behavior each day in his or her period by completing a form for any teasing and a form for any nonteasing (positive comments to peers) behavior. After several days of recording, the material is summarized to identify whether teasing and nonteasing are more frequent at certain times (in certain class periods), during certain activities, or in the presence of selected peers. For example, teasing might be much more frequent in some classes, during or after selected activities, and in the presence of two specific boys. This suggests a hypothesis about what might be controlling teasing behavior and based on that, an intervention can be implemented. Teachers can modify activities that appear to promote teasing or incorporate activities or conditions associated with lower rates of teasing. A reinforcement program can focus on those periods in which behavior is problematic or when interaction with the specific boys is likely. In a graduated fashion, conditions that were associated with teasing can be reintroduced while positive comments to peers can be reinforced.

Direct observations can be completed using the form in Figure 3–3 or some variant by persons in the client's everyday life (for example, parents, teachers, or staff). At the same time, this method does not provide a precise assessment of ongoing behavior and the specific events with which they are

Form To Report Functional Relations

Day, Date, & Time (Class Period): _____

Location (Classroom): _____

TEASING

Defined as negative comments to others about something they have done, how they look, or a threat.

SETTING EVENTS/ANTECEDENTS

    Activity when teasing occurred: _____

    Others near-by: _____

    Activity before present activity: _____

    Any other events before that seem relevant: _____

CONSEQUENCES

    Actions of teacher: _____

    Actions of peers: _____

    Any other consequences: _____

NON-TEASING

Peer-directed comments that are positive or neutral. Comments about external activities or events (e.g., sports, class), compliments, statements of fact (e.g., about the assignment) not about the peer.

SETTING EVENTS/ANTECEDENTS

    Activity when nonteasing occurred: _____

    Others near-by: _____

    Activity before present activity: _____

    Any other events before that seem relevant: _____

CONSEQUENCES

    Actions of teacher: _____

    Actions of peers: _____

    Other: _____

Each day the teacher fills out a report on incidents of teasing, if one occurs in his or her classroom, and on nonteasing behavior. After a week of observations across all classes, an effort is made to see if there are systematic patterns. It is likely that teasing is not randomly, i.e., dispersed equally across all activities, teachers, time periods, and persons present in the situation, and consequences. Tallying the pattern gives rise to hypotheses about setting and consequent events that control behavior.

FIGURE 3–3

Observations for Functional Assessment: Report of Behavior to Identify Functional Relations Over Several Days and Time Periods associated. A more demanding, but often more informative, method of direct observation is to have observers monitor ongoing behavior and record multiple events when the behavior occurs. The form in Figure 3–4 demonstrates this method of observation (see O'Neill et al., 1990). The form allows one to enter the behavior(s) of interest as well as any special setting events, functions, and consequences that might be relevant. Several possible setting events and functions are listed already. The client is observed during various time periods (to be written in) and then whatever happens in a given interval is checked off on the form. For example, if the client teased another child in the classroom during transition periods (after a lesson but immediately before recess) and received attention from the teacher, this pattern might emerge over several time periods of observation.

Direct assessment of ongoing behavior in a situation is clearly the preferred method of functional analysis because it provides more precise information about the behavior, setting, and functions. The relations identified by direct observation can lead to data-based hypotheses about what might be maintaining the behavior. Of course, there might be several hypotheses and any one or none of them might be correct. There is one further level of functional analysis that sometimes is completed in which the hypotheses are tested directly.

Direct Observation and Manipulation of Conditions

Another method of functional analysis includes direct observation but goes beyond it in a significant way. Specifically, in this method direct observations are made to examine behaviors, setting events, and consequences, and, as before, the information is used to develop hypotheses about what is maintaining behavior. The new feature is to test the alternative hypotheses. The test is conducted by experimentally manipulating (changing) the conditions during baseline assessment to see whether, in fact, behavior systematically varies. Different outcomes or contingencies in each of the conditions may lead to varied (higher, lower) levels of the behavior. Support for the functional relation is established by systematic changes in behavior as a function of the conditions. The information obtained from experimental manipulations provides a very strong test of maintaining conditions (Iwata, Dorsey, Slifer, Bauman, & Richman, 1982). Once the conditions are identified, the intervention is then implemented directly on the basis of this information. For example, Wacker and his colleagues (1990) assessed behavior of clients (children and adults) diagnosed with autism. Assessment was conducted at an outpatient clinic under analogue conditions, that is, special circumstances designed to resemble conditions in everyday life. The purpose was to identify factors that might maintain self-injurious behavior. One case was a 20-year-old man named Roy who had a lengthy history of self-injurious behavior (headbanging, arm and hand biting). Assessment of these behaviors was conducted under three brief conditions referred to as alone, escape, and social attention condition. In the *alone*

FIGURE 3–4
Functional analysis observation form.
SOURCE: O'Neill, R. E., Horner, R. H., Albin, R. W., Storey, K., & Sprague, J. R. (1990).

Person: ——— to ———
Dates: ———

84

condition, Roy was led to a room and left alone with no tasks or intervention. This condition was designed to simulate everyday life in which he might be left alone. An alone condition is important because self-injurious behavior is sometimes maintained by the stimulation (sensory stimulation) it produces (Iwata et al., 1982). In the *escape* condition, Roy was given a task to perform (folding and sorting towels) in the presence of a therapist who provided guidance and assistance. If any self-injury occurred, the behavior was ignored but the task was removed (terminated). This condition was designed to simulate circumstances in which tasks or activities are terminated when the individual engages in self-injury. Perhaps Roy's behavior was maintained in everyday life by negative reinforcement—that is, escape from unpleasant tasks or activities. In the *social attention* condition, no tasks or activities were presented. The therapist sat near Roy. When there was self-injury, the therapist provided attention (mild reprimands such as, "Please do not do that.") and a light touch on the shoulder. This condition was designed to stimulate situations in which care givers attend to self-injury and give little or no attention for appropriate (noninjurious) behavior. If social attention were maintaining behavior, more frequent self-injury probably would be evident.

Assessment under the varied conditions revealed that Roy's self-injury was much higher (35% of the intervals) in the escape condition than in the alone and social isolation conditions (less than 10% of the intervals). In other words, self-injury served the function of allowing Roy to escape from activities. For the intervention, the contingency was altered so that escape followed appropriate behavior (non-self-injury). This led to a reduction of self-injurious behavior.

The increased use of direct observation and manipulation of experimental conditions has shown the very important role of functional analysis in designing treatment. At this point, the method is noted here with emphasis on the assessment features. We shall return to this method of functional analysis as the chapters focus increasingly on interventions.

Special Considerations

There are several advantages to conducting a functional analysis. First, the analysis can suggest specific antecedent conditions that promote or give rise to the behavior. In the case of an undesirable behavior this may mean that reduction of the behavior may require rearranging antecedent conditions. As an example, two children (brother and sister) fight and scream daily over an early evening television show. The antecedent arrangements, such as allowing the two to come to the den, to argue each day, and to foster "survival of the fittest," are setting events that in part promote the problem. Rearrangement of the selection, choice, and alternation procedure between the siblings are a few among many stimulus rearrangements that might decrease this fighting.

Second, a functional analysis often suggests the type of contingency arrangement that is likely to be effective. Once identified, reinforcers operating in the situation might be rearranged to support the behavior of interest. For example, the brother's arguing and fighting with his sister each day may lead to their watching his choice of show. Arguing and fighting may be reinforced by choice of the television show. This contingency could be rearranged so that choice of the show followed prosocial and cooperative behavior and not arguing and fighting. A functional analysis in this case has suggested where to intervene and how to redeploy the reinforcers to support the behavior of interest.

Third, a functional analysis may suggest the contingencies that are likely to be ineffective. In our present example, praise for cooperative behavior for the brother and sister on days when there is cooperation or low rates of arguing may have some positive effect. Yet, a functional analysis might suggest that other reinforcers are operative (choice selection, sibling submission). Praise alone without rearranging other behavior stimuli relations in the setting is not likely to be effective.

A functional analysis that identifies setting and stimulus events and maintaining conditions is not always possible. A range of factors may influence behavior, both close to and distant from that behavior in time. For example, a child's aggressive behavior is known to be influenced by a number of factors including the history of aggressive behavior of the parents and grandparents, the child's temperament at birth, the parents' current and past use of harsh physical punishment of the child, and many other factors (Kazdin, 1987a). A functional analysis may observe only current antecedents and consequences and of course not provide a complete account of factors leading to aggressive acts. Even so, details of current functioning can generate hypotheses about factors that sustain current behavior and guide selection of the interventions. A complete explanation of all factors related to the behavior may not be needed to intervene effectively.

A related issue pertains to the feasibility of conducting a functional analysis. Many analyses have been conducted in well-controlled research where careful observations have been conducted or different stimulus arrangements have been made before intervening (for example, Cooper, Wacker, Thursby, Plagmann, Harding, Millard, & Derby, 1992; Wacker, McMahon, Steege, Berg, Sasso, & Melloy, 1990). In some cases, investigators have relied on computer technology to record ongoing behavior and antecedent events and to see immediately relations between behavior and these events (Repp & Karsh, 1990). Careful control and analyses of stimulus arrangements have greatly helped our understanding of the salient role of antecedents. Of course, in many instances in everyday life in settings such as home and school, such detailed analyses and extended observations may not be feasible, either because resources for observation are limited or because of the urgency to intervene (for example, to stop a child's fighting). Here, too, a functional analysis is still relevant and useful.

A functional analysis is not merely a method of assessment but also a way of thinking about behavior. In cases where it may not be feasible to *do* the analysis, it remains critically important to consider antecedents, consequences, and the varied circumstances related to performance of behavior. For example, consider developing completion of homework in a 12-year-old. A simplistic way to proceed would be to begin a reinforcement program (such as points exchangeable for privileges) for working on homework after school. It is possible that such a program would increase the time spent on homework and the completion of homework assignments. It is also possible that this is an oversimplistic analysis and that "throwing consequences" at the behavior, even if contingent, would have little effect.

A functional analytic perspective leads one to consider arranging conditions to promote homework completion. For example, perhaps the program would include a parent sitting with the child when both are not too tired, when there has not been an argument or conflict between them, when the child is not missing an important event (for example, a party or game) he or she would otherwise prefer, and so on. Arranging setting events to promote entry into the sequences of behaviors (of doing homework) is important.

Similarly, a functional analysis type of thinking draws attention to reinforcers likely to be related to the behavior. One could provide food and snacks for homework completion, but they may not be related to the behavior. However, expressions of interest by parents and teachers, the physical proximity and contact of parents and child during homework, praises, and struggling together to understand or to complete an assignment are more likely to foster the behavior of interest. In this example, a functional analysis was not completed formally. Yet, thinking about contingencies from the standpoint of such an analysis is valuable in its own right as a way of developing effective programs.

CONDUCTING OBSERVATIONS

Issues and Problems in Sampling Behavior

The purpose of assessment is to sample the extent to which behavior is performed over the total period of time that behavior change is desired. Performance fluctuates over time on a given day and across days and weeks. It is important to determine the level of behavior without allowing the fluctuations to misrepresent the overall rate. If behavior were unvarying in its level over each hour and each day, any sample of that behavior (for example, one hour) would be representative of behavior at all other times. However, behavior is rarely performed at a consistent rate. (The only time there is such complete consistency is when the behavior is never performed and the rate is zero.) Thus, to obtain a representative sample, assessment must be carried out over an extended period of time.

Three decisions need to be made regarding the observations that are required. First, the *number of times* that data will be collected must be decided. When possible, it is desirable to observe behavior each day or during each session (for example, in a classroom) that the target behavior may occur. The frequency of observation depends on such factors as the variation of behavior over time, the availability of observers, and scheduling exigencies in the setting. If the target behavior is very stable from one day to the next, daily assessment becomes less essential than if the target behavior fluctuates radically. As a general rule, behavior should be observed on as many occasions as possible, and preferably daily.

A second decision to be made before beginning assessment is the *length of time* set aside for a given observation period. The guiding general rule is that behavior should be observed for a period of time that will yield data representative of typical performance over the entire period of interest. For example, if it is desirable to alter behavior in the classroom, observational data should reflect performance over a relatively long period (such as one hour) or for several short periods throughout the day, rather than for just a few minutes during a brief block of time.

For some behavioral problems or in some settings, the target behavior may occur only during a specific period of the day. For example, child behaviors at home, such as getting dressed for school, completing chores, or going to bed without a tantrum, all occur at brief and specific times during the day. In other cases, a functional analysis may suggest that behaviors are more likely or more problematic at selected times. In such cases, observation periods of the target behavior need not be long. They can focus on the times when occurrences of the behavior are more important or especially relevant, given the goals of the program.

For practical reasons, it is usually unfeasible to observe behavior over an extended period or over several shorter periods throughout the day. In such instances, behavior might be observed for a single block of time during the period in which behavior change is most obviously required. An initial assessment at different times over a few days can determine which periods require the greatest attention. Subsequently, assessment can focus on those periods.

A third decision related to the length of the time that behavior is observed is *when the observations are conducted.* Observations using frequency, interval, or duration methods can record behavior in a block of time in a single day or at different times throughout the day. The advantage of sampling behavior at various times over the entire day is that the observed behavior is more likely to be representative of behavior over different time periods.

If interval assessment is used, in addition to the above decisions, the duration of the interval has to be decided. Although observations may be made for 30 minutes or one hour each day, the length of the intervals within that period must be decided. If behavior occurs at a high rate or is an ongoing response, relatively short intervals are recommended (for example, 10 or 15 seconds). Longer intervals (such as 60 seconds) would exclude much of the responding, because the interval is recorded for the presence or absence of only one response. If the behavior occurs 20 times during one 60-second interval, the interval is scored on the occurrence of the first response and the behavior cannot be scored again until the next interval. Thus, a great deal of behavior goes unrecorded. As a result of a behavior modification program, behavior may change from 20 times to 10 times per 60-second interval. However, this change will not be reflected in the data because the interval will continue to be scored merely for the presence or absence of the response.

There are several considerations that dictate the duration of intervals. First, interval duration should be relatively short (10 or 15 seconds) for discrete behaviors that occur frequently. Second, very short intervals (5 or fewer seconds) are sometimes difficult to score reliably because observers have difficulty in synchronizing observations. The interval is so short that it is not clear in which interval the behavior was performed. Third, the length of the interval may be less important when behavior is continuous (such as reading or watching television) than when it is discrete, because shorter or longer intervals are not likely to exclude "instances" of behavior. Many studies have used 10-second intervals, whereas others have reported intervals of one or a few minutes. Because there are no fixed rules for interval length, a wide range of durations has been employed.

Conditions Under Which Observations Are Obtained

Observations are usually completed by placing one or more observers in a position to see the client. Occasionally, the observer may be out of sight, such as behind a one-way mirror in an observation booth adjacent to a classroom or a hospital ward. At other times, observations may be taken from videotapes, so the observer is not present in the situation. In most studies, however, observers and clients are in the same situation, such as the home or the classroom.

If the client is aware of the observer's presence, the assessment procedure is said to be obtrusive. A potential problem with obtrusive assessment is that the client's behavior may be affected by knowing that observations are being made. Assessment is reactive if the observer's presence alters the client's behavior. Several investigations have shown that the presence of an observer may alter the behaviors of the persons who are observed (see Haynes & Horn, 1982; Kazdin, 1982b). But in most cases, the effects are temporary if they occur at all. For example, a wife may observe the amount of time that her husband engages in communication. (Insufficient communication is a spouse complaint that frequently emerges in marital therapy.) Once the husband is aware of the observation focus and procedure, the amount of his communication may temporarily increase. That increase is not likely to continue as the husband adapts to the novelty of the observations. Without new antecedents or consequences for the behavior, long-term behavior change would not be expected.

In situations where external observers enter into a situation to collect observations (for example, enter a classroom to record child behavior), reactivity can be minimized by avoiding interactions between the observer and the persons being observed. Thus, in the classroom, an observer would avoid behavior that might maintain the children's interest, such as eye contact, smiles, and conversation. To minimize reactivity by helping the clients to adapt to the novelty of the new person, many investigators place the observer into the situation on several occasions before actual assessment begins.

Several considerations in conducting observations pertain to the observers and the manner in which they are trained and supervised (see Foster, Bell-Dolan, & Burge, 1988). First, in some cases, many observers are used. When the observers are first trained to record behavior, they may adhere to the same definition of behavior. Over time and after training is finished, observers may "drift" or gradually depart from the original definition. The criteria for scoring behavior (for example, being out of the seat in class, talking when one should be working) may change slightly and influence the data. To ensure that observers adhere to the definitions, periodic retraining, review of videotapes, and feedback regarding the accuracy of recording during the sessions can help minimize or eliminate drift.

Second, observer expectations may influence their recordings. If observers expect change once they see a program in effect, these expectations may influence their recordings. If the investigator conveys expectations and then unwittingly fosters biased observations by praising data in the expected direction, biased observations are more likely. To reduce the likelihood of biased recording, periodic retraining throughout the project and emphasis on recording accuracy are important.

In general, clarity of the definition, careful training of observers, and monitoring observers over the course of assessment are protections against biased recording. In research studies, these practices are commonly used. In addition, periodic sessions may be videotaped and rated by other observers. The original data obtained from live recording can be compared to the data from videotapes. The comparison can indicate whether the conclusions about the frequency behavior or the impact of treatment would be any different.

Reliability of Assessment

Need for Reliability
It is important for individuals who observe the target behavior to agree on the occurrence of the response. Interobserver agreement, often referred to as *reliability of assessment,* is important for three major reasons.[2] First,

assessment is useful only when it can be achieved with some consistency. For example, if frequency counts differ greatly depending on who is counting, it will be difficult to know what the client's actual performance is. The client may be scored as performing a response frequently on some days and infrequently on other days as a function of who scores behavior, rather than of differences in actual client performance. Inconsistent measurement introduces variation in the data that adds to the variation stemming from normal fluctuations in client performance. If measurement variation is large, there may appear to be no systematic pattern to the behavior. If a behavior modification program is implemented, it may be difficult to determine whether behavior is changing, because the data are highly variable as a function of inconsistent recording. Stable patterns of behavior are required to reflect behavior change. Hence, reliable recording is essential.

Second, assessing agreement is important because it minimizes or circumvents the biases of any individual observer. If a single observer records the target behavior, any recorded change in behavior may result from a change over time in the observer's definition of the target behavior, rather than in the actual behavior of the client. The observer may become lenient or stringent over time. For example, the observer may expect and perceive improvement in the target behavior, even though no improvement actually occurs. If two or more observers are used, one can see whether the pattern in the data varies as a function of who completes the observations. Agreement between observers provides a check on the consistency of their recording of behavior.

Finally, assessing agreement is important because agreement reflects whether the target behavior is well defined. If observers readily agree on the occurrence of the behavior, it will be easier for the persons who eventually carry out the program to agree on the behavior and to apply the intervention (for example, reinforcing consequences) contingently.

Conducting Checks on Agreement

To ensure that the behavior is agreed upon, reliability checks can be made before baseline data are gathered. A few days of prebaseline observation generally are useful to finalize the rules for observing behavior and to handle instances in which it is not clear whether the target behavior has occurred. Once baseline begins, it is advisable to continue reliability checks intermittently throughout the program to ensure that behavior is consistently observed. If such checks are made only at the inception of the program, observers may over time become increasingly lax in their scoring or drift away from the definitions that they should be using. Hence, observers may become less reliable over time.

Agreement has to achieve an acceptable level before baseline observations are begun and has to maintain that level throughout the project. Although no single criterion for acceptable agreement has been set, convention dictates that agreement be between 80 and 100 percent. Interobserver agreement lower than 80 percent suggests that a moderate amount of error occurs in recording. Obtaining low agreement before a program is begun is no reason to be discouraged. In many instances, low agreement signals that the response definition should be more carefully specified. It is desirable to find this out early, so that the response definition can be clarified for those who administer the program as well as those who observe behavior.

How the reliability checks are conducted may influence the level of interobserver agreement. Hence, in addition to specifying the level of agreement, it is important to ensure that this level is determined under carefully conducted conditions. A major factor that may influence interobserver agreement is whether observers know that their agreement is being checked. When observers know their observations are being checked, they may show higher agreement than when they believe their observations are not being checked (see Foster, Bell-Dolan, & Burge, 1988). They may even record behaviors differently (for example, less disruptive behavior) if they believe their observations are being checked by a superviser. As a general rule, it is important to make the conditions of assessment similar on both assessed and unassessed days. It may be useful to convey the impression that all observations are being checked, so that the data obtained on checked days will not differ from the data obtained on unchecked days. Because observers tend to be more accurate when they believe that their agreement is being assessed, keeping them aware and informed of frequent reliability checks may be advantageous even on days on which no checks are made.

General guidelines for conducting reliability assessment are (1) to ensure that observers work independently without access to one another's recording sheets, (2) to supervise observers carefully during a reliability check, (3) not to convey expectations of the experimenter or the extent to which incoming data are consistent with these expectations, and (4) to have persons other than observers calculate reliability. These practices are in response to studies occasionally showing biases introduced by not engaging in careful reliability procedures (Foster, Bell-Dolan, & Burge, 1988; Kazdin, 1977b). Perhaps even more important than the specific practices is conveying to observers that careful and accurate recording and overall integrity of the procedures are the highest priorities.

Estimating Agreement

Interobserver agreement provides an estimate of how consistently behavior is observed and scored. The procedures for estimating agreement differ somewhat depending on the assessment method used. The procedures that estimate agreement for frequency and interval methods are highlighted here because they can be adapted readily to the other assessment procedures.[3]

Agreement for frequency measures requires that two observers simultaneously, but independently, count the target response during the time set aside for observation. At the end of the observation period, the frequencies obtained by the observers are compared. The major interest is whether the observers record the target behavior with equal frequency. A percentage of agreement can be formed to measure the degree to which two observers agree in their final counts.

It is likely that no two observers will agree perfectly in their recorded frequencies. To determine the percentage of agreement, a fraction is formed from the frequency obtained by each observer. *Interobserver agreement is determined by dividing the smaller frequency by the larger frequency and multiplying by 100.* For example, in the home, parents may count the number of times that a child spills food on the floor during a meal. During a reliability check, both parents independently count food spills. By the end of the meal, one parent has counted 20 instances of spilling, whereas the other parent has counted 18 instances. To form a percentage of agreement, the smaller number (18) is divided by the larger number (20) and the quotient is multiplied by 100. Agreement for this observation period was 90 percent (18/20 × 100).

Interpretation of this percentage must be made cautiously. The figure indicates that the observers agree on the total frequency of the behavior with a 10 percent (100 percent minus 90 percent) margin of error. This does not mean that the observers agree 90 percent of the time. Although one observer recorded 18 responses and the other recorded 20 responses, there is no way of knowing whether they recorded the *same* responses. Thus, reliability reflects agreement on the total number of responses, rather than agreement in any specific instance. A potential disadvantage in using a frequency measure is that when the behavior is not carefully defined, a high percentage of agreement for frequency data may still conceal a substantial amount of disagreement.

Calculation of agreement is different when an interval method of assessment is used. Interobserver agreement is usually computed on the basis of the proportion of intervals in which two observers agree on the occurrence of a target response. An agreement is scored if both observers record the occurrence of behavior in the same interval. A disagreement is scored when one observer scores a behavior in an interval and the other does not. For example, in a reliability check made between two observers independently recording the aggressive behavior of a child in an elementary school classroom, both observers are required to observe the child at the same time. Each observer records behaviors for several intervals. During each interval that the child is observed, the observer marks the occurrence or nonoccurrence of aggressive behavior. When the observers finish recording, reliability can be calculated.

Interobserver agreement is determined by dividing the number of intervals in which both observers mark the behavior as occurring (agreements) by the number of agreements plus the number of intervals in which one observer scored the behavior and the other did not (disagreements) and multiplying by 100. For example, if two observers recorded behavior for 50

10-second intervals and both observers agreed on the occurrence of the behavior in 20 intervals and disagreed in 5 intervals, overall agreement would be 20/(20 + 5) × 100, or 80 percent.

Although the observers recorded behavior for 50 intervals, not all of the intervals are used to calculate reliability. An interval is counted only if at least one observer recorded the *occurrence* of the target behavior. Excluding intervals in which neither observer recorded the target behavior is based on the following reasoning. If these intervals were counted, they would be considered agreements because both observers "agree" that the response did not occur. Yet in observing behavior, many intervals may be marked without the occurrence of the target behavior. If these were included as agreements, the reliability estimate would be inflated beyond the level obtained when occurrences alone are counted as agreements. To avoid this increase, most investigators restrict agreements to response occurrence intervals.

The above formula for estimating interobserver agreement for interval assessment is very commonly used. Yet many investigators have questioned its adequacy. The main concern is whether agreement should be restricted to intervals for which both observers record an occurrence of the behavior or should also include intervals for which both observers record a nonoccurrence. In one sense, both of these situations indicate that the observers were in agreement for a particular interval. The issue is important because the estimate of reliability depends on the frequency of the client's behavior and on whether occurrence and/or nonoccurrence agreements are included in the formula. If the client performs the target behavior relatively frequently or infrequently, observers are likely to have a high proportion of agreements on occurrences or nonoccurrences, respectively. Hence, the estimate of reliability may differ greatly depending on what is counted as an agreement between observers. Several investigators have discussed the problem of deciding what should be counted as an agreement and have suggested additional formulas for possible ways of using both occurrence and nonoccurrence intervals (see Kazdin, 1982c).

SUMMARY AND CONCLUSION

Identifying the goals of a behavior modification program and translating these into concrete, operational terms are critical steps preceding intervention. Selecting the goals is usually based on criteria related to client adjustment. Most often goals are designed to bring individuals to within normative levels of functioning or to reduce risk of injury, maladjustment, or felt problems in relation to themselves or to others. Once the goal is identified, the constituent behaviors need to be specified in concrete terms. Specification of target behaviors, the focus of the intervention, is often facilitated by *task analysis.* This procedure identifies the steps that constitute the behavior and helps specify and define concrete behaviors. Whether a single behavior or several different behaviors are identified as the target(s) of the intervention, the definition has to be concrete. The definition should ensure that few inferences need to be made by observers who assess behavior and others who ultimately will be responsible for providing consequences to alter behavior.

Assessment entails more than evaluation of the target behavior. *Functional analysis* is an assessment approach that examines antecedents, stimulus events, behaviors, and consequences. The goal is to identify factors that control the behavior, to generate hypotheses about these variables, and to translate these hypotheses into alternative interventions. Functional analysis conveys the very strong connection between assessment and treatment.

Assessment of target behaviors as well as other events in the situation can be completed in many different ways. Commonly used methods include frequency counts, discrete categorization, the number of clients who perform the response, interval assessment, and response duration. Once the assessment strategy is selected, it is important to evaluate the extent to which observers agree when scoring the response. Interobserver agreement or reliability of assessment is evaluated, although observers record the response independently. The exact formula in which reliability is estimated varies depending upon the assessment method. Periodic retraining and constant reliability assessment help ensure consistency in observing behavior among observers. In general, assessment plays a central role in behavioral research. Delineation of the target behavior and the conditions with which it is associated provide an important basis from which to launch treatment.

Notes

1. In discussions of functional analysis, investigators sometimes speak of identifying *causes* of behavior. This term is useful to convey the goal and focus of functional analysis—namely, to identify conditions that control the occurrence and maintenance of behavior. If these factors can be identified and then altered, behavior is more easily treated. Yet, the notion of "cause" can have many meanings and can easily imply more than what functional analysis is designed to accomplish. Functional analysis can be used to identify *current* factors that influence behavior. The causes of behavior can have many different factors, presumably, beginning with the onset of the behavior, perhaps early in life (for example, self-injury, tics, aggressive acts). Functional analysis focuses on current factors that influence behavior rather than on historical causes or underpinnings of behavior.

2. Among terms, *interobserver agreement* more accurately reflects the issue of interest in applied behavior analysis. *Reliability* is a much broader term in psychological assessment and reflects a number of different characteristics of measurement, most of which have been used in the context of developing and evaluating questionnaires and various inventories. However, the term *reliability*

continues to be used as interchangeable with the term *interobserver agreement* in published studies of behavioral programs. Hence, the convention is continued here.

3. The methods of estimating agreement between and among observers extend beyond the material provided here. For a more technical discussion of these methods and how they are used, other sources should be consulted (Iwata, Bailey, Fuqua, Neef, Page, & Reid, 1989; Kazdin, 1982c).

For Further Reading

Barrett, B. H., Johnston, J. M., & Pennypacker, H. S. (1986). Behavior: Its units, dimensions, and measurement. In R. O. Nelson & S. C. Hayes (Eds.), *Conceptual foundations of behavioral assessment* (pp. 156–200). New York: Guilford.

Bellack, A. S., & Hersen, M. (Eds.). (1988). *Behavioral assessment: A practical handbook.* Needham Heights, MA: Allyn & Bacon.

Hartmann, D. P. (Ed.). (1985). Mini-series: Target behavior selection. *Behavioral Assessment, 7,* 1–78.

Haynes, S. N., & O'Brien, W. H. (1990). Functional analysis in behavior therapy. *Clinical Psychology Review, 10,* 649–668.

O'Neill, R. E., Horner, R. H., Albin, R. W., Storey, K., & Sprague, J. R. (1990). *Functional analysis of problem behavior: A practical assessment guide.* Sycamore, IL: Sycamore.

CHAPTER FOUR

HOW TO EVALUATE A BEHAVIOR MODIFICATION PROGRAM

Assessment of behavior change is essential in behavior modification. Assessment may reveal that behavior has changed, but it does *not* show what caused the change. Proponents of behavior modification are extremely interested in determining the cause of behavior change. Once the cause is clear, our knowledge about the factors that influence behavior is increased. Also, if treatment can be shown to be responsible for change, it can be applied to the same person in the future and to clients in other settings, with increased confidence that behavior will change in the new applications as well.

In many cases, the person who conducts the program may be interested only in changing behavior and not in isolating the cause of the change. Yet, even in such a case, it may be important to identify what was responsible for behavior change. For example, a program may be carried out by a parent to reduce the fighting of two children at home. After fighting has been assessed (baseline), a program may be implemented (for example, praising the children for playing cooperatively). Once this has been done, assessment may reveal that the behavior has changed. Did the praise cause the behavior change? Perhaps the change occurred because one of the children was no longer physically ill when the program began and was therefore less irritable and less likely to get into fights. Or perhaps other events (in addition to praising the children) for one or both of the children— such as a new friend in the neighborhood, new after-school activities, or changes in the behavior of the children's peers or parents—contributed to the change. All of these explanations can be ruled out to determine whether delivery of praise was responsible for the change.

The cause of behavior change can be demonstrated in different ways. The program designer usually plans the situation so the program's specific contribution to behavior change can be demonstrated. The plan of the program used to demonstrate the cause of behavior change is referred to as the *experimental design.* The purpose of the design is to identify the variables that influence, control, or are responsible for behavior change. In behavioral research, this is referred to as the demonstration of a *functional relation* between the target behavior and the intervention or other factor. A functional relation is demonstrated when altering the experimental condition or contingency systematically changes behavior. Behavior is shown to be a *function* of the environmental events that produced change.

Different experimental designs can be used to show that the program, rather than extraneous events, altered behavior. The designs are usually referred to as single-case experimental designs. Although such designs can be used with large groups of individuals, their unique characteristic is that they can be used with individual cases (for example, one patient or student). Commonly used single-case designs are presented next to illustrate both the experimental arrangements themselves as well as the overall method of evaluating interventions in applied settings.[1]

REVERSAL OR ABAB DESIGNS

Reversal designs refer to a large number of arrangements in which different conditions are presented or removed over time with a client or group of clients. The designs illustrate very nicely the rationale underlying single-case research and the demonstration of functional relations. The version that illustrates the design most clearly includes four phases during which behavior is observed. The design begins with the assessment of the target behavior to obtain the baseline rate of performance before implementing specific contingencies. The baseline period or phase (referred to as the *A phase*) is continued until the rate of the response appears to be stable or until it is evident that the response does not improve over time. A stable rate of behavior during baseline serves as a basis for evaluating subsequent change. Baseline provides an estimate of what behavior would be in the future if the program were not introduced. After behavior stabilizes and follows a consistent pattern (several days are usually sufficient), the experimental phase is begun. During the experimental phase, the intervention (for example, reinforcement, punishment, extinction, or some combination of procedures) is implemented. The experimental or intervention phase (referred to as the *B phase*) is continued until behavior reaches a stable level or diverges from the level predicted by the baseline rate.

Figure 4–1 provides a hypothetical example of observations of some desirable behavior plotted over several days. Baseline data suggest that the behavior of interest falls within a fairly narrow range. In the immediate future, one would expect the behavior to continue roughly at this level. A dashed line has been added to show an extrapolation of baseline or the predicted level of performance if baseline conditions were to continue. Next, we intervene by adding a treatment (for example, reinforcement of the target behavior). During the intervention phase, (B phase), there is an increase in performance. Up to this point in the program, the *change* in behavior is evident. We say that the change is evident because it seems to be a departure from what we had projected (dashed line) from baseline. In the B phase, the frequency of behavior has increased and the slope or trend has shifted upward. If treatment were not effective, we would have expected the baseline pattern and level to have continued. At this point, using information from the first two phases, we have shown that there is a change. However, the *cause* of the change is unclear. Because the change in behavior coincides with implementation of the program, it is likely that the program accounts for the change. Yet, one cannot be sure that change in behavior is a function of the conditions we have altered.

After behavior attains a stable level, the experimental condition is withdrawn and the baseline condition (A phase) is reinstated. During the baseline condition, of course, no program or intervention is used to control behavior. A return to baseline conditions is called a *reversal* phase because the experimental condition is withdrawn and behavior usually reverses (that

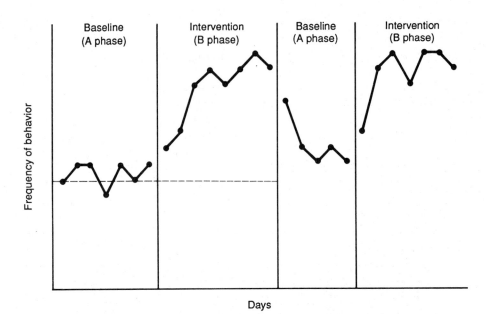

F I G U R E 4–1
Hypothetical rate of some behavior, plotted over baseline (A) and intervention (B) phases.

is, returns to or near the level of the original baseline). The purpose of the reversal phase is to determine whether performance would have remained unchanged (relative to baseline) had the program not been introduced. In Figure 4–1, the second A phase shows this reversal of behavior toward baseline. When behavior reverts to or near baseline levels, the experimental phase (B phase) is reinstated. If the intervention is responsible for the change, behavior should change again in the second experimental or B phase.

Changes in A and B conditions from one phase to another are not made until performance during a given phase is stable or is clearly different from performance during the previous phase. When changes are evident after the pattern of performance is clear within a phase, the results are easy to interpret. The pattern in Figure 4–1 suggests that the intervention was responsible for change. The reason is that whenever the intervention was in effect (B phases), behavior improved; whenever there was no intervention (A phases), behavior remained at a stable but lower rate. It is possible that something other than the intervention caused the change. However, the intervention is the most plausible cause.

The design is referred to as a reversal design because phases in the design are reversed to demonstrate the effect of the program. The design is also referred to as an ABAB design because A and B phases are alternated. If performance changes in the experimental phase relative to baseline, reverts to baseline or near baseline levels during the second baseline phase, and again changes in the final experimental phase, this provides a clear demonstration of the effectiveness of the experimental condition.

Examples of reversal designs are abundant. One program clearly illustrating the design focused on the aggressive behavior of elementary school children (Murphy, Hutchison, & Bailey, 1983). The children were 344 first- and second-graders who played outside before school began. The purpose of the study was to develop and evaluate an intervention to reduce the relatively high rates of aggressive behavior (such as striking, slapping, tripping, kicking, pushing, or punching others) on the playground. During baseline, the children were observed for 12 days to assess the number of aggressive behaviors during the 20-minute period before school began. The intervention, which included several components, began after baseline. The major component was organized game activities, including rope jumping and foot races supervised by playground aides. Aides led these activities, which structured the play of the children. Aides were also instructed to praise appropriate play behavior (reinforcement) and to use a mild punishment procedure (placing disruptive children on a bench for two minutes for particularly unruly behavior). The intervention was discontinued after seven days in a reversal phase to see whether the program was responsible for behavior change. Finally, the intervention was reinstated. The results are presented in Figure 4–2. The figure shows that the number of aggressive incidents during each intervention phase decreased relative to the baseline and reversal phases. This demonstrated that behavior improved only when nonverbal approval increased. From the changes in behavior that occurred when the experimental condition was presented, withdrawn, and re-presented, it could be concluded that other influences probably did not account for the results.

Design Variations

There are many variations of the design. The number and type of treatments can vary within the design. The ABAB version includes a particular treatment (in the B phase). Yet, sometimes the treatment is not effective or not sufficiently effective to achieve the intervention goals. A second treatment or variation of the first treatment (C phase) might be added. This might be summarized as ABCAC, in which once an effective intervention is identified (C), it is evaluated in the usual way. An important feature of continuous assessment in single-case research is the ability to see whether behavior is changing and changing sufficiently. If it is not, treatment can be modified to improve the effects achieved for the client.

The order of presenting the conditions is another dimension along which the designs can vary. The reversal design requires that the experimental condition be presented and temporarily withdrawn at some point in time. There are variations of this basic design. Sometimes it is undesirable

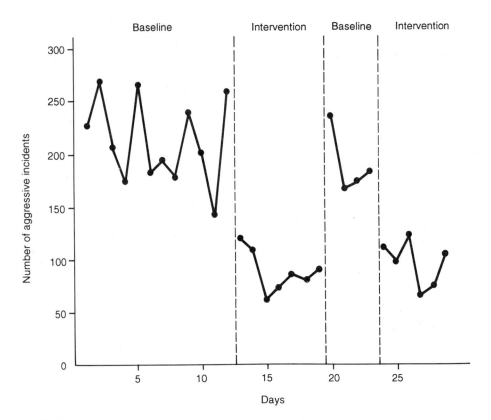

FIGURE 4–2

Number of incidents of aggressive behavior recorded on the playground before school started. Baseline—no intervention. Intervention—organized activities, praise, and time out. Reversal—return to baseline conditions. Intervention—return to the activities, praise, and time-out procedures.

SOURCE: Murphy, H. A., Hutchison, J. M., & Bailey, J. S. (1983).

to begin with a baseline phase because some immediate intervention is urgently required. For example, if fighting among delinquents is frequent and intense in a given setting, it might be undesirable to begin with a baseline period because some immediate therapeutic intervention is needed. In other situations, it also might be reasonable to forgo the initial baseline phase. In some other cases, target behaviors, such as exercising, completing homework, or saving money, may have exceedingly low rates or not have been performed at all, so that baseline might not be the first phase of the program. In these instances where baseline is not employed initially, a BABA design might be used. This is the reversal design beginning with the experimental phase (B) followed by baseline or reversal (A) phases.[2]

Finally, ABAB designs vary by precisely what is implemented in the reversal phase. The most commonly used alternative in the reversal phase is to withdraw the intervention. This usually restores the conditions to baseline. Understandably, behavior would likely revert to baseline levels when the intervention is withdrawn.

Another alternative during the reversal phase is *noncontingent delivery of the reinforcer.* Essentially, this refers to delivery of the consequences independent of behavior. This strategy is selected to show that it is not the event per se (for example, praise) that results in behavior change but rather the relationship of the event to behavior. For example, to change teasing among two siblings at home, parents may use praise as the reinforcer for cooperative behavior. During the intervention, when the children are playing nicely in the same room, praise is delivered by one of the parents. In other words, praise is contingent on the appropriate behavior. During the reversal phase, praise could be removed (withdrawal of the intervention and return to baseline conditions). Alternatively, praise could be continued but delivered noncontingently. Periodically, the parent might provide praise independent of what the children are doing. It is likely that cooperative behavior would decline because it is not reinforced or not reinforced very consistently. The results would show that it is not delivery of the praise per se that alters behavior but rather the delivery of praise contingent on the desired behavior.

The variations in the presentation of different treatments, the ordering of the phases, and the procedures used in the reversal phase lead to a large number of design permutations. In each case, the impact of the intervention is shown by changes in the pattern of the target behavior over time.

Problems and Considerations

Reversal designs nicely illustrate the underlying basis of experimental research by showing how one can draw conclusions by isolating the effect of the intervention. With these designs, the investigator can demonstrate that the intervention, rather than extraneous influences (such as changes in other events, maturation of the client, random fluctuations in performance), probably accounts for the change. The design very usefully shows how research with the single case can contribute to understanding the effects of treatment.

From the standpoint of helping an individual change behavior, one can see immediately that the design may be limited. Problems in the design emerge in the reversal phase. If it is possible to demonstrate a reversal of behavior, the reversal is usually *undesirable.* For example, autistic and mentally retarded children sometimes severely injure themselves by banging their heads for extended periods of time. If a program decreased this behavior, it would be undesirable to show that head banging would return in a reversal phase. Even when behavior is not dangerous, it is usually undesirable to make behavior worse after gains have been made. Behavioral programs are designed to focus on behaviors that are clinically or socially important to the clients and to those with whom they interact. Once some improvements are made, it would be difficult to justify a reversal phase, even if only for a short period.

Relatedly, ethical issues obviously arise when implementing a reversal phase. A reversal phase essentially is designed to make the client's behavior worse in some way. Whether behavior should be made worse and when such a goal would be justified are difficult issues to resolve. In a given clinical situation, the consequences of making the client worse need to be weighed carefully for the client and for those in contact with the client. In fact, when reversal phases are used, they tend to be relatively brief—even for only one or a few days. Yet, the problems of reversing behavior may still arise.

Apart from clinical and ethical issues, there is the experimental design issue. Sometimes when a program is withdrawn and a reversal phase is implemented, behavior does not return to the baseline rate of performance. When there is no reversal in behavior, it is not clear whether the experimental condition or some other event led to the initial behavior change. For example, in one report, electric shock was used as a desperate effort to decrease the coughing of a 14-year-old boy who had not responded to medical treatment or to attempts to ignore the coughing (Creer, Chai, & Hoffman, 1977). The cough was so disruptive and distracting to others that the boy was expelled from school until his cough could be controlled. Treatment consisted of applying a mild electric shock to the boy's forearm for coughing. After only one shock, the behavior was completely eliminated. The boy returned to school and did not suffer episodes of coughing for up to two and a half years after treatment. Stopping the punishment after one shock amounts to a reversal phase. Fortunately for the child, cessation of the shock did not lead to a return of the behavior. It is highly likely that treatment accounted for the change, especially given the history of the behavior and the rapidity of the change. Yet, in general, without such dramatic and rapid effects, it would be difficult to attribute the change to treatment if no reversal in behavior were shown when treatment is withdrawn.

In other situations, a reversal design should not be used because behavior would not be expected to reverse. Once certain behaviors are developed or altered, they may be maintained by favorable consequences that result directly from their performance. For example, increasing a child's social behavior may not reverse once the intervention is suspended because the behavior is now maintained by peer reinforcement rather than by the teacher praise that initiated the behavior. Generally, reversal of behavior may be difficult to achieve in situations where the behavior is maintained by naturally occurring events in the environment that are not directly manipulated by the teacher, parent, therapist, or investigator.

In general, a reversal design can raise obstacles. If a reversal does occur, that may be problematic if the behavior is important for the clients or for those in contact with them. If a reversal does not occur, this raises obstacles in concluding that the intervention led to the change. Fortunately, other designs are available to demonstrate the effects of the program without using a reversal of conditions.

MULTIPLE-BASELINE DESIGNS

In *multiple-baseline designs,* the effect of the contingency is demonstrated by showing that behavior change is associated with introduction of the contingency at different points in time. The key feature is showing these changes across different baselines. Usually, two or more behaviors are observed and serve as separate baselines. The intervention is introduced to one of the behaviors and later to the other behavior(s). The effect of the intervention is demonstrated by showing a pattern of change as the intervention is introduced. Multiple-baseline designs do not rely on or require a reversal of conditions to show the effect of an intervention. They do require the collection of data on more than one behavior, person, or situation, as illustrated below.

Variations: Behaviors, Persons, Settings, and Time

Multiple-baseline designs vary depending on the collection of data on more than one behavior, person, setting, or time. Two of the more commonly used variations illustrate the method and utility of the designs. In the *multiple-baseline design across behaviors,* baseline data are collected across two or more behaviors of a given individual or group of individuals. After each baseline has reached a stable rate, the experimental condition is implemented for only one of the behaviors, whereas baseline conditions are continued for the other behavior(s). The initial behavior subjected to the experimental condition is expected to change, whereas the other behaviors are expected to remain at baseline levels. When rates are stable for all behaviors, the second behavior is included in the contingency. This procedure is continued until all behaviors for which baseline data were gathered are included in the contingency. Ideally, each behavior changes only as it is included in the experimental contingency and not before. Control of the specific experimental contingency is demonstrated when behavior change is associated in each case with the introduction of the contingency. The multiple-baseline design across behaviors is useful when an individual or group has a number of behaviors that are to be changed.

A multiple-baseline design across behaviors was illustrated in a program designed for a 4-year-old girl who had sleep problems (Ronen, 1991). The child would not fall asleep in her bed and would awaken and engage in tantrums throughout the night when placed in her bed. A reinforcement program was developed in consultation with a therapist but was carried out by the child's parents at home. The intervention consisted of reinforcement (praise, attention, candy) for more appropriate sleep behaviors and extinction of tantrums, and time out for inappropriate behaviors. Observations by the parents were obtained daily for several behaviors. After baseline information was obtained, the intervention was applied to the separate behaviors in sequence, in accord with the multiple-baseline design. Figure 4–3 illustrates the behaviors, observations, and points in time when the intervention was introduced. The figure shows child performance during baseline before the intervention was implemented (Phase I). The intervention (Phase II) was introduced to each behavior at different points in time. The pattern of change suggests that the intervention was responsible for change; the reason is that each behavior changed when the intervention was introduced. The most plausible interpretation of this pattern is that the intervention rather than some other event occurring in time led to change. Assessment continued over a period of weeks to evaluate follow-up (Phase III). The follow-up assessment suggests that the gains were maintained.

The requirements of the multiple-baseline design were clearly met in this report. If all behaviors had changed when only the first one was included into the contingency, it would have been unclear whether the contingency caused the change. In that case, an extraneous event may have influenced all behaviors simultaneously. Yet, the specific effects obtained in this report strongly suggest the influence of training on each behavior.

As another variation, the multiple-baseline design can be conducted across individuals or clients. In the *multiple-baseline design across individuals,* baseline data are collected for a particular behavior across *two or more individuals.* After the behavior of each individual has reached a stable rate, the experimental condition is implemented for only one of the individuals, while baseline conditions are continued for the other(s). The behavior of the person exposed to the experimental condition should change whereas the behavior of the other individual(s) should not. When behavior stabilizes for all individuals, the contingency is extended to another person. This procedure is continued until all individuals for whom baseline data were collected are included in the contingency. As with other multiple-baseline designs, no reversal of the experimental condition (that is, return

---

F I G U R E   4–3 (*right*)
Change in sleep habits of a 4-year-old girl with sleep disorder. The impact of the intervention is demonstrated in a multiple-baseline design across behaviors. After baseline data were obtained on each behavior (Phase I), the intervention was introduced (Phase II) separately across each of the different behaviors. Each behavior changed when the intervention was introduced; with some exceptions behavior change closely followed the application of the intervention to that behavior. Consequently, the pattern of change suggests that the intervention, rather than more general extraneous influences, accounted for the changes. In the final phase (III), follow-up data were gathered.
SOURCE: Ronen, T. (1991).

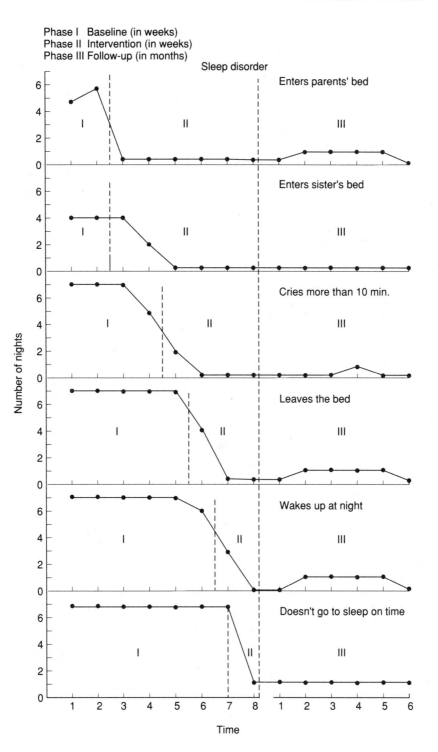

Phase I   Baseline (in weeks)
Phase II   Intervention (in weeks)
Phase III   Follow-up (in months)

to baseline) is required to demonstrate that the contingency was responsible for behavior change. The multiple-baseline design across individuals is useful when a given behavior is to be altered across a number of clients in a group.

A multiple-baseline design across individuals was used in a study designed to increase the extent to which emergency room nurses wore gloves during medical procedures to protect against human immunodeficiency virus (HIV) (DeVries, Burnette, & Redmon, 1991). Hospitals have many procedures and practices to protect health care workers from contact with patients' bodily fluids—for example, through accidental needle punctures and handling of blood—to prevent infection with HIV. Wearing protective gloves during emergency room at-risk (or potential-risk) situations was observed for four nurses across different nursing shifts. After baseline observations, assessed by other nurses working in the hospital, a feedback program was implemented as the intervention. During the feedback (intervention) phase, each nurse was seen briefly and individually. She was told how many times (in percentage of opportunities) she had worn protective gloves among the at-risk situations, was shown the daily data in graphical form, was informed of the at-risk situations in which gloves were to be worn, was praised for use of the gloves, and was encouraged to increase this frequency. Feedback sessions required five minutes each and were given periodically through the intervention phase.

The intervention was introduced in a multiple-baseline design fashion across four nurses. As shown in Figure 4–4, baseline rates varied for the individuals. Even so, in each case, introduction of the intervention was associated with an increase in the wearing of protective gloves. Other events that might have influenced the behavior, such as repeated observation over time, seeing others wear gloves, or changes in hospital life, could not easily explain the change. The results strongly argue for the role of the feedback intervention in changing behavior.

The multiple-baseline designs across behaviors and individuals are the more commonly used variations. There are other variations as well in which baseline data are gathered across several situations (for example, in class, on the playground), settings (for example, home, school), or times (for example, morning, afternoon, evening). The variations are similar in the introduction of the intervention at different points in time. As with other variations, the design is useful when there is interest in achieving behavior change across different baselines.

F I G U R E   4–4 (*right*)
Percentage of contact (at risk for bodily fluid contact) situations in which protective gloves were worn by four emergency room nurses for consecutive ten-hour work shifts. The intervention (feedback) was introduced in a multiple-baseline design across individuals. Arrows during the intervention phase indicate delivery of feedback by the nurse responsible for delivering the intervention.
SOURCE: De Vries, J. E., Burnette, M. M., & Redmon, W. K. (1991).

Problems and Considerations

Multiple-baseline designs demonstrate the effects of contingencies without using a reversal phase. With such designs, there is no need to return to baseline conditions and temporarily lose the gains made during the behavior modification program. Hence, these designs should be used when a reversal in behavior would be undesirable or unexpected. The designs require that there be two or more observable behaviors, individuals, or situations.

There are possible problems with multiple-baseline designs that should be mentioned. In the multiple-baseline design across behaviors, a clear demonstration of the effect of the contingency depends on showing that behavior changes *only* when the contingency is introduced. If a behavior changes before the contingency for that behavior is introduced (that is, during baseline), it is unclear whether the contingency is responsible for change. If changing the first behavior also changes the second behavior before the second behavior is included in the contingency, the specific effect of the contingency on behavior is unclear. Studies report that altering one behavior of an individual occasionally results in changes in behaviors that are not included in the contingency (for example, Parrish, Cataldo, Kolko, Neef, & Egel, 1986). In situations where generalization across responses occurs, a multiple-baseline design across behavior would not show the causal effect of the contingencies. There are analogous problems in the multiple-baseline designs across individuals or across situations. In these designs, changes in the behavior of one individual may alter the behavior of other individuals for whom baseline conditions are still in effect; or changes in behavior in one situation may be associated with changes in other situations even though the program has not been introduced in these situations (see Kazdin, 1982c).

In spite of the potential problems in demonstrating the specific effect of the contingencies in multiple-baseline designs, these designs are usually quite useful in demonstrating the relationship between a behavior and an experimental contingency. The problem appears to occur infrequently. But if it appears likely that altering one behavior (or behavior of one individual, or behavior in one situation) can produce generalized effects, a multiple-baseline design might be avoided.

An important consideration in using a multiple-baseline design is deciding how many baselines will be needed. Two baselines are a minimum, but more are usually desirable. As a general rule, the more baselines across which the effect of the intervention is demonstrated, the more convincing is the demonstration of a causal relationship. Whether an investigation provides a convincing demonstration across a given set of baselines depends on such factors as the duration of the baselines, the presence of trends or excessive variability during baseline, the rapidity of behavior change after the intervention, and the magnitude of behavior change. Usually two or three baselines are enough if the baseline data are stable and the intervention produces marked effects. Because it is difficult to predict the magnitude of behavior change and the stability of behavior within phases, it is often safer to choose a minimum of three baselines.

CHANGING-CRITERION DESIGN

The effect of a contingency can be demonstrated without using a reversal or multiple-baseline design. The *changing-criterion design* demonstrates the effect of the contingency by showing that behavior matches a criterion that is set for either reinforcement or punishment. As the criterion is repeatedly changed, behavior increases or decreases to match the criterion.

The changing-criterion design begins with a baseline period of observation. After baseline, the experimental contingency is introduced so that a certain level of performance is required to earn reinforcement. For example, the behavior may have to be performed a certain number of times per day to earn the reinforcer. When performance consistently meets or surpasses that criterion over a few days, the criterion is made more stringent. The criterion is repeatedly changed in a gradual fashion until the goal is achieved. The effect of the contingency is demonstrated if the behavior appears to match the criterion repeatedly as that criterion is changed.

A changing-criterion design was used to evaluate an exercise program for 11-year-old boys, some of whom were obese (DeLuca & Holborn, 1992). Exercise consisted of riding a stationary bicycle during a time of the day at their elementary school. During baseline, each child was told he could exercise as long as he liked (without an intervention). After baseline, the intervention, which consisted of the opportunity to earn points based on the amount of exercise, was introduced. The points could be traded for different backup reinforcers, such as model cars, planes, puzzles, books, handheld games, and other items, at the end of the session. The amount of exercise was measured in terms of the number of revolutions (wheel turns) on the bicycle. When a youth was pedaling at the level that would earn points, a bell rang and a light on the bicycle went on. The changing criterion feature of the design was intended to develop increasingly vigorous exercise. The baseline rate was used to decide the first criterion level that would be used in the intervention phase. When the intervention began, each child was required to increase exercise (revolutions) by 15 percent over baseline to earn reinforcement. When performance met this criterion, the criterion was shifted to 30 percent of baseline and then shifted to 45 percent of baseline rate when performance met 30 percent of baseline.

The effects of the program for five of the boys are presented in Figure 4–5. The figure shows that, during the intervention phase, exercise rates shifted to the new criterion that was invoked to earn points. There was a brief return to baseline in the study and then a reinstatement of the highest criterion. (The return to baseline is not needed for the design but further suggests that the intervention was responsible for change.) The results

indicated that exercise consistently followed the criterion. Accordingly, it is plausible that the reinforcement program, rather than extraneous influences, accounted for behavior change. As an aside, the boys rated the program very favorably, expressed greater interest in biking in general, and became involved in some athletics at school.

Problems and Considerations

The changing-criterion design is especially well suited to responses that are shaped gradually rather than acquired in one or a few trials. If performance shows a marked improvement or attainment of the final goal when the criterion is not set at that level, the relationship between the intervention and behavior change is unclear. To show that alteration of the criterion accounts for changes in behavior, the rate of behavior has to be such that it allows several changes to be made in the criterion before the terminal goal is achieved. Thus, a behavior to be decreased may need to be performed at a high rate so that several changes can be made in reaching the terminal level. A behavior to be increased may need to have a potential number that is high enough to permit several criterion levels.

The changing-criterion design is less satisfactory than reversal and multiple-baseline designs in ruling out the influence of extraneous events that might account for behavior change. Even if a behavior matches a criterion, the behavior may be changing as a function of some other event in the person's life that led to a directional change (that is, a decrease or an increase) in the behavior over time. A clear relationship is demonstrated only when performance matches the criterion very closely.

The design can be strengthened by making bidirectional changes in the criterion during the intervention phase. Rather than simply making the criterion increasingly stringent, it can be made more stringent at some points and slightly less stringent at others. This does not mean that a reversal (return to baseline) phase is implemented. Instead, the criterion could be shifted to a previous criterion level. If behavior improves as the criterion is made less stringent for a brief period, it is extremely unlikely that extraneous events could account for the results.

From the standpoint of clinical or applied priorities, the changing-criterion design is quite useful. The focus on gradual change is consistent

---

F I G U R E   4–5 (left)
Mean (average) number of revolutions pedaled per minute during baseline and intervention (15 percent increase, 30 percent increase, 45 percent increase over baseline), return to baseline (BL) and intervention (45 percent increase) for obese and non-obese boys aged 11. The changing criterion is specified above the phase and reflects a variable ratio schedule (or the average number of revolutions required for reinforcement for that child).
SOURCE: DeLuca, R. V., & Holborn, S. W. (1992).

with the goals of many behavior change programs in which shaping is used. As noted previously, shaping is the reinforcement of approximations toward the final goal behavior. The changing-criterion design can be used in cases in which the requirements for reinforcement and task completion can be increased in this gradual way.

ALTERNATING- OR SIMULTANEOUS-TREATMENT DESIGN

The *alternating- or simultaneous-treatment design* examines the effects of different interventions, each of which is implemented during the same phase. The interventions are implemented concurrently but under different conditions or at different times. Different patterns of performance under the different conditions are used to identify whether one or more conditions is more or most effective. The design is especially useful when the investigator is interested in determining *which* among two or more experimental conditions is more or most effective. Also, the design does not require a reversal or return to baseline as part of the demonstration.

Design Variations

The critical feature of the design is the simultaneous or concurrent comparison of two or more conditions in the same phase. This can be accomplished in many different ways. In one variation, the design begins with a baseline phase. After baseline, two or more interventions are implemented to alter the response. The different interventions are administered during the same phase but under varied and alternating stimulus conditions. For example, two interventions could be compared by implementing both of them on the same day but at different periods (morning and afternoon). The different interventions are *balanced* across all of the conditions so that their effects can be separated from those conditions until the response stabilizes under the separate interventions. If the response stabilizes at different levels during the intervention phase, the interventions differ in effectiveness. Once the differential effectiveness of the interventions has been demonstrated, a phase may be implemented in which the more (or most) effective intervention is given under all of the conditions (for example, each period).

A simultaneous-treatment design was used to evaluate different interventions designed to reduce the frequency of stereotyped repetitive movements among hospitalized mentally retarded children (Ollendick, Shapiro, & Barrett, 1981). Three children, ages 7 to 8 years, exhibited stereotypical behaviors, such as repetitive hand gestures and hair twirling. Observations of each child were made in a classroom setting while the child performed various visual-motor tasks (for example, puzzles). The behavior of the child was observed each day for three sessions, after which the intervention phase was implemented.

During the intervention phase, three conditions were compared—two active interventions and a continuation of baseline conditions. One of the treatment procedures consisted of physically restraining the child's hands on the table for 30 seconds, so that he or she could not perform the repetitive behaviors. The second treatment procedure consisted of physically guiding the child to engage in the appropriate use of the task materials. Instead of merely restraining the child, this procedure was designed to develop appropriate alternative behaviors that the child could perform with his or her hands. The final condition during the intervention phase was a continuation of baseline. Physical restraint, positive practice, and continuation of baseline were implemented each day across three time periods.

Figure 4–6 illustrates the results for a child who engaged in hand-posturing gestures. As is evident from the first intervention phase, both physical restraint and positive practice led to reductions in performance; positive practice was more effective. The extent of the reduction is especially clear in light of the continuation of baseline as a third condition during

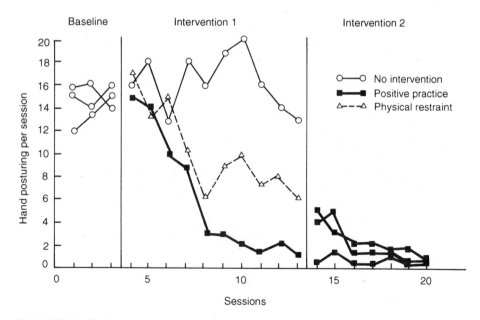

FIGURE 4–6
Stereotypical hand posturing across experimental conditions. The three separate lines in each phase represent the three separate time periods of each session. Only in the initial intervention phase (Intervention 1) were the three separate conditions in effect. In the second intervention phase (Intervention 2), positive practice was in effect for all three periods.
SOURCE: Ollendick, T. H., Shapiro, E. S., & Barrett, R. P. (1981).

the intervention phase. When baseline (no-treatment) conditions were in effect during the intervention phase, performance remained at the approximate level of the original baseline phase. In the final phase, positive practice was applied to all of the daily time periods. Positive practice, which had proven to be the most effective condition in the previous phase, also led to dramatic reductions in performance when it was implemented across all of the time periods. Thus, the strength of this intervention is especially clear from the design.

The design does not require an initial baseline as long as two or more conditions are compared in one of the phases. For example, an interesting variation of the design was reported in the treatment of a mentally retarded child who engaged in self-injurious behavior (Wacker, McMahon, Steege, Berg, Sasso, & Melloy, 1990). The child seemed to engage in higher levels of self-injury during activities in which tasks were done for the child. Consequently, different task conditions were implemented in the same phase to see whether self-injury levels differed. In the active condition, the child was required to participate and to engage in the activity with some assistance. In the passive condition, the task was done to or for the child without active child participation. Active and passive conditions were completed in the initial phase. The comparisons of passive and active conditions were completed across different tasks the child performed. Figure 4–7 shows that rates of self-injury were much higher in the passive condition. Consequently, the active condition was introduced in the second phase to achieve consistent reductions in self-injurious behavior. As evident in the figure, there are features of alternating conditions and multiple-baselines in this design.

Problems and Considerations

The main feature of the design is that it permits comparison of different interventions implemented in a single treatment phase for a given client. The design addresses a very practical question of which among alternative treatments is the most effective for a particular client. Also, the design is extremely useful prior to developing a program when an initial functional analysis is performed. As seen in one of the above examples (Wacker et al., 1990), if the target behavior varies as a function of setting conditions, tasks, or facets related to the environment, these can be altered to achieved desired changes in behavior.

F I G U R E   4–7 (*right*)
Performance of self-injurious behavior of a mentally retarded child across different (alternating) task conditions. The active condition (in which the child participated in the activity) was associated with less self-injurious behavior and hence was introduced in the second and final phase.
SOURCE: Wacker, D., McMahon, C., Steege, M., Berg, W., Sasso, G., & Melloy, K. (1990).

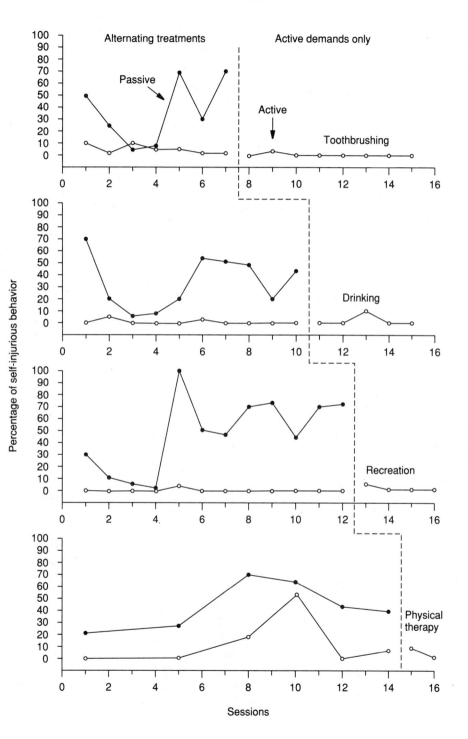

If several different conditions are compared in the design, it is some-times difficult to implement them in the same phase or to collect data across several different occasions or conditions on the same day. Also, the designs depend on showing that a given behavior changes in response to changes in treatment on a given day. It is important that there is no carryover effect from one intervention to another. For example, drug and behavioral treatments might not be easily compared in an alternating-treatment design because the influence of the drug might not be eliminated if the behavioral treatment were implemented later in the day. Also, the behavior selected for the design must be able to change rapidly. The re-sponse must occur frequently enough during the observation periods to reflect change for each intervention and a differential amount of change across interventions if the interventions have different effects. Despite the potential obstacles in practice, the design has been quite useful in identi-fying differences among alternative interventions (for example, Blake, Owens, & Keane, 1990; Singh, Watson, & Winton, 1986). Once the more or most effective intervention is identified for a given client, it can be imple-mented for all of the time periods to maximize the impact on the client.

Group Designs

Group designs represent another way to demonstrate the effect of an inter-vention. There are a variety of control-group designs suitable for applied settings (Kazdin, 1992). The basic design requires at least two groups: one receives the intervention (the experimental group) and the other does not (the control group). To determine whether the intervention is effective, rates of the target behavior in the experimental and control groups are compared. For example, a reinforcement program might be conducted in one school classroom but not in another. Immediately before and after the program, the behavior of all students in both classrooms is assessed. To determine whether the program is effective, the averages in performance for the groups are compared at the end of the program. If the group averages are different, this finding suggests that the program was respon-sible for the change.

To be sure that any difference between the two groups is the result of the program, the groups must be similar to begin with. Before the program is implemented, the best procedure to control for systematic differences between groups is to assign clients *randomly* to one of the two groups. If subjects are not randomly assigned to groups, the likelihood is greater that the groups may be different in their performance of the target behavior before the program is implemented and may differentially change in the target behavior over time for some reason other than the effect of the program.

The basic feature of the group design is the presentation of different conditions to two or more groups. An illustration of the design can be seen in a program to evaluate interventions for pregnant women who smoked cigarettes (Burling, Bigelow, Robinson, & Mead, 1991). Many of the negative consequences of cigarette smoking to the person who smokes are well known. There are, of course, added consequences for the unborn child and later for the infant of the mother who smokes during pregnancy and after giving birth (for example, reduced birth weight, increased risk for sudden infant death). The study included pregnant women who were cigarette smokers and who were seen at an obstetrics and gynecology clinic at a large hospital. All women received the standard care during their weekly visits, which included information about smoking from a nurse. The information was designed to increase positive health-related behaviors, including the reduction of smoking.

Through random assignment, half of the women also received a follow-up letter designed to make the importance of smoking cessation more salient. The letter noted that chronic abnormalities and health problems of the child were increased by cigarette smoke and urged the woman to stop smoking. Further information from the American Cancer Society, including guidelines for a self-directed smoking cessation program, was also enclosed. The 139 women who participated were assigned to one of two groups: standard care and standard care plus further information (the letter about the dangers of smoking that urged the recipient to stop). Cigarette smoking was measured by self-reports of the women and by taking breath samples to assess blood gasses (carbon monoxide), which measure the level of recent smoking. Weekly contacts were made. Figure 4–8 shows that at the initial assessment, before the intervention, groups were no different. By the second and final assessment, the percentage of women who had ceased smoking was greater for those who received standard care and the letter/information.

In passing, it is worth noting that interventions based primarily or exclusively on information alone, as this study shows, often are not very potent in the effects they produce. The investigators, well aware of this, noted that such interventions have compensatory advantages, including the ease of dissemination to large numbers of individuals and low cost relative to most other interventions. Indeed, merely mailing a letter and sending information augmented the standard program at relatively low cost. Of course, a stronger intervention based on more potent behavior change techniques would be worthwhile as well, given the serious consequences of adverse health styles during pregnancy. For present purposes, the study shows the use of comparisons between groups as a way of evaluating intervention programs.

In many instances, group and single-case designs are combined. For example, treatment was evaluated in a combined design for ten individuals (ages 6–36) who were diagnosed with Tourette's syndrome (Azrin & Peterson, 1990). The disorder, considered to be neurologically based, consists of multiple motor and vocal tics such as head, neck, and hand twitching, eye rolling, shouting of profane words, grunting, repetitive

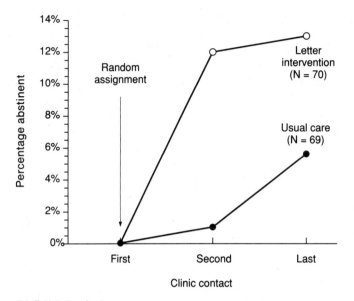

FIGURE 4–8
Percentage of mothers abstinent from smoking in the standard (usual) care program and the standard care program with the additional information (letter).
SOURCE: Burling, T. A., Bigelow, G. E., Robinson, J. C., & Mead, A. M. (1991).

coughing or throat clearing, or other utterances. The tics, which begin in childhood, usually are quite conspicuous. In this program, a combined control group and multiple-baseline design was used. The ten cases were assigned either to receive treatment or to wait for a 3-month period (waiting-list control group). The assignments were made on a random basis. For all cases, daily home recordings of tics were made, as well as periodic videotapes at the clinic, to assess tics. The treatment consisted of *habit reversal,* which includes several different behavior therapy treatments, such as being made more aware of the behavior, self-monitoring, relaxation training, practicing a response that competed with the tic (that is, is incompatible with the tic, such as contracting the muscles in a different way, or breathing in a way that prevents making certain sounds), and family members reinforcing improved performance at home. Many of the components have been used as separate interventions for various problems, as detailed in subsequent chapters. Observations were conducted at home and at the clinic (during treatment).

The results are shown in Figure 4–9, which graphs the number of tics per hour at home and at the clinic for the treatment group and the waiting-list control group. The baseline phase for the waiting-list group is longer because of the wait period. Hence, the continuous observations over baseline and treatment also meet criteria for a multiple-baseline design (across

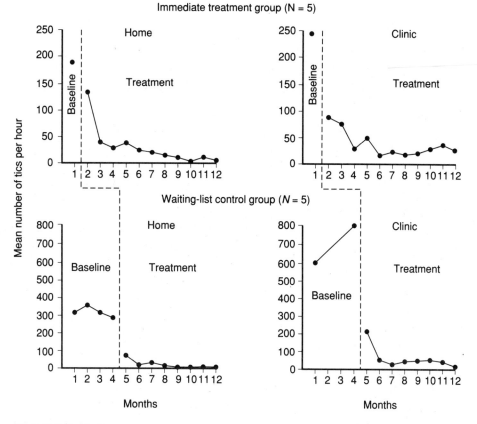

FIGURE 4-9

Monthly mean (average) of Tourette's syndrome tics per hour measured in clinic and home settings for subjects in the immediate treatment (upper panel) and waiting-list (lower panel) groups. The data illustrate the combined multiple-baseline design across two groups: one that received treatment immediately and one that waited for an initial period.

SOURCE: Azrin, N. H., & Peterson, A. L. (1990).

groups). The results indicate that the intervention clearly showed marked impact on tics. This is important because Tourette's syndrome has not been effectively treated with various psychotherapy or pharmacological treatments. The demonstration is persuasive in large part because of the comparisons within groups and between groups afforded by the combination of multiple-baseline and group-design strategies, even though either one of these designs alone would have been sufficient. The use of a control group provided useful information about the likely changes over time without an intervention during the waiting-list period.

Problems and Considerations

Group designs have not been applied as extensively as have single-case designs in programs on reinforcement, punishment, extinction, and other contingency-based interventions used in applied settings. The major reason is that these designs emphasize the behavior of groups rather than the behavior of individuals. When the group study is completed, the average frequency of behavior of individuals in the control group is compared with the average frequency of behavior of individuals in the intervention group. The focus on averages hides the behavior of individual clients. Thus, the average performance of a group may change, although only a few individuals in the group may actually have been affected by the program. Behavior modification programs in applied settings usually have been concerned with achieving relatively large changes in the behavior of individuals in such settings as the home, hospitals, classrooms, and institutions. This point is a matter of emphasis rather than of fixed differences. In recent years, more applications have been evaluated in settings such as the community at large, where the focus often has been on large groups rather than on individuals (see Chapter 12). In such instances, group designs alone or combined with single-case designs have been used more frequently.

Group designs are often used in many areas of behavior modification research, especially to evaluate outpatient treatment for such problems as anxiety, obesity, marital discord, and excessive alcohol consumption. In fact, one of the salient characteristics of behavior modification is a strong commitment to assessment, experimental design, and evaluation of treatment. Within the overall field of behavior modification, evaluation of behavior-change techniques based on operant conditioning principles have relied more heavily upon the single-case designs highlighted in this chapter. Of course, the particular type of design selected depends upon many factors, such as the purpose of treatment and the questions of interest to the investigator, rather than on the type of techniques that are used.

For many questions, a control group can provide valuable information that is difficult to obtain with single-case designs (Kazdin, 1992). For example, comparing the effectiveness of different experimental programs is readily accomplished by using different groups of clients who receive the different treatments. Group designs are especially useful for these comparisons. Also, when evaluating different treatments, it is possible and indeed likely that treatments will vary in effectiveness for different types of persons (for example, younger versus older, men versus women) or for different types of clinical problems (for example, depression versus aggression, social interaction versus instruction following). The large numbers of subjects characteristic of group designs are especially useful because they permit analyses of treatment for different subgroups of persons.

Assessment and Design in Clinical Work

Single-case experimental designs illustrated previously are used often in research and convey high standards for evaluating change and demonstrating the basis of the change. It is not always the case that the designs can be implemented in applied settings or in clinical work, often for practical reasons or because the priority is unequivocally to achieve immediate change in the client and design requirements often cannot be easily met. Evaluation in clinical work remains extremely important even if the designs themselves cannot be used (Kazdin, 1993a). More specifically, systematic assessment regarding changes in the target behavior or domains of functioning that serve as the focus of treatment provide valuable, if not absolutely essential, information.

The key to evaluation is the assessment of functioning on an ongoing basis. The situation may permit assessment on only a small number of occasions during baseline and over the course of treatment. This is equivalent to an AB design or the first part of the ABAB design noted previously. AB designs often are used in applications of treatment in clinic settings (for example, Eisen & Silverman, 1991; Erhardt & Baker, 1990). In such cases, one may not be able to infer a causal relation between the intervention and therapeutic change in a way that meets the rigors of experimental research. Even so, evaluation is no less important. First, it is important to document change in the client. Without such documentation, it may not be clear whether the client has improved, remained the same, or become worse in relation to the treatment focus. Assuming the client has improved, assessment is helpful in making judgments about the amount of change and whether that has been sufficient to have impact on the client's everyday life. Ongoing and continuous assessment provide information about client progress. Second, it is important to use the information from assessment to make decisions about treatment. The data can benefit the client when they are incorporated into decision making regarding more or different interventions used to achieve the goals or, when goals have been achieved, regarding what further treatment is needed, and so on. Thus, evaluation of behavioral programs is important, even if there are situations in which implementation of a specific experimental design or experimental arrangement is not feasible (see Kazdin, 1993a).

Evaluating Change

In each of the single-case designs, the degree of behavior change is evaluated by comparing performance during baseline with performance during the experimental phase. A major issue is the degree of change needed to provide a convincing demonstration that behavior has improved. The decision that change has occurred is important both in the execution of the design and in the evaluation of the overall effects of treatment. For example, in the reversal design, the experimental condition may be withdrawn, altered, or reinstated at different points based on evidence that behavior has changed or failed to change. To decide whether alterations should be made in the phases and, more important, whether the client has improved sufficiently, behavior change must be evaluated.

Deciding Whether Behavior Has Reliably Changed

In many instances in single-case research, behavior change is dramatic. Indeed, the usual purpose of the intervention is to obtain strong treatment effects. If these are obtained, they are usually quite evident from visual inspection, that is, from merely looking at the graphs to evaluate whether the change was reliable. In practice, a few guidelines are used to help decide whether behavior change has occurred and whether behavior has changed systematically from baseline. These guidelines are based on evaluating graphs on which performance is plotted across phases.

The first guideline is to see whether the *level of behavior during the experimental or intervention phase overlaps with the level of performance during baseline.* During the program, the data points may not even approach the data points obtained during baseline. Figure 4–10 (upper panel) shows such a data pattern. When there is *no overlap* of performance in the baseline and intervention phases, there would be general agreement that behavior change has occurred.

A second guideline for assessing the reliability of behavior change is to see whether there are *changes in the trend (slope) of the data.* For example, behavior may show a clear trend toward improvement during the intervention. Figure 4–10 (middle panel) shows such a pattern, with behavior decreasing during baseline and increasing during the intervention phase. If the data continued to be collected, the trend would be expected to change as the intervention was withdrawn and eventually reinstated.

Another guideline for evaluating behavior change is to see whether the *mean (arithmetic average) level of performance during the intervention phase differs from the average level of performance during baseline.* The mean may show a change even if only a slight change in behavior is evident. Figure 4–10 (bottom panel) shows a change in mean performance from one phase to the next. A change in means across phases may be difficult to evaluate, depending, of course, on the degree of change. Also, if it is not obvious that a change has taken place, this probably indicates that a more potent intervention is needed to help the client in relation to the target goals of the program. As a general rule, evidence that the means have changed

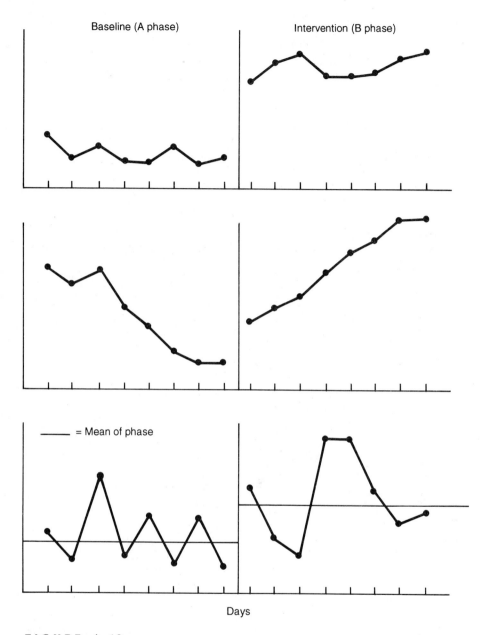

Days

FIGURE 4–10

Hypothetical illustration of patterns of data that help in deciding whether a systematic change has occurred from baseline (A) to the intervention (B) phase. These patterns are shown: nonoverlapping data in separate phases (upper panel); changes in the trend—the slope of the lines representing data in each phase (middle panel); and changes in mean (average) performance in separate phases (lower panel).

across phases, when the other criteria regarding overlap and trend have not been met, provides only a tenuous demonstration of the reliable effects of the program.[3]

Change of Applied or Clinical Significance

Demonstrating that a reliable or genuine change has occurred is important but by itself does not address the question of whether the change is important. A major criterion for evaluating change is the *applied or clinical significance* of the effects of treatment. The effects produced by the intervention should be large enough to be of practical value. Also, the help of individuals in constant contact with the patient, resident, or client who was in the program is needed to evaluate whether an important change was obtained (Wolf, 1978).

It is not enough to demonstrate that behavior change occurred, because the change may be too weak to be of any practical value. For example, treatment may reduce the frequency with which an autistic boy hits himself in the head from 100 times per hour to 50 times per hour. Change has been achieved, but a much larger change is needed. Self-injurious behavior is maladaptive and potentially dangerous, and it needs to be eliminated.

In general, applied behavior analysis programs seek treatment effects that clearly improve the level of client functioning in everyday situations. Of course, seeking clinically significant effects is a goal of any intervention approach. The special feature of behavioral research is an effort to integrate criteria to evaluate the importance of therapeutic change in the assessment of intervention effects. Several criteria are used to evaluate the clinical significance of change. One criterion, for example, consists of showing that the individual client's behavior change places him or her within the normative range of functioning. Prior to the intervention, the individual may be extreme in level or type of behavior (for example, aggressive acts, social withdrawal). In many instances, a clinically important change would be evident if the intervention returned the client to the level of functioning of persons in everyday life who have not been identified as in need of treatment.

The criteria for evaluating the clinical significance of change involve several issues related to the social context of behavioral research. The appropriate focus of treatment, the acceptability of the procedures that are used to achieve therapeutic change, and the adequacy or importance of the changes all involve evaluations of the community at large. Clinical significance will be discussed later in the broader social context of evaluating treatment and its effects.

SUMMARY AND CONCLUSION

In this chapter, experimental designs that are used to evaluate the effects of intervention programs were discussed. Experimental designs are used to determine whether the intervention was responsible for change. Several designs are used in behavior modification. A number of the commonly used designs were presented to illustrate the role of assessment and evaluation in applied behavior analysis. These designs include reversal (or ABAB) design, multiple-baseline design, changing-criterion design, alternating- or simultaneous-treatment design, and group designs. The designs and their many variations reflect several ways of demonstrating the relation between the intervention and behavior change.

Design selection may be determined by the population and behaviors of interest, demands of the clinical situation, the purposes of the intervention, and various advantages and disadvantages of specific designs. Considerations related to the use of individual designs were also discussed. In some cases, application of one of the experimental designs is not feasible because of the demands of the situation, practical limitations, or immediate priorities regarding implementation of the intervention. Even if one of the specific experimental design strategies cannot be applied, assessment and use of the assessment information to evaluate client progress are critically important. Thus, evaluation and collection of data on client progress play a central role in intervention research.

The purpose of the intervention is to achieve changes in behavior. Whether change has actually been achieved usually is judged by visually inspecting the graphed results to assess whether treatment was consistently associated with marked changes or differences in trends across phases. Ongoing assessment and use of one of the research designs facilitate evaluation of the change or the degree of change. The applied or clinical significance of change is also important to ensure that the intervention has made a difference in the life of the client.

In general, the methods of assessing and evaluating behavior modification programs, as discussed in this and the previous chapter, provide tools that are essential for designing effective treatments. Identifying techniques to change behavior and obtaining clinically important effects depend on measuring the extent of the client's behavior prior to intervening, seeing whether or how much change is obtained with the intervention, making adjustments in the intervention accordingly, and determining whether the intervention is responsible for change. Now that these important features have been discussed, we can turn to the many behavioral techniques that have been developed and identified in this fashion.

Notes

1. For a detailed discussion of various single-case designs that are used to evaluate behavioral programs and of the rationale underlying their use, other sources can be consulted (Kazdin, 1982c).
2. Many other versions of the ABAB design have been used (Barlow & Hersen, 1984; Kazdin, 1982c). For example, several treatments may be used in an $AB_1B_2B_3AB_3$ design. The different treatments $(B_1B_2B_3)$ may be needed if the first one did not work or did not work well enough to attain the desired level of change. Even when many interventions are used, the demonstration is a reversal design if it meets the basic requirement—evaluating the effect of the intervention(s) by implementing a phase that is intended to reverse behavior in the direction of the original baseline.
3. Several statistical techniques have been proposed to evaluate the effects of treatment in single-case designs (see Kazdin, 1982c). The use of statistical techniques has been controversial. Some investigators have suggested that developing an effective technology of behavior change requires that very strong treatment effects should be sought. Visually inspecting graphed results allows one to see only extremely strong treatment effects. In contrast, statistical analysis may identify intervention effects that are generally weak but meet a statistical criterion of significance. Visual inspection is still the primary criterion for evaluating programs using single-case designs. However, use of statistical analyses has increased in recent years.

For Further Reading

Barlow, D. H., & Hersen, M. (1984). *Single-case experimental designs: Strategies for studying behavior change* (2nd ed.). New York: Pergamon Press.

Iwata, B. A., Bailey, J. S., Fuqua, R. W., Neef, N. A., Page, T. J., & Reid, D. H. (Eds.). (1989). *Methodological and conceptual issues in applied behavior analysis.* Lawrence, KS: Society of the Experimental Analysis of Behavior.

Kazdin, A. E. (1982). *Single-case research designs: Methods for clinical and applied settings.* New York: Oxford University Press.

Kazdin, A. E. (1992). *Research design in clinical psychology* (2nd ed.). Needham Heights, MA: Allyn & Bacon.

Kazdin, A. E. (1993). Evaluation in clinical practice: Clinically sensitive and systematic methods of treatment delivery. *Behavior Therapy, 24,* 11–45.

POSITIVE AND NEGATIVE REINFORCEMENT

Various populations in treatment, education, and rehabilitation settings are often identified for special intervention because of their behavioral deficits or their lack of appropriate skills. For example, autistic and mentally retarded children often lack a variety of appropriate personal, social, and intellectual skills. Other individuals are identified for intervention because of disruptive and deviant behaviors, but they may also lack such skills. For example, delinquents may engage in aggressive behaviors whose elimination will not ensure the performance of socially appropriate behaviors. Such behaviors need to be developed. Still other individuals whose behavior is identified as problematic may possess appropriate skills but perform them under conditions different from those in which they should be performed in everyday life. For example, a "hyperactive" child may "know" how to sit down but may rarely do so in a classroom setting. In society at large, increases may be desirable in a number of adaptive behaviors such as eating nutritious foods, preventing illness and injury, driving safely, and working productively at a job. These are not problem behaviors of special populations but behaviors whose increase can improve life for the individual.

In the above cases, low-frequency behaviors have to be increased, new behaviors have to be established, or behaviors have to be developed in new situations. Because these goals entail developing or increasing behavior, reinforcement techniques are appropriate. Moreover, even in cases where the primary intent is to eliminate undesirable behaviors, reinforcement can play a major role. Reinforcement can develop socially appropriate behaviors that replace the undesirable behaviors. The present chapter considers positive and negative reinforcement. Greater attention is given to positive reinforcement because it plays a central role in almost all behavioral interventions in applied settings.

POSITIVE REINFORCEMENT

Positive reinforcement refers to an increase in the frequency of a response following the presentation of a positive reinforcer. Whether a particular event is a positive reinforcer is defined by its effects on behavior. If response frequency increases when followed by the event, it is a positive reinforcer. Defining a reinforcer by effects on behavior appears to be circular. However, the effectiveness of a reinforcer need not be limited to a particular behavior in a single situation. A reinforcer effective in altering one response in one situation may be effective in altering other behaviors in other situations as well. In addition, the Premack principle, discussed earlier, provides a way to assess whether an event is a reinforcer independent of the effects on behavior. Reinforcing consequences are the behaviors in a person's repertoire that have a relatively high probability.

TYPES OF REINFORCERS

There are a number of different types of reinforcers. Selecting one or more of them represents an initial consideration. The different types of reinforcers vary in their effects on behavior and in their ease of administration in applied settings.

Food and Other Consumables

Food qualifies as a primary reinforcer because its reinforcing value is unlearned. Of course, food preferences are learned, which make some foods more reinforcing than others and some foods not reinforcing at all unless the individual has been deprived of all food. Because food is a primary reinforcer, it is very powerful. Studies have occasionally used food as a reinforcer, including cereal, candy, cookies, crackers, soft drinks, and ice cream. Nonfood consumables (for example, chewing gum) have also been used as reinforcers.

Because food is a primary reinforcer, its effects should apply widely among different client populations. However, food is not used very frequently in applied settings. The major reason is that food is not ordinarily present at, or a part of, the everyday situations in which behavioral interventions are applied. Introducing food into the situation is not necessary to change behavior, given the availability, effectiveness, and ease of delivering other reinforcers. Food is noted here because it represents an important type (primary) of reinforcer and because it sensitizes us to states of the individual (deprivation, satiation) relevant to reinforcer delivery.

Occasionally, food can be used in some applied settings, particularly, institutional facilities for developmentally disabled individuals, where snacks and food can be used in specific training sessions to train specific behaviors (for example, speaking). For example, an interesting use of food as a reinforcer was reported with hospitalized physically handicapped children 1 to $3\frac{1}{2}$ years of age (Riordan, Iwata, Finney, Wohl, & Stanley, 1984). These children also suffered from food refusal or high food selectivity. They would not eat enough food, would spit out food fed to them, or would eat a limited range of foods that were not sufficient in vitamins or minerals. During mealtime, several different foods were fed to the children (presented one bite at a time) to identify the foods that they ate and preferred. The preferred foods were used as a reinforcer for eating a bite of other foods. For example, one of the children preferred dry cereal and graham crackers. These were used as reinforcers. When the child ate a bite of some other food (fruit, vegetable, meat, or starch), the preferred food was immediately delivered. At first, the preferred food was presented with the target food for a few bites; then the preferred food was delivered immediately after a bite of a target food. After several trials, the preferred food (reinforcer) was administered only intermittently. The use of preferred food increased the bites and consumption of a broader range of nutritionally balanced food.

   Important considerations.   The effectiveness of food and other consumables depends heavily on the deprivation state of the individual. If the individual is not at least partially deprived, food may be a weak reinforcer. Investigators sometimes use food reinforcement prior to mealtime or during mealtime itself. A difficulty with food as a reinforcer is that its reinforcement value may decline rather quickly. Even if the individual is hungry before training, as training proceeds on a given day, hunger and the reinforcing value of food may decline.

   The effectiveness of food reinforcement depends on the type of food used. Specific foods used in a given program may not be reinforcing for particular individuals. For example, although ice cream may serve as a reinforcer for most children, the flavor will influence its reinforcing properties for many individuals. When a single food or consumable is relied on, the possibility exists that the event will not be effective with a number of people. Moreover, the preferences of a given individual change from time to time, so a single food or other consumable may have short-lived reinforcing properties.

   There are potential problems in the administration of food reinforcers. The delivery and consumption of food after a response sometimes interrupt ongoing behavior. For example, if a special education classroom teacher distributed candy to her students while they were working attentively on an assignment, they might be distracted momentarily from the task. Also, the consumption of the reinforcer may temporarily distract the students.

   Moreover, it may be difficult to dispense food and other consumables immediately because they are cumbersome to carry or dispense. The setting in which food is used dictates the ease with which a particular type of food can be dispensed. Parents at home and staff in some institutions may be able to dispense food readily, depending on the type of food and on the ease of carrying a supply (for example, small candies). However, in everyday life, parents, teachers, peers, employers, and others cannot easily carry food or other consumables with them all of the time for use as reinforcers.

   A related problem is that food is not easily administered to several individuals in a group immediately after behavior has been performed. Because its administration to several individuals takes some time (for example, selecting the quantity of food or passing a piece to each individual), food is not particularly well suited to group situations in which everyone receives reinforcers. Many programs using food have been conducted on an individual basis rather than in groups.

   Finally, ethical and legal concerns restrict the use of food and consumable items. These reinforcers are most effective when clients are deprived. Yet, deprivation of food is ethically objectionable. Such deprivation also violates legal rights of clients. Hence, food deprivation is not a viable treatment alternative. When food is used as a reinforcer, clients ought not and cannot be deprived of food they would normally receive. Thus, food and consumables are often given over and above the items normally available to clients. Because clients normally have access to food, the extra food used as a reinforcer may be less potent than it would be if they were deprived.

Relatedly, people often object to the use of food. Adding food to a setting where it would not otherwise be used, for example, in the classroom or on the playground, has potential health consequences (such as in-creased sugar intake if candy is used) that raise concerns of both those who implement and those who are the consumers (for example, parents or teachers) of behavior modification programs. In light of ethical, legal, and preferential concerns, food is not used very often. Also, much of applied research is conducted in community settings, business and industry, and in everyday social intercourse. Administering a mouthful of this or that is not feasible or desirable.

Food and other consumables are used in situations where other events such as approval are not effective. For example, in institutions for severely and profoundly mentally retarded persons, food reinforcement is used to develop such behaviors as feeding oneself or using sounds, words, or gestures to communicate. In these applications, other reinforcers are often not available. Perhaps as important, food is useful in establishing the reinforcing properties of other events, such as praise, feedback, attention, smiles, and physical contact. Programs using food and other consumables invariably pair the delivery of the reinforcer with praise and other social events, so that these latter events can be used to change behavior.

Social Reinforcers

Social reinforcers such as verbal praise, attention, physical contact (includ-ing affectionate or approving touches, pats, and hand holding), and facial expressions (including smiles, eye contact, nods of approval, and winks) are conditioned reinforcers. Numerous studies have shown that attention or praise from a parent, teacher, or peer exerts considerable control over behavior.

For example, in one program, praise was used to alter the behavior of a 13-year-old boy named Tom in a seventh-grade classroom (Kirby & Shields, 1972). Tom was of average intelligence but was doing poorly on his class assignments, particularly the arithmetic assignments. Also, he rarely paid attention to the lesson and constantly had to be reminded to work. Praise was used to improve his performance on arithmetic assign-ments. Each day in class, after he completed the arithmetic assignment, he was praised for correct answers on his arithmetic worksheet. At first, every couple of responses were praised, but the number of correct problems required for praise was gradually increased. The praise consisted merely of saying, "Good work," "Excellent job," and similar things. Figure 5–1 (upper portion) shows the improvements in Tom's rate of correct answers per minute in the treatment phases of an ABAB design. The lower portion shows that his attentive behavior also improved even though it was not focused on directly.

A number of other investigations have shown that reinforcing academic performance not only improves the specific target behaviors but also increases classroom attentiveness and reduces disruptive behavior (Ruggles & LeBlanc, 1982). In most classroom studies, teacher attention consists primarily of verbal praise supplemented with facial expressions and physical contact. However, nonverbal teacher attention alone (consisting of smiles, physical contact, and approving nods contingent upon appropriate behavior) also improves classroom deportment (Kazdin & Klock, 1973).

Important considerations.   Social consequences have a variety of advantages as reinforcers. First, they are easily administered in everyday life and in a large number of situations. Providing praise takes little time, so there is no delay in praising a number of individuals immediately. Indeed, praise can be delivered to a group as a whole, as in a classroom. Second, praise need not disrupt the behavior that is reinforced. A person can be praised or receive a pat on the back while continuing to engage in appropriate behavior. Third, praise is a generalized conditioned reinforcer because it has been paired with many reinforcing events. Conditioned reinforcers may be less subject to satiation than food and other consumable items. Fourth, attention and praise are "naturally occurring" reinforcers employed in everyday life. Some reinforcers (such as food and other consumables) do not normally follow desirable behavior such as paying attention in a classroom, interacting socially with others, or working on a job. In contrast, social reinforcers such as attention from others or credit for a job well done occasionally do follow socially adaptive behaviors. Finally, because social reinforcers in everyday life may continue to follow those behaviors developed with social reinforcers in a treatment or training program, these behaviors may be more readily maintained outside the program setting than behaviors developed with other reinforcers may be.

In general, social reinforcers are not objected to and are consistent with what many persons in everyday life believe are acceptable as reinforcers. In addition, although social reinforcers are used, they are not delivered that frequently. During the course of a day, few of us receive or deliver praise contingent on behavior. This quasi-deprivation state may augment the effectiveness of social reinforcement when implemented to change behavior (Vollmer & Iwata, 1991).

Before embarking on a program employing social reinforcement, it is important to bear a few considerations in mind. Praise, approval, and physical contact are not reinforcing for everyone. Indeed, for some individuals, praise may even be aversive (Walker, Hops, & Greenwood, 1981). Because social events (praise, approval, and physical contact) are em-

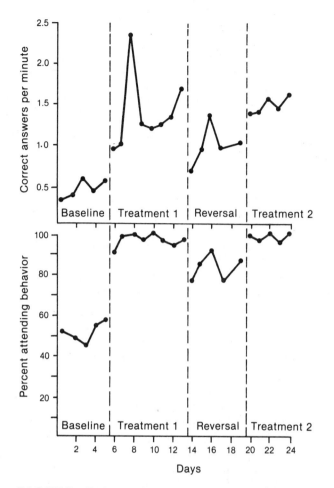

FIGURE 5–1
Number of correct arithmetic answers per minute and percentage of times scored as attending behavior as a function of baseline and treatment conditions.
SOURCE: Kirby, F. D., & Shields, F. (1972).

ployed in everyday life, it is important to establish them as reinforcers by pairing them with events that are already reinforcers.

High-Probability Behaviors

When persons are given the opportunity to engage in various behaviors, they will select certain activities with a higher frequency than they select other activities. Activities selected with a higher frequency can often serve as reinforcers for activities selected with a lower frequency. As a practical guide, allowing persons to engage in preferred activities and to earn various privileges can reinforce behavior. Laboratory research has attempted to identify higher-frequency behaviors by observing performance or by depriving animals of certain sorts of activities and thereby making such activities more likely in the future. In clinical applications, higher-probability behaviors are often inferred from the client's expressed verbal preferences or from seeing what the client actually does in his or her free time.

High-probability behaviors have been used effectively in several applied programs. For example, Allen and Iwata (1980) increased the extent to which mentally retarded adults engaged in daily exercise as part of their rehabilitation program. During baseline, opportunities and prompts were provided to encourage these clients to exercise (for example, do knee bends, sit-ups) and to play games involving physical activity (such as various ball games). Playing games, the more frequent activity, was used to reinforce exercising. A group contingency was implemented in which everyone had to complete a minimum number of exercises before the games could be played. Exercising (lower-probability behavior) increased in frequency when playing games (higher-probability behavior) was contingent upon this behavior.

Important considerations.   High-probability behaviors offer distinct advantages as reinforcers. In most settings, activities are privileges that are readily available. For example, in the home, access to television, peers, or the family automobile is likely to be associated with high-probability behaviors, depending on the person's age. At school, access to recess, free time, games, and entertaining reading materials may serve a similar function. In hospital and rehabilitation facilities, engaging in special recreational events or access to more desirable living quarters can also be used as reinforcers. In short, activities, and privileges that can be made contingent upon performance are usually available in any setting. Hence, extra reinforcers (for example, candy or money) need not be introduced into the setting.

There are limitations in using high-probability behaviors as reinforcing events. First, access to an activity cannot always immediately follow low-probability behavior. For example, in a classroom setting, access to recess or games cannot readily be used to reinforce behavior immediately. Such access may need to be delayed, so that the reinforcing activity (for example, games) does not interrupt the task (for example, writing a story). After the lower-probability behavior has been established, access to the higher-probability behavior can usually be delayed to a more convenient time without loss of the behavior. Also, intermediate rewards such as praise or a token (exchangeable for the activity) can help bridge the delay between behavior and the reinforcing activity, so that some reinforcement is provided immediately. Thus, the child can be told by the parent that because a specific behavior (playing cooperatively with a sibling) was "Great!" (praise), he or she can stay up 15 minutes extra at bedtime. The praise is delivered immediately, an important condition for effective reinforcement delivery. The praise may in fact be sufficient to develop the behavior at a high rate. However, the extra bedtime privilege may well add to the effectiveness by introducing an important reinforcer.

Second, providing an activity is sometimes an all-or-none enterprise, so that it is either earned or not earned. This can limit flexibility in administering the reinforcer. For example, in institutions for psychiatric patients or delinquents, access to overnight passes and trips to a nearby town are sometimes used as reinforcing activities. These activities cannot be parceled out so that "portions" of them are earned. They have to be given in their entirety or not at all. If a client's behavior comes very near but does not quite meet the performance criterion for reinforcement, a decision has to be made whether to provide the reinforcer. One solution is to shape behavior by initially setting low criteria for earning the activity. Gradually, the criteria for earning the reinforcer are increased. Another solution is to incorporate many privileges and activities into the contingency system. Different behaviors or varying degrees of a given behavior can then be reinforced with different privileges or with a choice among privileges.

Third, relying on one or two activities as reinforcers runs the risk that some individuals may not find them reinforcing. Since preferences for activities may be idiosyncratic, different activities need to be available. One alternative is to provide free time as the reinforcer, so that individuals can choose from a variety of activities.

A final consideration in using activities and privileges is that in many institutions activities must be freely available to the clients. Activities that might be made contingent upon performance are delivered independently of the client's performance. For example, it is required by law that many activities (such as opportunities for exercise, socialization) be provided noncontingently to ensure that institutionalized persons such as psychiatric patients, delinquents, and mentally retarded children and adults are not deprived of basic human rights. Hence, the person who develops a behavior change program has to provide special activities over and above those offered as part of routine care.

Feedback

Providing information about how a person has performed can serve as a reinforcer. Such *feedback* is a conditioned reinforcer because it is usually associated with the delivery of other reinforcing events. Feedback is implicit in the delivery of any reinforcer because it indicates which responses those who provide reinforcement regard as appropriate or desirable. Thus, when reinforcers such as food, praise, activities, or points are provided, a client receives feedback on how well he or she is doing. However, feedback can be employed independently of explicit approval or other reinforcers. Individuals can be informed of their behavior or of the extent to which their behavior has changed. Feedback refers to *knowledge of results* of one's performance and does not necessarily include additional events that may be reinforcing in their own right.

In one project, feedback was used to control the speeding of drivers on a highway entering a residential area (Van Houten, Nau, & Marini, 1980). Speeding was measured by a radar unit concealed in a litter can near the highway. After baseline observations, feedback was provided in the form of a conspicuous road sign that indicated the percentage of drivers not speeding on the previous day and the best percentage record obtained to date. The speed limit was 50 kilometers (31 miles) per hour. However, the police felt that 66 kilometers (41 miles) per hour was still safe, so this speed was used to define whether someone was speeding. The effects of feedback (posting the percentage of drivers who sped) are illustrated in Figure 5–2. The figure shows that speeding was reduced each time the feedback system was in effect. During the 26-week follow-up period, when the feedback system was used on a weekly rather than on a daily basis (a randomly chosen day each week), the effects of the program were maintained. Interestingly, during the feedback phase, a 57 percent reduction in the number of accidents was also noted, compared with the 2-year period before feedback had been implemented.

An important area involving feedback is *biofeedback*. Biofeedback consists of providing information to people about various physiological processes such as blood pressure, heart rate, muscle tension, and brain waves. Immediate information is provided to help clients learn to control various bodily processes. Biofeedback represents an important area of research in its own right and will be discussed later (Chapter 9).

Important considerations. Because of the ease with which feedback can be applied, it has been employed with a variety of client populations and in a variety of settings. Feedback can be employed readily when there is an explicit performance criterion, such as academic achievement or work productivity. In other situations, various criteria can be set, such as cigarettes smoked, calories consumed, or days of exercise. Daily feedback can convey how well the client is doing in relation to the criterion set. Specifying a criterion for performance is essential so the desired level of performance is clear.

An extremely important consideration in using feedback is that its effects often are equivocal. For example, the feedback controlling driving speed and car accidents, as noted in the prior example, is not always effective (for example, Roqué & Roberts, 1989). In other contexts, feedback has been effective but its effects are moderate. In general, feedback is usually less effective alone than it is in combination with other reinforcers, such as praise or tokens that can be used to purchase tangible backup reinforcers. Hence, feedback is not one of the more potent methods of altering behavior. The moderate effects of feedback are not an argument against its use. In most settings, feedback is not given for performance. If it is given, the schedule is very intermittent (for example, periodic work evalu-

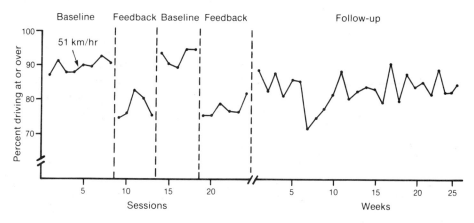

FIGURE 5–2
Percentage of motorists driving above the speed limit (50 km/hr or 31 mph) across baseline and feedback conditions. During the follow-up phase, the feedback procedure was conducted on a weekly basis rather than on a daily basis.
SOURCE: Van Houten, R., Nau, P., & Marini, Z. (1980).

ations, end-of-term grades, adherence to safety rules on the job). In such cases, use of feedback for behavior is likely to lead to reliable and important changes in behavior.

Programs based on feedback are often easier to implement than are other reinforcement programs, such as token economies. Also, people who implement a feedback program may be more favorably disposed to delivering feedback alone than to providing extrinsic reinforcers. For these reasons, it may be useful to begin with a program based on feedback, perhaps paired with praise, and then to resort to a more potent source of reinforcement and a more complex program if the desired goals have not been achieved.

Tokens

Tokens are conditioned reinforcers such as poker chips, coins, tickets, stars, points, or check marks. They are generalized reinforcers because they can be exchanged for a variety of reinforcing events referred to as *backup reinforcers.* A reinforcement system based on tokens is referred to as a *token economy.* In a token economy, tokens function in the same way that money does in national economic systems. Earned tokens are used to purchase backup reinforcers, including various goods and services. The backup reinforcers usually include food and other consumables, activities, and privileges. The rate at which tokens can be exchanged for backup reinforcers must be specified, so that it is clear how many tokens are required to purchase various reinforcers. The target behaviors are made explicit, as in most programs, along with the number of tokens that are administered for their performance.

The tokens need to be established as conditioned reinforcers because they have no reinforcing properties in their own right. For some populations, it is sufficient to explain that the tokens can be exchanged for various goods. After the explanation, the tokens take on a value that is maintained by the actual exchange of tokens for other reinforcers. For individuals whose behavior is not controlled by instructions about the value of tokens, the tokens can be given noncontingently a few times. Immediately after they have been delivered, they can be exchanged or traded for a backup reinforcer.

The use of tokens has a history antedating behavior modification in institutional settings such as schools, hospitals, and prisons (Kazdin, 1978). Current applications reflect a greater understanding of how reinforcement operates and how behavior changes are attained and maintained. Seminal work leading to current applications can be traced to the token economy begun in a psychiatric hospital in the early 1960s (see Ayllon & Azrin, 1968b). Psychiatric patients earned tokens (coins) for a variety of jobs and tasks on the ward (such as assisting with meals, doing chores), leading other patients in activities, and self-care. The tokens could be exchanged for various privileges (for example, opportunities for social interaction with staff, movies, trips to the nearby town), improved room facilities, and articles at a store on the ward. This initial program established the feasibility of a system of rewards that included several individuals, behaviors, and backup rewards. The program was shown to improve patient behavior and stimulated the development of a number of other programs.

Another program that has exerted major influence is a token economy used to rehabilitate predelinquent boys who have committed various offenses (for example, thefts, fighting, school truancy, academic failure) (Fixsen, Phillips, Phillips, & Wolf, 1976). The program was conducted at a home-style cottage setting called Achievement Place and was managed by two houseparents. The boys could earn points for such behaviors as watching the news, reading newspapers, keeping oneself neat and clean, performing chores around the house, and receiving good grades at school. Points could be lost for poor grades, aggressive talk (making threats), disobeying rules, lying, stealing, being late, fighting, and other disruptive behaviors. Points were used to purchase privileges such as staying up late, going downtown, watching television, using tools, riding a bicycle, and receiving an allowance. Interestingly, the boys actively participated in running the program by supervising one another's work, recording their own behavior, and developing and enforcing rules among their peers. The program has been shown to alter a variety of behaviors (for example, social interaction, completion of homework, chores) in the home setting. Youths participating in the program committed fewer criminal offenses in the community and had fewer contacts with police than did delinquents placed on probation or in other settings where this program was not in effect (Kirigin, Braukmann, Atwater, & Wolf, 1982; Kirigin, Wolf, Braukmann, Fixsen, & Phillips, 1979). Longer-term evaluations have indicated that the gains are not maintained (see Chapter 11).

Token economies have been used extensively in psychiatric hospitals. For example, in one of the most carefully evaluated programs, patients received tokens (colored plastic strips) for such behaviors as attending activities on the ward, group meetings, and therapy sessions and for grooming, making one's bed, showering, engaging in appropriate meal-time behaviors, and socially interacting (Paul & Lentz, 1977). Tokens could be exchanged for a variety of backup events such as purchasing cosmetics, candy, cigarettes, and clothing; renting chairs or bedside stands for one's room; ordering items from a mail-order catalog; using a piano, record player, or radio; spending time in a lounge; watching television; and having a private room and sleeping late. As patients improved in the ward, they advanced to higher levels within the program, in which more reinforcers were available and higher criteria were set for performance. Patients could "buy" themselves off the system by doing well, and each carried a "credit card" that allowed free access to all of the available reinforcers as long as personal performance was up to standards. The program was very success-ful in reducing bizarre behaviors, improving social interaction and commu-nication skills, and developing participation in activities. The gains were reflected in the number of patients discharged and in their adjustment in the community from one and a half to five years after termination of the program.

Token economies have been used as part of treatment for a wide range of groups of individuals and individuals in diverse settings. As an example, a token system was used to treat patients referred for drug addiction (Bud-ney, Higgins, Delaney, Kent, and Bickel, 1991). Two adult males (Phil, age 28; Mike, age 35) were seen separately for cocaine addiction. Both also used marijuana, which the authors report is the case for 40 to 50 percent of persons who are addicted to cocaine. Assessment of cocaine and marijuana use was accomplished by urinalyses that detected use within the previous 72 hours. Assessment was conducted four times a week to provide opportu-nities for earning tokens. No sign of cocaine use was rewarded with points. Bonus points were given for extended periods without a sign of drug use. Points could be exchanged for small amounts of money or goods and services, including movie tickets, sporting events, ski-lift tickets, dinner certificates, and others. The purpose of using these backup rewards was not only to imbue the points with value but also to involve the individuals in prosocial activities and, it was hoped, to develop a reinforcing drug-free lifestyle. After 12 weeks of the program, a maintenance phase was initiated to reduce the frequency of the checks. In the final phase, marijuana was added to the program. To earn tokens, the tests had to show that the individual did not use cocaine *or* marijuana.

Figure 5–3 plots the number of negative (no sign of drug use) urine

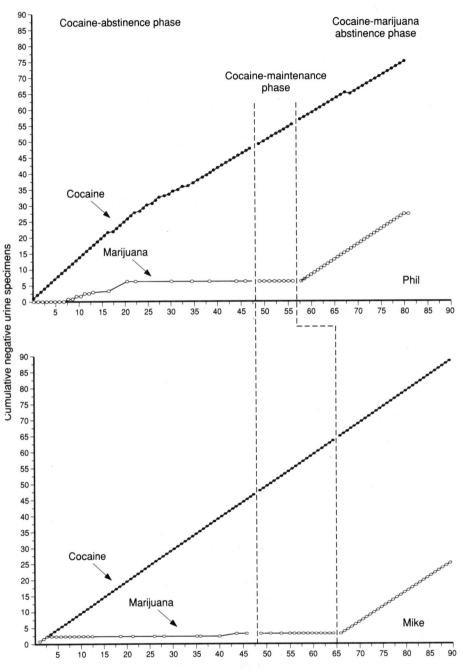

Cocaine-abstinence phase

Cocaine-marijuana
abstinence phase

Cocaine-maintenance
phase

Cocaine

Marijuana

Phil

Cocaine

Marijuana

Mike

Cumulative negative urine specimens

Consecutive urinalysis tests

specimens in a cumulative graph for each person.[1] The figure shows that when reinforcement was given for cocaine abstinence, tests for cocaine were negative. Marijuana continued to be used until the final phase, in which abstinence from both cocaine and marijuana were reinforced. The sequence of interventions across two individuals seen at the clinic and across two drugs follows the criteria of a multiple-baseline design. The pattern suggests that the token reinforcement program was responsible for the change. Follow-up assessment, including reports from others (girl-friend, roommate) and from the clients themselves, indicated no use of cocaine but some occasional use of marijuana.

Token economies have been used with a variety of populations other than those illustrated here, including the mentally retarded, prisoners, geriatric or nursing-home residents, alcoholics and drug addicts, and out-patient children and adults (see Glynn, 1990; Kazdin, 1982d). Similarly, the various settings in which token economies have been applied include the home, schools, institutions, hospitals, day-care centers, nursing homes, and business and industry. Also, as evident in a later chapter, applications of reinforcement techniques to social problems have frequently relied on token economies to alter behavior in everyday life.

Important considerations. Tokens offer advantages over other rein-forcers. First, tokens are potent reinforcers and can often develop behav-iors at a higher level than those developed by other conditioned reinforcers such as praise, approval, and feedback. Thus, it is often useful to begin with a token reinforcement program to obtain high levels of performance. After performance is consistently high, it can be maintained with praise, which is more easily administered. Second, tokens bridge the delay between the target response and backup reinforcement. If a reinforcer other than tokens (such as an activity) cannot be delivered immediately after the target re-sponse has been performed, tokens can be delivered instead and used to purchase a backup reinforcer later. Third, because tokens are backed up by a variety of reinforcers, they are less subject to satiation than are other reinforcers. If a client is no longer interested in one or two backup rein-forcers, usually there are many other reinforcers that are of value to the client. Fourth, tokens can be easily administered without interrupting the target response. Tokens do not require consumption (as do such rein-forcers as food) or the performance of behaviors that may interrupt the target response (for example, participating in a special activity). Fifth, to-

---

F I G U R E 5–3 (*left*)

Cumulative number of negative cocaine and marijuana urinalysis results obtained with Phil and Mike during three phases of treatment as a function of tests conducted throughout treatment. Cocaine and marijuana test results are presented by closed and open symbols, respectively. Steep slopes in the cumulative record indicate change; horizontal lines indicate no change.

SOURCE: Budney, A. J., Higgins, S. T., Delaney, D. D., Kent, L., & Bickel, W. K. (1991).

kens permit administering a single reinforcer (tokens) to individuals who ordinarily have different reinforcer preferences. Those preferences can be exercised in the exchange of backup reinforcers. Hence, with tokens, there is less likelihood that the reinforcers will be of value to only a few of the individuals in the setting. Finally, tokens permit parceling out of other reinforcers (such as activities) that have to be earned in an all-or-none fashion. Tokens can be earned toward the purchase of a large or valuable backup reinforcer.

There are potential disadvantages in employing tokens. In some programs, backup reinforcers extraneous to the setting are introduced. For example, in a classroom program, tokens may be backed up with food. A potential problem is removing the token system after behavioral gains have been made and transferring the control of behavior to naturally occurring events such as privileges and activities. Food is not normally presented in a class and eventually needs to be eliminated. Of course, in a token economy, backup reinforcers normally unavailable in the setting need not be introduced. Tokens can be used to purchase access to ordinary privileges, activities, and other events. Introducing tokens may itself be disadvantageous. Tokens (except for such tokens as money and grades) constitute a reinforcing event not available in most settings. Because the delivery of tokens is clearly associated with reinforcement of desirable behavior, they may exert stimulus control over that behavior. Clients learn that the presence of tokens signals that desirable behavior will be reinforced; the absence of tokens signals that desirable behavior will not be reinforced or be reinforced less often and with less potent reinforcers (for example, intermittent praise). Consequently, desirable behavior may decline. However, specific procedures are available to withdraw token reinforcement programs without a loss of behavioral gains (see Chapter 11).

Another possible disadvantage of tokens is that individuals in token economies may obtain them in unauthorized ways. For example, clients may steal tokens from one another. If tokens can be obtained without performing the target responses, their effect on behavior will diminish. To combat the stealing of tokens, tokens can be individually coded so that they differ for each individual.

General Comments

The variety of reinforcers provides a great deal of flexibility in devising reinforcement programs. At the very minimum, praise, activities, and privileges can be used in virtually any setting. The use of consumables may be limited by restrictions of the setting. For example, food may be too difficult to administer in a large group. Although tokens are usually the most powerful positive reinforcer in applied settings, they may not be needed in most settings. Praise, privileges, and feedback may be very effective. A token economy is somewhat more difficult to implement than other reinforcement programs (for example, it requires delivering tokens plus backup reinforcers and keeping track of token earnings), and it introduces problems (such as stealing or hoarding tokens, withdrawing tokens from the setting) that may not occur with other programs. Hence, in some applications, tokens may be introduced only if more easily implemented reinforcers have not been effective. On the other hand, token programs are used from the beginning in many cases because they provide a clear way of specifying the relations among several target behaviors and different types of reinforcers.

The discussion of types of reinforcers should not imply that the various types of reinforcers have to be used independently. A program that incorporates a variety of reinforcers, such as a token economy, is likely to be more effective than one that uses only a few reinforcers. More than one type of reinforcer should be used for an additional reason. Programs using activities, feedback, consumables, or tokens should pair these events with praise and attention. Developing responsiveness to social reinforcers is important because social consequences are likely to be the major source of reinforcement once the client functions outside the treatment setting.

BASIC REQUIREMENTS FOR EFFECTIVE APPLICATION

In the development of a reinforcement program, often the primary concern is with the type of reinforcer used. Clearly, the reinforcer is important and some reinforcers (for example, tokens), tend to be more effective than others (for example, feedback). Yet, the effectiveness of the program depends on a variety of other factors as well. Prominent among these is how the reinforcer is delivered.

Contingent Application of Consequences

The most fundamental condition for the effective application of a reinforcer is that the reinforcer be *contingent* on behavior. This means that the reinforcer is provided only if the desired response is performed. If the reinforcer is not provided contingently, behavior is not likely to change. Technically, *noncontingent* application of the reinforcer would not constitute reinforcement.

The contingent application of reinforcers is not necessarily an all-or-none matter. For example, when reinforcement is described to parents, teachers, and others who wish to implement behavioral programs, they often state that they have already used reinforcement, and with little or no success. However, reinforcement is usually carried out haphazardly in everyday situations. It is delivered contingently on some occasions and noncontingently on other occasions.

The differences between contingent and noncontingent reinforcement are dramatic and clear. Contingent reinforcement usually leads to marked behavior change; noncontingent reinforcement leads to little or no change; and reinforcement administered contingently on some occasions but not on others leads to performance somewhere in the middle (Baer & Wolf, 1970; Kazdin, 1973a; Redd & Birnbrauer, 1969). One might ask how noncontingent reinforcement can lead to any change in behavior. The reason is that noncontingent reinforcement accidentally follows the desired behavior on some occasions and hence constitutes weak and intermittent reinforcement for the behavior. Nevertheless, when the goal is to change behavior, noncontingent reinforcement should be avoided.

Delay of Reinforcement

The effectiveness of reinforcement depends on the *delay* between the behavior and the delivery of reinforcing consequences (food, praise, or points). Responses in close proximity to reinforcement are learned better than are responses remote from reinforcement. Thus, to maximize the effect of reinforcement, a reinforcer should be delivered *immediately* after the target response. If this is not done, a response different from the target response may be performed during the intervening period. If that happens, the intervening response will be immediately reinforced, whereas the target response will be reinforced after a delay. For example, children are often praised (or punished) for a behavior long after the behavior has been performed. If a child straightens up his or her room, a parent would do well to provide praise immediately. If praise is postponed until the end of the day, a variety of intervening responses may occur (including, perhaps, messing up the room). Similarly, in classroom settings, children are often told how "good" they are when they are on the verge of becoming restless or disruptive. The teacher may say that the class was well behaved in the morning and that she hopes it will remain well behaved. Such praise will be minimally effective because of the delay in delivering it.

Immediate reinforcement is especially important when the target response is being developed. After a response has been performed consistently, the amount of time between the response and reinforcement can be increased without a decrement in performance. For example, in classroom settings, students sometimes receive points or privileges daily while high rates of academic behavior are developing. After such behavior has stabilized, the reinforcers can be delivered every other day or every few days without a deleterious effect on performance. If a program begins with delayed reinforcement, behavior may not change at all or may change less rapidly than it would if reinforcement were immediate. After a behavior has been well developed, it is desirable to change from immediate to delayed reinforcement so that the behavior is not dependent on immediate consequences. A great many consequences in everyday life (accomplishments, wages, grades, and fame) follow long after a series of responses has been completed.

Magnitude or Amount of the Reinforcer

The amount of reinforcement delivered for a response also determines the extent to which the response will be performed. The greater the amount of the reinforcer delivered for a response, the more frequent the response will be. The amount of the reinforcer can usually be specified in such terms as quantity of food, number of points, or amount of money.

Although the magnitude of reinforcement is directly related to performance, there are limits to this relationship. An unlimited amount of reinforcement does not necessarily maintain a high rate of performance. A reinforcer loses its effect when it is given in excessive amounts. This phenomenon is referred to as *satiation*. Hence, the effect of increasing reinforcement is limited by the point at which the individual becomes satiated. Satiation is especially evident with primary reinforcers such as food, water, and sex. In excessive amounts, each of these reinforcers quickly loses its reinforcing properties and may even become aversive. Of course, satiation of primary reinforcers is temporary; they regain their reinforcing value as deprivation increases. Secondary, or conditioned, reinforcers, such as praise, attention, and tokens, are also subject to satiation, but to a lesser extent than are primary reinforcers.

The effect of the amount of a reinforcer on behavior depends on the satiation and deprivation states of the individual with respect to that reinforcer. An event (for example, money) is not likely to be very effective as a reinforcer if an individual has unlimited access to it. If an individual is partially deprived of an event, a smaller amount of a reinforcer is needed to change behavior. In most everyday situations, people do not have unlimited access to reinforcing events (such as free time in a classroom situation or time with friends or children), and thus they normally undergo various mild forms of deprivation. This means that a variety of events can be effective as reinforcers without introducing deprivation.

Quality or Type of the Reinforcer

The quality of a reinforcer, unlike the amount of a reinforcer, is not usually specifiable in physical terms. Rather, quality usually is determined by the preference of the client. This has been tested by asking individuals which of two or more reinforcers are preferred and then testing the reinforcer's value on performance (see Green, Reid, Canipe, & Gardner, 1991; Neef, Mace, Shea, & Shade, 1992). In general, reinforcers that are highly preferred lead to greater performance than do those that are less preferred. For a given client, it is usually not difficult to specify highly preferred activities. Behaviors frequently engaged in provide a helpful indication of highly preferred reinforcers. However, preference for a particular reinforcer may change over time. Yet, certain types of reinforcers, elaborated later, tend to result in higher performance than do others and thus better determine the extent of behavior change. For example, token reinforcement is often more effective than praise in altering behavior, and both of these are usually more effective than feedback is.

Schedule of Reinforcement

Schedule of reinforcement refers to the rule denoting how many or which specific responses will be reinforced. Reinforcers are always administered according to some schedule. In the simplest schedule, a response is reinforced each time it occurs. This schedule is referred to as *continuous reinforcement.* For example, to train a child to follow instructions, reinforcement can be given each time the child responds appropriately. On the other hand, reinforcement may be delivered after only some of the appropriate responses. This is referred to as *intermittent reinforcement.*

There are important differences between continuous and intermittent reinforcement while the behaviors are being reinforced and after reinforcement has been withdrawn. During the acquisition or reinforcement phase, a behavior developed with continuous reinforcement is performed at a higher rate than is a behavior developed with intermittent reinforcement. Thus, while a behavior is developing, a continuous or "generous" schedule of reinforcement should be used. However, the advantage of continuous reinforcement is compensated after the reinforcement ceases. In extinction, behaviors that were continuously reinforced diminish at a much more rapid rate than do behaviors that were reinforced intermittently.

Figure 5–4 plots the general relationship between schedules of reinforcement during acquisition (reinforcement phase) and during extinction (no further reinforcement). As shown in the figure, the advantage of continuous reinforcement is that performance occurs at a high level while behavior is reinforced. The advantage of intermittent reinforcement is that resistance to extinction is greater when reinforcement is discontinued. Both advantages can be obtained by developing behavior with continuous reinforcement until a high rate of behavior has been well established and then, to foster response maintenance, changing the schedule to intermittent reinforcement and making it increasingly intermittent.

The difference between responses developed with continuous reinforcement and responses developed with intermittent reinforcement is apparent in examples from everyday experience. A familiar response that is reinforced every time is depositing coins in a vending machine and pressing the lever or button. Barring mechanical failure, the response is followed by the reinforcer (for example, soda, candy) almost every time. Once reinforcement no longer occurs, this response (depositing coins) follows a pattern identical to that of continuous reinforcement. As soon as the reinforcer (that is, the product) is no longer delivered, extinction is almost immediate. If a vending machine does not deliver the reinforcer, few individuals will repeatedly put coins into it unless there is some evidence that it has been repaired. *For behaviors previously developed with continuous reinforcement, extinction is rapid.*

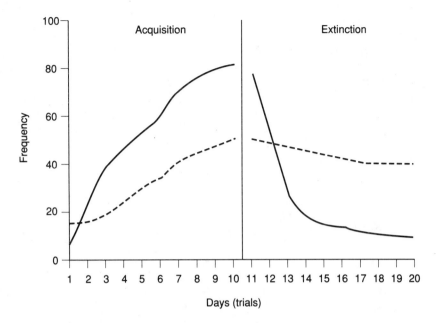

FIGURE 5–4
Effects on behavior of continuous reinforcement (solid line) and intermittent reinforcement (dashed line) while behavior is being reinforced (acquisition or reinforcement phase) and when reinforcement is no longer provided (extinction phase).

A similar response—putting coins into a machine and pulling a lever—
might be maintained by intermittent reinforcement, as in the case of slot
machines. Sometimes putting money into a slot machine is reinforced (with
money); many other times it is not. If money were no longer delivered
(extinction), the response would continue to be performed at a high rate
before extinguishing. It is difficult to discriminate when extinction begins
on a highly intermittent schedule of reinforcement. The resistance of a
response to extinction depends on how intermittent or *thin* the reinforcement schedule is. *Resistance to extinction is greater if very few responses
are reinforced than it is if many responses are reinforced.*

Another advantage of intermittent reinforcement is its efficient use of
available reinforcers. Intermittent reinforcement allows delivery of a few
reinforcers for a large number of responses. Moreover, if reinforcers are
administered only a few times, satiation is less likely to occur. For example,
with intermittent food reinforcement, the client is not likely to become full
quickly and thus temporarily unresponsive to food. A further advantage of
intermittent reinforcement is that it requires less time for administering
reinforcers than does continuous reinforcement.

Intermittent reinforcement can be scheduled in many ways, only a few
of which will be considered here. Two simple types of reinforcement schedules can be distinguished. Reinforcement can be contingent upon the emis-
sion of a certain *number of responses.* This is referred to as a *ratio schedule*

because the schedule specifies the ratio of the total number of responses to the one that is reinforced. Reinforcement can also be contingent upon the *amount of time* that passes. This is referred to as an *interval schedule.* With a ratio schedule, the amount of time that passes before the subject performs the response is irrelevant. The behavior of the subject controls the frequency of reinforcement. With an interval schedule, the number of responses performed is irrelevant as long as one response is performed after the prescribed amount of time has elapsed. The frequency of reinforcement is partially determined by the clock.

In both ratio and interval schedules of reinforcement, the requirement for reinforcement can be *fixed,* so that it is the same requirement every time. On the other hand, the requirement can be *variable,* so that it is different from time to time. Four simple schedules of reinforcement will be discussed: fixed ratio (FR), variable ratio (VR), fixed interval (FI), and variable interval (VI).

A *fixed-ratio schedule* requires that an unvarying number of responses be performed before a response is reinforced. The number following FR specifies which response will be reinforced. For example, FR: 1 specifies that only one response is required for the reinforcer to be delivered. (FR: 1 is also called continuous reinforcement, because every response is reinforced.) FR: 10 denotes that every tenth response is reinforced.

Performance under fixed-ratio schedules differs to some extent depending on whether the ratios are small or large. Characteristically, there is a temporary pause in responding after reinforcement is delivered, and then a rapid rise in response rate until the ratio is completed and reinforcement is again delivered. The pause after responding is a function of the ratio, with large ratios (when few responses are reinforced) producing longer pauses. Once the responses resume, reinforcement is maximized by performing all of the responses as quickly as possible. Examples of an FR schedule include any instance in which the reinforcer is delivered for a certain number of responses. For example, the behavior of factory workers who are paid according to how much they produce is reinforced on an FR schedule (commonly referred to as piecework). For every certain number of responses (products produced), the reinforcer (money) is earned. If several responses are required for reinforcement, there may be a temporary pause (no production) immediately after reinforcement.

A *variable-ratio schedule* specifies that reinforcement is to occur after a certain number of responses. That number *varies* unpredictably from occasion to occasion. On the average, a certain number of responses are performed before reinforcement is delivered. The number following VR specifies the average number of responses required for reinforcement. For example, VR: 5 indicates that, on the average, five responses are to be performed before the reinforcer is delivered. The second response may be reinforced on some occasions, whereas the eighth response may be reinforced on other occasions. A different number of responses may be required each time. Across all occasions, however, reinforcement is delivered on the average of the number specified (for example, five in the VR:5 schedule). Of course, the number 1 cannot be used in a VR schedule because using that number would be equivalent to reinforcing every response, which is a continuous reinforcement or FR:1 schedule.

Performance under VR schedules is consistently high. The pauses after responding in FR schedules can be virtually eliminated with a VR schedule unless the average ratio is very long. Immediately after a response is reinforced, the subject begins to respond because the next reinforcer may follow only a few responses. Performance continues at a high rate until reinforcement is delivered, and immediately resumes again. Behavior previously maintained under a VR schedule extinguishes more slowly than behavior previously maintained under an FR schedule, particularly if the variable schedule requires many responses for reinforcement. Performance is relatively persistent and consistent following a VR schedule. Thus, VR schedules are highly suited to forestalling extinction. Before reinforcement is withdrawn, the ratio can gradually be made very *thin* by increasing the number of responses required for reinforcement.

Examples of VR schedules are abundant in everyday experience. The behavior of a fisherman is controlled, in part, by VR reinforcement. A fish (reinforcer) is not caught every time a line is tossed into the water (response). The response is reinforced only some of the time, and the variable nature of the schedule ensures that extinction will not take place rapidly. Slot machines, mentioned earlier, represent a dramatic application of VR schedules. Since any response can be reinforced, the person playing the slot machine usually performs at a consistently high rate. His or her performance is unlikely to extinguish for long periods of time.

A *fixed-interval schedule* requires that an interval of time (usually expressed in minutes) pass before the reinforcer is available. The first response that occurs after the interval passes is reinforced. In such a schedule, of course, the interval is unvarying. For example, in an FI:1 schedule, the first response after one minute passes is reinforced. An *interval schedule* requires that only one response be performed after the prescribed interval has elapsed. Although this efficiency in responding rarely occurs, the characteristics of responses to FI schedules are distinct. Following reinforcement, there is usually a pronounced pause, during which responses are performed. This does not interfere with receiving reinforcement because a response before the appropriate time elapses is never reinforced. Only if the pause is longer than the fixed interval will the subject postpone reinforcement. FI schedules lead to less consistent rates of responding than do FR schedules because nonresponding immediately after reinforcement during an FI schedule does not postpone reinforcement, as it does with an FR schedule.

An example of an FI response pattern in everyday experience is looking to see whether one's mail has arrived. For most individuals, mail delivery is once a day, with (fairly) fixed periods of time (24 hours) before deliveries. The response (looking for mail in the mailbox) is reinforced (finding mail) daily. Immediately after reinforcement, there is no longer a response. One does not resume looking for mail again until the next day, when the 24-hour interval is almost complete. Looking for mail then increases until reinforcement is obtained, at which time the pause after reinforcement is again evident.

A *variable-interval* schedule specifies the *average length* of the intervals required for reinforcement. For example, a VI : 10 schedule denotes that, on the average, 10 minutes must elapse before a response is reinforced. On any given occasion, the interval may be more or less than 10 minutes. The reinforcer is delivered for the first response *after* the interval elapses. The studying behavior of students follows a pattern characteristic of a VI schedule if the instructor gives "pop quizzes." The interval between quizzes is unpredictable and varies from quiz to quiz. Studying tends to be relatively consistent under such a schedule. In general, responding tends to be higher under VI schedules than it is under FI schedules.

As already mentioned, it is desirable to reinforce continuously at the beginning of a behavior change program. In practice, it may be impossible to closely observe behavior constantly to ensure that every instance of the target behavior is reinforced. However, an almost continuous or rich schedule can be used initially before changing to increasingly intermittent schedules.

In selecting an intermittent schedule, both the characteristic response pattern of the schedule and practical exigencies should be considered. Although fixed schedules may be convenient to administer, the characteristic response pattern under such schedules includes pauses or lapses in performance of the reinforced behavior. For example, in an elementary school classroom, the teacher who wishes to increase attentive student behavior may decide to increase the frequency of reinforcement. The teacher may deliver praise every 30 minutes to children who are paying attention (FI : 30 schedule). The teacher may select 30 minutes because this is easy to track on the clock in the room. At the end of 30 minutes, the teacher may praise and mention by name each student who is behaving appropriately. Given the fixed-interval schedule, it is very likely that the desired performance (such as sitting, working quietly) will be high near the end of the interval with pauses (lapses in appropriate behavior) immediately after reinforcement. The teacher probably would conclude that praise "works" but does not really have any more than a temporary effect. Actually, the schedule fosters inconsistent performance. A better procedure would be to shift to a VI schedule. This can be accomplished by using a kitchen timer (as used in cooking) that sounds a ring when the timer is up. The teacher can turn the dial to different periods—some short (for example, 3 to 5 minutes), some long (for example, 60 minutes), and some in between. When the timer rings on this intermittent schedule, the teacher would praise attentive students. Behavior would be much more consistent over time throughout the day. In general, variable schedules can reduce inconsistency in performance. Interval schedules tend to be easily administered, but client performance is usually higher under ratio schedules. Under ratio schedules, high rates of responding speed up the delivery of reinforcement.

Intermittent reinforcement has many advantages. Mentioned already is the likelihood that resistance to extinction will be greater with intermittent reinforcement, a topic discussed later in Chapter 11. Also, intermittent reinforcement is an efficient use of reinforcers. Few reinforcers are delivered for many responses. Also, less time is required to administer the reinforcer and reinforcement delivery will interrupt ongoing behavior (for example, studying) on fewer occasions. Finally, satiation is less likely with intermittent reinforcement because the delivery is less often.

It is important not to overstate the case for intermittent reinforcement. When the goal is to develop a behavior of interest, usually the initial purpose of developing a behavior modification program, continuous reinforcement is the schedule of choice. If continuous reinforcement is not feasible (for example, in a classroom with one teacher, or in the home with a parent away at work), the schedule that provides the most frequent reinforcement of the behavior of interest is preferred. Intermittent reinforcement is useful to maintain the desired behavior once high levels have been achieved.

In general, the basic requirements of administering reinforcement noted previously exert a remarkable impact on behavior. The effectiveness of a program is not guaranteed if all of the requirements are met, since there are no other considerations beyond positive reinforcement. Yet, if these requirements are not met or are not met very well, little or no behavior change can be expected.

Persons in applied settings often report that they have tried the use of positive reinforcement and it really does not work. The reports are often correct. The novelty of behavior modification in this regard is not the introduction of procedures that have never been conceived previously. Rather, the evaluation of behavior to assess change and the elucidation of critical requirements to achieve change are central bases for the successful application of reinforcement techniques.

CONTINGENCY CONTRACTS

Often reinforcement contingencies are designed in the form of behavioral contracts between individuals who wish behavior to change (parents, teachers, hospital attendants) and clients whose behavior is to be changed (students, children, patients). An actual contract is signed by both parties indicating that they agree to the terms. *The contingency contract specifies the relationship between behaviors and their consequences.* Specifically, the contract specifies the reinforcers desired by the client and the behavior desired by the individual who wishes behavior change. Any of the reinforcers discussed previously, as well as idiosyncratic rewards, may be specified in the contract.

Ideally, contingency contracts contain five elements (Stuart, 1971). First, they detail what each party expects to gain. For example, parents may want a child to complete his or her work or attend school regularly. The child may want free time with friends, extra allowance, and other reinforcers. Second, the stipulated behaviors of the client are readily observable. If parents cannot determine whether a responsibility has been met, they cannot grant a privilege. Thus, some behaviors may not be readily incorporated into a contingency contract. For example, parents often cannot easily monitor whether an adolescent visits certain friends, so it would not be advisable to include a stipulation regarding such visits in the contract. Third, contingency contracts provide sanctions for a failure to meet their terms. The aversive consequences for not meeting the contract terms are systematic and planned in advance (agreed to by all parties), not arbitrary and after the fact. Fourth, contingency contracts include a bonus clause that reinforces consistent compliance with their terms. Bonuses (extra privilege, activity, or extension of curfew limit) can be used to reinforce consistent performance over an extended period. For someone whose behavior was recently developed, bonuses for consistent performance may be especially important. Fifth, contingency contracts provide a means of monitoring the rate of positive reinforcement given and received. The records inform each party when reinforcement is to occur and provide constant feedback. Moreover, the records may cue individuals to make favorable comments about desirable behavior when earning of the backup reinforcer is about to occur.

Contingency contracts need not be elaborate or complex. A sample contingency contract is illustrated in Figure 5–5. This contract was used to alter the behavior of an 8-year-old, second-grade boy named Andrew who constantly fought at school (Bristol, 1976). The program involved the teacher, parents, and Andrew. Each morning, Andrew received a card with a smiling face on it. In the morning, after lunch, and at the end of the day (as specified in the contract), the teacher signed the card if Andrew had not engaged in fighting. The teacher's signatures served as points that could be accumulated toward the purchase of a reward, also specified in the contract. The parents provided Andrew with praise, posted the cards in a conspicuous place, and gave extra rewards (staying up 15 minutes later at bedtime) for the signatures he received. As shown in Figure 5–6, Andrew averaged about nine fights per week before entering into the contingency contract and fewer fights while the contract was in effect. When the contract procedure was withdrawn, the number of fights increased. In the final phase, when the contract was reinstated, there were at first fewer fights, and for the last three weeks of the program, there were none. A report obtained 7 months after the end of the program indicated that Andrew was doing well without any special assistance.

Date
_____

Contract no.
_____

Mrs. Harris will initial a smiley card for Andrew each time he does one of the following:

1. Comes into school, hangs up his wraps, and takes his seat without arguing or fighting with another child.
2. Eats his lunch and has his noon recess without arguing or fighting with another child.
3. Clears his desk, gets his wraps, and goes to the bus without arguing or fighting with another child.

When Andrew has received 15 signatures from Mrs. Harris and has had his cards signed by one of his parents, he may choose one of the following rewards:

> Read a story to someone.
> Be first in line for lunch.
> Pass out supplies.
> Get notes from the office.
> Bring a treat from home for the class.
> Go to the library for free reading.
> Choose a book for Mrs. Harris to read to the class.
> Choose a friend for a math game.
> Bring a carrot for Chopper and get a chance to hold him.
> Be a student helper in math for 30 minutes.

I, Andrew, agree to the terms of the above agreement,

_____

I, the classroom teacher, agree to provide Andrew with the reinforcers specified above if Andrew keeps his part of the agreement. I also agree not to provide Andrew with any of the above reinforcers during the term of the contract if he does not earn the necessary signatures.

_____

I, Andrew's parent, agree to sign each card that Andrew brings home, to post the cards where Andrew can see them, and to help Andrew keep track of the number of signatures he has earned. Andrew can earn 15 minutes of extra "stay up" time by bringing home 3 signatures.

_____

WE UNDERSTAND THAT THIS IS NOT A LEGALLY BINDING CONTRACT, BUT RATHER A FIRM COMMITMENT OF GOOD WILL AMONG PARTIES WHO CARE ABOUT EACH OTHER.

FIGURE 5–5
Sample contingency contract.
SOURCE: Bristol, M. M. (1976).

Contingency contracts have been used successfully to alter a variety of problems, such as overeating, alcohol and drug abuse, cigarette smoking, problem behaviors of delinquents, academic and disruptive behavior of elementary school children, and studying in college students. Various authors have described procedures for developing contingency contracts that

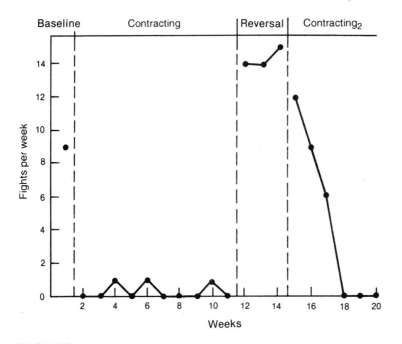

FIGURE 5–6

Weekly summary of the total number of fights occurring out of a possible maximum of 15.

SOURCE: Bristol, M. M. (1976).

can be applied to a wide range of problems and have illustrated additional applications (see DeRisi & Butz, 1975; O'Banion & Whaley, 1981).

Advantages of Using Contingency Contracts

Contingency contracts have several distinct advantages. First, the performance of clients may be better if they are allowed to have some input into designing or implementing a program than it is if a program is imposed on them. Even if the program is not more effective, active participation by the clients is likely to make the program more acceptable to them (Kazdin, 1980a). Second, the contingencies specified in a contract are less likely to be aversive to the client. The client can negotiate the consequences and the requirements for reinforcement. If the system is minimally aversive, the client is less likely to attempt to escape from the contingencies or from those who administer them. Third, contingency contracts are usually flexible in that participants can renegotiate their terms. The reinforcers delivered for particular responses can be adjusted, response requirements can be increased, and so on. Fourth, the contract makes the contingencies explicit. The specification of the contingencies serves as rules or instructions for the client on how to behave and defines the consequences that will follow behavior. Although explicit instructions alone may not produce durable changes in performance, they often increase the effectiveness of reinforcement. Fifth, contingency contracts are particularly useful in structuring the relationship among persons whose interactions may be maladaptive. For example, when compared to the families of "normal" children, the families of delinquent and behavior-problem children engage in a lower rate of positive social exchanges and inadequately reinforce socially appropriate behavior (see Patterson, Reid, & Dishion, 1992). Contingency contracts make explicit the requirements for delivering positive consequences and increase the likelihood that reinforcement for the desired behaviors will actually be provided. Putting the contingencies in writing makes it easier to monitor whether they are carried out in the desired fashion.

Contingency contracts have been used frequently. However, extensive research has not been completed to guide many of the specific details to make contracts maximally effective or acceptable to clients. Even so, the use of contracts to structure reinforcement programs, to make the requirements explicit to all parties, and to encourage negotiation among the parties is to be strongly encouraged.

REINFORCEMENT TECHNIQUES TO REDUCE UNDESIRABLE RESPONSES

In many situations, the major goal of the reinforcement program is to reduce undesirable behavior. Because reinforcement is a technique for increasing behavior, people often believe that employing it to decrease behavior is inappropriate. Hence, punishment and extinction, discussed in the next chapters, are used because they decrease response frequency directly. However, undesirable target responses can be decreased or eliminated by reinforcement. Indeed, reinforcement techniques for suppressing behavior are available and effective (LaVigna & Donnellan, 1986; O'Brien & Repp, in press).

Reinforcement of Other Behavior

One way to decrease undesirable behavior is to provide reinforcement when the client engages in any behavior other than the target response. *Differential reinforcement of other behavior* (DRO) consists of providing the reinforcing consequences of all responses *except* for the undesirable behavior of interest. The effect of this schedule is to decrease the target behavior. For example, a DRO schedule was used to reduce self-injury (facial hitting, hand biting) in a 16-year-old mentally retarded male named Donald (Iwata, Pace, Kalsher, Cowdery, & Cataldo, 1990). An edible reinforcer (sips of soda) was used to reinforce noninjurious behavior. At the end of 1-minute intervals in which no self-injury had occurred, Donald received a sip of soda. This is a DRO contingency because any behavior that occurred, other than self-injury, earned the reinforcer. The amount of time without self-injury needed to earn the soda was gradually extended (2, 4, 15 minutes). Self-injury declined from approximately 20 percent of the intervals in baseline to 0 percent during the DRO phase.

In another application, DRO was used with an adult psychiatric patient with seizure activity (Burgio & Tice, 1985). The purpose was to evaluate whether seizures could be controlled by behavioral intervention rather than the more commonly used anticonvulsive medication. A program was devised in which the patient could earn a walk outside the hospital with a staff member at the end of a 24-hour period with no seizures. An ABAB design showed that seizures systematically declined when reinforcement was provided for other (nonseizure) behavior.

A DRO schedule provides reinforcement for *not* engaging in a behavior. The reinforcer is delivered as long as the client is not performing the undesired response. Thus, when the reinforcer is delivered, the person may be doing virtually anything except the target behavior. For example, a DRO schedule to eliminate a child's hitting of peers would provide reinforcement for periods of nonaggression. The child may earn the reinforcer even when sitting alone and not interacting. It might be useful to provide reinforcement for positive behaviors, such as playing cooperatively with others, rather than just for not engaging in the undesirable response.

Reinforcement of Incompatible or Alternative Behavior

Reinforcement of the nonoccurrence of a response or any other behavior (DRO) is useful when there are very high rates of the undesired target behavior and one wishes to provide reinforcement anytime the response is not evident. For example, if autistic children are hitting themselves at high rates, reinforcement might be delivered whenever this behavior does not occur. In most situations, it is useful to identify specific positive behaviors that are reinforced. These behaviors are selected because they directly or indirectly interfere with performance of the undesired behavior. Usually specific positive behaviors in the setting (for example, working at one's desk at school or completing a chore at home) that the behavior change agent wishes to develop can be identified. Two differential reinforcement schedules are suited to this purpose.

In one of these schedules, reinforcement is provided for behaviors *directly incompatible* with the undesired response. An incompatible behavior is any behavior that directly interferes and cannot be performed with the undesired behavior. The incompatible behavior is often the direct *opposite* of the undesired behavior. Increasing the frequency of an incompatible behavior decreases the undesired behavior. This procedure, sometimes referred to as the *differential reinforcement of incompatible behavior* (DRI), focuses on reinforcing behaviors that are incompatible or that compete with the undesired behavior.

Usually, it is quite easy to select an incompatible response that can be reinforced. For example, if a child fights with siblings at home, reinforcement can be delivered for such behaviors as playing games cooperatively. If an institutionalized patient has violent outbursts and tantrums, reinforcement can be delivered for talking and sitting quietly and for calmly interacting with peers, which are incompatible with the undesired responses.

The effects of reinforcing a behavior incompatible with the undesired response were demonstrated in a program developed to reduce pica among three institutionalized mentally retarded adults (Donnelly & Olczak, 1990). Pica consists of eating nonfood and nonnutritive objects and can lead to injury, illness, and death. The individuals in this program ate cigarette butts, a form of pica that is particularly bothersome because of the toxicity and addictive properties of nicotine. The intervention was carried out in a room where a fake cigarette butt made of bread was placed in an ash tray and replaced each time it was removed. The fake butt was used to permit careful assessment without jeopardizing the health of the individuals. Each adult was treated separately and was invited to come into a room where the cigarette butt was available. The amount of time (latency) until the butt was eaten was the measure to evaluate the program. The program consisted of a DRI schedule in which chewing gum was the response considered to be incompatible with eating. Chewing gum was given to the individual and periods of checking were reinforced with sips of decaffinated and sweetened coffee. Initially short periods of engaging in the incompatible behavior were reinforced, then longer periods were.

Figure 5–7 illustrates the effects of the program for one of the adults. Baseline shows that this individual immediately consumed cigarette butts when he entered the room and kept doing so as these butts were replaced. With the DRI schedule, behavior changed markedly. In the final phase, the program was extended to the ward by staff. Improvements were maintained, although not to the level in the special sessions in which behavior was monitored and carefully assessed.

It is not always possible or necessary to identify a behavior that is physically incompatible with an undesired behavior that one wishes to decrease. A host of positive behaviors that serve as alternatives to the undesired behavior might be reinforced. These alternatives are behaviors whose performance decreases the likelihood that the undesired behavior will occur. Increasing the frequency of alternative behaviors, whether or not they are incompatible with the undesired behavior, decreases the undesired behavior. This procedure is referred to as the *differential reinforcement of alternative behavior* (DRA).

Because of the many alternatives that are available, examples of DRA are somewhat easier to identify than are examples of DRI. To suppress fighting among siblings, as noted above, playing cooperatively could be

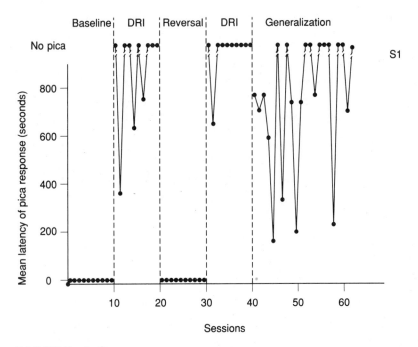

FIGURE 5–7

Mean (average) latency of pica responses within the session when the child was given the opportunity for baseline, DRI, reversal (return to baseline), DRI, and generalization (on the ward) phases. Low scores mean the individual consumed the fake cigarette butts immediately when the opportunity was provided; high scores mean the individual either had a long latency before consuming the butts or did not consume them at all. (No pica at top of graph).

SOURCE: Donnelly, D. R., & Olczak, P. V. (1990).

reinforced. Playing cooperatively is incompatible with fighting and constitutes a DRI. Other alternative behaviors could be reinforced, such as watching television together or completing a chore together. Neither of these behaviors is necessarily incompatible with fighting, yet their reinforcement is likely to decrease the frequency of fighting. These responses are part of a general class of behaviors that might, in casual terms, be referred to as "getting along." More opportunities for positive reinforcement are made available by identifying many alternative behaviors rather than only the alternative behaviors that are physically incompatible with the undesired response.

As an illustration, in one program, an adolescent, mentally retarded student spoke out excessively in class (Deitz, Repp, & Deitz, 1976). A DRI schedule reinforcing an incompatible response (being quiet) could have been used here. However, merely being quiet does not mean that the student is developing the behaviors that are important in a classroom setting. Given the goal of the setting, a DRA schedule was used in which reinforcement was provided for working on academic tasks. This response is not incompatible with talking out because a person can do both. Yet if one is working at a task, the chances are that he or she is not talking. In this program, reinforcement of working at a task decreased talking out.

As may be evident, DRI and DRA are closely related. Actually, DRA refers to reinforcing any alternative positive responses that decrease the likelihood that the undesired behavior will be performed. DRI is a subtype of DRA in which the alternative behavior is one that is incompatible with the undesired response. In practice and in working with parents, teachers, and others, it is useful to develop a DRA schedule where a few specific alternative behaviors are identified as the target response. In our own work with parents, for example, we tell them that whenever there is a behavior they wish to suppress or eliminate, they should think of a *positive opposite*. A positive opposite is a behavior that is an alternative to and preferably incompatible with the undesired behavior. As will become more clear in the discussion of punishment in the next chapter, the suppression of behavior can be greatly enhanced when a reinforcement program is designed to develop a positive, prosocial, opposite behavior.

Reinforcement of incompatible or alternative behaviors has been used effectively in many programs (see O'Brien & Repp, in press). For example, the behaviors of hyperactive children in the classroom and at home have been altered by using reinforcement techniques. Hyperactive behaviors include disturbing others excessively, blurting out statements, being out of one's seat, speaking rapidly, running around the room, not complying with the requests of parents or teachers, and generally engaging in very high levels of inappropriate activity. Rather than punish these behaviors, many programs have been designed to reinforce alternative behaviors. Typically, programs of this kind provide tokens, praise, and consumable rewards (for example, food) for such behaviors as correct responses on academic tasks, remaining in one's seat to work on specific tasks, and engaging in more restrained and quieter types of activity. Such programs have reduced hyperactive behaviors and increased the performance of on-task and academic behaviors.

Reinforcement of Functionally Equivalent Behavior

Behaviors can be examined from the standpoint of the functions they serve. The functions refer to the broader purposes, goals, and consequences that are achieved. For example, a child's tantrums might have different (and multiple) functions for different children. Tantrums might divert adult attention from a sibling, stop parents from arguing with each other, or cease demands that are being placed on the child. If the undesired, deviant, or inappropriate response is serving some function, perhaps another response can be identified that serves the same function but is more socially appropriate. *Reinforcement of functionally equivalent behavior* refers to reinforcement of a prosocial, acceptable behavior that attains the same goals and consequences as does the problem behavior. The effect of this procedure is to reduce or eliminate the undesirable behavior.

In passing, it is important to note that the functional role of behavior has long been recognized by nonbehavioral approaches to the study of behavior. For example, psychoanalytic and family therapy conceptualizations of behavior have routinely maintained that a given behavior is of less interest in its own right than are the specific functions it serves (for example, in relation to the individual's personality or in relation to family interactions and dynamics). Also, more atheoretical research has shown that many problem behaviors in children and adolescents (for example, delinquent acts, drug use, precocious sexual activity) in fact often go together. That is, individuals who show one of these are likely to show several others as well (Elliott, Huizinga, & Menard, 1988; Jessor, Donovan, & Costa, 1991). The hypothesized reasons for clusters of problem behaviors is that they serve similar functions in relation to development. Autonomy from parents and bonding with peers are two of the functions that may be served by such behaviors.

In the context of behavioral interventions, analysis of the functions of behavior provides an alternative method of suppressing undesired target behaviors. By identifying functions of behavior, one can develop socially acceptable behaviors that attain the same functions. For example, in one demonstration, different conditions that were related to aggression, tantrums, noncompliance, and self-injury were studied in four youths aged 7 to 14 with developmental disabilities (Carr & Durand, 1985). They were individually exposed to different task conditions (easy versus difficult) and to different amounts of adult attention (high versus low). A functional analysis revealed that problem behavior led to different consequences and hence appeared to serve different functions for the children. For some children, problem behaviors were high when they received little adult attention. That is, when attention was high, problem behavior was low. This suggests that problem behavior for these children may function as a way of obtaining adult attention. An appropriate behavior was trained that served the same function for these children. Specifically, the children were trained to ask the teacher, "Am I doing good work?" This prompt by the children led to attention from the teacher and hence the function (attaining attention) would be served. The results showed that identifying the function of problem behavior individually for the children and then training an appropriate behavior to serve that function significantly decreased problem behavior. Other studies have shown that reinforcing functionally equivalent responses can readily reduce problem behaviors such as tantrums, self-injury, and aggression (for example, Carr, Taylor, & Robinson, 1991; Wacker, McMahon, Steege, Berg, Sasso, & Melloy, 1990).

Reinforcement of functionally equivalent responses can be regarded as a special case of reinforcing alternative responses. The added feature, over and above a DRA, is systematically assessing the consequences of the problem behavior, that is, searching for the function(s) of that behavior, and then selecting a behavior that achieves these consequences. Because this assessment may not be feasible in many applied settings, it is reassuring to note that DRA schedules without this feature have worked well. At the same time, if the function can be identified and served by the new behavior that is developed, the likelihood of achieving the desired changes in behavior may be increased.

Reinforcement of Low Response Rates

Another reinforcement technique for suppressing behavior is to provide reinforcing consequences for reductions in the frequency of the undesired behavior or for increases in the time in which that behavior does *not* occur. These procedures, referred to as *differential reinforcement of low rates of responding* (DRL), can effectively suppress behavior.

In one variation of a DRL schedule, the client receives reinforcing consequences for showing a *reduction in the frequency of target behavior*. For example, Deitz (1977, Exp. 2) decreased the inappropriate talking out of an educable mentally retarded male adolescent who attended a special education class. After baseline observations of talking out, the teacher told the student that if he emitted three or fewer "talk-outs" during a 55-minute period, she would spend extra time working with him. The youth would receive the reinforcing consequence only if he showed a low rate of disruptive behavior. This DRL contingency was evaluated in an ABAB design. The results, shown in Figure 5–8, demonstrate that talking out decreased whenever the DRL contingency was in effect.

The DRL schedule can completely eliminate a behavior by making the requirements for reinforcement increasingly stringent. A client may be allowed a certain number of instances of the undesired behavior within a given period to earn the reinforcer, and in order to eliminate the behavior, this number may be decreased over time. Alternatively, a client may receive reinforcing consequences for going longer and longer periods without performing the undesired behavior. For example, in separate programs, reinforcement has increased the amount of elapsed time between one response and the next to reduce stereotypical behaviors and rapid eating (see Lennox, Miltenberger, & Donnelly, 1987; Singh, Dawson, & Manning, 1981). In other variations, reinforcement for performance of a few or no instances of the response has effectively suppressed behavior (LaVigna & Donnellan, 1986; Repp & Singh, 1990).

Advantages of Using Positive Reinforcement

Reinforcement techniques using the schedules discussed previously have reduced or eliminated a wide range of undesirable and maladaptive behaviors in children and adults. The procedures appear to be at least as effective as various punishment procedures in their capacity to decrease undesirable

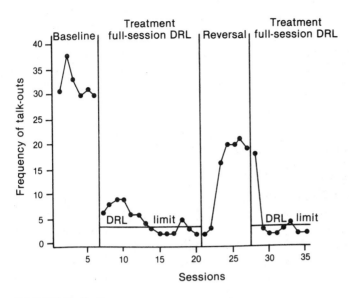

FIGURE 5–8
The frequency of talk-outs per 55-minute session of an educable mentally retarded male. During treatment, if the client emitted three or fewer talk-outs per session, the teacher spent 15 minutes working with him.
SOURCE: Deitz, S. M. (1977).

behaviors. Although punishment and extinction can decrease behavior, these procedures do not train people in socially appropriate alternative behaviors. Even if punishment or extinction is used, effects can be greatly enhanced by incorporating reinforcement for appropriate behavior into the program. Also, many ethical concerns and negative client reactions raised by punishment procedures are largely circumvented if the program is based on positive reinforcement. Given these benefits, reinforcement techniques should be used whenever the goal is to decrease behavior.

NEGATIVE REINFORCEMENT

Negative reinforcement can also be used to develop behavior. A behavior is increased or strengthened through negative reinforcement when it results in *escape* from or *avoidance* of an aversive event. Escape occurs when the individual comes in contact with the aversive event and the appropriate behavior eliminates the event. Many behaviors in everyday life are maintained by negative reinforcement through escape. For example, leaving the house to escape from an argument with one's roommate or spouse, turning off an alarm to escape from a loud noise, screaming to quiet noisy neighbors, and taking medicine to alleviate pain all represent escape.

Avoidance behavior allows the individual to prevent or indefinitely postpone contact with an aversive event. As mentioned in Chapter 2, avoidance learning may develop after an individual learns to escape an aversive event. Through classical conditioning, a previously neutral event acquires the capacity to elicit escape behavior. The escape behavior is automatically reinforced by terminating the conditioned aversive event. Thus, avoidance involves classical and operant conditioning. Avoidance refers to escape from a conditioned aversive event.

Most avoidance behavior is acquired without direct experience with the aversive event. Verbal cues from other individuals instruct us that certain consequences are to be avoided. The cues are discriminative stimuli indicating that certain untoward consequences may follow if we behave in a particular way. Examples of avoidance based on verbal cues are present in everyday experience. For example, one can avoid personal harm by responding to the threat of an impending hurricane. Avoidance of the hurricane is escape from or elimination of the threat. Behavior that reduces the threat is strengthened through negative reinforcement. Other examples of negative reinforcement through avoidance are parking one's car in a particular place to avoid a traffic fine, wearing a coat to avoid a chill, drinking alcohol sparingly to avoid a driving mishap, and leaving a sinking ship to avoid drowning.

Negative reinforcement, in the form of escape from an aversive event, has not been widely used in applied settings for various reasons. First, negative reinforcement requires an ongoing aversive event (nagging, noise) that can be terminated when the desired target behavior occurs. This means that the aversive event must be delivered frequently before reinforcement can occur. The use of aversive events is ethically indefensible if positive events (through positive reinforcement) have not been attempted first. Because there are many types of positive reinforcement programs (token economies, contingency contracts), there is rarely a need to employ negative reinforcement. Second, the use of aversive events often produces undesirable side effects. Corporal punishment, physical restraint, reprimands, isolation, and other aversive consequences lead the client to escape from the situation, to avoid the persons who administer these events, and even to aggress against them. These side effects can be avoided by relying on positive reinforcement. Third, negative reinforcement is often difficult to administer. The aversive stimulus must be carefully controlled, so that it can be terminated immediately after the appropriate behavior occurs. Usually this requires carefully monitoring behavior, often with certain apparatus. For these reasons, it is no surprise that negative reinforcement has been used quite sparingly.

An interesting example of the use of escape focused on disruptive behavior in a dentist's office (Allen, Loiben, Allen, & Stanley, 1992). Approximately 25 percent of children are behavioral management problems when they undergo dental procedures. When children are uncooperative, dentists usually stop for a moment until they settle down. Yet, momentarily stopping could serve as negative reinforcement for the child, namely, termination of the aversive event (the dental procedure itself) contingent on behavior (being disruptive or uncooperative). Essentially, an escape contingency is provided for undesired behavior. In this study, this contingency was altered and examined with four children, aged 3 to 7, who required ongoing dental (restorative) procedures and several visits to the dentist. Disruptive behavior (crying, moaning, complaining, squirming) was observed directly, using interval assessment. Videotapes were also made for later evaluation. After baseline, the escape procedure was altered. The dentist was trained to make escape contingent on positive (cooperative behavior). When the child was cooperative, the dentist told the child that he was so good in lying still that they would take a "little rest break." A brief break was taken. If disruptive behavior occurred during dental work, it was ignored or the child was reminded that there would be a break for lying still.

The negative reinforcement (escape) procedure was evaluated in a multiple-baseline design across the four children. Figure 5–9 shows the average amount of disruptive behavior (solid bars) for each child over consecutive dental visits. The graph also shows the use of contingent escape (open bars), with the average percentage of time the dentist used the escape procedure contingent on cooperative behavior. The escape procedure clearly reduced disruptive behavior. Moreover, two dentists unfamiliar with the program rated videotapes of baseline and intervention sessions and rated the children as much more cooperative during the intervention phases.

Negative reinforcement requires the presence of an aversive event in the situation that can be terminated quickly and contingently after appropriate behavior. One would not want to introduce a negative event into a situation. The above example is instructive in this regard. It is often the case that negative events and indeed negative reinforcement are already present in the situation. In the case of the dental program, negative reinforcement was being used in baseline to reinforce *uncooperative* behavior by providing escape contingent on this behavior. If dental work is aversive to a child and momentary rest (escape) periods are to be used, the contingency can be altered so that cooperative rather than disruptive behavior is reinforced.

Negative reinforcement may be present in many situations and may contribute to inappropriate or deviant behavior. In such cases, adding aversive events or introducing negative reinforcement are not at issue. Rather, the contingency can be altered to ensure that desired behavior is fostered. For example, negative reinforcement has been shown to exacerbate and maintain self-injurious behavior among mentally retarded children and adolescents. In one study, tasks and educational activities, such as puzzle completion and stacking or sorting objects, were performed by the client and experimenter (Iwata et al., 1990). When self-injurious behavior (for example, head banging) occurred, the experimenter terminated the activity, removed the materials, and turned away from the client. Over

FIGURE 5–9

Percentage changes in mean (average) disruptive behavior of the child and percent-age changes in the use of the escape contingency for appropriate behavior on the part of the dentist. The solid bars represent average disruptive child behavior per dental visit; the open bars represent the average use of appropriate contingent escape procedure by the dentist.

SOURCE: Allen, K. D., Loiben, T., Allen, S. J., & Stanley, R. T. (1992).

several trials, the procedure led to an *increase* in self-injury, compared to other conditions that were tested (for example, playing alone, giving reprimands for self-injury). That is, self-injury increased contingent on termination of the task. This information is important to learn because one can then rearrange the contingency so that activity is contingent on periods of not engaging in self-injury, which is an effective away to reduce the undesirable behavior (Steege et al., 1990).

There are separate points here that inform us about the way contingencies can operate. First, whether an event is a positive or negative reinforcer is an empirical matter and cannot always be discerned on intuitive grounds. In the above example, one would not expect that working on a task is an aversive task and termination could systematically increase self-injury. Second, in some instances the natural reinforcement in the situation (for example, the dentist terminating the procedure for uncooperative behavior) supports the very behavior one wishes to reduce. In such cases, introducing new procedures is not required; rather, the contingency can be rearranged so that reinforcers in the situation support the desired behaviors.

In the above examples, it is quite likely that positive reinforcement would have been effective in achieving the desired ends. Positive reinforcement has many variations, and they are usually effective. Consequently, negative reinforcement is a technique that should probably be employed as a last resort. There are possible exceptions that warrant consideration. In some situations, an aversive event is presented to the client as part of a punishment program. If punishment (presentation of an aversive event after behavior) is to be used, it is more effective if it is combined with reinforcement than if it is presented alone. Negative reinforcement can increase adaptive behavior and thereby increase the efficacy of punishment.

Occasionally, negative reinforcement is combined with positive reinforcement. As noted already, negative reinforcement might be considered if there is an aversive event inherent in the situation. For example, another application focused on children who were highly disruptive during their visits to the dentist (Allen & Stokes, 1987). Behaviors such as kicking, screaming, hitting, and noncompliance interfered with restorative dental treatment. It was assumed that the treatment procedure itself (that is, remaining in the dental chair, having a drill turned on) was aversive. In special practice sessions immediately before dental treatment, the children were individually instructed that they could practice being "big helpers," which meant sitting quietly. The behavior (sitting quietly) was negatively reinforced by terminating the procedure. For example, when the child sat quietly for only three seconds, the aversive event (having the drill on) was quickly terminated. This is an example of negative reinforcement. This response (sitting quietly) was gradually extended (shaping) to 6 minutes. Positive reinforcement was also used; it consisted of praise and stickers for increased cooperative behavior. The effect of the combined negative and positive reinforcement contingency markedly reduced disruptive behavior and permitted completion of the dental session.

Negative reinforcement has occasionally been applied as part of therapy techniques to alter such behaviors as excessive alcohol consumption, overeating, and sexual deviance, including transvestism and fetishism. For example, one form of treatment for alcoholics that involves punishment and negative reinforcement requires the client to ingest the drug disulfiram (Antabuse). If the client drinks alcohol less than 24 hours after ingesting the drug, intense nausea results. Nausea can be *avoided* by not consuming alcohol. Of course, the client can also avoid the aversive contingency by failing to take the drug.

Evaluation of Negative Reinforcement

A major restriction in using negative reinforcement is the risk of undesirable side effects. One such side effect is trying to escape or avoid the behavior change program and those associated with it. It is easy to see how this could happen. If parents, teachers, or supervisors administer aversive events (and not positive ones as well), they become aversive. Escape from such persons by leaving home, exiting the classroom, or changing jobs is negatively reinforced. Programs based on positive reinforcement do not foster this type of escape and avoidance behavior.

From the standpoint of designing a behavior modification program, aversive stimuli should be avoided or minimized. When they are used, emphasis should be placed on positive reinforcement for desirable behavior. In many applications of negative reinforcement, strong aversive stimuli are required because other procedures have failed or because the response (for example, sexual deviance) is strongly reinforced. In such instances, aversive stimuli, including punishment and/or negative reinforcement, constitute a last resort.

SUMMARY AND CONCLUSION

Positive reinforcement represents the major basis for behavioral techniques in applied settings. Several different types of reinforcers have been used effectively, such as food and other consumables, praise and attention, high-probability behaviors, feedback, and token reinforcement. Each reinforcer has its own advantages and limitations, such as dependence upon deprivation and satiation states, ease of administration, and relative effectiveness. Token economies usually incorporate a variety of backup reinforcers and thus overcome the limitations that accrue to the use of any single reinforcer.

Although reinforcers themselves can vary in their impact on behavior, the effectiveness of any reinforcement depends heavily on the manner in which it is administered. Program effectiveness depends on the delay of reinforcement, the magnitude or amount of reinforcement, the quality or type of reinforcer, and the schedule of reinforcement. To maximize performance, reinforcement should be delivered contingently and immediately after a response. Moreover, a highly preferred reinforcer should be used. During acquisition, continuous reinforcement should be used until the response is well established. Subsequently, intermittent reinforcement can be substituted to maintain behavior.

Contingency contracting refers to a way of structuring a reinforcement program. Each participant in the program negotiates and then formally agrees to the terms of the contract. The reinforcers for performing the target behaviors and penalties for failing to perform the behaviors are made explicit and are agreed upon in writing in advance of the program. The primary advantage of a contract arrangement is that clients have an opportunity to develop their own behavior change programs and to ensure that the terms are not coercive.

Positive reinforcement, and indeed reinforcement in general, refers to ways of increasing behavior. Yet, positive reinforcement plays a central role when the goal of a program is to decrease or eliminate undesirable behaviors. To accomplish the latter goal, several variations of reinforcement can be used, including differential reinforcement of other behaviors, of incompatible or alternate behaviors, of functionally equivalent behaviors, or of low rates of behavior.

Negative reinforcement is an alternative procedure to increase behavior. It has not been used widely as a behavior change technique in most applied settings. This is largely due to the undesirability of introducing aversive events if alternative procedures based on positive reinforcement can be applied. Interestingly, negative reinforcement contingencies often are already operative in everyday life, as when, for example, escape or avoidance serves to reinforce undesirable behavior (such as self-injury or aggression). In such instances, identifying the negative reinforcement contingency through functional analysis and altering the contingency so that positive, prosocial rather than deviant behavior is reinforced have been used successfully in a number of applications. We shall return to positive and negative reinforcement throughout remaining chapters, given the critical role they play in developing adaptive behavior.

Note

1. In a cumulative graph, the number of data points for a given day is added to the accumulated number of all of the previous days. Thus, the numbers cumulate over time. An increase in behavior is seen in an accelerated slope: the steeper the slope, the faster the behavior change. No change in behavior is shown by a horizontal line; no numbers or instances of the behavior are being added to the graph. In a cumulative graph, the slope cannot decelerate ("go down").

For Further Reading

Cooper, J. O., Heron, T. E., & Heward, W. L. (1987). *Applied behavior analysis.* Columbus, OH: Merrill.

Hall, R. V., & Hall, M. C. (1980). *How to negotiate a behavioral contract.* Austin, TX: Pro-Ed.

Iwata, B. A. (1987). Negative reinforcement in applied behavior analysis: An emerging technology. *Journal of Applied Behavior Analysis, 20,* 361–378.

Kazdin, A. E. (1977). *The token economy: A review and evaluation.* New York: Plenum.

O'Brien, S., & Repp, A. C. (In press). A review of 30 years of research on the use of differential reinforcement to reduce inappropriate responding. *Behavior Modification.*

Sulzer-Azaroff, B., & Mayer, G. R. (1991). *Behavior analysis for lasting change.* Fort Worth: Holt, Rinehart & Winston.

CHAPTER SIX

PUNISHMENT

CHARACTERISTICS OF THE PUNISHMENT PROCESS
Immediacy of Effects
Specificity of Effects
Recovery After Punishment Withdrawal

CONTROVERSY: PUNISHMENT AND ITS USE
Source of Controversy
Punishment Redefined
Alternatives

WHEN AND HOW TO USE PUNISHMENT

SUMMARY AND CONCLUSION

Aversive events play a major role in everyday life. Indeed, aversive techniques are deeply enmeshed in many social institutions, including government and law (fines and imprisonment), education (failing grades and expulsion), religion (damnation), international relations (military coercion), and normal social intercourse (for example, discrimination, disapproval, and social stigma). Routine interactions of most individuals with both physical and social environments result in aversive events ranging from a burn from a hot stove to verbal abuse from an acquaintance.

In behavior modification, the types of aversive events used and how they are applied differ greatly from punishment practices in everyday life. Before applications are discussed, a few prefatory comments are in order. To begin with, proponents of behavior modification generally avoid the use of punishment whenever possible. One reason, noted in the previous chapter, is that alternative procedures based on positive reinforcement are usually available. Consequently, there may be no need to use aversive consequences. There are many other reasons as well. Punishment is often associated with undesirable side effects, such as emotional reactions (crying), escape from and avoidance of situations (for example, staying away from a punitive parent), and aggression (for example, hitting others).

In addition, punishment can foster undesirable associations with regard to various agents (parents, teachers), situations (home, school), and behaviors (doing homework). An important objective in child rearing, education, and socialization in general is to develop positive attitudes and responses toward these agents, situations, and behaviors; their frequent association with punishment may be counterproductive. For example, screaming at a child to practice a musical instrument is not likely to develop a love of music. The constant pairing of aversive events (threats, reprimands, loss of privileges) and the ensuing reactions (child crying) are undesirable and unnecessary for developing the target behavior. As will become clear in this chapter, however, punishment can be beneficial when it is used infrequently and carefully and as part of a more comprehensive program that emphasizes positive reinforcement.

Proponents of behavioral techniques are extremely concerned with abuse and misuse of punishment. Such abuse and misuse have been shown to foster serious problems in children and adolescents. For example, families of deviant children tend to use harsher and more frequent punishment than is used by families of children who function well in everyday life (Kazdin, 1987a). More frequent punishment is not associated with improved behavior. Indeed, both physical and verbal punishment (reprimands) can increase the very behaviors (noncompliance, aggression) that parents, teachers, and others wish to suppress. Unfortunately, the old adage "Spare the rod and spoil the child" still has many adherents. This is unfortunate because a strong case might be made for an opposite contention, "Use the rod and spoil the child."

To be sure, there are many occasions when mild punishment can be useful as part of a behavior change program. And in some cases, people—for example, parents who engage in child abuse to control their children—may need to be trained to administer punishment (and reinforcement) judiciously (Wolfe, 1987). However, the types of punishment procedures, how they are used, and their combination with reinforcement programs make therapeutic applications of punishment very different from its applications in everyday life. The present chapter discusses the various types of punishment techniques, their effects and side effects, and their place in a behavior change program.

Types of Punishment

Punishment in the technical sense refers solely to the empirical operation (presentation or removal of events) that reduces the frequency of a response. Punishment does not necessarily involve physical pain. Indeed, painful events (such as spankings) may not decrease the responses they are designed to punish and thus may not qualify as punishing events. Alternatively, a variety of procedures that serve as punishment do not entail physical discomfort and are not odious to the client.

In behavior modification, several forms of punishment have been developed based on whether aversive events are presented, positive events are withdrawn, or the client's work or effort is required after performance of a particular behavior. Some of the techniques are familiar because they are commonly used in everyday life (for example, reprimands). However, other techniques, such as withdrawing reinforcing events for very brief periods or requiring clients to practice appropriate behavior, are probably less familiar. Although many of the techniques may be familiar, the ways in which they are implemented and the features that contribute to their effectiveness are not usually appreciated or practiced in everyday life. We shall examine the effectiveness of different techniques and the manner in which those techniques are most effectively administered.

Presentation of Aversive Events

After a response has been performed, an aversive event such as a spanking or a reprimand may be applied. There are two types of aversive events, primary aversive stimuli and secondary, or conditioned, aversive stimuli. Primary aversive stimuli are inherently aversive events. Such stimuli as electric shock, intense physical assault, bright lights, and loud noises are primary aversive stimuli. Their aversive properties are unlearned. Secondary, or conditioned, aversive stimuli acquire their aversive properties by being paired with events that are already aversive. For example, the word *no* serves as a conditioned aversive stimulus for many individuals. The word acquires its aversive value by being paired with such other aversive events as physical pain and loss of privileges. Conditioned aversive stimuli that typically control behavior include gestures, nods, frowns, and traffic tickets.

Stimuli may become aversive even if they are not paired with specific aversive stimuli. A stimulus consistently associated with the absence of reinforcement may become aversive. An event signaling that reinforcement will *not* be forthcoming, referred to earlier as an S^Δ, may serve as an aversive event (Azrin & Holz, 1966). The S^Δ serves as a signal that a period of nonreinforcement is in effect. For example, when a child breaks a valuable object, a parent may make a particular facial expression, become silent, and not respond to the child for a while. The parent's nonresponsiveness denotes that the child will not receive reinforcement. During parental silence, virtually no behavior receives approval. The signal or cue (for example, a facial expression) associated with the parent's nonreinforcement (silence) becomes aversive in its own right.

Verbal Statements

Verbal statements in the form of reprimands, warnings, disapproval, saying no, and threats are often used in everyday interactions between teacher and student, parent and child and among siblings, spouses, friends, and enemies. Occasionally verbal statements have been used to suppress behavior in applied research. For example, reprimands and disapproving statements have been applied in classroom settings to reduce playing during lessons, being out of one's seat, talking without permission, and other disruptive behaviors. Reprimands and disapproval in general have had inconsistent effects. In some cases, for example, disruptive student behavior has been suppressed relatively quickly by saying no after instances of disruptive behavior (Hall et al., 1971). In other cases, reprimands have served as a positive reinforcer rather than as a punisher. In one classroom, the teacher reprimanded the children by saying "Sit down" when students were out of their seats (Madsen, Becker, Thomas, Koser, & Plager, 1970). Interestingly, the reprimands *increased* the frequency of standing, serving as a positive reinforcer for the behavior they were designed to suppress.

The manner in which verbal statements are delivered may influence their effectiveness. For example, in classroom applications, reprimands are more effective in suppressing child behavior when they are accompanied by looking directly at and grasping the child (Van Houten, Nau, MacKenzie-Keating, Sameoto, & Colavecchia, 1982). Nonverbal components, such as glaring or staring at the child, pointing at him or her, or holding the child's arm, have been used in several studies in which reprimands have been applied (for example, Doleys, Wells, Hobbs, Roberts, & Cartelli, 1976; Forehand, Roberts, Doleys, Hobbs, & Resick, 1976). Reprimands are also more effective when they are delivered in close proximity to the child rather than from the other end of the room (Van Houten, Nau, MacKenzie-Keating, Sameoto, & Colavecchia, 1982). In general, reprimands can be effective, especially when accompanied by gestures and other features that may add to their salience or intensity.

Verbal punishment is likely to lose its effectiveness over time. For example, threats occasionally have been used to suppress behavior. When threats signal that some other aversive consequence will follow, they become conditioned aversive events whether the behavior is or is not performed. Yet, some threats are "idle"—not backed by the threatened consequence. Such threats tend to lose their effects quickly (for example, Kazdin, 1971). Verbal statements generally are likely to produce temporary effects if they are not followed by other consequences, or they are likely to require increases in intensity to sustain their effects if they are used by themselves.

Considerations in using verbal statements. Reprimands and threats are easily administered and, hence, from a practical standpoint are readily available for use as a punishment technique. Also, verbal forms of punishment cause no physical discomfort to the client. Receiving a reprimand may be unpleasant, but such unpleasantness is very different from the kind resulting from more extreme procedures such as corporal punishment. Yet, as mentioned previously, reprimands have been more effective when a child is grasped while reprimanded. The risk of using this procedure is that, in practice, grasping a child is likely to become more intense and may unnecessarily hurt the child. Physical contact with reprimands would need to be supervised closely to avoid misuse. Reprimands alone are commonly used in everyday life and are less objectionable than many other forms of punishment. However, their overuse probably makes them relatively ineffective in ordinary applications.

The major limitation of verbal statements as punishing events is their inconsistent effects; often they produce little or no behavior change. For most of the behaviors brought to treatment, the weak or inconsistent effects of verbal reprimands are not sufficient to achieve therapeutic change.

A related consideration is that parents and teachers use reprimands frequently. For some time, it has been known that reinforcement contingencies in the classroom do not support many of the behaviors that parents, teachers, and others would like to develop. Specifically, observations of teachers throughout elementary and high school grades have shown relatively high rates of disapproval and low rates of approval in regular classrooms (Thomas, Presland, Grant, & Glynn, 1978; White, 1975). The high rates of disapproval may attest in part to the likely long-term ineffectiveness of reprimands. This is exacerbated by the paucity of reinforcement, because reinforcement for positive behaviors can augment the effectiveness of otherwise weak punishment. To improve teacher effectiveness, one might want not to increase reprimands but rather to examine other reinforcement contingencies that might be used in the classroom to support positive student behavior and other reinforcement contingencies to be used outside the classroom to support positive teacher behavior.

An important consideration is that reprimands and verbal admonitions in one form or another compose a large part of naturally occurring events in everyday life. Hence, in treatment settings, it may be desirable to train clients to respond to disapproval, if they do not already respond to it. Verbal statements can be made to function as aversive events by pairing them with other events such as physical restraint or removal of positive events. Here the purpose of the program is to develop responsiveness to naturally occurring events.

Electric Shock

Shock is another aversive event that can be presented after behavior. Although shock is rarely used, its unique characteristics and effects deserve comment. Most applications of shock have been restricted to persons who engage in behaviors dangerous to themselves or to others and who have not responded to other procedures. When shock has been used in these extraordinary situations, usually it has consisted of a brief shock to the finger or arm. Because shock is a primary aversive event, even its brief application usually produces rapid and marked suppression of behavior.

Shock may be an alternative when rapid suppression of a serious behavior is needed and when other efforts have failed. For example, electric shock was used to eliminate self-injurious behavior among five individuals (aged 11 to 24) residing in an institution (Linscheid, Iwata, Ricketts, Williams, & Griffin, 1990). These individuals showed chronic self-injury involving forceful contact with the head (face and head hitting, head banging) that produced tissue damage, had a history of other treatments that had failed (for example, medication, overcorrection, physical restraint), and currently engaged in self-injury that required physical restraint or medication to control. Each individual, studied separately, was fitted with a special device worn over the head (a headband with a small apparatus) that automatically detected blows to the head, recorded these blows, and when programmed, delivered a brief shock to the arm or leg. In carefully evaluated experimental designs for each individual, contingent shock was shown to markedly reduce the behavior. In this study, shock was effective in reducing and in some cases eliminating self-injurious behavior that was dangerous and that did not respond to a number of other treatments.

The use of shock to suppress dangerous and life-threatening behavior was also illustrated in a program with a 9-month-old infant who engaged in chronic ruminative vomiting (Linscheid & Cunningham, 1977). Constant vomiting after meals had resulted in severe weight loss, malnutrition, and potentially fatal medical complications. The shock was intense enough to evoke a startle reaction but not intense enough to elicit crying. When shock was applied (to the leg) at the onset of vomiting, vomiting dropped from an average of over 100 instances per day to 1 instance per day after only 3 days of treatment. Follow-up evaluation, nine months after the infant was released from the hospital, revealed that ruminative vomiting no longer occurred and weight gain had increased.

In other applications, shock has occasionally been used to suppress such potentially harmful behaviors as self-injury, playing with dangerous equipment, and climbing dangerous places. The rapid and often durable effects of shock have led to its occasional use. Currently, shock is rarely used, partly because its use raises ethical and legal issues but also because many less objectionable but effective alternatives are available. With adults, usually in outpatient treatment, shock has been occasionally used to reduce or eliminate such behaviors as cigarette smoking, overeating, alcohol consumption, and various sexual behaviors, such as fetishes (for example, McConaghy, 1990). Shock has not been particularly effective in these instances, and less objectionable procedures with equal or greater effectiveness are readily available.

Considerations in using electric shock. Shock has been used in cases in which dangerous behavior needs to be suppressed rapidly and alternative procedures have not been effective. Because the procedure is painful, it is usually not resorted to unless alternative procedures have been unsuccessful. Indeed, in the examples provided above, shock was used only after several other procedures had failed to change behavior (for example, chronic vomiting and uncontrollable sneezing). In recent years, major advances have been made in elaborating alternatives to punishment and in understanding the factors that maintain self-injurious and dangerous behavior to which shock and other forms of punishment might be applied (see Repp & Singh, 1990). This has led to an expansion of interventions to reduce or eliminate dangerous behavior without resorting to aversive procedures such as shock. Given the range of effective alternative techniques, based on both punishment and reinforcement, serious ethical and legal objections would be warranted if shock were the first treatment to be considered.

Omitting for a moment the appropriateness and necessity of shock, a number of practical limitations would militate against the widespread use of shock in applied settings. To begin with, the administration of shock requires special equipment. Hence, shock has generally been restricted to laboratory or treatment settings where clients are seen individually and are closely supervised. In settings where clients are treated in groups, it is not readily feasible to employ shock. In addition, the person using shock must be well trained so that its intensity is not severe and so that accidents due to misuse of equipment do not occur. Even if shock could be applied, professionals and clients are likely to view it as unacceptable for treatment purposes (Kazdin, 1980b). Hence, independent of its effectiveness, its use is restricted to very special cases in which extreme procedures appear to be warranted.

Other Aversive Consequences

A variety of other aversive consequences, somewhat less well studied than reprimands and less controversial than shock, have also been used. For example, squirting lemon juice into the client's mouth has been used in a few treatment cases. In one application, lemon juice was used to suppress life-threatening vomiting in a 6-month-old infant (Sajwaj, Libert, & Agras, 1974). When the tongue movements that preceded vomiting occurred, lemon juice was squirted (using a syringe) into her mouth. The procedure markedly suppressed episodes of vomiting. At follow-up several months after treatment, it was found that the infant had continued to gain weight and that vomiting had not recurred. Similarly, in another report, squirting lemon juice from a plastic squirt bottle into the mouth of a severely retarded boy effectively eliminated public masturbation (Cook, Altman, Shaw, & Blaylock, 1978).

Another punishment technique that has been used is introducing the smell of aromatic ammonia (smelling salts) contingent upon undesirable behavior. For example, in one report, ammonia was used to suppress self-injurious behavior in two children (Altman, Haavik, & Cook, 1978). Severe hair pulling of a 4-year-old girl (who had made herself partially bald) and hand biting of a 3-year-old boy (who had damaged the tissues of his fingers) were suppressed by breaking a capsule of aromatic ammonia and placing it under the child's nose for a few seconds contingent upon the performance of self-injurious behaviors.

Other punishment procedures are occasionally used. Two of these procedures are spraying a mist of water in the client's face (water mist) and briefly covering the client's face with a piece of cloth or something else that blocks vision (facial screening). For example, water mist and facial screening have reduced self-injurious behavior (face punching, jaw hitting, self-biting) in mentally retarded adolescents (Singh, Watson, & Winton, 1986). The spray of water (at room temperature) or the brief facial screening (5 seconds) was contingent upon instances of self-injurious behavior.

The rationale behind many techniques of this kind has been to develop procedures that provide minimal discomfort but can effectively suppress behavior. The use of lemon juice as an aversive event illustrates this rationale. Although the taste of lemon juice is obviously unattractive to most people, its use as an aversive event is probably more socially acceptable than such other procedures as electric shock. Indeed, in one example above, lemon juice was used to suppress severely dangerous behaviors where shock might have been considered as an alternative.

Withdrawal of Positive Consequences

Punishment often takes the form of withdrawing positive events rather than of presenting aversive events after behavior. Familiar examples include the loss of privileges, money, or one's driver's license after behavior. Events that are positively valued and that may even have served as positive reinforcers are taken away as a form of penalty. The two major techniques, each with several variations, are time out from reinforcement and response cost.

Time Out from Reinforcement

Punishment often takes the form of removing a positive event. One procedure for removing a positive event is *time out from reinforcement* (or simply time out), *which refers to the removal of all positive reinforcers for a certain period of time.* During the time-out interval, the client does not have access to the positive reinforcers that are normally available in the setting. For example, a child may be isolated from others in class for 10 minutes. During that time, he or she will not have access to peer interaction, activities, privileges, and other reinforcers that are usually available.

The crucial ingredient of time out is delineating a brief period during which reinforcement is unavailable. Ideally, during this period, *all* sources of reinforcement are withdrawn. This ideal is not always attained. For example, if a child is sent to his or her room as punishment, removal from the existing sources of reinforcement qualifies as time out. However, all reinforcement may not be withheld; the child may engage in a number of reinforcing activities such as playing, listening to music, sleeping, or talking to himself or herself. Despite these possibilities, time out usually consists of making reinforcing events unavailable to the client for a brief period.

A variety of time-out procedures have been used effectively in treatment. In many variations, the client is physically isolated or excluded in some way from the situation. The client may be sent to a time-out room or booth, a special place that is partitioned off. For example, noncompliance with requests among mentally retarded residents was suppressed by requiring a child to sit in the corner of the room for 40 seconds for an instance of noncompliance (Doleys et al., 1976). Similarly, alcohol consumption among hospitalized chronic alcoholics was suppressed with time out (Bigelow, Liebson, & Griffiths, 1974). The patients were allowed free access to alcoholic beverages on the ward. During time out, they were placed in an isolation booth for 10–15 minutes contingent upon drinking.

Although many programs using time out have employed isolation (removal from the situation) as the time-out procedure, alternative procedures are available that still meet the definition of time out. One time out procedure that does not involve removing the individual from the situation was used to suppress disruptive behavior among children (ranging in age from 1 to 3 years) who attended a day-care center (Porterfield, Herbert-Jackson, & Risley, 1976). Disruptive behaviors, such as hitting or pushing peers, crying and fussing, engaging in tantrums, and breaking toys, were punished with time-out procedures while the children engaged in free-play activities. When disruptive behavior occurred, the child was told that the behavior was inappropriate and removed to the periphery of the other children's activity. While away from the center of activity in the room, the child was still allowed to observe the activity and the other children. However, the child was not allowed to play with toys. After a brief period, usually less than 1 minute, the child was allowed to return to his or her activities in the center of the room. Partial removal of children from their activities markedly decreased their disruptive behavior.

Variations of time out have been used in which the client is not even partially removed from the situation. For example, in one program, time out was used as part of a reinforcement program for boys in a special education class for mentally retarded children in a state institution (Foxx & Shapiro, 1978). As part of the reinforcement system, the children received praise and smiles (social reinforcement) for performing their work. Each child in the class was given a ribbon to wear around his neck. The ribbon signified to the child and the teacher that the child could receive social and, occasionally, food reinforcers that were administered while the children worked. When any disruptive behavior was performed, a time-out procedure was used. Time out consisted of removing the child's ribbon for three minutes. Without the ribbon, the child could not receive any of the reinforcers normally administered. This time-out procedure effectively reduced disruptive classroom behavior.

Positive reinforcers have been made unavailable in other ways to accomplish time out from reinforcement. For example, Mansdorf (1977) applied time out to a mentally retarded adult who refused to comply with staff requests to take a shower. When this resident did not comply, she would simply sit in the dayroom and watch television, listen to music, or go back to bed. Time out was used for noncompliance by removing her opportunities for reinforcement for a brief period. If she did not comply, television or music was turned off, peers were asked to leave the dayroom, and the pillow and bedding were removed. Essentially, the reinforcers she usually utilized were made temporarily unavailable. If she did comply, these reinforcing events were restored. The procedure was very effective in reducing the number of incidents of noncompliance, as shown in Figure 6–1. The effects were maintained six months after the program had been terminated.

Considerations in using time out.   Time out from reinforcement has been very effective in altering a number of behaviors, including psychotic

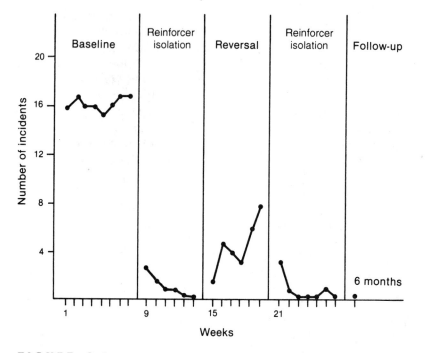

FIGURE 6-1

Number of noncompliant incidents per 5-day workweek for each experimental condition.

SOURCE: Mansdorf, I. J. (1977).

speech, toileting accidents, thumb sucking, and self-stimulatory and self-injurious behavior (see Hobbs & Forehand, 1977). Usually short time-out durations, such as several seconds or a few minutes, are effective in suppressing behavior. Longer time-out periods do not necessarily increase the effectiveness of the procedure.

Obvious advantages of time out are that it can be relatively brief and that it does not involve pain. Additional advantages and disadvantages of time out depend on the specific form it takes. Removing individuals from the situation in which deviant behavior occurs (such as sending individuals to a time-out room), particularly for extended periods, has potential disadvantages. Removing individuals from the situation in which their performance is a problem reduces opportunities for positive reinforcement in that situation. Hence, the client cannot learn the desired behaviors and the conditions under which those behaviors are appropriate. Also, in some cases, it may be undesirable to leave the client isolated from others because of the opportunity that isolation provides for engaging in maladaptive behaviors. For example, self-stimulatory behaviors are often maintained by the sensory stimulation they produce. Thus, it is not externally presented reinforcers (such as staff attention) that maintains the behavior but, rather, reinforcement that derives from the behavior itself. Understandably, a client in isolation may simply continue to engage in undesired self-stimulatory behavior (Solnick, Rincover, & Peterson, 1977).

Isolation from others may also be undesirable for clients who are socially withdrawn. Removal from the social situation may further isolate clients who already have only minimal interaction with others. A main goal of treatment should be to develop prosocial behaviors in the presence of other individuals and not to foster any more isolation, whether physical or social, than may already result from the client's interpersonal deficits.

Many of the objections to time out are resolved with variations that do not remove the client from the situation. Leaving the client in the situation (such as a classroom) but setting aside brief periods in which reinforcers are not available has many advantages. A client who is allowed to remain in the situation can continue to participate in activities and can perhaps even observe others who receive desirable consequences for appropriate behavior. Of course, an individual's behavior may be so disruptive that he or she has to be removed from the situation so as not to disturb or interfere with the activities of others. To handle this possible problem, some programs have allowed individuals to remain in the situation during time out unless their behavior becomes very disruptive (LeBlanc, Busby, & Thomson, 1974; Porterfield, Herbert-Jackson, & Risley, 1976). Using social isolation to back up a less severe form of time out is an excellent strategy because when this strategy is used the client is removed from the situation only if necessary.

The extent to which time out will be effective is likely to depend on the situation from which the client is removed. That ongoing situation, sometimes referred to as "time in," denotes the situation and reinforcing consequences from which the client is withdrawn. If the environment is highly reinforcing (for example, frequent praise, earning of points, peer interaction), a brief period of time out is likely to be more effective than it would be if the environment were devoid of reinforcing consequences (Solnick, Rincover, & Peterson, 1977). In practice, time out does not require that an ongoing reinforcement program or richly rewarding environment be in effect during the time-in period. During any punishment program, some reinforcement should be provided to develop positive and prosocial behavior. Consequently, reinforcement plus time out is likely to be more effective than is time out alone.

In general, time out provides an excellent alternative to many of the forms of punishment used in everyday life, such as reprimands and corporal punishment. Very brief time out, for several seconds or a few minutes, has been effective. Time out has been especially effective when many reinforcers are available in the setting, so that time out from these reinforcing events is especially aversive (Solnick, Rincover, & Peterson, 1977, Exp. 2). Occasionally, time out has been ineffective for some individuals and has even served as a positive reinforcer (Foxx & Azrin, 1972; Plummer, Baer, &

LeBlanc, 1977; Solnick, Rincover, & Peterson, 1977, Exp. 1). However, these findings are exceptions. The many currently available variations of time out provide alternatives that are adaptable to most clients and settings.

Response Cost

Response cost refers to a loss of a positive reinforcer. With response cost, there is no period during which positive events are unavailable, as is the case with time out from reinforcement (Kazdin, 1972). Response cost requires a penalty of some sort, usually in the form of a fine. Examples of response cost in everyday experience include fines for traffic violations, fees for late filing of income tax or for registering for classes beyond the due date, and charges for checks that "bounce."

In applied settings, response cost usually takes the form of a fine. For example, response cost was used as part of a contingency contract for an adult male alcoholic and his wife (Miller, 1972). The husband's excessive drinking was a major source of marital conflict. The contract specified that he could have only one to three drinks a day (instead of the average of seven to eight that he consumed during baseline) and that these could be consumed only before dinner. Any other drinking would require him to pay his wife $20 that she would spend as frivolously as possible, something that was very aversive to him. The wife agreed to refrain from negative verbal responses for her husband's drinking. She was required to pay him a $20 fine if she failed to do this. The husband's drinking decreased quickly and stabilized at a rate within the contract agreement. The effects were maintained up to six months when last observed.

Response cost was used to alter the classroom behavior of two second-grade hyperactive boys (Rapport, Murphy, & Bailey, 1982). The boys had poor attentiveness, high rates of disruptive behavior, and did not complete their academic seatwork. They were informed that they would receive 20 minutes of free time for working on their tasks without disruption but that they would lose 1 minute for each instance of inattentiveness. For example, for one of the boys, numbers from 20 to 1 were listed on cards near the teacher, with each number standing for the number of minutes of free time that remained. For each instance of inattentiveness, the teacher flipped the cards to the next lower value (from 20 to 19, and so on). The number remaining at the end of the lesson constituted the minutes of free time. Contingently withdrawing minutes of free time markedly improved the boys' attentiveness and academic performance. Medication (Ritalin) commonly used for hyperactive children also improved behavior but was less effective than response cost.

Response cost has often been used as part of token economies in which tokens are delivered for some behaviors and taken away for others. For example, in one program with psychiatric patients, fines were levied whenever patients violated a rule of the ward (Upper, 1973). Infractions included such behaviors as getting up late in the morning, undressing or exposing oneself, and shouting. Violations dropped below baseline rates when a fine was subtracted from token earnings. Whether implemented alone or in conjunction with token economies, response cost has altered a wide variety of behaviors such as overeating, disruptive classroom behavior, speech disfluencies, psychotic speech, thumb sucking, and toileting accidents (see Kazdin, 1977a).

Considerations in using response cost. Response cost, particularly in the form of withdrawing points or tokens after behavior, is relatively easy to implement. One problem that may arise is that clients who lose many points may soon have no further points to lose. Yet, more points or tokens could be earned for positive behaviors to ensure that points can be withdrawn contingent on the undesired behavior.

Providing points raises the clear benefit of response cost in the form of fines. If tokens or points are to be withdrawn, they have to be delivered to the client. Behavior change is likely to be more rapid if the tokens are delivered for behaviors incompatible with the responses that are to be suppressed. Hence, when points or tokens are used, reinforcement and punishment in the form of response cost can easily be implemented as part of a single program. Moreover, token reinforcement and response cost combined are more effective than either procedure alone (for example, Bierman, Miller, & Stabb, 1987; Walker, Hops, & Fiegenbaum, 1976).

Punishing Consequences Based on Effort

As a consequence for undesirable behavior, a client can be required to engage in responses that entail work or effort. This is different from presenting the client with an aversive stimulus (for example, reprimand) or withdrawing a positive event from the client (for example, response cost). Here the client is required to engage in aversive behavior.

Overcorrection

With *overcorrection,* the penalty for engaging in an undesirable behavior is performing some other behaviors in the situation. Two components of overcorrection can be distinguished. The first component, referred to as *restitution,* consists of correcting the environmental effects of the inappropriate behavior. Thus, if a child throws food at the dinner table, he or she would be required to clean it up completely. The second component, referred to as *positive practice,* consists of repeatedly practicing the appropriate behavior. For example, the child would be required to place food on his or her plate appropriately several times in a row and perhaps to serve others food as well. These responses are some of the "correct" ways of serving and managing food at the table. Restitution and positive practice are sometimes combined and sometimes used alone, depending on the behaviors that are to be suppressed.

In an initial application of the procedure, Foxx and Azrin (1972) used restitution and positive practice with a profoundly retarded 50-year-old female who had been hospitalized for 46 years. For several years, this client had engaged in severely disruptive and aggressive behavior, especially throwing things. When she performed a disruptive behavior, such as overturning a bed, she was required to correct the physical effects of her behavior on the environment (that is, turn the bed to its correct position and straighten the spread and pillows). In addition, she was required to rehearse the correct behavior by straightening all of the other beds on the ward. Thus, she had to correct the immediate consequence of whatever inappropriate behavior she performed (restitution) and then to practice repeatedly the correct behavior throughout the ward (positive practice). After 11 weeks of training, she no longer threw objects.

An interesting application of overcorrection was used to eliminate stealing among hospitalized mentally retarded adults (Azrin & Wesolowski, 1974). The residents had a high rate of stealing from one another, especially food during meal and snack times when they purchased items at a commissary (store) in the hospital. A staff member simply required the resident to return the food or the remaining portion if it had been partially consumed. Return of the food did not completely restore the original situation if the food had been partially consumed. With this procedure (called simple correction), stealing remained at a high rate. An overcorrection procedure was implemented that required the resident not only to return the food but also to purchase more of that food and give it to the victim. The results, illustrated in Figure 6–2, show that theft was eliminated among the 34 residents within a matter of a few days.

It is not possible to have individuals "correct" the environmental consequences of many behaviors that are to be suppressed. The behaviors may not have altered the environment. For example, if a child whines, hits himself, rocks back and forth, or stutters, there are no clear environmental consequences that can be corrected. For such behaviors, positive practice is often used alone. After the undesired behavior has been performed, the client is required to practice positively an appropriate or incompatible behavior. For example, positive practice was used to alter the classroom behavior of six disruptive boys enrolled in a special summer class (Azrin & Powers, 1975). Talking out and being out of one's seat were decreased by having the children who engaged in these behaviors remain in at recess. During this recess period, a child would practice appropriate classroom behavior by sitting in his seat, raising his hand, being recognized by the teacher, and asking permission to get up. This entire sequence was repeated for approximately five minutes, a procedure that markedly improved classroom performance. Loss of recess without engaging in positive practice did not achieve the marked changes associated with positive practice.

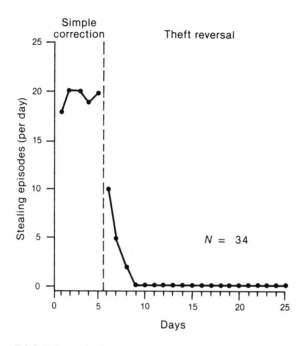

FIGURE 6–2

Number of stealing episodes that occurred each day among 34 mentally retarded adult residents in an institution. During the five days of simple correction, the thief was required to return the stolen item. During the theft-reversal (overcorrection) procedure (subsequent to the vertical dashed line), the thief was required to return the stolen item and to give the victim an additional item identical to the one stolen. The stealing episodes consisted of stealing food items from other mentally retarded residents during commissary periods.

SOURCE: Azrin, N. H., & Wesolowski, M. D. (1974).

Considerations in using overcorrection. Overcorrection alone or in combination with other procedures has altered a variety of behaviors such as toileting accidents, aggressive acts, self-stimulatory behaviors, tantrums, nail biting, and table manners (Foxx & Bechtel, 1983). Overcorrection procedures vary widely, depending on the specific behavior that is suppressed and the desired behavior that is developed in its place. The procedures are developed from the general principle of having individuals correct environmental consequences of their actions, where such consequences exist, and practicing the desired behavior repeatedly after each instance of the undesired behavior. The results of a few minutes of corrective training after the undesired behavior have often led to rapid and long-lasting therapeutic effects.

Certainly, the distinguishing feature of overcorrection, in relation to other punishment techniques, is that it focuses on the appropriate behavior that is incompatible with the undesired response. Most forms of punishment do not convey to the client the behaviors that are appropriate. The positive practice component of overcorrection trains desirable behaviors and thus serves an educative function not included in other aversive techniques. Indeed, research has shown that unlike other punishment procedures, overcorrection not only suppresses inappropriate behavior but also develops positive appropriate behaviors (Carey & Bucher, 1981). There is a related benefit of the procedure. In the usual punishment procedure, parents, teachers, or staff focus their attention on undesirable behaviors that need to be suppressed. Overcorrection shifts attention to desirable behaviors that need to be developed, the priority of any behavior change program.

For use of overcorrection, one must identify both the behavior that will correct the environment and the appropriate behavior that should be performed. When the undesired behavior is performed, the client is immediately required to engage in the sequence of behaviors that restore and overcorrect the action. If simple instructions to complete the requisite behaviors prove insufficient, the client may need to be physically guided (assisted) by the parent or teacher to go through these behaviors. Guiding the client through requisite behaviors can be problematic if the client resists or becomes aggressive (Foxx, 1982). If physical force is necessary, alternative procedures may need to be used.

Another consideration in using overcorrection is the supervision the procedure often requires. The person in charge of the program must ensure that the client goes through the overcorrection sequence for the allotted time and must provide physical prompts if necessary. In some situations, it may not be feasible to provide one-to-one client supervision to conduct overcorrection. For example, in a classroom situation, overcorrection has on occasion been discontinued in part because of the difficulties in supervising overcorrection while managing the rest of the class (Kelly & Drabman, 1977). On the other hand, applications have shown that in a classroom situation overcorrection can be delayed and conducted at recess time or during free periods, when direct supervision of the client need not detract from others in the room (Azrin & Powers, 1975; Barton & Osborne, 1978).

Overall, the rapid and dramatic effects of overcorrection have made this a viable treatment technique for a variety of problems. In many studies, overcorrection has achieved changes in behaviors where other techniques (such as time out, reprimands, reinforcement of other behavior, and physical restraint) have not proven effective. Although definitive statements about the relative effectiveness of alternative punishment techniques cannot be made at this time, overcorrection appears to be very effective in its own right. In addition, evidence suggests that parents, teachers, and children view overcorrection as a punishment procedure that is more acceptable than such alternatives as isolation (Kazdin, French, & Sherick, 1981).

Other Effort-Based Consequences

The unique feature of overcorrection is that the behaviors that the client must perform as part of restitution and positive practice are directly related to the behavior that is to be suppressed. Behaviors involving effort that bear no logical connection to the target behavior have also been effective. The effectiveness of such applications can be expected, based on a variation of the Premack principle. The principle was discussed previously in the context of positive reinforcement in which high-probability (or highly preferred) behaviors (such as playing) serve as reinforcers for low-probability (or less preferred) behaviors (such as working). The principle also suggests an arrangement of the contingency that can suppress behavior and be used as punishment. Low-probability behaviors can be used as consequences for an undesirable response.

For example, in one program, verbal and physical aggression were suppressed in two emotionally disturbed children in a special education classroom (Luce, Delquadri, & Hall, 1980). One of the children, a 7-year-old boy named Ben, engaged in aggression, severe tantrums, and self-stimulatory behavior. Ben's hitting of other children at school was the target behavior that was to be suppressed. Engaging in exercise was used as the aversive consequence. When Ben hit someone, he was required to stand up and sit down on the floor 10 times (which required less than 30 seconds). Initially, he was physically prompted by the teacher, who helped him up and down. Then, verbal prompts alone were sufficient to ensure that he completed the exercise. The effects of the program, illustrated in Figure 6–3, show that low rates of aggressive behavior were obtained when the exercise contingency was in effect. At a follow-up assessment one and a half years after the program was terminated, Ben's hitting had been completely eliminated.

In a somewhat different procedure, individuals can be required to engage in various aversive chores. For example, Fischer and Nehs (1978) altered the excessive swearing of an 11-year-old boy. The boy was told that each time he swore, he would be required to wash windows in the residential facility for 10 minutes. The procedure effectively suppressed his swearing. It remained at a low frequency two weeks after the program had been terminated.

Considerations in using effort. The use of effort-based activities as aversive consequences has advantages. The activities (exercises, chores) are quite familiar to parents, teachers, staff, and clients. Consequently, less training is needed in using effort than in using other procedures such as overcorrection, where novel behaviors of the behavior change agent (for example, special prompting) and the client (for example, special routine to practice new behavior) may need to be trained and closely supervised.

An important consideration with exercise of other effort-based procedures is whether performing the aversive behavior may interrupt ongoing

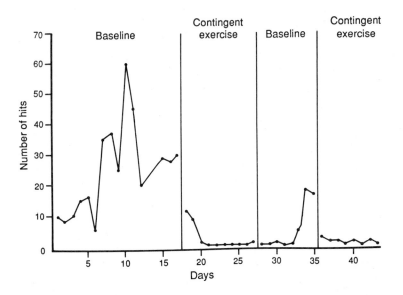

FIGURE   6–3

Number of instances of hitting by Ben while at school. During baseline, the aggressive behavior was ignored and no special program was provided to alter it. During the contingent-exercise phase, Ben was required to stand up and sit down on the floor for instances of hitting.

SOURCE: Luce, S. C., Delquadri, J., & Hall, R. V. (1980).

behavior or be disruptive in the situation. For example, in one study, contingent exercise was used to reduce a boy's inappropriate and bizarre verbalizations in a classroom (Luce & Hall, 1981). Instances of these behaviors were followed by a brief run (20 seconds) around the playground. Although such a procedure suppresses behavior, it may also interrupt sitting at one's desk, remaining in the situation, and possibly receiving reinforcement for remaining at a task. Another potential problem, not yet reported, is that engaging in exercise or leaving the situation (going to the playground) may actually serve as a reinforcer (escape from an aversive task or situation) for some children.

Effort-based procedures, such as exercise or chores, focus on suppressing undesirable behaviors. With such procedures, unlike overcorrection, no attempt is made to teach an appropriate behavior to replace the target response. For example, one does not want a child to exercise in the classroom or to run around the playground in the middle of a lesson. Overcorrection focuses on developing positive alternative behaviors in addition to suppressing the target response. If feasible in the situation, it may be the most preferable of the effort-based procedures.

Selecting Procedures to Suppress Behaviors

The precise punishment procedure selected in any instance may be determined by several considerations, including severity of the behavior, the danger of the behavior to the client or others, the ease of implementing the procedure in a particular setting, and the training required of the person(s) administering the behavior modification program. For example, response cost might be relatively easily administered and effective with many behaviors and require less time and supervision than would overcorrection. Overcorrection, if more difficult to implement, might be reserved for cases in which less complex procedures proved ineffective. The punishment procedures selected should be the least restrictive or intrusive among those available. Although shock or physical restraint might be effective in suppressing behavior, the severity of the procedures make them ethically unacceptable unless less restrictive procedures (for example, reinforcement of functionally equivalent responses, time out, response cost) have failed.

When aversive consequences are used to suppress behavior, special consideration might be given to the specific events used and to the possible long-range consequences of using them. Procedures commonly used in everyday life (but usually not in behavior modification programs) often require individuals to engage in tasks that should probably not be used as aversive events. For example, requiring children to stay in from recess or to remain after school, to write "I shall not swear" 500 times on the blackboard, to complete extra homework, or to see the principal when they are disruptive may defeat many of the inherent goals of school. Presumably, we do not want children to learn that these events are aversive. The fact that behavioral programs have occasionally used escape from the classroom as a reinforcer and completion of academic tasks as a punisher (for example, Harris & Sherman, 1973; MacPherson, Candee, & Hohman, 1974) suggests that important characteristics associated with school are already imbued with aversive properties. Nevertheless, an important goal is to develop positive attitudes and approach responses to these and similar events. To treat various activities or staff as aversive consequences may make school aversive, especially for students who are not obtaining other rewards (for example, good grades, achievement, peer status and popularity.)

At present, the long-term consequences of using particular aversive events are not known. Hence, considerations about selection of the events need to be based on information about the individual case and about possible consequences that might result. In short, common sense as well as scientific evidence should enter into the selection of specific punishing consequences.

Behavior modification research has developed and evaluated a large number of aversive techniques. This may seem ironic, given the evidence that, if at all possible, punishment should not be used, and then only as a supplement to a reinforcement program. Yet, research on punishment in applied settings has several obligations. Not only should such research develop effective procedures, but the procedures should be humane, socially acceptable to clients, relatively easy to implement, and not readily subject to abuse. The development of various punishment procedures has often been based on these considerations.

The present comments pertain to the selection among alternative punishment techniques. Consideration of alternatives among aversive events is important in the context of punishment techniques used in everyday life. Punishment used in everyday life is often harsh (for example, hitting or paddling children) and the way punishment is often administered is likely to render the intervention minimally effective. Punishment procedures highlighted in this chapter do not rely on physical punishment and are less severe or harsh than are those used in everyday life. Also, punishment is invariably used in behavior modification with positive reinforcement to develop positive, prosocial, or adaptive behavior. Thus, punishment in behavior modification is quite different from applications in everyday life.

In a broader context, there is the issue of whether punishment of any kind should be used and, if so, under what conditions. If the goal is to reduce undesirable behavior, there are many alternative procedures that do not rely on punishment. Before considering punishment in the context of these other procedures, it is important to describe punishment more fully.

Factors That Influence the Effectiveness of Punishment

The effectiveness of punishment, like that of reinforcement, depends on several conditions. Although punishment has been evaluated extensively in the laboratory (Azrin & Holz, 1966; Hutchinson, 1977), most of the laboratory research dealt with the presentation of aversive events. The removal of positive events has been less well studied. Nevertheless, general statements regarding the conditions that maximize the effectiveness of punishment can be extrapolated from laboratory and applied research.

Delay of Punishment

Punishment is more effective as positive reinforcement when it is delivered immediately after the target response than it is when it is delayed. If punishment of the undesirable response is delayed, it immediately follows some other behavior that may be desirable. For example, if a parent punishes a child for some behavior performed earlier that day ("Wait until your father [or mother] comes home"), the delayed punishment would have a weak effect on the undesirable behavior. Moreover, a desirable behavior (for example, helping with chores) may have been performed in close contiguity with that punishment and may thus inadvertently be suppressed by the punishment. Independent of the specific response that occurs during the delay, if punishment is delayed, it is not likely to be associated with the response that is to be suppressed.

In some cases, punishment is delayed because the undesirable response, such as theft or lying, cannot be detected immediately. The fact that the consequences would be so delayed may raise questions about their likely effects. There are ways to bring the consequences in closer proximity to the undesired behaviors. One method is to reenact portions of the previously performed behaviors that occurred and to apply aversive consequences immediately to the reenactment. Such procedures appear to bring the consequences closer to the behavior and lead to response suppression (Van Houten & Rolider, 1989).

Schedule of Punishment

Punishment is more effective when the punishing consequence occurs every time (continuous punishment), rather than once in a while (intermittent punishment). The greater the proportion of punished responses, the greater is the response reduction. However, when punishment is discontinued, recovery of the response is greater with continuous punishment than it is with intermittent punishment. For example, if time out is to be used in the home, it should be delivered every time the behavior occurs (continuous schedule). Administering time out intermittently, rather than after each occurrence of the response, usually leads to less response suppression (Hobbs & Forehand, 1977). After a response has been effectively suppressed, punishment can be delivered only intermittently to maintain low rates of the behavior (Calhoun & Lima, 1977; Clark, Rowbury, Baer, & Baer, 1973). In some circumstances and in the use of electric shock, the relationship between punishment schedule and response suppression does *not* hold. There may be no recovery even if punishment was previously delivered on a continuous schedule.

Source of Reinforcement

If a punished response is also positively reinforced, punishment is less effective than if that response is not reinforced. That a punished behavior is performed at all suggests that some reinforcer is maintaining it; otherwise, the behavior would have extinguished. The effect of punishment can be enhanced by removing the source of reinforcement for the punished response. For example, delinquents frequently provide peer social reinforcement for the commission of deviant acts. Punishment of deviant acts is likely to be less effective when there is such reinforcement.

When punishment is used, potential sources of reinforcement for the punished response should be identified and eliminated if possible. In practice, it is sometimes difficult to identify the source of the reinforcement that is maintaining a deviant behavior. In many instances, it is evident that teachers and parents socially reinforce behaviors that they wish to suppress. In situations such as the classroom, peers probably reinforce inappropriate behaviors (for example, clowning, teasing). Punishing disruptive behavior would be expected to have less effect if peers provide reinforcement for those behaviors.

Timing of Punishment in the Response Sequence

The earlier in the response sequence punishment is delivered, the more effective it tends to be. An undesirable response is not a single behavior but a chain or sequence of behaviors that culminates in an act considered undesirable. For example, a child's "theft" of a cookie prior to dinner may consist of a series (chain) of behaviors that includes walking into the kitchen, climbing onto a chair, reaching for the cookie jar, opening the jar, taking a cookie, and eating it. Punishment for going into the kitchen or climbing onto a chair will reduce cookie theft to a greater extent than will punishment after the cookie has been taken and eaten.

The importance of the timing of punishment can be readily explained. If the response chain is completed, the terminal behavior (for example, cookie consumption) is positively reinforced. Punishment imposed at that time is being used to suppress a response that has just been reinforced. This is not likely to be effective. Moreover, if the chain is completed, the reinforcement of the undesirable response is more immediate than is the punishment. As mentioned previously, punishment is more effective when the response to be suppressed is not reinforced than when it is reinforced. Hence, if a response is punished before it is reinforced, punishment should be more effective. Responses early in the chain of behavior may still be reinforced, since behaviors in a chain reinforce prior behaviors in that chain. But the further from the terminal reinforcer a behavior is, the less potent is the reinforcement. Behaviors early in a sequence are further removed from the terminal reinforcer, so their conditioned reinforcing properties are weaker and they are more readily suppressed when punishment is applied. Thus, a punishing consequence (reprimand) that might be ineffective at the end of the response sequence might well lead to suppression if administered earlier in the sequence.

A potential problem in applying punishment to initial behaviors in a response chain is that the behaviors at this point in the chain may be part of other response chains that constitute appropriate behavior. To continue our example, punishment of cookie theft might be very effective if it is delivered when the child enters the kitchen. However, entering the kitchen may be a part of appropriate chains, such as washing dishes, feeding a pet, washing one's hands, or hugging one's parents.

Variation of Punishment

Application of aversive events usually consists of a contingency in which a particular consequence (for example, reprimand or time out) is applied after the behavior. Research suggests that the effects of punishment can be enhanced by varying the punishers that follow behavior (Charlop, Burgio, Iwata, & Ivancic, 1988). For example, rather than using overcorrection, brief time out, or a reprimand after behavior, the specific consequence can be varied. Thus, on some occasions one of the consequences (time out) might be used, whereas on other occasions another consequence (reprimand) would be used. Variation of the aversive consequence leads to greater suppression of the responses than does use of any of the individual consequences applied to the behavior. Apparently, there is an adaptation to repeated use of the same consequence that is obviated by variation of the consequence.

The importance of varying the consequences after behavior raises an important point. The effectiveness of mild punishers, such as reprimands and time out, can be enhanced by varying the consequences that are presented. Thus, less severe punishers can be used to suppress behavior if they are varied. An important caution is in order. *Variation* of consequences is to be distinguished from the *combination* of consequences. The findings suggest that application of a consequence after behavior is more effective when that consequence changes; this does not mean in any way that several consequences should be given at the same time after an instance of behavior. The combination of many aversive procedures as a penalty for performance is a misplaced focus and is objectionable for ethical as well as practical reasons.

Reinforcement of Alternative Responses

Punishment is most effective when it is accompanied by reinforcement for performing desirable or prosocial behaviors. *Aversive events of relatively weak intensity can effectively suppress behavior if reinforcement is also provided for an alternative positive response.* Thus, intense punishment is not required to suppress behavior. Mildly aversive events (for example, grimaces, statements of disapproval, or saying no) may only temporarily suppress undesired behavior. However, their suppressive effect will be enhanced if reinforcement is delivered for positive behaviors.

Even aversive consequences that are not effective by themselves can be effective when they are combined with reinforcement for alternative forms of behavior. As an example, in one program, an attempt was made to train a profoundly retarded child to walk rather than crawl. Whenever the child crawled, he was restrained (held at the waist for 5 seconds) (O'Brien, Azrin, & Bugle, 1972). This procedure did not decrease crawling or increase walking. Then the investigators added a positive aspect to the restraint procedure. Whenever the child crawled, he was restrained as before, but he was also aided in walking for a few seconds. Reinforcing an alternative response (continued movement in an upright position), resulted in a dramatic decrease in crawling and an increase in walking. Restraint alone was effective once walking had been established.

Most applications of punishment in behavior modification include reinforcement for desirable behavior. For example, in one program, toddlers were required to sit during the activities in a day-care center as a time-out procedure for disruptive behavior (Porterfield, Herbert-Jackson, & Risley, 1976). In addition, approval was provided when a child was playing appropriately. In this and other studies, punishment alone might have been used to suppress behavior. Yet, suppressing an undesirable behavior does not guarantee that a desirable behavior will take its place. *Punishment usually trains a person in what not to do rather than in what to do.* For example, suppression of fighting in a delinquent does not guarantee the appearance of desirable social behavior.

Overcorrection, as a punishment technique, includes the practice of appropriate behavior to help make punishment more educative than is ordinarily the case. However, the behaviors that are positively practiced in overcorrection are not always desirable prosocial responses. Rather, they are often behaviors that appear to be incompatible with the response that is to be suppressed. For example, one study reported the use of overcorrection to eliminate self-injurious behavior in a psychotic and severely retarded adult (Azrin, Gottlieb, Hughart, Wesolowski, & Rahn, 1975). The positive practice component of the procedure included engaging in fixed bodily postures (for example, practice in holding the hands away from the body in a sequence of exercises) that were incompatible with hitting oneself. Since these behaviors were not socially desirable in their own right, separate reinforcement contingencies were included to develop appropriate social behaviors and participation in activities on the ward.

For at least three reasons, it is advisable to use positive reinforcement whenever punishment is employed. First, reinforcement for alternative responses increases the efficacy of punishment. Second, reinforcement can develop appropriate behaviors to displace the inappropriate behaviors that are to be eliminated. Third, positive reinforcement combined with punishment may eliminate undesirable side effects that might result from the use of punishment alone (see below). As a general rule, whether the goal is to increase or decrease a particular behavior, reinforcement techniques should constitute the primary basis of the behavior change program. Any of the various punishment techniques may be a valuable adjunct to reinforcement techniques but perhaps should not be used alone.

General Comments

In the discussion of the factors that influence the effectiveness of punishment, one of the more familiar dimensions considered in everyday life, namely, intensity of punishment, was omitted. In everyday applications, such as child rearing, it is often assumed that the greater the intensity of punishment, the greater is the suppression of behavior. Thus, advocates of "spare the rod and spoil the child" often believe that a "really good" spanking is needed to teach a lesson. In general, however, laboratory and applied evidence does *not* support the view that increased intensity of punishment results in increased suppression of a response. There is an exception in laboratory research: the presentation of electric shock at higher intensities has suppressed behavior more quickly than its presentation at lower intensities (Azrin & Holz, 1966). This relation does not hold for other aversive events in the laboratory (for example, noise) or for the many events that are studied in applied settings. For example, louder reprimands, shouts, or threats do not show more suppressive effects than do milder forms of these events.

In the withdrawal of positive reinforcers, the more intense punishments are not needed. Even when a reinforcer is withdrawn for a short period (time out), which does not seem to be an "intense" aversive consequence, response suppression may be dramatic. Occasionally, an increase in the duration of time out, up to several minutes, has led to greater suppression of behavior (for example, Hobbs, Forehand, & Murray, 1978). Similarly, for response cost (loss of tokens), larger fines have occasionally suppressed behavior more effectively than have smaller fines (Kazdin, 1971). However, these findings do *not* justify long periods of time out or large fines because far milder consequences are quite effective. For example, with time out, extremely brief periods, including periods ranging from 15 to 90 *seconds,* have been very effective in several studies. This is quite different from sending children to their rooms for 30 to 60 minutes, as parents often do, or for 8 or 9 hours, as abusive parents occasionally do. Such harsh punishments are not only unnecessary but likely to be ineffective for the child and frustrating for the parents. Much milder punishments, included as part of a program that reinforces prosocial or positive behaviors, can accomplish the goals much more effectively.

SIDE EFFECTS OF PUNISHMENT

Types of Effects

An argument against the use of punishment is that it often results in undesirable side effects. Even though punishment may eliminate the target behavior, it may have other consequences that are worse than the original behavior or are at least problematic in their own right. Laboratory research, usually with infrahuman subjects, provides evidence for a variety of undesirable side effects of punishment (Azrin & Holz, 1966; Hutchinson, 1977; Linscheid & Meinhold, 1990). These side effects also arise in applied situations where punishment is used.

Emotional Reactions

Undesirable emotional reactions may result from punishment. These reactions may be temporarily disruptive to the individual. For example, when a child receives a spanking, crying, anger, and similar emotional reactions will probably occur. These reactions are not essential ingredients of punishment but are undesirable concomitant effects. They are undesirable, in part, because they may interfere with new learning. The child may be unresponsive to the social environment until he or she is no longer upset or angry. An additional consideration is that undesirable emotional reactions are frequently paired with cues in the punishment situation. Eventually, the cues themselves (for example, parent or teacher or a given situation such as the home) may produce similar reactions in the absence of punishment.

Escape and Avoidance

Another side effect of punishment is that it can lead to escape from or avoidance of the punishment situation. If a situation is aversive, an individual can terminate the aversive condition by escaping. Successful escape from the situation is negatively reinforced because it terminates an aversive condition. Even if the punishing event is only mildly aversive and too weak to suppress behavior, it may still lead to escape behavior (Azrin & Holz, 1966). Hence, the use of aversive stimuli fosters escape and reinforcement of escape behaviors. For example, reliance on punishment in the home may result in attempts to avoid or escape from the home.

Stimuli associated with an aversive situation may also lead to escape. Recall that any event consistently associated with an aversive event becomes aversive in its own right. If one individual is constantly punishing another individual, the punishing agent will take on properties of a conditioned aversive stimulus. The individual whose behavior is punished will attempt to escape from or avoid the punishing agent because of these properties. This side effect is undesirable because if individuals (for example, children) escape or avoid punishing agents (for example, parents and teachers), the punishing agents will be unable to provide reinforcement to train desirable responses.

Aggression

In laboratory work with a variety of species, punishment sometimes results in attacks by one animal on another animal or on the source of punishment (Hutchinson, 1977). In applied programs using punishment, there is the possibility that the punished individual will aggress toward the punishing agent. Attacking the agent may remove the source of punishment, at least temporarily. Hence, the individual's aggression toward the punishing agent is *negatively reinforced* by terminating an aversive event. For example, if an adolescent fights back when being severely beaten by a parent, this may terminate the parental assault. Fighting back, if effective, terminates the aversive consequence by the parent and is negatively reinforced. (Unfortunately, if fighting back is effective, the adolescent's aggressive behavior is reinforced for severe aggressive behavior.)

Modeled Punishment

The punishing agent *models* (or provides an example of) certain behaviors, namely the use of aversive control techniques that the punished individual may learn. If a parent uses physical punishment with a child, especially harsh punishment, this increases the likelihood that the child will engage in physically aggressive behaviors (Timberlake, 1981). Adults provide models for how to interact with others. Thus, in interactions with their peers, children are likely to use behavioral control techniques similar to the techniques that their parents use to control them. It is no surprise, then, that children who are referred clinically for severely aggressive behaviors often come from homes where child and spouse abuse have been evident (see Kazdin, 1987a). Unfortunately, abuse in the home provides effective models that may help train children to become aggressive, apart from other influences operating in the environment. Certainly, caution is required in using aversive techniques—particularly physical punishment—because of the modeling influences of their use.

Perpetuation of Punishment

Another undesirable side effect of punishment is that its use is reinforced in the person who administers it. Punishment usually results in rapid (though temporary) reduction of the target response. If a parent shouts at a child, the child's behavior is usually altered immediately. Thus, the parent's behavior (shout) is *negatively reinforced* (termination of some undesirable child behavior). Because reinforcement is a powerful technique, particularly if it is immediate, the frequency with which the parent delivers punishment is likely to increase. Even though the punishment is not likely to alter the child's behavior for very long, the failure of the punishment is delayed, whereas the short-term effect is immediate. Hence, the parent is likely to rely increasingly on punishment and runs the risk of encountering the side effects discussed above.

Often there is frustration on the part of the punishing agent (parent, teacher) associated with the continued use of punishment. The agent continues to use punishment, no doubt due in part to the fact that use of punishment is immediately reinforced (by momentary suppression of behavior through negative reinforcement). Over time, parents and teachers invariably recognize that the child's behavior is not changing and that punishment, even harsh punishment, is "not working." In our own clinical work, this has led some of our abusive parents to very harsh physical abuse (burning children with cigarettes, hitting them with wooden boards) and unusual procedures they consider to reflect time out (for example, keeping a young child outside the house for four days while he looked in, asking for food and shelter; locking a child in his room without meals for two days). The parents often state that they increase the amount of intensity of punishment to "teach the child a lesson once and for all." The ineffectiveness of these procedures, recognized by all parties, does not lead to their disuse. The long-term effectiveness of such procedures does not cancel the effects of other contingencies that operate, such as the immediate negative reinforcement that the parent may experience, satisfaction that some effort was made on the part of the parent to teach the child a lesson, and reduction of parent frustration that applying punishment may afford. The reasons for using punishment in behavior modification are always to suppress behavior and to develop another behavior; the reasons in everyday life are much more complex because they are not necessarily aimed at suppressing behavior (for example, revenge, expression of frustration) nor are evaluated systematically with that purpose in mind.

Illustrations from Applied Settings

Negative Side Effects

Side effects of punishment have been reported in many applications and across a wide range of aversive techniques. For example, in one program, mentally retarded children received verbal reprimands for noncompliance with requests (Doleys, Wells, Hobbs, Roberts, & Cartelli, 1976). Some of the children showed brief periods of crying and soiling and wetting their pants. Similarly, reports of programs using overcorrection, response cost, time out, and shock have occasionally noted that the crying, tantrums, and emotional outbursts of the clients increased and that the clients were generally upset (for example, Carey & Bucher, 1981; Matson & Ollendick, 1977). These reports clearly suggest that *emotional side effects* may be associated with punishment.

Studies have also demonstrated that *avoidance* may be associated with punishment. For example, in two studies, children were exposed to adults who administered different consequences during play activities (Morris & Redd, 1975; Redd, Morris, & Martin, 1975). Subsequently, the children were asked to choose the adults with whom they wished to interact. The adults who had been associated with the delivery of punishment (reprimands) were generally not selected for further interaction, whereas those who had been associated with positive reinforcement (praise) were the most frequently selected for further interaction. This research suggests a clear preference for agents who administer reinforcing consequences rather than punishing consequences. Agents who primarily administer punishment are not sought out when clients are given the opportunity for additional interaction. If these findings extend to education and child rearing, children's avoidance of their teacher or parents may be fostered in part by the types of consequences that teachers or parents administer.

Aggression has also been found to be a side effect of punishment. Applications of overcorrection, reprimands, and brief slaps to the hand have effectively suppressed behavior (for example, Foxx & Azrin, 1972; Mayhew & Harris, 1978). However, increases in attacks on the trainer (for example, hitting, pinching, throwing things) have been reported early in training. Occasionally, the aggression associated with punishment has been self-inflicted. For example, applications of overcorrection have been associated with increases in self-injurious behavior in some clients (Azrin, Gottieb, Hughart, Wesolowski, & Rahn, 1975; Rollings, Baumeister, & Baumeister, 1977).

The negative side effects obtained in using punishment programs appear to be exceptions rather than the rule. And when undesirable side effects appear, they are usually temporary and they usually subside over the course of treatment.

Positive Side Effects

Occasionally, suppression of behavior leads to positive side effects. For example, mentioned previously was the use of electric shock to reduce chronic self-injury (Linscheid et al., 1990). Shock was extremely effective after a number of other interventions had failed. The target behaviors changed but what about side effects? Actually, positive side effects were evident. Systematic assessment showed reductions in other self-injurious behaviors (for example, hair pulling, biting, hitting objects) that were not punished. Moreover, vocalizations considered to reflect distress and measures of agitation also decreased systematically. Anecdotal (unsystematic) reports from others in contact with the cases suggested improvements in social interaction, greater compliance with instructions, and more independent self-care behavior (self-feeding) following punishment. These reports suggest that the positive side effects reflected behaviors that improved everyday life and interactions with others.

The positive side effects reported in this example are not restricted to specific forms of punishment such as shock. Social behaviors, including smiling, communication, and laughing with another resident or a staff member, increased as self-injurious behavior was decreased by the contingent application of water mist or facial screening (Singh, Watson, & Winton, 1986). Several studies have found that use of punishment techniques such as overcorrection and time out are associated with decreases in such behaviors as aggressiveness, whining, and fussing and with increases in participation in activities, attentiveness to others, and smiling.

The positive side effects of punishment have been less well investigated than have the negative side effects, both in laboratory and applied research. In general, negative side effects appear to be much more likely than positive side effects. The reason has to do with the effects of aversive events on behavior. Negative side effects, such as escape and emotional reactions, emerge from mild aversive consequences, even when these consequences are ineffective in suppressing behavior.

General Comments

Negative side effects do not necessarily emerge from the use of punishment. However, the side effects have been well documented in animal laboratory research spanning decades of research (Azrin & Holz, 1966; Hutchinson, 1977). Some authors have suggested that special features of the laboratory may maximize the likelihood of negative side effects. For example, aggression as a side effect in animal laboratory research might be due in part to the fact that animals often are in very close proximity to one another, are confined, and cannot control or escape from the delivery of the aversive event (Linscheid & Meinhold, 1990). These are very different circumstances from applied settings. In applied research, negative side effects may be less frequent. A systematic evaluation of applications of punishment over a period spanning two decades of research has suggested that positive side effects of punishment are reported over ten times more frequently than are negative side effects (Matson & Taras, 1989). Thus, negative side effects may emerge but do not appear to be common.

Perhaps a major reason that undesirable side effects have been less apparent in applied settings than in laboratory studies is that reinforcement for alternate responses is usually used in conjunction with punishment. For example, if some behavior is reinforced even though others are punished, it is less likely that the situation and punishing agent will be as aversive as the punishment would be if adminstered by itself. Hence, less escape and avoidance on the part of the client would be evident. In fact, fewer emotional side effects, such as avoidance, emotional reactions, and aggression, are found when punishment is combined with reinforcement for positive behaviors than when punishment is used alone (for example, Carey & Bucher, 1986). Another reason that undesirable side effects have not been widely found may be that mild and brief forms of punishment are usually used in applied settings. Mild forms of punishment are effective in suppressing behavior when reinforcement is delivered for other behaviors. Emotional disruption and aggressive behavior are less likely to result from mild forms of punishment than from intense forms resulting from painful stimuli.

The emergence of side effects, positive or negative, warrants much greater attention in research. Most studies report side effects anecdotally. More systematic assessment would be very important. Also, it will be important to study the conditions that lead to the emergence of one type of effect versus another. One study has suggested that positive effects are more likely to occur when deviant behavior is completely, rather then partially, suppressed (Van Houten & Rolider, 1989). This kind of research shows that there are interesting features to be studied. At present, one can only alert individuals to the possibility of side effects during punishment.

CHARACTERISTICS OF THE PUNISHMENT PROCESS

Immediacy of Effects

A reduction in response rate usually occurs immediately following punishment. Using punishment for prolonged periods may result in further suppression. If there is no immediate effect, it is probably not advantageous to continue the aversive contingency. It is difficult to specify precisely how immediate the effect of punishment should be to justify being continued. Laboratory work has shown that some response suppression occurs as soon as the punishing stimulus is delivered a few times (Azrin & Holz, 1966).

In applied settings, the rapidity of punishment effects has been especially evident with shock. In a matter of only a few sessions or even one application of shock, behaviors are reduced and sometimes completely eliminated. The rapid and dramatic effects of shock were illustrated in a 14-year-old boy who had a chronic cough (Creer, Chai, & Hoffman, 1977). The cough did not respond to medical treatment or to attempts to remove attention for coughing and to provide praise for periods of not coughing. The cough was so disruptive and distracting to others that the child was expelled from school until his cough could be controlled. After further medical tests proved negative, a punishment procedure was used. Baseline observations revealed that the boy coughed 22 times in a 1-hour period. Treatment began by applying a mild electric shock (to the forearm) for coughing. Application of one shock after the first cough eliminated the behavior. The boy immediately returned to school, and he did not suffer episodes of coughing for up to two and a half years after treatment. Since shock is rarely used as an aversive event in applied settings, its effects are not a helpful guide in characterizing the effects of punishment. Nevertheless, the general rule about immediacy of effect holds and is applicable to less intense forms of punishment.

Applications of time out, verbal reprimands, overcorrection, lemon juice, and other procedures have shown that reductions in behavior occur after one or a few days of punishment (for example, Marholin & Townsend, 1978; Singh, Watson, & Winton, 1986; Wilson, Robertson, Herlong, & Haynes, 1979). Although exceptions to these results can be found, the general pattern is a reduction in behavior relatively soon after treatment is applied. This does not mean that the behavior will be eliminated or suppressed to the desired level in only a few days, but it does mean that beneficial effects of punishment, when they occur, should be evident in client behavior within a relatively brief period (for example, a few days). If signs of progress are not soon evident, perhaps alternative procedures should be attempted. One would not want to continue punishment without clear signs of progress. Consequently, assessment of behavior is essential as part of a punishment program.

Specificity of Effects

Punishment often leads to effects that are specific to the situation in which the response is punished. Punishing a response in one setting or during one period may not carry over to other settings or other periods. For example, punishment effects achieved in special training sessions in a small room off a ward in an institution may not be evident in the same room after the sessions are over (Marholin & Townsend, 1978) or on the ward after the client leaves the sessions (Rollings, Baumeister, & Baumeister, 1977). Behaviors suppressed in the treatment setting may continue unless punishment is implemented in the new setting.

The specificity of punishment effects has been evident in other ways. The effect of punishment may be restricted to the person who previously administered it. For example, if two individuals are present and only one of them administers punishment (for example, reprimands), the behavior may decrease only in the presence of that person (for example, Rolider, Cummings, & Van Houten, 1991). In general, response suppression may be limited to the specific conditions associated with punishment. However, the specificity of punishment effects can be overcome by extending the contingency to other conditions.

Recovery After Punishment Withdrawal

The effects of punishment are often quite rapid, so that the frequency of a behavior is reduced in a short time. However, the effect of punishment may not last; when the punishment contingency is withdrawn, the punished behavior may recover or return to its baseline rate. Recovery is likely to occur when punishment has not completely suppressed the response while the contingency was in effect and when reinforcement has not been used to develop an alternative response. As mentioned earlier, whether punishment is highly effective in suppressing behavior depends on a variety of factors. For example, a few electric shocks can completely eliminate self-destructive behavior. Moreover, the suppression is complete and the response does not recover even though the contingency is withdrawn.

Ordinarily, mild forms of punishment will result in recovery after the punishment contingency is withdrawn. Indeed, even when punishment is in effect, the individual may adapt to mild punishment, so that it loses its suppressive effects. For example, the more frequently threats are used, the more they lose their suppressive effects (Phillips, Phillips, Fixsen, & Wolf,

1971). To maximize response suppression with punishment and to minimize recovery, positive reinforcement can be provided for behaviors incompatible with the punished response. When the punishment contingency is removed, the reinforced response will be of a higher relative frequency than is the punished response. It will have replaced the previously punished response, and it can be maintained with continued reinforcement.

CONTROVERSY: PUNISHMENT AND ITS USE

Source of Controversy

The use of punishment in behavior modification has been a major source of controversy and debate (see Repp & Singh, 1990). Much of the debate has emerged in the discussion of individuals who engage in self-injurious behavior where there may be severe self-injury (for example, permanent physical damage), where painful events (self-injury itself) are already going on, and where the need to intervene is urgent, as illustrated in examples earlier in the chapter. Confronted with a child who is gouging his or her eyes, which is threatening vision, is obviously an urgent situation. The usual response to such an individual in an institutional setting is to use some form of physical restraint (for example, a jacket that completely restricts use of hands and arms, or a helmet that does not permit hand contact with the face). Such restraint, of course, is restrictive. A question is whether some behavioral (or any other) procedure might be used to eliminate the behavior and to permit the individual to function more normally and with greater freedom in everyday life. Using punishment in this situation could appear to be quite justified or unjustified to most people, depending on further details of the case, such as the nature of the punishing event and alternatives that had been tried unsuccessfully. The issues raised by punishment are not restricted to self-injurious behavior or any particular treatment population or focus, even though special issues might emerge in each case.

Punishment raises special ethical, legal, humanistic, and value issues because of the aversive nature of the interventions. Questions are raised of whether punishment techniques ought to be used in principle, apart from their effects; whether they are necessary to use, given alternative procedures; and if they are to be used, at what point, when, and with what procedures. It is fairly easy to take an extreme or one-sided view of whether punishment ought to be used to change behavior. Also, case examples are plentiful in which one view (punishment seemed necessary or unnecessary) led to an intervention that reduced significant suffering. The complexities of the issue derive from the manifold definitions of *punishment,* inconsistencies in society's views and uses of punishment, and incomplete information about the optimal ways of changing behavior. More general ethical and legal issues are raised in Chapter 13. For the present chapter, it is useful to consider punishment as a behavior change procedure more concretely.

Punishment Redefined

The meaning and use of punishment in everyday life and in behavior modification are different in important ways relevant to the controversy. In everyday life, *punishment* refers to applying aversive events to behavior. The meaning is complex because it includes a number of notions such as retribution, retaliation, and inflicting pain. Although these are not necessary features of punishment, they are related in everyday usage, in the etymology of the word *punishment* (as noted previously), and in cultural beliefs. For example, the "an eye for an eye" philosophy of punishment focuses more on the notion of justice and suitable penalties than it does on actually changing behavior.

In behavior modification, the definition and focus of punishment are very different from the term in everyday life. *Punishment* refers to a decrease in the frequency of a behavior when a consequence is provided contingent on that behavior. Punishment includes such procedures as time out and response cost, usually in extremely low magnitudes (for example, 1 to 5 minutes of time out). These are examples of punishment, to be sure, and one may object in principle to aversive events. At the same time, they may not deserve the emotionally laden reactions more appropriately applied to corporal punishment. Because punishing events are defined by their effects, many events commonly viewed as rewarding (praise, time with a parent or another adult, and indeed tokens) can serve as punishing consequences for some individuals. When the definition refers to a decrease in behavior rather than retaliation, retribution, pain, or providing "justice," what is used as a punishing event can be very different.

Alternatives

A goal is to identify interventions that are effective and acceptable to society at large (for example, those who use and who receive them). Effectiveness and acceptability are not simple criteria. For example, many measures of effectiveness can be identified, including the rapidity of change, the range of responses (such as several or just the one punished) and settings (such as change in several or just the one setting in which treatment was provided), the durability of change (short versus long-term change), and others (see Kazdin, 1992). The different criteria do not always go together, so that different conclusions would be reached depending on the criterion to judge effectiveness.

Behavior modification programs often assess a target behavior to be sure that change is occurring. Yet, this greatly oversimplifies the full nature of change. A change in one behavior is often related to several other behaviors of the individual and changes across different settings, whether or not they are assessed. Thus, deciding whether one intervention is more effective than another is not merely comparing their impacts on a single target behavior. The notion of effectiveness is relevant to discussion of punishment because whether some interventions are more or less effective depends on the specific criterion used to draw conclusions. Other criteria might yield different conclusions.

There are many alternatives to punishment, although in any instance it is not possible to be certain in advance whether one will be more effective than another or sufficiently effective to achieve the desired change. Thus, it is important to keep in mind the portfolio of intervention techniques that can be used. In the present context, consider that we have interest in reducing or eliminating a particular behavior, a situation in which we might first consider one of the many punishment procedures already discussed. There are several alternatives that might be quite effective, without ever considering punishment (see LaVigna & Donnellan, 1986; O'Brien & Repp, in press). Prominent examples have been described and illustrated previously and hence are mentioned here only in passing.

The identification and modification of setting and stimulus events can suppress behavior. A functional analysis may reveal that events presented in advance of behavior (for example, comments from a relative, activity in a certain situation) increases the undesired (for example, aggressive) behavior. The undesired behavior can be reduced and eliminated by altering the situation or antecedents that serve as the occasion for the behavior.

A large number of positive reinforcement procedures can be used as alternatives to punishment. In the previous chapter, we discussed differential reinforcement of other behavior, of incompatible behavior, of alternative behavior, of functionally equivalent behavior, and of low rates of behavior. These methods of providing reinforcement provide multiple options that are often quite effective in reducing behavior and in developing appropriate behavior in its stead.

Negative reinforcement too can be used to reduce undesired behavior. It is possible that the undesired behavior is maintained by an aversive contingency already operative in the situation. Specifically, escape may be contingent on undesired behavior. An example in the previous chapter showed how uncooperative and disruptive behavior of children receiving dental treatment temporarily terminated the treatment (negative reinforcement for disruptive behavior). Negative reinforcement contingencies that support maladaptive behavior are not, of course, restricted to pediatric dentistry. The point is that an undesired behavior can be reduced or eliminated by rearranging the existing events so that they promote desired behavior. No punishment is used in this case; negative reinforcement is used to obtain behaviors that are incompatible with or are an alternative to the undesired behavior.

Extinction, detailed in the next chapter, represents an alternative to punishment as well. During extinction, reinforcers previously provided for the behavior are no longer given. If the reinforcer(s) that maintains the behavior can be identified and controlled, behavior can be reduced through extinction.

The above procedures can be implemented in many ways and in many combinations. Thus, one cannot say there is a fixed number of alternative interventions to punishment. Moreover, our understanding of factors that control behavior and the reciprocal relations among motivation, behavior, and consequences is far from complete (see Iwata et al., 1990). Procedures that can change behavior, options beyond those enumerated here, are likely to develop even further. But even at present, there are alternatives to the use of punishment, if one wishes to avoid punishment entirely.

When and How to Use Punishment

Punishment is a procedure to be used cautiously for many reasons, ranging from broad ethical and social issues (for example, Should it be used? Is the procedure or practice acceptable?) to more concrete caveats, such as possibly undesirable side effects. The evidence simply is not available to argue for a strong position that punishment is absolutely essential to achieve a particular goal in the general case. As a general rule, other procedures should be employed in advance of punishment. An initial question that should be asked is whether punishment is needed at all. *The fact that a goal may be to suppress behavior does not necessarily mean that the program should be based upon punishment.* Response suppression can be achieved with many other interventions, as noted previously. In particular, the many reinforcement techniques are especially viable alternatives.

Even though reinforcement techniques present viable alternatives to punishment, several situations are likely to arise in which punishment will be useful, required, and possibly even essential. First and perhaps most obviously, punishment is a viable alternative when the inappropriate behavior may be physically dangerous to oneself or others. Some immediate intervention is required to suppress responses before the relatively delayed effects of reinforcement and extinction might operate. Not all professionals would agree that this situation requires the use of punishment, because evidence is not available that other procedures are necessarily less effective (Donnellan & LaVigna, 1990). Even so, in some cases life-threatening behavior (for example, ruminative vomiting in an infant) can be immediately eliminated, and discussions about alternative procedures seem moot at the level of clinical care.

Second, punishment is useful when reinforcement of a behavior incompatible with the disruptive behavior cannot be administered easily. For example, if a hyperactive student is literally out of his or her seat all of the time, it may be impossible or unfeasible to reinforce in-seat behavior. Punishment (for example, response cost along with shaping) may be helpful in initially obtaining the desired response. Eventually, of course, punishment can be faded or eliminated completely with increased reliance upon shaping with positive reinforcement.

Third, punishment is useful in temporarily suppressing a behavior while another behavior is reinforced. This latter use may be the most common application of punishment in applied settings. However, it should be remembered that mild forms of punishment (for example, mild reprimands, brief time-out durations, and small penalties or costs) usually are sufficient to suppress behavior as long as reinforcement for alternate responses is provided. Indeed, mild punishment can sometimes enhance the effectiveness of reinforcement. In several programs attempts have been made to decrease disruptive child behavior (for example, noncompliance, aggressiveness) at home or at school by having parents and teachers provide approval, attention, and praise for appropriate behavior (for example, following instructions, playing cooperatively). Appropriate child behavior may show little or no improvement. When mild punishment is added in the form of a brief time out or response cost, behavior change is often dramatic (Roberts, Hatzenbuehler, & Bean, 1981; Wahler, Hops, & Greenwood, 1981). In general, studies have shown that the combination of mild punishment and positive reinforcement is more effective than either procedure used alone (for example, Bierman, Miller, & Stabb, 1987; Carey & Bucher, 1986; Pfiffner & O'Leary, 1987).

It should be clear that the best use of punishment in applied settings is as an *ancillary* technique to accompany positive reinforcement. Usually, punishment will suppress undesirable responses but will not train desirable behaviors. Reinforcement is essential to develop appropriate behaviors that replace the suppressed behaviors. This is widely recognized in clinical and applied research, where the vast majority of studies that use punishment also employ positive reinforcement as part of the program (Matson & Taras, 1989).

Several considerations are important to address if aversive techniques are to be used. First and perhaps foremost, the availability of alternative interventions is critical to consider before aversive techniques are used. Behavior change might be attained with positive reinforcement alone or combined with mild punishment (for example, response cost). Reliance on aversive techniques can be justified only if positive reinforcement procedures have proven unsuccessful. Second and related, if aversive techniques are to be used, they should be the least severe or restrictive interventions possible to achieve therapeutic ends. Relatively more severe or restrictive events (for example, shock, physical restraint) can be justified only if aversive events of lesser intensity or severity have been unsuccessful. Third, the duration of the program is an important consideration. A program that includes aversive events should have well-specified limits regarding how long it is to be in effect and what the conditions are that will lead to its termination or continuation. A final consideration is whether there are clear benefits to the clients that result from treatment. If behavior does not change or show a trend in the direction of change, continuation of aversive events is not justified. The above points convey minimal guidelines regarding the use of aversive events; they do not exhaust the issues that need to be addressed. Also important are ethical and legal guidelines as means of protecting client rights; these are highlighted in Chapter 13.

SUMMARY AND CONCLUSION

Punishment consists of reducing behavior by presenting aversive events (such as verbal reprimands and disapproval), removing positive events (as in time out or response cost), and requiring effort and alternative behaviors (as in overcorrection or contingent exercise). Several factors influence the effective application of punishment related to the delay of punishment, schedule of administration, sources of reinforcement, timing of punishment in the response sequence, and, most important, reinforcement of alternative behaviors. By reinforcing an alternate response, even mild forms of punishment can change behavior dramatically.

Use of punishment can lead to undesirable side effects, such as emotional reactions, escape from the situation or from the person who administers punishment, aggression, the use of punishment by the individual who is punished, and overreliance upon aversive control procedures. Positive side effects, such as increased socialization, are more common in applications of punishment in applied settings. Even so, the possibility of adverse side effects makes extensive reliance upon aversive procedures somewhat hazardous. Additionally, punishment effects may be very specific, both in the responses that are altered and in the situations in which behavior change occurs.

In general, there is a place for punishment in behavior modification programs, namely, as a supplement to reinforcement programs designed to develop other appropriate behaviors. Emphasis of the present chapter was on the procedures, their effective application, and the characteristics of the punishment process. Controversial issues, highlighted only briefly in the present chapter, will be discussed further in a broader context of guidelines for treatment.

For Further Reading

Axelrod, S., & Apsche, J. (Eds.). (1983). *The effects of punishment on human behavior.* New York: Academic Press.

Cooper, J. O., Heron, T. E., & Heward, W. L. (1987). *Applied behavior analysis.* Columbus, OH: Merrill.

LaVigna, G. W., & Donnellan, A. M. (1986). *Alternatives to punishment: Solving behavior problems with non-aversive strategies.* New York: Irvington.

Repp, A. E., & Singh, N. N. (Eds.). (1990). *Perspectives on the use of nonaversive and aversive interventions for persons with developmental disabilities.* Sycamore, IL: Sycamore.

CHAPTER SEVEN

EXTINCTION

In the previous chapter, punishment was discussed as a technique for reducing or eliminating a response. Applying specific punishing consequences can reduce the frequency of behavior, particularly when those consequences are accompanied by a reinforcement program designed to develop positive behaviors. The frequency of behavior can be reduced without presenting punishing consequences. Many maladaptive behaviors are maintained by consequences that follow from them. For example, temper tantrums or interrupting others during conversations are often unwittingly reinforced by the attention they receive. When there is interest in reducing behavior, extinction can be used by eliminating the connection between the behavior and the consequences that follow. *Extinction refers to withholding reinforcement from a previously reinforced response.* A response undergoing extinction eventually decreases in frequency until it returns to its prereinforcement level or is eliminated.

Extinction in applied settings usually is used for behaviors that have been maintained by *positive* reinforcement. In such cases, eliminating the connection between behavior (for example, tantrums) and positive reinforcement (for example, parent attention) can help reduce or eliminate the behavior. There are other uses of extinction for responses that are developed or maintained by *negative* reinforcement. These latter applications refer to behaviors that are performed to *escape* or *avoid* aversive consequences.

Extinction of Positively Reinforced Behavior

As already mentioned, in applied settings the usual focus of extinction is in relation to behaviors that have been positively reinforced. Positive consequences that follow the behavior are no longer forthcoming. There are many examples from everyday life in which extinction of positively reinforced responses occurs. For example, trying to start a defective automobile ceases (extinguishes) after several unsuccessful attempts; warmly greeting an acquaintance each day decreases if he or she repeatedly ignores these efforts; and raising one's hand in class will cease if it is never followed by teacher attention. In each case, the behavior decreases because the reinforcing consequence no longer occurs.

Extinction refers to a specific relation between behavior and the events after the behavior. The principle relates the occurrence of a behavior that has been reinforced in the past and the cessation of reinforcing consequences. Although application of the principle can be used to change behavior, extinction often operates in everyday life to foster problem behaviors. For example, in elementary school classrooms extinction often operates with reinforcement to sustain inappropriate behavior. As an illustration, raising one's hand to ask a question is often not attended to by the teacher. The absence of reinforcement is likely to result in extinction of hand raising. Extinction of this behavior that many teachers like is augmented if the teacher reinforces (provides attention to) children who shout out questions or answers. In fact, it is very easy to reinforce disruptive behavior in a class because it receives teacher and peer attention (social reinforcement). On the other hand, quiet and prosocial behaviors, such as hand raising or working quietly, are often ignored. Although quite simple, this example conveys how appropriate or desirable behavior in a setting may be inadvertently extinguished while undesirable behavior may be systematically, albeit unwittingly, reinforced. The present chapter discusses how to utilize extinction as a way of changing behavior in applied settings.

Factors That Influence the Effectiveness of Extinction

Extinction of positively reinforced behaviors is almost always used in a behavior modification program. For example, in a reinforcement program, when a target response is reinforced, nontarget responses that are no longer reinforced are implicitly undergoing extinction. Although extinction is an ingredient in most programs, it may be used as the major technique to decrease undesirable behavior. When extinction is relied on as the major technique, various factors determine whether it will be effective.

Schedule of Reinforcement

The efficacy of extinction and the speed with which the reduction of a response is achieved depend on the schedule of reinforcement that previously maintained the response. A response that has been reinforced every time (continuous reinforcement) rapidly extinguishes when the reinforcer is no longer provided. In contrast, a response that has been reinforced once in a while (intermittent reinforcement) extinguishes less rapidly when the reinforcer is withheld. The more intermittent the schedule (or the less frequent the previous reinforcement), the greater is the resistance of the response to extinction.

The relationship between reinforcement schedules and extinction creates a major problem for behavior change programs that rely exclusively on extinction because many behaviors are maintained by intermittent reinforcement. For example, incoherent verbalizations of psychiatric patients are often attended to by peers and staff but are sometimes ignored. Decreasing the frequency of these behaviors may be difficult because of the intermittent schedule on which they have been maintained. If all the sources of reinforcement were removed from a behavior previously maintained by intermittent reinforcement, the behavior would eventually decrease and perhaps be eliminated. Intermittent reinforcement *delays* the extinction process, and the delay may be unfortunate. While the long extinction process is under way, it is possible that the response will be *acciden-*

tally reinforced. The possibility of accidental reinforcement during extinction is always a problem—and that problem is exacerbated by a long extinction period.

Other Variables Affecting Extinction

The effects of reinforcement schedules on extinction have been more thoroughly studied than the effects of other variables. Yet general statements can be extrapolated from laboratory research on variables that contribute to resistance to extinction. First, the amount or magnitude of the reinforcement used to develop the response affects extinction. The greater the amount of a particular reinforcer given for a response, the greater is the resistance of the response to extinction. Similarly, the longer the response has been reinforced, the greater is the resistance to extinction. Finally, the greater the number of times that extinction has been used in the past to reduce the behavior, the more rapid extinction will be. The individual learns to discriminate periods of reinforcement and extinction more rapidly. If a strong or powerful reinforcer maintained a response and if that response were sustained over a long period, it is likely to be more resistant to extinction than it would be if weak reinforcers had been used and those reinforcers had been delivered over a short period.

Identifying the Reinforcer Maintaining Behavior

Extinction requires that the reinforcer or reinforcers maintaining behavior be identified and that they be withheld when the behavior is performed. Although this appears simple enough, in practice it may be difficult to isolate those reinforcers. For example, an emotionally disturbed child's aggressive behavior with peers may be maintained by various reinforcers, such as the control that aggressive behavior exerts over peers, the submissive response of the victims, admiration from friends, or special attention from a teacher or parent. In such a situation, it is difficult to identify which potential reinforcer or combination of reinforcers is maintaining the aggressive behavior. Removing teacher and parent attention may fail to decrease that behavior because other reinforcers are operative. For example, in a classroom program, an attempt to extinguish disruptive behavior by withdrawing teacher attention may have inadvertently served as a reinforcer for that behavior (Madsen, Becker, & Thomas, 1968). The disruptive behavior increased, apparently because it was maintained by reinforcement resulting from peer attention or from the disruptive behavior itself.

Empirical observation is the only method for determining which reinforcer is maintaining a behavior. If the consequence is withheld and the behavior declines, this suggests that the consequence served as a positive reinforcer and maintained the behavior. That possibility can be evaluated systematically by using a reversal or other experimental design, as outlined earlier. The difficulty in carrying out this approach is that the reinforcer is not easily identified if it follows the behavior infrequently (intermittently). For example, in a psychiatric hospital, disruptive patient behavior may be maintained by attention from a psychiatrist or psychologist. The psychiatrist or psychologist may have little interaction with the patient, yet that interaction may follow particularly bizarre patient behavior. The interaction may be so infrequent that it is assumed not to be responsible for maintaining the bizarre behavior. Consequently, identification of the reinforcer maintaining the behavior is likely to be delayed. If the reinforcer is not quickly identified, there can be considerable delay in beginning the extinction process.

In most instances in which extinction is used in applied settings, attention from adults or peers is assumed to be the reinforcer maintaining behavior. Attention can maintain inappropriate behavior in everyday life. For example, if someone interrupts a conversation, shouts out, or engages in a conspicuous deviant behavior, attention from others invariably is provided. Thus, as a general rule, attention is a viable and reasonable initial hypothesis regarding the reinforcer that might be controlling behavior. Yet attention is not necessarily the controlling reinforcer, and withholding it from the behavior may have little or no effect.

The way to evaluate which reinforcer is maintaining behavior is to conduct a functional analysis. As described earlier, a functional analysis is designed to provide data regarding the stimuli and consequences that influence performance of behavior. In the context of the present discussion of extinction, a functional analysis can identify the reinforcer that is maintaining behavior. Once identified, the connection between the deviant behavior and the reinforcer can be altered to achieve extinction and to reinforce prosocial behavior.

As an example, a recent study evaluated the aggressive behavior (hitting, kicking, scratching, pushing others) of a 7 1/2-year-old autistic child (named Molly) who was in a special classroom (Sasso et al., 1992). In experimental sessions with an investigator and then later in class with the teacher, a functional analysis was completed to identify the conditions influencing the frequency of aggressive behavior. In one condition, aggressive behavior was ignored. In another condition, attention was given for aggressive behavior by saying such things as "Please do not do that," "Stop that, you're hurting me"). In yet another condition, a task was presented to the child. Instances of aggression led to escape (termination) from the task and shift to another activity. Given the frequent use of removing attention (ignoring) in extinction programs, one might expect aggressive behavior to decline during the ignore condition. Yet, ignoring or providing attention did not affect the frequency of aggression in either laboratory sessions or the classroom. However, when termination of the task followed aggressive behavior, this behavior increased. Thus, the behavior was maintained (reinforced) by escaping from the task. Treatment was devised for Molly by permitting her to shift to a new task (escape) only for appropriate behavior; aggressive behavior did not lead to escape but to completion of more of the activity. This resulted in a dramatic decrease in aggressive behavior.

The example conveys that attention is not necessarily the reinforcer maintaining behavior in everyday situations. In the example, merely ignoring the behavior would not work as an intervention. This could lead an investigator, therapist, parent, teacher, or other person to say that "extinction did not work with this child." Yet, extinction is defined as no longer providing the reinforcer; if attention is not the reinforcer, withdrawing attention is not really extinction. The use of functional analysis of deviant behavior has increased in recent years in an effort to establish empirically the events controlling behavior so as to develop optimally effective intervention programs.

Controlling the Source of Reinforcement

Once the reinforcer maintaining an undesirable behavior has been identified, a major problem may be withholding the reinforcer after the behavior. Extinction requires very careful control over reinforcers. Any accidental reinforcement may rapidly reinstate the inappropriate behavior and prolong the extinction process.

An example of accidental reinforcement was reported in one of the earliest documented behavioral applications of extinction in a program designed to eliminate a child's bedtime tantrum behavior (Williams, 1959). When the child's parents followed instructions not to provide attention for this behavior, extinction proceeded uneventfully until tantrums were nearly eliminated within a few days. One night the child fussed when put to bed by his aunt. She provided a great deal of attention to the tantrum by staying with him until he went to sleep. As a result, the tantrums had to be extinguished a second time. After tantrums were eliminated the second time, they did not occur during the following two years. In this illustration, the accidental reinforcement of the behavior by the aunt merely slowed the extinction process. In more complex situations with many more opportunities for accidental reinforcement, such as classrooms where peers may reinforce an inappropriate behavior, extinction may be difficult to apply effectively.

Reinforcement is particularly difficult to control when it is delivered by peers. Parents, teachers, or staff members are often unaware that peers are providing reinforcing consequences for each other's behavior. Clowning in a classroom or stealing among delinquents in the community are examples of such peer reinforcement. Constant surveillance would be required to ensure that no such reinforcement occurred. From a practical standpoint, constant surveillance usually is not possible in either applied settings or the community at large.

One alternative is to enlist peers so that they ignore (extinguish) the deviant behavior of a particular individual. Peers can receive reinforcing consequences for systematically ignoring certain behaviors. If strong peer incentive for extinguishing a response is provided, it is likely that there will be little or no accidental reinforcement. For example, students in one elementary classroom received candy if they ignored a peer who had severe tantrums that consisted of profane screaming and throwing objects (Carlson, Arnold, Becker, & Madsen, 1968). By reinforcing peer behavior, these authors decreased the likelihood of uncontrolled reinforcement.

It is virtually impossible to control reinforcement for some behaviors. For example, autistic children frequently engage in self-stimulatory behaviors such as repetitively playing with objects or their fingers and rocking back and forth. As already mentioned, research has suggested that these behaviors are maintained in part by the sensory stimuli they generate (for example, auditory, visual, and tactile stimulation). The behaviors can be extinguished by reducing the stimuli they produce (for example, by blindfolding the children so that they cannot see what they are doing). However, reducing such stimuli is not feasible or desirable in most settings, so the behavior is likely to be reinforced automatically. Similarly, criminal, aggressive, and bizarre behaviors that one might like to reduce often yield immediate and intermittent reinforcement (for example, the material goods resulting from theft, the submission of a victim, attention from others). When the source of reinforcement is not easily controlled or eliminated, extinction is neither feasible nor likely to be effective.

CHARACTERISTICS OF THE EXTINCTION PROCESS

Gradual Reduction in Behavior

Although extinction effectively decreases and often eliminates behavior, the *process of extinction is usually gradual.* Unlike punishment, extinction typically does not result in an immediate response reduction. Rather, several unreinforced responses are performed before an effect is demonstrated.

When the undesirable behaviors are dangerous or severely disruptive, the delayed effects of extinction can be deleterious either to the individual or to others. Consider self-injurious behavior among austistic and mentally retarded children. It is possible that attention from others would maintain the behavior. In this case, ignoring the behavior may reduce its frequency. Yet, if the extinction process is gradual, significant physical damage may result from self-injury. For example, in one attempt to use extinction, the limits of the procedure were clearly shown. One child who engaged in self-inflicted head banging had multiple scars over his head and face from the injuries (Lovaas & Simmons, 1969). During extinction, the child was taken out of physical restraints and placed in a small room with no adults who could reinforce (attend to) the destructive behavior. The child's behavior, observed through a one-way mirror, eventually extinguished in ten sessions over a total of 15 hours. However, from the beginning of extinction until the response finally decreased to zero, the child had hit himself almost 9,000 times. Thus, a great deal of self-inflicted injury occurred during the course of extinction. Although extinction can reduce behavior, dangerous behavior may require an intervention with more rapid results than extinction usually provides.

The example warrants comment in light of recent advances in behavioral research. Early in the development of behavioral treatments (1960s), there was no consistent attempt to identify which reinforcers were maintaining behavior. Assumptions were made that commonly occurring reinforcers, such as attention, may inadvertently sustain deviant behavior, as in the above example. In fact, attention often maintains deviant behavior, but this cannot be assumed. In contemporary work, functional analyses are completed that are designed to test hypotheses about what is maintaining behavior. As discussed further in this chapter, results often reveal that attention is not the reinforcer for self-injurious behavior or not the main or sole reinforcer of that behavior. It is still the case that extinction by itself tends to be gradual in its effects. However, only recently have systematic efforts been made to identify empirically what the reinforcers are to maximize the effectiveness of extinction. Clearly, the process of reducing behavior can be augmented by using other procedures along with extinction (for example, differential reinforcement procedures).

Extinction Burst

At the beginning of extinction, the frequency of a response may become greater than it was while the response was being reinforced. The increase in responding at the beginning of extinction is referred to as a burst of responses. Numerous examples of such a burst at the beginning of extinction pervade everyday experience. For example, turning on a radio is usually followed by some sound. If the radio no longer works—so that no reinforcement (sound) occurs—attempts to turn on the radio will eventually extinguish. However, before this occurs, the response may temporarily increase in frequency (several on/off turns) and in intensity or vigor.

A burst of responses at the beginning of extinction has occasionally been reported in behavior modification programs. For example, Neisworth and Moore (1972) used extinction to reduce the frequent asthmatic attacks of a 7-year-old boy. The boy's prolonged wheezing, coughing, gasping, and similar responses were usually associated with excessive verbal and physical attention at bedtime. During extinction, his asthmatic attacks when he was put to bed were ignored. When those attacks were shorter than they had been on the previous night, he was rewarded in the morning with lunch money so that he could purchase his lunch at school rather than take his lunch. The results of the program are plotted in Figure 7–1. Of special

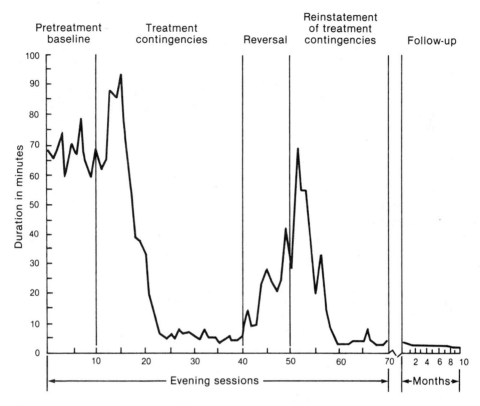

FIGURE 7–1
Duration of bedtime asthmatic responding as a function of contingency changes.
SOURCE: Neisworth, J. T., & Moore, F. (1972).

note is the first phase of extinction (treatment contingencies). At the beginning of extinction, the asthmatic attacks lasted longer than they did during baseline. A similar burst of responses was evident the second time extinction was begun. Eventually, the asthmatic attacks were eliminated, but not before temporarily becoming worse.

A burst of responses is especially serious with behaviors that threaten the client's physical well-being. For example, Wright, Brown, and Andrews (1978) treated a 9-month-old girl who constantly engaged in ruminative vomiting (regurgitating food after eating and between meals). The girl weighed only 8 pounds (her normal weight would have been about 20 pounds) because she received little nourishment from her meals. Because of the excessive staff attention that the girl received from vomiting, an extinction contingency was implemented. Staff were instructed to leave the girl's presence immediately when she began to vomit. When she was not vomiting, staff engaged in normal interaction with her, such as holding and looking at her. At the beginning of extinction, there was a burst of vomiting responses. This was especially unfortunate because it meant even greater food deprivation than the girl experienced during baseline. Fortunately, the burst lasted only two days and was followed by a decrease in vomiting and an increase in weight. The benefits of treatment were evident over a year later, when follow-up data were obtained.

A burst of responses may be undesirable even with behaviors that are not physically dangerous. It may be exceedingly difficult for someone to tolerate the undesirable behavior as it intensifies at the beginning of extinction. Thus, during a burst of responses, there is a greater likelihood that these other persons will provide reinforcement for the behavior. For example, if a child's tantrum becomes worse when parents systematically ignore the behavior, the parents may give in to the child and provide attention and comfort. Such parental reinforcement will increase the probability of intense tantrums because it is provided when the behavior is worse than usual. To the parents, of course, extinction may appear to be failing because the behavior has become worse. In reality, however, the effects of extinction are merely beginning.

It is likely that reinforcement during a burst of responses is a basis for undesirable behaviors often seen in children, such as protracted whining and excessive demands for attention. Parents, teachers, or other persons who may be involved in the extinction program need to be prepared for the possibility of a burst of responses so that they do not overreact to a temporary increase in behavior. An initial burst of responses does not always occur. However, when it does occur, the possibility of reinforcement adds to the risk in relying on extinction in the absence of other procedures.

Spontaneous Recovery

After extinction has progressed, a response may temporarily reappear, even though it has not been reinforced. *The temporary recurrence of a nonreinforced response during extinction is referred to as spontaneous recovery.* When a response recovers during extinction, its strength is ordinarily less than it was prior to extinction. For example, if a child's tantrums are ignored, the frequency of tantrums will probably decrease over time, possibly after an initial burst of responses. However, a tantrum may occur after extinction has progressed for some time. Such a tantrum is likely to be of a lower intensity than that of the tantrums during baseline.

As with extinction burst, a major concern with spontaneous recovery is that the response will be accidentally reinforced. Spontaneous recovery occurs after several responses have not been reinforced. If reinforcement is provided, it follows a long series of nonreinforced responses. This is tantamount to a highly intermittent reinforcement schedule, which may further increase resistance to extinction. If extinction continues and no accidental reinforcement occurs, the frequency and intensity of the spontaneously recovered response decrease. It is important to realize that the spontaneous recurrence of a response during extinction does not necessarily reflect the ineffectiveness of the procedure. Such recurrences often characterize the extinction process.

Possible Side Effects

Another characteristic of extinction is that the cessation of reinforcement may result in "emotional responses," such as agitation, frustration, feelings of failure, rage, and aggression (Rilling, 1977). Apparently, the transition from positive reinforcement to extinction is aversive and leads to side effects similar to those evident with punishment. Instances of emotional reactions in response to extinction abound in everyday experience. For example, after individuals place money into a malfunctioning vending machine (reinforcement is no longer delivered), statements of anger, swearing, and aggressive attacks on the machine are common. Individuals who have experienced repeated reinforcement of certain responses may view the cessation of such reinforcement as a failure. When an athlete performs poorly, for example, he or she may swear, express feelings of failure, and throw something to the ground in disgust. The notion of a "poor loser" signifies a person who engages in emotional behavior when his or her responses are not reinforced in a contest—that is, when he or she loses.

Adverse side effects of extinction have occasionally been reported in behavioral programs. For example, to eliminate the effeminate behavior of a boy with a gender identity problem, Rekers and Lovaas (1974) instructed the boy's mother to ignore him whenever he engaged in so-called "feminine" play (with girls' toys). When the mother failed to provide attention for his play behavior, he cried excessively and engaged in aggressive behavior toward her. In fact, a session had to be stopped to reassure the mother that she was doing what she was supposed to and that extinction should be continued.

In general, adverse side effects of extinction have not been well studied in applied settings. Laboratory evidence and reports from some applications suggest that when side effects occur, they are likely to be temporary and to diminish as the target response extinguishes. It is important to be aware that any situation in which reinforcement is no longer provided may become aversive. An aversive situation may result in escape and avoidance and thus reduce the opportunity for providing the client with positive reinforcement for desirable behavior. To avoid this, reinforcement should be delivered for a response other than the one to be eliminated. Thus, there is no net loss in reinforcement for the client. Rather, reinforcement is provided for a new or alternative behavior.

APPLICATIONS OF EXTINCTION

Extinction has been successfully applied to diverse problems. In one of the first demonstrations of this technique, it was used to reduce the frequency with which a psychiatric patient visited the nurses' office (Ayllon & Michael, 1959). The visits had been going on for two years and interfered with the nurses' work. The nurses usually paid attention to the patient when she visited and frequently pushed her back into the ward. After baseline observations, the nurses were instructed not to provide attention to the patient when she visited. Extinction decreased her visits from 16 times a day during baseline to 2 times a day at the end of 7 weeks.

Extinction was also used to reduce awakening in the middle of the night among infants (France & Hudson, 1990). Nighttime waking, exhibited by 20 percent to 50 percent of infants often is noted as a significant problem for parents. Parents may play a role in sustaining night waking by attending to the infant in ways that reinforce the behavior. In this study, parents with infants (8 to 20 months old) participated in an extinction-based program to decrease nighttime awakening. Waking up during the night was defined as a sustained noise (more than 1 minute) of the infant between onset of sleep and an agreed-upon waking time (such as 6:00 A.M.). Over the course of the project, several assessment procedures were used, including parent recording of sleep periods, telephone calls to the parents to check on these reports, and a voice-activated recording device near the child's bed. After baseline observations, parents were instructed to modify the way in which they attended to night wakings. Specifically, parents were told to ignore night wakings. If the parent had a concern about the health or safety of the child, the parent was instructed to enter the room, check the child quietly and in silence with a minimum of light, and to leave immediately if there was no problem.

The program was implemented separately for seven infants in a multiple-baseline design. Figure 7–2 shows the frequency of night wakings each week for the children during the baseline and intervention periods; frequency decreased during the intervention period. Follow-up consisted of assessment approximately three months later and then two years later, which showed maintenance of the changes. The figure is instructive for other reasons. The gradual nature of extinction and repeated instances of spontaneous remission are suggested both during the intervention and follow-up phases. The prospect of accidental reinforcement during these periods requires special caution on the part of parents to ensure that the behavior is not reinforced.

A related issue pertains to Child 3 (in Figure 7–2), who did not profit from the program. Parents reported difficulty in distinguishing the usual night wakings from those associated with illness of their child. Additional data revealed that these parents attended relatively frequently to nonillness awakenings during the intervention but improved during the first follow-up phase. The parents cannot be faulted. The pattern of behavior and eventual improvement draw attention to the difficulty in ignoring behavior contingently and discriminating when behavior does and does not warrant attention. In any case, the demonstration is clear in showing that extinction generally was quite effective in decreasing night waking among infants.

Generally, extinction is used in conjunction with other procedures, especially positive reinforcement. For example, in a preschool classroom, extinction and reinforcement were used to alter the aggressive behavior of a $3\frac{1}{2}$-year-old boy named Cain who would choke, push, bite, hit, kick, and poke his peers (Pinkston, Reese, LeBlanc, & Baer, 1973). The teacher usually reprimanded the boy, which seemed to have little effect. An extinction program was initiated whereby the teacher ignored his aggressive behavior. Of course, a problem with doing this was that he might seriously injure the victims of his aggression. To avoid that possibility, the teacher immediately interrupted Cain's aggressive activity by attending to the victim and helping the victim begin another activity away from him. While doing this, she ignored Cain. Thus, he did not receive attention from the teacher or submission and adverse reactions from the victim, which also might have helped reinforce his aggressive behavior.

Along with the extinction program, the teacher provided attention (social reinforcement) to Cain whenever he initiated appropriate (nonaggressive) interaction with his peers. The effects of the extinction and reinforcement program appear in Figure 7–3. Extinction reduced Cain's aggressive behavior, as shown in the ABAB design (upper portion of the figure). His aggressive behavior remained low one month after the program (last data point), even though no special procedures remained in effect. The effects of extinction of aggressive behavior were probably enhanced by the reinforcement program (lower portion of the figure), which increased appropriate peer interaction.

Extinction was combined with reinforcement to reduce the delusional speech of four psychiatric patients (Liberman, Teigen, Patterson, & Baker, 1973). The delusional speech included comments about being persecuted, being poisoned by the staff, being injected with monkey blood, being James Bond or an agent of the FBI, and so on. In daily individual interviews with the staff, extinction was used by having the staff simply leave the room (no longer pay attention) when delusional speech began. Each patient could also earn reinforcement that involved an evening chat with a therapist. During the chat, the patient and the therapist were in a comfortable room in which snacks were served. The amount of time earned toward the evening chat depended on how much rational (nondelusional) conversation the patient engaged in during interviews earlier that day. The effects of extinguishing irrational speech and rewarding rational speech can be seen in Figure 7–4. In a multiple-baseline design across four patients, the effects of treatment appear clear. Rational speech increased when the program was introduced.

Many other reports have shown the successful application of extinction alone or in conjunction with other procedures (particularly reinforcement).

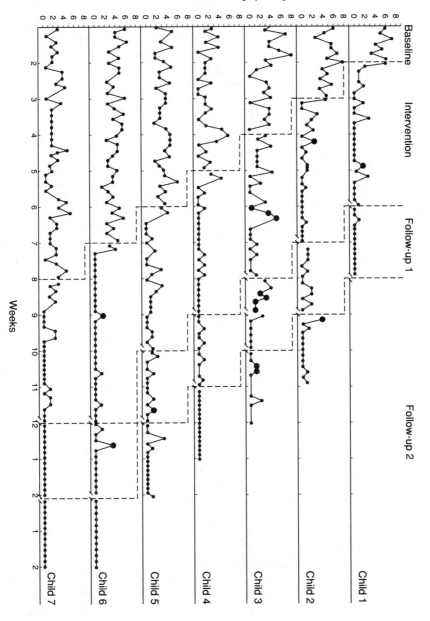

FIGURE 7-2

Frequency of night wakings per week for seven infants treated with extinction. The program was evaluated in a multiple-baseline design across infants. Follow-up 1 and Follow-up 2 represent evaluation at three months and two years after the initial intervention program, respectively. The solid, large dots denote nights in which the infant was ill.

SOURCE: France, K. G., & Hudson, S. M. (1990)

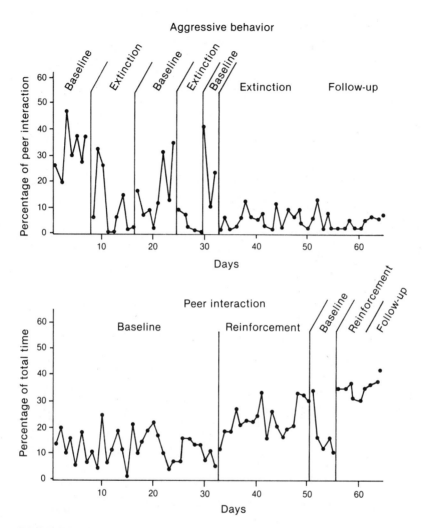

FIGURE 7–3

Subject's daily aggressive behaviors as a percentage of all peer interaction observed (top) and his daily peer interaction as a percentage of time observed (bottom).

SOURCE: Pinkston, E. M., Reese, N. M., LeBlanc, J. M., & Baer, D. M. (1973).

Hypochondriacal complaints, vomiting, obsessive comments, compulsive rituals, and excessive conversation in the classroom are among the diverse problems that have been treated with extinction and reinforcement. Such applications are particularly noteworthy because they reveal that a number of maladaptive behaviors may be maintained by their social consequences.

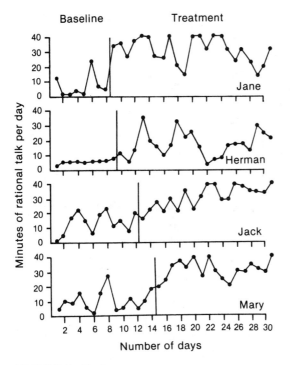

FIGURE 7–4
Duration of rational speech before onset of delusions in daily interviews during baseline and treatment (extinction and reinforcement) conditions.
SOURCE: Liberman, R. P., Teigen, J., Patterson, R., & Baker, V. (1973).

WHEN AND HOW TO USE EXTINCTION

Extinction is useful in situations in which the reinforcer that maintains behavior can be readily identified and controlled. In some situations, it is likely that only one or a few reinforcers maintain behavior. For example, parents may attend to a child's tantrum before the child goes to bed. The reinforcers for tantrums may be attention and food, if a snack is given to placate the child. In this example, the reinforcers maintaining behavior are probably limited to attention and food. Each can readily be withdrawn to test this notion. Of course, if there are other relatives in the house (for example, siblings and grandparents) who can inadvertently provide reinforcement, identifying and controlling the available reinforcers are more difficult. Another consideration in using extinction is whether the burst that may occur will be harmful to the client or to others or intolerable to the agents responsible for the client. If the above conditions for extinction can be satisfied, extinction may eliminate the target behavior, so that it is unnecessary to employ other procedures (such as punishment).

Extinction is enhanced tremendously when it is combined with positive reinforcement for behavior incompatible with the response to be extinguished. There are many reasons to combine reinforcement with extinction. First, the problems of effectively executing extinction are mitigated. Identifying and controlling reinforcement that maintains the undesirable response are less essential if other reinforcers are provided to develop desirable behavior. Second, the potential undesirable side effects of extinction and the problematic characteristics of the course of extinction are less likely to occur if reinforcement is provided for alternative responses. Providing reinforcement should prevent the side effects that result from reinforcer loss. In addition, a burst of responses and spontaneous recovery may not occur if the reinforced response replaces the extinguished response. Third, extinction may effectively decrease behavior, but it does not ensure that a desirable behavior will replace the eliminated behavior. However, reinforcement can effectively strengthen behavior. If certain undesirable behaviors are extinguished and desirable behaviors are not simultaneously reinforced, extinction may not be very effective. When extinction is terminated, the undesirable behavior is likely to return because no alternative responses have been developed and no alternative means of obtaining reinforcement have been provided. *When extinction or punishment is used, reinforcement should be delivered to develop a behavior that will replace the response to be eliminated.*

Various reinforcement procedures (for example, differential reinforcement of other behavior, of functionally equivalent responses, and so on) can be used in conjunction with extinction, as discussed in the chapter on punishment. In this regard, the reinforcer and the specific contingency used to develop behavior deserve comment. When reinforcement is used along with extinction, it is advisable to provide the same reinforcer to the client but for appropriate rather than for inappropriate behavior. Thus, if attention is the reinforcer, then the extinction procedure consists of no longer providing attention for the maladaptive or disruptive behavior. The reinforcer (attention) can still be given, but instead for appropriate or prosocial behavior. In this way, a new reinforcer (food, tokens) is not introduced; rather, an existing reinforcer can be redeployed to promote prosocial behavior. In other words, maladaptive behavior serves a function for the client, which is to obtain a particular reinforcer, such as attention or escape from an undesirable situation. A behavior that is adaptive or appropriate is more likely to develop if the positive behavior serves the same function and attains the reinforcement (see Durand & Carr, 1991; Wacker, McMahon, Steege, Berg, Sasso, & Melloy, 1990). Extinction is particularly effective when the reinforcer maintaining behavior is identified, when the connection between the behavior and that reinforcer is terminated, and when that reinforcer is deployed to follow positive, prosocial behavior.

EXTINCTION OF NEGATIVELY REINFORCED BEHAVIOR

Operant Behavior and Escape Extinction

In applied settings, extinction has been used primarily for behaviors that were previously maintained by *positive* reinforcement. No longer providing positive reinforcement (for example, parental attention) for behavior (for example, tantrums) is a common example and useful way to remember the procedure. Extinction also is used for negatively reinforced behavior. These instances refer to behaviors that are maintained because they *escape or avoid* an event or consequences. Essentially, the event or consequence serves as an aversive event to the individual. Engaging in some inappropriate behavior is reinforced by terminating the event. For example, a parent may demand that a child complete a chore (such as cleaning his or her room). The child may shout back or scream at the parent to leave him or her alone. The aversive stimulus for the child in this example is the parent's demand to perform a task. The child can escape the demand by shouting and getting the parent to stop talking and perhaps to leave the room. Child shouting (behavior) is negatively reinforced (termination of aversive condition). So far, we have merely described negative reinforcement. Extinction of negatively reinforced behavior means that the behavior occurs (shouting of the child) but does not lead to reinforcement (the parent does not stop talking or leave and the demand is not stopped). If the behavior is no longer reinforced, one would expect the behavior (shouting of the child) to decline.

In general, negative reinforcement often is more difficult to remember than positive reinforcement. Extinction of negatively reinforced responses may also seem to be a bit more complex. However, the principle of extinction is the same; no longer providing reinforcement for a response. Consider some examples of extinction of negatively reinforced behavior.

Throughout previous chapters, examples have been given of youths who engage in self-injurious behavior, such as hitting themselves or banging their heads. Several studies have conducted functional analyses of these behaviors to identify what is maintaining them. For example, in a study of children and adolescents (aged 5 to 16) already mentioned, several developmentally delayed youths engaged in self-injurious behavior (Iwata, Pace, Kalsher, Cowdery, & Cataldo, 1990). Youths were individually exposed to different conditions in brief (15 minute) sessions to see which conditions increased or decreased their self-injurious behavior. In a demand condition, the child worked on educational tasks; the "demand" was for the child to work educational tasks. The experimenter was not literally demanding, nasty, or negative—characteristics that might be connotations of "demand." In fact, praise and pats on the back were given for correct task performance. However, instances of self-injurious behavior were followed by termination of the task. If task termination is a negative reinforcer, then self-injurious behavior would increase. The results for several children showed that demand conditions in fact increased self-injury and that other conditions generally did not (playing with the child, providing attention for instances of self-injury). Having identified the reinforcer (escape from demand), the authors then used an extinction procedure in which the youths could not escape from demand with self-injurious behavior. When self-injury occurred, the task continued. The experimenter provided guidance (prompts, physical assistance) to complete the task. Self-injurious behavior decreased substantially across youths when extinction was implemented.

The procedure illustrated above is extinction because the reinforcer (escape) did not follow the inappropriate behavior. Sometimes this is referred to as *escape extinction,* and it is a useful way to remember extinction of negatively reinforced operant behavior. The reinforcer (escape) is no longer forthcoming. Several studies of self-injurious, aggressive, and disruptive behavior have shown that escape extinction alone or in combination with prompting (for example, physical guidance and assistance to complete the tasks) and positive reinforcement techniques can effectively eliminate deviant behavior (for example, Repp, Felce, & Barton, 1988; Sasso et al., 1992).

Anxiety Treatment and Outpatient Therapy

There are other uses of extinction for responses that are developed or maintained by *negative* reinforcement. These latter applications have to do with behaviors that are performed to *avoid* anticipated aversive consequences. For example, individuals who have intense fear related to heights (acrophobia) avoid high places in their everyday lives. There is a connection between heights and aversive consequences (perceived danger). Although there may be little or no real danger in many of the situations the individuals fear, certainly the anxiety or panic they experience when they approach heights or are actually in situations involving heights is a deeply felt and genuinely aversive consequence.

It is possible to extinguish responses developed or maintained through negative reinforcement. In such cases, the extinction procedures are generally used in the context of individual therapy for persons who seek treatment rather than in applied settings such as the home, the school, institutions, and the community. Nevertheless, because such procedures are widely practiced in the context of behavior therapy, it is useful to mention techniques in which the extinction of avoidance behavior is considered to be operative.

Everyday experience teaches us that avoidance behaviors such as fears and phobias are difficult to overcome. The resistance of avoidance behaviors to extinction has been demonstrated in laboratory animal research. In classic experiments, dogs were trained to avoid brief electric shocks by responding to a buzzer that preceded a shock (Solomon, Kamin, & Wynne, 1953). A dog could avoid the shock by jumping over a barrier in the middle of the compartment when the buzzer sounded. The avoidance training procedure was repeated in each side of the compartment. At the beginning of training, the dog was shocked and escaped over the barrier. In a short time, it repeatedly jumped back and forth over the barrier in response to the buzzer. Although the shock was eventually withdrawn from the situation, the avoidance response did not extinguish. The dog never remained in the situation long enough to find out that extinction (removal of shock) began.

Anxiety is presumed to play a role in the development and maintenance of avoidance responses. A previously neutral stimulus elicits anxiety and escape through classical conditioning, described earlier. Cues associated with the unconditioned aversive event can elicit the anxiety and escape response. In the case of avoidance in animals, anxiety or fear increases when the buzzer sounds because the buzzer preceded shock. Escape from the buzzer reduces fear. Thus, anxiety reduction, by termination of the unconditioned aversive event, negatively reinforces escape. Although the unconditioned aversive event (shock) no longer occurs, successful escape from the anxiety-arousing conditioned aversive event maintains avoidance behavior.

Fear and anxiety in human behavior have often been conceptualized on the basis of avoidance conditioning studied in laboratory research. With humans, it is not clear how most fears develop, as it is in animal research that specific fear reactions are induced. However, like laboratory-induced fear, human avoidance behavior is highly resistant to extinction. Fearful persons rarely place themselves in the fear-provoking situation. If they did, escape and avoidance behaviors might extinguish, as described below. Anxiety can be reduced by remaining in the provoking situation long enough to allow the conditioned anxiety to extinguish. Most people do not gain the benefit of extinction because they either do not enter into the situation they fear or only remain in it for a brief period. Thus, avoidance of or escape from the situation is reinforced by anxiety reduction.

Several techniques have been effective in extinguishing avoidance responses. One of the more widely practiced techniques is *systematic desensitization,* which was derived from a classical conditioning framework (Wolpe, 1958). As mentioned earlier, desensitization alters the valence of the conditioned stimuli so that they no longer elicit anxiety. Anxiety-eliciting conditioned stimuli are paired with nonanxiety states of the client. To achieve a nonanxiety state, the client is usually trained to relax very deeply. Relaxation is eventually paired with actually being in the anxiety-provoking situation or imagining that one is in that situation. For example, in the more commonly used variation of desensitization, the client imagines approaching only mildly provoking situations while he or she is deeply relaxed. As treatment progresses and the client has successfully associated relaxation with these situations, he or she imagines increasingly arousing situations. Eventually, the client can imagine these situations without anxiety. Stimuli that previously elicited anxiety no longer do so. Moreover, the changes in the client's anxiety responses are not restricted to images or thoughts about the situation but eventually extend to the actual situation.

Another technique often used to extinguish avoidance reactions is *flooding.* Flooding nicely illustrates the rationale for extinguishing anxiety responses because it involves exposing the client to anxiety-eliciting stimuli for prolonged periods. Like desensitization, flooding can be conducted in imagination or in the actual situations themselves. The procedure consists of exposing the client to the fear-provoking stimuli directly. For example, a client who is afraid of heights might imagine being in very high places. When the client first imagines such a situation, intense anxiety is produced. However, as he or she continues to imagine the situation for a prolonged period (several minutes or even an hour or more), anxiety decreases. Repeated presentation of the same situation is likely to evoke much less anxiety. As the situation is repeated and others are presented, anxiety is completely eliminated. The conditioned stimuli have lost their capacity to evoke anxiety.

Systematic desensitization, flooding, and related techniques have been successfully used in many programs to overcome anxiety (Barlow, 1988; Emmelkamp, 1990). Each of these techniques exposes the individual to a situation that usually is avoided and prevents or minimizes the need for an avoidance response. Avoidance behavior extinguishes because no untoward consequences actually occur in the situation, and contact with the feared stimuli is actually encouraged. Extinction of avoidance responses may occur inadvertently in the context of counseling or psychotherapy. In therapy, clients frequently express feelings and thoughts that elicit anxiety and guilt in themselves. These feelings and thoughts may be avoided at the beginning of therapy precisely because they evoke anxiety. Therapists typically respond in a permissive and nonpunitive fashion so that maladaptive emotional responses extinguish. As therapy progresses, self-reported and physiological arousal associated with anxiety-provoking topics, such as sex, may decrease over time.

Behavior therapy techniques have been effective in treating a variety of avoidance and anxiety reactions. Phobias in which specific events or situations are avoided (for example, heights, flying, open spaces), obsessions (repetitive thoughts), and compulsions (repetitive and ritualistic acts) have been successfully treated with behavioral techniques based on imaginal or real-life (in vivo) exposure. The techniques merely place persons in the situations that arouse anxiety. The situation is presented in special ways, often in conjunction with the use of other techniques for overcoming anxiety (for example, relaxation training). Many of the behavioral techniques, such as desensitization and flooding, have been quite effective.

SUMMARY AND CONCLUSION

Extinction often is an effective procedure to eliminate behavior. The effectiveness of withholding reinforcement for a response depends primarily upon the schedule of reinforcement that has been maintaining the response. Behavior maintained with highly intermittent reinforcement is particularly resistant to extinction. In practice, extinction can be difficult to implement because the source of reinforcement maintaining behavior cannot always be readily identified and controlled. Several features of extinction warrant consideration.

1. For behaviors that are dangerous (for example, self-destructive) or highly disruptive (for example, shouting and screaming), extinction is not recommended. Even if the precise reinforcer maintaining behavior has been identified (for example, through functional analysis), extinction alone may not be suitable. Because the decrease in behavior is usually gradual during extinction, a large number of responses may be performed before the undesirable behavior is eliminated. If an immediate intervention is required, extinction may be too slow to produce change.
2. Responses may increase at the beginning of extinction. If behavior is inadvertently reinforced when it becomes worse, increasingly deviant behavior may result.
3. Extinguished behaviors sometimes recover spontaneously, even though responses are not reinforced. Again, a potential problem is that inadvertent reinforcement will reinstate the behavior when spontaneous recovery occurs.
4. Extinction may be accompanied by undesirable emotional side effects such as anger or frustration. These states are not necessarily inherent in response reduction but are side effects that are likely to occur when alternate means of obtaining reinforcement are not provided. In applied settings, positive side effects have been documented as more frequent than the negative side effects. Yet, the specific side effects that emerge are not entirely predictable and hence the potential for negative side effects raises special cautions.

Although extinction can decrease or eliminate behaviors, it cannot develop new prosocial behaviors to replace those responses that have been extinguished. The most effective use of extinction is in combination with reinforcement for behaviors that are incompatible with or that will replace the undesirable behavior. In most cases, positive reinforcement for desired behavior is used. Yet, in a number of instances, negative reinforcement already in the situation is responsible for deviant behavior; altering the contingency so that prosocial behavior is reinforced is used to achieve therapeutic change. The use of reinforcement along with extinction is the most frequent use of extinction in behavior modification programs.

Apart from operant extinction, several behavioral techniques are based on extinction of anxiety-based reactions. These reactions are usually conceptualized from a classical conditioning paradigm. Systematic desensitization, flooding, and exposure-based treatments in general have been effective in the treatment of many anxiety disorders. Most of these applications are conducted individually with clients who seek outpatient therapy.

For Further Reading

Cooper, J. O., Heron, T. E., & Heward, W. L. (1987). *Applied behavior analysis.* Columbus, OH: Merrill.

Hall, R. V., & Hall, M. C. (1980). *How to use planned ignoring (extinction).* Austin, TX: Pro-Ed.

Iwata, B. A., Vollmer, T. R., & Zarcone, J. R. (1990). The experimental (functional) analysis of behavior disorders: Methodology, applications, and limitations. In A. C. Repp & N. N. Singh (Eds.), *Perspectives on the use of nonaversive and aversive interventions for persons with developmental disabilities* (pp. 301–330). Sycamore, IL: Sycamore.

CHAPTER EIGHT

SPECIAL TECHNIQUE VARIATIONS TO ENHANCE CLIENT PERFORMANCE

In previous chapters, reinforcement, punishment, and extinction procedures were discussed. By and large, the applications illustrated individual techniques such as the use of token reinforcement or time out. The illustrations showed that relatively simple and straightforward applications of the procedures are often effective in altering behavior. Actually, the procedures can be applied in a very large number of ways alone and in combination.

For several reasons, it is important to examine variations in the ways behavioral programs can be implemented. To begin with, behavioral programs are not invariably effective when they are applied or as effective as one would like them to be. For example, the behavior of a hyperactive child may improve with a token reinforcement program, but the improvement may not be great enough to make an important difference to his teachers. Similarly, in a group therapy situation, reinforcement may have increased the extent to which many of the patients participate, yet some of the patients may not have even begun to participate. Or a program may have been designed to change several behaviors but may not have succeeded in changing all of them. In such instances, it is important to be alert to variations in programs that can be implemented.

A major strength of behavioral procedures is that they lend themselves well to evaluation. The effects of a program can be readily evaluated so that one can determine when procedures are not working well. This permits altering the procedures or implementing new procedures to see whether they can produce the desired changes. In many applications, behavioral programs have not worked well initially. Often, varying the programs, perhaps by altering the magnitude or type of reinforcement or by adding procedures (for example, response cost), has led to significant increments in client performance (Kazdin, 1983). There is a host of options for improving client performance.

Another reason for considering program variations is to convey the range of options available. Different settings have different demands, often practical in nature, that need to be considered when a program is being developed. For example, at home, it may seem reasonable to instruct and train parents to provide reinforcers, such as tokens exchangeable for special privileges, for a child who is having special problems. This program must be implemented in such a way as not to have an adverse impact on their other children. For larger-scale programs, however, such as programs conducted in day camps, at industrial sites, or in entire cities, it may not be feasible to provide reinforcers based on the performance of each individual because of difficulties in monitoring individual performance or because not enough persons can be deployed to administer such reinforcers. In such circumstances, equally effective variations can be used.

The present chapter considers a number of technique variations that go beyond the variations discussed previously. These variations can be used to enhance client performance when a behavior modification program is not working well or is not working well enough to meet the goals. The present chapter also considers a number of techniques for adapting programs to special characteristics or limitations of various settings.

ENHANCING CLIENT PERFORMANCE

Although behavior modification programs have been effective, occasionally some individuals do not respond to the contingencies or respond only minimally. When a program does not appear to be working or working well, there are a number of components of the program that should be checked. In most instances, the problem stems from how the program is implemented. Features that maximize the effectiveness of a program, such as delivery of reinforcers contingent on behavior, immediately after behavior, and on as continuous a schedule as possible, are not always easy to implement or to implement consistently. Consequently, ensuring that these features are in place may be all that is needed to improve a program. Similarly, punishment programs based on time out or reprimands may not work very well initially but can usually be improved by ensuring that the reinforcement program for desirable behavior also is in effect. Prior to implementation of the contingencies, a functional analysis can be helpful in identifying factors that might be maintaining behavior. The results of the analysis would also have direct implications for ensuring the program is effective.

Assume for a moment that the initial steps of identifying reinforcers were accomplished, that the program was implemented adequately, and that behavior was changing reasonably well. There may still be a need for further techniques to enhance performance and to incorporate into the program. Several such techniques are discussed in the present chapter.

Prompting

In some cases, the client does not perform the behavior, so the target response cannot be reinforced. Although prompting and shaping have already been discussed, they warrant further consideration here because of their complexities and because of their importance and limitations in developing behavior.

Antecedents That Guide and Direct Behavior
Performance can be enhanced by increasing the use of prompts and efforts to guide behavior. Prompts, as discussed earlier, can include verbal statements, gestures, guided assistance, modeling, or other interventions to help the individual initiate the response. For example, a child may not clean up his or her room even though a reinforcement program has been put into place. Prompts to initiate the behavior might include helping the child clean the room, picking up one or two items to model the desired

behavior, gently reminding the child, or keeping the child company while he or she does it. Prompts help the individual begin or complete the response and are especially useful at the beginning of a program. Eventually, the prompts can be faded.

Parents, teachers, and others often note that they prompt behavior in everyday life and the prompts do not "work." Examples of the ineffective use of prompts are fairly common. Familiar examples include nagging children to clean up their rooms or to complete their homework. Prompts of this kind are likely to be ineffective in part because they are not associated with consequences (reinforcing) when the desired behavior occurs. Moreover, the aversiveness of repeated prompts (constant reminders) probably leads to other behaviors (side effects of aversive procedures) such as escape or avoidance, as reflected in not listening, "tuning out," leaving the situation, or staying away from the person who provides the prompts. Nevertheless, prompts can be effective in initiating and occasionally in sustaining behavior.

Instructions

Oral and written instructions are the prompts most frequently studied in applied settings and used in everyday life. Instructions can help guide performance in different ways. Instructions serve as discriminative stimuli and can tell which behaviors will and will not receive consequences, when to initiate a response, and how to complete the response. Statements about how to perform the behavior can greatly speed development of the behavior and minimize errors. For example, teaching a person to drive a car utilizes different types of prompts such as modeling (viewing others) and instructions. Instructions are especially useful in directing behavior (for example, "release the emergency break," "gently press your foot to the gas pedal").

The usual use of instructions and other prompts is to initiate behavior so the behavior can be reinforced. In this use, instructions are a part of the intervention program. Occasionally, instructions have been used in their own right as the primary basis for the intervention. A novel example of the use of instructions in this fashion was to influence cartoonists who drew well-known syndicated comic strips (Mathews & Dix, 1992). The goal was to increase the extent to which cartoonists of different strips portrayed passengers wearing seat belts when passengers were depicted. Comic strips in daily papers were examined. If passengers and cars were depicted, data were recorded regarding whether passengers were shown to be wearing seat belts. After baseline, written prompts were used in an effort to alter cartoonist behavior. The intervention consisted of a letter advocating the use of seat belts in the strips (advocacy letter). The letter was mailed after the appearance of an unbelted passenger in a particular strip, along with a copy of the strip and a statement of the desirability of seat belt use. The letter was sent from the director of a head and spinal cord injury prevention program to help underscore the importance of the issue. Comic strips were subsequently monitored to see whether there were any effect on the behavior of the cartoonists. The effects of the written instructional prompt can be seen in Figure 8–1. As shown, a multiple-baseline design was used in which the letter was introduced at different points in time among eight cartoonists. Clearly, some of the cartoonists changed their behavior (see "Cathy," "Mark Trail," "Blondie"). Yet, the effects of written instructions were not uniformly strong or consistent among cartoonists, a point to which we shall return. Even so, some changes were made.

There have been many novel applications of instructions, especially in community settings to increase use of seat belts, to conserve energy and water, to encourage recycling, and to reduce littering (for example, Geller, Winett, & Everett, 1982). Oral and written prompts have been effective in many cases, but by themselves they are inconsistent in their effects. Prompts appear to be more effective when (1) they are delivered immediately before the opportunity to engage in the desired behavior, (2) they specify the precise behaviors that are to be performed, (3) they are provided in a nondemanding and polite fashion, and (4) the prompted behaviors are followed by immediate reinforcement.

The effective use of prompts is illustrated in a community-based study to promote seat belt use (Geller, Bruff, & Nimmer, 1985). The prompts were administered by a car passenger (referred to as a "flasher"). A prompt was delivered when the flasher's car and an adjacent car pulled up at an intersection at which both cars were stopped. If the driver of the adjacent car did not have a seat belt on (as evident by an unused shoulder belt in the car), the flasher held up (flashed) a sign (11 × 14 inches) that stated "Please buckle up—I care" and depicted an almost-buckled seat belt. Conditions designed to maximize the effect of prompts were present in this situation. The prompt was closely associated with the opportunity to engage in the desired behavior (while in one's car), identified and illustrated the desired behavior (with words and a picture), and was delivered in a nondemanding fashion. If the driver buckled up after the prompt, the prompting card was turned over—the other side stated "Thank you"—to provide social reinforcement. Thus, the prompted behavior was immediately reinforced. Data on buckling were gathered by observers in the back seat of the car from which the prompts were delivered. About 21.5 percent of the prompted drivers buckled their seat belts before leaving the intersection and almost 80 percent did not. Of course those who were influenced by the prompt did not necessarily maintain the behavior. However, the point is only to note that prompts delivered in special ways can help initiate behavior.

General Comments

It is important to distinguish the varied uses of prompts in changing behavior. First, prompts such as instructions and other forms of guidance can be used to initiate behavior. In this use, prompts are *part* of a behavior change program; other aspects of the program, such as reinforcement of the prompted behavior, play a pivotal role in the program. Second, prompts

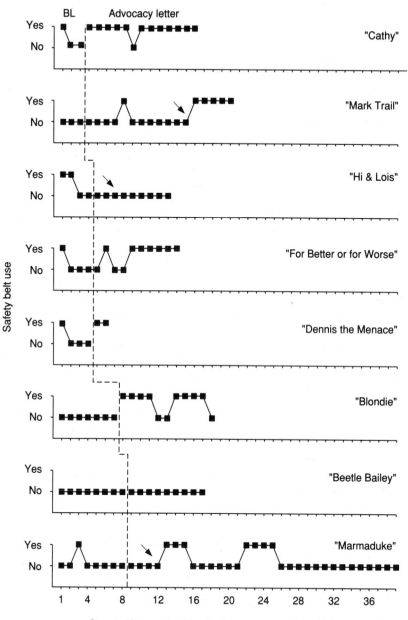

FIGURE 8–1

Seat-belt use as depicted in comic strips in which characters occupied motor vehicles. Baseline (BL) included recording how characteristics were depicted prior to the intervention. During the intervention (advocacy letter), a letter was sent to cartoonists encouraging depiction of passengers using safety belts in future cartoons. Arrows indicate the point at which a second letter was sent. The name of the cartoon is depicted to the right of individual portions of the figure.

SOURCE: Mathews, R. M., & Dix, M. (1992).

can be used as the intervention. In this use, the prompt (for example, instructions, or exposure to a model who performs the behavior) is not necessarily followed by reinforcement of the desired behavior in the client. In everyday life, instructions are often relied on in this latter way, that is, as an intervention in its own right. Commands given to people—"Do not smoke, drink, lie, cheat," "Do your chores," "Do your homework," "Just say no to drugs"—and commands codified in religious codes (for example, commandments) reflect oral or written instructions. Instructions on what and how to perform often change behavior, as illustrated by prior examples and by our experience in everyday life. Yet, prompts alone as the sole or primary basis of an intervention, without consequences for the prompted behavior, often generate weak, inconsistent, and short-lived effects.

The weak intervention effects of prompts serve as a source of frustration in everyday life. For example, in reference to another person, someone might say, "I told her (him) a thousand times and it is like talking to a wall. S(he) knows what to do, but doesn't do it." These expressions and the frustration they reflect derive in part from the fact that instructions, reminders, and explanations by themselves may not be potent. The relative ineffectiveness of such interventions is known. The frustration stems from continued beliefs that telling people what to do by itself is sufficient to change behavior. Sometimes it is; invariably, it is more effective to combine instructions and other antecedents and consequences to develop the behavior.

If behavior is not changing or is not being performed consistently in a behavior modification program, one of the first lines of attack is to examine the use of prompts. It is important to ensure that the prompts are provided and that they meet the conditions noted previously. Prompts can usually be altered, expanded upon, or provided more consistently to help initiate behavior. At the same time, it is critical to bear their limitations in mind. Prompts are designed to initiate performance. Whether performance is sustained and behavior improves depends on the consequences that follow.

Shaping

Prompting and instructions of course focus on the setting and antecedent events. Many facets of the behavior and delivery of consequences can influence and improve the effectiveness of the program. One of the initial areas to examine in enhancing the impact of the program is the behavior required for reinforcement. Often "too much behavior" or too stringent demands for behavior change are placed on the person at the beginning of a program. For example, your college roommate may not exercise at all, but, learning of your newly acquired knowledge of behavioral principles and techniques, he or she begs you to develop a behavioral program. Your roommate *can* exercise—he or she used to play tennis or jog five or six days a week. You reason that this is merely a matter of providing some incentive, because your roommate already has the necessary behaviors in his or her repertoire.

You begin the program by telling your roommate that in exchange for exercising four days a week, you will take him or her out for dinner or "happy hour" on Saturday. You know that it is critical to define "exercise" so that it can be recorded and so that the reinforcer can be delivered contingently for the behavior when it is performed. You and your roommate agree to define exercise to be *at least* 20 minutes of jogging, playing tennis, or engaging in some similar activity on which you both agree. As for the incentives, perhaps you wish to include several reinforcers, so you use a token or point economy. If your roommate exercises for four days, he or she earns 20 points. Any day of exercise over that earns 10 additional points. At the end of the week, your roommate can exchange these points for dinner (20 points) or "happy hour" (30 points) or save them toward some event that requires more points than can be accumulated in a week, such as $10 (70 points) or a ticket to a live concert (150 points). Because the cause is very worthy, you of course agree to pay for these backup events as they are earned.

There are a few potential problems with this program. The first is the amount of response (exercise) that is being required. If your roommate has not exercised at all during the previous weeks, the first task is to develop *some* exercise. An attempt to develop a lot of exercise is likely to fail. Perhaps points should be given for 10 rather than 20 minutes of exercise. As a general rule, a short response is more likely to occur than a long one. Also, a 10-minute response is closer to the baseline level (0 minutes per day) and thus is more likely to be performed. Also, the program requires at least four days of exercise to earn any reinforcers. This means that exercise for one, two, or three days in a given week will not earn points. At the beginning of a program, when the behavior is developing, reinforcers should be provided for any day of exercise.

Also, the points earned in this program are exchanged for backup events at the end of the week. Although this may be convenient from your standpoint (for example, you do not have to go out to dinner in the middle of the week), the consequences are too delayed. Behaviors performed early in the week are not associated with the backup reinforcers. It would be better to include some back up events that can be provided on a daily basis, such as doing the dishes or running errands for your roommate, in addition to the other reinforcers.[1]

If your program did not increase exercise or had short-lived effects, this would be understandable. The program may need to be revised further so that any short period of exercise is rewarded with points and so that some of the backup rewards can be bought on any given day. The revised program shapes behavior better by making the demands smaller. It increases the likelihood that the behavior will occur and that the behavior can be reinforced. After a few days of consistent exercise, longer periods of exercise or more days of exercise could be associated with special bonuses. For example, any exercise period of at least 20 minutes could receive an extra token or any week of four or more exercise days could be followed with a 20-point bonus. In this way, one can move toward the original goals. One begins a program by reinforcing behavior close to what the person already does. Program failures often result from not shaping behavior gradually and from not moving to more stringent demands only after behavior has become consistent at less stringent levels.

Response Priming

In many instances, the client readily performs the response and has often done so on recent occasions. In such instances, extensive shaping may not be required. The response merely has to be primed in some way. *Response priming refers to any procedure that initiates early steps in a sequence or chain of responses.* Prompts, such as instructions, serve a response-priming function because they initiate performance. However, response priming encompasses more than prompts. As noted earlier, any act can be broken down into a sequence or chain of responses. A difficulty with initiating a sequence of responses is that the final reinforcement (at the end of the chain) is remote. For example, a frequent difficulty with completing a term paper, writing a book, or doing a chore is merely beginning the task. Once the task is begun, the prospect of reinforcement is less remote and the sequence of the requisite behaviors is more likely to be performed.[2] Response priming consists of requiring the client to engage in the initial components of the sequence. Engaging in responses that are early in a sequence increases the probability of performing the final behaviors in the sequence.

Response priming has been used to initiate responses that otherwise have an exceedingly low frequency. For example, a priming procedure was used to increase the frequency with which residents of a nursing home engaged in various activities (McClannahan & Risley, 1975). Several of the residents were physically disabled and confined to wheelchairs or beds, some were mentally retarded, and most had medical disorders. Typically, residents remained in their rooms, did not engage in many activities, sat around the facility, and avoided social interaction. Activities were increased by making equipment and recreational materials (puzzles and games) available in the lounge. As a resident entered the lounge, he or she was given some materials, even if the materials were not requested. An activity leader demonstrated how to use the materials and provided assistance until the resident began working on them. The priming procedure led to very marked increases in the percentage of residents participating in activities. This procedure illustrates the use of response priming, because residents were encouraged to engage in the initial steps of the response—namely, to take the materials and to begin work with them. Once the behavior was begun, it continued.

Priming procedures achieve their effects by making the initial responses easier or more likely. In programs in which the target responses are performed infrequently even though they are in the repertoire of the clients, a priming procedure can be used. Even if the responses are not in the clients' repertoire of responses, the priming procedure can initiate early response components and facilitate shaping.

Reinforcer Sampling

Reinforcer sampling refers to procedures that provide a brief or small sample of the reinforcing event in order to promote greater utilization of that event. Reinforcer sampling is a special case of response priming, but it warrants discussion in its own right. The responses primed are those involving the use of a potentially reinforcing event. In reinforcement programs, it is very important that the clients utilize the available reinforcers. The more frequently the reinforcers are used, the more the clients will engage in the target behaviors required to obtain them. The utilization of a reinforcer can be viewed as a sequence of responses. If the initial responses in the sequence can be primed, the likelihood of completing the sequence is increased. To initiate the sequence, a client can engage in the initial part of, or briefly sample, the reinforcing event.

Reinforcer sampling has been used relatively infrequently despite the apparently consistent evidence attesting to its effects. In one of the first reports of the procedure, Ayllon and Azrin (1968a) used reinforcer sampling to increase the frequency with which psychiatric patients engaged in various ward activities. The activities were included in a list of backup reinforcers that could be purchased with tokens. The patients were told twice daily that they could go for a walk on the hospital grounds. Payment of tokens was required to engage in the walk. After a few days of baseline, the reinforcer-sampling procedure was implemented. Not only were walks announced but all of the patients were required to assemble outside the ward for a few minutes before deciding whether they would purchase the walk. Essentially, by being required to go outside, the patients *sampled* many of the cues and reinforcers associated with the activity (for example, outdoor sights, sounds, fresh air). While outside, the patients were asked whether they wished to go for a walk. Those who decided not to go for a walk returned to the ward. The reinforcer sampling procedure increased the utilization of walks. More walks were purchased by patients who had or had not engaged in walks during baseline. During a reversal phase, when the sampling procedure was discontinued, the frequency of walks decreased. Some patients still continued to engage in more walks than they had engaged in during baseline. In other applications, reinforcer sampling was used to increase the use of recreational and social events (Ayllon & Azrin, 1968b). In each instance, a small sample of the event was provided by entering persons in the activity for a brief period before asking them whether they wished to engage in the full activity.

In general, reinforcer sampling appears to initiate performance among individuals who previously did not engage in the event. For these individuals, reinforcer sampling provides familiarity with the reinforcer, which subsequently augments its use. Reinforcer sampling also affects individuals who are already quite familiar with the reinforcer and have utilized it on previous occasions. After reinforcer sampling is terminated, clients may continue to utilize the reinforcer to a greater extent than they did during baseline. Thus, the effects of the sample procedure are maintained.

In any situation in which it is possible to provide a small sample of a reinforcer, the sampling procedure should enhance performance. In utilizing reinforcer sampling, it is usually important to provide only a small sample of the event so as to avoid satiation. If an individual samples a large portion of the event, such as food or an activity, this may amount to noncontingent reinforcement and thus will not increase the behaviors that are required to earn the reinforcer. In applied settings, the effect of a reinforcement program may be relatively weak, in part because the "reinforcers" provide little incentive to engage in the target behaviors. If the activity that is designed to serve as a reinforcer can be made more "valuable" to the client, the likelihood of the client's engaging in the target behaviors to earn that activity is increased.

Vicarious Processes

Performance of a client can be altered by having the client observe the consequences that follow the behavior of other individuals. Individuals are more likely to engage in certain behaviors after observing others (models) receive reinforcing consequences for engaging in those behaviors. In contrast, individuals who observe models receive punishing consequences for engaging in certain behaviors are less likely to engage in those behaviors. These two processes are referred to as *vicarious reinforcement* and *vicarious punishment,* respectively.

Reinforcement
Vicarious reinforcement is readily familiar in everyday life. For example, as has been mentioned, slot machines utilize intermittent reinforcement to maintain high rates of behavior (depositing coins) with little payoff (reinforcement). Actually, the behavior is also cleverly maintained by the use of vicarious reinforcement. When playing the slot machines, one invariably sees and hears other players win. Indeed, when someone wins, the slot machine makes loud noises and flashes lights so that the consequences will be conspicuous to others. Similarly, when contests are advertised,

reports of happy previous winners are provided to help convey vicarious reinforcement and its effects.

In behavior modification, vicarious reinforcement has been studied in classrooms, the home, and various rehabilitation settings (see Kazdin, 1979a). Investigations have shown that the behavior of one person can be altered by providing reinforcing consequences to others. For example, in a class for behaviorally handicapped children, administering praise to three children for social interaction led to increases in social interaction among children who did not receive praise (Strain, Shores, & Kerr, 1976). Similarly, in another program, praising compliance with parental instructions and imposing time out for noncompliance not only altered the behavior of an uncooperative boy in his home but also improved some behaviors of the boy's brother, although these were not directly praised or punished (Resick, Forehand, & McWhorter, 1976).

Although vicarious reinforcement has been demonstrated in several studies, its effects have occasionally been weak or inconsistent. For example, persons may not respond when they see others receive reinforcing consequences; for those who do respond, the effects of vicarious reinforcement may be quite temporary (Budd & Stokes, 1977; Fantuzzo & Clement, 1981). How reinforcement is administered to the client may influence whether others show vicarious effects. For example, vicarious reinforcement effects are enhanced by delivering reinforcement in a conspicuous fashion and by providing individuals with many opportunities to see others receive reinforcing consequences (Kazdin, Silverman, & Sittler, 1975; Strain, Shores, & Kerr, 1976).

It is not entirely clear why vicarious reinforcement achieves beneficial effects. The most obvious explanation is that of modeling, in which others see a person receive reinforcing consequences for a particular behavior and then engage in that same behavior to obtain reinforcing consequences. Yet, copying a model may not account for all of the findings because the person who is responding vicariously is not always looking at or imitating the person who receives direct consequences (see Kazdin, 1973b, 1977d). For example, in a classroom, it may be that seeing or hearing the delivery of reinforcement (for example, praise) is a cue to others that the teacher is looking and might also administer reinforcement to them. Praise of one child may serve as a signal (S^D) that other children will be praised if they are behaving appropriately. Hence, children hearing praise may improve their behavior to increase the likelihood that they too will receive praise. Vicarious reinforcement may also draw attention to the specific behaviors that are desired. Delivery of the reinforcing consequences, especially when noting the target behaviors in a conspicuous fashion (for example, "Look what he did, that's great!"), may help prompt the behavior in persons who do not receive the consequences (Lancioni, 1982).

The cueing function of vicarious consequences is suggested by everyday experience. For example, when one is driving on a highway, seeing a police car and another passenger car next to the road serves as a cue to slow down. The cue suggests that one's driving is being monitored and that a similar consequence (presumably a traffic ticket) might be forthcoming.

Punishment

Vicarious punishment has been less well studied than vicarious reinforcement. Nevertheless, research suggests that when the target behavior of one person is punished, the target behavior may decrease both in that person and in other persons (Van Houten, Nau, MacKenzie-Keating, Sameoto, & Colavecchia, 1982). For example, in one study, the vicarious effects of time out from reinforcement were evaluated in a kindergarten class (Wilson, Robertson, Herlong, & Haynes, 1979). One boy with a high rate of aggressive behaviors (tripping, kicking, throwing things at others) was placed in time out for instances of these behaviors. His time out consisted of sitting for five minutes in a booth in class from which he could not see his peers. When time out was used, both the boy and his classmates showed a decrease in aggressive acts, even though his classmates never experienced time out for their aggressive behaviors.

In general, the performance of a client may be improved by providing reinforcing and/or punishing consequences to others who are engaging in the target behavior. Of course, vicarious reinforcement and punishment are not substitutes for providing direct consequences to the client. However, they can serve to prompt behaviors by signaling that these behaviors may be reinforced. Once the client has performed the behaviors, they can be reinforced directly to ensure that they are developed and sustained at high levels (Egel, Richman, & Koegel, 1981; Lancioni, 1982).

GROUP-BASED PROGRAMS

In most of the programs discussed in previous chapters, reinforcing and punishing consequences were applied to individual clients. Even when programs are conducted with groups of individuals, such as a class of students or a ward of patients, consequences are typically provided to individual clients based on their own performance. Although most programs are individualized in this sense, it is possible and often desirable to administer programs in such a way that the peer group is involved in the contingencies. Programs utilizing the peer group can be implemented in several ways (see Greenwood & Hops, 1981; Kazdin, 1977a). Three major methods of using the group are group consequences, team competition, and consequence sharing.

Group Contingencies

Group contingencies refer to programs in which the criterion for reinforcement is based on the performance of the group as a whole. The group must perform in a particular way for the reinforcing consequences to be delivered. For example, a group contingency was used to reduce stealing in three second-grade classes (Switzer, Deal, & Bailey, 1977). Students in these classes frequently stole things (money, pens, toys) from one another and from the teacher. The investigators assessed the frequency of theft by placing such items as money, magic markers, and gum around the room each day and monitoring their loss. Before initiating the group contingency, the teacher lectured the students by telling them the virtues of honesty and told them they should be "good boys and girls." Later, when the group contingency was implemented, the teacher told the students that if nothing was missing from the classroom the class as a whole could have 10 extra minutes of free time. This was a group contingency because the consequences were based on how the class as a group responded. The group contingency was introduced in a multiple-baseline design. As shown in Figure 8–2, the number of items stolen was not affected by the lecture (weak prompts) emphasizing honesty. On the other hand, whenever the group contingency was introduced into one of the classes, marked reductions in theft were obtained.

FIGURE 8–2

Number of items stolen per day in each of three second-grade classrooms.
SOURCE: Switzer, E. B., Deal, T. E., & Bailey, J. S. (1977).

A group contingency was used to reduce the shortage of cash in the register of a family-style restaurant (Marholin & Gray, 1976). Cash register receipts were carefully monitored. At the end of each day, the cash in the register was lower than the amount automatically recorded on an internal record of the register. After a baseline period of recording the shortages, a group response cost contingency was devised. If a cash shortage was equal to or greater than 1 percent of a day's cash receipts, the shortage was subtracted from the salaries of all the employees who worked at the register that day. The total shortage was simply divided by the number of individuals who worked at the register. Cash shortages were greatly reduced by this procedure, which monitored the performance of all the cashiers as a group and assessed a fine on the basis of the group's performance.

Group contingencies are obviously well suited to situations in which there is a peer group and in which there is interest in fostering similar responses in its members. The previous examples illustrate two areas in which a group contingency was useful—classroom performance and the behavior of employees in a small business. In large-scale community and work applications, group contingencies may play an especially important role. For example, in some business organizations, special incentives are provided if a group (for example, 90 percent of all employees) engages in a behavior of interest (for example, donates to a charity, attends an exercise period designed to improve health). In these situations, the interest in developing a particular behavior across many people lends itself well to group contingencies. The effectiveness of such contingencies is evaluated by charting the behavior of the group rather than the performance of one or a few individuals.

Team-Based Contingencies

Team-based contingencies represent a special type of group contingency but are worthy of separate treatment because of their effectiveness. *In a team-based contingency, a group is divided into two or more subgroups (or teams). Each subgroup functions on a separate group contingency.* As with group contingencies, an individual client can earn or lose for the group and the collective behavior of the group determines the consequences the individual receives. However, the subgroups compete against each other. The consequences are delivered to the subgroup or team with better performance. For example, Maloney and Hopkins (1973) evaluated the effect of a team contingency on the writing skills of elementary school students attending a remedial summer school session. The students were on one of two teams. They received points for writing behaviors that would improve their compositions, such as increasing the use of different adjectives, action verbs, and novel sentence beginnings. The team that earned the higher number of points (by adding the points for each of its individual members) was allowed to go to recess five minutes early and received small pieces of candy. To ensure that excellent performance was reinforced, both teams could win on a given day if their performance met a prespecified high criterion. The team contingency markedly increased the specific writing skills focused on.

Another program using a team-based contingency focused on the dental hygiene of children in a first-grade class and a second-grade class (Swain, Allard, & Holborn, 1982). The purpose of the program was to increase the cleanliness of their teeth, which was assessed by standard dental procedures measuring the amount of debris or plaque on the teeth. Before baseline, the children were taught how to brush and were provided with a dental kit (toothbrush, toothpaste, and "redcote" tablets that allowed them to detect debris). Daily observations were made on random samples of children in each of the two classes. After baseline, a team contingency was introduced by dividing each class into two teams. Each day, the team that had cleaner teeth received praise, posting of its members' names, and stickers. As shown in Figure 8–3, when the team-based contingency was introduced, the average amount of debris and plaque decreased. Moreover, nine months after the program had been terminated, an unannounced check of the children revealed that the gains had been maintained.

The above programs may have been effective independent of the division into teams because group contingencies are generally very effective. However, evidence indicates that dividing groups into teams leads to greater changes than does focusing on the group as a whole (Harris & Sherman, 1973). Thus, team competition appears to enhance the effectiveness of group contingencies.

Consequence Sharing

Another type of contingency that involves the group is consequence sharing. *With consequence sharing, the client's peers are involved because they share in the reinforcing consequences earned by the client.* The group members earn the reinforcers not for their behavior but when the target client performs certain behaviors.

Consequence sharing is particularly useful in situations in which there is a need to focus on the behavior of one or a few persons. A reinforcement system can be developed for one person, but the consequences earned can be provided to the person and his or her peers. When peers share in the consequences, they become involved with the program indirectly and can support and contribute to the client's improvement. For example, the effect of consequence sharing on the behavior of two mentally retarded elementary school children in a special education class was examined (Kazdin & Geesey, 1977). Tokens were provided for working on academic tasks and paying attention to the lesson. When a predetermined number of tokens were earned, each of the two children earned a reinforcer selected from a list of reinforcers (such as extra recess) that had been developed in advance

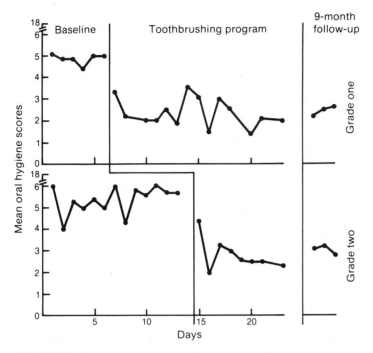

FIGURE 8–3
The effects of a team-based contingency on oral hygiene in which lower scores reflect less dental debris and plaque (that is, cleaner teeth).
SOURCE: Swain, J. J., Allard, G. B., & Holborn, S. W. (1982).

of the program. As might be expected, contingent token reinforcement improved appropriate classroom performance. However, the token program proved markedly more effective when the reinforcers earned by the two children were given to everyone in the class (consequence sharing) and not just to them.

In another example, consequence sharing was used to improve the behavior of a 50-year-old female psychiatric patient diagnosed with schizophrenia and brain damage (Feingold & Migler, 1972). The patient participated in a token economy that did not have much impact on her behavior. She engaged in little social interaction, completed her work infrequently, did not keep herself well groomed, and showed inappropriate verbal behavior. To increase her responsiveness to the program, a consequence-sharing contingency was developed in which two other patients on the ward received the same number of tokens as she earned. In an ABA design, the target patient's responsiveness to the contingencies was evaluated when she was in the program in which she earned tokens only for herself and when she was in the program in which she earned tokens for both herself and her peers. As shown in Figure 8–4, the number of tokens she earned,

FIGURE 8–4

Token earnings during baseline, consequence-sharing, and return-to-baseline phases. During baseline, the patient earned tokens only for herself. During the consequence-sharing phase, she earned tokens for her peers as well as for herself. SOURCE: Feingold, L., & Migler, B. (1972).

and hence the extent of her appropriate job and self-care behaviors, greatly increased during the consequence-sharing contingency.

Consequence sharing is a convenient way to include persons in a program who might otherwise not be included (for example, classmates, siblings, other family members). One reason that the contingency may be effective is that it increases the cooperative behavior of group members. Indeed, in a recent demonstration in a classroom setting, cooperative behaviors, such as working with and seeking help from others (friends, teachers) and working as a team, were greater among youths who were involved in a consequence-sharing contingency relative to those who were not (Williamson, Williamson, Watkins, & Hughes, 1992). Thus, consequence sharing may be particularly useful when there is interest in mobilizing the group to help develop the target behavior.

Lotteries

Another type of group program involves a lottery. A lottery *is a way of arranging reinforcement contingencies to develop specific behaviors in a group of persons.* It is a token economy in which behaviors earn tokens (tickets) that are exchangeable for backup reinforcers (the prize). In a lottery, there is usually only one backup reinforcer and not everyone earns it.

Hence, a lottery is often used to maximize the amount of behavior generated by a small number of rewards. A lottery is usually group-based in the sense that it is applied to large groups of persons. However, in a lottery, unlike the group arrangements discussed previously, each person's behavior is usually unrelated to that of others in the group.

Lotteries are a familiar technique used in everyday life to raise money. In the usual lottery, numerous tickets are sold, after which there is a drawing of one or more tickets. The persons whose tickets are drawn earn money or a prize, such as a vacation or a car. In everyday life, "buying a lottery ticket" is the behavior that makes one eligible for the prize. In behavioral programs, engaging in some specific target behavior earns a lottery ticket. Thus, a critical difference between lotteries in everyday life and in behavior modification is in the target behavior. In behavior modification, the tickets are contingent on behaviors that are designed to improve the behavioral repertoire of the client (for example, improve homework, use of seat belts).

In one application in industry, a lottery was used to reduce absenteeism (Pedalino & Gamboa, 1974). The program was conducted in a manufacturing distribution center. The intervention consisted of a lottery in which an employee who came to work on time received an opportunity to choose a card from a deck of playing cards. At the end of each week, the employee would, ideally, have five cards, which were used as a poker hand. Several of the employees with the highest poker hands received $20. The lottery reduced absenteeism whether it was administered every week or every other week.

Lotteries have been used extensively in community applications of behavioral techniques. Programs concerned with energy conservation, littering, waste recycling, and other community-relevant behaviors have used lottery-based programs. For example, in an effort to reduce the consumption of gasoline, several studies provide lottery tickets to persons who decreased the use of their cars. Reductions in mileage, as measured by odometer readings, are rewarded with tickets that are drawn at the end of the week or month to provide small prizes, money, or, in one study, a free keg of beer (see Geller, Winett, & Everett, 1982).

Lotteries are convenient ways to administer reinforcers in group settings. One advantage of lotteries is their ability to dispense relatively large rewards because few rewards are actually provided. The impact of large rewards is especially evident in state lotteries, in which millions of dollars may be provided in a single lottery drawing. That incentive leads to a great deal of behavior (ticket buying). Similarly, but perhaps less dramatically, lotteries can promote a large amount of behavior in a group with relatively few rewards. A potential problem is that such lotteries may not affect the individuals whose behavior is in the need of greatest change because they will not enter the lottery, not earn tickets for the drawing, or not receive the rewarding consequences when they do. This is not a disadvantage of lotteries per se. If the goal is to alter the behavior of particular individuals, this has to be specified in the contingency. The use of lotteries has been most frequent in cases where the primary interest is in overall group behavior. In such cases, lotteries can be adapted to individuals by combining them with other procedures. For example, individuals could be allowed to earn lottery tickets for themselves and their peers on the basis of their own behavior.

Considerations in Using Group-Based Programs

Group-based contingencies have several advantages. To begin with, they provide an extremely convenient way to implement behavior modification programs. It is easier to administer reinforcing and punishing consequences when the clients are considered as a group than when each client is focused on individually. Indeed, in many of the settings in which behavior modification programs are implemented, few persons are available to conduct individual programs. Hence, group contingencies often can be implemented more readily than individual programs can. If individualized contingencies are needed to handle special behaviors of a few clients, those contingencies can be added to the overall group program. The ease of administering group contingencies may explain why people who implement contingencies often prefer group over individualized programs.

Another advantage of group-based contingencies is that they help bring to bear peer sources of reinforcement for behavior. Peers often actively support appropriate behavior so that the group or team can earn the reinforcers. Similarly, with consequence sharing, peers may encourage appropriate behavior so that they can earn the reinforcers (Williamson, Williamson, Watkins, & Hughes, 1992). Occasionally, it has been reported that peers brought pressure to bear on other group members or clients whose performance determined their own reinforcers. For example, peers may make threatening verbalizations or gestures or may reprimand target subjects for not earning the reinforcers. More often, group contingencies have been associated with positive side effects, such as increased prompting among peers and reinforcement of one another for appropriate behavior, verbal and nonverbal gestures of friendship (for example, back patting), and helping behavior (for example, Greenwood & Hops, 1981; Kohler & Greenwood, 1990).

The interactions resulting from group-based contingencies may depend on how the program is implemented. Aversive peer interactions may be more likely to result if available reinforcers in the setting are lost when the group does not meet the criterion for performance. Reinforcers normally available in the setting should not depend on group performance because, if they do, individuals may lose events that they would normally receive when their performance is up to standard. Group consequences should include special events or extra privileges over and above what individuals would normally receive, so that reinforcers are not lost because someone else in the group or the target subject did not perform adequately.

Contingencies for the group as well as for individual members are often combined to ensure that individual performance is reinforced and to obtain the added advantages of group incentives. For example, in a program for aggressive elementary school children, selected children received praise and earned points for appropriate social behavior and lost points (response cost) for aggressive acts as part of individual contingencies (Walker, Hops, & Greenwood, 1981). The points that each of these children had left at the end of the day could be exchanged for back-up rewards that the parents agreed to provide at home. A group contingency was also in effect at school, where a special activity was earned by classmates if a child met a specific level of appropriate performance. The group contingency in this program may be especially useful in encouraging and developing appropriate social interaction among aggressive children and their peers.

In another program with group and individual contingencies, seventh-grade students received points for participating in a classroom discussion and were given bonus points for especially well-reasoned discussion statements (Smith, Schumaker, Schaeffer, & Sherman, 1982). In addition to this individual contingency, extra tokens could be earned if all of the students in a given row of seats participated in the discussion. The individual contingency increased participation, and this effect was enhanced by the addition of the group contingency.

PEER-ADMINISTERED CONTINGENCIES

The use of group-based contingencies illustrates an indirect way in which peers are involved in the behavior modification program. The contingencies structure the situation so as to increase peer investment in appropriate behavior. A more direct way to involve peers in the program is to have them administer reinforcing and punishing consequences (Foot, Morgan, & Shute, 1990; Kohler & Strain, 1990). With peer-administered contingencies, the peers serve as the behavior change agents and provide direct consequences to the target subjects.

Illustrations

Peers have been used in a variety of programs, with considerable success. For example, in one program, peers were utilized to alter disruptive behavior (noncompliance with teacher instructions, not putting away materials, running, shouting, fighting) in a kindergarten class for children with behavior problems (Smith & Fowler, 1984). Peers provided tokens to a teammate, a child with whom each was paired. Tokens were exchanged for opportunities to participate in special outdoor activities (kite flying, softball). The peers' tasks were to watch their teammates, to remind them of the appropriate behaviors, and to award tokens. The peers in charge of these responsibilities changed daily. Each day, the children who had earned the maximum number of tokens were entered into a lottery from which the names of peer monitors were drawn the next day. The results indicated that disruptive behaviors decreased with the peer-monitored token reinforcement system.

Peers have been used in the Achievement Place program for predelinquents (Phillips, Phillips, Wolf, & Fixsen, 1973). One of the boys served as a manager of his peers and delivered or fined tokens to develop room-cleaning behavior among them. The manager was responsible for ensuring that the room-cleaning behaviors were completed. He assigned the jobs and provided tokens or fines for the performance of the tasks. When the room was checked by the teaching parents in the facility, he earned or lost tokens based on how well the task had been completed. The peer-manager system of administering consequences was even more effective in obtaining high rates of room cleaning than was the system of having contingencies administered by the teaching parents.

In addition to peers, siblings have been used to alter behavior. For example, in one program, children (aged 6 to 8) were trained to increase the social interactions of their siblings with physical and mental handicaps (James & Egel, 1986). The nonhandicapped siblings were trained, using prompting and modeling, to initiate and reinforce social interactions. The training consisted of brief sessions that totaled about one to one and a half hours for each nonhandicapped child. The results, presented in Figure 8–5, show the increase in interactions as training was introduced in a multiple-baseline design across sibling pairs. The final assessment was conducted six months after the program ended and showed maintenance of the behavior.

In the above examples, peers or siblings were used to provide reinforcing consequences. Peers can also be utilized as models for appropriate behaviors and can help prompt such behaviors in others. For example, in a preschool program for "normal" children and children with mental retardation, "normal" children were used by the teacher as models to prompt appropriate use of classroom materials (Peck, Apolloni, Cooke, & Raver, 1978). During free play, the teacher drew attention to the appropriate behavior of the peer by saying to the child with mental retardation, "Look! See what he is doing? You do it." When the child with mental retardation performed the behavior, his behavior was directly reinforced with praise. Interestingly, peers can be used as models without being trained for this purpose. The teacher or other staff member can merely draw attention to the appropriate peer behavior when it occurs, conveying that such behavior will be directly reinforced if a target child models it.

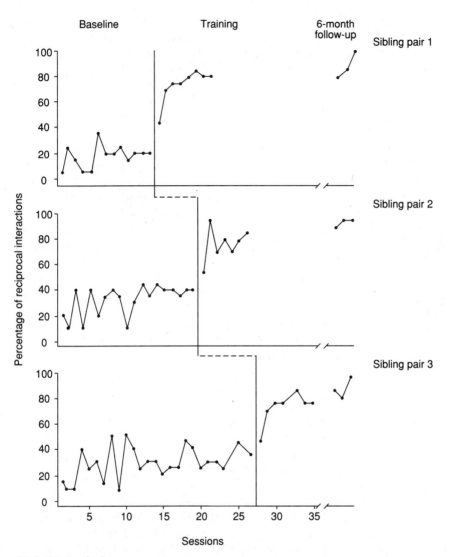

FIGURE 8–5

Positive reciprocal interactions (percentage of intervals of interactions) between handicapped and nonhandicapped siblings over the course of baseline, training, and six-month follow-up.

SOURCE: James, S. D., & Egel, A. L. (1986).

Considerations in Using Peer-Administered Contingencies

Several advantages have been reported to result from peer administration of the contingencies (Strain, 1981). To begin with, having *the opportunity to work with one's peers* is often a positive reinforcer. For example, in one program, second-grade students decreased their disruptive behavior to earn the opportunity to work with a peer tutor (from the fifth grade) on reading tasks (Robertson, DeReus, and Drabman, 1976). When opportunities to work with a peer tutor were contingent upon classroom performance, marked changes in student behavior were obtained.

A second and related advantage of peer-administered contingencies is that *the opportunity to serve as a peer behavior change agent* can itself be a reinforcer. Peers often work and pay (in tokens) for the opportunity to participate in the training of another client. For example, in one token economy with predelinquents, youths would bid for the privilege of serving as a manager in the program (Phillips, Phillips, Wolf, & Fixsen, 1973). The privilege was periodically auctioned to the highest bidder—the person who offered the highest number of tokens to purchase it.

A third advantage is that peers who serve as trainers often *improve the target behaviors* they are changing in the trainees. For example, elementary school students who serve as peer trainers and administer a reinforcement program related to prosocial classroom behavior and academic performance improve in these areas as well (Dougherty, Fowler, & Paine, 1985; Stern, Fowler, & Kohler, 1988). Similarly, peers who monitor appropriate playground behavior improve in their own interactions on the playground (Fowler, Dougherty, Kirby, & Kohler, 1986). Thus, using peers can serve an important training function for both the trainers and trainees.

A fourth advantage is the ancillary side effects on social behavior. Occasionally, peer-administered contingencies have *improved the social interaction among clients.* For example, peers who administer reinforcing consequences or participate in peer tutoring may show an increase in their social contacts or social status (McGee, Almeida, Sulzer-Azaroff, & Feldman, 1992; Pigott, Fantuzzo, & Clement, 1986). In addition, peers are evaluated more favorably by clients if they are associated with reinforcing consequences (Sanders & Glynn, 1977). Thus, utilizing peers as behavior change agents can improve aspects of the relationships among peers and target clients.

A fifth advantage is that peer-administered contingencies occasionally *facilitate maintenance and transfer of the behavior.* Behaviors developed by peers may be maintained even when the peer-administered contingencies are not in effect and may transfer to new settings after the program is terminated (for example, Stokes & Baer, 1976). When peers administer the contingencies, they may continue to exert stimulus control over the client. The client maintains the behavior in their presence.

Finally, the use of peers as behavior change agents has obvious practical advantages. Utilizing peers *enables clients to receive more individualized attention and training* than can be provided by the staff in the setting. For example, in one program, high school students served as peer trainers to provide driver education to individuals who needed remedial training in mastering information about driving skills (Bell, Young, Salzberg, & West, 1991). The use of peers as a resource permitted more individualized attention and training than would otherwise have been available. In cases where there are limited staff resources (for example, classrooms), peers may be an important resource. Given the other benefits of peer-administered contingencies, peers may be relied on even when the resource question is not at issue.

Potential disadvantages are associated with the use of peer-administered contingencies. Peers may not monitor others as well as external agents do (teachers, parents). For example, in one program, children who delivered tokens to their peers did not withhold tokens as often as they should have when performance did not meet the criteria (Smith & Fowler, 1984). This behavior occurred only on occasion. Nevertheless, it constituted reinforcing relatively poor performance or noncontingent reinforcement. In the long run, such contingencies might not produce consistent changes in behavior. However, this problem has been reported infrequently, perhaps because feedback and monitoring of peers by an external agent are usually included in a program to ensure that the contingencies are administered as intended. In general, the advantages of peer-based contingencies appear to far outweigh the possible disadvantages. Such contingencies have a variety of side effects that are favorable both to the peers who administer the program and to the recipients of their ministrations.

SUMMARY AND CONCLUSION

Numerous technique variations can be derived from the principles of reinforcement, punishment, and extinction. In the present chapter, some of these variations were illustrated. The different variations have special uses, such as aiding the program when the initial efforts to change behavior have not been effective or taking advantage of special limitations (for example, difficulties in monitoring behavior for all members in a group) or influences (for example, the availability of peers as possible aides) to change behavior.

In many behavior modification programs, a small number of persons may not respond to the contingencies or may respond minimally. Several techniques can be implemented to enhance performance. The first step that should be taken is to examine the basic features of the contingencies. The use of prompts represents an initial line of attack. Prompts are likely to initiate the responses of interest if they clearly specify the desired behavior and are provided in close proximity to opportunities to perform that behavior.

In addition to prompts, it is important to evaluate whether the demands placed on performance are too stringent as a point of departure. It is critical to consider shaping in developing behavior even if the client has shown on occasion that he or she can perform the terminal behavior. Building small early segments of the behavior and developing these segments so that they are performed consistently are an initial tactic to enhance performance.

Also discussed were response priming (to help initiate early steps in a response sequence) and reinforcer sampling (providing a sample of the reinforcing event to increase its utilization). Administering positive or negative consequences to others—referred to as vicarious reinforcement and punishment, respectively—can enhance the performance of persons who do not receive the consequences directly.

Special contingency arrangements that can enhance performance and provide many practical advantages rely on the client's peer group. Group contingencies (in which criteria met by the group serve as the basis of positive reinforcement), team-based contingencies (in which groups may compete against one another), and consequence sharing (in which clients earn consequences for themselves that are shared with others) are primary examples of group-based programs.

Peers provide a potentially valuable resource for the administration of contingencies. Peers can directly administer reinforcing consequences to alter behavior. A variety of benefits accrue from incorporating peers into the administration of reinforcement. Peers who administer reinforcing consequences often improve their own behavior in doing so.

Notes

1. In passing, there is another point to mention about the reinforcer in this example. One of the backup reinforcers is going to a "happy hour"; that is, having an opportunity to drink alcoholic beverages. The events used for backup reinforcers need to be considered. Alcohol consumption (at a "happy hour") may be reinforcing but in a given case (for example, excess drinking) may be objectionable because of the breadth of potential adverse consequences (such as an automobile accident driving home). The specific concerns of a given reinforcer or program can be circumvented with practical solutions, but the broader issue is critical here. It is important to consider consequences of the reinforcers that are used, whether they bear liabilities that are undesirable or themselves contribute to undesirable behavior. In the extreme, the point is easily seen. For example, it would be unwise to use handguns as backup reinforcers in a token economy for prisoners. Among the problems: handguns support, contribute, or increase the risk of behaviors that are undesirable.

2. The effectiveness of response priming is based on chaining, as discussed in Chapter 2. In a chain of responses, each behavior further along in the chain is closer to the final reinforcing consequence. Each response in the chain serves to reinforce the previous response and provides an S^D for subsequent responses. Thus, once the chain of responses begins, it is more likely to be completed. Response priming attempts to begin the early responses in the chain so as to start the sequence.

For Further Reading

Cooper, J. O., Heron, T. E., & Heward, W. L. (1987). *Applied behavior analysis.* Columbus, OH: Merrill.

Kazdin, A. E. (1983). Failure of persons to respond to the token economy. In E. B. Foa & P. M. G. Emmelkamp (Eds.), *Failures in behavior therapy* (pp. 335–354). New York: Wiley.

Kohler, F. W., & Strain, P. S. (1990). Peer-assisted interventions: Early promises, notable achievements, and future aspirations. *Clinical Psychology Review, 10,* 441–452.

Sulzer-Azaroff, B., & Mayer, G. R. (1991). *Behavior analysis for lasting change.* Fort Worth: Holt, Rinehart & Winston.

CHAPTER NINE

SELF-CONTROL TECHNIQUES

The principles of behavior modification describe lawful relations among various environmental conditions and behaviors. The techniques discussed previously represent instances in which one individual (the behavior change agent) manages the contingencies to alter the behavior of another individual (the client). Those techniques can also be applied by the client to control his or her own behavior. When techniques are applied to alter one's own behavior, they are referred to as *self-control* or *self-management techniques.* The present chapter discusses self-control techniques and how they are applied.

Interest in Self-Control

There are several reasons for interest in self-control techniques within behavior modification. To begin with, self-control techniques can increase the range of applications beyond those available with externally managed procedures. Some of the problems for which people seek therapy—for example, overeating, deviant sexual behavior, obsessive thoughts, and phobic responses—are not readily accessible to the therapist. In such cases, it may be important to have the client help monitor behavior and apply techniques to control behavior in the natural environment. Many of the problems for which individuals seek therapy entail covert or private events (including thoughts, images, fantasies, hallucinations, and dreams) that are not "observable" by anyone other than the individual to whom they occur. It has been suggested that covert events can be viewed as covert operant responses (referred to as *coverants*) (Homme, 1965). Perhaps covert responses, like overt behavior, can be altered by varying the consequences that follow them. Because the client is the only one who can identify the occurrence of coverants, he or she is in the best position to provide contingent consequences for them. Self-control techniques extend behavior modification procedures to events that are not observable (for example, thoughts) or are not always readily observed (for example, eating in everyday situations).

Self-control techniques are also of interest because they help overcome some of the potential limitations and disadvantages of externally administered contingencies. In virtually every behavior modification program, external agents administer the reinforcing or punishing consequences. There are potential disadvantages in relying entirely on externally administered contingencies. First, teachers, parents, and other agents usually miss a great deal of behavior when applying reinforcement. Monitoring several clients in a group situation or one client whose actions extend across many situations makes it virtually impossible to notice, not to mention reinforce, all instances of a target response. Second, the agents who administer contingencies may become a cue for performance of the target behavior because of their association with reinforcement and punishment. That behavior may be performed only in the presence of those who administer reinforcers. Third, and related to the above, the client may perform behaviors less readily in situations in which external agents are not administering reinforcement because the client can easily discriminate different contingencies across situations. Fourth, individuals sometimes perform better when, instead of having the contingencies imposed on them, they are allowed to contribute to the planning of the program or to choose the behaviors they are to perform (as in contingency contracting).

Yet another reason for interest in self-control is that the goal of behavior modification is to train individuals to control their own behavior and to achieve self-selected goals. Continuous control over a client by an external agent is not an end in itself. Whenever possible, external control is a means for achieving self-control. Self-control and external control can be viewed as opposite ends of a continuum rather than as discrete procedures. Behavior modification programs vary in the degree to which clients exert control over the contingencies and over the administration of reinforcing or punishing consequences. Self-control techniques attempt to maximize the control that individuals have over the behavior change program. Of course, external control in some form is essential to initiate the program. Therapists train clients to exert self-control by providing recommendations, strong advice, systematic praise, and feedback, all of which are external influences on client behavior. It is hoped that after training has been completed, the clients can apply techniques to themselves to alter new behaviors across different situations. When this final stage is reached, self-control has been achieved.

Self-Control in Everyday Life

People exert control over their own everyday behaviors, such as selecting courses of action, abstaining from particular excesses, adhering to various rituals intended to sustain or recover health, and acting in ways that appear to violate self-interest. In controlling their own behaviors, people use many of the techniques used to control the behaviors of others—that is, they alter the antecedent and consequence conditions.

Individuals have a variety of techniques to control their own behavior in everyday life (Skinner, 1953). First, use is made of *physical restraint,* such as clasping one's mouth to stifle a laugh, covering one's eyes to avoid seeing something, and clasping one's hands to avoid nail biting. With this technique, individuals place physical restrictions on themselves to achieve a particular end. Second, *changing the stimulus conditions* (or cues) that occasion the response is used to control behavior. For example, one lists appointments or important dates on a calendar so that these stimuli will increase the probability of engaging in certain behaviors at a later date. Third, *depriving or satiating* oneself can be used as a self-control technique. An individual may deprive himself or herself of lunch in anticipation of a special dinner or prior to participation in an athletic event. Fourth, *emotional reactions* can be altered. An individual can prevent an emotional reaction (such as laughing) by eliciting an incompatible response (such as biting one's tongue). Pleasant or unpleasant feelings can be reinstated by conjuring up emotive memories and images. Fifth, individuals use *aversive events* in the environment to control behavior. For example, setting an alarm clock ensures that an aversive event (noise) will be presented. Individuals may also make threatening statements to themselves, such as "If I don't do this, I'll be late." Sixth, *drugs, alcohol, and stimulants* may be ingested for self-control purposes. Alcohol may be consumed to alter one's mood or alleviate one's anxiety. Coffee may be consumed to increase one's alertness during studying or driving. Seventh, *self-reinforcing and self-punishing* operations are employed to control behaviors. A man may derogate himself after failing to achieve a goal or praise himself after accomplishing a feat. Finally, *doing something else* is a technique commonly used to control one's own behavior. An individual can engage in behaviors other than the one that leads to aversive consequences. For example, one can alter topics in the middle of a conversation to avoid an argument or whistle a happy tune whenever one feels afraid.

The above techniques used in everyday life allow individuals to control their own behavior. Most of the techniques operate by having individuals perform one behavior (a *controlling* response) to alter the probability of another behavior (a *controlled* response). Thus, a person may chew gum (controlling response) to reduce the likelihood of smoking cigarettes (controlled response). Similarly, a person may wear a blindfold (controlling response) in a well-lighted room to increase the likelihood of sleeping (controlled response). In self-control training, the client is taught how to control a response or to apply a particular technique. The client can then extend the procedure as needed to new situations and behaviors.

Definition of Self-Control

As a general definition, *self-control* usually refers to those behaviors that a person deliberately undertakes to achieve self-selected outcomes. The person must choose the goals and implement the procedures to achieve them. Debates have frequently emerged in defining self-control (see Brigham, 1982). It has been argued that a person can never "really" control his or her own behavior. When a person appears to be the source of control over a particular behavior, it is possible to explain that behavior on the basis of events in the person's past that have perhaps determined his or her current decision. Hence, a discussion of self-control can easily lead to the perennial debate about free will versus determinism. Yet, it is unlikely that behavior is entirely dictated by forces outside the individual's control (for example, heredity, early home environment) or that the individual acts or chooses a particular course of action entirely free from all external influences.

In behavior modification, self-control is considered to be a matter of degree rather than an all-or-none phenomenon. Behavior change procedures can readily be distinguished by the extent to which the client is in charge and bears responsibility for carrying out the program. The person can be a complete *object* of a treatment procedure that others administer (external control), or can completely design and implement treatment for himself or herself (self-control). Also, the person or external agents of change may be involved in varying degrees, so that self-control and external control both operate. *Self-control procedures in behavior modification refer primarily to techniques in which the client plays an active part and occasionally the sole part in administering treatment.*

The notion of self-control usually refers to regulating behaviors that have conflicting consequences—that is, both positive reinforcement and punishment. The reinforcing consequences that follow the behaviors may be immediate, and the punishing consequences may be delayed. Behaviors in this category include excessive consumption of food, cigarettes, alcohol, and drugs. For example, excessive eating results in immediate positive reinforcement derived from the food. However, the aversive consequences that follow overeating, such as physical discomfort, obesity, and the social ostracism attendant upon being overweight, are delayed. Alternatively, the aversive or potentially aversive consequences that follow behaviors may be immediate, and the reinforcing consequences (if present at all) may be delayed. Behaviors in this category include heroic, altruistic, and charitable acts.

Acts of self-control often appear to forgo immediate rewards for future rewards. Thus, a student may forgo the opportunity to attend a party on a Friday night, an apparent act of self-control. The student may sacrifice immediate rewards (entertainment, time with friends) for the prospect of future rewards (doing well in courses that will increase the chances of getting into graduate school). Similarly, people often undergo moderate discomfort in the present to avoid potentially greater discomfort in the future. For example, going to the dentist for cleanings, checkups, and occasional fillings may be uncomfortable in the present. But doing this reduces the chances of much greater discomfort in the distant future, when serious dental problems might otherwise warrant attention.

In the context of treatment, self-control procedures have been applied primarily to behaviors that appear to have immediate positive consequences and delayed aversive consequences. A person performs a response that counteracts or appears to counteract the effects that would be expected from external reinforcers. Thus, refusing a rich dessert after a meal appears to run counter to the expected contingencies. Of course, self-control is often invoked when simplistic accounts of behavior are proposed. Behaviors may normally be controlled by a variety of positive and aversive consequences in the present, past, and future (anticipated consequences). Simply refusing dessert may result from all sorts of influences that are not immediately apparent (pain from eating too much, previous experiences of nausea when overeating, allergic reactions to ingredients in the dessert, anticipation of not being able to get into one's clothes). In applications of self-control, the issue is not whether the individual or other events account for certain sorts of responses. Rather, the focus is on helping the individual bring to bear influences to achieve ends that he or she would like to attain.

Development of Self-Control

Self-control is assumed to reflect a set of behaviors that are learned in much the same way as other behaviors. In early development, a child's behavior is controlled by external agents such as parents and teachers, who set standards and provide consequences for performance. The standards vary for different behaviors. Some parents set high standards for musical or academic achievement but not for mechanical or social skills or household chores. Indeed, standards may vary for different-sex siblings within the same home. Positive reinforcement is provided when the child achieves the standard, whereas punishment (or lack of reward) is provided for performance below the standard. As training continues, achieving a particular standard may take on reinforcing consequences because achievement in the past was paired with external reinforcement. Conversely, the failure to achieve a standard may become aversive by being paired with punishment or lack of reward. Thus, attainment or lack of attainment of an externally or self-imposed standard may contain its own reward or punishment. Through early training, the process of setting standards and providing consequences of achievement eventually becomes independent of external consequences.

The above interpretation of how self-reinforcement and self-punishment patterns of behavior develop has received some support (see Bandura, 1977). Laboratory research has shown that patterns of standard setting and self-reinforcement can be transmitted in ways consistent with that interpretation. For example, individuals can learn to evaluate their own performance based on how others evaluate that performance. Individuals who are rewarded generously by others are more generous in rewarding themselves. Thus, one administers reinforcers to oneself consistent with the way in which others have provided reinforcement.

Modeling is also extremely important in transmitting self-control patterns. For example, children adopt standards of reinforcement that they observe in someone else (a model). If a child is exposed to a model who sets high or low standards for self-reinforcement, the child adopts similar standards for himself or herself (see Bandura, 1977). Individuals exposed to models with low achievement standards tend to reward themselves for relatively mediocre performance. The self-rewarding and self-critical statements made by a model are transmitted to and made by observers.

Self-held standards and self-administered consequences for achievement are also regulated by others in everyday interaction. For example, self-reinforcement for achieving consensually low standards of performance is not looked upon favorably. Students rarely flaunt a D grade point average, in part because the standard is consensually low. Thus, standards of performance in self-reinforcing patterns are conveyed through direct reinforcement, modeling, and social control.

TECHNIQUES OF SELF-CONTROL

Self-control patterns can be developed through behavior modification techniques to achieve specific therapeutic ends. Several of the major techniques for training people to control their own behavior can be identified. These techniques are stimulus control, self-monitoring, self-reinforcement and self-punishment, alternative response training, biofeedback, and self-help manuals.[1]

Stimulus Control

Specific behaviors are performed in the presence of specific stimuli. Eventually, the stimuli regularly associated with a behavior serve as cues and increase the probability that the behavior will be performed. Three related types of behavioral problems result from maladaptive stimulus control. First, some behaviors are under the control of stimuli that the client wishes to change. For example, cigarette smoking may be under the control of many stimuli, such as getting up in the morning, drinking coffee, talking with friends, studying, and being alone. It is cued by a variety of situations because it has been repeatedly associated with these situations. Because of these associations, the individual is likely to smoke a cigarette as situations are presented. The therapeutic goal is to eliminate the control that these stimuli exert over smoking.

Second, some behaviors are not controlled by particular stimuli when such control would be desirable. For example, students who have difficulty in studying often have no particular setting, time, or cues associated with studying. Their studying is not consistently performed in the presence of any particular stimuli. The problem is experienced as difficulty in studying at one's desk or as being easily distracted wherever one studies. The therapeutic goal is to develop stimulus control over study behavior.

Third, some behaviors are under the control of inappropriate stimuli. Sexual deviance such as exhibitionism and fetishism is included in this category. With these behaviors, sexual responses are controlled by stimuli that deviate from appropriate stimuli as determined by social standards. The goal of treatment is to alter the control that some stimuli exert over behavior.

A person who is aware of how certain stimuli control behavior can structure his or her environment to maximize the likelihood that the desired behavior will occur. For example, avoiding a bakery is one example of using stimulus control as a self-control technique. When going by a bakery window, a person unable to "control himself" may enter the bakery and purchase pastries. However, not walking by the bakery or crossing the street just before approaching the bakery can remove the sight of the tempting stimuli (pastries) in the window, so that they cannot exert their influence. Self-control can be attained in the actual tempting situation by gradually approximating the original controlling stimulus in mild doses. The individual tempted by the bakery window can pass the window when the bakery is closed, walk by the window quickly when the bakery is crowded, walk by the window while looking away, and stop by the window after eating a large meal. If the person does not enter the bakery in the presence of increasingly tempting cues, the bakery may no longer exert its influence over his or her behavior.

The use of stimulus control ordinarily requires that a therapist initially consult with the client to explain how stimulus control operates and to help the client identify events that control or fail to control his or her behavior. Actual treatment may consist of helping the client begin to perform behavior under a narrow or new set of stimuli to develop stimulus control or of helping the client to perform new behaviors under familiar stimuli to eliminate existing sources of control. For example, in early applications of stimulus control in behavioral research, clients who failed to study or who ate excessively were instructed to perform the behavior only under certain stimulus conditions (for example, studying in a special place and at a certain time of the day or eating only at the table and with a full place setting) (Fox, 1962; Goldiamond, 1965). Such procedures were designed to bring behavior under the control of specific stimuli to help increase studying when the clients were in certain situations or to decrease eating when the clients were not in specific situations ordinarily associated with eating.

Insomnia has been treated using stimulus control procedures. For whatever reason insomnia develops, it follows a familiar pattern. A person may be tired before retiring, but as soon as the person goes to bed, he or she may begin to worry about the day's activities. Thus, the stimuli usually associated with sleeping (bed, darkness, and a specific time and place) become associated with behaviors incompatible with sleeping. One adult insomniac went to bed about midnight but was unable to fall asleep until approximately 3:00 or 4:00 A.M. (Bootzin, 1972). Before sleeping, he would worry about several mundane problems and finally turn on the television. He would fall asleep while the television was still on. Treatment attempted to bring sleep under control of the stimuli associated with going to bed. The client was told to go to bed when he felt sleepy but not to read or watch television. If unable to sleep, he was to go into another room and stay up as long as he liked. When he again felt sleepy, he was to go back to bed. If he still could not sleep, he was to repeat the procedure. For the first few days of treatment, the client got up four or five times each night before going to sleep. Yet after two weeks, he no longer got up at all. When he went to bed, he stayed there and fell asleep. The client reported sleeping much better and getting much more sleep each night. During a follow-up period conducted up to two months after treatment began, the client got up during the night less than once a week. Thus, the treatment appeared to work very well.

Although stimulus control requires the therapist to explain the principles, techniques, and recommended applications, the clients themselves apply the procedures in their daily lives. Ideally, the clients can extend the use of stimulus control techniques beyond the area that served as the impetus for seeking treatment.

Self-Monitoring

Self-monitoring, or self-observation, consists of systematically observing one's own behavior. Most people are not entirely aware of the extent to which they engage in various behaviors. Habitual behaviors are automatic. People rarely observe their own behavior in a systematic fashion. However, when people are provided with the opportunity to observe their own behavior carefully, dramatic changes often occur.

The reasons that self-monitoring alters behavior are not completely understood. The information obtained through careful observation may provide important feedback about the person's level of behavior. The information conveys whether the behavior departs from a culturally or self-imposed standard of performance. If behavior departs from an acceptable level, corrective action may be initiated until the level has been met (Kanfer, 1977). For example, weighing oneself may provide information that one is overweight and initiate other actions (avoiding snacks, exercising) until the desired weight has been achieved. Thus, although self-monitoring does not itself alter weight, it initiates other behaviors that do.

Self-monitoring may be effective because the act of observation itself may take on reinforcing or punishing properties. For example, for the individual who records hours of study behavior or miles of jogging, each hour or mile tallied may provide reinforcement. Here the act of self-monitoring may operate by providing reinforcement for the behavior.

Although it is not entirely clear why self-monitoring is effective, it has been widely applied as a therapy technique (Kazdin, 1974; Nelson & Hayes, 1981). The use of self-monitoring was illustrated in a program with a 25-year-old woman who complained of obsessive thoughts about cancer of the breast and stomach (Frederiksen, 1975). She was very upset about these frequent thoughts, which appeared to become worse over a six-year period prior to treatment. She was instructed to monitor the frequency of the obsessive thoughts while at home. Keeping a daily tally of the thoughts was associated with a rapid reduction in their frequency from a high of 13 per day to about 2 per day. The woman was then instructed to monitor her thoughts in a more detailed fashion by recording the time of the thought, what she was doing at that time, the specific content of each thought, and so on. When this more detailed assessment procedure was used, her obsessive thoughts decreased further. They did not recur up to four months after treatment.

Self-monitoring has been effectively used with young children in classroom settings. For example, in one study, four learning-disabled children (aged 9 to 10) who were behind in academic areas participated in a program in which they self-monitored their classroom behavior (Harris, 1986). In one condition, they monitored whether they were paying attention (by marking yes or no on a sheet) whenever a sound was randomly emitted from a tape recorder. In another condition, they recorded and graphed the number of words they had written at the end of the work period. In general, when one of the behaviors was monitored (that is, paying attention or words written), on-task behavior and work performance improved.

Investigations have shown that self-recording behavior can influence smoking, overeating, tics, studying, nail biting, and several other behaviors. However, the effectiveness of self-observation has been inconsistent. A number of studies have shown that self-monitoring does not alter behavior; others have shown that when self-monitoring does alter behavior, the effects are transient. Consequently, self-monitoring is used infrequently as a technique in its own right. It is usually combined with such techniques as self-reinforcement and self-punishment.

Self-Reinforcement and Self-Punishment

Reinforcing and punishing consequences administered to oneself have been used rather extensively as self-control techniques (Gross & Drabman, 1982; Jones, Nelson, & Kazdin, 1977). Clients are trained to administer consequences to themselves contingent upon behavior rather than receiving consequences from an external agent. Self-reinforcement has received more attention than self-punishment has.

The major requirement of *self-reinforcement* is that the individual be free to reward himself or herself at *any time,* whether or not a particular response is performed (Skinner, 1953). The person who self-administers reinforcers must not be constrained by external pressures to perform a response or to deliver or withhold consequences. An additional requirement to qualify as reinforcement is that the behavior followed by a self-administered consequence must increase in frequency.

In most applications of self-reinforcement, two procedures can be delineated. First, the client can determine the response requirements needed for a given amount of reinforcement. The client controls when to deliver reinforcement and the amount of reinforcement to be delivered. When the client determines the criteria for reinforcement, this is referred to as *self-determined reinforcement* (Glynn, 1970). Second, the client can dispense reinforcement for achieving a particular criterion, which may or may not be self-determined. When the client administers reinforcers to himself or herself, this is referred to as *self-administered reinforcement.* Who administers the reinforcers (oneself or someone else) may not be crucial. The crucial elements are determining *when* to deliver reinforcement and for *what* behaviors. Yet, if a person is not permitted to self-administer reinforcers, there may be external agents who influence the self-reinforcement process. Self-reinforcement is probably best achieved when the client self-determines and self-administers the reinforcers. Self-reinforcement usually requires the client to observe and record his or her behavior so as to determine whether it has met a criterion. Thus, self-monitoring is an ingredient of the procedure.

Self-reinforcement has been used in several behavior programs conducted in classroom settings. For example, self-reinforcement was used to improve the story writing of elementary school children (Ballard & Glynn, 1975). The children self-recorded the number of sentences, the number of different descriptive words, and the number of different action words on a special sheet. Self-recording did not alter these behaviors. Self-reinforcement was added in which the children were told to administer one point to themselves for increases in the number of sentences they had written. The points were exchangeable for such activities as free time; access to games, art materials, and books; and public display of one's story. The number of sentences increased markedly with self-reinforcement. An extension of the self-reinforcement contingency to the other writing behaviors also showed increases. Interestingly, the quality and interest value of the stories were rated as better during the self-reinforcement phases than during baseline by two university faculty in English who were unaware of the program.

In a quite different context, self-reinforcement was used with middle-management men working for large businesses (Nakano, 1990). The focus of the intervention was on Type A behavior, which refers to a behavioral pattern characterized by impatience, competitiveness, time urgency, anger, and hostility. Type A behavior is a significant focus because the pattern has been linked to coronary disease. In the present study, assessment began by having individuals monitor several Type A behaviors (for example, eating fast, not relaxing after a meal, hurrying others to reach a point when they were speaking). During baseline, the men monitored their behavior (self-monitoring) and were told to set goals for taking more time to eat meals and to relax. Spouses of the men also assessed various behaviors related to impatience to provide a further check on the program. Self-reinforcement programs were introduced in which each individual constructed a reward menu (reinforcers they would like to earn) and set prices for each reward (as in a token economy).

As evident in Figure 9–1, the effect of self-reinforcement was examined in a multiple-baseline design across the six men. When the intervention was introduced, the amount of time the men engaged in eating and relaxing (taking more time for each) increased. Measures from the spouses showed similar changes. The results for both sets of data indicated that the positive changes were maintained at the six-week follow-up assessment. Other measures of Type A behavior and of physical health symptoms also showed improvements with treatment.

Self-punishment has been used relatively infrequently in behavior modification programs. The reasons are similar to those outlined in the previous discussion of punishment, namely, that reinforcement techniques are usually viable alternatives and are less likely to evoke undesirable side effects. Also mentioned before was the central role of positive reinforcement for appropriate behavior whenever punishment for inappropriate behavior is used. In keeping with this recommendation, self-control programs that use punishment usually incorporate positive reinforcement. For example, self-reinforcement and self-punishment were combined to control the cigarette smoking of a 65-year-old male (Belles & Bradlyn, 1987). The client lived 200 miles from the clinic, so treatment was planned over the telephone. A self-control program was devised to decrease the number of cigarettes that he smoked. This was corroborated by counts that his wife made unobtrusively. After baseline, Joe rewarded himself for smoking a reduced number of cigarettes. Specifically, for each day on which he met or fell below the criterion number of cigarettes smoked, he provided $3 to a fund for items that he wished to buy. For each day on which he exceeded the criterion, he agreed to send a personal check for $25 to a charity he disliked. To verify this procedure, the check was to be mailed to the investigator, who would then forward the contribution to the charity.

The program was implemented and evaluated in a changing-criterion design so that in many separate phases the criterion for the number of cigarettes was set progressively lower. As shown in Figure 9–2, the criterion (horizontal line) was closely approximated in each phase (B through U). When Joe reached the criterion of five cigarettes per day, he indicated that he wished to remain at that level. The level was maintained and the program was terminated. Follow-up conducted up to 18 months later indicated that smoking remained at this level, obviously well below and much safer than the rate of 80 to 100 cigarettes each day before the study and baseline (A) phase began.

Self-reinforcement and self-punishment techniques have been applied to a wide range of problems—a craving for drugs, deviant sexual behavior, cigarette smoking, inadequate dating skills, and so on. In many applications, clients do not administer an overt consequence, such as money or points. Rather, clients may *imagine* various events or consequences. Imagery-based procedures are addressed later (Chapter 10) because they encompass a variety of techniques in addition to self-reinforcement and self-punishment.

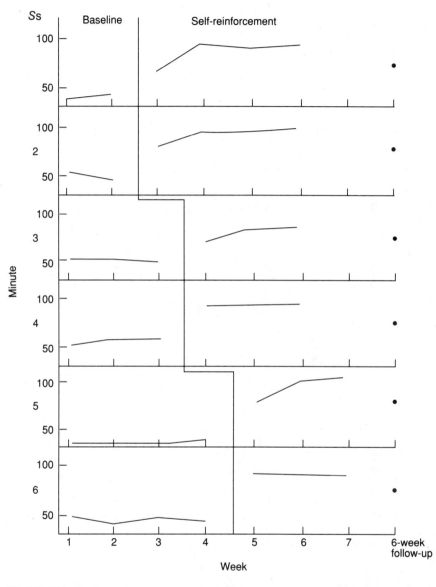

FIGURE 9–1
Amount of time spent eating and relaxing each day (averaged per week) over the course of baseline (self-monitoring and self-evaluation were included in baseline) and self-reinforcement. The effects are shown in a multiple-baseline design across six subjects (Ss). The final assessment was a six-week follow-up after the program had ended.
SOURCE: Nakano, K. (1990).

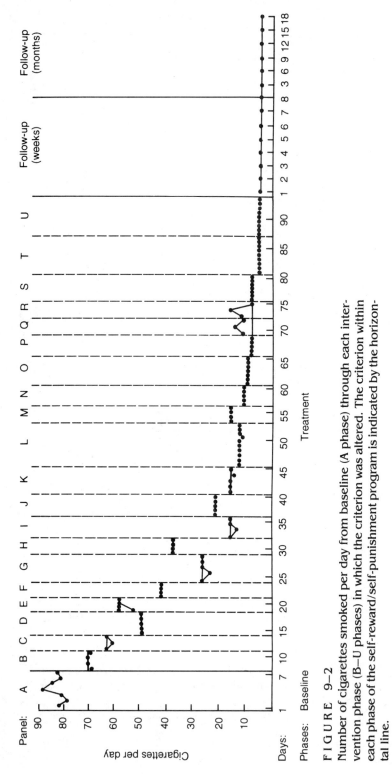

FIGURE 9–2

Number of cigarettes smoked per day from baseline (A phase) through each intervention phase (B–U phases) in which the criterion was altered. The criterion within each phase of the self-reward/self-punishment program is indicated by the horizontal line.

SOURCE: Belles, D., & Bradlyn, A. S. (1987).

Alternate Response Training

Another self-control technique is training a person to engage in responses that interfere with or replace an undesired response. Essentially, the person is trained to replace one behavior with another. Of course, to accomplish this, the person must have an alternate response in which to engage. For example, people can think pleasant thoughts to control worrying or they can relax to control tension.

The most common focus of *alternate response training* is the control of anxiety. Relaxation has been widely used as a response that is incompatible with, and therefore an alternative to, anxiety. Typically, a client is trained by a therapist to relax deeply. Many methods for achieving relaxation are available. In behavior therapy, a client is usually trained to tense and relax individual muscle groups. Alternatively tensing and relaxing helps the person discriminate different levels of muscle relaxation. Another relaxation procedure that has been used is to have the client make suggestions to himself or herself (self-instructions) of feeling warmth and heaviness in the muscles. Various forms of meditation can also be used to develop relaxation skills. Once relaxation has been learned, it can be used as a self-control technique. The person can use it to overcome anxiety in a variety of situations. Individuals have applied relaxation to themselves effectively in dealing with anxiety regarding interactions with the opposite sex, natural childbirth, public speaking, interviews, and many other problems (see Lichstein, 1988).

Relaxation training also has been used effectively to decrease headaches, from mild tension to more severe migraine headaches. As an illustration, three adults (aged 24 to 48) were treated with relaxation for headaches (Gutkin, Holborn, Walker, & Anderson, 1992). Their histories of headaches extended from six to twenty-three years. Medical evaluations ruled out the possibility that their headaches were caused by a current medical problem. The patients were seen and treated individually at the clinic. Each began by keeping a diary, a commonly used assessment strategy, in which a daily record was made of headache frequency, intensity, and duration. After weeks of baseline observation, each patient was given ten training sessions in relaxation, including tensing and contracting individual muscle groups. An audiotape of the instructions was provided to guide practice of relaxation at home. Practice at home was checked by having the patient squeeze and release a hand-control device while carrying out the tension-relaxation sequences; the procedure helped to ensure home practice. Patients could relax themselves in a very brief period (1 to 2 minutes), and were instructed to continue the procedure. Each achieved a reduction in the number of weekly headaches and an increase in the number of days free from headaches. Figure 9–3 presents the data for one of the patients. The figure shows improvement during the treatment (when relaxation training was provided) and maintenance phases (when individ-

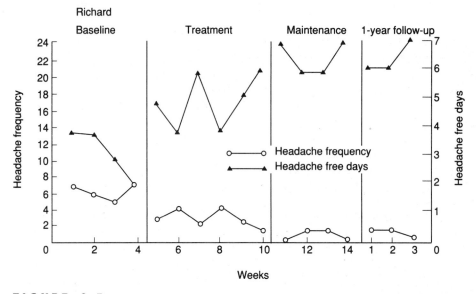

FIGURE 9–3

Headache frequency and number of headache-free days for one case (adult male) during baseline, treatment (relaxation training), maintenance (completion of training but with instructions to continue relaxation at home), and 1-year follow-up. The intervention was evaluated with three cases with staggered baselines as in a multiple-baseline design across cases, although this figure presents data for only one of the cases.

SOURCE: Gutkin, A. J., Holborn, S. W., Walker, J. R., & Anderson, B. A. (1992).

uals were instructed to continue the program on their own). Moreover, follow-up assessment one year later indicated that the gains had continued.

Varni (1981) used relaxation to treat three hemophiliac patients who suffered from severe arthritic pain.[2] The pain resulted from recurrent internal bleeding that affected the joints and caused cartilage and bone damage. Because of possible drug dependency, medication is of limited value in controlling chronic pain. To help control pain, a self-control strategy was developed in which the patients were trained to relax deeply, to engage in deep breathing while saying the word *relax* to themselves, and to imagine themselves in situations previously associated with relief of pain. The patients' reports of pain, illustrated in Figure 9–4, decreased when the self-control training was introduced. The effects were maintained from 7 to 14 months after treatment. Moreover, after treatment, the patients decreased their use of medication to control pain.

FIGURE 9–4 (*right*)

Days of arthritic pain reported per week during baseline, self-regulation training, and follow-up for each of three patients.

SOURCE: Varni, J. W. (1981).

Relaxation training is significant as an intervention for several reasons. To begin with, various procedures to induce relaxation (for example, progressive relaxation, exercises, meditation, biofeedback) have been studied in relation to a number of clinical problems and have been shown to produce change. In addition, relaxation training has been effective in altering a wide range of problems, as already noted. Perhaps relaxation is of special interest because of accumulating evidence regarding the role of stress in placing individuals at risk for physical disease and psychological dysfunction (such as depression). For example, research has suggested that relaxation training enhances the strength of the immune system and reduces the biological impact of stressors (see Kiecolt-Glaser & Glaser, 1992). Such research raises the possibility that relaxation training may affect functioning in a way that is directly related to bodily defenses against disease.

Biofeedback

Many physiological processes are directly involved in problems brought for treatment, including hypertension, headaches, epileptic seizures, muscle spasms, cardiac arrhythmias (irregular heartbeats), and anxiety. Management, reduction, and occasionally elimination of the problem can be aided by control of the processes. Indeed, various medications that are used for treatment control medical problems by interrupting the specific processes (for example, blocking transmission of neurotransmitters or chemical reactions) that directly contribute to the problem. Nonmedical procedures can also be used to alter, interrupt, or influence physiological processes that influence behavior.

Biofeedback refers to a number of intervention techniques that are designed to alter physiological processes (for example, heart rate, brainwave activity) through training. Generally, biofeedback consists of providing information to individuals about their ongoing physiological processes. The information is displayed to the client so that moment-to-moment changes in these processes can be monitored. The goal is to produce a change in the specific response influence or to control the physiological process. Several different biofeedback procedures can be distinguished, depending precisely on what physiological processes are monitored and how feedback is administered.

Biofeedback is included here as a self-control procedure because the goal of many biofeedback procedures is to teach clients specific techniques for regulating their own responses in the natural environment. For example, biofeedback may be used to control blood pressure. In treatment sessions, the client may be connected to a device that monitors blood pressure and provides visual feedback (on a TV screen or a digital counter) or auditory feedback (tone) when the blood pressure is above or below a specified criterion. The client can be instructed to decrease the blood pressure and will receive immediate feedback on the extent to which this has been successfully accomplished. Ideally, the client will learn to engage in responses (for example, pleasant thoughts, relaxation) that are effective in decreasing blood pressure. These responses, it is hoped, will be extended to everyday situations long after biofeedback training has been completed.

Biofeedback was used to control the tension headaches of a 39-year-old male who had a 16-year history of severe headaches (Epstein, Hersen, & Hemphill, 1974). A neurological examination failed to reveal organic causes of the headaches. Since research had shown that tension headaches are often associated with contraction of the frontalis (forehead) muscle, muscle relaxation of the frontalis was focused on in this case. To provide feedback, electrodes placed above the client's eyebrows were attached to an electromyograph, which measured muscle tension. The biofeedback consisted of playing music to the client (recordings of his favorite music) whenever the muscle tension was lower than a specified criterion level. He was told that the music was played whenever low levels of muscle tension occurred and that he was to try to keep the music on as much as possible. In an ABAB design, baseline sessions (no feedback) were alternated with biofeedback sessions. As shown in Figure 9–5, biofeedback reduced the client's overall muscle tension. In addition, the client reported a decrease in headaches. To ensure that the client would maintain relaxation when he returned to his normal routine, he was trained to engage in relaxation exercises that he could perform on his own after treatment. Up to a 7-month follow-up, the client reported a low incidence of headaches. Other studies have shown that electromyographic feedback of the frontalis muscles can produce general relaxation that affects responses other than headaches, such as improved respiratory flow among asthmatics, reduced blood pressure among hypertensive patients, reduced sleep latency among clients with insomnia, and reduced tension among individuals suffering from phobias or chronic anxiety (Surwit & Keefe, 1978).

In another example, biofeedback was used to help train relaxation as a means of managing stress in a 36-year-old woman with insulin-dependent diabetes (McGrady & Gerstenmaier, 1990). Control of blood glucose levels is attained through careful diet, regular exercise, and insulin injections. Diabetic patients monitor their glucose levels daily to ensure that glucose remains within a normative range. In this case, glucose levels were erratic and not completely controlled, even though the patient complied with the prescribed regimen. Several stressors were identified that might be contributing to this because it is known that stress can influence control of glucose in diabetics. Biofeedback and relaxation together were the treatments and were used in conjunction to control stress.

Treatment was provided in sessions over a 10-month period. The client was trained to engage in relaxation. Biofeedback consisted of muscle and temperature feedback while she was relaxed. Biofeedback was used by providing a tone based on muscle tension (forehead and neck) and hand temperature. Reduction of muscle tension and increases in hand temperature were the goals to reach a more relaxed state. Biofeedback was trained

FIGURE 9–5
Mean seconds per minute that contained integrated responses above the criterion microvolt level during baseline and feedback phases.
SOURCE: Epstein, L. H., Hersen, M., & Hemphill, D. P. (1974).

in the laboratory. However, as mentioned, a goal is to provide self-control strategies for clients in many applications of biofeedback. In this case, the client was encouraged to practice relaxation at home and to use a portable, hand-held thermometer to monitor her hand temperature. She was encouraged to carry out relaxation sessions whenever she was aware of increased muscle tension or a cooling of her hands. For most people, this might be difficult to detect. Indeed, one of the purposes of biofeedback is to permit improved monitoring of such states. Over the course of treatment, the blood glucose levels were monitored, given that this was the focus of initiating treatment. The results indicated that her blood glucose levels were more controlled and less variable (less frequently outside the desired range). That is, both the mean (average) and variability of blood glucose scores were positively affected. The case illustrates the use of biofeedback in training sessions and the extension of the procedures to manage stress in everyday life.

Clinical applications of biofeedback have focused on a variety of responses, including cardiac arrhythmia, tachycardia (accelerated heart rate), hypertension, muscle paralysis and inactivity, seizure activity, sexual arousal, and anxiety (see White & Tursky, 1982). Biofeedback has been provided in ways that convey muscle tension, blood pressure, skin temperature, heart rate, brain waves, blood volume, and galvanic skin responses. Although biofeedback has been successful in many reports, researchers have suggested that treatment effects can be more easily obtained with relaxation training, a technique that is easier to implement (because no equipment is required) and more readily extended to the natural environment (Lichstein, 1988). Also, relaxation training can be more readily applied to a wider range of problems because the technology for assessing various physiological processes cannot be applied to measure selected clinical problems (for example, obsessive thoughts).

Another issue has been whether the effects of feedback are sustained after training is completed. Several reports have shown that feedback does not invariably provide a technique that clients implement on their own. Nevertheless, biofeedback has often been shown to result in sustained treatment effects. However, like other self-control methods, biofeedback techniques designed to change behavior have developed to a greater extent than have the methods of ensuring that subjects apply the skills they learn in treatment to their everyday lives.

Self-Help Manuals

Many of the self-control techniques discussed to this point develop skills in clients during treatment sessions. After the skills have been developed, the clients can extend these to the environment to control their own behaviors in a variety of situations. Several self-help techniques have been developed that clients implement for themselves with minimal or no therapist assistance. The techniques have occasionally been referred to as *bibliotherapy* because the procedures are conveyed to potential clients in written form, usually as self-help books or manuals that can be purchased in stores or are made available at clinics. Bibliotherapy, or the use of self-help manuals, has been applied to an extraordinary range of problems, including fear reduction, overeating, depression, cigarette smoking, social skills, toileting accidents, sexual dysfunction, and excessive alcohol consumption (Glasgow & Rosen, 1984; Rosen, 1987). The techniques included in these manuals encompass a variety of procedures, alone and in combination. The manuals describe in a step-by-step fashion how the client should proceed to alter his or her problem.

Self-help manuals have been used in adult treatment for a variety of problems. One of the more well-investigated applications is the self-administration of systematic desensitization, a treatment designed to reduce anxiety. Rosen, Glasgow, and Barrera (1976, 1977) evaluated the extent to which clients who feared snakes could self-administer desensitization without therapist contact. Desensitization as usually practiced is administered by a therapist. The client is trained to relax deeply and to imagine situations related to the fear while relaxed. By imagining a series of situations related to the fear (such as snakes) while deeply relaxed, the client is eventually no longer anxious in the presence of the actual situations. Rosen and his colleagues provided clients with a written manual that explained how to conduct systematic desensitization. A record was included that trained clients in relaxation. Also provided were instructions to develop scenes that could be imagined and paired with relaxation. The results indicated that completely self-administered desensitization was as effective as therapist-administered desensitization on self-report, overt be-havior, and physiological measures of anxiety. Self- and therapist-administered groups were more successful than subjects who received either no treatment or a manual that simply contained information about snakes. These results were maintained up to two years of follow-up.

Self-help manuals have been effectively applied to help parents alter the behavior of their children. For example, McMahon and Forehand (1978) examined the effectiveness of a self-help brochure for parents in training appropriate mealtime behaviors in their children. Three normal preschool children from different families participated on the basis of their parents' interest in changing such inappropriate behaviors as playing with food, throwing or stealing food, and leaving the table prior to the end of the meal. An initial consultation in the parents' home explained the procedures. At this point, the parents received a brochure of two and a half pages describ-ing how to provide attention and praise for appropriate mealtime behavior and how to use time out from reinforcement (isolating the child in another room) for inappropriate behaviors that the child did not cease to engage in when asked. With only this brief description of reinforcement and time out, the parents implemented training. The results of training were evaluated by observations of actual eating behaviors in the home. The program was very effective, as shown in the multiple-baseline design across different chil-dren, plotted in Figure 9–6. The effects of the program were maintained at follow-up assessment approximately six weeks after treatment. These re-sults are impressive because of the ability of the parents to administer treatment completely on their own.

One of the most widely circulated self-help manuals was developed several years ago for parents who wish to toilet train their children quickly (Azrin & Foxx, 1974). The manual included a series of procedures based on many of the techniques that have been reviewed: prompting, positive prac-tice, reinforcement, and so on. Instructions, edible rewards, praise, feed-back, guidance, and occasional punishment (positive practice) are inter-twined to develop the child's self-initiation of toileting skills. The specific procedures on which the manual is based have been carefully researched in experimental studies in which those procedures have produced rapid re-sults. Indeed, the manual suggested that toilet training can be conducted in "less than a day" (average time about four hours). Investigations of how parents actually perform with the manual in training their children have been generally positive. Yet, evidence suggests that implementing the pro-cedures from reading the book alone is not very effective in developing toileting skills, unless someone is available to provide parents with super-vision on how to use the procedures (Matson & Ollendick, 1977).

Self-help manuals have proliferated in recent years. The manuals have important advantages. Because they can be widely disseminated, treat-ment can be provided to many individuals. This may improve the quality of life for a number of people who might not otherwise seek or receive treat-ment. Relatedly, control over one's treatment is likely to be preferred by

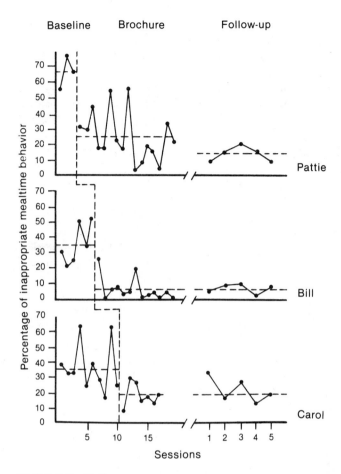

FIGURE 9–6

Percentage of intervals scored as inappropriate mealtime behavior. The broken horizontal line in each phase indicates the mean percentage of intervals scored as inappropriate mealtime behavior across sessions for that phase.

SOURCE: McMahon, R. J., & Forehand, R. (1978).

many people over other treatment options. The ease, promised simplicity, and disseminability of self-help manuals also raise a number of caveats about their use (see Rosen, 1987).

To begin, manuals often make exaggerated claims and promises about improving virtually all facets of functioning including sleep, happiness, self-esteem, marital and sexual relations, and so on. Because self-help manuals are often sold commercially, they are promoted in the usual way one would expect from advertising and marketing. That is, claims are made to boost sales, and there is no regulation of the claims. Thus, the titles of several manuals include promises for *effective, permanent,* and *rapid* change (see Rosen, 1987, for a listing).

Second, the vast majority of the self-help books and manuals are un-tested. It is simply not known whether the effects that are promised in fact can be achieved. The problem is not merely that the manuals might be ineffective, or not produce the promised result; in some cases, there might be harm. For example, dieting manuals might lead to temporary weight loss but fail to point out that repeated dieting and weight loss, or repeatedly losing and gaining weight (referred to as yo-yo dieting), can be harmful to one's health (for example, increase the risk for coronary heart disease) (see Brownell, 1991). Thus, understanding the effects of using manuals is im-portant. Manuals are likely to vary in their effectiveness and in their effects and to be differentially effective for different individuals. Research designed to address these matters is important.

Third, tests of several manuals have shown that individuals often fail to comply with manuals aimed at overcoming fears, controlling eating, or eliminating sexual dysfunction (see Rosen, 1987). That is, the manuals might be effective, but people do not in fact execute the procedures. Evi-dence suggests that some contact with a professional to help guide the use of the self-help manual is likely to be more effective than is use of the manual without such help. Thus, some data already suggest that for many problems, manuals are a useful component of treatment but perhaps insuf-ficient by themselves.

The popularity of the self-help manuals stems from the promises they often provide to the public, such as large and permanent amounts of weight loss, cessation of smoking, elimination of sexual dysfunction, and others. The appeal of self-help manuals is augmented by the rapid, inexpensive, and marvelously effective cures they suggest. They promote the equivalent of a "get-rich-quick" scheme for one's emotional and behavioral problems. Yet, as a general rule, most of the manuals remain untested and are unlikely to produce the sorts of changes the strong claims suggest.

IMPORTANT CONSIDERATIONS OF SELF-CONTROL TECHNIQUES

Who Is in Control?

To what extent do clients really control their own behavior when self-control techniques are used? These techniques vary considerably in the role they accord clients in implementing treatment. Self-help manuals provide the greatest client autonomy because, when these are used, the therapist ex-erts little or no direct influence and the clients are left on their own to carry out the procedures. Other self-control techniques, such as self-reinforcement and self-punishment, imply much greater client autonomy than often exists. Even though the clients may play a role in deciding when or how to administer consequences to themselves, many external constraints may strongly influence how the consequences are administered and for what behaviors (Gross & Wojnilower, 1984; Jones, Nelson, & Kazdin, 1977). For example, clients are often told *when* to administer consequences and *what* the standards for performance should be. The client may be told that he or she can deliver a reinforcer for *interacting socially,* for performing *correctly* on a task, or for *losing* weight. Self-reinforcement and self-punishment usually require that the client be allowed to administer or not administer the consequences at any time and for any behaviors that he or she sees fit. For reasons that are made clear below, behavior modification programs have usually placed strong constraints on clients so that they have less than complete control over the contingencies.

As has been noted, in terms of the role that clients are given in changing their behavior, self-controlled and externally controlled procedures can be viewed as opposite ends of a continuum. In most techniques, clients exert some control by being involved in selecting the problem focused on in treatment. Beyond this, clients may have some role in implementing the techniques themselves. The degree of involvement that clients can have in their own treatment is an important consideration in deciding which technique to use. Obviously, the amount of control that therapy can delegate to clients is related to such variables as client age, the type of problem focused on, and the setting in which treatment is conducted. Young children would not be expected to control their own hyperactivity with a self-help manual, and prisoners who are repeated sex offenders would not be expected to alter their behaviors by self-monitoring instances of their undesirable behaviors for a few weeks. Problems discussed below, which occasionally arise with various self-control procedures, determine in part whether the self-control technique should be applied or should be expected to accomplish the desired goal.

As a general rule, involving the client in treatment probably is advisable whenever possible. Evidence suggests that clients often prefer techniques that they help design or implement (Kazdin, 1980a). Also, in the case of self-reinforcement, clients occasionally perform better when they dictate the criteria for reinforcement or administer the rewards than when others administer the contingencies (Dickerson & Creedon, 1981). The importance of involving clients was evident in a report on the exercise programs of burn victims (Hegel, Ayllon, VanderPlate, & Spiro-Hawkins, 1986). Exercise is critical among burn patients because it prevents skin from contracting over the joints during healing and thus severely limiting the mobility of muscles and joints. The necessary exercise is often stressful and painful. In this successful project, patients engaged in a self-exercise regimen as an alternative to engaging in a program administered by the hospital staff.

Other advantages of involving clients in their behavior modification program are that this may help ensure that the gains achieved are maintained over time and extended to a variety of situations in the client's life. The effects of treatment might be enhanced by training clients to analyze

the environmental influences that will arise and to implement specific procedures that will sustain performance. Hence, self-control may be useful in
maintaining behaviors once change has been achieved (see Chapter 11).

Adherence to Treatment

An issue that arises in any treatment technique is the extent to which clients
will adhere to or carry out the procedures. Self-reinforcement and self-
punishment techniques have led to problems in adherence. If an individual
is completely free to deliver rewarding or punishing consequences for
behavior, will those consequences be administered contingently? The natural contingencies (that is, the contingencies normally fostered by the
environment) may discourage adherence to self-reinforcement and self-
punishment contingencies. For example, if a client does not meet a self-
imposed performance criterion for self-reward (such as studying for two
hours), he or she can still self-administer the reward (such as going out with
friends). If the standards for self-reinforcement are lowered, no immediate
penalty will result from an external agent. Essentially, the client might be
rewarded for ignoring the performance standard and the entire self-
reinforcement contingency. Thus, noncontingent reinforcement and suspension of the contingencies are probably much more likely in self-control
programs than in externally managed programs.

In many self-reinforcement studies, the contingencies have not been
consistently adhered to over time. For example, in one study, self-
reinforcement was used to develop the study skills of college students with
low grades (McReynolds & Church, 1973). The students devised "self-
contracts" in which they specified small response requirements (for example, study for a few minutes each day) to acquire reinforcers (for example,
cigarettes or attending a sports event). A new contract was drawn up at the
end of a few days as behavior met the previously specified criteria. Despite
the fact that the students devised the response criteria themselves—or
perhaps because of it—many of them rewarded themselves even though
they had not met the requirements for the behavioral contract. These
students did not adhere to the contingencies; hence, behavior change
should not have been expected.

Self-reinforcement has been most extensively used in classroom settings, where students are permitted to provide reinforcing consequences to
themselves for studying and paying attention to the lesson. When students
are allowed to determine the number of reinforcers or to decide when they
have earned a given number of reinforcers, their standards often diminish.
Children become increasingly lenient over time and eventually provide
reinforcing consequences to themselves for relatively disruptive behavior
(see Gross & Drabman, 1982).

In self-reinforcement and self-punishment programs, several procedures have been used to decrease noncontingent or lenient administration

of consequences. Such programs usually begin with external reinforcement (by a teacher or parent) to identify the behaviors that should be self-rewarded. This initial phase of externally managed contingencies increases the likelihood that the person will self-administer reinforcement contingently later (O'Brien, Riner, & Budd, 1983). During the self-reinforcement phase, other procedures have been employed to maintain contingent administration of consequences. For example, in classroom programs, external reinforcers are provided by explicitly instructing the children to give themselves rewards only when they have met stringent criteria or by checking the children to see whether they self-reward correctly and threatening punishment if they do not (for example, Hundert & Bastone, 1978; Robertson, Simon, Pachman, & Drabman, 1979). Although student behavior is effectively controlled by providing externally controlled reinforcing or punishing events or by setting the standards for self-reward, the use of such procedures challenges the notion of *self*-control.

Delivering aversive events to oneself also introduces the problem of leniency. As mentioned earlier, an aversive event administered by an external agent may result in escape or avoidance. There is no reason to believe that this will not happen if aversive events are self-administered. Individuals may avoid applying an aversive event to themselves in one of two ways: by not performing the undesirable behavior or by simply performing the behavior but not applying the aversive event afterward. Programs using self-administered punishment have reported that clients do not administer the consequences to themselves as they should (James, 1981; Wilson, Leaf, & Nathan, 1975). Hence, it is not likely that clients will widely adhere to self-punishment alone.

With both self-reinforcement and self-punishment, clients may discontinue the contingency at any time because it is under their control. If a client suspends the contingency, even temporarily, that behavior will be reinforced (obtain the positive reinforcer or avoid the aversive event). Hence, a concern with self-control procedures is what will maintain adherence to the contingency. It is hoped that the delayed reinforcing consequences or intended goal of the program (for example, losing weight) will sustain self-control. However, everyday experience suggests that delayed consequences are not sufficient to maintain adherence to self-imposed contingencies. More often than not, individuals appear to go off diets, resume cigarette smoking, or give up some other contingency that they originally designed. It may be essential to provide individuals with some external reinforcement (perhaps delivered by friend, relative, or spouse) for adherence to the "self-control" contingency. Gradually, external reinforcement might be delivered intermittently and then eliminated altogether. External influences may be critical to the effects of self-reinforcement in other ways. Setting goals publicly (so that others know about them) has been shown to be important in obtaining behavior change in self-reinforcement programs (Hayes et al., 1985). When the contingencies are known to others, social consequences may implicitly serve as an external influence by ensuring that the self-reinforcement program is conducted as intended.

Adherence to treatment has been somewhat of a problem when clients are given self-help manuals and left to their own devices to implement treatment. First, persons left entirely on their own to conduct treatment have relatively high rates of attrition (dropping out of treatment), a finding shown in self-help training for such problems as anxiety associated with public speaking, fears, and sexual dysfunction (Marshall, Presse, & Andrews, 1976; Rosen, Glasgow, & Barrera, 1976; Zeiss, 1978). Second, clients who stay in treatment often do not carry out the required procedures when they are left on their own with a self-help manual. For example, investigators have reported that 50 percent or more of the clients who used a self-help manual for the treatment of anxiety failed to complete the procedures that they were instructed to perform (Marshall, Presse, & Andrews, 1976; Rosen, Glasgow, & Barrera, 1976). In a study on the treatment of problem drinkers, approximately one-third of the clients said that they had not even read the self-help manual that was used to help maintain treatment gains (Miller, 1977, Exp. 2). For many problems and clients, self-control may provide an adjunct to treatment; however, therapist contact or supervision may be necessary to ensure that the program is carried out. Indeed, research has suggested that reading the materials in a self-help manual and carrying out the prescribed activities are enhanced by contact with a therapist (Glasgow & Rosen, 1984; Holroyd, 1986). At this point, research has not determined which problems or clients are most likely to benefit from self-control strategies and what level of involvement of therapists or other external agents is required to maximize behavior change.

USE OF SELF-CONTROL PROCEDURES

Self-control procedures have been applied to diverse populations, including children and adolescents in classroom settings; inpatient and outpatient clients treated for anxiety, overeating, and alcohol consumption; and parents interested in altering a variety of their children's behaviors at home. Several advantages accrue from the development of self-control procedures. First, such procedures permit various techniques to be more widely extended to the public than would ordinarily be the case with techniques completely carried out by trained professional therapists. In self-control techniques such as stimulus control, self-monitoring, and alternate response training, clients have initial contact with a therapist but carry out the procedures on their own. The initial contact means that little professional time and client expense are involved in beginning and carrying out treatment. With self-help manuals, the potential for widespread dissemination of treatment is even greater than with other self-control techniques. If readers carry out behavior modification techniques presented in manuals, a large number of people might be reached who ordinarily would not even seek treatment.

A second advantage of self-control procedures is that they may be preferred by clients over a therapist-administered treatment. People may prefer implementing a treatment on their own because self-administered treatment may be less expensive and more efficient and because it enables them to play a more direct role in their own treatment. Many clients might be more apt to undergo treatment if they could self-administer the procedures. For example, a Gallup opinion survey indicated that only about 34 percent of cigarette smokers would come for treatment at a clinic and that most cigarette smokers preferred self-help methods (Glasgow & Rosen, 1984). The preference for self-help procedures may extend to a variety of problems.

The application of self-control techniques raises important questions that remain to be resolved. To begin with, the range of clients for whom self-control procedures can be applied has not been elaborated. Perhaps self-control techniques are readily applied to clients who already have enough control to initiate them. Many of the self-control procedures have been carried out on an adult outpatient basis. Inpatient populations, such as developmentally disabled persons, psychiatric patients, delinquents, and prisoners, warrant further study in relation to self-control. For many of these groups, treatment is not self-initiated but imposed by the agency or setting. This may reduce the incentives to carry out self-control procedures.

The range of problems for which self-control procedures are effective needs to be evaluated. Currently, applications of self-control procedures encompass a variety of problems, including anxiety, depression, sexual dysfunction, overeating, cigarette smoking, alcohol abuse, and the management of diseases (Holroyd & Creer, 1986; Karoly & Kanfer, 1982). The extent to which various problem areas are amenable to self-control training remains to be researched.

Self-control techniques vary in the extent to which the therapist or some other external agent plays a role in treatment. Contact with the therapist may be important to ensure that treatment is conducted properly, to provide encouragement when problems arise or when the client begins to discontinue the procedures, and to help decide when other procedures should be tried. The role of therapist contact in various self-control procedures needs to be evaluated further.

Although many questions about self-control remain to be resolved, its accomplishments have already been impressive. The available techniques provide clients with a number of alternative means so that they can implement treatment for themselves. Although techniques for controlling one's own behavior have been advocated throughout the history of psychotherapy, only recently have such techniques been evaluated experimentally to establish their effectiveness. The results have demonstrated that for many applications various procedures can help people gain control over their own behavior.

Summary and Conclusion

Self-control refers to the behaviors that an individual deliberately undertakes to achieve self-selected outcomes. Behavioral techniques are applied by the individual rather than by an external agent. Several self-control techniques are discussed. *Stimulus control* allows individuals to control their own behavior by altering environmental and situational events that serve as cues for behavior. *Self-monitoring* requires that individuals keep a careful record of the target response. Merely observing one's own behavior often leads to a systematic change. *Self-reinforcement* and *self-punishment* require that individuals apply certain events to themselves following behavior. The crucial aspect of self-reinforcement or self-punishment is the freedom to partake of the reinforcer or to not apply the punishing event.

Alternate response training requires that a client engage in a response that interferes with or replaces the response that the client wishes to control. *Biofeedback* procedures provide information to clients about their physiological processes. Ideally, clients can learn to control the bodily processes related to the problem for which they sought change. *Self-help manuals* comprise a variety of techniques that have in common the manner in which they are presented to clients. Clients receive written material in brochure or book form that conveys how they are to conduct treatment for themselves. They can use this material to conduct treatment on their own with minimal or no contact with a therapist or consultant.

In many of the self-control techniques, some preliminary training may be needed to convey both the principle behind a technique and the requirements for effective application. Once the basic principle is understood and the initial training has been completed, the client can implement the treatment intervention and determine the range of behaviors or situations to which it will be applied.

Three major issues pertaining to self-control techniques were discussed. First, in some applications, questions can be raised about the extent to which the client is permitted to self-control. Some of the self-control techniques are embedded in strong external contingencies from a therapist or other agent. Other self-control techniques, such as self-help manuals, often give the client complete autonomy. Second, adherence to treatment has been an issue in various self-control techniques. Clients often do not carry out the procedures on their own, and the contingencies may deteriorate over time. Also, many clients drop out of some self-control programs, and the result may be a lower success rate than might be achieved with therapist-administered treatment.

Finally, self-control techniques have advantages that argue for their use. The techniques allow for widespread extension of treatment to the public in ways that cannot be readily accomplished with traditional therapist-administered treatment. The costs of treatment are minimal, as in the case of self-help manuals. Contact with a therapist, if any, is brief as well. In addition, clients often prefer to have a role in their own treatment; self-control techniques foster direct involvement and application of treatment that may increase adherence to the procedures as well as their effectiveness.

Notes

1. There are other self-control techniques that cannot be treated here. Additional sources, noted below, detail the full range of self-control techniques.
2. Hemophilia is an inherited disorder of blood coagulation in which there is frequent and difficult-to-control bleeding.

For Further Reading

Holroyd, K. A., & Creer, T. L. (Eds.). (1986). *Self-management of chronic disease: Handbook of clinical interventions and research.* New York: Academic Press.

Karoly, P., & Kanfer, F. H. (Eds.). (1982). *Self management and behavior change: From theory to practice.* New York: Pergamon Press.

Lichstein, K. L. (1988). *Clinical relaxation strategies.* New York: Wiley.

Rosen, G. M. (1987). Self-help treatment books and the commercialization of psychotherapy. *American Psychologist, 42,* 46–51.

Watson, D. L., & Tharp, R. G. (1992). *Self-directed behavior: Self-modification for personal adjustment* (6th ed.). Pacific Grove, CA: Brooks/Cole.

CHAPTER TEN

COGNITIVELY BASED TREATMENT

Cognitively based techniques are a family of procedures that adhere to the general notion that behavior change can be achieved by altering cognitive processes. The *cognitive processes* that serve as the focus of treatment include perceptions, self-statements, attributions, expectations, beliefs, and images. The assumptions underlying cognitively based techniques are that maladaptive cognitive processes lead to maladaptive behaviors and that changing these processes can lead to behavior change.

Previous chapters have emphasized the importance of environmental changes and how individuals respond to these changes. For example, *positive reinforcement* and *punishment* refer largely to external events that are applied to individuals to influence their behavior. Consideration of cognitive processes is a significant addition to treatment approaches because these processes emphasize how the individual perceives the environment. How the environment is perceived can greatly influence the impact of environmental events.

Everyday experience conveys the obvious impact of perceptions. For example, two persons riding a roller coaster may react quite differently, in part because of the different ways in which they perceive the experience. For both persons, the physical characteristics of the ride itself—the "environmental factors"—are essentially the same. Yet, one of them may believe that the ride is dangerous and life threatening and feel extremely anxious, whereas the other may believe that the ride is safe and feel excited and exhilarated. During the ride itself, the former may say to himself or herself that something horrible might happen any minute, whereas the latter may say to himself or herself that the ride is wonderful and exciting. The ride can have a different impact on the two persons because of the differences in their perceptions, beliefs, and self-statements.

Differences in perceptions are not to be regarded lightly. The arousal, stress, anxiety, dread, and other biological and psychological signs of these two persons may be dramatically different. Moreover, the events are not just different "in their minds." Their perceptions can have a direct impact on the safety of the experience. The person who views the experience as entirely free from risk might become careless and not take advisable safety precautions. This might increase the risk of injury. The person who views the experience as dangerous might consume alcohol or tranquilizers and thus be unresponsive if an untoward eventuality occurred. Perceptions are significant not only in their own right but also through their influence on behavior.

The interrelationships among cognitive processes, environmental events, and behavior are perhaps more clearly conveyed in the context of social behavior. For example, a person who believes that other people are very friendly may initiate social responses (greetings, conversations) with acquaintances and strangers. The belief (cognitive process) leads to greeting and chatting with others (behavior), which in turn generate environmental consequences (attention, praise, and other sources of reinforcement from others). These consequences are likely to affect the person's perceptions and behaviors in the future. This small-scale example conveys how cognitive processes and environmental events mutually influence each other.

INTEREST IN COGNITIVE PROCESSES

Interest in cognitive processes as behavior change procedures can be traced to many influences in both basic and clinical research. Basic research in developmental psychology has been especially significant—in particular, research within psychology. Core areas of psychological research focus on cognitive processes and how they influence perception, motivation, learning, attitude formation, and social interaction. Basic research in developmental psychology illustrates the broad interest in cognitive processes. Research in developmental psychology focuses on such topics as how cognitive processes and language emerge in childhood and on how language affects behavior. It has been shown that early in childhood children often talk out loud to describe what they are doing and to regulate or influence their own actions (Zivin, 1979). This can be observed in situations in which children seem to be narrating what they are doing as they play with toys or dolls and engage them in various activities. Over the course of development, speech becomes internalized and private, so that adults have private thoughts before or during their actions. Private speech can be observed by having children and adults say out loud what they are thinking or by having them answer questions about what they are thinking as they engage in various activities. Theory and research in child development have elaborated the emergence and importance of cognitive processes over the course of childhood (for example, Kohlberg, Yaeger, & Hjerthuim, 1968; Piaget, 1928).

Cognitive processes have been shown to relate to a number of clinical disorders, including depression, schizophrenia, anxiety, and others (for example, Stein & Young, 1992). As an example, consider depression, a disorder characterized by sadness, lack of interest in activities, and often other symptoms such as disturbances of sleep and eating. Several cognitive attributional processes are associated with depression. For example, depressed individuals tend to view themselves as failures, to see their world as filled with loss, to feel pessimistic and hopeless about the future, and to attribute stressful events and negative occurrences to their own actions (see Alloy, 1988). These beliefs are related to the various symptoms of depression as well as to reduced interactions with others and a lack of interest in activities. Suicidal thoughts or attempts, which are often associated with depression, have been identified with even more specific beliefs. In both children and adults the belief that the future is hopeless, more than other characteristics of depression (such as sadness) and more than the severity of depression, is related to suicide ideation, attempt, and completion (Beck, Kovacs, & Weissman, 1975; Kazdin, French, Unis, Esveldt-Dawson,

& Sherick, 1983). Many forms of psychotherapy and medication are available for depressed persons. One effective treatment, referred to as *cognitive therapy,* focuses directly on altering the belief system of depressed persons (Beck, Rush, Shaw, & Emery, 1979).

Many other clinical problems appear to have important cognitive features that may lead to maladaptive behavior. For example, aggressive children appear to have a predisposition to perceive their interpersonal environment in ways that help promote their aggressive reactions. Such children often perceive as hostile ambiguous social situations in which the intent of others is not clear (Dodge, 1993). Thus, if an aggressive child is accidentally bumped in the hall while walking to class, he is more likely than a nonaggressive child to see this as an act of aggression. Understandably, when such situations are perceived as hostile, the child is more likely to respond aggressively. A number of other cognitive processes have been shown to relate to aggressive behavior (Kazdin, 1985b), and some of these will be illustrated in the discussion of specific techniques later in the chapter.

Most cognitively based techniques are applied in the context of psychotherapy sessions in which children, adolescents, or adults are seen individually or in a group by professional therapists. Treatment focuses on specific processes that are designed to alter behavior. This context is different from that of applied settings where contingencies in the environment are managed by parents, teachers, hospital staff, peers, or others directly in the situations in which problem behaviors have emerged. However, it is not easy to delineate clearly how and by whom cognitively based techniques are administered. These techniques are often used as self-control procedures in which individuals learn a particular technique that they can apply as needed to situations in everyday life. Also, in many applications, parents and teachers have been trained to help children at home and at school. For example, cognitively based treatments are sometimes used in school classrooms as a method of preventing dysfunctional behavior and promoting prosocial competence (Weissberg, Caplan, & Harwood, 1991). Finally, cognitively based techniques are often used in combination with reinforcement and punishment techniques in applied settings. Selected applications of cognitively based techniques are also illustrated in the present chapter.

ILLUSTRATIVE TECHNIQUES
Imagery-Based Exposure Treatments

Early in the development of behavior modification, systematic desensitization and flooding were procedures developed for the treatment of anxiety. These treatments have been mentioned previously, but it is worthwhile to reintroduce them because variations of the procedures rely on imagery. As such, they might be considered as cognitively based treatments. Systematic desensitization and flooding are procedures that expose the individual to stimuli that provoke anxiety. For example, a person who fears high places (acrophobia) might be exposed to varied situations that evoked anxiety. Images of looking up at a skyscraper, climbing stairs, going up in an elevator, looking down from a skyscraper, and so on might evoke anxiety. Images of these events can be used in treatment.

The work of Joseph Wolpe (1958) is particularly noteworthy because of the development of *systematic desensitization* as a treatment for anxiety. As mentioned earlier, systematic desensitization consists of training someone to be deeply relaxed and pairing relaxation with exposure to the situations that evoke anxiety. The situations can be presented in imagery or the person can approach these with the therapist in real life. The characteristic of desensitization is to approach these anxiety situations gradually, beginning with those that evoke little or no anxiety. As these can be imagined or approached in everyday life, situations that provoke more anxiety are presented. All of the situations are imagined while the person is deeply relaxed. Repeated images of the situations while relaxed reduces and can eventually eliminate the anxiety that the situations evoke. At the end of treatment, those situations that evoked the greatest anxiety can be approached with little or no anxiety.

In *flooding*, the client is not trained to engage in relaxation. Also, only the most anxiety-provoking situations are presented. The idea, as discussed earlier, is to evoke anxiety and to keep the situation present so that the person habituates to it. The situation, when presented repeatedly, eventually loses its ability to evoke anxiety. In our hypothetical example with fear of heights, the client might imagine looking down from a skyscraper or actually do this (in real life) for several minutes or hours until anxiety (physiological arousal, behavioral signs of anxiety, reported distress) subsides. Repeated exposure in this way diminishes anxiety.

In general, desensitization and flooding represent exposure-based treatment methods. They can be conducted by having individuals imagine the anxiety-provoking situations or by exposing individuals to the actual situations themselves. Exposure to the actual situations, referred to as in vivo treatment (for example, in vivo desensitization) tends to be more effective than exposure in imagery. In clinical practice, sometimes imagery is used in the treatment sessions and clients are given practice assignments where they approach actual situations in everyday life. The advantage of imagery is the ease of presenting a wide range of situations and controlling the presentation of these situations.

For example, an *imagery-based flooding procedure* was used to treat Joseph, a 6½-year-old boy, who suffered from posttraumatic stress disorder (Saigh, 1986). This disorder is a reaction to a highly stressful event or experience. Its symptoms include persistently reexperiencing the trauma (for example, in thoughts and dreams), avoidance of stimuli associated with the trauma, numbing of responsiveness, outbursts of anger, difficulty in sleeping, and exaggerated startle responses. Joseph was a Lebanese boy who experienced the disorder after exposure to a bomb blast. His symptoms included trauma-related nightmares, recollections of the trauma, depression, and avoidance behavior.

To treat Joseph, five scenes were developed that evoked anxiety (for example, seeing injured people and debris, approaching specific shopping areas). He rated his discomfort as each scene was described to him. After Joseph was trained to relax, the scenes were presented to him for extended periods (over 20 minutes). During this exposure period, he was asked to imagine the exact details of the scenes. The five scenes were incorporated into treatment in a multiple-baseline design, so that exposure to the scenes occurred in sequence or at different points in time. In each session, Joseph rated his discomfort in response to all of the scenes.

The results are presented in Figure 10–1. As evident, Joseph improved markedly after only ten sessions (one session of baseline assessment, ten sessions of treatment). Assessment immediately after treatment and six months later indicated that the scenes no longer caused discomfort. Perhaps more important are the results from other measures. Before and after treatment, Joseph was assessed in the marketplace where the bomb blast had occurred. After treatment, he showed less avoidance of the area and remained in it longer. Other measures, including assessment of anxiety, depression, and classroom performance at school, also indicated improvement after treatment. Thus, imagery-based treatment appeared to affect several important areas of functioning.

Covert Conditioning

The use and application of imagery in desensitization led to the development of a broader set of imagery-based behavioral techniques. In the 1960s, Joseph Cautela developed a set of techniques referred to as *covert conditioning*. The treatments were called covert because the client is asked to imagine target behaviors and consequences. They are referred to as conditioning because they draw on learning, including classical conditioning, operant conditioning, and observational learning. The techniques assume that there is an interaction between overt and covert (imagined) behaviors and that changes in one are likely to influence the other.

Table 10–1 lists several of the techniques and what they attempt to accomplish. A few procedures can illustrate how covert conditioning proceeds. In general, clients imagine various events in specific ways that lead to change in their behavior. For most of the techniques, clients imagine a specific behavior and positive or negative consequences to develop or to suppress behaviors. The rehearsal of various behaviors in imagery has been shown to influence actual behavior in a number of circumstances (see Cautela & Kearney, 1986, 1993). A few examples of covert conditioning techniques convey use of the techniques.

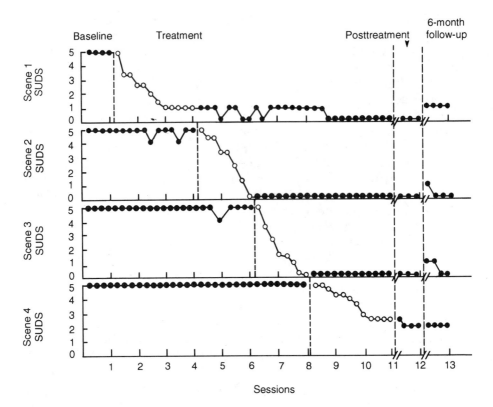

FIGURE 10–1

Joseph's ratings of discomfort, referred to as Subject Units of Disturbance (SUDS), in which 5 = maximum discomfort and 0 = no discomfort. Assessment was conducted to measure the discomfort caused by each scene during the treatment sessions. Treatment reflects the period in which imagery-based exposure (flooding) focused on the specific scene.

SOURCE: Saigh, P. A. (1986).

One procedure based on imagery is referred to as *covert sensitization.* The procedure consists of having clients imagine themselves engaging in an undesirable behavior (for example, overeating or excessive alcohol consumption). When this image is vivid, the clients imagine an aversive consequence associated with the behavior (for example, nauseated). The purpose of treatment is to build up an aversion toward stimuli that previously served as a source of attraction. The procedure is referred to as *covert* because it is conducted in imagination. The clients do not have to engage in behavior but only to imagine it as associated with particular consequences. The effects of treatment, however, carry over to actual behavior.

Covert sensitization was used with an adult male who was in a psychiatric facility because of his multiple sexual deviations (Hayes, Brownell, &

TABLE 10–1
Major Covert Conditioning Techniques

Technique	Procedure
Covert sensitization	The client is instructed to image engaging in the target behavior to be eliminated (for example, consuming alcohol) and then to imagine an aversive consequence.
Covert extinction	The client imagines the target behavior to be reduced (for example, acting obnoxiously) and then imagines that the reinforcer maintaining behavior (attention from others) is not forthcoming.
Covert response cost	The client imagines the target behavior to be decreased and then imagines loss of a reinforcer (for example, money, valuable item).
Covert positive reinforcement	The client imagines the target behavior (for example, approaching an employer) and then is asked to imagine a pleasant scene (for example, listening to music) that is assumed to be reinforcing.
Covert negative reinforcement	The client imagines an aversive stimulus (for example, nagging from a peer) and then is asked to terminate the aversive scene and to imagine the response that is to be increased (for example, responding assertively to the peer).
Covert modeling	The client imagines a model (another person) who performs the behavior. Reinforcing (positive or negative) can be added to the scenes but strictly speaking is not central to the defining procedure.

Barlow, 1978). His history included attempted rape, multiple fantasies involving sadistic sexual acts (for example, forced sexual acts with bound women, the use of pins and whips during intercourse), and exhibitionism. He had been arrested for both attempted rape and exhibitionism. Treatment consisted of having him imagine aversive consequences associated with situations in which exhibitionistic and sadistic acts are performed. This was a typical exhibitionistic scene with aversive consequences (Hayes et al., 1978):

> "I call her over to the car. She doesn't see what I'm doing. I say, 'Can you please help me with this?' She looks down and sees my dick. It's hard and she's really shocked. Her face looks all kinds of distorted. I quick drive away. As I drive away, I see her look back. I think, 'Oh, shit, she's seen my license plate!' I begin to worry that she might call the police. . . . I get

home and I'm still worried. My wife keeps saying, 'What's wrong?' . . . As we all sit down to dinner, I hear a knock on the door. I go open it, and there are four pigs. They come charging in and throw me up against the wall and say, 'You're under arrest for indecent exposure!' My wife starts to cry and says, 'This is it! This is the last straw!' "

After several days of treatment, similar scenes were developed to associate imagined aversive consequences with sadistic acts. Over the course of treatment, sexual arousal was directly measured by the degree of the client's erection (penile blood volume) as the client viewed slides of exhibitionistic, sadistic, and heterosexual scenes. For example, heterosexual slides displayed pictures of nude females and sadistic slides displayed nude females tied or chained down in a number of provocative positions. The client also reported his degree of arousal to cards describing various sexual situations.

The effects of covert sensitization were evaluated in a multiple-baseline design, since the procedure was introduced at different points in time for scenes related to exhibitionism and sadism. As shown in Figure 10–2, both physiological arousal and self-reported attraction to deviant sexual stimuli decreased as a function of treatment. On the other hand, arousal to heterosexual stimuli was never focused on and did not change. Moreover, these effects were maintained up to eight weeks after treatment.

As another illustration, covert positive reinforcement was used with a developmentally disabled 29-year-old male (moderate level) with limited language ability, including both comprehension and speech (Groden, 1993). The client lived in a community-based group home and came for treatment at an institution during the day. He had an extended history of violence and aggression, and was often restrained (for example, with handcuffs) because of his aggressive behavior. The facility included a number of programs for vocational and academic training as well as reinforcement contingencies, such as contingency contracts. Of interest here is the use of covert positive reinforcement to develop nonviolent behavior. Situations were developed in which appropriate behavior could be imagined followed by a pleasant (presumably reinforcing) scene. Over the course of treatment, situations were presented in different forms including tape-recorded vignettes as well as pictures that would instruct him to carry out the procedure. Here are two sample scenes that illustrate covert positive reinforcement.

> *Change in the schedule:* Imagine that it's time to work at the food bank. The food bank has just called and said there is no work today. You feel disappointed but you take a deep breath and relax your whole body and you say to yourself, "I can go next time and today I will do some contract work." You feel relaxed and comfortable. Now imagine listening to your radio. You enjoy the music and you have a nice smile on your face.
> *Feeling tense:* Imagine yourself starting to get tense. You feel yourself beginning to rock and you feel yourself getting angry. You tell yourself to relax, to take a deep breath, and keep your hands at your sides. You feel

FIGURE 10–2
Percentage of full erection and self-reported arousal in response to exhibitionistic, sadistic, and heterosexual stimuli during baseline, treatment, and follow-up phases. Card sort data are daily averages in the baseline and treatment phases and weekly averages in the follow-up phase.
SOURCE: Hayes, S. C., Brownell, K. D., & Barlow, D. H. (1978).

yourself getting very comfortable and relaxed. You continue what you are doing, feeling very cool and comfortable. When you can imagine that, signal to me. Now imagine being up in the gym, shooting baskets, sinking the baskets. You feel great; you have a smile on your face; you feel happy. (Groden, 1993, p. 147)

After a year, aggression was markedly reduced, and indeed in one of the settings decreased to zero over the next five years. In another setting, aggression was still a problem but was decreased with further treatment.

The case is useful in illustrating covert positive reinforcement scenes. Without a formal evaluation of the treatment and of any other treatments operative in the setting, one cannot be assured that the changes that occurred were due to covert positive reinforcement.

Covert conditioning techniques have been applied to a variety of problems, such as anxiety, sexual deviation, inassertiveness, obsessions, and alcohol consumption, to mention a few (Cautela & Kearney, 1993). Nevertheless, evidence on the effectiveness of these procedures with clinic samples is limited to a small number of problems. The procedures are usually conducted in treatment sessions in the presence of a therapist. Yet, the treatments can also be viewed as self-control techniques because clients can imagine various scenes in their everyday life to handle problems that arise long after contact with the therapist has been terminated. By rehearsing (in imagination) behaviors that may be difficult to perform, or by imagining rewarding or aversive consequences to facilitate or inhibit a response, clients can control their own behavior.

Modeling

Modeling, or observational learning, refers to learning by observing the performance of someone who engages in the behaviors that one wishes to develop. Through observation, clients acquire desired responses without performing these responses. Whether one includes modeling as a cognitively based technique has much to do with the interpretation of how modeling leads to therapeutic change. Albert Bandura (1977) has proposed that modeling achieves its effects by altering cognitive processes. The observer sees the model perform but does not engage in the behavior. An assumption is that the modeled behaviors are acquired by altering cognitive mental processes that code the observed events. Whether the behavior is performed may depend on a variety of circumstances, such as incentives to perform the response. But the coding of these behaviors (their storage in memory) is often viewed as the basis for modeling effects.

There are several variations of modeling treatment. In the usual method, live or film models are used to convey the desired target behaviors. For example, in live modeling, a therapist might demonstrate (model) the desired behaviors. Live modeling has the advantage of flexibility in modeling the specific behaviors that need to be developed in the client and in repeating the modeling situations based on how well the client is doing.

The use of live modeling is nicely illustrated in the treatment of a 3-year-old girl with a debilitating fear of animals (Matson, 1983). The girl would not go places where she thought an animal would be present. Upon seeing a dog or cat, she would freeze, shake visibly, go into a fetal position, and report fear of harm. Assessment was conducted to measure these signs of fear when the girl was in the presence of a dog and a cat.

Treatment was carried out by the girl's mother in the backyard of their home. Prior to the treatment sessions, the mother was coached by a therapist on how to conduct the modeling sessions. Each day, treatment began with the mother and child spending a few minutes playing with a stuffed dog and cat. The mother modeled petting and holding the stuffed animal. The child was encouraged to pet and hold the animal as well and was praised for doing so. After time with the stuffed animals, a live dog and cat were then introduced in each session. The child was told that she would not be required to move toward or to touch the live animal. The mother modeled approach behavior and petting. The child then was encouraged to walk over and to engage in these behaviors as well. The mother encouraged the child to try the behaviors. Gradually, the child engaged in increased approach behaviors modeled by the mother.

Assessment of the child's fear was completed in brief sessions (approximately 10 minutes) during baseline and each day prior to the treatment sessions once treatment began. For this assessment a live dog and cat were introduced, but the arrangement of the fences in the yard precluded the possibility of physical contact with the animals during assessment. The data for the different measures of fear in the presence of the live dog and cat are shown in Figure 10–3. As indicated by the figure, training was first completed on approach to a dog and then to a cat. The results show that introduction of treatment led to reductions in fear. The results were maintained after a one-year follow-up. The impact of treatment is suggested by the pattern of effects during the multiple-baseline portion of the design.

Modeling can also be carried out using imagery. One of the covert conditioning techniques noted previously (Table 10–1) is referred to as covert modeling (Cautela & Kearney, 1986). In covert modeling, clients *imagine* rather than observe models. Covert modeling has been used in outpatient treatment to train shy adults to act more assertively in a variety of social situations (Kazdin, 1984). In treatment, these clients imagine a person similar to themselves behaving assertively in such situations as returning merchandise at a store, asking an apartment landlord to make needed repairs, responding to high-pressure salespersons, and asking one's employer for a raise. This enabled the clients to effect changes in their overt behavior.

In applied settings such as the home and school, modeling has been used more frequently as a component of a larger intervention package than as a behavior change procedure by itself. Modeling in this context is particularly useful to demonstrate the behavior or task requirements. Once the behavior is demonstrated, the individual then performs the behavior and consequences can be applied directly to reinforce performance. For example, modeling is often used to develop social skills in children and adults. The skills may focus on speaking with another person, making requests, and responding to requests of others, and may entail both verbal and nonverbal behaviors (for example, facing others, standing upright). Modeling would consist of the therapist's or trainer's showing a socially appro-

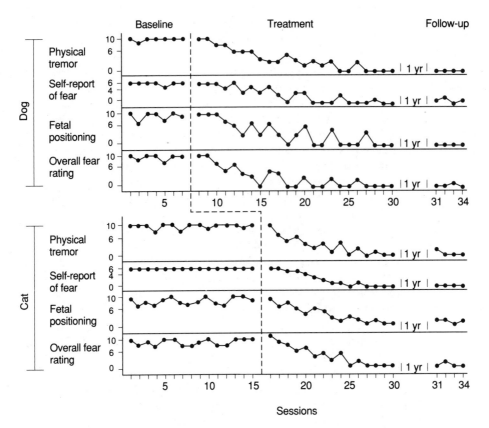

F I G U R E 10–3
Ratings of fear behavior observed each day as the child was exposed to a tame dog (upper portion) and cat (lower portion) during baseline, treatment (modeling), and follow-up.
SOURCE: Matson, J. L. (1983).

priate response by actually doing it with the client. Modeling is only the beginning of teaching the desired behaviors. After the behaviors are modeled, the client then rehearses or practices the behaviors (role-playing) that were modeled. Feedback and social reinforcement are then provided by the trainer to shape behavior. Further modeling is completed by the trainer to develop behavior as needed. Thus, modeling, practice, and reinforcement are combined to develop behavior.

Although live modeling is the most frequent use in the context of treatment, film modeling has also been used. Films are made that show, for example, individuals engaging in prosocial behavior, such as interacting with others or approaching a feared stimulus. Film models permit standardizations of presenting modeling situations to ensure that the situations are constant. The potential of film modeling as an intervention deserves special comment. The use of films and videotapes would permit large-scale dissemination of effective interventions. Also, videotapes can be standardized so that optimally effective variations can be placed on tape and delivered in diverse settings. In fact, videotaped models have been used in training in behavioral research. For example, in one program videotaped models are used to train parents how to manage their oppositional and aggressive children. Videotaped models of parents using behavioral techniques has been shown to improve child performance at home and at school (see Webster-Stratton, 1992).

Rational-Emotive Psychotherapy

Rational-emotive therapy, developed by Albert Ellis (1979), is based on the view that psychological problems arise from faulty or irrational thought patterns. These patterns are evident in implicit verbalizations that people make, that is, things people say to themselves. These verbalizations arise from assumptions that we make about the world and the events that happen to us. More specifically, some event occurs in our lives and in response to that, we have a series of thoughts (implicit self-verbalizations). These self-verbalizations then lead to a series of emotions (for example, anger, disgust) and behaviors (for example, vengeful acts, suicide attempt). For example, a man might lose his job because of a layoff. This event may be followed by any number of implicit verbalizations. He may say that these are difficult economic times, that things are "tough," and so on. Alternatively, he may say that his boss and co-workers are behind the layoff, that they never liked him, and he did not deserve this. The latter set of implicit verbalizations may lead to vengeful behavior, such as getting back at the company, the boss, and co-workers. In everyday life, the experience of stress and other events are fostered or fueled by the verbalizations we make to ourselves (for example, we are "no good"). The purpose of rational-emotive therapy is to examine the implicit self-verbalizations that people make, to challenge them and to point to their irrationality, and, importantly, to substitute more adaptive self-verbalizations.

Several irrational beliefs are common to our culture and contribute to emotional and behavioral problems. Examples of common beliefs are that

- it is necessary for an adult to be loved or approved of by virtually every other important person in his or her life
- an adult must be totally competent, adequate, and efficient to be worthwhile
- life is miserable and disastrous when events are not turning out the way one would like
- human unhappiness depends on external forces beyond an individual's control.

These beliefs, and others like them, lead to emotions and behaviors that are maladaptive. Therapy challenges these beliefs, substitutes other types of self-statements, and practices appropriate self-statements in everyday life.

Rational-emotive therapy was used with a 17-year-old adolescent girl who chronically engaged in pulling her own hair (referred to as trichotillomania) (Bernard, Kratochwill, & Keefauver, 1983). The behavior had been ongoing since the age of 12 and had led to her wearing a wig to cover bald spots. Initial evaluation revealed that the behavior was not a problem at school but was a problem at home when she was studying schoolwork alone. At these times she felt worried, anxious, and depressed. The authors hypothesized that hair pulling was a reaction to stress that itself could be traced to irrational cognitions. Assessment revealed that the girl engaged in various irrational cognitions (for example, that she was worthless unless she was competent in school, that she must be approved of by her father for her work, that it was awful when performance at school did not meet her expectations). Rational-emotive therapy was used to dispute the cognitions and to try alternative cognitions in their stead. The client recorded hair pulling at home (numbers of hairs pulled within a given time period) while studying. After baseline assessment, therapy was conducted weekly for 12 weeks.

Figure 10—4 presents the amount of hair pulling on a daily basis. After baseline (A phase), rational-emotive therapy sessions were conducted (B phases) and led to reductions in hair pulling. A suspension of the procedure (return to baseline during week 6) and a return to rational-emotive therapy suggested that the treatment was associated with reductions in behavior. However, during weeks 7 and 8, the behavior still was not eliminated. Another intervention (self-instruction training) was added. This intervention (C) was used with rational-emotive therapy and focused on having the client instruct herself to cope with anxiety, to focus attention on her work, to relax, and to provide self-praise for completed work and for not engaging in hair pulling. The results indicated that hair pulling was substantially reduced. During session 15 all treatments were ended. Follow-up assessment several weeks later indicated that the behavior had not returned.

Rational-emotive psychotherapy has been applied to a number of clinical problems (Lyons & Woods, 1991). The primary focus of research has been on anxiety-based disorders (for example, social anxiety, phobias) and in the context of psychotherapy. Work in applied settings is less frequent, although as the above example illustrates, treatment can be extended to everyday situations. Rational-emotive therapy and many other treatments discussed in this chapter rely on what individuals say to themselves. The structure and content of these statements can be examined and challenged in the context of treatment sessions. Yet, application of the treatment (for example, substituting more adaptive self-statements) can be carried out in everyday life.

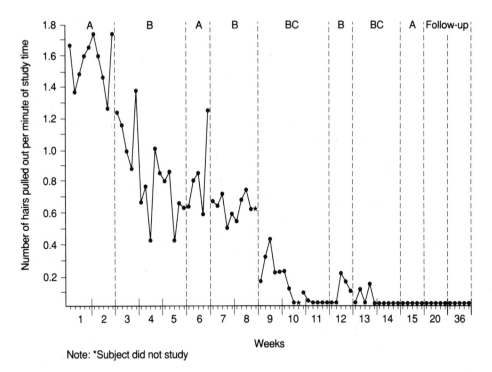

Note: *Subject did not study

FIGURE 10–4

Number of hairs pulled per minute of study time over baseline (A phases), treatment (B, BC phases), and follow-up phases. During B phases, rational-emotive therapy was used. To increase the impact of treatment, self-instruction training (referred to as C in the figure) was added.

SOURCE: Bernard, M. E., Kratochwill, T. R., & Keefauver, L. W. (1983).

Self-Instructions and Self-Statements

What people say to themselves has been considered important in controlling their own behavior (Zivin, 1979). It has been suggested that the influence of one's own speech on behavior results from childhood learning. The speech of external agents (for example, parents) controls and directs behavior in early childhood. The child eventually develops a self-directed and verbal repertoire that derives from the speech of these external agents. For example, children praise and criticize themselves in ways that they observe in adult models. Similarly, children verbally administer self-instructional statements to guide their actions. While the instructions of others continue to influence behavior throughout life, self-instructional statements also exert control. Self-instructional statements, while usually private or covert, are sometimes evident in everyday life when an individual "thinks out loud" and describes a course of action that he or she believes should be personally pursued. For example, in preparing to ask an employer for a raise, an individual may tell himself or herself what to say when the situation arises. Indeed, the individual may use self-verbalization while engaging in the actual conversation.

Self-instruction training has been used as a behavior change technique. Individuals are trained to make suggestions and specific comments that guide their own behavior in a fashion similar to being instructed by someone else. Investigations have shown that children and adults can be trained to make statements to themselves that guide their behavior.

Self-instruction training was initially developed and investigated in the context of treating schoolchildren identified as impulsive (Meichenbaum & Goodman, 1971). Training involves several steps that the therapist and child alternately execute while performing simple tasks. The basic steps include the therapist's performing a task first while talking aloud to himself or herself and then having the child perform the same task while the therapist is providing instructions, then while giving self-instructions aloud with no therapist help, and finally while making covert (internalized and inaudible) self-instructions. Training includes several tasks such as coloring figures and copying lines. Self-instructional statements help to guide performance on the task. The beginning step in which the therapist modeled self-statements is illustrated by the following comments the therapist makes aloud:

> Okay, what is it I have to do? You want me to copy the picture with the different lines. I have to go slow and be careful. Okay, draw the line down, down, good; then to the right, that's it; now down some more and to the left. Good, I'm doing fine so far. Remember go slow. Now back up again. No, I was supposed to go down. That's okay. Just erase the line carefully. . . . Good. Even if I make an error I can go on slowly and carefully. Okay, I have to go down now. Finished. I did it. (Meichenbaum & Goodman, 1971, p. 117).

In the original study (Meichenbaum & Goodman, 1971) and others that followed, self-instruction training was shown to decrease impulsive responding and errors on tasks and to improve performance on a number of cognitive tests (for example, intelligence-test subscales) and laboratory tests (for example, completing mazes). Initial evidence did not show consistent changes in everyday life, as reflected in behavior at home and at school. Since this initial focus, the range of problems, populations, and procedural variations to which self-instruction training has been applied has increased substantially. In many studies, benefits have been evident on clinically relevant—that is, everyday—measures (Kendall & Braswell, 1993). For example, in one application, self-statements were used to treat headaches (Holroyd, Andrasik, & Westbrook, 1977). Adult clients reporting a history of headaches (average of six years) were trained to identify thoughts about events or situations that precipitated stress. They practiced reappraising stressful events with self-statements (such as, "What am I thinking to induce my distress?") and emitting self-instructions that helped cope with these situations (such as, "Calm down, concentrate on the present," "Imagine myself for a moment carefree, at the beach"). They were encouraged to implement their coping skills at the first sign of a headache. Treatment resulted in reported reductions in headaches. These self-instruction clients showed greater reductions than did persons who received biofeedback or no treatment. The effects were maintained up to a 15-week follow-up assessment.

Self-statements have also been used to control anxiety. For example, the effects of different types of self-instruction were compared in helping young children handle fear of the dark (Kanfer, Karoly, & Newman, 1975). Children trained to make self-statements reflecting competence ("I can take care of myself in the dark") were better able to remain in the dark than were children instructed to make statements that reevaluated the situation ("The dark is a fun place to be") or distract themselves with other types of statements ("Mary had a little lamb"). Thus, the types of self-statements that individuals make may determine the effectiveness of training.

The above examples show how self-statements are used to develop a particular type of behavior. A number of self-statement procedures are used to decrease intrusive or maladaptive thoughts. One such treatment, referred to as thought stopping, warrants separate comment. The technique is used to help individuals control undesirable and repetitive thoughts, urges, and actions. The client is trained to stop his or her bothersome thoughts. The technique proceeds similarly to self-instruction training in which the therapist first models the desired statement, then the client states the instruction aloud and, gradually, covertly. Eventually, the client takes over the self-instructions and can utilize the treatment as needed to control thoughts.

For example, Hackmann and McLean (1975) used thought stopping to treat obsessive-compulsive clients. When a client had an obsessive thought or imagined a ritualistic behavior, the therapist hit the desk with a ruler and shouted, "Stop!" in order to interrupt the obsessive thought. After a few trials, the therapist said, "Stop," without using the ruler. The client was instructed to shout, "Stop!" aloud to interrupt obsessive thoughts. Later, the client was instructed to say, "Stop," in a whisper and then subvocally. In this way, the client learned how to interrupt obsessive thoughts effectively without the aid of the therapist. Treatment effectively reduced obsessive thoughts in a matter of only a few sessions. Other applications of thought stopping have attested to its efficacy, but the technique is less well researched than are other self-statement methods.

Another type of treatment challenges maladaptive beliefs and self-statements that individuals may make to themselves. For example, delusions, or falsely held beliefs about oneself or others, are characteristic of severely disturbed psychiatric patients. Such patients may believe they are being controlled by others, that they are a special religious leader (for example, Jesus), or have direct contact with "God," and so on. The beliefs may be held tenaciously and guide large segments of the individual's behavior. Merely challenging or denying the accuracy of the beliefs is not likely to be effective. However, therapeutic challenges to delusional self-statements have reported some successes.

In one report, two adult psychiatric patients with delusions were treated by challenging their beliefs (Lowe & Chadwick, 1990). One of the patients, a 29-year-old male, had three delusional beliefs: namely, that he was married to a woman named Amanda who was reading his mind and controlling many events that happened to him; that he had been Jesus Christ in a prior life; and that he had been Leonardo da Vinci in a prior life. The intensity of conviction was assessed in an interview in which the patient ranked how likely it was that each belief was true, how preoccupied he was with it, and how much anxiety was caused by thinking about it. Treatment consisted of conveying to the client how beliefs influence much of behavior. Then, in a gradual and nonconfrontational way, the sessions focused on temporarily suspending each belief to consider alternative ways of thinking. Evidence that the patient cited in support of the veracity of each belief was challenged and alternative interpretations were proposed. A delusional belief was not presented as a sign of illness but, rather, as one way to react to events and experiences that had occurred. With the patient, the irrationality of the belief was challenged.

The impact of the verbal challenge to the individual's beliefs was evaluated in a multiple-baseline design across beliefs. Figure 10–5 presents the data for this patient. The shaded area shows the period in which a particular belief was challenged during treatment. Belief in being married to Amanda, who controlled his behavior, decreased when the belief was the focus of treatment. Beliefs in having been Jesus also declined when treatment was extended to this delusion. The belief in having been da Vinci also declined, but before treatment was introduced. This might suggest that when the belief of having been Jesus in another life was challenged, the effect extended to a similar belief of having been da Vinci in another life. In any case, the delusional beliefs were changed over the course of treatment. Follow-up data indicated that one of the delusional beliefs had returned, although the others remained low. Further treatment and the application of additional treatment might have been warranted. In a separate demonstration with a different patient and different delusions, treatment was effective and the effects were maintained up to six months. The differential effectiveness underscores the importances of obtaining follow-up data in general.

Problem-Solving Skills Training

Cognitively based treatment has been applied extensively to children and adolescents in programs that develop interpersonal *problem-solving skills* (Durlak, Fuhrman, & Lampman, 1991; Kendall & Braswell, 1993). The programs are based on evidence that children and adolescents with ad-

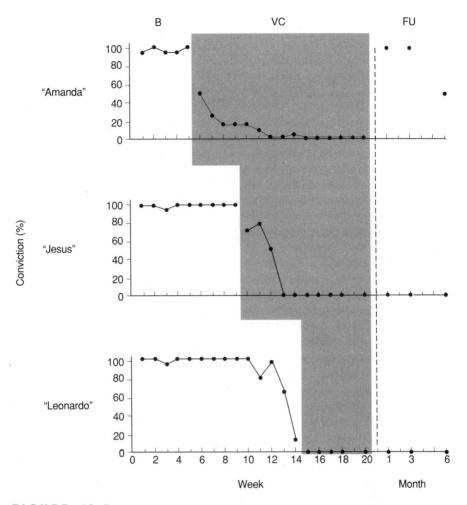

FIGURE 10–5

Percentage (strength) of conviction in delusional beliefs: that the patient was married to Amanda, who controlled his life; that he had been Jesus Christ in another life; that he had been Leonardo da Vinci in another life. Baseline (B) consisted of assessment; verbal challenge (VC) consisted of nonconfrontational challenging of these beliefs, and follow-up (FU) consisted of assessment months after treatment. The shaded portion of the figure shows the multiple-baseline feature of the design. SOURCE: Lowe, C. F., & Chadwick, P. D. J. (1990).

justment problems have deficits in various cognitive processes that underlie social behavior. Specific problem-solving skills that have been well studied and in which deficits are evident among maladjusted children are listed in Table 10–2. These skills are considered the basis for social behaviors that individuals perform in everyday situations. For example, children with adjustment problems often have difficulty in identifying alternative solu-

TABLE 10–2
Problem-Solving Skills That Relate to Adjustment

1. *Alternative solution thinking*—the ability to generate different options (solutions) that can solve problems in interpersonal situations.

2. *Means-end thinking*—awareness of the intermediate steps required to achieve a particular goal.

3. *Consequential thinking*—the ability to identify what might happen as a direct result of acting in a particular way or choosing a particular solution.

4. *Causal thinking*—the ability to relate one event to another over time and to understand why one event led to a particular action of other persons.

5. *Sensitivity to interpersonal problems*—the ability to perceive a problem when it exists and to identify the interpersonal aspects of the confrontation that may emerge.

SOURCE: Adapted from Spivack, G., Platt, J. J., & Shure, M. B. (1976).

tions to interpersonal problems (for example, resolving an argument), the consequences of their behaviors (for example, the reactions of others), and the steps that need to be taken to achieve a goal (for example, how to make friends). These and related skills can be developed by training the children to use problem-solving steps and self-statements in various games, academic tasks, and real-life situations. Training helps the children to think about the particular task, problem, or situation, the behaviors that need to be performed, and the alternative courses of action that are available, and then to select a particular solution. As in self-instruction training, the children ask specific questions or make specific self-statements to help themselves develop problem-solving skills (such as, "What am I supposed to do? What is my plan? How do I do it?"). They are trained to answer these questions when confronted with interpersonal situations in which their behavior is problematic and to identify and carry out socially appropriate solutions to problems.

A number of studies have shown that problem-solving skills training can decrease disruptive and impulsive behavior and increase peer popularity among children and adolescents (see Kazdin, 1985a; Kendall & Braswell, 1993; Spivack & Shure, 1982). Many of these studies have focused on children who are mildly disruptive or impulsive at school. With such children, the effects of training are maintained up to two years later (Shure & Spivack, 1982). With more severely disturbed children and adolescents, such as those who show aggressive or delinquent behavior, cognitively based treatment that focuses on problem-solving skills training has led to significant changes at home, at school, and in the community, and these gains are evident up to one year later (see Durlak, Fuhrman, & Lampman, 1991; Kazdin, 1993b; Kendall & Braswell, 1993).

For example, in one project, problem-solving skills training was used with children (aged 7 to 13) referred for outpatient treatment because of their severe aggressive and antisocial behavior (fighting at school, stealing, lying, truancy, cruelty to animals) (Kazdin, Siegel, & Bass, 1992). Children were seen individually on a weekly basis and trained to engage in problem-solving steps in a variety of interpersonal situations, such as interactions with parents, teachers, peers, and siblings. Parents were also involved in treatment by learning the problem-solving skills and practicing their application to situations at home and at school. The results showed that training children in problem-solving skills led to reductions in aggressive and antisocial behavior at home, at school, and in the community, and that the effects are maintained up to one year after treatment. Several studies by others have also shown reliable changes in aggressive and antisocial behavior (see Kazdin, 1993b; Kendall & Braswell, 1993). Although children who learn problem-solving skills are less aggressive than similar children who do not receive treatment, they are still more aggressive than children who are functioning well at home and at school and who have not been referred for treatment. Thus, treatment does not invariably place aggressive youth into the range of others without problems in their functioning at home and at school. Because severely disturbed aggressive children often do not respond to various forms of treatment, the gains shown with problem-solving skills training are promising.

Problem-solving skills training has been used in a variety of areas. For example, the approach has been effectively applied with mothers who neglect their children. *Parental neglect* refers to a chronic failure of parents to meet their children's needs with regard to physical safety, health, nutrition, and emotional development. For legal purposes, neglect is often considered with physical abuse in the sense that they both reflect extreme, harmful, and maladaptive child-rearing practices. Neglectful parents may have deficits in judgment and behavior because they fail to anticipate the needs of their children and the consequences of their neglect. Problem-solving training was applied to mothers whose neglect had been adjudicated (Dawson, de Armas, McGrath, & Kelly, 1986). This project focused on three mothers (aged 20 to 27) who had been identified by child-protective services as neglectful and referred for treatment. Several vignettes related to the care of children were constructed based on past reports and the mothers' descriptions of situations in which they failed to meet their children's needs. Each of the vignettes was read aloud to the parent, who was asked to engage in the problem-solving approach—to define the problem, to consider possible solutions, to describe the consequences and obstacles of each solution, and to choose the best solution. Here is a sample vignette:

> You and your mother have an argument on the phone. She tells you that you can just forget about bringing your children over tonight for her to baby-sit while you go out with your boyfriend (husband). It's 5 P.M. You don't have any money to hire a baby-sitter. The story ends with you and your boyfriend (husband) going out for the evening. (Dawson et al., 1986, p. 213)

During baseline, problem situations were presented to see how each mother managed the care of her children—whether she identified a plan to solve the problem, selected various means or steps toward the goal, and identified obstacles that would interfere with completing appropriate behaviors. The problem-solving skills training approach was then taught individually to each mother, using modeling, shaping, and feedback. The effects of training were evaluated in a multiple-baseline design. As shown in Figure 10–6, each mother's solutions to the problems (vignettes) included more of the problem-solving-skills components than did her baseline performance. Effectiveness ratings were also completed by social workers associated with each case to assess the extent to which the mother improved in her child-rearing practices, as reflected in such activities as solving child-related problems in the home, performing responsibilities, and providing food, clothing, and child care. Effectiveness ratings increased after treatment for each of the mothers. At follow-up 15 months later, only one of the mothers was available for reassessment on the vignettes. She continued to show high levels of problem-solving skills. The other two mothers, who had moved, had had full custody of their children restored by the child welfare department, with no further reports of neglect.

Stress Inoculation Training

Stress inoculation training is designed to help individuals cope with stressful events, such as situations in which anxiety, anger, or pain arise (Meichenbaum, 1985). The approach teaches a variety of cognitive and self-control skills to reduce the impact of these events. The medical notion of "inoculation" is used to convey the idea that clients are exposed to small or manageable doses of the stressful event that do not overwhelm their defenses (Novaco, 1979).

Treatment helps clients to identify stressful events and the cognitions that arise when clients are confronted with these events; to evaluate the events differently by applying various coping strategies, including relaxation, imagery, and adaptive self-statements; and to practice the coping skills in both treatment sessions and everyday life. Training helps clients replace maladaptive cognitive appraisals (interpretations) of the events with positive evaluations and self-statements. To accomplish this, self-control and cognitive components are included in treatment.

Because of the relevance of stress in several areas of life and the importance of coping skills, stress inoculation has been applied to a broad range of problems, such as controlling anger among hospitalized patients or delinquents and reducing stress among persons whose jobs expose them to frequent crises (for example, law enforcement officers, probation counselors). Several applications have utilized stress inoculation training to help individuals cope with stressful medical procedures.

For example, the technique has been used effectively for patients (aged

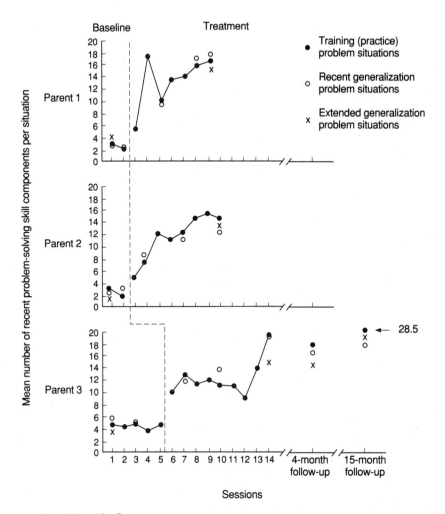

FIGURE 10–6
Mean (average) number of problem-solving skill elements included in responses to
problem situations for each parent.
SOURCE: Dawson, B., de Armas, A., McGrath, M. L., & Kelly, J. A. (1986).

14 to 62) who were undergoing elective surgery (Wells, Howard, Nowlin, &
Vargas, 1986). The anxiety and pain associated with surgery make the
notion of inoculation against stress particularly relevant. In this project,
patients were assigned either to the stress inoculation or to a control condition that was the standard hospital preparation for surgery. Stress inoculation patients were instructed about the stress associated with surgery and
taught to identify cognitive and physical cues associated with or leading to
stress (for example, increased heart rate, negative self-statements). They
were also instructed in the use of relaxation, deep breathing, pleasant

imagery, and coping and positive self-statements. Training was completed prior to surgery. Assessment revealed that before and after training, but prior to surgery, the anxiety of the patients in the stress inoculation training group decreased. In contrast, the anxiety of the patients in the control group increased. After surgery, the patients who had received stress inoculation reported less anxiety during their recovery in the hospital and lower pain intensity than did the patients in the control group. Moreover, the patients who had received stress inoculation were rated by nurses as having adjusted better to their hospitalization. Thus, the study demonstrated that stress inoculation reduced both preoperative and postoperative distress.

Stress inoculation training has also been applied to children who were undergoing stressful medical procedures. One program focused on children with leukemia who were being given a special medical test (bone marrow aspiration) to identify whether cancer cells were present (Jay, Elliot, Katz, & Siegel, 1987). The test, which requires the injection of a needle through bone and the suction of bone marrow, is both stressful and painful, despite the use of local anesthetics. Distress, reports of pain, and blood pressure were significantly lower for the children who received stress inoculation training than for the children who received mild tranquilizers.

Special populations have also received stress inoculation training to help them cope with the complications of physical disease. For example, a recent program focused on adults who suffered from multiple sclerosis, a physical disease of the central nervous system (Foley, Bedell, LaRocca, Scheinberg, & Reznikoff, 1987). The physical symptoms of this disease include impairment of sensory, motor, visual, bladder, and other functions. Many patients are restricted to wheelchairs or the use of crutches. Apart from the physical symptoms of multiple sclerosis, its psychological complications may include anxiety, depression, poor body image, and low self-esteem. Stress inoculation training was used to increase coping skills and to reduce psychological symptoms. Patients were randomly assigned to stress inoculation training or to routine care, which included various forms of psychotherapy and medication. The stress inoculation patients were trained in muscle relaxation; self-monitoring of stressors, thoughts, feelings, and behavior; the use of imagery and reinterpretation or cognitive reappraisals of the situation; and role-play of these coping strategies. Stress inoculation training led to reductions in anxiety and depression and to improved ability to cope with stressors. These effects were maintained at a six-month follow-up assessment. The patients who had been given routine care did not improve on these measures and hence were eventually given stress inoculation training.

Combined Procedures

As already noted, cognitively based techniques are often used in the context of psychotherapy. In applied settings, select cognitively based techniques are used by themselves or, more often, in combination with various reinforcement and punishment procedures. Cognitive procedures such as the use of self-statements to control behavior may be combined with direct reinforcement of the desired behaviors.

For example, cognitive treatment, self-control, and reinforcement were combined in a study to treat two girls (aged 8 and 10) who experienced separation anxiety (Ollendick, Hagopian, & Huntzinger, 1991). Separation anxiety in children refers to their concern about time away from their parents, worry about the welfare of their parents, and interest in constant reassurance about their parents. The concern becomes worthy of treatment when it interferes with daily functioning. In the case of Mary and Lucy, the two girls treated in this program, refusal to sleep in their own beds because of their fears and concerns were problems for their families. For baseline assessment, each girl and her mother recorded when the child went to bed, whether she slept in her own bed through the night, and related behaviors. After several days of observation, cognitively based and self-control procedures were implemented. Each girl was trained to use self-instructions to help her manage and cope with anxiety, to apply relaxation exercises to help reduce anxiety, and to administer self-praise for using these approaches to control anxiety. Parents also provided praise when the girls used these strategies in treatment sessions as well as at home. After this phase of self-control training, reinforcement was added when the girls actually slept in their own beds. Reinforcement was provided in the morning (verbal praise, or earning earrings, video rentals) based on whether the child slept in her own bed at night. A graduated approach (shaping) was used as needed to increase the number of nights each girl slept in her bed.

The effectiveness of the program was evaluated in a multiple-baseline design across the two children. Figure 10–7 shows the number of nights each girl spent in her own bed (out of seven nights for each week). For example, during baseline, Mary never slept in her bed in a 2-week period; Lucy slept in her own bed 2 times in a 4-week period. Self-control training (cognitive self-instructions and self-control training) led to weak and inconsistent effects. When positive reinforcement was added to the procedure, both girls increased in the number of nights in their own beds. Essentially, there was no problem because both slept seven nights in their own beds during each week. These effects were maintained in follow-up assessment two years and one year later for Mary and Lucy, respectively. The program shows that sleeping in one's bed could be increased, but did the program also reduce anxiety? Several standardized measures indicated that treatment was associated with reductions in anxiety. Moreover, before treatment both girls met criteria for separation anxiety, as delineated as a psychiatric disorder of childhood, based on the number and severity of their symptoms. Neither met the criteria for the disorder after treatment. Thus, the combined treatment seemed to have had a significant effect on their daily functioning.

Cognitively based treatment and reinforcement contingencies were combined in a program for adolescents who were considered to be in need of controlling their anger (Feindler, Ecton, Kingsley, & Dubey, 1986). These

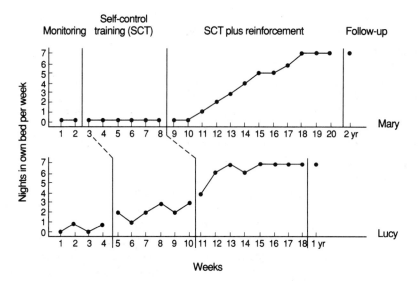

FIGURE 10–7
Number of nights each girl slept in her own bed during each week. During baseline, the children and parents observed their sleep behavior. In the self-control training phase, self-instruction training, relaxation, and self-praise were used. Parent praise was also provided for using the self-control techniques (but not for going to bed). In the final phase, self-control plus reinforcement, each girl received reinforcing consequences for sleeping in her own bed. Follow-up assessment one or two years after treatment showed that program effects were maintained.
SOURCE: Ollendick, T. H., Hagopian, L. P., & Huntzinger, R. M. (1991).

adolescents were hospitalized as part of an inpatient program for behaviorally and emotionally disturbed youths. The intervention consisted of eight weeks of training in relaxation, self-instruction, use of coping statements, self-monitoring of anger and conflict experiences, and problem-solving skills. Modeling, rehearsal, and practice were used to train the skills. In addition, a reinforcement system was invoked in which points were provided for patient compliance and participation. At the end of treatment, those who were given the training engaged in fewer rule violations in the hospital and received fewer restrictions to their room than did those who were not given the training. Additional measures, such as reduced impulsiveness and increased ratings of self-control by staff, improved for those who were given the cognitive-behavioral training. Further assessment indicated that the effects of training were maintained two months later.

Programs similar to the above have been reported in which cognitively based interventions are combined with reinforcement (for example, Kazdin et al., 1992; Sanders et al., 1989). Although research has shown that combined procedures are often effective, relatively few studies have shown that combinations are more effective than the individual components (for example, reinforcement procedures without cognitive procedures or vice versa) used by themselves. In the context of clinical care, combined procedures often are used to maximize the likelihood of achieving change. Yet, further tests are needed to evaluate the benefits of adding one type of treatment to another.

ISSUES AND CURRENT STATUS

Scope and Characteristics of the Techniques

Cognitively based techniques include a wide range of interventions, only some of which were sampled here. The techniques are usually applied in the context of therapy in which individuals meet with a therapist to learn the approach and to apply what they have learned to everyday situations. A wide array of clinical problems (anxiety, depression, aggression, headaches, chronic pain, eating disorders, or substance use) and populations (children through adults, persons with clinical problems, or persons at risk for problems) are encompassed by such techniques (Hollon & Beck, 1994).[1]

Although there are many techniques, it is obvious from the present examples that many of them overlap. For example, self-instruction training and problem-solving skills training are very similar: both believe that what individuals say to themselves is important to guide behavior, both alter what individuals say, and both often encourage practice in everyday situations. The overlap of techniques is not necessarily problematic. The individual techniques emerged separately to address particular clinical issues. Many of the techniques have drawn upon similar theory and research and are understandably similar.

In remembering the techniques, it may be useful to bear in mind three characteristics of the treatment: the conceptual basis of the technique, the problem(s) or behaviors to which the technique is applied, and the procedures themselves or what is actually done with the client in treatment. These characteristics can help to make salient similarities and differences among techniques. For example, both self-instruction training and problem-solving skills training draw on important conceptual advances regarding self-statements and self-regulation; both are similar in the procedures on which they rely (such as practice, overt and covert rehearsal of self-statements). However, the techniques tend to differ on how they are applied. Problem-solving skills training tends to focus on interpersonal interactions and relations with others (for example, behaving in prosocial rather than aggressive ways with peers), which has not been the usual focus of self-instruction training.

Cognitively based techniques are often referred to as *cognitive-behavior modification*. There is no consistent use in the field in distinguishing among the terms *cognitively based treatment, cognitive therapy,* and *cognitive-behavior modification*. Book titles, journal articles, and professional conferences, for example, vary in how these terms are used even when their content is virtually identical. The matter of terminology is not as critical for us as is the basis for the notion of *cognitive-behavior modification.* Techniques are considered to be cognitive if they rely on cognitive processes in the theory underlying the emergence of problem behavior, in explaining how treatment works, or in attempting to alter such processes as beliefs, attributions, and self-statements during treatment. At a technique or procedural level, many of the cognitively based treatments rely heavily on direct overt behavior-change methods. For example, in cognitive therapies, role-playing, practice, feedback, positive reinforcement, shaping, and related procedures are often used.

As an example, problem-solving skills training with aggressive children teaches them to apply various problem-solving steps to interpersonal situations. Say we have an 8-year-old boy who argues when his teacher asks him to do something. In the session, a vignette (situation) individualized to address this problem area might be presented to the boy. He will be asked to apply the problem-solving steps to identify an appropriate (for example, nonaggressive) solution to the problem—that is, to select an appropriate way to interact with the teacher. After this is identified while both therapist and child are sitting and talking in the session, the therapist might then say, "OK, let's get up and act it out." At this point, the therapist pretends to be the teacher and makes a request of the boy. The boy goes through the problem-solving steps and selects an appropriate solution, and then acts it out. During this process the therapist might use prompts (instructions, reminders, gestures) to encourage use of the steps and selection of an appropriate solution. Any prosocial solution is likely to be reinforced with praise or maybe even tokens. Then, the therapist may provide feedback, prompts for even better performance, and so on. At this point, the situation may be practiced again and better performance, presumably, would be reinforced. It is possible that the boy and therapist will reverse roles; that is, the therapist pretends to be the boy to model good problem solving in this situation.

Without getting lost in the example, the overriding point is clear. Cognitively based techniques often rely heavily on noncognitive (behavioral) procedures. This is not a problem in understanding or describing the techniques. Cognitions still play a central role in the techniques. The term *cognitive-behavior modification* captures the fact that many cognitively based techniques encompass behavioral procedures as well.

Evidence and Illustrations

As mentioned already, there are many cognitive-behavior therapy techniques. The evidence for their effectiveness cannot be summarized easily because one must examine the techniques individually as applied to specific clinical problems. In the context of psychotherapy research, cognitively based techniques have been shown to be effective when several studies are combined across different problem domains (for example, Hollon & Beck, 1994; Lyons & Woods, 1991). Thus, in the general case, evidence on the therapeutic effectiveness of cognitively based psychotherapies is favorable.

In applied settings such as the home and school, rather than in the context of psychotherapy, the impact of cognitively based treatment is less well established. In applied work, cognitively based interventions have been used primarily to control disruptive behavior of young children. In this context, some ambiguities have emerged. Consider two examples.

Self-Instruction Training

Several years ago, self-instruction training was used effectively with three Head Start children who were highly disruptive in class (Bornstein & Quevillon, 1976). After baseline data on in-class behavior were obtained, self-instruction training was administered. Training was conducted for two hours outside the classroom, where the children worked on tasks (copying figures, solving problems). For each task, an experimenter modeled the type of question that the child should ask (for example, "What does the teacher want me to do?"), directions (for example, "I'm supposed to copy that picture"), and self-praise (for example, "I really did that one well"). In general, the instructions were designed to convey how to complete work successfully for a variety of tasks. The children were instructed to administer instructions to themselves—first aloud, then in a whisper, and finally without sound (covertly). As shown in Figure 10–8, self-instruction training was administered in a multiple-baseline design across children and was associated with marked increases in on-task behavior. Classroom performance clearly improved. Moreover, these effects were maintained several weeks after treatment was initiated.

It might be expected that the immediacy, magnitude, and durability of the effects illustrated in the figure would be cause for tremendous encouragement. However, several investigators have tried to repeat this demonstration, a process referred to as replication, with little or no success (for example, Bryant & Budd, 1982; Friedling & O'Leary, 1979). For example, Billings and Wasik (1985) tried to follow closely the procedures implemented in the original study. They provided self-instruction training to Head Start children who were disruptive in class and evaluated the training in a multiple-baseline design across children. Figure 10–9 presents the results for three children (Brian, Elliott, and John) who received training and for a fourth child (Andy) who did not. With an effective intervention, classroom behavior would have been expected to improve after training was introduced, as in the original study of Bornstein and Quevillon (1976). The effects are unclear. In this study, as in a number of others, self-instruction training did not alter performance.

The ambiguities surrounding the effects of self-instruction training have been a topic of continued research. Investigators have focused on identifying the conditions under which self-instruction training leads to

FIGURE 10–8
Daily percentage of on-task behaviors for three Head Start children (Scott, Rod, and Tim) across experimental conditions.
SOURCE: Bornstein, P. H., & Quevillon, R. P. (1976).

change and the bases of or reasons that these changes may occur. For example, in one study, self-instruction was carried out with children in a private preschool (Guevremont, Osnes, & Stokes, 1988). Performance on tasks during special training sessions changed with self-instruction training. The instructions were not used by the children in the classroom on similar tasks. When the children were prompted to use self-instructions in the classroom, the gains evident in the training sessions then also were made in the regular classroom.

In another study of the process, first- and second-grade children re-

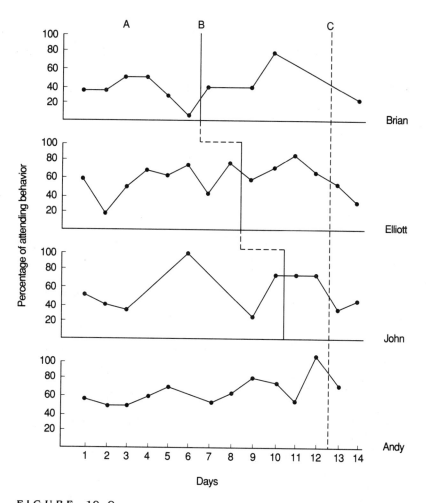

FIGURE 10–9
Daily percentage of attending behavior in class across baseline (A phase), training
(B phase), and follow-up (C phase).
SOURCE: Billings, D. C., & Wasik, B. H. (1985).

ceived self-instruction training to improve their performance on arithmetic
tasks (Roberts, Nelson, & Olson, 1987). The training focused on how to
approach the task and complete the problems. The children who received
self-instruction training improved, but further analyses revealed that the
improvement was not associated with using the self-instructions after training. In fact, the children tended not to use self-instructions unless they
received reinforcers (tokens) for doing so. The investigators suggested that
self-instructions may improve performance by providing clear instructions
on how to approach a task rather than by altering cognitive processes that
putatively underlie behavior. This suggestion is consistent with other work

showing that instructions from an external agent, such as a parent or teacher, can speed up the acquisition of behavior (for example, Resick, Forehand, & Peed, 1974). The findings raise questions about how self-instructions work and about whether they provide an intervention that operates differently from instructions provided by an external agent.

Problem-Solving Skills Training

Problem-solving skills training, as discussed earlier, has enjoyed wide-spread application and some success. An issue that has emerged in many studies has to do with the effects of such training on performance in applied settings. In many studies, evaluation of the effects of the training on a number of laboratory-based measures has shown that children do utilize the problem-solving skills in which they have been trained. Additional measures have focused on behavior and measures of adjustment at home and at school. On measures of behavior in applied settings, the effectiveness of problem-solving procedures has been less consistent.

For example, problem-solving skills training was incorporated into the curriculum for elementary school children in grades 2 to 4 (Weissberg & Gesten, 1982). In one variation of the program, children received 34 lessons (20–30 minutes each) and opportunities to review skills and practice in resolving interpersonal conflicts. Major areas of the training were recognizing feelings in oneself and others, identifying interpersonal problems, generating alternative solutions, considering consequences, and integrating problem-solving skills. Use of the skills covered in these lessons was integrated with classroom activities, such as solving minor problems between children. Several evaluations of the program showed that the children who received training in problem-solving skills improved significantly as compared with the children who did not receive such training. However, the impact of problem-solving skills training on teacher ratings of classroom adjustment has been equivocal; some studies have shown gains, but other studies have not (for example, Gesten et al., 1982; Weissberg et al., 1981).

Two studies evaluated the impact of problem-solving skills training on elementary school children (Nelson & Carson, 1988). The results from both studies indicated that improvement in performance on measures reflecting knowledge of and skills in the problem-solving approach was greater for the children who received the training than for the children who did not receive it. However, measures of behavioral adjustment, peer acceptance, and children's views about themselves were not consistently altered. The study raises questions about the extent to which problem-solving skills can effect changes in behavior in the home, at school, and in the community. Mentioned earlier were studies of problem-solving skills for treatment of antisocial behavior in children. Here changes in behavioral adjustment have been achieved, yet the effects have been weaker than one would like. In a significant proportion of cases, children do not improve or do not improve sufficiently to function normally in everyday life. Thus, the studies raise questions about the cases for whom the interventions are effective.

General Comments

The ambiguities surrounding self-instruction training and problem-solving skills training result from the presence of positive outcome effects on some occasions but not on other occasions. Occasional exceptions or studies that do not obtain identical results are not rare in scientific research. One reason for seeming inconsistencies is that the effects can depend on a variety of conditions that are not well understood, such as characteristics of the clients, the persons who administer the intervention, and the setting. When there are conflicting findings, one set of findings is not necessarily "true" and the other necessarily "false." One need not decide whom to believe. From the standpoint of developing interventions for classroom or other applied settings, the inconsistent effects reflect an important statement regarding the status of the interventions.

Self-instruction training and problem-solving skills training as interventions for applied settings are not yet sufficiently well understood, and the variables that make these interventions effective are not yet clear. Factors on which their effectiveness may depend include the age, intelligence, race, gender, and developmental level of the clients and many characteristics related to how the interventions are implemented. For example, cognitively based treatment (self-instruction training, problem-solving skills) tends to be more effective with older (aged 11 to 13) rather than younger (5 to 11) children (Durlak, Fuhrman, & Lampman, 1991). One reason might be that older children have attained higher levels of cognitive development and hence can more readily profit from treatment that relies on cognitive processes. This explanation is plausible but not known to be true. It is important to know the reasons that treatment produces changes and the persons for whom treatments are optimally effective so that treatment effects can be more reliably produced.

In contrast, a great deal is known about the application of positive reinforcement and about many of the conditions that contribute to its effectiveness. For example, and as detailed in Chapter 5, it is known that delay, magnitude, type, and schedule of reinforcement can contribute to the extent of behavior change. If favorable conditions are not carefully implemented, as when very delayed or intermittent consequences are used, reinforcement programs are not likely to change behavior. Cognitively based interventions have been less well studied than positive reinforcement in applied settings. Parallel information about the factors to ensure their effectiveness is not yet available. Thus, when a given study shows that a cognitively based intervention has produced some behavior change, this suggests that the intervention holds promise. However, more needs to be understood before the intervention can be used reliably to produce change.

Summary and Conclusion

Cognitively based techniques include a broad range of interventions. Their common feature is the view that cognitive processes (perceptions, self-statements, attributions, expectations, beliefs, and images) relate in significant ways to behavior, and that change in these processes leads to behavior change. Many of the cognitively based techniques are applied in the context of psychotherapy, where the client is seen by a therapist in individual or group treatment sessions. A number of techniques have been extended to applied settings as well.

Several cognitively based treatments were illustrated. *Imagery-based exposure treatments* were discussed in the context of treatment of anxiety disorders. Systematic desensitization and flooding, in which anxiety-provoking stimuli are presented in imagery, are prime examples of the treatments.

Covert conditioning refers to a family of intervention techniques in which various principles of learning (reinforcement, punishment, extinction) were used as a basis to develop imagery-based treatments.

Modeling was discussed in part because a prominent interpretation of the procedure in behavior modification has been based on cognitive processes assumed to underlie behavior. Modeling is used often as part of behavioral interventions that combine a number of other procedures. Typically, these procedures consist of having individuals imagine various behaviors and consequences that are designed to alter the behaviors.

A number of cognitively based treatments emphasize what clients say to themselves. In *rational-emotive* therapy, irrational cognitions are assumed to underlie maladaptive patterns of functioning. Treatment alters these cognitions as a way to develop prosocial behavior. In a somewhat similar vein, *self-instructions and self-statement training* develop patterns of instructing oneself how to perform. The statements allow individuals to analyze a situation and to specify the requirements for their own behavior. The instructions are designed to prompt and guide performance.

Problem-solving skills training develops cognitive problem-solving processes that underlie interpersonal behavior. The individual uses a specific type of self-statement to identify effective solutions and approaches to interpersonal situations. *Stress inoculation training* focuses on developing cognitive and self-control skills to reduce the impact of stress. Individuals are trained to monitor events and their evaluations of them, to use coping strategies such as relaxation, imagery, and positive self-statements, and to apply coping skills in everyday life.

Cognitively based procedures are used in applied settings either by themselves or in combination with reinforcement and punishment techniques. The most common application has been self-instruction training or problem-solving skills training in the schools to improve classroom deportment and child adjustment. Applications of cognitive techniques in applied settings have not been as extensively evaluated as have reinforcement or punishment techniques. Their effects have been promising but somewhat inconsistent. Whether they increase the effectiveness of reinforcement and punishment procedures has been suggested but warrants further research.

Note

1. Research on cognitively based treatments is published in several journals in clinical psychology and behavior therapy. A journal devoted exclusively to cognitive-behavioral techniques is *Cognitive Therapy and Research.*

For Further Reading

Cautela, J. R., & Kearney, A. J. (Eds.). (1993). *Covert conditioning casebook.* Pacific Grove, CA: Brooks/Cole.

Kendall, P. C. (Ed.). (1991). *Child and adolescent therapy: Cognitive-behavioral procedures.* New York: Guilford.

Meichenbaum, D. (1985). *Stress inoculation training.* Elmsford, NY: Pergamon Press.

Spivack, G., & Shure, M. B. (1982). The cognition of social adjustment: Interpersonal cognitive problem-solving thinking. In B. B. Lahey & A. E. Kazdin (Eds.), *Advances in clinical child psychology* (Vol. 5, 323–372). New York: Plenum.

Stein, D. J., & Young, J. E. (Eds.). (1992). *Cognitive science and clinical disorders.* San Diego: Academic Press.

CHAPTER ELEVEN

RESPONSE MAINTENANCE AND TRANSFER OF TRAINING

RESPONSE MAINTENANCE

TRANSFER OF TRAINING

PROGRAMMING RESPONSE MAINTENANCE AND TRANSFER
Bringing Behavior Under Control of the Natural Contingencies
Programming Naturally Occurring Reinforcers
Gradually Removing or Fading the Contingencies
Expanding Stimulus Control
Training Individuals to Respond to the "General Case"
Schedules of Reinforcement
Delay of Reinforcement
Peer Facilitators
Self-Control Procedures
Cognitively Based Procedures
Duration of Intervention Programs
Procedures Used in Combination

SUMMARY AND CONCLUSION

Techniques discussed in previous chapters have altered many behaviors among a wide range of clients. Dramatic changes in behavior are obviously impressive, but do those changes last? What happens when behavioral programs are discontinued or when clients leave the special settings in which the programs have been conducted? The issues raised by these questions, often referred to as generalization, constitute the topic of the present chapter.

The term *generalization* has been employed very loosely to signify that behavior changes carry over (or generalize) to conditions other than those included in training. However, generalization can include a variety of phenomena, among them behavior changes that carry over to situations, periods, or settings other than those in which the behavioral program was implemented (Allen, Tarnowski, Simonian, Elliott, & Drabman, 1991; Stokes & Baer, 1977). The extension of behavior changes over time is usually referred to as response maintenance or resistance to extinction. The question addressed by response maintenance is whether behavior change is maintained after the program has been terminated. The extension of behavior changes to new situations and settings is usually referred to as *transfer of training.* The question addressed by transfer of training is whether behavior change extends to situations not included in the program (for example, to the home when the program is conducted in the classroom). Transfer of training can also mean the extension of behavior changes to the presence of other persons. For example, behaviors trained in the presence of parents may not carry over to other adults (guests, teachers), siblings, or peers.

Response maintenance and transfer of training are not uniquely relevant to behavior modification. They apply to any enterprise or activity in which behavior change is a goal. Thus, they represent critical issues for child rearing, education, religion, psychotherapy, and many other areas aside from behavior modification. For example, a major issue in psychotherapy is whether positive changes that take place in the therapist's presence (for example, reduced anxiety in talking about a particular topic, improved communication between marital partners) are maintained when the clients complete therapy and interact socially in everyday situations. Similarly, in education, a major hope is that after completing formal education, people will continue to read and educate themselves (maintenance) outside the classroom situation (transfer). Governments are interested in having citizens maintain their law-abiding behaviors (for example, traveling within the speed limit) even when the contingencies (for example, surveillance by police officers) are not in effect.

Response maintenance and transfer of training have received special attention in behavior modification for three reasons. First, an obvious priority for treatment is developing ways of changing behavior. Only after effective procedures for changing behavior have been developed is it meaningful to raise questions about response maintenance and transfer of behavior. Until recently, few effective procedures were available to alter many of the problem behaviors to which behavioral procedures have been effectively applied. For example, until recently, few effective procedures were available to increase the use of seat belts among automobile drivers and passengers. Evidence emerged noting that special reinforcement contingencies could markedly increase seat belt use (for example, Roberts & Fanurik, 1986). After it has been shown that initial changes are quite possible, maintaining behavior and ensuring the transfer of behavior to other situations (for example, when the person is a driver or a passenger, when the person is in his or her car or in the car of others) take on primary importance. Indeed, other studies have shown that the maintenance and extension of seat belt use is feasible (for example, Sowers-Hoag, Thyer, & Bailey, 1987). In any case, an initial task is to show that behavior change can be reliably achieved. For many applied problems, evidence attests to such changes. Behavior modification has expanded the research focus to study maintenance and transfer to sustain and to extend these changes.

Second, evaluations of behavioral techniques have often suggested that maintenance and transfer may not occur after treatment. For example, many studies have used an ABAB (or reversal) design, in which treatment is temporarily withdrawn in a return-to-baseline phase. When this is done, behavior usually reverts to or near baseline levels. Such loss of behavior during a reversal phase may provide a preview of coming attractions, namely, loss of the acquired behavior once the behavior change program has been terminated. Similarly, in multiple-baseline designs, contingencies are often introduced, one situation at a time, into different situations, such as the home, the classroom, and the playground. Behavior change in one situation usually occurs without behavior changes in other situations until the program (for example, reinforcement) has been introduced into those situations. This suggests that newly developed behaviors are not likely to transfer to new situations without special contingencies.

Third, behavior modification programs usually require the use of reinforcement and other contingencies that differ from the contingencies available in everyday life. For example, children who have behavioral and academic problems at school or psychiatric patients who engage in bizarre behaviors may be placed in a special classroom or ward where the contingencies are highly conducive to behavior change. This raises the obvious question of what will happen to these persons when they return to ordinary settings, where the contingencies are not programmed to promote desirable behaviors.

In some situations, response maintenance is not an issue because the program is intended to remain in effect. For example, employees are often provided with incentives, such as bonuses for exceeding a sales quota or bonuses for using exercise facilities (because improved fitness reduces employee absenteeism). The reinforcement contingencies may remain in effect permanently. In such situations, special procedures for maintaining behavior may not be required.

In most of the programs in which behavioral techniques are applied, the program is intended to be a temporary tool for developing behavior so that it is performed consistently. In such programs, the assumption is that the person will return to a setting or situation in which the specific contingencies are not present. Maintenance of the behavior in that setting or situation is obviously critical and must be planned before the contingencies are withdrawn.

Response maintenance and transfer of training can readily be distinguished in the abstract, but in practice they often go together. For example, if a special education student attends a special classroom where a token reinforcement system is in effect and then returns to a regular classroom, both response maintenance and transfer of training are important. Conditions of the special education classroom, such as frequent reinforcement of specific target behaviors, may no longer be used in the regular classroom (that is, extinction of those behaviors). Understandably, such behaviors may not be maintained. At the same time, the setting is different, so the acquired behaviors may not transfer to the regular classroom. The extent to which the behaviors are maintained and transferred determine the success of the child's return to the regular classroom.

Response maintenance and transfer need not always go together. For example, in classroom situations, reinforcement programs are often implemented at one time of day (for example, morning). Transfer of training can refer to whether behavior also changes during times of day (for example, afternoon) or in situations (for example, the playground) in which the reinforcement program has not been implemented. Response maintenance or resistance to extinction is not relevant here because the target behaviors are still reinforced in the morning. The issue is whether the reinforced behaviors transfer or generalize to other situations while the program is in effect. The present chapter examines the evidence bearing on both response maintenance and transfer of training. It also discusses techniques to increase the likelihood that behaviors will be maintained and will carry over to new situations.

RESPONSE MAINTENANCE

At the outset, it is important to note that behaviors do not always revert to preprogram or baseline levels when the contingencies are withdrawn. Behaviors are often maintained after a program has been terminated. Thus, loss of behavior is by no means inevitable. For example, token reinforcement and response cost were used to alter behavior (using abusive language, not attending activities such as therapy sessions, and neglecting personal grooming) of hospitalized schizophrenic patients (Peniston, 1988). The program lasted 12 weeks. The marked improvements evident during treatment were maintained 6 and 12 months later, when performance was again assessed. Thus, the gains were clearly sustained long after treatment had ended.

When responses are maintained after reinforcing or other conse-quences have been withdrawn, the reason is usually unclear. One would expect behaviors to reflect the contingencies that currently operate in the environment. When the contingencies are withdrawn, one can only specu-late why the behaviors are maintained. Various explanations have been offered. First, it is possible that behaviors developed through a reinforce-ment program may come under the control of other reinforcers in the setting. For example, in a classroom, withdrawal of a token economy may not lead to the loss of appropriate behaviors. Because the teacher has been consistently paired with the delivery of token reinforcement, he or she may serve as a stimulus for appropriate behavior and may continue to serve as a powerful source of reinforcement after the token reinforcement has been withdrawn. Second, behaviors may be maintained because of reinforce-ment resulting directly from the behaviors themselves. Many behaviors result in their own reinforcement. For example, reading, social interaction, or eating skills may be maintained once they have been developed. Each of these behaviors may be reinforced by the consequences that naturally follow their execution.

Finally, behavior may be maintained after the reinforcers have been withdrawn because the behavior of the persons who administered the pro-gram (parents, teachers, peers, hospital staff) has changed in some per-manent fashion. For example, if a contingency contract system in the home is withdrawn, a child's desirable behavior may still be maintained at a high level because the parents may then provide reinforcement (allowance and praise) and punishment (loss of privileges) more systematically than they did prior to the contract system. Unfortunately, there is very little evidence that the behavior of those who administer a behavior modification program is permanently altered (see Kazdin & Moyer, 1976). As soon as a program is withdrawn, the agents who administer the program frequently revert to the behaviors they previously used to control client behavior.

Each of the above explanations of response maintenance is usually offered after the fact. After behavior fails to reverse when a program is withdrawn, an investigator may speculate why this occurred. Any of the explanations may be correct in a given instance. However, maintenance of behavior is more clearly understood when it is predicted in advance on the basis of the special procedures used to develop resistance to extinction rather than when extinction does not occur and has to be explained.

Despite the above examples and explanations of response mainte-nance, removal of the contingencies usually results in a decline of perfor-mance to or near baseline levels. This has led authors to state that if response maintenance is the goal of the behavior modification program, it has to be programmed systematically into the contingencies rather than merely hoped for as a desirable side effect (Baer, Wolf, & Risley, 1987; Stokes & Baer, 1977).

Transfer of Training

Transfer of training can refer to different phenomena, depending on whether one is speaking of transfer across situations, settings, or the persons who implement the contingencies. In most programs, changes of behavior in one situation do not result in a transfer of those changes to other situations or settings, either while the program is in effect or after it has been withdrawn. Indeed, the stimulus conditions controlling behavior are often quite narrow, so that behavior changes are restricted to the specific setting in which training has taken place and even to the persons who administered the program. As we shall see in the present chapter, changing behavior often requires procedures different from those used to develop maintenance and transfer of training. Even so, there are several occasions in which transfer of behavior to new situations and settings has been reported during treatment, before special procedures were implemented to develop transfer.

For example, in one program, parents were trained to use reinforcement and mild punishment (time out) to control disruptive behavior of their children (aged 2 to 7) (McNeil, Eyberg, Eisenstadt, Newcomb, & Funderburk, 1991). The behaviors (noncompliance, overactivity, and physical aggression) were selected because they were a problem at home. Treatment was carried out for 14 weeks. Youths who received the treatment, compared with control youths who did not, showed marked improvements. The gains were evident at home, which was expected because parents were trained to implement procedures to alter behaviors that were problematic at home. Interestingly, observations revealed that noncompliance and disruptive behavior decreased at school for these youths, even though performance at school was not included in the program. Thus, the gains transferred to the school setting.

Other examples might be mounted where gains obtained in one setting carried over to other settings. Yet, it would be important not to misrepresent the weight of the evidence. In general, transfer of behavior across situations and settings is unlikely to occur unless specific efforts are made to program generalization across the situations of interest. Without special procedures, transfer *may* occur—perhaps for some individuals in a program or across some situations of interest. Yet, to obtain reliable (consistent, predictable) changes in behavior and transfer of these changes, transfer of training usually has to be programmed directly.

Programming Response Maintenance and Transfer

The initial priority for behavior modification in applied settings has been to develop techniques that reliably alter behavior. Consequently, the technology for changing behavior has received much greater attention than the technology for developing maintenance and transfer of behavior. In the past several years, however, tremendous progress has been made in the areas of maintenance and transfer by identifying the different types of generalization that need to be developed, by elaborating the principles that suggest how these types of generalization might be developed, and by describing concrete methods of assessing and evaluating generalization (for example, Horner, Dunlap, & Koegel, 1988; Landrum & Lloyd, 1992; Stokes & Osnes, 1989). The present section reviews major techniques for achieving response maintenance and transfer of training. Techniques to achieve maintenance and transfer will be treated together because they are often focused on simultaneously in a given program and also because the techniques that accomplish one often affect the other. Procedures that are more suited to maintenance than to transfer, or vice versa, will be noted as such.

Bringing Behavior under Control of the Natural Contingencies

Perhaps the most obvious procedure for ensuring that behavior will be maintained and will transfer to new situations is to bring it under the control of the consequences that naturally occur in the environment. Reinforcing and punishing consequences that ordinarily follow behavior in everyday life may be sufficient to maintain behavior once it has been well established. Also, if behavior comes under the control of the natural contingencies, transfer of training will not be a problem because the consequences in the new situations may sustain the behavior. For example, praise and attention from others as well as the consequences that follow from the behavior itself, as in the case of eating and reading, may sustain performance.

The notion of *behavioral traps* was introduced to convey the rationale behind maintenance and transfer that result from the natural contingencies (Baer, Rowbury, & Goetz, 1976). According to this concept, once a client's behavior has been developed, it should be "trapped" into the system of reinforcers that is available in the environment. The purpose of behavioral interventions should be to bring the client's behavior up to the level sustained by the natural consequences. Initially, his or her behavior may be developed by extraneous reinforcers (for example, tokens, food and other consumables, praise) that the environment normally would not provide. After that behavior has been developed, other reinforcers (for example, contact with peers) may sustain its high level.

An example where behavior appeared to be maintained by natural reinforcers was reported in a preschool classroom (Baer, Rowbury, & Goetz, 1976). To increase social interaction in a withdrawn boy, the teacher provided social reinforcement (attention, expressions of interest) whenever he socialized with his peers. In several phases of an extended ABAB design, teacher praise was alternately delivered and withdrawn. Two results emerged from the program. First, the teacher's praise was responsible for the boy's increased interaction. Second, over time, his interaction was maintained even when the teacher did not deliver praise. Apparently, the reinforcement resulting from peer interaction tended to maintain his social behavior after it had been well developed. That behavior was, as it were, trapped into the network of peer interactions and thus no longer required the behavior modification program. Other research has shown that training such social behaviors as smiling and sharing, and providing positive physical contact among children changes the social behaviors of their peers (Cooke & Apolloni, 1976). Thus, behaviors may be maintained by mutual social reinforcement among peers and target subjects even when the contingencies administered by the persons who initiated the program have been withdrawn.

Ideally, behavioral programs would just develop positive, prosocial behavior and then these behaviors would be trapped and maintained. Years of research have taught us that this hope is infrequently fulfilled. Behaviors that appear to be of the kind that the natural environment will maintain are very often not maintained at all. For example, even social interaction (the subject of the above example of trapping) is usually not maintained in children or adults after the contingencies have been withdrawn (for example, Kazdin & Polster, 1973; Strain, Shores, & Timm, 1977). Similarly, behaviors that are followed by immediate reinforcement, such as appropriate eating skills (for example, O'Brien, Bugle, & Azrin, 1972) or smiling to others (for example, Reisinger, 1972), are not automatically maintained by the natural environment. At present, it is difficult to identify in advance which behaviors will be maintained by naturally occurring events in the environment or which situations will automatically support newly developed behaviors.

A related difficulty in relying on naturally occurring reinforcers to maintain behavior pertains to how the social environment operates. The natural network of reinforcers does not necessarily promote or maintain appropriate behavior. Deviant or disruptive behaviors are likely to receive attention or notice in everyday situations such as the home or the school. Parents, teachers, hospital staff, and peers often attend to and reinforce inappropriate behavior as a matter of course. For example, disruptive behaviors are likely to be directly reinforced by attention from one's peers. Thus, the natural contingencies often seem to operate against the maintenance and transfer of prosocial behavior.

Perhaps the major obstacle to using the natural contingencies as a way to support desirable behavior is the lack of clear guidelines as to how this should be done. The procedures for improving behaviors are well developed. But procedures have not been developed for structuring the situation so that the target behaviors are invariably trapped by the social environment.

For individuals functioning normally in society, many adaptive behaviors are maintained by the natural environment. Yet, most individuals have received extensive social training and respond to a variety of subtle external and self-imposed influences. In contrast, individuals in treatment, rehabilitation, and educational settings (for whom most behavior modification programs are conducted) are trained to respond to external consequences in carefully programmed situations. It is no surprise, therefore, that their behaviors are not maintained when the consequences are withdrawn and they are placed in social situations for which they have not been prepared. What often happens is that when a behavior modification program has been withdrawn, behaviors are maintained for a few persons but not for others. If behaviors continue, perhaps they are being maintained by the naturally occurring reinforcers. If behaviors are not maintained, specific procedures can be implemented to achieve response maintenance and transfer of training. Because unplanned and unprogrammed maintenance and transfer of behavior are exceptions rather than the rule, it is usually advisable to implement one or more of the procedures discussed next.

Programming Naturally Occurring Reinforcers

In many programs, the consequences used to alter behavior are not ordinarily available in the setting where clients will eventually function. For example, tokens usually do not follow behavior in the classroom or on a hospital ward. However, consequences that are normally available can replace the extraneous events that were used to alter behavior initially. Programming naturally occurring consequences, as does the technique discussed above, utilizes available events in the environment to maintain behavior or to achieve transfer. Instead of depending on the natural contingencies to support or trap behavior, naturally occurring events can be substituted systematically to sustain performance.

The programming of naturally occurring reinforcers has been used successfully in many programs that were concerned with both response maintenance and transfer of training. For example, Kallman, Hersen, and O'Toole (1975) treated a male patient who complained that he could not walk. Although the patient had no organic problem, he was hospitalized and confined to a wheelchair. Social reinforcement was used to develop his standing and walking in the hospital. Eventually, he walked by himself. He returned home, where the treatment effects were maintained for about a month. Then he said that he could not walk and he returned to the hospital. His walking was developed, and he again returned home. Videotaped interactions of the patient and his family revealed that his family had previously attended to his disability and had ignored his attempts to walk. Hence, to maintain walking, the patient's family was trained to reinforce walking and to ignore (extinguish) complaints of being unable to walk. After the family was trained, follow-up indicated that the behavior was maintained up to 12 weeks after treatment. In this program, social consequences in the natural environment were used to sustain the gains that had been achieved in treatment.

The importance of training relatives to ensure response maintenance and transfer has been emphasized in the treatment of autistic children (Lovaas, Koegel, Simmons, & Long, 1973). Follow-up assessment of the behavior of autistic children one to four years after treatment showed that children whose parents had been trained to carry out the behavioral procedures maintained their gains outside the treatment facility and indeed improved slightly. On the other hand, children who had been institutionalized where the contingencies were not continued lost the gains that they had achieved in treatment.

Teachers in regular classrooms have been trained to continue the contingencies initiated in a special setting to achieve both transfer and maintenance (Walker, Hops, & Johnson, 1975). Highly disruptive children participated in a token economy in a special education classroom to develop appropriate classroom behavior. After improvements had been achieved, the children were returned to their regular classrooms. In some of these classrooms, the teachers conducted a behavioral program to sustain the gains that had been achieved in the special education classroom. The children who returned to a classroom where some of the contingencies were continued maintained their behavior in the new settings to a much greater extent than did the children who returned to a classroom where no program was in effect. When the special contingencies in the regular classrooms had been terminated, the behavioral gains were maintained among the children who had continued the program in their regular classrooms. Thus, the substitution of one program for another helped maintain behavior transfer and helped transfer it to a new setting, even though the program was eventually discontinued.

In general, behaviors may need to be developed with special contingencies to achieve high and consistent levels of performance. After behavior has been developed, contingencies utilizing sources of influence available in the natural environment can be substituted. The natural contingencies may not automatically sustain appropriate behavior, as has been noted in the discussion of behavioral traps. Yet, if naturally occurring consequences are altered to support behavior, they provide a useful transition between highly programmed contingencies and the haphazard and often counterproductive contingencies of the natural environment.

Gradually Removing or Fading the Contingencies

Losses of behavioral gains following a behavior modification program may result from abruptly withdrawing the reinforcing and punishing consequences. Gradually removing or fading the program is likely to be less discriminable to the client than is the abrupt withdrawal of consequences.

Eventually, the consequences can be eliminated entirely without a return of behavior to its baseline rate.

Fading of the contingencies can be accomplished in many ways. One of the most frequently used ways has been reported in token economies in institutional settings. For example, with psychiatric patients, token economies are often divided into steps or levels. As patients progress, they pass through the various levels of the program. As patients perform the target behaviors consistently, they move to higher levels in the system, at which more reinforcers may be available (to encourage further progress). At the highest level, few or no contingencies may be in effect, so that the patients can learn to function without direct and immediate consequences.

Paul and Lentz (1977) used a leveled token economy to fade the contingencies for chronic psychiatric patients. At the first level, the patients needed to perform only minimal levels of behavior (such as attending activities) to earn tokens. As they moved to higher levels, they could earn more tokens and they had access to a larger range of backup reinforcers. At the highest level, they could buy themselves off the system. They used a credit card instead of tokens, and they had access to all of the available reinforcers as long as they continued to perform adequately.

The purpose of using levels is to develop higher levels of performance over time and to reduce the highly structured contingencies that maintain performance. Ideally, the highest level in the program will resemble the contingencies that one is likely to encounter outside the setting. To ensure that performance is maintained at a high level, clients can be given the privilege of earning themselves off the highly structured contingencies (as in a token economy) only if their performance meets a particular criterion (Kazdin & Mascitelli, 1980). If a client's performance continues at a high level with few or no contingencies, behavior is more likely to be maintained when the client leaves the setting.

The contingencies can be faded in ways other than using levels in a token reinforcement program. An alternative procedure is to check behavior and provide reinforcing consequences less often over time. For example, Rosen and Rosen (1983) reduced stealing in a 7-year-old boy who frequently took things from his classmates. Points (exchangeable for extra recess and other reinforcers) were provided if he did not have other children's possessions; fines were invoked if he did. The boy was checked every 15 minutes and received or lost points accordingly. This procedure effectively reduced his stealing. The program was then faded by checking and providing consequences only once every two hours. As shown in Figure 11−1, when the program was faded, virtually no stealing occurred. During the follow-up phase, checking, points, and fines were discontinued. The effects of the program were maintained over a 31-day follow-up period.

Gradually withdrawing contingencies may be very useful because it prepares clients for the conditions under which they must normally function. In everyday living, contingencies are often unsystematic and consequences for performance, if any, may be delayed. The gradual withdrawal

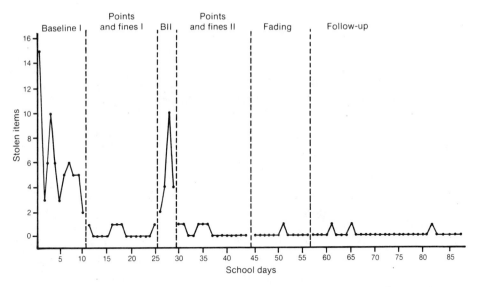

FIGURE 11–1
Number of items stolen each day during baseline and intervention (points and fines) phases. During the fading phase, consequences were provided less frequently for behavior. In the follow-up phase, the program was discontinued.
SOURCE: Rosen, H. S., & Rosen, L. A. (1983).

of contingencies provides a transition between a highly programmed environment and one that is less well programmed with regard to given target behaviors. At present, several other studies have shown that fading the consequences leads to maintenance of behavior (for example, Friman & Hove, 1987; Sullivan & O'Leary, 1990). Thus, fading represents a maintenance strategy that should probably be routinely incorporated into behavioral programs.

Expanding Stimulus Control

One reason that behaviors may not be maintained and may not transfer to new settings is that clients readily form a discrimination between the conditions in which reinforcement (or punishment) is (S^D) and is not delivered (S^Δ). Behavior becomes associated with a narrow range of cues that may include specific behavior change agents (for example, parents, teachers) who administer the program and the specific setting in which the contingencies are in effect (such as the classroom rather than the playground or the home). As soon as the program is withdrawn or the setting changes, clients discriminate that the desirable behavior is no longer associated with certain consequences. Thus, responses are not maintained and do not transfer to new situations.

Maintenance and transfer can be developed by expanding the breadth of the stimuli that exert control over behavior (Horner, Bellamy, & Colvin, 1984). The procedures used to expand stimulus control may vary as a function of the type of transfer that is of interest. For example, in some programs, client behavior may be restricted to the presence of the specific persons who conduct training and implement the contingencies. In these cases, the narrow control exerted by the staff may be expanded by introducing more staff into training. For example, Stokes, Baer, and Jackson (1974) trained four children with severe and profound retardation to engage in greeting responses (hand waving), using one staff member in the institution as the trainer in special experimental sessions. Although the behaviors were developed in this way, observations revealed that the children usually did not greet other staff members who approached them. The behavior was apparently under quite narrow stimulus control. The stimulus control was expanded by having a second staff member also conduct training. The additional training not only increased greeting responses to this staff member but also resulted in greeting responses to several other staff members who had not been associated with the training. Thus, the behavior was no longer under the narrow stimulus control of the trainer. Programs often introduce new trainers to ensure transfer of training (for example, Davis, Brady, Williams, & Hamilton, 1992). Only one or a few individuals may be needed; the behavior then generalizes to many new trainers, staff, and others.

Usually, it is of interest to ensure that behavior transfers simultaneously across several dimensions, including staff members, activities, situations, and settings. For example, in one study, praise and points (exchangeable for money) were used to develop positive interpersonal comments among four delinquent adolescents (Emshoff, Redd, & Davidson, 1976). To develop behavior that would transfer across a variety of stimulus conditions, two of the clients were trained under conditions that varied across activities (for example, during games and discussions), trainers, locations in the facility, and the time of day. Unlike the clients who were trained under constant training conditions, the clients who received this highly varied training made positive comments under several tests for generalization when tokens were delivered noncontingently, when a new trainer was introduced, and when the activity, setting, and trainer all varied. Not only was transfer of training improved by varying the training conditions, but the clients who were trained in this way also showed superior maintenance of the behavior three weeks after training had been terminated.

In a program with autistic children, several behaviors were developed, such as attending to a task, imitating, speaking, and recognizing words (Koegel & Rincover, 1974). Although these behaviors were increased, performance did not transfer beyond the one-to-one situation with the staff member used in the training sessions. When a child was placed with others in a group situation, the trained behaviors decreased. To develop transfer to the classroom situation, various stimulus conditions of the classroom were gradually introduced into training. Other children, the classroom teacher, and teacher aides were included in the training situation to associate performance of the target behavior with a variety of stimuli. After the stimulus conditions were expanded in training, behavior transferred to the classroom.

The above studies illustrate that transfer of training and response maintenance can be established by introducing various components of the situation in which transfer is desired or by expanding the range of the individuals who administer the contingencies. From these studies, it appears that the stimulus conditions of the transfer setting need to be introduced while training is still in effect. As the stimuli that exert control over behavior broaden, the likelihood that the behavior will be performed in new situations and in the presence of a variety of people is markedly increased. It is important to note that not all of the conditions across which transfer is desired need to be introduced into training. Only a few of the new stimulus conditions need to be introduced, after which transfer extends to new settings and to people who have had no association with the training.

Training Individuals to Respond to the "General Case"

Expanding stimulus control, which consists of introducing a broad range of stimuli into training, has been conducted for many years. Recently, this approach has been developed more systematically in a strategy referred to as *training the general case.* This strategy trains the individual to perform the target behavior across a variety of stimulus conditions so that the behavior does not come under the control of a narrow range of cues.

A number of specific steps are employed to teach the general case (Horner, Eberhard, & Sheehan, 1986). These steps are listed in Table 11–1. Consider the steps with a hypothetical program designed to teach a shy, withdrawn child to socialize with peers at school. The target behavior may consist of speaking with other children. In Step 1, we note the specific situations in which we wish the behavior to occur. In our example, we decide that we would like the child to engage in the behavior during recess, at lunch, and during free time in class. In Step 2, we identify the salient stimulus characteristics that vary among these conditions. Among such characteristics are differences in the number of children present, in daily activities, in settings, and in the amounts of structure provided in the situations. In this step, an indefinite number of characteristics might be identified, but the success of the strategy does not depend on identifying every conceivable characteristic on which the situations vary. The task is merely to identify some of the salient characteristics that differentiate the situations.

In Step 3, we specify the variations of the target behaviors that are required in these situations. The behaviors might include initiating conversation, approaching others, responding to initiations of others, joining a

TABLE 11–1
Requirements for Training the General Case

Step 1	Specify the set of stimulus situations across which a behavior is to be performed after training has been completed.
Step 2	Define the range of relevant dimensions or characteristics across which they vary.
Step 3	Define the range of response variations or the different behaviors required across the set of stimulus situations.
Step 4	Select and teach examples that sample from the range of the stimulus and response domains (as specified in Steps 2 and 3).

SOURCE: Adapted from Horner, R. H., Eberhard, J. M., & Sheehan, M. R. (1986).

group that is already engaged in an activity, and starting an activity with another person. Finally, in Step 4, we select for training exemplary situations that represent the stimulus and response domains of interest. Thus, training might be carried out in different social situations, with different persons present, and with different social cues. Using the overall approach, training systematically programs behaviors for performance in diverse situations.

Several studies have evaluated general-case training as a means of ensuring transfer of behaviors across stimulus conditions. One such study was designed to teach the simple skill of putting on a shirt to developmentally disabled persons (8 to 23 years old) who lived in community group homes (Day & Horner, 1986). Two training methods were used. The first method consisted of single-instance training, in which individuals were trained (prompts, praise) to put on a single type of shirt (T-shirt). The second method consisted of general-case training, in which additional types of shirts were presented in training (T-shirt, tank top, turtleneck). These shirts sampled a broader range of stimulus conditions (for example, type of collar, sleeve length, fit, fabric), and as a consequence they also required the broader range of responses entailed in "putting on a shirt." At different points in training, individuals were tested (without prompts or reinforcement) to see the extent to which they could put on a wide range of shirt types, including types that had not been part of training. General-case training led to a much broader performance across a range of new stimulus conditions than did single-instance training.

Other studies have used the general-case training approach to develop self-care and community-relevant skills among people with developmental disabilities as well as to train institutional staff working with special populations to use behavioral techniques with their clients (for example, Ducharme & Feldman, 1992; Horner, Albin, & Ralph, 1986; Neef, Lensbower, Hockersmith, DePalma, & Gray, 1990). The results have shown behavior transfers to a broader range of stimulus conditions with general-case training than from the usual single-case training. Few studies have shown the extent to which long-term assessment is aided by general-case training.

Maintenance up to six months in one program (for example, Ducharme & Feldman, 1992) is promising. Further work is needed. At this point, the strength of general-case training is in relation to transfer of training. General-case training is an important strategy to ensure that behaviors are not restricted to features of the training setting.

In some cases, practical obstacles may prevent introducing diverse stimuli conditions into training. For example, many behavioral programs focus on developing community-related skills among various populations. Training is often conducted in the community to help train the general case. It may be difficult to make diverse settings available for training purposes. One alternative may be to use videotaped vignettes illustrating the diverse settings in which the behaviors are to be performed, a procedure that also facilitates generalization across settings (Haring, Kennedy, Adams, & Pitts-Conway, 1987).

In general, training the general case is an exceedingly important strategy to enhance transfer of training across situations, settings, and trainers. A related feature of the strategy is worth mentioning in passing. Often it is useful to begin training in special laboratory sessions rather than in applied settings. For example, teaching a hyperactive student to work on school assignments without disrupting others may be readily achieved with a number of procedures, such as prompting, shaping, or self-instruction training. Training may be more easily accomplished, at least initially, by working with the child in a contrived situation, such as special sessions where a trainer works with the child outside the classroom. With a one-to-one trainer-student ratio and close supervision, behavior change is more easily achieved. Remember, of course, the initial task is to develop the desired behaviors. Once the desired behaviors are developed, general-case training provides a way to ensure transfer of behavior to everyday situations. As the behaviors are developed, new trainers, stimulus conditions, tasks, and other features of the natural environment can be introduced so that behavior transfers (for example, Neef, Lensbower, Hockersmith, De-Palma, & Gray, 1990).

Schedules of Reinforcement

As mentioned earlier, resistance to extinction can be enhanced by using intermittent reinforcement. After behavior has been well established, reinforcing consequences can be delivered intermittently. The intermittence of the reinforcement can be increased, so that very little reinforcement is provided for behavior. Resistance of behavior to extinction once reinforcement is withdrawn is a function of the intermittence of the reinforcement. The more intermittent (or thinner) the reinforcement schedule, the greater is the resistance to extinction.

Intermittent reinforcement has been used to maintain behavior. In a simple demonstration several years ago, reinforcement was used to develop social behavior of two adults with developmental disabilities who attended a sheltered workshop (Kazdin & Polster, 1973). Because these men had engaged in little social interaction, they received tokens for talking with their peers. They were told they would receive tokens for interacting with peers socially during three work breaks. Each client received a token for each of the peers with whom he had spoken during each break. Thus, every interaction was reinforced. Figure 11–2 shows that during the first phase in which reinforcement was given, the daily average number of both clients' interactions gradually increased. Then, during a reversal phase in which tokens were withdrawn, their interactions decreased. When reinforcement was reinstated, one of the clients (S_1) received tokens as he had before (that is, continuous reinforcement). The other client (S_2) was told that he would receive tokens only once in a while (that is, intermittent reinforcement). At first, the second client received tokens during two of the work breaks. Eventually, all of his token reinforcement was withdrawn. As Figure 11–2 shows, during a second reversal phase, the client whose behavior had been continuously reinforced showed an immediate decline in social interaction. However, the client whose behavior had been intermittently reinforced maintained a high rate of social interaction. Thus, intermittent reinforcement appeared to help maintain behavior.

Intermittent reinforcement was also shown to enhance maintenance in a project designed to increase the selection of nutritious snacks among three children (aged 4 to 5) enrolled in a day-care center (Baer, Blount, Detrick, & Stokes, 1987). Each day, the children were offered a choice of snacks that were considered nutritious (fruit, vegetable) or relatively non-nutritious (cookie, cracker). The children were trained to identify the nutritious snacks, to state that they would choose such snacks, and then to select such a snack afterward. If the children completed this sequence, they were allowed to draw from a grab bag that included cards listing consequences (reinforcers) that they would receive (for example, hugs, tickles, stickers). After the behavior had been developed, the opportunities to select from the grab bag were made increasingly intermittent. At first, consequences were given every day (100 percent of the days). This was faded over periods of 5 to 10 days so that the consequences were delivered only 67 percent and then 33 percent of the days. Eventually, no consequences were provided. The results indicated that behavior was maintained up to seven weeks after the reinforcement had been terminated.

Instead of eliminating reinforcement completely, some investigators continue the use of intermittent reinforcement to maintain behavior at a high level. Intermittent reinforcement is quite effective, of course, while the reinforcement is still in effect. For example, in the Achievement Place program points were given or withdrawn based on the degree to which predelinquent youth cleaned their rooms (Phillips, Phillips, Fixsen, and Wolf, 1971). After the behavior had been well established, the reinforcing and punishing consequences became increasingly intermittent. The rooms were checked daily, but reinforcement or punishment occurred only once in a while. Although the consequences were delivered on only 8 percent of the

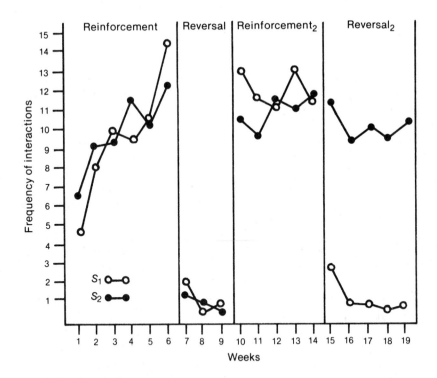

FIGURE 11–2

Mean frequency of interactions per day during reinforcement, reversal, reinforcement$_2$, and reversal$_2$ for Subject 1 (S$_1$) and Subject 2 (S$_2$).

SOURCE: Kazdin, A. E., & Polster, R. (1973).

days checked, the behavior was maintained at a high level. The consequences were not completely withdrawn, so the effect of intermittent reinforcement on extinction was not evaluated.

Intermittent reinforcement can be readily incorporated into most programs. It is important to make the schedule of reinforcement increasingly intermittent to increase resistance to extinction. It is unclear whether highly intermittent reinforcement forestalls extinction only temporarily or can virtually eliminate extinction even after a long extinction period. Behaviors reinforced intermittently have been maintained up to several months or a year after the intervention has been terminated (Hall, Cooper, Burmaster, & Polk, 1977; Morin, Ladouceur, & Cloutier, 1982).

Delay of Reinforcement

Behavior may also be maintained by gradually increasing the delay between reinforcement and the target behavior. When behavior is initially developed, immediate reinforcement is usually essential to ensure a high rate of responding. As behavior stabilizes and becomes well established, the delay between behavior and the reinforcing consequences can be increased without a loss in performance.

In maintaining behavior, the effectiveness of delaying reinforcement following a response has not been widely studied, although delay of reinforcement has often been used as part of other maintenance strategies, such as fading the contingencies and altering reinforcement schedules. An illustration of how delays can be used was provided in three classrooms where reinforcement was contingent upon the appropriate behavior of the group (Greenwood, Hops, Delquadri, & Guild, 1974). After behavior had achieved a relatively high level, a delay was introduced in earning the group consequences. The classes were required to perform high levels of behavior for an increasing number of consecutive sessions before the reinforcer was delivered. A maximum delay of ten sessions was attained before earning the reinforcer. Follow-up data three weeks after the program ended revealed that appropriate classroom behaviors were maintained.

A major purpose of delaying reinforcement is to maintain behavior after the program has been entirely withdrawn. Yet, while the program is in effect, delayed reinforcement may increase generalization of behavior over time or across situations. For example, the effects of immediate and delayed reinforcement in maintaining the behavior of preschool children were compared (Fowler & Baer, 1981). Individual target behaviors (sharing, cooperative play) were identified, depending on the problem areas of each child. Behavior was observed for two classroom periods each day. Reinforcement (stickers exchangeable for toys) and feedback for performance of the target behavior were provided for performance in the first class period each day. When reinforcement and feedback were provided immediately after that period, behavior improved; but the changes were not evident in the second period. When the consequences were delayed until the end of the day (even though they were provided only for how well the children did in the first period), performance improved in both periods. Thus, delayed reinforcement promoted maintenance of behavior across both periods. It is likely that with delayed reinforcement the children were less able to discriminate the behaviors and periods for which reinforcement was provided, so they sustained their behavior at high levels to maximize their chances of receiving reinforcement.

In general, delayed reinforcement is not a reliably effective method for changing behavior initially. Yet it can be effective in maintaining behavior over time (for example, Dunlap, Koegel, Johnson, & O'Neill, 1987). The shift from immediate to delayed reinforcement may be important in behavior change programs because most of the reinforcers available in the social environment are delayed. Hence, it is important to wean a client from immediate reinforcement. Behaviors should be well established before long delays are invoked. When delayed reinforcement is introduced, performance should be observed closely to ensure that there is no loss of behavioral gains. Eventually, reinforcement may be withdrawn entirely or delivered only after long delays without a loss in performance.

Peer Facilitators

Peers may be utilized to help maintain behavior and to develop transfer across a variety of situations. If behavior comes under the stimulus control of the persons who implement the contingencies, it may be important to involve peers in the administration of consequences. Because peers have contact with the client across a variety of situations, their presence may provide the client with cues to continue the target behavior across these situations. After the specific contingencies have been terminated, peers may still influence the client's behavior.

Many programs utilizing peers as behavior change agents have been conducted in classroom settings (see Strain, 1981). For example, Lancioni (1982, Exp. 1) trained normal fourth-grade children as tutors to help socially withdrawn children with developmental disabilities engage in cooperative play, activities, and self-help skills. The tutors were trained to model the target behaviors and to provide prompts and social reinforcement. For their assistance, the tutors received tokens. They worked with these children in activities in special sessions outside the classroom, which increased the social behavior of the developmentally disabled children. Moreover, the changes in the behavior of the developmentally disabled children transferred to social interaction with other children and to a play situation in which training had not been conducted. After training had been terminated, performance was maintained over a two-week follow-up period. These results suggest that the use of peers may facilitate both transfer of training and response maintenance.

Similarly, in another program, three junior high school students were trained to serve as tutors for children in need of remedial reading instruction (Greer & Polirstok, 1982). The tutors were trained to administer approval for on-task behavior and to ignore disruptive behavior. They received token reinforcement for their delivery of approval. The results indicated that the target children improved in their performance in reading assignments. After the tutors no longer received token reinforcement for helping the target children, they continued to provide approval and the target children maintained their improvements in reading. These results illustrate a potential advantage of peer-based reinforcement. Once peers have been trained, they may continue to provide reinforcement to persons under their charge. Alternatively, they may serve as discriminative stimuli and (through stimulus control) help promote the target behaviors altered in training.

Other investigations have shown that peer-administered contingencies sometimes lead to maintenance and transfer of behavior to situations other than those in which training has been conducted (Peck, Cooke, & Apolloni, 1981). However, the use of peers as facilitators of transfer and maintenance remains to be exploited. In many of the situations in which behavioral programs are conducted, peers, siblings, or other inmates or residents might be involved in monitoring the behavior of a target subject.

Self-Control Procedures

As noted earlier, one reason that changes in behavior are not maintained and do not transfer is that behavior comes under the stimulus control of external agents (for example, parents, teachers, staff) and the restricted situations (for example, home, classroom, ward) in which training is conducted. Perhaps, training clients to control their own behavior would prevent behavior changes from being lost when a program is withdrawn. Also, because the client implements the contingencies in self-administered programs, such programs can be executed across situations.

Few programs have carefully tested the effects of self-control strategies as a means of maintaining long-term gains or ensuring transfer of training. In one demonstration, self-control techniques were used with parents of preschool children who had been referred for treatment (Sanders & Glynn, 1981). The children were noncompliant, demanding, and difficult to manage at home. The parents were trained to provide prompts and praise for appropriate behavior, to deliver feedback, and to use reprimands and withdrawal of reinforcers for inappropriate behavior. Initially, training was conducted by a therapist who visited the home. After the parents' skills had been developed, a self-management training procedure was provided to help the parents maintain their skills. They were trained to monitor their own behavior, to structure the situation to foster appropriate child behavior, to identify target behaviors, and to monitor their children's progress. The initial training increased the parents' skills (for example, use of social reinforcement), which decreased disruptive child behavior in the home. With the self-management training, the parents' skills were maintained in the home and generalized to community settings (shopping trips, visits to relatives), where disruptive child behavior also decreased. Moreover, a three-month follow-up assessment indicated that the parents' skills and low rates of disruptive child behavior were maintained.

Self-control strategies have been used to achieve transfer of training across situations (Ninness, Fuerst, Rutherford, & Glenn, 1991). In this program, three emotionally disturbed adolescents in a special education classroom were trained to engage in on-task behavior and to reduce socially inappropriate behavior (fighting, throwing objects, cursing). Modeling, reinforcement, role-playing, and self-control training (self-monitoring, self-reinforcement, matching self-assessment to the assessment of the teacher) led to reduction of inappropriate behavior. Socially inappropriate behavior did not change during periods between classes as students walked to other classes, which was assessed by means of a hidden camera. When students were instructed to apply self-control and self-evaluation to the between-classes period, socially inappropriate behavior decreased, as it had in the classroom. The effects were evaluated for only a few days; consequently, whether the gains would have been sustained in the classroom or between classes without additional contingencies is not known. Yet, the results suggest that self-control can be used to enhance transfer.

In general, self-control strategies may be useful to enhance mainte-nance and transfer. Few demonstrations have examined long-term impact. There is a general concern that self-control techniques by themselves may be limited. Evidence, mostly from classroom settings with elementary school students, indicates that self-monitoring and self-reinforcement have short-lived effects unless external contingencies (for example, by the teacher) are applied to sustain behavior (see Jones, Nelson, & Kazdin, 1977). The value of self-control techniques does not depend on whether they maintain behavior or lead to transfer when used by themselves. The techniques may serve as a useful adjunct to help effect the transition from externally managed contingencies to the contingencies in the natural envi-ronment. Self-reinforcement, self-monitoring, and self-evaluation, alone or in combination, involve the client more directly in the program and provide less reliance on external agents such as parents or teachers. In this sense, self-control procedures may be considered part of a more general strategy of fading the contingencies (cf. Gardner, Cole, Berry, & Nowinski, 1983; Mank & Horner, 1987).

Cognitively Based Procedures

Cognitively based techniques, such as self-instruction training and problem-solving skills training, constitute special self-control procedures that may also be useful in maintaining behavior and promoting transfer. These procedures focus on developing skills that individuals can apply to a variety of situations and settings.

As mentioned in the previous chapter, self-instruction training was used to develop on-task behavior among preschool children (Guevremont, Os-nes, & Stokes, 1988). Training led to improvements in performance during the special training sessions but did not carry over to the classroom. Prompts (instructions, reminders) from the teachers to the children to use self-instructions in the classroom led to improvements in the classroom. Thus, increasing the use of self-instructions to a new situation led to trans-fer of training.

Apart from transfer of training, response maintenance occasionally results from self-instruction training. For example, in a classroom setting, Bornstein and Quevillon (1976) trained disruptive children to administer self-instructions to develop appropriate classroom behavior. Attentive be-havior markedly increased, and these effects were maintained several weeks after training. However, as discussed in Chapter 10, the effects of self-instruction in altering classroom behavior have been inconsistent.

Cognitively based interventions have frequently improved various problem-solving skills (for example, thinking of solutions to problems). In several studies, self-instruction training and problem-solving skills training have altered behavior in applied settings including the home, the school, and the community (see Durlak et al., 1991; Kazdin, 1993b). Also, the effects of treatment have been maintained up to one year after treatment has been terminated. In some cases, treatment emphasizes practice opportunities outside the sessions so that assignments are given during treatment to apply the techniques to problems as they emerge in these other settings. Insofar as maintenance and transfer are achieved, these may be due to other methods we have discussed in relation to generalization (for example, expansion of stimulus control) rather than to a special feature of cognitively based treatment. The use of cognitively based treatments as a means of promoting generalization has not been well studied. The rationale for its use is that cognitive changes may affect a broad range of situations and that the specific skills that are used can be a self-control strategy the individual applies to many different situations. These are reasonable bases for maintenance and transfer but await supporting evidence.

Duration of Intervention Programs

Many behavioral programs have been implemented in settings such as the classroom, home, or community for relatively brief periods (for example, several days or a few weeks). Marked changes in behavior can be achieved even in such brief periods. However, maintenance and transfer may be especially unlikely in programs implemented for relatively brief treatment periods. If one wishes to develop durable behaviors that are performed in many different situations, an extended period of training may be necessary.

The duration of the program appears to be related to response maintenance and transfer of training, though the effects of duration on maintenance and transfer have not been carefully tested. A number of programs that have become "classics" for the field have been carried out for protracted periods (from several months to a few years). In such instances, the results have suggested that the responses are maintained and transferred to new situations. For example, in the Paul and Lentz (1977) program, psychiatric patients who participated in a token economy over several months continued to show gains one and a half to five years after the program, and these gains were reflected in community adjustment. Thus, both maintenance and transfer appeared to have been achieved. As another example, a behavior modification program was implemented in elementary school grades over a period of several years and grade levels (Bushell, 1978). The program led to changes in behavior that were still evident two years after the program had been terminated and the children had entered classrooms where reinforcement programs were not in effect.

Programs in place for extended periods often provide intensive treatment effort. For example, in a program for autistic children (under 4 years of age), behavioral intervention was provided in the home, school, and community (Lovaas, 1987). Treatment focused on eliminating maladaptive behavior (for example, self-stimulation, aggression) and developing a variety of prosocial skills (for example, play) and cognitive-academic skills (for example, language, reading, writing). The program involved parents, teachers, and trained undergraduates so that almost all of each child's waking hours were devoted to developing adaptive behaviors. Treatment was provided for 40 hours a week, 365 days a year, for 2 to 6 years. The results indicated that 47 percent of the children were eventually placed in normal first-grade classes and improved markedly on standardized intelligence tests. These gains were not evident in control children who were not involved in the training program. Here the gains of the program appeared to transfer to regular public school functioning.

Follow-up was conducted for both treatment and control groups (McEachin, Smith, & Lovaas, 1993). At the time of follow-up, intervention youths had been out of treatment for a mean of five years (range zero to twelve years); control subjects were out of treatment for a mean of three years (range zero to nine years). The results indicated that the benefits of treatment were maintained. More youths in the intervention group remained in a regular class placement, mean IQ scores were higher, and adaptive behavior scores were superior to the control group. The original treatment and more follow-up results represent critically important findings suggesting the impact of intensive and long-term intervention.

The above programs do not show unequivocally that the longer a program is in effect, the more likely it is that behaviors will be maintained and will transfer to new settings. To obtain this information, research would need to compare the effects of a program applied to different children for different durations. Yet, some evidence has suggested that programs in effect for brief periods show little maintenance and that maintenance increases as treatment is continued. For example, in one program, peer interaction was developed among withdrawn elementary school children (Paine et al., 1982). The children received token reinforcement at recess and in-class training for social behavior. Behaviors improved, but the gains were lost in return-to-baseline phases. Treatment was introduced and withdrawn repeatedly in separate phases over time. With each successive treatment phase, less of the desired social behavior was lost when baseline conditions were reintroduced. By the end of the program, behaviors were maintained and the children remained within the normal range of social interaction without continuing treatment.

The reasons that behaviors were maintained are unclear. It is possible that as a behavior is performed for an extended period, reinforcers that naturally occur in the environment or are provided by the behavior itself begin to control the behavior. Indeed, such effects seem evident in everyday life. Engaging in exercise or eating special foods may initially require some special incentive program. However, once the behaviors have been performed for an extended period, they often seem to be maintained "on their own." Similarly, in behavioral programs, repeated opportunities to perform a behavior appear to influence maintenance (Greenwood, Delquadri, & Hall, 1984; Horner, Williams, & Knobbe, 1985). Thus, evidence points to the importance of such factors as repeated performance of the behavior over time. However, the process of developing behavior so that it becomes fixed in one's repertoire (that is, relatively impervious to moment-to-moment contingencies) is not well understood. Additional research is needed in the context of behavioral programs to examine whether, in fact, programs in effect for longer periods of time are related to maintenance of behavior change once the programs have been terminated.

Procedures Used in Combination

The previously discussed procedures for promoting response maintenance and transfer of training are not mutually exclusive. In fact, many of the procedures can be viewed as variations of a more general strategy. For example, many of the procedures are designed to make the training situation increasingly similar to the nontraining situations so that stimulus control over the desired behavior is relatively broad. Thus, altering the delivery of reinforcement so that it is increasingly intermittent and delayed, fading the contingencies altogether, fading the presence of the trainer, and using peers who are present in the natural settings might all be viewed as efforts to develop behavior so that it is not connected to, or performed exclusively in the presence of, a narrow range of conditions.

Another reason for not viewing the procedures for promoting maintenance and transfer as mutually exclusive is the way they are employed. Investigators frequently use several procedures simultaneously to maximize the likelihood that responses will be maintained and will transfer to new situations. For example, in one study adolescents in an institutional setting (nonspecified) received training in various social skills (responding politely, reacting prosocially to criticism or to confrontation from others) (Foxx, Faw, & Weber, 1991). Each youth had been identified with emotional and behavioral dysfunction. The skills were trained in special sessions in a novel part of the facility, although the goal was to develop skills that would generalize widely across others and to the youths' regular classroom. To achieve generalization and maintenance, several strategies discussed previously were combined. To begin, the responses (social skills) were considered to be important for natural interaction in the situation and hence would be supported by the natural contingencies; the contingencies were gradually faded from token (monetary) reinforcement to praise for the desired behaviors; stimulus control was expanded by including in training persons who would be present in the nontraining setting after training; also, prompting and reinforcement by the trainers were gradually decreased as social skills improved; subjects assumed a larger role over their own training by self-monitoring (self-control) their progress on a score card and administering self-instructions covertly (cognitively based strategies) to guide behavior. The results indicated that training effects generally were maintained up to the three-month follow-up assessment and generalized to the regular classroom. The use of several strategies to achieve maintenance and transfer means that it is difficult to know which strategy or combination of strategies was responsible for the favorable effect. In applied settings, the primary goal usually is to demonstrate that maintenance and transfer were achieved to ensure that clinically important changes were made to help the people who participated in the program. At the same time, other research in more-laboratory-based settings needs to analyze carefully what strategies lead to maintenance and transfer and how these effects can be maximized.

Similarly, Haney and Jones (1982) used several procedures to maintain behavior in a program designed to teach children with developmental disabilities how to escape from fires in their homes. The training consisted of instructions, modeling, rehearsal, and social and tangible (candy) reinforcement. Several complex sequences of behaviors were taught, so that the children could assess the danger of the situation and behave accordingly. After the behaviors had been well established, the training program was faded, using several procedures. First, prompts were gradually decreased to reduce reliance on the trainer. Second, reinforcement was provided for increasingly large sequences of correct behavior. Finally, external reinforcement from the trainer was replaced by self-reinforcement, under which the children took their rewards for correct completion of the appropriate escape behaviors. Assessment six months after the program had been terminated indicated that the behaviors were maintained.

Many other behavior modification programs have combined various techniques to promote response maintenance and transfer, such as substituting naturally occurring reinforcers for more contrived reinforcers and expanding stimulus control so that the training situation resembles natural stimulus conditions (Koegel, O'Dell, & Koegel, 1987); training in multiple settings to expand stimulus control and shifting to more intermittent reinforcement (Rasing & Duker, 1992); using delayed and intermittent reinforcement and fading the presence of the trainer (Dunlap, Koegel, Johnson, & O'Neill, 1987); and using peers, shifting from edible to social and from continuous to intermittent reinforcement, and increasing the delay of reinforcement (Lancioni, 1982).

In general, each of the procedures designed to promote maintenance and transfer emphasizes a different aspect of the contingencies that control behavior. The focus on any single factor, such as the stimuli that exert control over the response, the scheduling of consequences, and fading of the contingencies, may be limited when applied individually. In many of the situations in which maintenance and transfer are required, it is likely that several procedures would have to be programmed systematically. Current research represents an important beginning by looking at several specific techniques for achieving maintenance and transfer.

SUMMARY AND CONCLUSION

Two major issues in evaluating behavior modification programs are maintenance of behavior once the program has been withdrawn and transfer of the behavior to situations and settings other than those in which training has taken place. These issues are referred to as response maintenance and transfer of training. Maintenance and transfer are not automatic by-products of a behavior modification program. Rather, they usually have to be programmed directly by including specific procedures in the program.

Recently, advances have been made in developing techniques that help maintain behavior and help ensure its transfer. Major techniques of this kind are (1) bringing behavior under the control of the natural contingencies, (2) programming naturally occurring reinforcers, (3) gradually removing or fading the contingencies, (4) expanding stimulus control over behavior, (5) training individuals to respond to the general case, (6) altering the schedules of reinforcement, (7) increasing the delay of reinforcement, (8) using peer facilitators, (9) using self-control procedures, and (10) using cognitively based procedures. These techniques vary in the extent to which they have been evaluated and in the extent to which they achieve maintenance, transfer, or both. The techniques are often combined in many programs to maximize the likelihood that durable and broad changes in performance will be attained. Hence, the effectiveness of individual techniques is often difficult to determine. Nevertheless, present work suggests that several of the techniques can be implemented to maintain high levels of performance and to extend these levels to the new situations in which the client will function.

For Further Reading

Albin, R. W., Horner, R. H., Koegel, R. L., & Dunlap, G. (Eds.). (1987). *Extending competent performance: Applied research on generalization and maintenance.* Eugene, OR: University of Oregon.

Allen, J. S., Jr., Tarnowski, K. J., Simonian, S. J., Elliott, D., & Drabman, R. S. (1991). The generalization map revisited: Assessment of generalized treatment effects in child and adolescent behavior therapy. *Behavior Therapy, 23,* 393–405.

Horner, R. H., Dunlap, G., & Koegel, R. L. (Eds.). (1988). *Generalization and maintenance: Life-style changes in applied settings.* Baltimore: Paul Brookes.

Stokes, T. F., & Osnes, P. G. (1989). An operant pursuit of generalization. *Behavior Therapy, 20,* 337–355.

CHAPTER TWELVE

CURRENT APPLICATIONS OF BEHAVIORAL TECHNIQUES

Previous chapters have presented alternative techniques derived from operant conditioning principles and methods of assessing and evaluating the impact of these techniques on behavior. The techniques were illustrated by drawing on examples of behavioral problems with various populations, settings, and behaviors. As the illustrations may reflect, most behavior modification programs have been conducted in school classrooms, the home, institutional settings for people with developmental disabilities or psychiatric patients, and facilities for delinquents. The initial applications focused on clients and behaviors that were traditionally regarded as central to education, treatment, and rehabilitation. Understandably, these areas have been emphasized because of the long-recognized need for techniques to alter behavior.

Behavioral techniques have been extended to many other areas. The extensions were prompted by successes of the techniques in altering a variety of behaviors within traditional domains of treatment and education. In addition, if operant conditioning principles describe relations between environmental events and behavior with any degree of generality, the techniques should be relevant to a wide range of behaviors in diverse settings. The previous chapters have focused primarily on principles and techniques of behavior modification. Examples have illustrated diverse techniques. It is useful to shift the focus to *areas of research* where behavioral techniques have been systematically applied. By focusing on areas of application, the potential of addressing important issues in everyday settings becomes more clear. The present chapter conveys more explicitly the range of applications by sampling some of the salient areas of current work.

MEDICAL APPLICATIONS

Behavior modification techniques are being applied increasingly to problems that relate to physical health and illness. Applications of behavioral science to the prevention, diagnosis, and treatment of problems of physical health have recently emerged as an area referred to as *behavioral medicine* or, more generally, *health psychology*. The domain encompasses many foci, such as fostering healthy lifestyles (such as exercising and following dietary guidelines), reduction of behaviors that increase risk for disease or dysfunction (for example, unprotected sex and risk for AIDS), and the treatment of a variety of dysfunctions and disorders (for example, hypertension, headaches, pain, obesity) (see Blanchard, 1992; Glenwick & Jason, in press). Although examples throughout previous chapters have illustrated applications related to health, it is important to highlight the area here.

Prevention of Illness and Disease

In many cases, serious illness and disease can be averted by engaging in preventive behaviors. A number of studies have focused on developing behaviors to reduce risk of disease or to detect early onset of disease so that treatments can be effectively applied. Only a few of the many areas in which this has been accomplished can be sampled here.

Behavioral interventions have been applied to the prevention of life-threatening disease. For example, exposure to the sun is known to be a risk factor for skin cancer. The likelihood of skin cancer is increasing, which is assumed to be the result of a change in lifestyle, increased exposure to the sun, and depletion of the ozone layer. Individuals exposed to the sun rarely engage in sufficiently protective behavior. In a recent study, an effort was made to increase the extent to which individuals attending two private swimming pools engaged in protective behaviors (Lombard, Neubauer, Canfield, & Winett, 1991). The target behaviors included wearing a shirt to cover the upper body, wearing a hat, using a sunscreen, wearing zinc oxide (covering) on one's face, and other behaviors. An intervention was implemented by providing information posters to convey how to protect oneself, daily feedback posters noting the percentage of adults and children who had performed protective behaviors on the previous day, and a raffle for individuals who completed a form pledging to engage in "safe-sun" practices. The intervention was implemented at two pools at different points in time.

As shown in Figure 12–1, the intervention led to increases in the percentage of individuals who engaged in two or more protective behaviors. The results are instructive in showing that relatively simple informational and feedback interventions can lead to change. The magnitude of the results also suggests that more potent interventions are needed. Many individuals did not engage in the desired behaviors and hence placed themselves at risk for skin cancer. Even so, the changes reflect an important focus and show that behavior change can be achieved in behaviors in everyday settings.

There is considerable consensus that one of the best ways of reducing cancer deaths is early detection. Survival rates are greater for many cancers if the cancer is identified early and treated before it has spread (metastasized). Behavioral techniques have been applied to increase early detection through self-examination. Instructions, feedback, and reinforcement have been used to train women and men, respectively, to self-examine for early symptoms of breast or testicular cancer (see Friman, Finney, Glasscock, Weigel, & Christophersen, 1986; Hall et al., 1980). The relatively few studies in this area have shown that the requisite behaviors can be developed and maintained after training has been terminated.

Behavioral interventions have focused on a number of areas that are critical even if not life threatening. For example, considerable work has been conducted on dental care to prevent tooth decay, gum disease, and loss of teeth. Although environmental interventions (fluoridation of community water supplies) have helped, individual care of one's teeth remains critical. Interventions for different facets of dental care have been studied. Evaluating interventions has been facilitated by the availability of measures to assess various degrees of dental plaque. Such measurement permits evaluation of the extent to which persons are brushing and flossing effectively.

FIGURE   12–1
Percentage of children (upper graph) and adults (lower graph) who showed any two
or more protective behaviors on consecutive observation days. The intervention
was introduced in stages and in a multiple baseline design across the two pools.
SOURCE: Lombard, D., Neubauer, T. E., Canfield, D., & Winett, R. A. (1991).

In one project, children were trained to floss their teeth to reduce plaque. Instructions, prompts (reminder cards at home), self-monitoring, and intermittent reinforcement were quite effective in reducing plaque (Dahlquist & Gil, 1986). The intervention was maintained in the home by shifting the assessment and reinforcement procedures from an experimenter to the parents. Other studies have shown that behavioral techniques can increase the frequency and quality of toothbrushing and tooth flossing in children and adults (Claerhout & Lutzker, 1981; Iwata & Becksfort, 1981).

Eating Disorders and Dieting Habits

Behavioral techniques have been applied to a variety of eating disorders that can lead to or reflect physical disease, including obesity, ruminative vomiting, anorexia nervosa, and bulimia. For example, anorexia nervosa, a disorder invariably found in young women, involves reduced food consumption that results in extreme loss of weight. Women with anorexia nervosa lose at least 20 percent of their normal body weight, have a marked fear of becoming obese, and resist gaining weight. The physical consequences of significant weight loss include an emaciated appearance, cessation of menstruation, and, in severe cases, death.

In one program, several anorexia nervosa patients were treated using a contingency contract system (Pertschuk, Edwards, & Pomerleau, 1978). Hospitalized patients were told that a daily weight gain of one-half pound was required in order to earn certain privileges on the ward. Individualized contracts were drawn up in writing and signed by the therapist and the patient. The patients were told that they were responsible for gaining weight and that they could request nutritional counseling if they wished assistance. During baseline, the patients had generally continued to lose weight. However, during the contract period (about two weeks), they showed an average weight gain of about 4.2 kilograms (9.3 pounds). Follow-up assessment ranging from 3 to 28 months indicated that the patients had continued to gain weight after discharge from the hospital. Other reports have suggested successful treatment of anorexia nervosa with reinforcement and feedback techniques, contingency contracting, desensitization, and other behavioral procedures alone or in combination (see Brownell & Foreyt, 1986).

Another eating disorder is bulimia, which is characterized by self-induced vomiting and other methods of purging (for example, the use of laxatives). Individuals who are bulimic are greatly concerned with becoming obese. In a recent demonstration, cognitive behavioral techniques were used with 13 women who received outpatient treatment for bulimia (Kettlewell, Mizes, & Wasylyshyn, 1992). Treatment was evaluated in a multiple-baseline design across subsets of subjects. The treatment included engaging in competing behaviors when they were going to purge food, challenging and maladaptive cognitions (for example, "I must be thin"), setting goals to increase weight, engaging in coping activities (relaxation) to reduce the urge to binge, and others. Based on self-report measures of binging and purging, most (69 percent) of the individuals were symptom free by the end of treatment; at the three-month follow-up only 15 percent remained symptom free. The results are instructive in showing the effects of treatment but also in showing the limits. Clearly, further changes are needed to increase the short- and long-term impact of treatment. The duration of treatment was brief (eight group sessions lasting one and a half hours each). Consequently, it is reasonable to examine whether a much more intensive dose achieves more potent effects.

Not all interventions related to eating focus on disorders. Eating habits and styles relate to overall health. Hence, many programs focus on dieting for the general public. For example, high-fat and low-fiber diets are associated with a number of diseases including coronary heart disease and various forms of cancer. Behavioral programs in everyday settings have focused on increasing the selection and purchase of high-fiber and low-fat foods (such as cereals, grains, and vegetables). For example, interventions conducted in fast-food restaurants and grocery stores have been designed to increase the purchase of healthful foods (Wagner & Winett, 1988; Winett et al., 1991).

Pain

Behavioral techniques have been applied to treat pain associated with a variety of disorders. The techniques are usually applied to alter many of the behaviors associated with pain—for example, to increase the amount of time hospitalized patients remain out of bed; to reduce signs of pain, such as grimacing, moaning, complaining, and walking in a guarded or protective manner; and to decrease reliance on medication.

Pioneering work applying behavioral techniques to chronic pain was reported several years ago by Fordyce and his colleagues (Fordyce et al., 1974). In one of the studies, patients with back pain (due to a variety of physical disorders) participated in a treatment program for approximately seven weeks within the hospital. During treatment, the patients received social reinforcement from their families and from staff for engaging in increased activity (such as going on walks) in the hospital. Complaints, moaning, inactivity, and grimacing were ignored. After treatment, the patients reported less intense pain, reduced their intake of medication, and increased the amount of time they spent out of bed. Other studies have shown that reinforcement from staff can increase activities (for example, walking, riding a stationary bicycle) and reduce pain among hospitalized patients diagnosed with chronic back pain (Cairns & Pasino, 1977).

Behavioral treatments are often used to help individuals manage and cope with invasive and painful medical procedures. For example, one study of children (aged 3 to 13) with leukemia assisted with pain and stress management (Jay, Elliot, Katz, & Siegel, 1987). As part of their treatment and care, the children were routinely required to complete three bone marrow aspirations, a traumatic and aversive medical procedure. The test requires insertion of a large needle into the hip bone to extract bone marrow, and yields information critical to assess the presence or absence of cancer cells. Typically (in the United States), a local anesthetic is administered, but this does not alleviate the pain of the entire procedure.

A cognitive behavioral treatment was used that included viewing a modeling film of children coping with the procedure, breathing exercises, emotive imagery and distraction techniques, and behavioral rehearsal (for example, role-playing with the doctor). The effects of treatment were evaluated on direct observations of distress during the aspiration procedure, child self-support immediately after the procedure, and physiological measures (blood pressure, pulse rate). In general, the cognitive behavioral procedure led to significantly less fear than either a minimal treatment condition routinely provided to patients or medication (tranquilizers) did.

Other studies have demonstrated the effectiveness of various therapies to reduce stress among children undergoing medical procedures. For example, in one study children (aged 4 to 10) were prepared for surgery by viewing a modeling film and practicing coping responses or by taking part in routine hospital procedures, such as receiving information and seeing the equipment (Faust, Olson, & Rodriguez, 1991). Modeling led to significantly less stress during recovery from the operation. In another study, two interventions were compared to reduce stress among young children (aged 3 to 9) undergoing venipuncture as part of their cancer treatment (Manne et al., 1990). A behavioral intervention (parent coaching, attentional distraction, and positive reinforcement) led to less observed stress, parent ratings of child stress, and parental ratings of their own distress than did a control procedure (in which the parents tried to aid their children in any way they wished). Controlled trials of treatment techniques for children undergoing medical procedures have repeatedly shown the benefits of diverse procedures over the routine, standardized care that patients receive. Other reports have suggested that behavioral techniques, including biofeedback, relaxation training, incentive systems, and cognitive-behavioral strategies such as the use of self-statements, can be used to treat pain associated with chronic disease, menstruation, and intercourse (see Blanchard, 1992; Turk, Meichenbaum, & Genest, 1983). Specific disorders, such as headaches and back pain, represent areas in which several techniques have been studied.

Adherence and Compliance

Adherence to medical regimens is an important area of concern because many forms of medical and psychological treatment depend on client compliance with treatment recommendations. Yet, estimates have suggested that up to 50 percent of medical patients do not comply with their prescribed regimens (Gillum & Barsky, 1974).

Behavior modification has been used to increase adherence to a variety of treatment procedures. For example, Lowe and Lutzker (1979) treated a juvenile diabetic, named Amy, who had been hospitalized repeatedly as a result of not adhering to her prescribed medical regimen. To ensure a blood sugar balance, she had been prescribed a special diet, insulin injections, and exercise. She had been instructed to conduct urine tests several times daily to measure the effect of balancing diet, insulin, and exercise. She had also been told to maintain personal hygiene, especially with regard to foot care because of poor circulation to her feet, loss of sensation in her feet, and possible injuries that might become infected if not detected. Unfortunately, Amy did not follow the appropriate diet, conduct urine tests, or engage in foot care (wash and inspect for cuts and bruises).

To increase compliance with this medical regimen at home, the investigators gave Amy a "memo" (written instructions) that told her how to complete the desired behaviors and at what times this should be done each day. Later, a token economy was devised in which Amy earned points (exchangeable for rewards daily or at the end of the week) for engaging in the tasks required to manage her diabetes. The effects of the program are presented in Figure 12–2, which graphs Amy's daily percentage of completion of the desired tasks. Introducing the memo increased Amy's adherence to the diet (bottom portion of the figure) but did not affect her other behaviors. The token system, however, markedly improved her adherence to the requirements regarding foot care and urine tests. During the follow-up period, the experimenter was no longer formally involved in the program. Amy's parents continued the program, and her behaviors were maintained at a high rate.

Another program focused on improving the ability of 19 children (aged 8 to 12) to control their diabetes (Epstein et al., 1981). The children and their parents were trained to assess urine glucose levels, to adjust insulin doses as needed, to follow a special diet, and to exercise. When the children received points for accurately assessing their urine glucose levels and for following diet and exercise regimens, their control of their glucose levels increased substantially. The gains were maintained up to ten weeks after treatment had ended.

Reinforcement techniques have also been used to increase compliance with special diet, exercise, and medication regimens among patients with a variety of disorders, including renal dysfunction, hypertension, asthma, and coronary disease, to mention a few (see Russo & Varni, 1982; Stuart, 1982). These applications are especially significant because of the life-threatening consequences associated with failure to follow prescribed treatments.

PERSONAL SAFETY

Behavioral techniques have been increasingly applied to areas of safety to prevent injury and death in a variety of situations. The significance of safety-related behaviors can be attested to in many ways. For example,

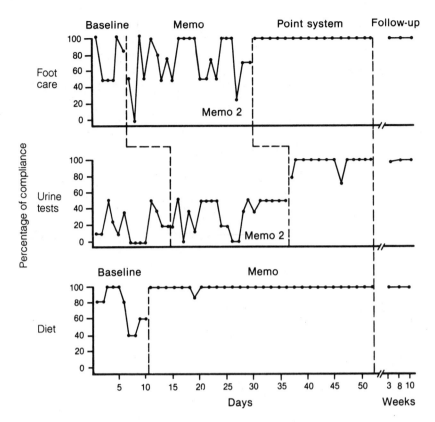

FIGURE 12–2
Percentage of compliance to medical regimen for foot care, urine tests, and diet.
SOURCE: Lowe, K., & Lutzker, J. R. (1979).

among adults, accidents are the fourth leading cause of death (after heart disease, cancer, and stroke). Accidents involving motor vehicles and work accidents are the two categories of accidents that result in the highest death rates. Interventions that can decrease the likelihood of injury and death from accidents are obviously important. The range of safety-related behaviors and situations to which behavioral techniques have been applied is extensive and can only be sampled here.

Seat Belt Use

The use of seat belts in automobiles is a major safety issue, given evidence that the practice can prevent approximately half of all the deaths and injuries that would occur in their absence among motor vehicle passengers. As one illustration of work in this area, seat belt use was increased among children who attended an after-school day-care program (Sowers-Hoag,

Thyer, & Bailey, 1987). Seat belt use was assessed at the end of each day as the parents picked up the children. Each parent drove to a loading zone, at which time a staff member went to get the child and bring the child to the car. Seat belt use was measured by noting whether the child had belted himself or herself before the car left the loading zone. The intervention to develop seat belt use included educational information for the children about the use of seat belts, assertiveness training through role-play to help children ask as needed where to find or how to fasten the seat belt, and practice in using different kinds of seat belts. Also, a reward system was used in which the children who used seat belts were eligible for a lottery on the next day in which they could earn a small prize (valued at between $0.24 and $0.59). A child's chances of earning a prize on the next day was relatively high (50 percent). After the program was in effect, the performance criterion for eligibility for the lottery was increased to two consecutive days of seat belt use.

Although the program was applied to all of the 158 children at the facility, the intervention was evaluated with only 16 of the children. The intervention was introduced in a multiple-baseline design across two groups of children. As is evident in Figure 12–3, child seat belt use was increased when the intervention was introduced. When the frequency of the lottery was reduced and two days of seat belt use was required, seat belt use remained high. A follow-up assessment was conducted three months after the program had been terminated. The results indicated a high level of seat belt use (75 to 86 percent).

Special Situations for Children

There is a host of situations in which children are at risk because of their age, lack of knowledge, inexperience, and stage of development. Several foci illustrate efforts to apply behavioral techniques to improve child safety at home and in the community. Child abduction is obviously a major social and parental concern. In one investigation, preschool children (3 to 5 years old) were trained to protect themselves against abduction by strangers (Poche, Brouwer, & Swearingen, 1981). Children were initially selected for participation if they were susceptible to abduction, which was assessed by having a stranger (actually someone working in the study) approach a child and ask whether he or she would leave the preschool with him. Unfortunately, approximately 90 percent of the children agreed to go with the stranger after being given simple verbal inducements, though no child was actually taken from the setting.

Training was conducted at various places around the school. Adults were trained to lure children by using verbal ploys to encourage children to leave with them. Physical force, of course, was not used to encourage the children to leave. (Such force is rarely used by persons who actually abduct children.) Such statements as these were made to the children: "Would you

FIGURE 12-3
Percentage of safety belt use by eight children in Group 1 and eight children in Group 2.
SOURCE: Sowers-Hoag, K. M., Thyer, B. A., & Bailey, J. S. (1987).

like to go with me for a walk?" and "I've got a nice surprise in my car." The target behaviors, derived from interviews with parents, consisted of making a brief verbal comment to the stranger and then getting away as quickly as possible. The training consisted of modeling the desired behaviors, having the child rehearse the desired behaviors, and providing the child with social and tangible reinforcement (for example, praise, stickers) for correct responding. Practice continued across different situations and across different types of approaches by the adults. The results indicated that the children learned the requisite behaviors and were not amenable to being lured by the adults. The effects generalized to assessment in a naturalistic situation out in the community and were maintained up to 12 weeks after training had been completed. Subsequent research has shown that children can be trained in skills to avoid abduction with a specially made videotape that presents the training sequence (Poche, Yoder, & Miltenberger, 1988). The program could be widely disseminated because of its videotape form, accompanied by instruction in its use.

In another program, elementary school children were trained to engage in behaviors that would enable them to escape from emergency fire situations in their home (Jones, Kazdin, & Haney, 1981). The children were trained in simulated bedrooms at school. The desired escape behaviors were selected from fire safety manuals and after consulting with fire-fighters, who identified problem situations and lifesaving behaviors. The target behaviors were extremely complex sequences of responses to avoid being overcome by smoke (for example, rolling out of bed, crawling to a door or window), to make decisions based on the extent and location of the hypothetical fire, and to select among alternative escape routes. Training included instructions, feedback, modeling, and both external reinforcement and self-reinforcement. The results indicated that the children did not have the requisite responses prior to training but developed them at a high level when the program was executed. Moreover, the responses were maintained at a two-week follow-up assessment. Other efforts to develop fire safety skills have focused on special populations, such as persons with profound mental retardation, visual impairment, and physical disability who are trained to exit their home safely (for example, Bannerman, Sheldon, & Sherman, 1991; Jones, Sissan, & Van Hasselt, 1984).

Child safety has been the focus of several other applications of behavioral techniques, such as interventions to reduce the number of child safety hazards (for example, fire, electricity, poisons) at home (Tertinger, Greene, & Lutzker, 1984) and to manage the situations of "latchkey children"—children who return to an unsupervised home after school (Peterson, 1984). In these studies, efforts have been made to increase the safety of the home or to help the children manage in situations in which an adult is not available.

Business and Industry

Many applications of behavior modification have been conducted in industry to promote safe practices on the part of employees (for example, wearing protective devices, using potentially dangerous equipment properly) and management (for example, removing work hazards). An excellent illustration can be seen in a study of safety in open-pit mining (Fox, Hopkins, & Anger, 1987). The study was conducted at two open-pit mines, one in Wyoming and the other in Arizona. Uranium was extracted and processed at one of the mines; coal was extracted and processed at the other. The two mines used similar equipment (trucks, bulldozers) and procedures (strip mining, crushing, storing materials). The goals of the program were to decrease job-related injuries, days lost from work due to such injuries, and costs (due to medical care, insurance, and equipment damage) among employees in each mine.

An incentive in the form of tokens (trading stamps) was provided at the end of each month to workers who had not been injured or had not required medical care because of an accident. Trading stamps were also given to all members of a group that worked under a particular supervisor if no one in the group had been injured. Bonus stamps were available to workers whose suggestions for improving safety in the facility were adopted. Trading stamps could also be lost (response cost) for missing work due to injury or for causing an accident. The trading stamps could be exchanged at a nearby redemption center that carried hundreds of items, such as small appliances, barbecue grills, spice racks, and clocks. The program was introduced to each mine in a multiple-baseline design and integrated with the mine's routine practices for several years. Figure 12–4 shows a marked reduction in the number of accidents among workers (upper panel) as well as a reduction in monetary costs to the company (lower panel). Also of interest is the long-term use of the program and the continuation of the improved safety.

Several other applications in industry have shown that behavioral techniques can enhance worker safety. The interventions have utilized feedback to workers, prompts and reinforcement for behaviors that promote safety, and modeling of safe work practices. These interventions have promoted employee practices to avoid injury and have effectively reduced hazards leading to accidents and exposure to toxic and potentially carcinogenic substances in the air (Alavosius & Sulzer-Azaroff, 1986; Hopkins et al., 1986; Sulzer-Azaroff & de Santamaria, 1980).

PARENTING AND PARENT-CHILD INTERACTION

Behavioral techniques have been applied to an extraordinarily wide range of parenting and child-rearing domains. The breadth of applications is understandable. Over the course of normal development, there are many behaviors that develop and need to be developed for the child's functioning in everyday life. Behavioral techniques can help negotiate many of the challenges of child rearing. In addition, often dysfunctional or maladaptive parenting emerges as reflected in physical abuse and neglect of children. Here, too, behavioral techniques have been applied. The range of applications of behavioral techniques to parenting and parent-child interaction is illustrated with examples of a few of the many domains of research.

A number of parents with disability and retardation have children and often are poorly equipped to care for them. Skill training is critically important because poor care for infants obviously can have serious consequences including illness and death. Child welfare agencies often identify such parents as at risk for neglect or poor care of their children. Identification of parents is useful only insofar as some intervention can be applied to help them and their children in some concrete way.

Behavioral interventions have been used to develop basic parenting skills with clear implications for welfare of the children. As an example, a recent study identified mothers with developmental disabilities (aged 21 to 39 with IQs less than 80) who had infants who were monitored by child protection agencies because of concerns over adequate child care (Feldman et al., 1992). A behavioral program was designed to train mothers to engage in such basic care skills as bathing the children, training in toi-

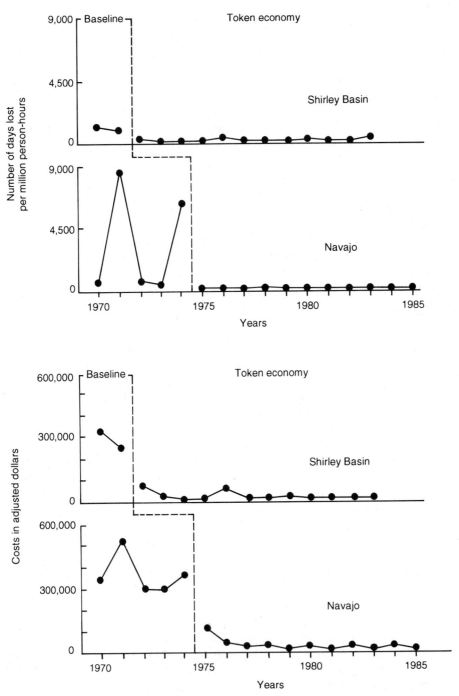

FIGURE 12–4

Yearly number of days lost from work, per million person-hours worked, because of work-related injuries (upper figure) and yearly cost, adjusted for hours worked and inflation, resulting from accidents and injuries (lower figure).

SOURCE: Fox, D. K., Hopkins, B. L., & Anger, W. K. (1987).

leting, cleaning bottles, preparing formulas, treating diaper rash, and ensuring crib and sleep safety of the children. Training was conducted in the homes of the mothers and used verbal instructions, modeling of the desired behavior, pictures to show the desired behaviors, physical guidance (prompts), feedback, and token reinforcements (coupons exchangeable for backup reinforcers). After performance on the requisite skills was 100 percent and was consistent, training ended. The results indicated that the gains were maintained over follow-up ranging from a few weeks to almost one and a half years. Moreover, concrete gains in the children were also evident during treatment (for example, elimination of diaper rash, weight gain in better-nourished children). With a similar population, mothers with developmental disabilities were trained to increase expressions of physical affection, praise, and imitations of child vocalization (to help stimulate interactions and to develop language) (Feldman, Case, Rincover, Towns, & Betel, 1989). Mothers learned the requisite behaviors and maintained these over months of follow-up assessment. Children with language delays improved in their speech.

Parent training has extended well beyond basic infant and child care. In many families, parent-offspring interactions become strained as the children enter adolescence. Adolescence marks a period of changing roles for parents and children, and negotiating these may raise communication difficulties related to parent control, youth autonomy, rules of the home, and interactions with peers and others. Behavioral techniques have been used to assist in developing positive communication patterns when programs have been identified. For example, in one demonstration, families who identified themselves as experiencing parent-adolescent communication problems participated in a program that focused on a variety of communication skills (for example, giving positive or negative feedback to others, accepting feedback, negotiating, problem solving, facilitating communication of the other person) (Serna, Schumaker, Sherman, & Sheldon, 1991). Adolescents were trained as a group; parents were trained as well in a separate group. Skills were then practiced in parent-adolescent dyads. Siblings and eventually the entire family were involved in training sessions and extensions of the sessions to the home.

The impact of training on specific skills is illustrated in Figure 12–5, which shows that specific skills were trained in parents (left column) and adolescents (right column) in a multiple-baseline design across behaviors. Over a period of months, this training continued to develop skills related to communication and interaction. Observations in the home revealed that family communication and interactions improved and generalized to a number of different (untrained) interactions. Parent and youth ratings indicated that they perceived communication to have improved from treatment.

Parent training has been used extensively in clinical applications with children who are identified as significantly impaired and referred for treatment. For example, parent training is used in the treatment of children referred for aggressive and antisocial behavior (Kazdin, 1985a; Miller &

FIGURE   12–5
Mean percentage of skill components performed correctly for each skill in individual testing situations for parents (left) and adolescents (right).
SOURCE: Serna, L. A., Schumaker, J. B., Sherman, J. A., & Sheldon, J. B. (1991).

Prinz, 1990). Treatment consists of training parents to utilize several of the procedures outined in previous chapters, including variations of prompting and shaping, reinforcement (for example, praise, tokens), reinforcement of incompatible behavior, and contingency contracts. Parents of aggressive and antisocial children have higher rates of harsh punishment (for example, beating their children). Parent training emphasizes positive reinforcement, minimal use of punishment, and only mild forms of punishment (for example, time out, small response costs). Although parent training is conducted in sessions with a trainer, the programs are implemented in the home and at school to change problem behaviors of the child. Scores of studies have shown that parent training can decrease aggressive and antisocial child behavior. Follow-up assessment has indicated that the gains are maintained up to one year later. Although the gains have been quite positive, parent training has not been equally effective for everyone. Families characterized by marital conflict, socioeconomic disadvantage, and parental depression have been less likely to show changes or to maintain the gains of treatment over time (see Kazdin, 1993b).

Behavioral techniques have been applied to many other facets of parent-child interaction and family life. Mentioned was parent training for aggressive and antisocial behavior. In addition, parent training has been applied to diverse clinical populations, including children with attention deficit disorder (hyperactivity), autism, mental retardation, learning delays, eating disorders, enuresis (involuntary urination), encopresis (involuntary defecation), and other problems. Parents who engage in abusive child-rearing practices also have served as the focus of parent training (Wolfe, 1987). Many other applications have focused on everyday concerns of parents that do not reflect extreme clinical problems. For example, applications have used reinforcement techniques to train fathers to better care for their newborn infants (Dachman, Alessi, Vrazo, Fuqua, & Kerr, 1986), to reduce television viewing and to increase reading of school-age children (Wolfe, Mendes, & Factor, 1984), and to increase family socialization and interaction when families go out to eat (Green, Hardison, & Greene, (1984).

CONTEMPORARY CONCERNS IN EVERYDAY LIFE

Behavioral techniques have been extended to several areas that reflect issues, concerns, and experiences in everyday life. Applications have extended to such problems as traffic control, energy, conservation, littering, waste recycling, employment, and job performance (see Geller, Winett, & Everett, 1982).

Traffic Control and Driving Practices

The control of automobile traffic has served as the focus of a number of studies designed to reduce accidents and injury. Applications in this area might also be conceived as extensions to safety and prevention. Several studies have focused on speeding because of the direct relation of speeding to automobile accidents and death. Already mentioned (Chapter 5) was the effect of feedback in reducing the number of drivers speeding on the highway (Van Houten, Nau, & Marini, 1980). The feedback consisted of a road sign that indicated the percentage of drivers not speeding on the previous day as well as the best percentage on all previous days. Both speeding and the number of traffic accidents were decreased. Extensions of programs to cities in other countries (such as Canada, Israel, and Iceland) have shown that feedback can reduce driving speed and accidents (for example, Ragnarsson & Björgvinsson, 1991; Van Houten, Malenfant, & Rolider, 1985). In the latter study, other procedures were added to the roadside feedback. Drivers were occasionally stopped and given either a warning fine for speeding or praise (a thank-you note) for adhering to the speed limit.

As mentioned (in Chapter 5), feedback is often inconsistent in its effects. In relation to traffic control, feedback has not always been effective (Roqué & Roberts, 1989). Thus, more effective interventions may be needed. The conditions under which feedback is optimally effective are not fully understood. However, the ease of implementation and the definite impact that feedback can exert on safety suggest that it should be used more routinely in everyday life.

Also related to traffic accidents is the manner in which drivers approach yellow and red lights. Increased accident risk is associated with approaching an intersection when the traffic light changes to yellow or red. The likelihood of going through a yellow or red light has to do in part with the timing of lights from one intersection to the next. One demonstration assessed the percentage of drivers leaving one intersection who went through a yellow or red light at the next intersection (Jason, Neal, & Marinakis, 1985). As a result of the assessment, the timing sequence of the traffic lights at the two intersections was altered so that the change to the yellow light occurred much sooner at the second intersection. Thus, drivers going through a green light at the first intersection were more likely to have a red light at the next intersection, and therefore to stop. Manipulating the timing sequence markedly increased the number of cars that stopped correctly at the second intersection. As a result of the change, accidents were reduced by approximately 33 percent.

Approximately 18 percent of the persons killed in traffic accidents are pedestrians (see Jason & Liotta, 1982). A question of applied significance is whether pedestrian behavior can be changed to reduce the number of accidents. A major source of pedestrian accidents is crossing the street outside the crosswalks (jaywalking) or stepping into traffic without warning. Studies have shown that such interventions as prompting, feedback, and reinforcement can effectively train children and adults to cross streets safely and provide warnings to drivers (for example, Van Houten, Malenfant, & Rolider, 1985; Yeaton & Bailey, 1978). Similarly, prompting procedures have increased pedestrian safety by increasing the extent to which motorists yield to pedestrians (that is, stop safely and further back from the crosswalk) (Van Houten, 1988).

Occasionally special populations of interest are identified in relation to driving safety. Persons who deliver pizza are one such group. The "fast-and-free" delivery advertised by some pizza services has been associated with claims of reckless driving and traffic accidents. The usual contingency for the drivers may inadvertently encourage fast driving. Typically, commissions and tips are related to the number of pizzas delivered, so that faster (and hence more) deliveries pay more. This is exacerbated by policies of some companies that prompt their drivers to make deliveries within a specific time period. Safer driving practices were trained among pizza deliverers by providing incentives for safer driving, such as using seat belts and using turn signals, and by monitoring driving practices (Ludwig & Geller, 1991). Thus, driving practices in such highly specialized situations as delivery service can be readily altered.

Energy Conservation

Consumption of electricity, gasoline, and home heating oil and gas has been a worldwide concern because of the limited energy resources available from usable fossil fuels and because of the increased demand for energy. Several investigations have examined whether behavioral techniques can be used to curb energy consumption. For example, in a four-month project designed to reduce fuel oil consumption in the home, Seaver and Patterson (1976) studied 180 households randomly drawn from rural communities. These households were assigned randomly to one of three conditions: feedback, feedback plus social commendations, and no treatment. At the time of fuel delivery, the feedback households were told how much fuel they had consumed relative to the same period in the previous year and how much money they had saved or lost. The feedback-plus-commendation households received the above feedback plus social recognition (in the form of a decal saying "We are saving oil") if they had reduced their fuel consumption. The feedback-plus-commendation households used significantly less fuel than did the other households. The feedback-alone households and the no-treatment households did not differ from each other. Several other studies have shown that interventions involving feedback, monetary reinforcement, and self-monitoring effectively reduce home energy consumption (Geller, Winett, & Everett, 1982).

A major source of fuel consumption is the use of automobile gasoline. A number of applications have used behavioral techniques, such as token reinforcement, feedback, or small incentives, to promote the use of mass transit (buses) instead of personal automobiles or to promote driving less than usual (Foxx & Hake, 1977; Geller, Winett, & Everett, 1982). For example, one study increased the use of car pools by providing token reinforcement and special parking privileges to university students who formed such pools (Jacobs, Fairbanks, Poche, & Bailey, 1982). Conservation of energy and a decrease in pollution are two benefits that can result from the extension of such programs to reduce one-person use of cars.

Waste Recycling

A concern related to littering is the accumulation of waste products in the environment. For some waste products, recycling is an alternative approach to litter control. If waste products, (such as metal cans, paper, and returnable bottles), can be recycled, they become a resource. In one program, the recycling of paper was increased on a university campus (Geller, Chaffee, & Ingram, 1975). Several dormitories had collected wastepaper to be sold to a paper mill at $15 per ton and eventually recycled. Different interventions were implemented to increase the collection of wastepaper. One intervention consisted of a "recycling contest" between men's and women's dormitories. The dorm that collected the most paper would receive a bonus of $15. Another intervention consisted of a raffle in which each student who brought paper to the collection room received a ticket. Tickets were drawn each week and earned prizes, including monetary certificates redeemable at retail stores for clothing, groceries, furniture, and other items varying in monetary value. Both the contest contingency and the raffle contingency increased the amount of paper that was brought to the collection rooms of the dormitories, but more paper was brought and more individuals brought paper when the raffle contingency was used.

Extrinsic reinforcers are not always necessary to increase recycling. In one project, residents of three apartment complexes were merely informed of the location of recycling containers that were being used to collect newspapers (Reid, Luyben, Rawers, & Bailey, 1976). Near the containers, which were placed in the laundry rooms of the apartment complexes, were instructions explaining their use. In addition, residents were interviewed briefly prior to the program and prompted about the use of the containers. Over a period of several weeks, the amount of newspapers collected increased relative to baseline levels.

Employment and Job-Related Skills

Obtaining and keeping a job entails problems of obvious social significance. Lack of employment, aside from its economic implications, is associated with a number of social ills including crime, "mental illness," alcoholism, medical neglect, and family dysfunction (Warr, 1987). Behavioral programs have improved job interview skills, success in obtaining employment, and on-the-job performance.

A few studies have examined procedures for helping individuals to obtain employment. For example, Azrin, Flores, and Kaplan (1975) developed a job-finding club to train unemployed persons in skills that would enhance their opportunities for obtaining jobs. Members were paired into dyads, so that each member would have someone to provide support and encouragement. Also, members were trained to search for jobs through various sources (for example, former employers, relatives), role-played job interviews, received instructions in dress and grooming, learned to prepare a résumé, and expanded their job interests. Persons who participated in the program found employment within a shorter time period and received higher wages than did persons who did not participate. Three months after participation in the program, 92 percent of the clients had obtained employment, compared with 60 percent of persons who did not participate.

Behavioral techniques have also improved job interview skills. For example, in one program, former hospitalized psychiatric patients were trained in interview skills (Furman, Geller, Simon, & Kelly, 1979). The clients were trained to provide positive information about themselves and their experiences, to make appropriate nonverbal gestures while speaking, to express interest in and enthusiasm for the potential position, and to ask appropriate questions. The training used role-playing, practice, videotaped feedback, prompts, and praise for appropriate behavior. The effects of training for one person are illustrated in Figure 12–6. At the end of training, an experienced job interviewer, unfamiliar with the training program, rated interview skills as improved. Similarly, adults with developmental disabilities have been trained in job interview skills so they could answer questions appropriately in relation to personal information, work, and education (Schloss, Santoro, Wood, & Bedner, 1988). Prompts, feedback, and reinforcement were shown to increase suitable interview behavior in response to interview questions obtained from a survey of business employers. Interview skills were maintained up to six months after treatment had ended.

On-the-job performance has been improved in several behavior modification programs. Emery Air Freight Corporation is a frequently cited example of the use of reinforcement in industry ("New Tool," 1971). To improve many aspects of company operations, Emery used feedback, praise, and social recognition to reinforce job performance. For example, in one application, the cost of delivering airfreight was reduced by shipping several smaller packages in a large container. Employees who worked on the loading dock received feedback and praise for shipping packages in larger containers, thus saving money. Use of the containers increased 95% and remained at a high level for almost two years, saving the company approximately $650,000 per year.

Many other businesses have relied on reinforcement contingencies to improve both employee performance and morale. For example, a small company that produced egg cartons used a token economy to recognize the efforts of employees and to increase productivity (Nelton, 1988). Employees earned 25 points a year for perfect attendance, 20 points a year if no disciplinary action was formally noted, and 15 points for working a year without lost time due to injury. Five points were deducted for each day of

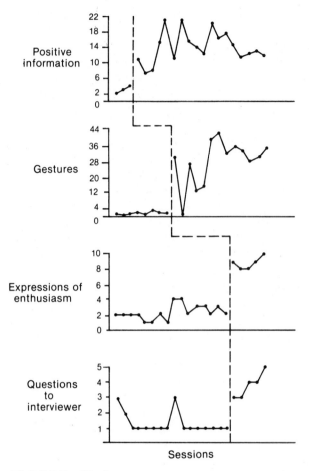

FIGURE 12–6

Job interview training for one client as evaluated in multiple-baseline introduction of giving positive information, gesturing, asking questions, and expressing enthusiasm for the position.

SOURCE: Furman, W., Geller, M., Simon, S. J., & Kelly, J. A. (1979).

absence. Points were also earned for cost-saving or safety suggestions and for community service. Employees who reached 100 points were awarded a jacket with the company logo and the words "The 100 Club." Reports from employees indicated that the program was well liked. Production improved as well, although the role of the token reinforcement program was not specifically evaluated.

The previous examples are only a sampling of a plethora of applications of behavioral techniques to business and industry. Feedback and incentive systems have altered absenteeism, tardiness, production and sales, and employee-customer interactions (see Frederiksen, 1982). Although most of the applications have focused on small businesses (such as a single store, restaurant, or local company), some of the programs have been implemented by large industries with offices throughout the United States (for example, Mirman, 1982).

ADDITIONAL APPLICATIONS

Extensions of behavior modification to social, environmental, health-related, and safety problems represent only a few of the innovative directions that the field has taken. Consider some of the other areas of application. Behavioral techniques have been applied to the *elderly,* such as nursing home residents and geriatric patients. Programs based on social or token reinforcement have increased their social interaction, physical activity, and recovery from physical injury. Their self-care skills (for example, bathing), eating habits, and leisure-time activities have been improved as well (see Burgio & Burgio, 1986).

Interventions have been extended to facets of *crime* other than the rehabilitation of delinquents and criminals. For example, prompting and police patrol techniques have effectively reduced shoplifting in department stores and burglary rates in communities (McNees et al., 1976; Schnelle et al., 1978). Shoplifting among employees (for example, in a large grocery store) was also reduced by informing employees of stolen items and providing feedback about amount of theft (Carter, Holmström, Simpanen, & Melin, 1988). For years, behavioral applications have focused on delinquent youths and adult criminals in various settings (Burchard & Lane, 1982).

Athletic performance has been the focus of several studies. Feedback, modeling, social and token reinforcement, relaxation training, self-control techniques (for example, self-monitoring), and cognitively based treatments (for example, self-instruction training, imagery) have improved the performance of athletes and increased the effectiveness of coaching (Meyers, 1991). The acquisition of skills related to the sport of interest (for example, executing football plays or engaging in exercises correctly) and the quality and speed of performance have been enhanced in applications to football, gymnastics, tennis, swimming, and track (for example, Hume & Crossman, 1992; Shapiro & Shapiro, 1985).

Overall, the above illustrations convey the breadth of behavioral applications. Some of these applications reflect areas of work that have not been within the traditional purview of psychological interventions. Indeed, these extensions have led to the emergence of new disciplines or subdisciplines or new areas of work in which behavioral techniques merge with other fields, as reflected in areas bearing such labels as behavioral medicine, behavioral pediatrics, behavioral ecology, and behavioral geriatrics.

Multicomponent Interventions

In previous chapters, many behavioral procedures and their variations were described. It was important to focus on individual procedures—such as token reinforcement, time out from reinforcement, and others—to illustrate their variations, the manner in which they are applied to maximize behavior change, and to identify their individual effects. In many instances, several behavior-change procedures are combined into a single program. These programs are referred to as multicomponent interventions because several different procedures (components) such as feedback, social and token reinforcement, and response cost are combined into a treatment "package."

There are several reasons to combine multiple procedures in a given behavioral program. The reasons pertain to the nature of the behaviors that serve as the focus of the intervention as well as the multiple influences and contexts in which these behaviors occur. Consider the reasons related to behavior. First, for many behaviors that serve as the focus of interventions, achieving marked and durable changes is difficult. The behaviors may have a long history and may be pervasive across a number of settings. Combining procedures that individually have been shown to be effective may increase their likelihood of having impact.

Second and related to the first reason, combining procedures may increase the rapidity of change. It is possible that a particular procedure (for example, token reinforcement) might lead to behavior change. Prompting, mild punishment (for example, response cost), and group contingencies, when added to token reinforcement, may speed the change.

Third, problem behaviors often go together so that individuals with one area of dysfunction often show multiple other problem behaviors. For example, in adolescents, drug use, unprotected sexual activity, and antisocial behaviors go together (Farrell, Danish, & Howard, 1992). This does not mean that every adolescent who engages in one of these behaviors also engages in the others. It does mean that these behaviors often go together, so that a person who engages in one is likely to engage in the others. From the standpoint of interventions, multicomponent interventions are sometimes used to help address a range of behaviors, with separate but related procedures used for the different behaviors.

Fourth, multicomponent interventions are also used because of the scope and complexity of influences that promote or sustain the behavior of interest. For example, children who engage in aggressive behavior are not likely to engage in this behavior merely because a reinforcer or two is maintaining aggressive acts. Parents of aggressive children often use harsh physical punishment and engage in interactions, such as spouse abuse or marital conflict, that contribute to child aggressive and antisocial behavior (Kazdin, 1987a). Moreover, poor peer relations are also likely among aggressive children. Multicomponent interventions are used to address a range of factors that may contribute to the problem (for example, parents' aggressive acts against each other as well as against the child) or facets of the problem that cannot be neglected in clinical care (for example, poor peer relations).

In applied behavior analysis programs, several components are routinely combined. Table 12–1 lists commonly used components and states the purposes toward which they are directed. The components address three facets of the contingency, namely antecedents, behaviors, and consequences. As a package, they focus on facets critical to the development of the target behavior (education, instructions, and modeling), correct execution and improved rendition of the target behavior (rehearsal, practice, and corrective feedback), and increased frequency or consistency of performance (reinforcement). These components in various forms have been used as a package in many studies, including studies designed to develop personal safety skills among children (Sowers-Hoag, Thyer, & Bailey, 1987), to train hospital staff to use behavioral techniques (Parsons, Schepis, Reid, McCarn, & Green, 1987), and to enhance conversational skills among nursing home residents (Praderas & MacDonald, 1986).

T A B L E   12–1
Components Commonly Used as Part of Behavioral Interventions in Applied Settings

Components of the intervention	Purpose
Antecedents	
1. Education	Description of the behaviors and the rationale for their importance.
2. Instructions	Verbal or written prompts designed to describe the behaviors and the conditions and way in which they are performed.
3. Modeling	Visual prompt to illustrate how the behavior is to be performed and to direct attention to difficult or complex portions of the behavior; illustration of the sequence or order of several behaviors that go together.
Behavior	
4. Rehearsal and practice	Opportunities to perform the behavior, so that instructions (prompts), feedback, and reinforcement can be provided.
Consequences	
5. Feedback	Information designed to correct or improve portions of the behavior.
6. Reinforcement	Consequences to increase the frequency of performance of the behavior or to develop consistency of performance.

Often multicomponent interventions combine reinforcement procedures of applied behavior analysis with cognitively based interventions. For example, in one of our own studies, we evaluated alternative treatments for aggressive and antisocial children (aged 7 to 13) who were referred for treatment at a child outpatient clinic (Kazdin, Siegel, & Bass, 1992). The effectiveness of three conditions was examined: cognitively based problem-solving skills training, parent management training, and the combination of both of these. Families were randomly assigned to receive one of the three treatments. Treatment was provided weekly to children and/or their parents individually for a period of six to eight months. The results indicated that each of the treatments led to improvements in child functioning at home and at school, based on measures completed by parents, teachers, and the children themselves. However, the combined treatment (both problem-solving skills training and parent training) led to the largest reductions in child dysfunction and improvements in parent functioning (reduced parental stress and depression). These effects were evident immediately after treatment as well as at a one-year follow-up. In this case, the combined treatment apparently was useful for addressing different components of antisocial behavior among children and their families.

The importance of combining different components can be seen with interventions for the prevention of the spread of AIDS (see Kelly & Murphy, 1992). Preventive efforts have focused on behaviors that place individuals at risk for contact with the HIV. There are several facets of the problem that require multiple interventions. For example, in one study gay men received a multicomponent behavioral intervention (Kelly, St. Lawrence, Hood, & Brasfield, 1989). Gay men were selected because they represent a high-risk group (that is, they have a disproportionally higher rate of AIDS cases than the general public in the United States). Treatment consisted of several components: an educational component (to teach information about behaviors that place individuals at risk for AIDS), self-management techniques (self-monitoring of antecedent events leading to at-risk sexual behavior, use of self-statements to prompt nonrisk behavior), assertiveness training (to discuss with partners the importance of protected sexual behavior, to respond assertively in coercive sexual situations), and problem-solving skills training (to foster steady relations and to handle potentially high-risk sexual encounters). Individuals were randomly assigned either to the treatment condition where they received each of the above components or to a waiting-list control group that received treatment after treatment ended for the other group. The impact of treatment can be seen in Figure 12–7, which shows three behaviors that place individuals at risk for contracting HIV. As evident in the figure, sexual practices changed markedly with the treatment program.

Many studies combine different components of treatment along the lines of the above examples. One of the objections that is raised is that once

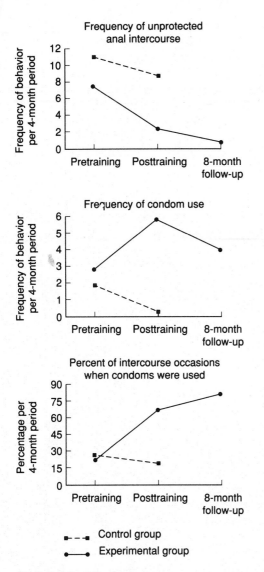

FIGURE 12–7

Frequency of unprotected anal intercourse, frequency of condom use during intercourse, and proportion of intercourse occasions protected by condoms among experimental and control (waiting-list) groups. After the intervention period (four months) the waiting-list group was then provided with treatment.

SOURCE: Kelly, J. A., St. Lawrence, J. S., Hood, H. V., & Brasfield, T. L. (1989).

a combined treatment is shown to be effective, one has no clear idea which component of the intervention was responsible for change or whether all were necessary. With complex and multifaceted problems, often multiple treatments are combined in an effort to exert initial impact. Obviously, in clinical and applied work, investigators are interested in developing interventions that lead to large and durable changes in behavior. There has been less interest in dissecting intervention packages by looking at the effect a program exerts with or without a particular component. Nonetheless, investigation of the individual treatments that are to be combined is very important.

Using a multicomponent treatment is not merely a matter of adding everything that might help into a treatment program. Mentioned earlier was the regrettable finding that many treatments have not been studied at all and therefore are not known to be effective. Adding such treatments together may not be very sound because individually there is no evidence that they help. It is desirable to combine components of treatment to alter different facets of a problem but also to know that the components themselves can have impact. Research on individual treatments and their contribution to behavior change is often a prior step before combinations of treatments are studied.

LARGE-SCALE APPLICATIONS

Most applications of behavioral techniques have been on a relatively small scale, as reflected in programs designed for one or a few individuals. The focus on individuals obviously is essential when particular clients require special treatment programs. Similarly, many demonstrations have focused on small groups or intact units of individuals, such as students in a classroom, patients on a psychiatric ward, or youths in a facility for delinquents. This focus is also essential because effective interventions are needed for a wide range of populations in special settings. In the past several years, behavioral techniques have been applied on a much larger scale. The large-scale extensions have followed naturally from the promising evidence of the small-scale demonstrations. Many of the areas to which behavioral techniques have been extended are relevant to large segments of the population, such as the community at large.

Education

Perhaps the largest extensions of behavioral techniques have been in the schools (see Sulzer-Azaroff et al., 1988). One program, referred to as Behavior Analysis, was developed for disadvantaged elementary school children (Bushell, 1978).[1] The program included more than 7,000 children in approximately 300 classrooms (from kindergarten through third grade) in 15 cities throughout the United States. The program relied heavily on token reinforcement to promote academic performance. It also included several other components, such as instructing children in small groups within the class, using academic curricula that permitted evaluation of student progress, specifying performance criteria for teachers and students, and providing special training and feedback to teachers regarding their performance and the progress of their students. The gains in academic performance of students who participated in the program were markedly greater than were the gains of students in traditional classrooms. Moreover, those gains were still evident two years after the program had been terminated and the children in the program had entered classrooms where token reinforcement was not in effect.

Another variation of treatment that relies on principles of behavior analysis is referred to as the Comprehensive Application of Behavior Analysis to Schooling model (CABAS) (Greer, 1992). The CABAS model utilizes behavioral principles to organize students, teachers, and supervisors and the instructional methods used to teach the students. More specifically, learning objectives for students are carefully specified as part of the curriculum (for example, what individuals are supposed to learn in a given subject matter). Student learning and progress toward the objectives in each subject matter are continually assessed as part of instruction. Teachers are trained in the use of prompts, feedback, shaping, and positive reinforcement. When student learning objectives are met, teachers move on to the next objectives.

Critical to the CABAS model is the role of persons who supervise the teachers. The supervisors are responsible for teacher training, assessing information on teachers and students, monitoring progress toward learning objectives, and teacher performance in the classroom. Data collected on the students as well as the teachers are used to evaluate progress over time. Continuous observation of teachers and students departs from the usual school program where achievement tests are administered once a year. Continuous assessment in the CABAS program permits one to see whether the learning objectives are being approached and met for individual students, and whether the procedures designed to train the students are implemented.

The impact of the CABAS model has been evaluated in different programs. In one demonstration in a small private school for multiply handicapped individuals (aged 3–21), training was implemented as described (Selinske, Greer, & Lodhi, 1991). Figure 12–8 shows that the program was implemented in a multiple-baseline design across different sets of teachers. The figure illustrates the trials of responding (opportunities for students to learn the material) over time. Baseline was followed by a period during which teachers were trained. After the training of the teachers, the full program was considered to be in effect. As evident in the figure, training increased the number of trials to which students were exposed and the number of correct trials. That is, learning of the academic material in-

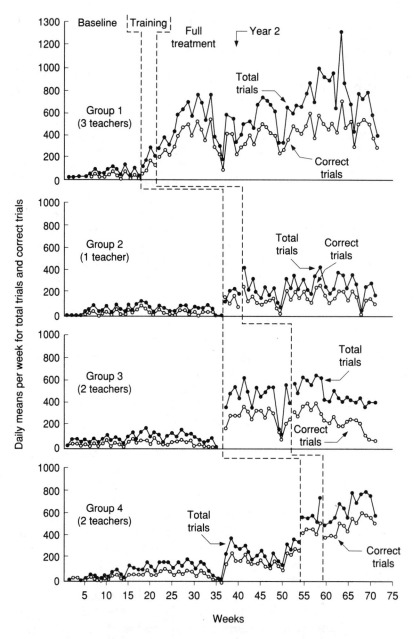

FIGURE   12–8

Daily means per week for the total number of trials taught, where a trial equals a training opportunity guided by the teacher and total number of correct trials. Training was introduced to sets of teachers in a multiple-baseline design. Baseline (no intervention) was followed by a period in which teachers were trained to administer the instruction and reinforcement procedures. Full treatment refers to the period when teachers had completed the training.

SOURCE: Selinske, J. E., Greer, R. D., & Lodhi, S. (1991).

creased. The program was carried out for an extended period (over 52 weeks for Group 1). Not shown in the figure are the follow-up data. Gains were reported to be maintained one year after the program had been implemented.

The CABAS model represents a program involving students, teachers, and supervisors, continuous assessment, direct training, and extensive student practice to learn the academic materials. Behavioral procedures (prompting, shaping, reinforcement) are used to increase correct responding and progress toward the learning goals. The initial successes of the program have led to its extension to a number of schools in the United States and abroad (Selinske, Greer, & Lodhi, 1991).

In other educational programs, behavioral techniques have been extended to encompass entire schools, entire school districts, or classrooms from several schools (for example, Boegli & Wasik, 1978; Greenwood et al., 1987; Rollins, McCandless, Thompson, & Brassell, 1974; Thompson, Brassell, Persons, Tucker, & Rollins, 1974). Favorable results from these programs indicate that academic performance and classroom deportment can be altered in large-scale applications of behavioral techniques.

Delinquent Youths

Programs for delinquent youths have also been extended on a relatively large scale. Approximately 20 years ago, a behavioral program for predelinquents was developed in a single home-style setting in Kansas (Achievement Place). The program consists of several components, including a token economy managed by a well-trained couple (teaching parents), programs to train children in several skill areas, and procedures to help reintegrate children into the community (Kirigin, Braukmann, Atwater, & Wolf, 1982). Multiple studies demonstrated the effects of various reinforcement and punishment techniques in altering behaviors in the facility, at school, and in the community. The program has since been extended to over 150 group homes throughout the United States and a few foreign countries (Jones, Weinrott, & Howard, 1981).

Work-Site Applications

Many applications of behavioral techniques have focused on health-related behaviors such as alcohol consumption, cigarette smoking, weight control, and nutrition. Although most of these programs have been implemented with small numbers of individuals as part of a special treatment project, large-scale extensions have increased. For example, incentive programs have been implemented in industrial settings (such as Dow Chemical

Company) to alter the cigarette smoking of hundreds of people (Danaher, 1980). The Dow Chemical program was initiated when the company discovered that it had lost $500,000 because of missed workdays due to the illness of persons who smoked. Cigarette smokers were given the opportunity to win a large prize (a boat and motor worth $42,400) for each month of not smoking. Smaller incentives ($1 each week and the opportunity to win $50 quarterly) were also provided for nonsmoking. Four hundred employees participated in the program. After one year of the program, abstinence from smoking was reported for 75 percent of these employees. Several programs have been reported in which work sites were used as the basis for recruiting large numbers of clients to control diet, weight, and hypertension and to manage stress (Brownell, 1982).

Long-Term Follow-Up

When behavior modification first emerged as an area of study, the primary question was whether interventions could change behavior and whether behavioral changes were due to the specific procedures. Small-scale projects were emphasized, and treatments were implemented and withdrawn in brief phases (as part of ABAB designs) to see whether the program was responsible for changes. Thus, preliminary work was largely restricted to short-term effects of treatment. The study of long-term effects of treatment was not the priority. In general, studies of various forms of treatment, whether or not they are behavioral, infrequently evaluate the long-term effects. For example, the majority of various forms of psychotherapy for children, adolescents, and adults do *not* assess whether the gains are maintained months or years later (Kazdin, Bass, Ayers, & Rodgers, 1990). It is difficult to follow clients over time, to obtain measures to assess how well they are doing, and then to be sure that the original treatment was responsible for change.

The progress of behavior modification in demonstrating change in behavior has become clear. For example, to mention only two areas, hundreds of studies have demonstrated the ability to alter readily the adaptive and deviant behaviors of hospitalized psychiatric patients and the academic performance and deportment of children and adolescents in the classroom. The need no longer exists to show that behavioral interventions can produce change in these populations and settings. What is needed is evidence that long-term gains can be sustained.

Several programs have focused on long-term maintenance of changes and on the transfer (generalization) of treatment effects. For example, in a program for hospitalized psychiatric patients, mentioned previously, a token economy was used to develop a variety of adaptive behaviors on the ward, such as attending activities, engaging in self-care behaviors, and engaging in social interaction (Paul & Lentz, 1977). The effects of the program, relative to routine hospital care or milieu treatment (provided to other groups), were marked. Patients who participated in the token economy showed greater changes while in the hospital and greater rates of discharge. Moreover, the gains were evident from one and a half to five years after the patients had left the hospital. The impact of treatment on long-term maintenance is an important extension over previous work.

In school settings, the assessment of long-term effects has increased over the past several years with quite promising results. For example, the Behavior Analysis program, already mentioned, indicated that the academic gains of elementary school students were maintained up to two years after the program had ended (Bushell, 1978). Similarly, in a junior high school program for adolescents with behavioral problems, token reinforcement led to reductions in expulsions, suspensions, and academic failure. At follow-up assessment three to four years later, gains were still evident (Heaton & Safer, 1982; Safer, Heaton, & Parker, 1981). Adolescents who participated in the program showed higher rates of entrance into high school and of school attendance, better classroom conduct, and lower rates of withdrawal from school, compared with adolescents who did not participate in the program.

The long-term impact of treatment has been evaluated in selected programs of research. For example, in an intensive behavioral program (Lovaas, 1987) mentioned previously, young autistic children (less than 4 years old) received a behavioral program that was conducted in the child's home, school, and community for an average of 40 hours per week for two or more years. Several college-student therapists who worked on a part-time basis administered the treatment over this period. In addition, parents were trained extensively, so that treatment could take place at home for almost all of the children's waking hours, 365 days a year. Treatment focused on eliminating maladaptive behavior (for example, self-stimulation, aggression) and developing a variety of prosocial skills (for example, play) and cognitive/academic skills (for example, language, reading, writing, and other tasks). A major goal of treatment was to place children into regular classrooms, where they would function largely as other children did. For children who entered a regular first-grade class, treatment was reduced from 40 hours a week to ten hours or fewer a week and eventually was terminated with minimal contact. For treated children who did not enter regular first grade, the intervention continued at 40 hours a week for more than a total of six years (more than 14,000 hours of one-to-one treatment per child).

The results indicated that 47% of the treated group achieved normal intellectual and educational functioning, as reflected by scoring within the normal range on standardized intelligence tests and successfully completing first grade in the public schools. Control children who did not receive the intensive treatment did not show these gains. The impact of treatment was dramatic; children gained an average of 30 points on standardized intelligence tests (WISC-R, Stanford Binet, or other measure) over control subjects who did not participate in the treatment. Follow-up data indicated that after several years (mean = 5), more of the treatment youth compared with controls remained in a regular classroom. Their IQ scores and adaptive behaviors were also higher (McEachin et al., 1993). Maintenance of gains over several years was clearly evident with this program.

As mentioned previously, follow-up data on various forms of treatment and intervention are rarely obtained. Thus, follow-up from the above reports represents exemplary research, even though many questions about the impact of treatment might remain. In the usual cases, data are simply incomplete or too sparse to draw conclusions. For example, parent management training is probably the most well investigated and established treatment for oppositional, aggressive, and antisocial children. An extraordinarily large number of studies have shown that parent training leads to therapeutic change relative to other treatment and control conditions (Kazdin, 1985a). Follow-up data, when obtained, usually do not evaluate how the children are doing beyond one year later. One year follow-up in many studies has shown that the effects of treatment are maintained. These results are promising because severe aggressive behavior in children and adolescents has been resistant to many forms of psychological treatment. At the same time, further information is needed over the course of follow-up. For example, if training is provided to parents of children aged 8 to 10, it would be important to see whether the gains are sustained through adolescence; if adolescents are treated, we wish to see whether they continue to show the benefits of treatment into young adulthood. For many areas of intervention research, long-term follow-up data are not available.

In some areas, follow-up data have shown that intervention effects are not sustained. For example, mentioned previously was the Achievement Place program. Delinquent youths who are in the program attend regular school and live in the community while they are in the special home. During the intervention period, Achievement Place youths show clear benefits of intervention in terms of decreased contact with the police and the courts. These benefits seem to be lost at follow-up one to two years later. The fact that the gains are not sustained at follow-up can be interpreted differently. One view is that the program is not particularly helpful because once youths leave, the gains are lost. Another view is that the program is very helpful (because of the consistent changes while the program is in effect) but that it needs to remain in effect for the youths. It may be the case that for some serious and chronic problems like delinquency, giving treatment and returning individuals to their original settings is not an appropriate model of treatment. Rather, treatment in some form may need to be continued for an extended period over the course of several years (Kazdin, 1988; Wolf, Braukmann, & Ramp, 1987). In any case, at present even the most effective interventions may not be sufficiently effective to attain the long-term gains we wish to obtain.

The above projects are significant because they address important problems in several applied areas. The work is especially noteworthy because it goes beyond demonstrating that behavior changes can be achieved. For the changes to be significant, evidence is needed that they can be maintained and that they enhance the long-term, everyday-life functioning of the persons who have achieved them.

SUMMARY AND CONCLUSION

The principles of operant conditioning describe relations between behavior and environmental events and hence should be generally applicable when there is interest in changing behavior. This does *not* mean that all behavior is the same, that behaviors in everyday life can be altered in a fashion identical to those under control in the laboratory, or that all people are alike. Rather, the general applicability of the principles means that arranging antecedent and consequent events in a systematic way is likely to change behavior. Extended applications of behavior modification have been possible in large part because of their method of evaluating interventions. The assessment of behavior over time in many different settings has permitted evaluation of the interventions and their effects. The behavioral approach to problem identification and evaluation has helped to translate significant problems into concrete behaviors that can be altered.

As evident in the present chapter, behavioral techniques and evaluation approaches have been widely extended. The chapter sampled a broad number of areas of application including interventions designed to

- prevent illness and disease;
- alter eating disorders and dieting habits;
- help individuals cope with and manage pain;
- increase adherence to and compliance with medical regimens;
- engage in safe behaviors in the community, at home, and in business settings;
- improve parenting and parent-child interactions; and
- address diverse concerns in everyday life (for example, energy conservation, waste recycling)

These areas of application, of course, are in addition to the more common foci in such settings as the classroom, home, community, and institutions for diverse populations as illustrated throughout previous chapters. In sampling extensions of behavior modification, the full range of applications could not be presented. Indeed, many areas (for example, applications by the military or in college teaching) were omitted entirely. The interests of society as well as of individuals in influencing behavior (for example, in education, health practices, and government) mean that the range of domains to which behavioral procedures can be applied is virtually unlimited. Consequently, it may be more important to convey the applicability of the interventions rather than to attempt to exhaust the range of applications themselves.

Apart from extensions to many different areas of everyday life, central characteristics of behavioral applications have changed in many ways. Although most projects have been small-scale demonstrations of what behavioral techniques can accomplish, many programs have been conducted on a large scale especially in education, in facilities for delinquent youths, and at work sites. Another change is the increased attention to long-term effects. Both large-scale applications and long-term effects of behavioral programs are in need of much further attention, a point that will be raised in the next and final chapter.

Note

1. The program was part of Project Follow Through, a demonstration project that was designed to follow up the gains provided in an early, federally funded program, Head Start. Project Follow Through tested the effects of several types of educational programs, one of which was behavior analysis.

For Further Reading

Blanchard, E. B. (Ed.). (1992). Special issue: Behavioral medicine: An update for the 1990s. *Journal of Consulting and Clinical Psychology, 60,* 491–643.

Geller, E. S. (1991). Special section: Behavioral community intervention. *Journal of Applied Behavior Analysis, 24,* 621–718.

Geller, E. S. (1991). Special section: Road safety: International perspectives. *Journal of Applied Behavior Analysis, 24,* 13–94.

Geller, E. S. (Ed.). (1992). Special issue: The education crisis: Issues, perspectives, and solutions. *Journal of Applied Behavior Analysis, 25,* 13–235.

Glenwick, D. S., & Jason, L. A. (Eds.). (In press). *Promoting health and mental health in children, youth, and families.* New York: Springer.

Greene, B. F., Winett, R. A., Van Houten, R., Geller, E. S., & Iwata, B. A. (Eds.). (1987). *Behavior analysis in the community.* Lawrence, KS: Society for the Experimental Analysis of Behavior.

Sulzer-Azaroff, B., Drabman, R. M., Greer, R. D., Hall, R. V., Iwata, B. A., & O'Leary, S. G. (Eds.). (1988). *Behavior analysis in education.* Lawrence, KS: Society for the Experimental Analysis of Behavior.

Williamson, D. A. (1987). Recent advances in behavioral medicine. *Behavior Modification, 11,* 259–263.

CHAPTER THIRTEEN

CRITICAL ISSUES AND FUTURE DIRECTIONS

Previous chapters have presented different principles and techniques of behavior change and illustrated a wide range of applications. It should be evident that behavioral techniques have been effectively applied to many areas of the functioning of children, adolescents, and adults. It is fairly safe to say that these techniques have been extended to more areas of human functioning than have any other approaches to therapy, education, or rehabilitation. However, behavioral techniques are not just a matter of applying techniques to behavior. A number of considerations relate to how the behavioral approach is carried out and to the social, ethical, and legal contexts in which behavioral programs are conducted. The present chapter considers critical features of the behavioral approach, the social context in which behavioral techniques are administered, and directions for future work.

CRITICAL ELEMENTS OF THE BEHAVIORAL APPROACH

At first blush, the success of behavioral interventions might be considered a result of the generality of operant conditioning principles and of the techniques derived from them. Indeed, it is true that positive reinforcement, for example, has considerable generality and can be used to alter behavior in the laboratory or applied settings and among many infrahuman species and humans. The effectiveness of behavioral interventions is only partially due to the behavior change techniques themselves. The approach toward conceptualizing the problem, and the assessment and evaluation derived from that conceptualization, contribute fundamentally to the effectiveness of treatment. It is useful to consider critical elements of the behavioral approach. Although the topics have been dealt with earlier in concrete terms, here a few of them will be examined briefly at a somewhat higher level of abstraction.

Task Analysis

Task analysis plays a central role in developing effective programs, prior to consideration of the interventions themselves. As detailed previously, task analysis consists of identifying the precise behaviors that need to be assessed and that serve as the focus of the intervention. The significance of task analysis is that it places the focus of treatment into concrete terms. The overall goal may include a somewhat general statement, such as improving social interaction among psychiatric patients living in a group home, increasing safe driving among high-risk populations, or following a complex medical regimen for patients with a chronic disease. Task analysis identifies the constituent behaviors in concrete stages or steps.

The significance of identifying the constituent behaviors is twofold. First, by making the behaviors concrete, one can evaluate progress systematically. One can evaluate whether: the person is learning the behaviors; the behavior is stable; an entire sequence of behaviors has been learned; the behavior extends to other settings and situations; and so on. Second, task analyses divide behaviors into small components so that shaping can be used. Training can proceed by reinforcing approximations of the final goals. The method of training and developing new behavior can be readily approached once the concrete steps are identified. The special contribution of task analysis is formulating the goals into units that can facilitate evaluation of progress.

Functional Analysis

Functional analysis, also discussed earlier, consists of identifying the relations between antecedents, consequences, and behaviors. More generally, functional analysis permits the investigator to pose and to test hypotheses about events in the environment that may bear a causal relation to the behavior. The effectiveness of a treatment derives from identifying what maintained the behavior or why the behavior was performed. Understandably, treatment is likely to be effective in changing behavior if the factors shown to maintain the behavior are altered.

An illustration of functional analysis places this broader issue into sharper light. Repp, Felce, and Barton (1988) tested alternative hypotheses regarding what maintained self-stimulatory and self-injurious behavior among retarded children in special education classrooms. For one of the clients, they tested two hypotheses, namely, that the behavior was maintained by *positive reinforcement* (consequences following the behavior, such as staff approach, eye contact, verbalizations, and touching) or by *negative reinforcement* (for example, demands placed on the child that led to the child's deviant behavior, which in turn stopped the demand—that is, removed the "aversive" consequence).

During baseline, both the behaviors and environmental events associated with them were measured. Baseline observations suggested that negative reinforcement was the critical contingency maintaining behavior. The authors, however, tested both hypotheses. In one classroom during the day, the negative reinforcement hypothesis was tested by extinction. Task demands (responding to simple commands) were made of the child and were not terminated when the child engaged in the undesirable response. If the child responded, positive reinforcers were provided. In short, extinction (no longer terminating commands when the child engaged in self-stimulation) and positive reinforcement for complying with the task were provided. In a second classroom, the positive reinforcement hypothesis was tested. Extinction was used by ensuring that all self-stimulation did not receive staff attention.

Figure 13–1 shows the results of the different treatments implemented in different classes each day. In the second phase, the program testing the negative reinforcement hypothesis was implemented during one class pe-

FIGURE   13–1

The number of head banging responses per hour in two classrooms. After baseline, the negative reinforcement hypothesis was tested in one classroom and the positive reinforcement hypothesis was tested in the other. In the third phase, the negative reinforcement hypothesis was put into effect in both classrooms.

SOURCE: Repp, A. C., Felce, D., Barton, L. E. (1988).

riod; the treatment testing the positive reinforcement hypothesis was implemented in the other class period. The results strongly supported the hypothesis that negative reinforcement was the contingency that maintained behavior. Consequently, in the third and final phase, the treatment based on the negative reinforcement hypothesis was implemented in both classroom periods.

At a very general level, the example illustrates the importance of identifying antecedents and consequences and manipulating them to achieve behavior change. The treatment was hypothesis driven—that is, based on educated guesses posed by the authors about which current influences were causing the behavior to occur. The treatments that were tested were based on these hypotheses. What is so special about treatments driven by hypotheses? The answer is very important for advances in treatment.

Functional analysis is an effort to *understand* the factors that influence behavior for a particular individual and then to alter them to achieve behavior change. It is possible to change behavior without this understanding. For many behavioral programs, reinforcement and punishment procedures are administered in an effort to achieve behavior change. For example, teachers may provide praise and token reinforcement to increase the frequency of homework completion, a contingency that is likely to change student behavior. The treatment is designed with a likelihood that the contingency would have impact. However, no effort is made to understand the behavior. A functional analysis is designed to understand behavior, to identify the basis for the behavior, to test the hypotheses, and to use the information to design effective treatment (see Carr, Robinson, & Palumbo, 1990). Much more effective treatments are likely when current maintaining conditions are understood. For example, medical treatments often are effective when they are applied even when the basis of the disease is not known (for example, chemotherapy, surgery, and radiation for various cancers). Treatment will be more effective when the factors that cause the disease are known. The interventions can then be directed specifically at the factors leading to and sustaining the disease. And, of course, once the understanding of a disorder increases, then preventive efforts are likely to be effective as well.

The general point is that functional analysis is a major feature of the behavioral approach. Functional analysis provides a procedure for identifying current factors that relate to performance. These factors are shown in a given case to be related to the target behavior in a causal way, that is, by showing that behavior is increased and decreased reliably as a function of the condition. Treatment consists of converting this information into an intervention to promote prosocial behavior. We shall return briefly to this topic in discussing program failures.

Assessment and Evaluation

The effectiveness of behavioral techniques depends heavily upon assessment and evaluation. *Assessment* refers to the systematic collection of data. The data permit one to describe the level of functioning and to examine progress over the course of treatment. Assessment in behavioral programs usually consists of direct measurement of the behaviors of interest. For example, if a task analysis reveals ten behaviors that constitute appropriate eating for severely retarded persons, current job performance of factory workers, or study skills of college students with academic difficulties, the specific behaviors are measured directly. Although behavioral assessment emphasizes overt behavior, clinical problems and targets for behavioral interventions are broad. Thus, assessment can include affect (feelings, moods) and cognitions (thoughts, beliefs, attributions) as well as overt behavior. The critical issue from the standpoint of intervention is systematic assessment of the focus of interest.

Systematic assessment of the target focus is a hallmark of behavioral research. Assessment is directly related to the ability to improve client behavior and to achieve change (Kazdin, 1993a). Under ideal conditions, continuous assessment is conducted before (baseline phase), during (intervention phase), and after (follow-up) the intervention. Baseline assessment is essential to identify the level of functioning or performance prior to training. If training produces the desired changes, assessment will reveal a departure from baseline levels of performance. By observing performance during baseline and intervention phases, one can see clearly whether the intervention is having the desired effects. A major reason that behavioral techniques are so effective is that it is relatively easy to tell when the programs are failing or not working as well as desired.

Assessment makes a major contribution to clinical and applied work even when baseline cannot be collected. With continuous measures over the course of treatment, the therapist, trainer, teacher, and so on can evaluate progress. Systematic and continuous assessment provide *feedback* to the trainer about how the program is working and whether more or different treatment is needed.

As a hypothetical example, a behavioral program might reduce the rate of fighting of an aggressive child from 20 fights a day to 5 fights a day. A change of this magnitude is likely to be quite clear when graphed over time. Yet, the results would also convey that the program needs to be changed. To be successful, virtual or complete elimination of fighting is required. The assessment provides essential *feedback* to the investigator about the program and whether alternative techniques need to be pursued. Indeed, in many behavioral programs, the procedures designed to alter behavior initially have been ineffective for the clients (see Kazdin, 1983). For example, defiant and aggressive child behavior in the home or at school often is unaffected by simply having parents or teachers praise appropriate child behavior (for example, Wahler & Fox, 1980; Walker, Hops, & Greenwood, 1981). The undesired behavior may not decrease until mild punishment (time out, response cost) is added to the contingencies. The decision to alter the contingencies in these and many other applications was made possible by the data obtained through direct assessment of behavior. Clear information that an intervention is not working serves as a prompt for the therapist, trainer, or investigator to do something differently. For many other approaches to treatment, information about the impact of the intervention is either provided after treatment is completed or not obtained at all. Consequently, one cannot alter treatment if it is not working.

One might ask whether one really needs systematic information to evaluate interventions. For example, in therapy it seems that the therapist and client could certainly tell whether there is improvement. Very dramatic changes (for example, elimination of all obsessions, compulsions, signs of sexual dysfunction) might be so clear as not to require systematic assessment. Yet, in the vast majority of cases, treatment effects are not likely to be so dramatic or unidimensional that they can be unequivocally determined without formal evaluation. The amount of change, the range of behaviors that have changed, and generalization of the changes to other situations require systematic assessment. Many studies have shown that human judgment, whether or not the humans in question are experts, is not able to perceive many of the changes or to identify the bases for the changes without systematic assessment (Nezu & Nezu, 1989).

A major difficulty with many approaches to therapy, education, and rehabilitation is that one cannot tell when programs are succeeding or failing (that is attaining or not attaining the goals) or falling somewhere in between. Programs are implemented that are designed to help—to help reduce crime in a city, to encourage healthful diets, to help people stop cigarette smoking, to promote safe sex, and so on. The merit of the programs does not derive from the well-motivated goals or intentions of those who implement the program. Programs with laudatory goals, such as the prevention of suicide or drug abuse and the treatment of delinquency, sometimes have no effect or actually make the problems worse (Bangert-Drowns, 1988; Shaffer et al., 1990). Such findings underscore the importance of evaluation in any situation in which there is interest in benefiting people (Kazdin, 1993a).

The value and utility of continuous assessment extend beyond behavior modification. Continuous evaluation of progress is relevant to any situation and intervention in which the goal is to improve some facet of functioning or performance. If one believes a specific intervention can produce change, then direct assessment of intervention effects is critical. Many interventions have been evaluated with continuous assessment over time, including the effects of medications on psychiatric problems and various nonbehavioral psychotherapy approaches (for example, psychoanalysis with children). Apart from the contribution of several behavior change principles and techniques, behavior modification has shown the importance of continuous assessment in aiding clients more generally. Assessment and evaluation have permitted the identification of effective treatment techniques and have been no less important than the techniques themselves.

THE SOCIAL CONTEXT OF TREATMENT

The approach toward intervening to change behavior refers to the manner of identifying behaviors and evaluating the impact of the intervention. Much broader considerations need to be taken into account in deciding which behaviors to alter, which techniques to use, and whether the outcomes attained are very important. The goal of clinical and applied research is not only to develop effective procedures but also to ensure that those procedures take into account the concerns of society and the concerns of the consumers of treatment (parents, teachers, clients).

Several years ago, Wolf (1978) introduced the notion of *social validation,* which drew attention to the social context of intervention research. As initially formulated, three types of questions were central to social validation:

- Are the goals of the behavioral program relevant to everyday life?
- Are the intervention procedures acceptable to consumers and to the community at large?

- Are the outcomes of the intervention (the changes) important, and do they make a difference in the everyday lives of individuals?

These questions are critically important to any intervention research, whether or not behavioral procedures are used. Social concerns have received considerable attention in applied behavior analysis and can be highlighted by examining the social context in relation to the focus of treatment, the acceptability of the procedures that are used to alter the focus, and the importance of the changes or whether the changes make a difference to the individual or the community at large.

Focus of Treatment

Considerable agreement exists regarding the goals of most therapeutic programs, whether or not they are behavioral programs. Thus, there is reasonable consensus that behavior change techniques should be applied to improve the academic behaviors of children who are doing poorly in school, to decrease the symptoms of depressed psychiatric patients, to eliminate the self-destructive behavior of autistic or mentally retarded children, to decrease antisocial behavior among delinquents, and to develop behaviors that prevent disease. In most instances, the focus of treatment does not raise major questions. However, situations occasionally arise that pose fundamental questions about the focus and social implications of treatment.

Social and moral questions about the focus of treatment (target behaviors) have been actively discussed. Two examples from the 1970s are historically interesting because the foci are relevant to contemporary discussions of stereotypes and acceptable behavior. The first example pertains to the application of behavioral techniques to a boy named Kraig who engaged in cross-gender behaviors (Rekers & Lovaas, 1974). As noted previously (Chapter 2), Kraig, who was almost 5 years old, engaged in several feminine behaviors, including dressing up as a girl, playing with cosmetics, and showing pronounced feminine mannerisms, gestures, and gait. He mimicked subtle feminine behaviors of an adult woman. Kraig's cross-gender behaviors appeared extreme, and they led to social isolation and ridicule. Also, because cross-gender behaviors in childhood are sometimes associated with sexual deviance in adulthood, the need to intervene seemed especially urgent. In any case, Kraig's parents sought treatment.

Rekers and Lovaas developed masculine behaviors such as playing with toys typical of little boys (soldiers, guns, airplanes), engaging in aggressive behaviors (playing cowboys and Indians, playing with a dart gun and a rubber knife), and dressing in masculine-typed clothes (army shirt, football helmet). Such behaviors as dressing in girls' clothes, playing with dolls, taking the role of the girl in games, and showing feminine gestures were decreased. In therapy sessions, Kraig's mother attended to his masculine behaviors and ignored his feminine behaviors; at home, his parents used token reinforcement to develop gender behaviors that were considered more sex appropriate. The program was very effective in altering Kraig's cross-gender behaviors, and 26 months after treatment, his sex-typed behaviors were considered to have become "normalized." Indeed, follow-up revealed not only the absence of pretreatment feminine behaviors but also expanded sex-role activities characteristic of boys (for example, more rough-and-tumble play and interest in camping out).

Fundamental questions were raised about the focus of this study (Nordyke, Baer, Etzel, & LeBlanc, 1977; Winkler, 1977). Developing masculine behaviors explicitly adheres to social stereotypes about how boys and girls—and later, men and women—ought to behave. Yet, traditional sex-role behaviors may be questioned—they are not necessarily psychologically "healthy" or natural. Indeed, the authors who raised the concerns cited studies noting that more highly sex-typed individuals (females who are high in femininity and males who are high in masculinity) often show such characteristics as high anxiety, low self-esteem, low social acceptance, and lower intelligence compared with less-sex-typed individuals. The important point here is that fostering sex-typed behavior reflects a value stance and the adjustment of the individual or the welfare of society may not necessarily be enhanced by stronger sex-typed behaviors.

On the other side of the issue, Rekers and Lovaas (1974; Rekers, 1977) noted that the severity of Kraig's cross-gender behavior, the possibility of his sexual deviance in adulthood, and his parents' concern over his social adjustment suggested the need to intervene. The issue extends beyond any particular case, and it raises questions about areas of treatment that are controversial and value laden. Scientific research cannot resolve the many questions that arise. For example, it is not known that children with cross-gender behaviors in fact later become deviant. If this were known, additional questions might be raised about whether the deviance (for example, transvestism) would necessarily harm the individual or society. Obtaining informed consent from the persons involved in treatment does not resolve the problem because neither the therapist nor the client (or the parents) can be truly informed. Insufficient information exists about the consequences of treating or failing to treat the behavior, so the long-term risks and benefits of treatment cannot be known.

In another example of historical and contemporary significance, issues were raised about whether some behaviors should be treated. In the 1970s, homosexuality was viewed as a clinical disorder. Challenging this view, Davison (1976) argued that treating homosexuality unwittingly acknowledged sexual preferences for the same sex as a "problem." Yet the problem may not be sexual preferences per se but adjusting to a world that has strong biases against homosexuality. Many homosexuals may be driven to treatment because of the tremendous pressures associated with "staying in the closet." Therapists are not apt to treat heterosexuals who wish to be homosexual or to expand their sexuality to include homosexual relations. So, it has been argued, perhaps homosexuals should not be treated for their sexual preferences. Independent of the stand that a particular person may take, this issue clearly illustrates the role that values may play in selecting target behaviors.

Concerns over the social value of target behaviors selected in behavioral and other forms of treatment also arose with behaviors that may evoke fewer emotional responses than are evoked by sex-role behaviors and sexual preferences. For example, classroom applications of behavioral techniques frequently focus on making children well behaved, so that they remain in their seats, do not speak without permission, and attend to their lessons (Winett & Winkler, 1972). Most of these applications have not included especially deviant children who engaged in severely disruptive or dangerous behavior (for example, hyperactivity, aggression). Yet, for many years, the focus on having mildly disruptive or inattentive children pay attention went unchallenged. A large number of investigations have since shown that improving attentiveness among students in the classroom does not improve academic performance. Perhaps proponents of behavior modification have been too apt to embrace goals selected by others—having "well-behaved and quiet children"—while neglecting major goals of education, such as improved academic performance. A shift in the research focus in educational settings has shown that improving academic performance frequently has, as a side effect, improved classroom attentiveness and reduced disruptive behavior (Kazdin, 1981a). Thus, concerns that many teachers have about discipline can be remedied by improving academic behaviors. Unless severe behaviors are apparent, the focus on classroom deportment might be appropriately redirected to academic accomplishment.

Concerns over the focus of treatment have been raised in studies where there might seem to be little reason to do so. Consider contemporary examples where the focus is on behavior related to risk of AIDS. Mentioned earlier was a study with emergency room nurses (DeVries, Burnette, & Redmon, 1991). The purpose of the study was to increase the frequency of wearing rubber gloves as a means of decreasing the risk of HIV exposure (by contact with bodily fluids). Feedback was shown to reliably increase glove wearing. What possible question could one raise about this focus? Actually, two questions were raised (Finney, 1991).

To begin, glove wearing is only one of the behaviors that is likely to decrease the risk of HIV exposure for hospital care workers. In fact, in the United States, several practices (target behaviors) are mandated for hospital workers (by the Occupational Safety and Health Administration [OSHA]), including using safe methods in disposing of sharp objects (for example, needles, scalpel blades), managing wastes (for example, products that may include blood or other bodily fluids), and wearing diverse protective barriers (such as gloves, eye protection, and face masks). Glove wearing is only one of the behaviors that protect health care workers. Hence, the case might be made that the target focus was insufficient to decrease risk, the original goal of the program.

One might reply that at least the study increased the frequency of one safe practice, and hence the target focus should not be challenged. Yet, wearing gloves does not prevent accidental needle sticks, one way that HIV is transmitted to health care workers. Moreover, wearing gloves might even increase the likelihood of needle sticks if the gloves are worn too often (Finney, 1991). Handling needles is more cumbersome while wearing gloves and may increase the risk of a needle stick. In short, to address the reduction of risk of exposure to HIV, a more comprehensive focus may be needed than increasing glove wearing alone.

As another example, a recent study was designed to encourage patrons in three "gay" bars to take free condoms from a container available in the area adjacent to where individuals purchased their drinks (Honnen & Kleinke, 1990). Carefully executed and evaluated prompting procedures (signs noting that condoms were available, the number of persons who died of AIDS in the state, and reminders of safe sex practices) were shown in an ABAB design to increase the number of condoms that were taken in each of the bars. The target behavior can be easily defended as important, because possession of a condom is a precondition for its use. At the same time, taking free condoms is not the same as engaging in safe sex or using the condoms. In fact, having more condoms in one's possession (two pockets full or two purses full) may not add to the probability of safe sex any more than having fewer of them (1 pocket full or 1 purse full). Dissemination of condoms is important even in laboratory or research contexts on a small scale (what might be called artificial dissemination). Yet, further assessment is needed to ensure that development of the target behavior, as operationalized, has impact on the original focus of interest.

The purpose of the above examples is not to derogate in any way the illustrations that were selected but, rather, to raise the larger questions. The target focus of an intervention—any intervention, whether from a behavioral or other perspective—can raise significant issues (see Kazdin, 1985b). The issues may reflect values (for example, how one ought to behave) and social perspectives (for example, what is deviant), as well as data (for example, what behaviors and levels of change actually improve an individual's functioning in everyday life or aid society overall). These issues are not easily resolved.

Mentioned previously (Chapter 3) were guidelines for selecting target behaviors. One of the guidelines was selecting behaviors that people in everyday life regard as important. People in everyday life include the client, persons in contact with the client, or society at large who might be affected by the outcome of treatment (Schwartz & Baer, 1991). Opinions of the appropriate target focus are a useful guide. Yet, opinions, whether from laypersons or professionals, are not always informed and at best provide an imperfect guide to what behaviors will be adaptive, appropriate, and of benefit in the short and long runs.

Treatment Acceptability

The selection of target behaviors raises issues about the focus and goals of treatment. The treatment techniques of course concern the means to obtain them. The social context is obviously relevant to the selection of the treatments. The techniques that can be used to alter behavior must consider people's opinions about what is appropriate and what should be done. It may be of little use to develop effective treatments if the procedures are highly objectionable to the people who need them (for example, parents, teachers, clients) or to the people for whom they will be used (for example, children, patients).

Attention has been given to the public reaction to the procedures used in treatments and to whether treatments are viewed as acceptable ways of changing behavior. The notion of *treatment acceptability* refers to judgments by laypersons, clients, and others of whether treatment procedures are appropriate, fair, and reasonable for the problem that is to be treated. There are a number of reasons for the interest in the acceptability of treatment. One reason is that client rights are protected if institutional review committees, laypeople, and clients themselves evaluate whether proposed treatment procedures are acceptable in light of the client's problem. A second reason is that procedures need to be designed that are not only effective but also desirable or preferred among alternative treatments that might produce change.

Moreover, treatment acceptability is likely to relate to adherence to procedures. Clients and therapists are more likely to carry out treatments that they view as highly acceptable. In outpatient treatment, clients are more likely to remain in treatment if the procedures used are palatable or positive. Indeed, aversion techniques often have high dropout rates, presumably because the techniques, even if effective, are not very acceptable.

Research has examined how people evaluate treatment and whether treatment procedures are acceptable. For example, in one project, young psychiatric inpatients, their parents, and hospital staff were asked to evaluate several procedures that were applied to children (hypothetical cases) for highly deviant and disruptive behavior at home and at school (Kazdin, French, & Sherick, 1981). The procedures were described in detail and the subjects rated the extent to which the different treatments were consistent with commonly held notions of what treatment should be, whether the treatments were fair or cruel, whether the treatments were appropriate for clients who could not give consent, and so on. Marked differences among the treatments were shown in a measure that assessed the overall acceptability of treatment. The children, parents, and staff agreed in their ordering of treatments. A reinforcement technique (in which appropriate behavior was reinforced as a way of reducing inappropriate behavior) was evaluated as much more acceptable than the alternative treatments. Time out (involving 10 minutes of isolation) was rated as the least acceptable treatment. Positive practice and medication to control disruptive behavior were intermediate in overall acceptability.

Evaluations of treatment acceptability have focused on several questions (see Elliott, 1988; O'Brien & Karsh, 1990). The most frequent focus has been to examine different procedures and their relative acceptability. Another line of research has been to examine differences in acceptability among different types of clients or consumers of treatment (such as children, parents, teachers, or the community at large) (for example, Blampied & Kahan, 1992). Different perspectives are likely to lead to different views about acceptable treatment. Characteristics of the treatments themselves can influence acceptability, and efforts have been made to isolate a number of these. For example, whether the individual client is permitted to play a role in planning the treatment and whether treatment has adverse side effects are two of the many factors that can influence acceptability ratings (for example, Kazdin, 1980b, 1981b).

People's views of treatment acceptability probably depend on many factors, such as how treatment is applied, who applies it, the severity of the problem, and the number of alternative treatments that have been previously tried. It is important to understand the factors that influence acceptability so that procedures incorporating the factors that potential consumers see as important can be developed. Apart from effectiveness, it is important to develop treatments that are sensitive to the interests, values, and lifestyles of those who are consumers of treatment. For example, there are cultural and ethnic differences in the seeking of treatment, utilization of clinical services, and treatment preferences (see Tharp, 1991). Understanding factors that influence acceptability of treatment services may be helpful in fostering increased utilization of treatment by making treatments more acceptable to diverse groups.

The other side of making treatments more acceptable is educating individuals about existing treatments that are effective but less familiar, such as response cost, time out, and positive practice. The acceptability of treatments known to be effective can be enhanced by clarifying the rationale underlying their use and describing the procedures in some detail (see O'Brien & Karsh, 1990). Thus, views of acceptability of treatment can be influenced by variations in the procedures themselves as well as by efforts to educate potential consumers more about the procedures.

Traditionally, treatment techniques have been evaluated by looking at how effective they are on various measures of personality and behavior. Obviously, the effectiveness of a treatment is extremely important. However, treatments, whether behavioral or nonbehavioral in orientation, need to be evaluated along many dimensions. Some of these dimensions reflect broader concerns than the extent of therapeutic improvement for a particular client. Client evaluations of procedures, the ease of implementing techniques, the costs of treatment, and similar considerations illustrate the expanded criteria that are being used to evaluate treatment. Within behavior modification, the criteria include concerns about the importance of the changes achieved as well as consumer satisfaction with the treatments themselves and how they are conducted.

Treatment Outcomes

The social context of behavioral treatment also arises in evaluating changes in performance. Although dramatic changes often result from behavioral interventions, it is still appropriate to ask whether the changes are really important and whether they make a difference in the lives of the clients. The social context in which the clients perform is an important consideration in answering these questions. *The social context* refers to evaluation of change in relation to other persons and in the contexts of everyday life.

In the past decade in particular, advances have been made in elaborating and using alternative criteria to evaluate the importance of changes. The term *clinical significance* has been used to denote whether the changes are important to the client. The context of behavior extends well beyond therapy and clinics (for example, to business and industry, everyday life, and education), but the issue is the same; namely, are the changes important, and do they make a difference in the client's functioning in everyday life? Several ways of measuring the importance of change in the client are illustrated below (see Kazdin, 1992).

Comparison Methods
Comparison methods, as the name suggests, examine the clinical significance of the change by directly comparing clients with others. The most commonly used method is to evaluate the functioning of clients relative to the "normal" functioning of others in everyday life. Prior to treatment, the client sample presumably would depart considerably from the peer sample that is functioning well in everyday life in the areas identified for treatment (for example, anxiety, depression, social withdrawal, aggression, tics). One measure of the extent to which treatment produced clinically important changes would be the demonstration that at the end of treatment the client sample was indistinguishable from or well within the range of a normative, well-functioning sample on the measures of interest.

Evaluating the extent to which individuals perform at or within the normative range is the most commonly used method of evaluating clinical significance. To invoke this criterion, a comparison is made between treated clients and peers who are functioning well or without significant problems in everyday life. For example, in a study mentioned earlier, alternative treatments were applied to help aggressive and antisocial children (Kazdin, Siegel, & Bass, 1992). The effectiveness of three conditions was examined: problem-solving skills training (PSST), parent management training (PMT), and both combined (PSST + PMT). Treatment was provided to children (PSST) and/or their parents (PMT) based on one of the three conditions to which families were assigned. Among the outcome measures were standardized scales (Child Behavior Checklist) completed by parents and teachers. The scales reflect a broad range of emotional and behavioral problems. Original development of the scales included normative data of children delineated separately by age and sex (Achenbach & Edelbrock, 1986). From this original work, analyses indicated that among the normative sample, the 90th percentile is the cutoff point that best delineated clinic from community (nonreferred) samples. In the treatment study, scores at this percentile were used to define the upper limit of the "normal range" of emotional and behavioral problem behavior. Change was considered to be clinically significant if children's scores were reduced to fall below this cutoff.

Figure 13–2 shows the means at pretreatment, posttreatment, and a one-year follow-up for antisocial children in the different treatment conditions. Both parent (upper panel) and teacher evaluations (lower panel) are presented and show some improvement of groups toward the normative range. The results in the figure provide group means (average performance of each group). However, clinically significant change is of equal if not greater interest in relation to individuals. One can compute how many individuals fall within the normative range at the end of treatment. In the present example, for the parent-based measure referred to in the figure, results at posttreatment indicated that 33%, 39%, and 64% of youths from PSST, PMT, and combined treatment, respectively, fell within the normal range. The percentage of youths returned to "normative" levels of functioning reflect one way to examine the clinical importance of the change.

In a very different context, the normative range was used as a way to evaluate the impact of treatment of insomnia (Jacobs, Benson, & Friedman, 1993). Behavioral treatment, based on relaxation training and stimulus control (for example, associating going to bed with drowsiness and relaxation rather than restlessness and worrying), was provided to adults (aged 18 to 52) who could not get to sleep. A sample of individuals without sleep problems was assessed on several sleep-related measures to provide a normative range to evaluate the effectiveness of treatment. After treatment, individuals who were treated fell within the range of the normative sample in terms of such measures as time required to get to sleep (sleep onset latency).

Several other reports have evaluated whether behaviors of deviant, socially disruptive, or withdrawn children; the behaviors of anxious, depressed, or socially withdrawn adults; speech patterns of psychiatric patients; and many other domains of functioning have achieved normative levels after behavioral treatment (for example, Kazdin, 1977c). In each case, the study depends on identifying nondeviant peers who can serve as a basis for comparison. The performance of these peers is assessed to iden-

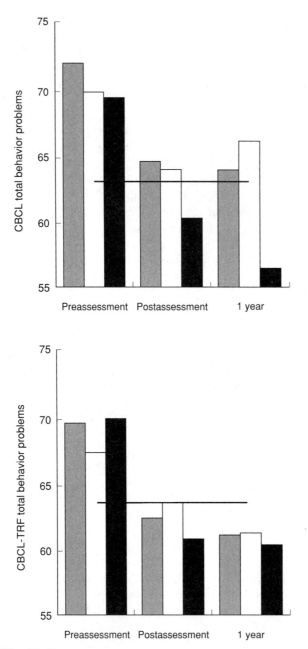

FIGURE 13–2

Mean scores for Problem-Solving Skills Training (PSST), Parent Management Training (PMT), and both combined (PSST + PMT) for the total behavior problem scales
of the parent-completed Child Behavior Checklist (CBCL, upper panel) and the Child
Behavior Checklist–Teacher Report Form (CBCL–TRF lower panel). The horizontal
line reflects the *upper* limit of the nonclinical ("normal") range of children of the
same age and sex. Scores *below* this line fall within the normal range.
SOURCE: Kazdin, A. E., Siegel, T., & Bass, D. (1992).

tify normative functioning. The mean and some interval about that mean are used to provide a window of functioning that is considered to represent persons in the normal range.

Another comparison that has been devised is a comparison of clients after treatment with a *dysfunctional sample* that has not received the intervention. The notion is that at the end of treatment, clients who have made a clinically significant change will depart markedly from the original sample of dysfunctional cases. A statistical criterion has been suggested. Specifically, for an individual to be considered to be improved in a clinically important way, he or she should have a score on the measure that is two standard deviations from the mean (average) of the dysfunctional sample (Jacobson & Revenstorf, 1988).[1] Thus, at posttreatment, individuals whose scores depart at least two standard deviations from the mean of the dysfunctional group (untreated cases with demonstrated dysfunction) would be regarded as having undergone an important change. To be considered as clinically significant, the changes of course must reflect a departure from the deviant sample in the direction of a decrease of symptoms or increase in prosocial functioning.

As an illustration, a recent study compared two variations of cognitive problem-solving therapy to treat depression in adults (Nezu & Perri, 1989). In evaluating the clinical significance of change, the investigators examined the proportion of cases in each group whose score on measures of depression fell two or more standard deviations below (that is, less depressed) the mean of the untreated sample. For example, on a standardized measure of depression commonly used in treatment research with adults (the Beck Depression Inventory), 85.7 percent of the cases who received the full problem-solving therapy regimen achieved this level of change. In contrast, only 50 percent of the cases who received the abbreviated problem-solving condition achieved this level of change. The comparisons add important information about the impact of treatment.

Subjective Evaluation

Another method for evaluating whether the behavior changes achieved are important is to ask people in contact with the client or in a position of expertise whether the changes have made a difference. For example, in one program treatment was provided to a college student named Steven who wished to eliminate two muscle tics (uncontrolled movements) (Wright & Miltenberger, 1987). The tics involved head movements and excessive eyebrow raising. Individual treatment sessions were conducted in which Steven was trained to monitor and identify when the tics occurred and in general to be more aware of their occurrence. In addition, he self-monitored the tics throughout the day. Assessment sessions were conducted in which he read at the clinic or the college library and observers recorded the tics. The impact of self-monitoring and awareness training procedures was evaluated in a multiple-baseline design in which the two muscle tics were focused on in sequence. As shown in Figure 13–3, both of the tics declined in frequency when treatment was applied.

F I G U R E   13–3

Percentage of intervals observed of two tics in the clinic sessions in which Steven sat and read for 25-minute periods and in generalization sessions (various places in the college library). Observers recorded the tics in these sessions across baseline and treatment phases.

SOURCE: Wright, K. M., & Miltenberger, R. G. (1987).

A central question is whether the reduction was very important or made a difference to either Steven or others. At the end of treatment, Steven's responses to a questionnaire indicated that he was no longer distressed by the tics and that he felt that they were no longer very noticeable to others. In addition, four observers rated randomly selected pretreatment and posttreatment videotapes. These were videotapes of assessment periods in which direct observations had been made of Steven's tics. The observers rated the tics from the posttreatment tapes as not at all distracting, normal to very normal in appearance, and small to very small in magnitude. In contrast, they rated the tics from the pretreatment tapes as much more severe on these dimensions. The observers were then told which video-tapes were the posttreatment tapes and were asked to report how satisfied they would have been if they had achieved the same results. All of the observers reported that they would have been satisfied with the treatment results. The evaluations from Steven and independent observers help attest to the importance of the changes achieved and provide information that cannot readily be discerned from the reductions graphed from direct obser-vations.

Subjective evaluation has been used to assess whether improvements in writing skills of children are reflected in ratings of creativity or interest value of the compositions; whether individuals who are trained in public speaking skills are evaluated more positively by the audience; and whether people in contact with deviant children see their behaviors differently after treatment (see Kazdin, 1977c). In many cases, the opinions of persons with special expertise is relevant. For example, skills developed in escaping from emergency fire situations in the home were viewed by firefighters as making a difference (Jones, Kazdin, & Haney, 1981). Evaluations indicated that youths would be much less likely to be fatally burned in emergency situations after than before treatment. In most cases, the opinions of persons in everyday life and in contact with the client (parents, teachers, peers) serve as the basis for obtaining measures of subjective evaluations. The opinions of others in contact with the client are important as a criterion in their own right because they often serve as a basis for seeking treatment in the first place and because they reflect the evaluations the client will encounter after leaving treatment.

Social Impact Measures

Another type of measure that helps to evaluate the clinical or applied importance of treatment outcomes is to see whether measures of social impact are altered. These measures refer to outcomes assessed in everyday life as of importance to parents, teachers, and society at large. They often are gross indices of change. For example, measures for programs designed to improve academic functioning, to decrease aggressive behavior, and to prevent coronary illness might include grades in school, arrest records, and mortality rates, respectively.

As an example, a recent treatment study evaluated parent management training with chronically offending adolescent delinquents (less than or 16 years old) (Bank, Marlowe, Reid, Patterson, & Weinrott, 1991). Parents were trained to monitor delinquent behavior better and to use more age-appropriate incentives and punishment (for example, work details, reporting law violations to authorities). Outcome measures included official offense reports, direct observation of home behavior, and parent reporting of problem behaviors. Parent training was compared to another group that received court-provided family treatment that included family therapy, group therapy, and drug counseling. The major results indicated that offense rates for both groups declined significantly after the onset of treatment. The decline was more rapid for the parent training group, as evident in lower offense rates for the adolescents during treatment and at the one-year follow-up assessment. Parent training cases spent significantly fewer days of incarceration during the first two follow-up years, which the authors note represented a significant cost saving favoring parent training. For the five-year period of the project, from initial assessment through the three-year follow-up, rates of nonstatus (more serious) offenses (for example, misdemeanors, felonies) but not status (age-related) offenses (for example, curfew violation, running away) were lower for the parent training condition. The measures of cost and of offense rates through juvenile court records represent important social impact measures.

Social impact measures have often been used in behavioral approaches. For example, in studies that improve safety practices in business and industry, the benefits are often reflected in the number of injuries and accidents (Fox, Hopkins, & Anger, 1987). Similarly, efforts to alter the habits of drivers not only have reduced speeding, the target behavior of interest, but also have been reflected in reductions in accidents (Van Houten, Malenfant, & Rolider, 1985). In these studies, injuries and accidents are measures of obvious social importance.

General Comments

The use of comparative data, subject evaluation, and social impact measures represents an important step toward quantifying the extent to which outcomes produced with treatment really have made a difference in the clients' everyday lives. The measures address somewhat different questions about the importance of change and hence provide different conclusions about the importance of change. Each of the methods raises a number of issues that are far from resolved (see Kazdin, 1992). For example, the use of normative comparisons, perhaps the most commonly used method to evaluate the clinical or applied significance of change, raises many questions. An initial question is, Who should serve as the normative group? With whom, say, should the developmentally disabled, chronic psychiatric patients, or prisoners be compared in evaluating treatment or training programs? Developing a normative level of performance might be an unrealistic ideal in treatment, if that level is based on individuals normally functioning in the community. Also, what variables would define a normative population?

It is unclear how to match subjects included in the normative group along the diverse variables. The normative group might well be defined differently. For example, in one program, social behaviors such as eye contact and verbalizations were developed in three hospitalized psychiatric patients whose social and verbal behaviors were deficient (Stahl, Thomson, Leitenberg, & Hasazi, 1974). Consider the results for one of the patients whose verbal behavior was altered after training. The patient's verbalizations increased to a level very close (within 9 percent) to that of other hospitalized psychiatric patients of similar education who were not considered verbally deficient. Yet the increase in verbalizations was very discrepant (about 30 percent away) from the level of intelligent normally functioning individuals. Thus, the clinical impact of treatment would be viewed differently depending upon the normative standard used for comparison.

Even if a normative group can be identified, exactly what range of members' behaviors would be defined as within the normative level? Among individuals whose behaviors are not identified as problematic, there will be a range of acceptable behaviors. It is relatively simple to identify deviant behavior that departs markedly from the behavior of "normal" peers. But as behavior becomes slightly less deviant, it is difficult to identify the point at which behavior is within the normative range. Is the normative range within some measure of variability of the average (mean) behavior of the normal peers, say, plus or minus one standard deviation? A subjective judgment is required to assess the point at which the individual has entered into the normal range of performance.

Another issue has to do with the criterion for normative functioning. For many behaviors and measures of interest, bringing individuals into the normative range is a questionable goal. Consider, for example, reading skills of elementary school children. A clinically significant change might well be to move children with reading dysfunction so that they fall within the normal range. However, perhaps the normal range itself should not be viewed as an unquestioned goal. The reading of most children might be accelerated from current normative levels. Thus, normative data themselves need to be critically evaluated. As a more general statement, what one's peers do in a given culture or context (for example, use drugs or weapons) is not necessarily a target at which treatment should aim.

There are interpretive issues regarding subjective evaluation as well. The greatest potential concern is the problem of relying upon the opinions of others for determining whether treatment effects were important. Subjective evaluations and the global ratings on which they depend appear to be more readily susceptible to biases on the part of raters than are overt behavioral measures. Thus, one must treat subjective evaluations cautiously; it is possible that subjective evaluations will reflect change when other measures of change do not. In addition, the fact that persons associated with a client assert that they notice a difference in behavior as a function of the client's treatment does not mean that the extent of the client's change is clinically important. Persons in contact with the client may perceive a small change and report this in their ratings. But this says nothing about whether treatment has accomplished enough to alleviate the problem for which treatment was sought or to bring the client within normative levels of behaving.

Measures of social impact raise special problems. The measures often rely on records of various agencies (for example, schools, the courts) that are often collected inconsistently (Kazdin, 1979b). Also, the measures may "miss" a great deal of important behavior. For example, any program designed to reduce delinquent behavior might measure the arrest record of a child or adolescent or the extent to which a child or adolescent has contact with the police or the courts. Yet, the police often do not count all of their contacts with youths, and even if they do, most delinquent acts are not detected by them (Empey, 1982). Consequently, their records cannot be expected to measure change accurately. Nevertheless, social impact data are a useful means of seeing whether the improvements identified on specific behaviors are reflected directly on measures of primary interest to consumers of treatment and society at large. When such measures show a change, they convey important evidence that the impact of an intervention was socially important.

THE ETHICAL AND LEGAL CONTEXT

Several ethical and legal issues must also be taken into account in designing and implementing interventions. Most of the ethical and legal issues associated with treatment apply broadly across disciplines (such as psychology, psychiatry, social work, and counseling) and treatment approaches (for example, family, humanistic, and other approaches). A few such issues have been raised in relation to behavioral techniques. These issues are highlighted here.

Behavior Control and Individual Freedom

The behavioral approach represents explicit attempts to alter specific behaviors in the context of education, treatment, rehabilitation, or everyday life. The focus on behavior and behavior change may raise special concerns about efforts to "control" people. The very term *behavior modification* may imply efforts to control, manipulate, or otherwise tinker with other people's lives. Indeed, the term, rather than the procedures it describes, is what seems to evoke negative reactions (Kazdin & Cole, 1981; Woolfolk, Woolfolk, & Wilson, 1977).

There are no inherent or unique control issues raised by behavioral techniques that are not also raised by other approaches to treatment. Behavioral techniques do not necessarily embrace particular goals or an agenda for changing society. The issue relevant to behavioral interventions is not "control" or the dictating of objectives but the bearing of behavioral interventions on the many goals of individuals, families, and society at large. Obvious examples of such goals are the education of young people, the minimization of crime, and the prevention of disease. The issue is whether behavioral or other forms of intervention can contribute something to facilitate the achievement of these goals. For example, in classroom settings, many of the attempts of teachers to control student behavior are based on corporal and verbal punishment. The issue here is not whether child behavior should be controlled to achieve certain goals. The goals of improved academic performance, appropriate classroom behavior, and increased enjoyment of specific activities such as reading are widely agreed upon. The issue is whether behavioral interventions have anything to offer that will improve attainment of these goals. Techniques discussed in previous chapters, especially those based on positive reinforcement, appear to offer means that can greatly improve upon many of the techniques ordinarily used in everyday life (for example, lectures, pleas, repeated instructions, threats, verbal and physical punishment).

Behavioral principles and techniques do not argue for a particular way of life or particular goals. Indeed, the same principles and techniques have been applied to quite different styles of living. For example, behavioral principles and techniques have been applied to communal living. Small communities (such as Twin Oaks in Virginia and Los Horcones in Sonora, Mexico) have been developed on the basis of operant conditioning principles and specific practices outlined in *Walden Two* (Skinner, 1948). For example, Twin Oaks, begun in 1967, is organized on the basis of a token economy in which credits are earned for performing the work and activities that the community requires in order to function. The lifestyle of the community embraces such values as sharing of assets, individual autonomy, and self-government in a way different from that of mainstream community life (Kinkade, 1973). But behavioral principles and techniques can also be used by individuals as part of self-control techniques for advancing personal rather than communal goals. In general, the goals of professionals concerned with the welfare of individuals is to increase effective living, personal choices, and freedom from behaviors that may restrict functioning in everyday life. The goals of behavior modification do not differ from the goals of other approaches to the welfare of individuals.

Misuse of Reinforcement and Aversive Techniques

Behavior change practices need to be used responsibly and ethically. One can readily conceive of ways of misusing techniques under the guise of laudatory purposes. In fact, outside the realm of behavior modification, there are many examples from everyday life where unacceptable practices (such as physical abuse of children) are designed to achieve reasonable goals (for example, improve child behavior). Behavioral techniques can be misused.

Contingent Consequences and Environmental Restraint
A basic feature of behavior modification programs is the contingent delivery of reinforcing events to alter behavior. The potential for abuse in withholding reinforcers (for example, food, activities) is readily conceivable. There are multiple sources for the protection of clients with whom such abuses might be practiced. Within the "helping" professions (such as psychology, psychiatry, social work, and counseling), various ethical codes are designed to protect the rights of clients. In addition, legal decisions have helped clarify the rights of the clients who are most vulnerable to abusive conditions.

Separate legal decisions have held that involuntarily confined populations, such as psychiatric patients, persons with developmental disabilities, and institutionalized delinquents, have the right to a variety of events and activities. For example, they have the right to receive nutritionally balanced meals, to receive visitors, to sleep in a comfortable bed, to be given a place for their clothes, to engage in regular exercise, and to watch television. As a rule, these basic events and activities cannot be used as reinforcers and made contingent upon behavior. However, this has not interfered with the development of effective programs. Reinforcement programs for involuntarily confined individuals can provide backup events beyond those to which these individuals are entitled by right and which the setting normally provides. In such instances, use is generally made of token economies in which a large number of backup events are provided, including *extra* privileges and activities and access to a store where tokens can purchase diverse items (for example, Paul & Lentz, 1977).

Most applications of behavioral techniques are made in cases where issues of constitutional and legal rights are not raised. For example, adults in their own behalf and in their children's behalf often seek treatment and agree to and help design the program that will be used in treatment, and they reserve the right to change their minds. In such cases, the participants provide their consent to engage in treatment. Other protections of the client, noted later, are aimed at ensuring that the program will not misuse contingent events.

Use of Aversive Techniques

Behavior modification relies much more heavily on positive reinforcement than on negative reinforcement and punishment. Yet, the punishment techniques of behavior modification have come under judicial review. Actually, the courts had been evaluating punishment long before the development of behavior modification because physical restraint, corporal punishment, and inhumane conditions were often used under the guise of treatment or rehabilitation. The courts seek to protect individuals from "cruel and unusual" punishment, as specified by the Eighth Amendment of the U.S. Constitution.

Most of the judicial rulings on punishment do not apply to the procedures used in behavior modification because the more dramatic and intrusive forms of punishment, such as chaining individuals or beating them, have never been part of the behavioral techniques. It is instructive to consider the judicial rulings on punishment procedures that may be a part of behavior modification. Court decisions reached about punishment, of course, depend heavily on the specific procedures that are used. Obviously, the considerations governing a few minutes of isolation (one form of time out) differ from those governing electric shock or very long periods of isolation. Indeed, the courts have ruled that extended periods of isolation are not permissible and that during brief periods of isolation the clients must have adequate access to food, lighting, and sanitation facilities (*Hancock* v. *Avery*, 1969).

Electric shock is rarely used as a punishing event, but the courts have delineated rather clear restrictions governing its use. For example, in one decision (*Wyatt* v. *Stickney*, 1972), shock was restricted to extraordinary circumstances, such as when a client is engaging in self-destructive behavior that is likely to inflict physical damage. Moreover, shock should be applied only when another procedure has been used unsuccessfully, when a committee on human rights within the institution has approved of the treatment, and when the client or a close relative has consented to its use.

The fact that the courts permit the use of mild shock under any circumstances probably reflects their recognition that the procedure can permanently eliminate a behavior (for example, self-injurious acts) after only a few applications.

The courts have not addressed most of the forms of punishment that are currently used in behavior modification, but some court rulings have focused on punishments that bear a resemblance to behavioral techniques. Isolation or seclusion, for example, resembles time out from reinforcement. However, several characteristics of time out make it different from the punishments that the courts consider. In particular, the brevity of time out (one minute to a few minutes), the multiple variations of the time-out procedures (for example, with and without isolation), the procedures used during the "time-in" period (for example, reinforcement of positive behaviors), and the settings in which time out is usually applied (such as the classroom or home) make the time out from reinforcement quite different from the isolation and seclusion considered by the courts. Many other behavioral procedures, such as overcorrection, positive practice, and response cost (all of which are in relatively common use), are not considered by the courts. These procedures are for milder forms of punishment than the types of aversive interventions that have come before the courts.

There has been extensive debate within the profession regarding the use of aversive events (see Repp & Singh, 1990). Many of the discussions have focused on self-injurious (for example, head banging, face slapping) and aggressive behavior (for example, fighting) for obvious reasons. Behaviors that are dangerous warrant immediate attention and require complete elimination if at all possible. Early in the development of behavior modification, electric shock was used (brief, mild, and delivered on few occasions) and was shown to be effective in eliminating self-injurious behavior. This was significant because in a number of instances the behavior was long-standing and had not responded to other treatments. Over the past several years, significant advances have been made in devising alternative procedures to reduce and eliminate dangerous behaviors.

In general in behavior modification, when punishment is used, it is mild (such as brief intervals of time out or small fines from one's earnings of token reinforcement). In fact, relative to punishment commonly used in everyday life (such as spanking, slaps, expulsions from school), the actual events in behavior modification are tame. As important, in behavior modification, punishment is invariably connected to a positive reinforcement program to develop prosocial behaviors. The use of a reinforcement program means that the overall environment is more positive for the client, that punishment occasions can be relatively less frequent (than if no reinforcement program were in place), that mild forms of punishment can be effective, that fewer side effects (for example, client tantrums) are likely to result, and that further punishment (for such tantrums) is less likely. Punishment is used in behavioral programs, and issues regarding its use are considered next.

Least Restrictive Alternative

Guideline for Use of Aversive Procedures

The use of aversive events and varying degrees of restraint they may pose for clients raises a broader issue. The use of aversive procedures has prompted many organizations and legislative bodies to adopt the *least-restrictive-alternative* doctrine of providing treatment.[2] The doctrine states that the least restrictive procedure is to be used to achieve therapeutic change. *Least restrictive* might refer to the least drastic or least aversive procedure.

Table 13–1 illustrates several procedures that vary in degree of restrictiveness and how the treatments might be applied to a child who engages in self-injurious behavior (Singh, Lloyd, & Kendall, 1990). The table lists procedures that move in ascending order from the least (reinforcement) to the most (restraint) restrictive procedure. Understandably, if a less aversive or drastic procedure can be effective, there is no justification for a more drastic procedure. There are two facets of the least-restrictive-alternative guideline. First, treatment ought to begin with a less restrictive (less aversive, drastic) procedure. Second and obviously related, more drastic procedures should be sought if evidence shows that the less restrictive procedure was ineffective.

The least-restrictive-alternative guideline has received greatest attention in the context of using aversive events (for example, time out, physical restraint, shock) and for individuals who may not be able to consent to procedures (such as individuals with developmental disabilities, young children, and severely impaired psychiatric patients) (Repp & Singh, 1990). For example, of considerable concern has been the treatment of individuals with developmental disabilities who engage in dangerous self-injurious behavior. A number of procedures might be used for this behavior. As mentioned previously, one candidate, not in very much use, is electric shock, which can eliminate self-injury in a relatively brief period. The question in relation to the least restrictive guideline is whether a less aversive, nonpainful, and indeed non-punishment-based procedure would be effective. If it would be, it ought to be tried first.

The least-restrictive-alternative guideline has received attention primarily in relation to the use of aversive events, where ethical issues, humane treatment, and abridgment of rights are most salient. The doctrine is part of a larger social context that reflects a general view that freedom and lack of restraint are rights to which individuals are automatically entitled. Exceptions to these rights are made when the freedom of one individual impinges on the rights of others (for example, dangerous criminal behavior that jeopardizes the freedom or safety of others). That individual's freedom is then restricted (for example, by going to prison). For many years, treatment of special populations (for example, psychiatric patients, individuals with developmental disabilities) relied heavily on hospitalization and institutionalization. Hospitalization of many individuals has decreased in part because less restrictive procedures could be used. Persons who can function in the community all or part of the time often do so because these are less restrictive living conditions.[3]

Considerations

The least-restrictive-alternative guideline would seem to be a reasonable way to proceed in relation to the use of aversive events. At the same time, the view has raised considerable controversy. To begin, the view implies that for behaviors that are dangerous or extreme, more restrictive techniques are likely to be more effective. Yet, the view that more restrictive interventions (for example, using electric shock, restraining someone from actually engaging in the behavior) are more effective than less restrictive procedures (for example, ignoring the behavior, giving attention for incompatible behaviors) is not supported by the data (Lennox, Miltenberger, Spengler, & Erfanian, 1988). In fact, some authors have argued and provided data to show that a variety of procedures that do not rely on aversive events can be effective in suppressing dangerous behavior such as self-injury (Donnellan & LaVigna, 1990). Thus, aversive procedures in general may be avoidable in treatment. Although the least-restrictive-alternative guideline seems reasonable, one should be cautioned against the assumption that more restrictive is "better" or even needed at all.

A second consideration with the doctrine has to do with the notion of restrictiveness. Clearly, some treatments are more drastic, extreme, and restrictive than others. Yet, how does one rate the restrictiveness of variations of response cost, time out, and positive practice? Presumably, restrictiveness might be measured by evaluating acceptability of treatment by consumers of treatment and the amount and speed of change that is likely to be produced. In short, the continuum of the restrictiveness of procedures is not entirely clear.

A final consideration rejects the doctrine as not particularly helpful in selecting treatment options (Pyles & Bailey, 1990). There may be *causes* of an individual's dangerous behaviors that can be identified through functional analysis. These causes, once identified, can then be used to identify effective treatment. The concern with the least restrictive alternative is that it suggests a continuum of selecting interventions that has little to do with identifying *effective* treatments. We do not wish to proceed from one procedure to the next based on the level of restrictiveness, particularly because more restrictive treatments are not more effective. The task is to understand the conditions that maintain behavior, to test these, and then to reduce behavior based on that understanding. In most instances in which this has been accomplished, as illustrated previously, aversive procedures that raise concerns about restrictiveness or individual rights are not even used. Functional analysis often reveals that a negative reinforcement contingency is maintaining behavior and can be used to alter the behavior. Restrictiveness is not the issue; understanding the factors that maintain behavior is the issue. Once these factors are understood in a given case, they can be used to treat effectively.

TABLE 13–1
Definitions and Examples of Some Procedures Commonly Used to Influence Maladaptive Behavior

Procedure	Definition	Example
Reinforcement[1]	The delivery of a consequence that increases the chances of the behavior recurring.	After every minute when Amy has kept her hands at her sides, the teacher stands near her, talks pleasantly to her, and gives her a token that she may use to "buy" special treats.
Punishment	The delivery of a consequence that decreases the changes of the behavior recurring. (Often these consequences are called aversives.)	When Amy pokes her finger into her eye socket, the teacher says "No," and holds smelling salts under Amy's nose.
Extinction	The discontinuation of an environmental event that has served as a reinforcer for behavior.[2] Extinction decreases the chances of the behavior recurring.	When Amy pokes her finger into her eye socket, the teacher turns away and stops talking.[3]
Response Cost	The removal of a reinforcer contingent upon the behavior occurring. This decreases the chances of the behavior recurring.	When Amy pokes her finger into her eye socket, the teacher takes away the tokens that Amy has accumulated.

[1] Reinforcement may be either positive or negative. In both cases, reinforcement increases behavior. Negative reinforcement is not the same as punishment.
[2] Technically, extinction also may include the discontinuation of a negative reinforcement contingency. The definition and example given here do not reflect this.
[3] This example assumes that eye-gouging is maintained by social attention. The details of extinction procedures vary, depending upon what feature of the environment maintains the behavior.

Alternative Guidelines

The least restrictive doctrine raises an important issue about one characteristic of treatment but itself does not guide treatment selection to help individual clients. This has led to alternative procedures to guide treatment (see Green, 1990). For example, one alternative has been the Behavioral Diagnostics model (Pyles & Bailey, 1990), which specifies a general strategy for identifying effective treatments. Table 13–2 presents the five steps for identifying effective treatments and a brief description of what they entail. They initial step consists of identifying the problem (direct observation) and proposing hypotheses about maintaining conditions. The second step consists of developing a treatment plan. Some of the plans may require manipulation of antecedent conditions rather than implemen-

T A B L E   13–1   *(continued)*

Procedure	Definition	Example
Time Out	The imposition of a brief time period when reinforcement is not available.	When Amy pokes her finger into her eye socket, the teacher stops awarding her tokens for three minutes.
Overcorrection	The institution of a more appropriate response and repeated practice of it contingent upon the behavior occurring. This decreases the chances of the behavior recurring.	When Amy pokes her finger into her eye socket, the teacher pulls Amy's hand away from her face, tells her to keep her hands down, and requires her to practice flexing and relaxing her hands repeatedly.
Visual or Facial Screening	The blocking of an individual's field of vision contingent upon the performance of a behavior. This decreases the chances of the behavior recurring.	When Amy pokes her finger into her eye socket, the teacher removes the poking finger and covers Amy's eyes with her hand (visual screening) or a terry-cloth bib (facial screening) for five seconds.
Restraint	The physical restriction of parts of the body involved in a behavior in order to make performance of the behavior impossible.	When Amy has been poking her finger into her eye frequently, the staff may decide to restrain her by wrapping a soft cloth around her wrists and running it behind her back. This "soft-tie" makes it impossible for Amy to raise her hands as high as her face.

SOURCE: Singh, N. N., Lloyd, J. W., & Kendall, K. A. (1990).

tation of any consequences (aversive or otherwise) to change behavior, as illustrated in other examples of functional analysis studies. The third step tests the plan about what is maintaining behavior and then makes environmental changes as needed to implement the plan. The fourth step evaluates the results. The fifth step then puts the program into place where needed (for example, in the home or institution) with continued observation and staff training.

Three key issues are raised by this model. One is the central role of functional analysis. The second is the importance of ongoing assessment of program effects. Both functional analysis and assessment have already been discussed. The third component has to do with staff (parent, teacher,

T A B L E   13–2
Behavioral Diagnostic Model of Developing Effective Treatment

Step 1: Diagnose the Problem
Directly observe the behavior and assess possible causes (stimulus conditions, antecedents, and consequences) that might be maintaining the behavior.

Step 2: Develop a Plan Based on the Diagnosis
Consider alternative interventions. Some of these may require merely altering the antecedent conditions, i.e., how instructions, requests, or task demands are made to the individual. Others may require the more usual programs In which consequences (e.g., reinforcement, punishment) are applied.

Step 3: Test the Plan Under Controlled Conditions
Arrange to run special (perhaps very brief) sessions in which changes in the plan are tested. Two or more different conditions or procedures might be tried for brief period that are varied in laboratory (off the ward, out of the classroom) sessions.

Step 4: Evaluate the Results
Measure the target behavior over the course of different conditions. Any related behaviors that might be of interest (e.g., side effects, prosocial behavior) might be assessed as well. From this evaluation, the more or most effective intervention can be identified or the steps can be initiated again (beginning with Step 1).

Step 5: Put the Program into Place
Train staff or persons who are to conduct the program in how to implement the procedures. Ensure that they can and do carry out the requisite behaviors to implement the program. Implement the contingency or program into the settings where needed. Continue to assess and monitor.

SOURCE: Adapted from Pyles, D. A. M., & Bailey, J. S. (1990).

institutional staff) training. The most effective and least restrictive procedure is not relevant if it is not implemented correctly. Consequently, procedures to ensure that those who administer the program implement it properly are critical.

General Comments

The general view embraced by the least-restrictive-alternative doctrine has obvious merit. We would not want to select an extreme procedure if a mild procedure would accomplish the same end. The critical feature of the guideline may be different from its primary emphasis. The primary emphasis is on procedures and how drastic, extreme, or restrictive they are. Yet, implicit in the doctrine is the importance of monitoring and evaluating the intervention and its effects. A more restrictive intervention is justified only if another alternative has not achieved change.

The notions of monitoring and evaluating the intervention in relation to change are critically important. In society at large, the impact of many, if not the vast majority, of the interventions used or promoted (such as many forms of individual psychotherapy, many educational practices and curricula) are not monitored or evaluated. Whether or not they are restrictive, the absence of assessment and evaluation raises ethical issues in its own right (see Kazdin, 1993a). The concern of the least-restrictive-alternative view is with client rights, including rights to effective intervention. Intervention without evaluation raises serious ethical issues. An intervention that places any restriction on a client, including seemingly innocuous interventions, might be unjustified if they are not shown to have some positive effect on behavior. Also, interventions may have untoward side effects so that absence of evaluation may increase risk for harming the individual in some way. The least-restrictive-alternative doctrine sensitizes us to procedures as well as to their impact and hence extends in relevance beyond the use of aversive events.

Ethical Guidelines and Protection of Client Rights

The ethical issues that can emerge in providing professional services and in conducting research extend well beyond the use of aversive techniques. Delivery of services requires weighing alternatives that balance the individual rights of the clients and potential for untoward consequences, harm, and effects of withholding treatments that may be of benefit. A number of safeguards have emerged to guide the behavior of professionals and to protect the clients whom they serve. These safeguards include international codes and national guidelines to cover treatment and intervention research (see Kazdin, 1978). In addition, organizations and professions involved in delivery of services have provided guidelines designed to protect clients and to establish standards of professional conduct. The full range of regulations, codes, and guidelines that govern professional behavior and interactions with the public is too extensive to review here. However, a few are illustrated.

At the most general level, professional organizations provide guidelines to cover a variety of responsibilities of the profession. For example, the American Psychological Association (APA) has provided a set of principles and guidelines that delineate professional responsibilities in relation to a variety of activities and situations, including assessment, therapy, research, contacts with the media, and others. Central principles cover obligations in relation to standards of professional competence, integrity, professional and scientific responsibility, respect for the rights and dignity of others, concern for others' welfare, and social responsibilities. Principles from the most recent revision of the codes (APA, 1992) appear in Table 13–3 to convey the type of statements that are provided. These broad guidelines are designed to identify considerations, obligations, priorities, and potential conflicts of interest in relation to the people with whom professionals interact. More specific ethical standards are also provided to address many situations in which psychologists are placed, such as inter-

TABLE 13–3
Principles of Psychologists

Principle A: Competence
Psychologists strive to maintain high standards of competence in their work. They recognize the boundaries of their particular competencies and the limitations of their expertise. They provide only those services and use only those techniques for which they are qualified by education, training, or experience.

Principle B: Integrity
Psychologists seek to promote integrity in the science, teaching, and practice of psychology. In these activities psychologists are honest, fair, and respectful of others. In describing or reporting their qualifications, services, products, fees, research, or teaching, they do not make statements that are false, misleading, or deceptive.

Principle C: Professional and Scientific Responsibility
Psychologists uphold professional standards of conduct, clarify their professional roles and obligations, accept appropriate responsibility for their behavior, and adapt their methods to the needs of different populations. Psychologists consult with, refer to, or cooperate with other professionals and institutions to the extent needed to serve the best interests of their patients, clients, or other recipients of their services.

Principle D: Respect for People's Rights and Dignity
Psychologists accord appropriate respect to the fundamental rights, dignity, and worth of all people. They respect the rights of individuals to privacy, confidentiality, self-determination, and autonomy, mindful that legal and other obligations may lead to inconsistency and conflict with the exercise of these rights.

Principle E: Concern for Others' Welfare
Psychologists seek to contribute to the welfare of those with whom they interact professionally. In their professional actions, psychologists weigh the welfare and rights of their patients or clients, students, supervisees, human research participants, and other affected persons, and the welfare of animal subjects of research.

Principle F: Social Responsibility
Psychologists are aware of their professional and scientific responsibilities to the community and the society in which they work and live. They apply and make public their knowledge of psychology in order to contribute to human welfare. Psychologists are concerned about and work to mitigate the causes of human suffering.

SOURCE: Adapted from American Psychological Association (1992).

preting psychological tests, providing psychotherapy, or testifying before the courts. Apart from professional guidelines, universities and many other institutions where research is conducted rely upon review committees to evaluate the extent to which research projects provide safeguards for subjects.

Professional ethical codes and review-committee evaluation serve as a point of departure for intervention research. That is, they are the basic standards for meeting professional responsibilities and providing care. Additional codes have been provided to further guide the use of interventions in clinical and applied settings. These do not replace professional codes but, rather, add other issues. One set of guidelines that directs attention specifically to intervention issues has been provided by the Association for Advancement of Behavior Therapy (AABT), and poses a number of questions that therapists (or persons who design and implement a program) should adequately address prior to implementing therapy. The questions, which appear in Table 13–4, are intended to ensure that the procedures are appropriate and that the client (or guardian) is fully aware of the intervention. These guidelines are not directed specifically toward behavior modification procedures because behavior change procedures in general, whether behavioral or not, raise similar ethical issues. The questions are intended to guide those who implement any form of psychological treatment.

T A B L E   13–4
Ethical Issues for Human Services: Selected Questions to Guide
Professional Practice

The questions related to each issue have deliberately been cast in a general manner that applies to all types of interventions, and not solely or specifically to the practice of behavior therapy. Issues directed specifically to behavior therapists might imply erroneously that behavior therapy was in some way more in need of ethical concern than non-behaviorally oriented therapies.

In the list of issues the term *client* is used to describe the person whose behavior is to be changed, and *therapist* is used to describe the professional in charge of the intervention; *treatment* and *problem,* although used in the singular, refer to any and all treatments and problems being formulated with this checklist. The issues are formulated so as to be relevant across as many settings and populations as possible. Thus, they need to be qualified when someone other than the person whose behavior is to be changed is paying the therapist, or when that person's competence or the voluntary nature of that person's consent is questioned. For example, if the therapist has found that the client does not understand the goals or methods being considered, the therapist should substitute the client's guardian or other responsible person for "client," when reviewing the issues below.

- A. Have the goals of treatment been adequately considered?
- B. Has the choice of treatment methods been adequately considered?
- C. Is the client's participation voluntary?
- D. When another person or an agency is empowered to arrange for therapy, have the interests of the client been sufficiently considered?
- E. Has the adequacy of treatment been evaluated?
- F. Has the confidentiality of the treatment relationship been protected?
- G. Does the therapist refer the clients to other therapists when necessary?
- H. Is the therapist qualified to provide treatment?

SOURCE: Association for Advancement of Behavior Therapy (1977).

T A B L E   13–5
Some Values Guiding Community Research and Actions

Values of community research and action	Research perspective	Community perspective
1. Researchers should form collaborative relationships with participants.	Research should be grounded in the local context.	Communities should exert some control over research that affects them.
2. Descriptive research should provide information about the variety of behavior-environmental relationships of importance to communities.	Research should contribute knowledge about naturally occurring events.	Research should contribute to understanding about strengths (as well as deficits) and the variety of ways that individual and community goals can be met.
3. Experimental research should provide information about the effects of environmental events on behaviors and outcomes of importance.	The effects of research interventions should be replicable, durable, and generalizable to other people and situations.	Research should help identify goals, procedures, and effects that are important and acceptable to clients.
4. The chosen setting, participants, and research measures should be appropriate to the community problem under investigation.	Applied research should use valid measures to examine real-world problems in the natural context of people actually experiencing the concerns.	Research should target all those who contribute to the problem and should leave improved valued aspects of the community.
5. The measurement system must be replicable, and measures should capture the dynamic or transactional nature of behavior-environmental relationships.	Measurement systems should be replicable by typically trained researchers.	Research findings should tell the complete story, including the role that participants play in changing their environments.

The guidelines listed to this point emphasize very broad professional responsibilities (APA, 1992) and treatment in the context of therapist-client settings (AABT, 1977). Applied settings (such as the community at large, schools, homes) in which behavioral interventions are implemented raise special considerations. A set of guidelines proposed by Fawcett (1991) conveys considerations that are raised by interventions in applied settings. The guidelines are provided as values to guide research in applied settings

TABLE 13–5 *(continued)*

Values of community research and action	Research perspective	Community perspective
6. Community interventions should be replicable and sustainable with local resources.	Interventions should be replicable by those available to implement them.	Community interventions should be sustainable with local resources and should build on local capacities for addressing community concerns.
7. Community action should occur at the level of change and timing likely to optimize beneficial outcomes.	Interventions should produce the maximum desired impact.	Interventions should be targeted to optimize benefits for the community and its members.
8. Researchers should develop a capacity to disseminate effective interventions and provide support for change agents.	Interventions should be disseminated cautiously so that their continued effectiveness is assured.	Interventions should be adapted to local conditions and their use should enhance local capacities for change.
9. Results should be communicated to clients, decision makers, and the broader public.	Research findings should be submitted for peer review and, if judged acceptable, disseminated to the broader scientific community.	Research findings should be communicated to participants and decision makers in understandable and maximally influential ways and these audiences should help assess what was valuable about the research.
10. Community research and action projects should contribute to fundamental change as well as understanding.	Community research should contribute to understanding of environmental events that affect behavior.	Community research should contribute to prevention of problems in living, capacity building, and empowerment of people of marginal status.

SOURCE: Fawcett, S. B. (1991).

and are presented in Table 13–5. The three columns of the table convey what the applied research ought to do, the perspective of the researcher or investigator who is conducting the research, and the community or consumer perspective. The different perspectives of the researcher and consumer (for example, school district, community, clients) are important to identify to make explicit the interests, goals, and potential responsibilities of the different parties involved in applied settings. The guidelines emphasize many issues discussed earlier in the chapter, such as seeking intervention effects that maximize behavior change (for example, clinically significant effects) and generalization.

Diverse guidelines have been illustrated. They are different in their focus and in the domains and issues to which they alert professionals in the context of treatment and intervention. At a higher level of abstraction, they specify broader values such as open communication between the professional (for example, the researcher or therapist) and the person who is served, adherence to ethical standards and the public interest, and integration of scientific tenets (measurement, replication of research findings) with socially important ends.

Although the above guidelines all include efforts to protect client rights, the topic warrants special comment. In most interventions in research and applied settings, clients or individuals acting in their behalf (such as parents) must provide informed consent. *Informed consent* refers to agreement to the intervention and to the conditions under which the intervention is provided. For consent to be informed, the individual must be competent to make rational decisions, must understand the intervention and the available options, and must act without duress. The issues of consent have been raised most frequently with involuntarily confined persons (for example, hospitalized psychiatric patients). The purpose of informed consent is to ensure understanding of and agreement with the procedures. Individuals in treatment can revoke their consent at any time.

In addition to requiring consent, institutions that provide treatment or rehabilitation services have institutional review boards that consider the procedures being proposed for treatment. These boards may include experts in the area of treatment as well as lawyers and laypersons who provide different perspectives regarding controversial applications of treatment. Many, if not most, of the procedures applied are considered standard and need not undergo special review. Special procedures (for example, aversive consequences) or applications involving special populations that cannot act on their own behalf are reviewed routinely to ensure that individual rights are protected.

Another means of protecting individual rights is the use of a contractual arrangement between the therapist and the client. A behavioral contract is used whenever possible to involve all of the parties that are included in the program. The contract can make explicit the goals of treatment, the procedures that will be used, and the likely risks and benefits. A useful feature of a contract is that it enables the client and his or her guardians to negotiate the final goals of treatment. Active client participation in the design of treatment is likely to make treatment fairer than it would be if treatment were unilaterally imposed on the client. Including the client in the development of the contract may have manifold benefits, such as making the treatment more acceptable and fostering communication (negotiation) between the parties involved (for example, parent and child, spouses) (cf. Barbrack & Maher, 1984; Kazdin, 1980a).

CURRENT ISSUES AND FUTURE DIRECTIONS

Extensions of behavioral techniques to a wide array of populations, efforts to implement behavioral programs on a relatively large scale, and evidence for the long-term effects of treatment suggest that behavioral techniques may be effective in addressing multiple personal and social problems. The evidence attesting to the effectiveness of behavioral techniques in many areas of treatment, rehabilitation, and education is truly impressive. Yet, the accomplishments of these techniques need to be viewed in perspective.

Limitations of the Approach

Behavioral techniques do not always achieve the desired outcomes, even in reasonably well circumscribed situations (such as the home or classroom) in which many contingencies can be carefully implemented and closely monitored. Behavioral techniques bring to bear important influences, such as various positive reinforcers. When these events are administered in special ways (for example, immediately after behavior, on a continuous or rich reinforcement schedule, and contingent upon behavior), behavior changes are often dramatic. Still, limitations should be expected in the effects that are produced. Antecedent events (for example, prompts) or consequences (for example, reinforcers) do not exhaust the range of the factors that influence normal and maladaptive behavior. The expansion of behavioral techniques to include cognitive events (self-statements, imagery) enhances the potential of treatment by increasing the range of the influences that can be brought to bear to produce therapeutic change. But even the addition of cognitive and environmental influences does not exhaust the range of the factors that control behavior. Biological predispositions (for example, temperament), genetic endowment, and environmental factors that usually cannot be controlled in treatment (for example, family living conditions, maladjustment of parents) may delimit the types of effects that any treatment can achieve. Thus, no single set of interventions can be expected to solve invariably the clinical and other problems to which it is applied.

As an example of the range of influences, consider the problems of antisocial behavior in children. Serious antisocial behaviors in children (aggression, stealing, tantrums, destructiveness, lying and related behaviors) is influenced by harsh child-rearing practices, serious psychological dysfunction (depression, antisocial behavior, alcoholism) in the parent(s), child temperament, genetic endowment, and many other factors (see Kazdin, 1987a). These and other influences do not invariably determine that a child will become antisocial, but they increase the risk that serious antisocial behavior will develop. Training parents in behavioral techniques (parent management training) has been one of the most effective interventions for treating antisocial children (Kazdin, 1993b). Yet, it would be quite understandable if changing parent-child interaction and altering the contingencies of reinforcement in the home did not totally eliminate the problems of such children. Antisocial behavior seems to be influenced by many factors other than the reinforcement contingencies in the home. Indeed, parent management training has been very effective in some applications but has produced mixed effects in others. Although further improvements in treatment are likely to be made, the complexity of the problem of child antisocial behavior and the number of factors that influence such behavior will probably continue to present obstacles to any treatment approach.

In general, the effects of behavioral techniques have been quite effective in altering a number of behaviors in the context of clinical treatment and of extensions to society. The influences of these techniques on behavior extend beyond the current contingencies of reinforcement. This does not mean that altering the contingencies will be ineffective. However, it does mean that limitations in the effects of any approach to intervention may be expected.

Program Failures

In many applications, behavioral programs initially fail to achieve the desired changes in behavior. The conclusion reached may be that behavior modification "does not work" or that the procedures "do not really apply" to the client. As a general and quite tentative rule, the less experience one has with behavioral techniques, the more likely one is to conclude that a program does not work. This may well reflect a bias against admitting failure among proponents of behavior modification. Yet, in several instances in which the issue of program failure arises, two alternative explanations are plausible.

The first reason that programs fail has to do with a misunderstanding of the current factors maintaining behavior. This explanation has been greatly supported in recent years with the more frequent use of functional analyses of behavior. As mentioned previously, functional analysis isolates specific factors that are controlling behavior by assessing behavior directly under different conditions. Patterns frequently emerge that indicate very clearly that behavior is influenced by one particular condition or set of conditions more than another.

For example, a functional analysis might be completed to examine factors that contribute to a child's tantrum in the home. The analysis may reveal that the tantrums are primarily on the weekends and come after parents ask the child to do chores or homework. After a request or comment about the task from the parents, the child becomes "moody," retreats to his or her room, and begins a tantrum. During the tantrum, the parents may attend to the child, nag a bit, threaten some punishment, and make further demands. A behavioral program based on the functional analysis might suggest that the antecedent conditions, rather than the attention and other consequences, play a central role. A program designed to address antecedents might include devising a contingency contract with the child each Friday (before the weekend), deciding how much time or work will be done, when during the weekend the work will be completed, what positive consequences will be provided, and so on. In this case, tantrums were largely precipitated by antecedents. A number of other factors might well be involved and different approaches or models of human behavior (for example, family therapy) might focus on such factors. However, the functional analysis identifies specific influences, obtains data to show their impact, and then alters these factors to obtain change. No other model or approach to treatment really tries to accomplish this and to evaluate the effects empirically. In any case, identifying the precipitating influence and altering it in the home are likely to have potent and immediate effects on behavior.

Consider an alternative approach to the tantrum. This alternative approach is one that still is the most common use of behavior modification. The general recommendation to alter the tantrum is to suggest that the tantrum is probably maintained by social reinforcement. The parents ought to ignore tantrums (extinction) and perhaps provide reinforcement for non-tantrum behavior (differential reinforcement of other behavior). A program might be developed in which demands of and requests to the child are not altered but incentives are provided for not having a tantrum. This program is designed without a functional analysis. It is important to underscore that this program in general is likely to work if the contingency is implemented consistently. Yet, without the benefit of a functional analysis, the precise factors that are controlling behavior are not identified. Understandably, the program may not work.

In recent years, functional analyses have been used increasingly. In the case of self-injurious behavior, where the analyses have been particularly well studied, it has become clear that factors maintaining behavior (such as negative rather than positive reinforcement) might have been missed or underestimated without the analyses. Altering the contingency quickly reduces self-injury.

Over the years, there have been many instances in which behavioral programs failed to achieved the desired changes. One could conclude that behavioral techniques did not work and leave it at that. Interestingly, several studies have shown that slight modifications in the program when clients have failed to respond (using some of the techniques discussed in Chapter 8) often produce the desired behaviors (Kazdin, 1983). Thus, an initial judgment that treatment has failed may be controverted by additional applications of treatment and additional evaluations of progress. For example, defiant and aggressive child behavior in the home or at school is often unaffected by simply having parents praise appropriate child behavior (Wahler & Fox, 1980; Walker, Hops, & Greenwood, 1981). The undesired behaviors may not decrease until mild punishment (response cost, time out) is added to the contingencies. These demonstrations, consistent with functional analyses, suggest that critical influences were not identified in the initial program. When confronted with a program failure, one could always *say* the critical variables were misidentified. What distinguishes the behavioral approach is a methodology that identifies the variables (functional analysis) and directly tests their effects. In many instances, documented here and in prior chapters, changes that do occur after program revision show that the misidentification notion is not just an excuse for an ineffective approach.

At the outset, we noted that program failures could occur for two primary reasons. The second one is that the behavioral contingencies are not implemented correctly. Part of the difficulty with behavioral procedures is that they are familiar to people in principle, and this provides the illusion that they have been implemented all of the time. For example, parents who are learning behavioral techniques for managing their children invariably note that these techniques are not new and that they have been using the techniques all along. They often assert that their use of reinforcement (praise or allowance) or time out (sending the child to his or her room) has not worked. Parents are usually correct in this assertion. Yet, careful inquiry or direct observation of their behavior in the home reveals that the procedures they have tried are not even close approximations of the ways in which reinforcing and punishing consequences are applied in behavioral programs. For example, parents often say that they have used reinforcement to alter behavior but that it has not helped. However, positive reinforcers need to be administered immediately after behavior, on a continuous or close to continuous schedule, and contingent upon performance. As important, the target behaviors need to be carefully specified, so that reinforcement can be applied consistently and the results measured to see whether the program is having impact. Once these and related conditions (for example, use of prompts, shaping) are faithfully observed, one may be in a better position to say that the procedures have not worked.

The principles of reinforcement, punishment, and extinction and the techniques derived from those principles are relatively simple. However, considerable skill is required to implement the techniques so as to attain the desired outcomes. The techniques need to be implemented systematically and consistently and with knowledge of the factors that influence their effects. Many successful programs have devoted considerable attention to ensuring that behavior change agents (parents, teachers, hospital staff) are well trained. Once these change agents have been trained, their behaviors are often monitored carefully to ensure that the contingencies are carried out correctly (for example, Bushell, 1978; Patterson, 1982; Paul & Lentz, 1977). Without careful training and monitoring, behavior change programs are likely to deteriorate over time (for example, Harchik, Sherman, Sheldon, & Strouse, 1992). It is likely that assessment and monitoring of staff or others who implement the behavior change procedures need to become a permanent part of the setting (for example, school, hospital). There are examples where training staff and monitoring staff and students are part of the ongoing program. As mentioned in the previous chapter, the CABAS (Comprehensive Application of Behavior Analysis to Schooling) program (Selinske, Greer, & Lodhi, 1991) includes assessment and monitoring of teacher and student behavior to ensure that the techniques are implemented correctly and that children are learning. The assessment and supervision practices are central to the effectiveness of the procedures, and hence their incorporation as part of the program is critically important.

In short, quality of program implementation is obviously important. In fact, what distinguishes behavior modification techniques from everyday uses of reward and punishment is *how* the techniques are applied and evaluated. The successful applications illustrated throughout this book depend on very careful implementation and evaluation of behavioral techniques.

Extensions of Behavioral Techniques

Extrapolation from present work in behavior modification suggests that the focus of treatments will continue to expand. Over the brief history of behavior modification as a formal movement, the trend toward an expanding focus can be readily identified. In early applications beginning over 30 years ago, behavioral techniques were directed primarily to special populations such as psychiatric patients, the developmentally disabled, autistic children, and delinquents. Applications with these populations have continued by extending the range of the techniques and target behaviors studied and by extending the duration of treatment effects. In the past decade, additional populations and settings have been investigated. Prominent examples include the applications of behavioral techniques to medical problems, geriatric populations, and business and industry.

Current work points toward continued expansion of applications in several directions. First, behavioral techniques are being increasingly applied to behavior in everyday life. At one level, such techniques are being used to deal with social and community problems (for example, crime, energy conservation) whose solution can affect the quality of life for society as a whole. At another level, they are increasingly available to help people improve the quality of their personal lives.

Second, large-scale applications are likely to continue in the foreseeable future. Applications to deal with social problems at the level of community, city, state, and country may raise concerns about attempts to control behavior and dictate goals to others. Efforts to regulate many behaviors are already being made. Behavioral techniques may be valuable in increasing the effectiveness of efforts to encourage behaviors that have been identified as desirable (for example, encouraging parents to obtain vaccinations for their children, encouraging children to eat well-balanced meals, and encouraging people not to drive when intoxicated).

Finally, for several years, further attention is likely to be devoted to the dissemination of current findings on behavioral techniques and their application. Identification of effective interventions is an obviously important step, but by itself is not enough. A major task is to disseminate what has been learned, so that treatments can be more widely applied. There have been efforts to disseminate techniques that have been shown to be effective. For example, books and manuals have been prepared for parents and teachers to help them learn behavioral techniques and apply them at home and in school (for example, Azrin & Foxx, 1974; Blechman, 1985; Clark, 1985; Forehand & McMahon, 1981). Also, behavioral programs for the treatment of psychiatric patients and delinquent youths have been disseminated to facilities other than those in which they were originally developed (see Bacher, Liberman, & Kuehnel, 1986). The obstacles to disseminating behavioral procedures are quite formidable. Among the obstacles are the difficulty of integrating new procedures within institutional structures that are hard to penetrate and the difficulty of ensuring that the procedures, if adopted, are implemented correctly.

Efforts to disseminate current findings do not mean that all of the questions regarding behavioral techniques have been answered or that the most effective approaches are known. Yet there are large numbers of people with behavioral problems for which effective treatments have already been identified and many everyday behaviors whose alteration could have a significant impact on education, interpersonal relations, health, and other areas. A source of frustration is the failure to disseminate current techniques widely. However, only recently has there been an accumulation of scientific knowledge about effective practices that warrant widespread dissemination.

Notes

1. Standard deviation reflects a measure of variation or spread of scores. The measure is used to provide a standard way of referring to how far away (in standard deviation units) a person's score is from the mean (average) of the group. A departure of two standard deviation units is arbitrary but reflects a rather large departure. For example, a person whose IQ score is two standard

deviations above the mean would have an IQ higher than approximately 98% of other people. For the present discussion, the critical point is not the standard deviation units but rather the comparison of the scores of different groups.

2. Several of the guidelines devised by professional organizations that include the least-restrictive-alternative doctrine and guidelines for use of aversive events are presented elsewhere (see Singh, Lloyd, & Kendall, 1990).

3. The issue is more complex than less restrictive alternatives. Cost of treatment and the use of medication on an outpatient basis to control symptoms of many patients have been important considerations in deinstitutionalization. Living in the community usually costs less per patient than does hospital care. These comments are provided only to convey a broader social context for the guideline.

For Further Reading

American Psychological Association. (1992). Ethical principles of psychologists and code of conduct. *American Psychologist, 47,* 1597–1611.

Fawcett, S. B. (1991). Some values guiding community research and action. *Journal of Applied Behavior Analysis, 24,* 621–636.

Geller, E. S. (Ed.). (1990). Special section: Social validity: Multiple perspectives. *Journal of Applied Behavior Analysis, 24,* 179–249.

Hopkins, B. L. (1987). Comments on the future of applied behavior analysis. *Journal of Applied Behavior Analysis, 20,* 339–346.

Kunkel, J. H. (1987). The future of JABA: A comment. *Journal of Applied Behavior Analysis, 20,* 329–334.

Repp, A. E., & Singh, N. N. (Eds.). (1990). *Perspectives on the use of nonaversive and aversive interventions for persons with developmental disabilities.* Sycamore, IL: Sycamore.

Glossary

A

ABAB design See **reversal design.**

alternate response training A technique used in therapy (such as desensitization) and as a self-control strategy in which the individual is trained to engage in a response (for example, relaxation) that interferes with or replaces another response that is to be controlled or eliminated.

alternating treatment design An experimental design in which two or more interventions are implemented concurrently in the same treatment phase. The interventions are balanced (varied) across different conditions such as the time period of the day in which treatment is implemented. The design is useful for comparing the relative effectiveness of two or more interventions.

aversive event A stimulus that suppresses a behavior that it follows or increases a behavior that results in its termination.

avoidance Performance of a behavior that postpones or averts the presentation of an aversive event.

B

back-up reinforcer An object, activity, or event (primary or secondary reinforcer) that can be purchased with tokens. A reinforcer that "backs up" the value of tokens.

baseline The frequency with which behavior is performed prior to initiating a behavior modification program. The performance rate used to evaluate the effect of a behavior modification program. Operant rate of behavior. The initial phase of reversal, multiple-baseline, changing-criterion, and simultaneous-treatment designs.

behavior Any observable or measurable response or act. (The terms *behavior* and *response* are used synonymously.) Behavior is occasionally broadly defined to include cognitions, psychophysiological reactions, and feelings, which may not be directly observable but are defined in terms that can be measured by means of various assessment strategies.

behavioral control Exerting power or influence over others by altering the environmental contingencies to achieve a definite end.

behavioral medicine The application of behavioral procedures to problems of physical health and illness. Applications of this kind focus on problems related to the prevention, diagnosis, and treatment of physical disorders or on behaviors with consequences related to health and illness.

behavioral trap   Refers to the notion that once a client's behavior has been developed, it may become entrenched in and maintained (that is, trapped) by the social system of available reinforcers in the client's everyday environment. That is, behaviors initially developed through special contingency arrangements may be maintained by ordinary, naturally occurring contingencies after the program has been withdrawn.

bibliotherapy   A form of self-help treatment that is conveyed to clients through written materials such as manuals and books. This form of treatment involves little or no therapist assistance.

biofeedback   Procedures that provide information to the client about his or her ongoing physiological processes. The information enables the client to monitor moment-to-moment changes in these processes.

C

chain   A sequence of behaviors that occurs in a fixed order. Each behavior in the sequence serves as a discriminative stimulus (S^D) for the next response. Each behavior in the sequence (except the first behavior) also serves as a conditioned reinforcer that reinforces the previous response.

chaining   Developing a sequence of responses in reverse order, so that the last response in the sequence is developed first, the next to the last response is trained second, and the remaining responses are trained in the reverse order of their performance once the sequence is finally performed. Developing a complex behavior by training individual components of the behavior in a reverse order.

changing-criterion design   An experimental design in which the effect of the program is evaluated by repeatedly altering the criterion for reinforcement or punishment. If the target behavior matches the criterion as the criterion is repeatedly altered, this suggests that the contingency is responsible for the behavior change.

classical (or respondent) conditioning   A type of learning in which a neutral (conditioned) stimulus is paired with an unconditioned stimulus that elicits a reflex response. After the conditioned stimulus is repeatedly followed by the unconditioned stimulus, the association between the two stimuli is learned. The conditioned stimulus alone will then elicit a reflex response. In classical conditioning, new stimuli gain the power to elicit respondent behavior.

client   The person for whom the behavior modification program has been designed and implemented. Used in the present text as a generic term to include the patient, student, subject, child, or other person for whom the intervention has been planned.

cognitively based treatment   An approach that considers cognitive processes, such as thoughts, beliefs, and perceptions, to play a major role in the conceptualization and treatment of clinical problems.

cognitive processes Internal events such as thoughts, beliefs, self-statements, perceptions, and images.

conditioned aversive stimulus An initially neutral event that acquires aversive properties by virtue of being paired with other aversive events or with a signal that no reinforcement will be forthcoming.

conditioned reinforcer See **secondary reinforcer.**

conditioned response A reflex response elicited by a conditioned stimulus in the absence of the unconditioned stimulus. This response resembles, but is not identical to, the unconditioned response. See **classical conditioning.**

conditioned stimulus A previously neutral stimulus that, through repeated associations with an unconditioned stimulus, elicits a reflex response. See **classical conditioning.**

consequence sharing A contingency arrangement in which the consequences earned by one person are provided to both that person and his or her peers.

contingency The relationship between a behavior (the response to be changed) and the events (consequences) that follow the behavior. Sometimes events that precede the behavior (antecedents) are also specified by a contingency.

contingency contract A behavior modification program in which an agreement or contract is made between a person who wishes behavior to change (for example, a parent) and the person whose behavior is to be changed (for example, a child). The contract specifies the relationship between behavior and its consequences.

contingent delivery of a reinforcer The delivery of a reinforcer only when a specified behavior has been performed. Contrast with **noncontingent delivery of a reinforcer.**

contingent upon behavior An event (for example, praise, tokens, time out) is contingent upon behavior when the event is delivered only if that behavior is performed.

continuous reinforcement A schedule of reinforcement in which a response is reinforced each time it is performed.

control group design An experimental design in which the effect of the program is evaluated by comparing (at least) two groups, a group that receives the program and a group that does not.

coverant A private event such as a thought, a fantasy, or an image that is not "observable" to anyone other than the individual who is experiencing it. Private events can be viewed as responses that can be altered by varying the consequences that follow them. The term *coverant* is a contraction of the terms *covert* and *operant.*

covert conditioning Imagery-based procedures that require a client to imagine target behaviors and consequences. They are referred to as conditioning because they draw on learning, including classical conditioning, operant conditioning, and observational learning. The techniques assume that there is an interaction between overt and covert (imagined) behaviors and that changes in one are likely to influence the other.

covert event   A private event such as a thought, a fantasy, or an image. See **coverant.**

covert sensitization   An imagery-based treatment in which clients imagine themselves engaging in an undesired behavior (such as overeating) and then imagine an aversive event or state (such as vomiting). The treatment is designed to decrease the undesired behavior.

cue   See **discriminative stimulus (S^D).**

D

delay of reinforcement   The time interval between a response and delivery of the reinforcer.

deprivation   Reducing the availability of, or access to, a reinforcer.

differential reinforcement   Reinforcing a response in the presence of one stimulus (S^D) and extinguishing the response in the presence of other stimuli (S^Δ). Eventually, the response is consistently performed in the presence of the S^D but not in the presence of the S^Δ.

differential reinforcement of alternative behavior (DRA)   Delivery of a reinforcer after any response that decreases the likelihood that an undesired behavior will occur. The reinforced response may be incompatible with the behavior that is to be reduced (DRI) or may be any behavior other than the one that is to be reduced (DRO).

differential reinforcement of incompatible behavior (DRI)   Delivery of a reinforcer after a response that is incompatible or competes with a target response that is to be suppressed. The effect is to increase the frequency of the incompatible response (for example, cooperative play) and to decrease the frequency of the undesirable target response (for example, fighting).

differential reinforcement of low rates (DRL)   Delivery of a reinforcer for reductions in performance of the target behavior. Reinforcers may be delivered for reduction in the overall frequency of a response within a particular period or for an increase in the amount of time that elapses between responses. A DRL schedule can reduce the frequency of a target response.

differential reinforcement of other behavior (DRO)   Delivery of a reinforcer after any response except the target response. The effect of reinforcing only behaviors other than the target response is to decrease the target (unreinforced) response.

discrete categorization   A method of assessing behavior in which behaviors are dichotomously scored as having occurred or not occurred. This method is very useful when several behaviors are to be scored.

discrimination   Responding differently in the presence of different cues or antecedent events. Control of behavior by discriminative stimuli. See **stimulus control.**

discriminative stimulus (S^D) An antecedent event or stimulus that signals that a certain response will be reinforced. A response is reinforced in the presence of an S^D. After an event becomes an S^D by being paired with reinforcement, its presence can increase the probability that the response will occur.

disease model A general approach in medicine in which symptoms (for example, fever) are viewed as a result of some underlying disease or pathology (for example, bacterial infection) and treatment, ideally, is directed at the underlying disease. This approach was transferred to abnormal behavior by positing an underlying "psychological disease." The intrapsychic model in psychology is consistent with the disease approach in medicine.

duration A method of recording behavior that measures the amount of time in which a behavior is performed.

E

elicit To bring about a response automatically. Respondent or reflex behaviors are elicited by unconditioned stimuli. Contrast with **emit** and **operant behavior.** See **classical conditioning.**

emit To perform a response spontaneously. Operant behaviors are emitted. They are controlled primarily by the consequences that follow them. Contrast with **elicit** and **respondent.** See **operant conditioning.**

escape Performance of a behavior that terminates an aversive event.

escape extinction Extinction of a response that was maintained (reinforced) by escape from the situation. Extinction of a negatively reinforced behavior when it no longer leads to escape from the situation.

experimental design The program plan that determines how the effect of the experimental contingency will be evaluated. The plan for evaluating whether the behavior modification program, rather than various extraneous factors, was responsible for behavior change.

extinction A procedure in which the reinforcer is no longer delivered for a previously reinforced response.

extinction burst An increase in the frequency and intensity of responding at the beginning of extinction.

F

fading The gradual removal of discriminative stimuli (S^D), including such prompts as instructions or physical guidance. Initially, developing behavior is often facilitated by prompts. However, in most situations, it is important to fade the prompt. Fading can also refer to the gradual removal of reinforcement, as in the progressive thinning of a reinforcement schedule.

feedback Knowledge of results of one's performance. Information is conveyed regarding how the person has performed.

fixed-interval schedule A schedule of administering reinforcement. In an FI schedule, reinforcement is given to the first occurrence of the target response after a fixed time interval elapses.

fixed-ratio schedule A schedule of administering reinforcement. In an FR schedule, an unvarying number of occurrences of the target response is required for reinforcement.

flooding A behavior therapy technique used for the treatment of anxiety-based disorders in which the individual is exposed in real life (*in vivo*) or in imagery to situations that provoke anxiety. Exposure is to situations that elicit relatively high levels of anxiety usually for prolonged periods until there is adaptation to the situation, as reflected in reductions in anxiety. Repeated exposure leads to diminished reactions and attenuation of anxiety.

frequency The number of times that a response occurs. See **rate of responding.**

functional analysis Evaluation of the behavior, and of antecedent and consequences associated with the behavior. A functional analysis is to identify the "causes" of behavior, that is, current conditions that are maintaining the behavior. These conditions are identified through assessment, and often by varying the conditions to demonstrate directly that the conditions cause the behavior. The information from functional analysis is then used to guide the intervention by direct alteration of conditions that sustain the behavior.

functional relation A relationship between behavior and the experimental condition or contingency. A functional relationship is demonstrated if behavior systematically changes when the contingency is applied, withdrawn, and reapplied.

functionally equivalent responses See **reinforcement of functionally equivalent behavior.**

G

generalized conditioned reinforcer A conditioned reinforcer that has acquired reinforcing value by being associated or paired with a variety of other reinforcers. Money is a generalized conditioned reinforcer.

group contingencies Contingencies in which the group participates. There are two major variations: (1) An individual's behavior can determine the consequences delivered to the group, and (2) the behavior of a group as a whole determines the consequences that each member of the group receives.

H

high-probability behavior A response that is performed with a relatively high frequency when the individual is given the opportunity to select among alternative behaviors. See **Premack principle.**

I

imagery-based techniques Cognitively based behavior modification procedures that rely on the presentation of events in imagination.

incompatible behavior A behavior that interferes with, or cannot be performed at the same time as, another behavior.

informed consent Agreeing to participate in a program with full knowledge about the nature of the treatment and about the program's risks, benefits, expected outcomes, and alternatives. Three elements are required for truly informed consent—competence, knowledge, and volition.

intermittent reinforcement A schedule of reinforcement in which only some occurrences of a response are reinforced.

interval recording An assessment strategy in which behavior is observed as having occurred or not occurred. Observations are usually made in a single period (for example, 30 minutes) that is divided into small intervals (for example, 15 seconds). Behavior is scored as having occurred or not occurred during each of the small intervals.

interval schedule of reinforcement A schedule in which reinforcement is delivered on the basis of the amount of time that passes before a response can be reinforced. Contrast with **ratio schedule of reinforcement.**

intrapsychic model The view that overt behavior, whether "normal" or "abnormal," is a result of underlying psychological processes and that the underlying processes must be treated before the overt behavior can be changed.

L

latency The time between the presentation or onset of a stimulus and the occurrence of behavior.

least restrictive alternative A guideline that has been used to guide treatment, particularly in the context of selecting among aversive (punishment) techniques that might be applied for therapeutic ends. The guideline states that the procedure to be used is the one that is the least restrictive necessary to achieve change. The least restrictive may include the least aversive, painful, or restrictive of freedom. Less restrictive procedures are to be tried first; more restrictive procedures are used only if the less restrictive procedures have not been effective.

M

model The person whose behavior is observed or imitated in observational learning.

modeling Learning by observing another individual (a model) engage in behavior. To learn from a model, the observer need not perform the behavior nor receive direct consequences for his or her performance.

multiple-baseline design Experimental designs that demonstrate the effect of a contingency by introducing the contingency across different behaviors, individuals, or situations at different points in time. A causal relationship between the experimental contingency and behavior is demonstrated if each of the behaviors (individual or situation) changes only when the contingency is introduced.

N

naturally occurring reinforcers Uncontrived reinforcing events that are usually available as part of the environment. Such events include attention, praise, completion of an activity, and mastery of a task.

negative reinforcement An increase in the frequency of a response that is followed by the termination or removal of a negative reinforcer. See **negative reinforcer.**

negative reinforcer An aversive event or stimulus whose termination increases the frequency of the preceding response. The increase in frequency of the response that terminates or removes the aversive event is called "negative reinforcement."

noncontingent delivery of a reinforcer The delivery of a reinforcer independent of behavior. The reinforcer is delivered without reference to how the individual is behaving. Contrast with **contingent delivery of a reinforcer.**

O

observational learning See **modeling.**

observer drift The gradual departure of observers from the definitions that they are supposed to use when they record behavior. If this happens, recorded changes in the target behavior may reflect changes in how responses are being scored rather than the effects of the program.

occasion Presenting an S^D and thus increasing the likelihood that a response will be performed. Certain cues in the environment (for example, music) occasion certain responses (for example, singing).

operant behavior Emitted behavior that is controlled by its consequences.

operant conditioning A type of learning in which behaviors are altered primarily by regulating the consequences that follow them. The frequency of operant behaviors is altered by the consequences that they produce.

operant rate See **baseline.**

operational definitions Defining a concept (for example, aggression, social skills) by referring to the specific operations that are to be used for assessment. The "operations" or methods of measuring the construct constitute the operational definition. The definitions represent the construct but are not considered to assess necessarily all facets that may be of interest.

overcorrection A punishment procedure that consists of two components. First, the environmental consequences of the undesirable behavior must be corrected (for example, cleaning up a mess). Second, correct forms of desirable behavior must be thoroughly rehearsed or practiced (for example, cleaning up messes made by several other people).

overt behavior Behavior that is publicly observable and measurable. Contrast with **covert event.**

P

paraprofessional A person, such as a parent, teacher, or peer, who works with the mental health professional to implement a treatment program.

positive opposite A behavior that is an alternative to and preferably incompatible with the undesired behavior. Suppression or elimination of an undesirable behavior can be achieved or accelerated by reinforcing a positive opposite. This is not a technical term but, rather, a useful way to approach the development of many behavioral programs. When the goal is to reduce or eliminate behavior, it is helpful to consider the positive opposite behaviors that are to be developed in its stead. See also **differential reinforcement of alternative behavior** and **differential reinforcement of incompatible behavior.**

positive practice Repeatedly practicing appropriate responses or responses incompatible with an undesirable response that is to be suppressed. This is a component of overcorrection, but it is often used alone as a punishment technique when the response that is to be suppressed (for example, a self-stimulatory behavior such as rocking) has no clear environmental consequences that can be corrected.

positive reinforcement An increase in the frequency of a response that is followed by a positive reinforcer. See **positive reinforcer.**

positive reinforcer An event whose presentation increases the probability of a response that it follows.

Premack principle Of any pair of responses or activities in which an individual freely engages, the more frequent one will reinforce the less frequent one.

primary reinforcer A reinforcing event that does not depend on learning to achieve its reinforcing properties. Food, water, and sex are primary reinforcers. Contrast with **secondary reinforcer.**

problem-solving skills training Cognitively based treatment in which individuals are trained to approach interpersonal situations; focuses on the requirements of a particular task or problem, the behaviors that need to be performed, the alternative courses of action that are available, the consequences of these actions, and then selection of a particular solution. Individuals engage in self-instruction to guide them through the problem-solving approach.

prompt An antecedent event that helps initiate a response. A discriminative stimulus that occasions a response. Instructions, gestures, physical guidance, and modeling cues serve as prompts.

psychodynamic view An explanation of personality that accounts for behavior by positing underlying psychological forces—drives, impulses, or personality dynamics.

punishment Presentation of an aversive event or removal of a positive event contingent upon a response that decreases the probability of the response.

R

rate of responding The frequency of responding is often expressed in relation to the amount of time that a behavior has been observed. The rate of responding equals frequency (number of occurrences of the behavior) divided by time (seconds or minutes).

ratio schedule of reinforcement A schedule in which reinforcement is delivered on the basis of the number of responses that are performed. Contrast with **interval schedule of reinforcement.**

rational-emotive psychotherapy Cognitively based treatment that considers psychological problems to arise from faulty or irrational thought patterns. These patterns are reflected in assumptions and self-verbalizations we make that lead to emotions and behaviors that are maladaptive. Treatment challenges these assumptions and verbalizations and substitutes more adaptive cognitions.

reinforcement An increase in the frequency of a response when the response is immediately followed by a particular consequence. The consequence can be either the presentation of a positive reinforcer or the removal of a negative reinforcer.

reinforcement of functionally equivalent behavior Reinforcement of a prosocial, acceptable behavior that attains the same goals and consequences as the problem behavior. The behaviors that are developed are functionally equivalent if they achieve the same environmental consequences as the original behavior.

reinforcer sampling A case of response priming in which the purpose is to develop or increase the utilization of an event as a reinforcer. Providing the client with a sample or small portion of the event increases the likelihood that the entire event can serve as a reinforcer.

reliability of assessment In behavioral research, this term usually refers to interobserver agreement, or the consistency with which different observers working independently score a target response. The method used to calculate agreement depends on the method used to assess behavior (for example, frequency, interval, or duration). The calculation usually yields a percentage of agreement between observers.

resistance to extinction The extent to which a response is maintained once reinforcement is no longer provided.

respondent Behavior that is elicited or controlled by antecedent stimuli. Reflexes are respondents because their performance automatically follows certain stimuli. The connection between such unconditioned respondents and the antecedent events that control them is unlearned. Through classical conditioning, respondents may come under the control of otherwise neutral stimuli.

response See **behavior.**

response cost A punishment procedure in which a positive reinforcer is lost contingent upon behavior. With this procedure, unlike time out from reinforcement, no time limit to the withdrawal of the reinforcer is specified. Fines are a common form of response cost.

response covariation   The tendency of several responses to change together, even when only one of the responses serves as the focus for change. In a person's repertoire, many behaviors may be correlated. If that is the case, changing one of those behaviors often changes behaviors with which it is correlated.

response deprivation hypothesis   The frequency of a target behavior can be increased if a preferred behavior is contingent upon first performing the target behavior. The effectiveness of this contingency is considered to depend on the fact that unless the target behavior is performed, the individual is deprived of performing the preferred behavior (that is, cannot engage in it freely at the baseline rate). See **Premack principle.**

response generalization   Reinforcement of one response increases the probability of other responses that are similar to that response. Contrast with **stimulus generalization.**

response priming   Any procedure that initiates early steps in a sequence of responses. By initiating early steps, response priming increases the likelihood that the terminal response in the sequence will be performed.

restitution   A component of overcorrection that consists of correcting the environmental effects of the undesired or inappropriate behavior. See **overcorrection.**

reversal design   An experimental design in which the target behavior of a subject or a group of subjects is assessed to determine baseline performance. The experimental condition is then introduced, and it is maintained until the target behavior changes. A reversal phase follows in which the experimental condition is withdrawn. Finally, the experimental condition is reintroduced. A functional relationship is demonstrated if the target behavior changes during each of the phases in which the experimental condition is presented and if it reverts to baseline or near baseline levels when the experimental condition is withdrawn. Also called an *ABAB design.*

reversal phase   A phase in the reversal design in which the program is withdrawn or altered to determine whether the target behavior reverts to baseline or near baseline levels.

S

satiation   Providing an excessive amount of the reinforcer. A loss of effectiveness that occurs after a large amount of the reinforcer has been delivered.

schedule of reinforcement   The rule denoting how many or which responses will be reinforced.

S^D   See **discriminative stimulus.**

S$^\Delta$ An antecedent event or stimulus that signals that a certain response will not be reinforced.

secondary (or conditioned) reinforcer An event that becomes reinforcing through learning. An event becomes a secondary reinforcer by being paired with other events (primary or conditioned) that are already reinforcing. Praise and attention are examples of secondary reinforcers. Contrast with **primary reinforcer.**

self-administered reinforcement Refers to the client's delivery of the reinforcer to himself or herself.

self-control Refers to those behaviors in which an individual deliberately undertakes to achieve self-selected outcomes by manipulating antecedent and consequent events.

self-determined reinforcement Refers to the client's specification of the criteria for reinforcement.

self-help manuals Books, manuals, or brochures that are designed to teach clients how to implement treatments for themselves. Usually little or no therapist contact is required. The client merely applies the specified techniques in a step-by-step fashion.

self-instruction training A self-control technique in which individuals prompt their own behavior by providing covert self-instructions or statements that direct and guide it.

self-monitoring Assessing or recording one's own behavior. Sometimes used as a self-control technique.

self-punishment Providing oneself with punishing consequences contingent upon behavior.

self-reinforcement Providing oneself with reinforcing consequences contingent upon behavior. For a procedure to qualify as self-reinforcement, the client must be free to partake of the reinforcer at any time, whether or not a particular response has been performed.

self-statements The statements that people make to themselves either aloud or privately (covertly). Self-statements are utilized in various treatment techniques, such as self-instruction training.

setting events Antecedent events that refer to context, conditions, or situational influences that affect the contingencies that follow. Such events set the stage for behavior-consequence sequences that are likely to occur.

shaping Developing a new behavior by reinforcing successive approximations toward the terminal response. See **successive approximations.**

simultaneous-treatment design See **alternating treatment design.**

social learning theory A conceptual framework within behavioral research that integrates the influence of different types of learning (classical, operant, and observational learning) in explaining how behavior develops and is maintained and altered. Social learning theory emphasizes the significance of cognitive processes in mediating the influence of environmental events and in actively influencing performance, the interrelationship of cognitions and the environment, and the influence that cognitions and the environment have on each other.

social reinforcers   Reinforcers that result from interpersonal interaction, such as attention, praise and approval, smiles, and physical contact.

social validation   Refers to the evaluation of the social importance of both the behavior focused on in treatment and the changes achieved in treatment. The applied or clinical significance of behavioral programs is often evaluated after treatment by comparing the behavior of the target subject with that of persons who perform adaptively or by soliciting the opinions of persons in the community with whom the client interacts.

spontaneous recovery   The temporary recurrence of a behavior during extinction. A response that has not been reinforced may reappear temporarily during the course of extinction. The magnitude of such a response is usually lower than its magnitude prior to extinction.

stimulus   A measurable event that may have an effect on a behavior.

stimulus control   The presence of a particular stimulus serves as an occasion for a particular response. The response is performed only when it is in the presence of a particular stimulus. See **discriminative stimulus.**

stimulus generalization   Transfer of a trained response to situations or stimulus conditions other than those in which training has taken place. The behavior generalizes to other situations. Contrast with **response generalization.**

stress inoculation training   A cognitively based treatment that focuses on developing cognitive and self-control skills to reduce the impact of stress. Individuals are trained to monitor events and their evaluations of them; to use coping strategies such as relaxation, imagery, and positive self-statements; and to apply coping skills in everyday life.

subjective evaluation   A method used to evaluate whether the changes achieved by a behavioral program make an important difference to various consumers of treatment, including the clients themselves, persons in contact with them, and persons who are in a position to evaluate the behaviors of interest. This method solicits the opinions and subjective evaluations of potential consumers to help decide whether these changes are important or make a difference in everyday situations.

successive approximations   Responses that more and more closely resemble the terminal behavior that is being shaped. See **shaping.**

systematic desensitization   A behavior therapy technique used for the treatment of anxiety-based disorders in which the client is exposed in real life (*in vivo*) or in imagery to situations that provoke anxiety. A central feature of the procedure is exposure to the anxiety-provoking situations in a gradual fashion while the individual engages in a response such as relaxation. Exposure to the stimuli in a gradual fashion (beginning with situations that evoke only small amounts of anxiety) while the client is relaxed leads to attenuation of anxiety.

T

target behavior   The behavior to be altered or focused on during a behavior modification program. The behavior that has been assessed and is to be changed.

task analysis   An initial stage in developing a program. The stage consists of identifying the precise behaviors that need to be developed, dividing those behaviors into concrete steps that can be trained, and setting the sequence (or order) in which the training will take place.

team-based contingency   A group contingency in which the members of a group earn reinforcers on the basis of the group's performance. In addition, use is made of subgroups or teams that compete to earn reinforcers between the teams.

terminal response   The final goal of shaping or the behavior that is achieved at the end of shaping. See **shaping.**

time in   The situation from which a person is removed when time out from reinforcement is used and access to available reinforcers is thus withdrawn for a brief period. The effectiveness of time out depends in part on how reinforcing that situation is.

time out from reinforcement   A punishment procedure in which, contingent upon behavior, access to positive reinforcement is withdrawn for a brief period. Isolation from a group exemplifies time out from reinforcement.

token   A tangible object that serves as a generalized conditioned reinforcer. It can be exchanged for backup reinforcers from which it derives its value. Poker chips, coins, tickets, stars, points, and check marks are commonly used as tokens. See **token economy.**

token economy   A reinforcement system in which tokens are earned for a variety of behaviors and are used to purchase a variety of backup reinforcers. A token economy is analogous to a national economy, in which money serves as a medium of exchange and can be earned and spent in numerous ways.

training the general case   A strategy designed to ensure that behaviors are performed across a variety of stimulus conditions (for example, in different situations, in the presence of different persons) in which the behaviors will be required. The strategy requires that variations of different stimulus conditions be included during training.

transfer of training   The extent to which responses trained in one setting transfer to settings other than the one in which training took place. See **stimulus generalization.**

U

unconditioned response   A reflex response elicited by an unconditioned stimulus. See **classical conditioning** and **respondent.**

V

variable-interval schedule   A schedule of administering reinforcement. In a VI schedule, the first occurrence of the target response after a given interval has elapsed is reinforced. However, the time interval changes each time that reinforcement is delivered; the interval is variable. The schedule is denoted by the average time that must elapse before a response can be reinforced.

variable-ratio schedule   A schedule of administering reinforcement. In a VR schedule, a number of occurrences of the target response are required for reinforcement. The number of required responses varies each time that reinforcement is delivered. The schedule is denoted by the average number of times that the response must occur before reinforcement is delivered.

vicarious punishment   Punishment of one individual sometimes decreases performance of the punished behavior in individuals who have not been directly punished. A spread of punishment effects to individuals whose behaviors have not been directly punished.

vicarious reinforcement   Reinforcement of one individual sometimes increases performance of the reinforced behavior in individuals who have not been directly reinforced. A spread of reinforcement effects to individuals whose behaviors have not been directly reinforced.

REFERENCES

Achenbach, T. M., & Edelbrock, C. S. (1986). *Manual for the Teacher's Report Form and teacher version of the Child Behavior Profile.* Burlington: University of Vermont.

Alavosius, M. P., & Sulzer-Azaroff, B. (1986). The effects of performance feedback on the safety of client lifting and transfer. *Journal of Applied Behavior Analysis, 19,* 261–268.

Albin, R. W., Horner, R. H., Koegel, R. L., & Dunlap, G. (Eds.). (1987, September). *Extending competent performance: Applied research on generalization and maintenance.* Eugene, OR: University of Oregon.

Allen, J. S., Jr., Tarnowski, K. J., Simonian, S. J., Elliott, D. S., & Drabman, R. S. (1991). The generalization map revisited: Assessment of generalized treatment effects in child and adolescent behavior therapy. *Behavior Therapy, 22,* 393–405.

Allen, K. D., Loiben, T., Allen, S. J., & Stanley, R. T. (1992). Dentist-implemented contingent escape for management of disruptive child behavior. *Journal of Applied Behavior Analysis, 25,* 629–636.

Allen, K. D., & Stokes, T. F. (1987). Use of escape and reward in the management of young children during dental treatment. *Journal of Applied Behavior Analysis, 20,* 381–390.

Allen, L. D., & Iwata, B. A. (1980). Reinforcing exercise maintenance: Using existing high-rate activities. *Behavior Modification, 4,* 337–354.

Alloy, L. R. (Ed.). (1988). *Cognitive processes in depression.* New York: Guilford.

Altman, K., Haavik, S., & Cook, J. W. (1978). Punishment of self-injurious behavior in natural settings, using contingent aromatic ammonia. *Behaviour Research and Therapy, 16,* 85–96.

American Psychological Association. (1992). Ethical principles of psychologists and code of conduct. *American Psychologist, 47,* 1597–1611.

Association for Advancement of Behavior Therapy. (1977). Ethical issues for human services. *Behavior Therapy, 8,* v–vi.

Axelrod, S., & Apsche, J. (Eds.). (1983). *The effects of punishment on human behavior.* New York: Academic Press.

Ayllon, T., & Azrin, N. H. (1968a). Reinforcer sampling: A technique for increasing the behavior of mental patients. *Journal of Applied Behavior Analysis, 1,* 13–20.

Ayllon, T., & Azrin, N. H. (1968b). *The token economy: A motivational system for therapy and rehabilitation.* New York: Appleton-Century-Crofts.

Ayllon, T., & Haughton, E. (1964). Modification of symptomatic verbal behaviour of mental patients. *Behaviour Research and Therapy, 2,* 87–97.

Allyon, T., & Michael, J. (1959). The psychiatric nurse as a behavior engineer. *Journal of the Experimental Analysis of Behavior, 2*, 323–334.

Azrin, N. H., Flores, T., & Kaplan, S. (1975). Job-finding club: A group-assisted program for obtaining employment. *Behaviour Research and Therapy, 13*, 17–27.

Azrin, N. H., & Foxx, R. M. (1971). A rapid method of toilet training the institutionalized retarded. *Journal of Applied Behavior Analysis, 4*, 89–99.

Azrin, N. H., & Foxx, R. M. (1974). *Toilet training in less than a day.* New York: Simon & Schuster.

Azrin, N. H., Gottlieb, L., Hughart, L., Wesolowski, M. D., & Rahn, T. (1975). Eliminating self-injurious behavior by educative procedures. *Behaviour Research and Therapy, 13*, 101–111.

Azrin, N. H., & Holz, W. C. (1966). Punishment. In W. K. Honig (Ed.), *Operant behavior: Areas of research and application* (pp. 380–447). New York: Appleton-Century-Crofts.

Azrin, N. H., & Peterson, A. L. (1990). Treatment of Tourette Syndrome by habit reversal: A waiting-list control group. *Behavior Therapy, 21*, 305–318.

Azrin, N. H., & Powers, M. A. (1975). Eliminating classroom disturbances of emotionally disturbed children by positive practice procedures. *Behavior Therapy, 6*, 525–534.

Azrin, N. H., & Wesolowski, M. D. (1974). Theft reversal: An overcorrection procedure for eliminating stealing by retarded persons. *Journal of Applied Behavior Analysis, 7*, 577–581.

Bacher, T. E., Liberman, R. P., & Kuehnel, T. G. (1986). Dissemination and adoption of innovative psychosocial interventions. *Journal of Consulting and Clinical Psychology, 54*, 111–118.

Baer, D. M., Rowbury, T. G., & Goetz, E. M. (1976). Behavioral traps in the preschool: A proposal for research. *Minnesota Symposia on Child Psychology, 10*, 3–27.

Baer, D. M., & Wolf, M. M. (1970). The entry into natural communities of reinforcement. In R. Ulrich, T. Stachnik, & J. Mabry (Eds.), *Control of human behavior* (Vol. 2). Glenview, IL: Scott, Foresman.

Baer, D. M., Wolf, M. M., & Risley, T. R. (1968). Some current dimensions of applied behavior analysis. *Journal of Applied Behavior Analysis, 1*, 91–97.

Baer, D. M., Wolf, M. M., & Risley, T. R. (1987). Some still-current dimensions of applied behavior analysis. *Journal of Applied Behavior Analysis, 20*, 313–328.

Baer, R. A., Blount, R. L., Detrick, R., & Stokes, T. F. (1987). Using intermittent reinforcement to program maintenance of verbal/nonverbal correspondence. *Journal of Applied Behavior Analysis, 20*, 179–184.

Ballard, K. D., & Glynn, G. (1975). Behavioral self-management in story writing with elementary school children. *Journal of Applied Behavior Analysis, 8*, 387–398.

Bandura, A. (1965). Influence of models' reinforcement contingencies on the acquisition of imitative responses. *Journal of Personality and Social Psychology, 1*, 589–595.

Bandura, A. (1977). *Social learning theory.* Englewood Cliffs, NJ: Prentice-Hall.

Bandura, A. (1986). *Social foundations of thought and action: A social cognitive perspective.* Englewood Cliffs, NJ: Prentice-Hall.

Bangert-Drowns, R. L. (1988). The effects of school-based substance abuse education: A meta-analysis. *Journal of Drug Education, 18*, 243–264.

Bank, L., Marlowe, J. H., Reid, J. B., Patterson, G. R., & Weinrott, M. R. (1991). A comparative evaluation of parent-training interventions for families of chronic delinquents. *Journal of Abnormal Child Psychology, 19,* 15–33.

Bannerman, D. J., Sheldon, J. B., & Sherman, J. A. (1991). Teaching adults with severe and profound retardation to exit their homes upon hearing the fire alarm. *Journal of Applied Behavior Analysis, 24,* 571–577.

Barbrack, C. R., & Maher, C. A. (1984). Effects of involving conduct problem adolescents in the setting of counseling goals. *Child and Family Behavior Therapy, 6,* 33–43.

Barlow, D. H. (1988). *Anxiety and its disorders: The nature and treatment of anxiety and panic.* New York: Guilford.

Barlow, D. H., & Hersen, M. (1984). *Single-case experimental designs. Strategies for studying behavior change* (2nd ed.). New York: Pergamon Press.

Barrett, B. H., Johnston, J. M., & Pennypacker, H. S. (1986). Behavior: Its units, dimensions, and measurement. In R. O. Nelson & S. C. Hayes (Eds.), *Conceptual foundations of behavioral assessment* (pp. 156–200). New York: Guilford.

Barton, E. J., & Osborne, J. G. (1978). The development of classroom sharing by a teacher using positive practice. *Behavior Modification, 2,* 231–250.

Beck, A. T., Kovacs, M., & Weissman, A. (1975). Hopelessness and suicidal behavior. An overview. *Journal of the American Medical Association, 234,* 1146–1149.

Beck, A. T., Rush, A. J., Shaw, B. F., & Emery, G. (1979). *Cognitive therapy of depression.* New York: Guilford.

Bell, K. E., Young, K. R., Salzberg, C. L., & West, R. P. (1991). High school driver education using peer tutors, direct instruction, and precision teaching. *Journal of Applied Behavior Analysis, 24,* 45–51.

Bellack, A. S., & Hersen, M. (Eds.). (1988). *Behavioral assessment: A practical handbook.* Needham Heights, MA: Allyn & Bacon.

Belles, D., & Bradlyn, A. S. (1987). The use of the changing criterion design in achieving controlled smoking in a heavy smoker: A controlled study. *Journal of Behavior Therapy and Experimental Psychiatry, 18,* 77–82.

Bergin, A. E., & Garfield, S. L. (Eds.). (1994). *Handbook of psychotherapy and behavior change* (4th ed.). New York: Wiley.

Bernard, M. E., Kratochwill, T. R., & Keefauver, L. W. (1983). The effects of rational-emotive-therapy and self-instructional training on chronic hair-pulling. *Cognitive Therapy and Research, 7,* 273–280.

Bierman, K. L., Miller, C. L., & Stabb, S. D. (1987). Improving the social behavior and peer acceptance of rejected boys: Effects of social skill training with instructions and prohibitions. *Journal of Consulting and Clinical Psychology, 55,* 194–200.

Bigelow, G. E., Liebson, I., & Griffiths, R. (1974). Alcoholic drinking: Suppression by a brief time-out procedure. *Behaviour Research and Therapy, 12,* 107–115.

Billings, D. C., & Wasik, B. H. (1985). Self-instructional training with preschoolers: An attempt to replicate. *Journal of Applied Behavior Analysis, 18,* 61–67.

Blake, D. D., Owens, M. D., & Keane, T. M. (1990). Increasing group attendance on a psychiatric unit: An alternating treatments design comparison. *Journal of Behavior Therapy and Experimental Psychiatry, 21,* 15–20.

Blampied, N. M., & Kahan, E. (1992). Acceptability of alternative punishments: A community survey. *Behavior Modification, 16,* 400–413.

Blanchard, E. B. (Ed.). (1992). Special issue: Behavioral medicine: An update for the 1990s. *Journal of Consulting and Clinical Psychology, 60,* 491–643.

Blechman, E. A. (1985). *Solving child behavior problems—At home and at school.* Champaign, IL: Research Press.

Boegli, R. G., & Wasik, B. H. (1978). Use of the token-economy system to intervene on a schoolwide level. *Psychology in the Schools, 15,* 72–78.

Bootzin, R. R. (1972). Stimulus control treatment for insomnia. *Proceedings of the 80th Annual Convention of the American Psychological Association, 7,* 395–396.

Bornstein, P. H., & Quevillon, R. P. (1976). The effects of a self-instructional package on overactive preschool boys. *Journal of Applied Behavior Analysis, 9,* 179–188.

Brigham, T. A. (1982). Self-management: A radical behavioral perspective. In P. Karoly & F. H. Kanfer (Eds.), *Self-management and behavior change: From theory to practice.* Elmsford, NY: Pergamon Press.

Bristol, M. M. (1976). Control of physical aggression through school- and home-based reinforcement. In J. D. Krumboltz & C. E. Thoresen (Eds.), *Counseling methods* (pp. 180–186). New York: Holt, Rinehart & Winston.

Brown, J. (1987). A review of meta-analyses conducted on psychotherapy outcome research. *Clinical Psychology Review, 7,* 1–23.

Brownell, K. D. (1982). Behavioral medicine. In C. M. Franks, G. T. Wilson, P. C. Kendall, & K. D. Brownell (Eds.), *Annual review of behavior therapy, Vol. 8, Theory and practice* (pp. 156–207). New York: Guilford.

Brownell, K. D. (1991). Dieting and the search for the perfect body: Where physiology and culture collide. *Behavior Therapy, 22,* 1–12.

Brownell, K. D., & Foreyt, J. P. (Eds.). (1986). *Handbook of eating disorders: Physiology, psychology, and treatment of obesity, anorexia, and bulimia.* New York: Basic Books.

Bryant, L. E., & Budd, K. S. (1982). Self-instructional training to increase independent work performance in preschoolers. *Journal of Applied Behavior Analysis, 15,* 259–271.

Budd, K. S., & Stokes, T. F. (1977, August). *Cue properties of praise in vicarious reinforcement with preschoolers.* Paper presented at meeting of the American Psychological Association, San Francisco.

Budney, A. J., Higgins, S. T., Delaney, D. D., Kent, L., & Bickel, W. K. (1991). Contingent reinforcement of abstinence with individuals abusing cocaine and marijuana. *Journal of Applied Behavior Analysis, 24,* 657–665.

Burchard, J. D., & Lane, T. W. (1982). Crime and delinquency. In A. S. Bellack, M. Hersen, & A. E. Kazdin (Eds.), *International handbook of behavior modification and therapy* (pp. 613–652). New York: Plenum.

Burgio, L. D., & Burgio, K. L. (1986). Behavioral gerontology: Application of behavioral methods to the problems of older adults. *Journal of Applied Behavior Analysis, 19,* 321–328.

Burgio, L. D., & Tice, L. (1985). The reduction of seizure-like behaviors through contingency management. *Journal of Behavior Therapy and Experimental Psychiatry, 16,* 71–75.

Burling, T. A., Bigelow, G. E., Robinson, J. C., & Mead, A. M. (1991). Smoking during pregnancy: Reduction via objective assessment and directive advice. *Behavior Therapy, 22,* 31–40.

Bushell, D., Jr. (1978). An engineering approach to the elementary classroom: The Behavior Analysis Follow Through project. In A. C. Catania & T. A. Brigham (Eds.), *Handbook of applied behavior analysis: Social and instructional processes* (pp. 525–563). New York: Irvington.

Cairns, D., & Pasino, J. A. (1977). Comparison of verbal reinforcement and feedback in the operant treatment of disability due to chronic low back pain. *Behavior Therapy, 8,* 621–630.

Calhoun, K. S., & Lima, P. P. (1977). Effects of varying schedules of time out on high- and low-rate behaviors. *Journal of Behavior Therapy and Experimental Psychiatry, 8,* 189–194.

Calvert, S. C., & McMahon, R. J. (1987). The treatment acceptability of a behavioral parent training program and its components. *Behavior Therapy, 18,* 165–179.

Carey, R. G., & Bucher, B. B. (1981). Identifying the educative and suppressive effects of positive practice and restitutional overcorrection. *Journal of Applied Behavior Analysis, 14,* 71–80.

Carey, R. G., & Bucher, B. B. (1986). Positive practice overcorrection: Effects of reinforcing correct performance. *Behavior Modification, 10,* 73–92.

Carlson, C. S., Arnold, C. R., Becker, W. C., & Madsen, C. H. (1968). The elimination of tantrum behavior of a child in an elementary classroom. *Behaviour Research and Therapy, 6,* 117–119.

Carr, E. G., & Durand, V. M. (1985). Reducing behavior problems through functional communication training. *Journal of Applied Behavior Analysis, 18,* 111–126.

Carr, E. G., Robinson, S., & Palumbo, L. W. (1990). The wrong issue: Aversive versus nonaversive treatment. The right issue: Functional versus nonfunctional treatment. In A. Repp & N. Singh (Eds.), *Perspectives on the use of nonaversive and aversive interventions for persons with developmental disabilities* (pp. 361–379). Sycamore, IL: Sycamore.

Carr, E. G., Taylor, J. C., & Robinson, S. (1991). The effects of severe behavior problems in children on the teaching behavior of adults. *Journal of Applied Behavior Analysis, 24,* 523–535.

Carter, N., Holmström, A., Simpanen, M., & Melin, L. (1988). Theft reduction in a grocery store through product identification and graphing of losses for employees. *Journal of Applied Behavior Analysis, 21,* 385–389.

Catania, A. C. (1992). *Learning* (3rd ed.). Englewood Cliffs, NJ: Prentice-Hall.

Cautela, J. R., & Kearney, A. J. (Eds.). (1986). *The covert conditioning handbook.* New York: Springer.

Cautela, J. R., & Kearney, A. J. (Eds.). (1993). *Covert conditioning casebook.* Pacific Grove, CA: Brooks/Cole.

Charlop, M. H., Burgio, L. D., Iwata, B. A., & Ivancic, M. T. (1988). Stimulus variation as a means of enhancing punishment effects. *Journal of Applied Behavior Analysis, 21,* 89–95.

Christophersen, E. R., Arnold, C. M., Hill, D. W., & Quilitch, H. R. (1972). The home point system: Token reinforcement procedures for applications by parents of children with behavior problems. *Journal of Applied Behavior Analysis, 5,* 485–497.

Claerhout, S., & Lutzker, J. D. (1981). Increasing children's self-initiated compliance to dental requirements. *Behavior Therapy, 12,* 165–170.

Clark, H. B., Greene, B. F., Macrae, J. W., McNees, M. P., Davis, J. L., & Risley, T. R. (1977). A parent advice package for family shopping trips: Development and evaluation. *Journal of Applied Behavior Analysis, 10,* 605–624.

Clark, H. B., Rowbury, T. G., Baer, A. M., & Baer, D. M. (1973). Time out as a punishing stimulus in continuous and intermittent schedules. *Journal of Applied Behavior Analysis, 6,* 443–455.

Clark, L. (1985). *SOS: Help for parents.* Bowling Green, KY: Parents Press.

Cole, P. M., & Kazdin, A. E. (1980). Critical issues in self-instruction training with children. *Child Behavior Therapy, 2,* 1–23.

Cook, J. W., Altman, K., Shaw, J., & Blaylock, M. (1978). Use of contingent lemon juice to eliminate public masturbation by a severely retarded boy. *Behaviour Research and Therapy, 16,* 131–134.

Cooke, T. P. & Apolloni, T. (1976). Developing positive social-emotional behaviors: A study of training and generalization effects. *Journal of Applied Behavior Analysis, 9,* 65–78.

Cooper, J. O., Heron, T. E., & Heward, W. L. (1987). *Applied behavior analysis.* Columbus, OH: Merrill.

Cooper, L. J., Wacker, D. P., Thursby, D., Plagmann, L. A., Harding, J., Millard, T., & Derby, M. (1992). Analysis of the effects of task preferences, task demands, and adult attention on child behavior in outpatient and classroom settings. *Journal of Applied Behavior Analysis, 25,* 823–840.

Creer, T. L., Chai, H., & Hoffman, A. (1977). A single application of an aversive stimulus to eliminate chronic cough. *Journal of Behavior Therapy and Experimental Psychiatry, 8,* 107–109.

Dachman, R. S., Alessi, G. J., Vrazo, G. J., Fuqua, R. W., & Kerr, R. H. (1986). Development and evaluation of an infant-care training program with first-time fathers. *Journal of Applied Behavior Analysis, 19,* 221–230.

Dahlquist, L. M., & Gil, K. M. (1986). Using parents to maintain improved dental flossing skills in children. *Journal of Applied Behavior Analysis, 19,* 255–260.

Danaher, B. G. (1980). Smoking-cessation programs in occupational settings. *Public Health Reports, 95,* 149–157.

Davis, C. A., Brady, M. P., Williams, R. E., & Hamilton, R. (1992). Effects of high-probability requests on the acquisition and generalization of responses to requests in young children with behavior disorders. *Journal of Applied Behavior Analysis, 25,* 905–916.

Davison, G. C. (1976). Homosexuality: The ethical challenge. *Journal of Consulting and Clinical Psychology, 44,* 157–162.

Dawson, B., de Armas, A., McGrath, M. L., & Kelly, J. A. (1986). Cognitive problem-solving training to improve the child-care judgment of child neglectful parents. *Journal of Family Violence, 1,* 209–221.

Day, H. M., & Horner, R. H. (1986). Response variation and the generalization of a dressing skill: Comparison of single instance and general case instruction. *Applied Research in Mental Retardation, 7,* 189–202.

Deitz, S. M. (1977). An analysis of programming DRL schedules in educational settings. *Behaviour Research and Therapy, 15,* 103–111.

Deitz, S. M., Repp, A. C., & Deitz, D. E. D. (1976). Reducing inappropriate classroom behavior of retarded students through three procedures of differential reinforcement. *Journal of Mental Deficiency Research, 20,* 155–170.

DeLuca, R. V., & Holborn, S. W. (1992). Effects of a variable-ratio reinforcement schedule with changing criteria on exercise in obese and nonobese boys. *Journal of Applied Behavior Analysis, 25,* 671–679.

DeRisi, W. J., & Butz, G. (1975). *Writing behavioral contracts: A case simulation practice manual.* Champaign, IL: Research Press.

DeVries, J. E., Burnette, M. M., & Redmon, W. K. (1991). AIDS prevention: Improving nurses' compliance with glove wearing through performance feedback. *Journal of Applied Behavior Analysis, 24,* 705–711.

Dickerson, E. A., & Creedon, C. F. (1981). Self-selection of standards by children:

The relative effectiveness of pupil-selected and teacher-selected standards of performance. *Journal of Applied Behavior Analysis, 14,* 425–433.

Dodge, K. A. (1993). Social-cognitive mechanisms in the development of conduct disorder and depression. *Annual Review of Psychology, 44,* 559–584.

Doleys, D. M., Wells, K. C., Hobbs, S. A., Roberts, M. W., & Cartelli, L. M. (1976). The effects of social punishment on noncompliance: A comparison with time out and positive practice. *Journal of Applied Behavior Analysis, 9,* 471–482.

Donnellan, A. M., & LaVinga, G. W. (1990). Myths about punishment. In A. C. Repp & N. N. Singh (Eds.), *Perspectives on the use of nonaversive and aversive interventions for persons with developmental disabilities* (pp. 33–57). Sycamore, IL: Sycamore.

Donnelly, D. R., & Olczak, P. V. (1990). The effect of differential reinforcement of incompatible behaviors (DRI) on pica for cigarettes in persons with intellectual disability. *Behavior Modification, 14,* 81–96.

Dorsey, M. F., Iwata, B. A., Ong, P., & McSween, T. E. (1980). Treatment of self-injurious behavior using a water mist: Initial response suppression and generalization. *Journal of Applied Behavior Analysis, 13,* 343–353.

Dougherty, S. B., Fowler, S. A., & Paine, S. C. (1985). The use of peer monitors to reduce negative interaction during recess. *Journal of Applied Behavior Analysis, 18,* 141–153.

Ducharme, J. M., & Feldman, M. A. (1992). Comparison of staff training strategies to promote generalized teaching skills. *Journal of Applied Behavior Analysis, 25,* 165–179.

Dunlap, G., Koegel, R. L., Johnson, J., & O'Neill, R. E. (1987). Maintaining performance of autistic clients in community settings with delayed contingencies. *Journal of Applied Behavior Analysis, 20,* 179–184.

Durand, V. M., & Carr, E. G. (1991). Functional communication training to reduce challenging behavior: Maintenance and application in new settings. *Journal of Applied Behavior Analysis, 24,* 251–264.

Durlak, J. A., Fuhrman, T., & Lampman, C. (1991). Effectiveness of cognitive-behavioral therapy for maladapting children: A meta-analysis. *Psychological Bulletin, 110,* 204–214.

Egel, A. L., Richman, G. S., & Koegel, R. L. (1981). Normal peer models and autistic children's learning. *Journal of Applied Behavior Analysis, 14,* 3–12.

Eisen, A. R., & Silverman, W. K. (1991). Treatment of an adolescent with bowel movement phobia using self-control therapy. *Journal of Behavior Therapy and Experimental Psychiatry, 22,* 45–51.

Elliott, D. S., Huizinga, D., & Menard, S. (1988). *Multiple problem youth: Delinquency, substance abuse, and mental health problems.* New York: Springer-Verlag.

Elliott, S. N. (1988). Acceptability of behavioral treatments: Review of variables that influence treatment selection. *Professional Psychology: Research and Practice, 19,* 68–80.

Ellis, A. (1979). *New developments in rational-emotive therapy.* Pacific Grove, CA: Brooks/Cole.

Emmelkamp, P. M. G. (1990). Anxiety and fear. In A. S. Bellack, M. Hersen, & A. E. Kazdin (Eds.), *International handbook of behavior modification and therapy* (2nd ed.; pp. 283–305). New York: Plenum.

Empey, L. T. (1982). *American delinquency: Its meaning and construction.* Homewood, IL: Brooks/Cole.

Emshoff, J. G., Redd, W. H., & Davidson, W. S. (1976). Generalization training and the transfer of treatment effects with delinquent adolescents. *Journal of Behavior Therapy and Experimental Psychiatry, 7,* 141–144.

Endler, N. S., & Magnusson, D. (1976). Toward an interactional psychology of personality. *Psychological Bulletin, 83,* 956–974.

Ennis, B. J., & Friedman, P. R. (Eds.). (1973). *Legal rights of the mentally handicapped. Vols. 1 and 2.* Practicing Law Institute, The Mental Health Law Project.

Epstein, L. H., Beck, S., Figueroa, J., Farkas, G., Kazdin, A. E., Daneman, D., & Becker, D. (1981). The effects of targeting improvements in urine glucose on metabolic control in children with insulin-dependent diabetes. *Journal of Applied Behavior Analysis, 14,* 365–375.

Epstein, L. H., Hersen, M., & Hemphill, D. P. (1974). Music feedback in the treatment of tension headache: An experimental case study. *Journal of Behavior Therapy and Experimental Psychiatry, 5,* 59–63.

Erhardt, D., & Baker, B. L. (1990). The effects of behavioral parent training on families with young hyperactive children. *Journal of Behavior Therapy and Experimental Psychiatry, 21,* 121–132.

Eysenck, H. J. (1952). The effects of psychotherapy: An evaluation. *Journal of Consulting Psychology, 16,* 319–324.

Eysenck, H. J. (1959). Learning theory and behaviour therapy. *Journal of Mental Science, 105,* 61–75.

Fantuzzo, J. W., & Clement, P. W. (1981). Generalization of the effects of teacher- and self-administered token reinforcers to nontreated students. *Journal of Applied Behavior Analysis, 14,* 435–447.

Farrell, A. D., Danish, S. J., & Howard, C. W. (1992). Relationship between drug use and other problem behaviors in urban adolescents. *Journal of Consulting and Clinical Psychology, 60,* 705–712.

Faust, J., Olson, R., & Rodriguez, H. (1991). Same-day surgery preparation: Reduction of pediatric patient arousal and distress through participant modeling. *Journal of Consulting and Clinical Psychology, 59,* 475–478.

Favell, J. E., McGimsey, J. F., & Jones, M. L. (1978). The use of physical restraint in the treatment of self-injury and as positive reinforcement. *Journal of Applied Behavior Analysis, 11,* 225–241.

Fawcett, S. B. (1991). Some values guiding community research and action. *Journal of Applied Behavior Analysis, 24,* 621–636.

Feindler, E. L., Ecton, R. B., Kingsley, D., & Dubey, D. R. (1986). Group anger-control training for institutionalized psychiatric male adolescents. *Behavior Therapy, 17,* 109–123.

Feingold, L., & Migler, B. (1972). The use of experimental dependency relationships as a motivating procedure on a token-economy ward. In R. D. Rubin, H. Fensterheim, J. D. Henderson, & L. P. Ullmann (Eds.), *Advances in behavior therapy* (pp. 121–127). New York: Academic Press.

Feldman, M. A., Case, L., Garrick, M., MacIntyre-Grande, W., Carnwell, J., & Sparks, B. (1992). Teaching child-care skills to mothers with developmental disabilities. *Journal of Applied Behavior Analysis, 25,* 205–215.

Feldman, M. A., Case, L., Rincover, A., Towns, F., & Betel, J. (1989). Parent education project III: Increasing affection and responsivity in developmentally handicapped mothers: Component analysis, generalization, and effects on child language. *Journal of Applied Behavior Analysis, 22,* 211–222.

Fichter, M. M., Wallace, C. J., Liberman, R. P., & Davis, J. R. (1976). Improving social interaction in a chronic psychotic using discriminated avoidance ("nagging"): Experimental analysis and generalization. *Journal of Applied Behavior Analysis, 9,* 337–386.

Finney, J. W. (1991). Selection of target behaviors and interventions: A case of necessary but insufficient choices. *Journal of Applied Behavior Analysis, 24,* 713–715.

Fischer, J., & Nehs, R. (1978). Use of a commonly available chore to reduce a boy's rate of swearing. *Journal of Behavior Therapy and Experimental Psychiatry, 9,* 81–83.

Fishman, D. B., Rotgers, F., & Franks, C. M. (Eds.). (1988). *Paradigms in behavior therapy.* New York: Springer.

Fixsen, D. L., Phillips, E. L., Phillips, E. A., & Wolf, M. M. (1976). The teaching-family model of group home treatment. In W. E. Craighead, A. E. Kazdin, & M. J. Mahoney (Eds.), *Behavior modification: Principles, issues, and applications.* Boston: Houghton Mifflin.

Foley, F. W., Bedell, J. R., LaRocca, N. G., Scheinberg, L. C., & Reznikoff, M. (1987). Efficacy of stress-inoculation training in coping with multiple sclerosis. *Journal of Consulting and Clinical Psychology, 55,* 919–922.

Foot, H., Morgan, M., & Shute, R. (Eds.). (1990). *Children helping children.* Chichester, England: Wiley.

Fordyce, W. E., Fowler, R. S., Lehmann, J. F., DeLateur, B. J., Sand, P. L., & Trieschmann, R. B. (1974). Operant conditioning in the treatment of chronic pain. *Archives of Physical Medicine and Rehabilitation, 54,* 399–408.

Forehand, R., & McMahon, R. J. (1981). *Helping the noncompliant child: A clinician's guide to parent training.* New York: Guilford.

Forehand, R., Roberts, M. W., Doleys, D. M., Hobbs, S. A., & Resick, P. A. (1976). An examination of disciplinary procedures with children. *Journal of Experimental Child Psychology, 21,* 109–120.

Foster, S. L., Bell-Dolan, D. J., & Burge, D. A. (1988). Behavioral observation. In A. S. Bellack & M. Hersen (Eds.), *Behavioral assessment: A practical handbook* (pp. 119–160). Needham Heights, MA: Allyn & Bacon.

Fowler, S. A., & Baer, D. M. (1981). "Do I have to be good all day?": The timing of delayed reinforcement as a factor in generalization. *Journal of Applied Behavior Analysis, 14,* 13–24.

Fowler, S. A., Dougherty, B. S., Kirby, K. C., & Kohler, F. W. (1986). Role reversals: An analysis of therapeutic effects achieved with disruptive boys during their appointments as peer monitors. *Journal of Applied Behavior Analysis, 19,* 437–444.

Fox, D. K., Hopkins, B. L., & Anger, W. K. (1987). The long-term effects of a token economy on safety performance in open-pit mining. *Journal of Applied Behavior Analysis, 20,* 215–224.

Fox, L. (1962). Effecting the use of efficient study habits. *Journal of Mathematics, 1,* 75–86.

Foxx, R. M. (1982). *Decreasing behaviors of severely retarded and autistic persons.* Champaign, IL: Research Press.

Foxx, R. M., & Azrin, N. H. (1972). Restitution: A method of eliminating aggressive-disruptive behavior of retarded and brain damaged patients. *Behaviour Research and Therapy, 10,* 15–27.

Foxx, R. M., & Bechtel, D. R. (1983). Overcorrection: A review and analysis. In S.

Axelrod & J. Apsche (Eds.), *The effects of punishment on human behavior* (pp. 133–220). New York: Academic Press.

Foxx, R. M., Faw, G. D., & Weber, G. (1991). Producing generalization of inpatient adolescents' social skills with significant adults in a natural environment. *Behavior Therapy, 22,* 85–99.

Foxx, R. M., & Hake, D. F. (1977). Gasoline conservation: A procedure for measuring and reducing the driving of college students. *Journal of Applied Behavior Analysis, 10,* 61–74.

Foxx, R. M., & Shapiro, S. T. (1978). The time out ribbon: A nonexclusionary time out procedure. *Journal of Applied Behavior Analysis, 11,* 125–136.

France, K. G., & Hudson, S. M. (1990). Behavior management of infant sleep disturbance. *Journal of Applied Behavior Analysis, 23,* 91–98.

Frederiksen, L. W. (1975). Treatment of ruminative thinking by self-monitoring. *Journal of Behavior Therapy and Experimental Psychiatry, 6,* 258–259.

Frederiksen, L. W. (Ed.). (1982). *Handbook of organizational behavior management.* New York: Wiley.

Frederiksen, L. W., Jenkins, J. O., Foy, D. W., & Eisler, R. M. (1976). Social-skills training to modify abusive verbal outbursts in adults. *Journal of Applied Behavior Analysis, 9,* 117–125.

Friedling, C., & O'Leary, S. G. (1979). Effects of self-instructional training on second- and third-grade hyperactive children: A failure to replicate. *Journal of Applied Behavior Analysis, 12,* 211–219.

Friman, P. C., Finney, J. W., Glasscock, S. T., Weigel, J. W., & Christophersen, E. R. (1986). Testicular self-examination: Validation of a training strategy for early cancer detection. *Journal of Applied Behavior Analysis, 19,* 87–92.

Friman, P. C., & Hove, G. (1987). Apparent covariation between child habit disorders: Effects of successful treatment for thumb sucking on untargeted chronic hair pulling. *Journal of Applied Behavior Analysis, 20,* 421–426.

Furman, W., Geller, M., Simon, S. J., & Kelly, J. A. (1979). The use of a behavioral rehearsal procedure for teaching job interviewing skills to psychiatric patients. *Behavior Therapy, 10,* 157–167.

Gardner, W. I., Cole, C. L., Berry, D. L., & Nowinski, J. M. (1983). Reduction of disruptive behaviors in mentally retarded adults: A self-management approach. *Behavior Modification, 7,* 76–96.

Geller, E. S. (Ed.). (1990). Special section: Social validity: Multiple perspectives. *Journal of Applied Behavior Analysis, 24,* 179–249.

Geller, E. S. (1991). Special section: Behavioral community intervention. *Journal of Applied Behavior Analysis, 24,* 621–718.

Geller, E. S. (1991). Special section: Road safety: International perspectives. *Journal of Applied Behavior Analylsis, 24,* 13–94.

Geller, E. S. (Ed.). (1992). Special issue: The education crisis: Issues, perspectives, and solutions. *Journal of Applied Behavior Analysis, 25,* 13–235.

Geller, E. S., Bruff, C. D., & Nimmer, J. G. (1985). "Flash for life": Community-based prompting for safety belt promotion. *Journal of Applied Behavior Analysis, 18,* 309–314.

Geller, E. S., Chaffee, J. L., & Ingram, R. E. (1975). Promoting paper recycling on a university campus. *Journal of Environmental Systems, 5,* 39–57.

Geller, E. S., Winett, R. A., & Everett, P. B. (1982). *Preserving the environment: New strategies for behavior change.* New York: Pergamon Press.

Gesten, E. L., Rains, M., Rapkin, B. D., Weissberg, R. G., Flores de Apodaca, R., Cowen, E. L., & Bowen, G. (1982). Training children in social problem-solving competencies: A first and second look. *American Journal of Community Psychology, 10,* 95–115.

Gillum, R. R., & Barsky, A. J. (1974). Diagnosis and management of patient noncompliance. *Journal of the American Medical Association, 12,* 1563–1567.

Glasgow, R. E., & Rosen, G. M. (1984). Self-help behavior therapy manuals: Recent developments and clinical usage. In C. M. Franks (Ed.), *New developments in behavior therapy: From research to clinical application* (pp. 525–570). New York: Haworth Press.

Glenwick, D. S., & Jason, L. A. (Eds.). (In press). *Promoting health and mental health in children, youth, and families.* New York: Springer.

Glynn, E. L. (1970). Classroom applications of self-determined reinforcement. *Journal of Applied Behavior Analysis, 3,* 123–132.

Glynn, S. M. (1990). Token economy approaches for psychiatric patients. *Behavior Modification, 14,* 383–407.

Goldiamond, I. (1965). Self-control procedures in personal behavior problems. *Psychological Reports, 17,* 851–868.

Green, C. W., Reid, D. H., Canipe, V. S., & Gardner, S. M. (1991). A comprehensive evaluation of reinforcer identification processes for persons with profound multiple handicaps. *Journal of Applied Behavior Analysis, 24,* 537–552.

Green, G. (1990). Least restrictive use of reductive procedures: Guidelines and competencies. In A. C. Repp & N. N. Singh (Eds.), *Perspectives on the use of nonaversive and aversive interventions for persons with developmental disabilities* (pp. 479–493). Sycamore, IL: Sycamore.

Green, G. R., Linsk, N. L., & Pinkston, E. M. (1986). Modification of verbal behavior of the mentally impaired elderly by their spouses. *Journal of Applied Behavior Analysis, 19,* 329–336.

Green, R. B., Hardison, W. L., & Greene, B. F. (1984). Turning the table on advice programs for parents: Using placements to enhance family interaction at restaurants. *Journal of Applied Behavior Analysis, 17,* 497–508.

Greene, B. F., Winett, R. A., Van Houten, R., Geller, E. S., & Iwata, B. A. (Eds.). (1987). *Behavior analysis in the community.* Lawrence, KS: Society for the Experimental Analysis of Behavior.

Greenwood, C. R., Delquadri, J. C., & Hall, R. V. (1984). Opportunity to respond and student academic performance. In W. L. Heward, T. E. Heron, D. S. Hill, & J. Trap-Porter (Eds.), *Focus on behavior analysis in education* (pp. 58–88). Columbus, OH: Merrill.

Greenwood, C. R., Dinwiddie, G., Bailey, V., Carta, J. J., Dorsey, D., Kohler, F. W., Nelson, C., Rotholz, D., & Schulte, D. (1987). Field replication of classwide peer tutoring. *Journal of Applied Behavior Analysis, 20,* 151–160.

Greenwood, C. R., & Hops, H. (1981). Group-oriented contingencies and peer behavior change. In P. S. Strain (Ed.), *The utilization of classroom peers as behavior change agents.* New York: Plenum.

Greenwood, C. R., Hops, H., Delquadri, J., & Guild, J. J. (1974). Group contingencies for group consequences in classroom management: A further analysis. *Journal of Applied Behavior Analysis, 7,* 413–425.

Greer, R. D. (1992). *L'enfant terrible* meets the educational crisis. *Journal of Applied Behavior Analysis, 25,* 65–69.

Greer, R. D., & Polirstok, S. R. (1982). Collateral gains and short-term maintenance in reading and on-task responses by inner-city adolescents as a function of their use of social reinforcement while tutoring. *Journal of Applied Behavior Analysis, 15,* 123–139.

Griffen, A. K., Wolery, M., & Schuster, J. W. (1992). Triadic instruction of chained food preparation responses: Acquisition of observational learning. *Journal of Applied Behavior Analysis, 25,* 193–204.

Groden, J. (1993). The use of covert procedures to reduce severe aggression in a person with retardation and behavioral disorders. In J. R. Cautela & A. J. Kearney (Eds.), *Covert conditioning casebook* (pp. 144–152). Pacific Grove, CA: Brooks/Cole.

Gross, A. M., & Drabman, R. S. (1982). Teaching self-recording, self-evaluation, and self-reward to nonclinic children and adolescents. In P. Karoly & F. H. Kanfer (Eds.), *Self-management and behavior change: From theory to practice.* (pp. 285–314). New York: Pergamon Press.

Gross, A. M., & Wojnilower, D. A. (1984). Self-directed behavior change in children: Is it self-directed? *Behavior Therapy, 15,* 501–514.

Guevremont, D. C., Osnes, P. G., & Stokes, T. F. (1988). The functional role of preschoolers' verbalizations in the generalizations of self-instructional training. *Journal of Applied Behavior Analysis, 21,* 45–55.

Gutkin, A. J., Holborn, S. W., Walker, J. R., & Anderson, B. A. (1992). Treatment integrity of relaxation training for tension headaches. *Journal of Behavior Therapy and Experimental Psychiatry, 23,* 191–198.

Hackmann, A., & McLean, C. A. (1975). A comparison of flooding thought stopping in the treatment of obsessional neurosis. *Behaviour Research and Therapy, 13,* 263–269.

Hall, D. C., Adams, C. K., Stein, G. H., Stephenson, H. S., Goldstein, M. K., & Pennypacker, H. S. (1980). Improved detection of human breast lesions following experimental training. *Cancer, 46,* 408–414.

Hall, R. V., Axelrod, S., Foundopoulos, M., Shellman, J., Campbell, R. A., & Cranston, S. (1971). The effective use of punishment to modify behavior in the classroom. *Educational Technology, 11,* 24–26.

Hall, R. V., & Hall, M. C. (1980). *How to use planned ignoring (extinction).* Austin, TX: Pro-Ed:

Hall, R. V., & Hall, M. C. (1982). *How to negotiate a behavioral contract.* Austin, TX: Pro-Ed.

Hall, S. M., Cooper, J. L., Burmaster, S., & Polk, A. (1977). Contingency contracting as a therapeutic tool with methadone maintenance clients: Six single-subject studies. *Behavior Research and Therapy, 15,* 438–441.

Hancock v. *Avery,* 301 F. Supp. (M.D. Tenn. 1969).

Haney, J. I., & Jones, R. T. (1982). Programming maintenance as a major component of a community-centered preventive effort: Escape from fire. *Behavior Therapy, 13,* 47–62.

Harchik, A. E., Sherman, J. A., Sheldon, J. B., & Strouse, M. C. (1992). Ongoing consultation as a method of improving performance of staff members in a group home. *Journal of Applied Behavior Analysis, 25,* 599–610.

Haring, T. G., Kennedy, C. H., Adams, M. J., & Pitts-Conway, V. (1987). Teaching generalization of purchasing skills across community settings to autistic youth using videotape modeling. *Journal of Applied Behavior Analysis, 20,* 89–96.

Harris, K. R. (1986). Self-monitoring of attentional behavior versus self-monitoring of productivity: Effects on on-task behavior and academic response rate among learning disabled children. *Journal of Applied Behavior Analysis, 19,* 417–424.

Harris, V. W., & Sherman, J. A. (1973). Use and analysis of the "good-behavior game" to reduce disruptive classroom behavior. *Journal of Applied Behavior Analysis, 6,* 405–417.

Hartmann, D. P. (Ed.). (1985). Mini-series: Target behavior selection. *Behavioral Assessment, 7,* 1–78.

Hawkins, R. P. (1986). Selection of target behaviors. In R. O. Nelson & S. C. Hayes (Eds.), *Conceptual foundations of behavioral assessment* (pp. 331–385). New York: Guilford.

Hawkins, R. P., & Dobes, R. W. (1975). Behavioral definitions in applied behavior analysis: Explicit or implicit. In B. C. Etzel, J. M. LeBlanc, & D. M. Baer (Eds.), *New developments in behavioral research: Theory, methods, and applications: In honor of Sidney W. Bijou.* Hillsdale, NJ: Erlbaum.

Hayes, S. C., Brownell, K. D., & Barlow, D. H. (1978). The use of self-administered covert sensitization in the treatment of exhibitionism and sadism. *Behavior Therapy, 9,* 283–289.

Hayes, S. C., Rosenfarb, I., Wulfert, E., Munt, E. D., Korn, Z., & Zettle, R. D. (1985). Self-reinforcement effects: An artifact of social standard setting? *Journal of Applied Behavior Analysis, 18,* 201–214.

Haynes, S. N., & Horn, W. F. (1982). Reactivity in behavioral observation: A methodological and conceptual critique. *Behavioral Assessment, 4,* 369–385.

Haynes, S. N., & O'Brien, W. H. (1990). Functional analysis in behavior therapy. *Clinical Psychology Review, 10,* 649–668.

Heaton, R. C., & Safer, D. J. (1982). Secondary school outcome following a junior high school behavioral program. *Behavior Therapy, 13,* 226–231.

Hegel, M. T., Ayllon, T., VanderPlate, C., & Spiro-Hawkins, H. (1986). A behavioral procedure for increasing compliance with self-exercise regimens in severely burn-injured patients. *Behaviour Research and Therapy, 24,* 521–528.

Herbert, E. W., Pinkston, E. M., Hayden, M., Sajwaj, T. E., Pinkston, S., Cordua, G., & Jackson, C. (1973). Adverse effects of differential parental attention. *Journal of Applied Behavior Analysis, 6,* 15–30.

Hineline, P. N. (1977). Negative reinforcement and avoidance. In W. K. Honig & J. E. R. Staddon (Eds.), *Handbook of operant behavior* (pp. 364–414). Englewood Cliffs, NJ: Prentice-Hall.

Hobbs, S. A., & Forehand, R. (1977). Important parameters in the use of time out with children: A reexamination. *Journal of Behavior Therapy and Experimental Psychiatry, 8,* 365–370.

Hobbs, S. A., Forehand, R., & Murray, R. G. (1978). Effects of various durations of time out on the noncompliant behavior of children. *Behavior Therapy, 9,* 652–656.

Hollon, S. D., & Beck, A. T. (1994). In A. E. Bergen & S. L. Garfield (Eds.), *Handbook of psychotherapy and behavior change: An empirical analysis* (4th ed.). New York: Wiley.

Holroyd, K. A. (1986). Recurrent headache. In K. A. Holroyd, & T. L. Creer (Eds.), *Self-management of chronic disease: Handbook of clinical interventions and research* (pp. 373–413). New York: Academic Press.

Holroyd, K. A., Andrasik, R., & Westbrook, T. (1977). Cognitive control of tension headache. *Cognitive Therapy and Research, 1,* 121–133.

Holroyd, K. A., & Creer, T. L. (Eds.). (1986). *Self-management of chronic disease: Handbook of clinical interventions and research.* New York: Academic Press.

Homme, L. E. (1965). Perspectives in psychology: XXIV. Control of coverants, the operants of the mind. *Psychological Record, 15,* 501–511.

Honnen, T. J., & Kleinke, C. L. (1990). Prompting bar patrons with signs to take free condoms. *Journal of Applied Behavior Analysis, 23,* 215–217.

Hopkins, B. L. (1987). Comments on the future of applied behavioral analysis. *Journal of Applied Behavior Analysis, 20,* 339–346.

Hopkins, B. L., Conrad, R. J., Dangel, R. F., Fitch, H. G., Smith, M. J., & Anger, W. K. (1986). Behavioral technology for reducing occupational exposures to styrene. *Journal of Applied Behavior Analysis, 19,* 3–12.

Horner, R. H., Albin, R. W., & Ralph, G. (1986). Generalization with precision: The role of negative teaching examples in the instruction of generalized grocery item selection. *Journal of the Association for Persons with Severe Handicaps, 11,* 300–308.

Horner, R. H., Bellamy, G. T., & Colvin, G. T. (1984). Responding in the presence of nontrained stimuli: Implications of generalization error patterns. *Journal of the Association for Persons with Severe Handicaps, 9,* 287–295.

Horner, R. H., Dunlap, G., & Koegel, R. L. (Eds.). (1988). *Generalization and maintenance: Life-style changes in applied settings.* Baltimore: Paul Brookes.

Horner, R. H., Eberhard, J. M., & Sheehan, M. R. (1986). Teaching generalized table bussing: The importance of negative teaching examples. *Behavior Modification, 10,* 457–471.

Horner, R. H., & Keilitz, I. (1975). Training mentally retarded adolescents to brush their teeth. *Journal of Applied Behavior Analysis, 8,* 301–309.

Horner, R. H., Williams, J. A., & Knobbe, C. A. (1985). The effects of "opportunity to perform" on the maintenance of skills learned by high school students with severe handicaps. *Journal of the Association for Persons with Severe Handicaps, 10,* 172–175.

Hume, K. M., & Crosssman, J. (1992). Musical reinforcement of practice behaviors among competitive swimmers. *Journal of Applied Behavior Analysis, 25,* 665–670.

Hundert, J., & Bastone, D. (1978). A practical procedure to maintain pupils' accurate self-rating in a classroom token program. *Behavior Modification, 2,* 93–112.

Hutchinson, R. R. (1977). By-products of aversive control. In W. K. Honig & J. E. R. Staddon (Eds.), *Handbook of operant behavior* (pp. 415–431). Englewood Cliffs, NJ: Prentice-Hall.

Iwata, B. A. (1987). Negative reinforcement in applied behavior analysis: An emerging technology. *Journal of Applied Behavior Analysis, 20,* 361–378.

Iwata, B. A., Bailey, J. S., Fuqua, R. W., Neef, N. A., Pae, T. J., & Reid, D. H. (Eds.). (1989). *Methodological and conceptual issues in applied behavior analysis.* Lawrence, KS: Society of the Experimental Analysis of Behavior.

Iwata, B. A., & Becksfort, C. M. (1981). Behavioral research in preventive dentistry: Educational and contingency management approaches to the problem of patient compliance. *Journal of Applied Behavior Analysis, 14,* 111–120.

Iwata, B. A., Dorsey, M. F., Slifer, K. J., Bauman, K. E., & Richman, G. S. (1982). Toward a functional analysis of self-injury. *Analysis and Intervention in Developmental Disabilities, 2,* 3–20.

Iwata, B. A., Pace, G. M., Kalsher, M. J., Cowdery, G. E., & Cataldo, M. F. (1990). Experimental analysis and extinction of self-injurious escape behavior. *Journal of Applied Behavior Analysis, 23,* 11–27.

Iwata, B. A., Vollmer, T. R., & Zarcone, J. R. (1990). The experimental (functional) analysis of behavior disorders: Methodology, applications, and limitations. In A. C. Repp & N. N. Singh (Eds.), *Perspectives on the use of nonaversive and aversive interventions for persons with developmental disabilities* (pp. 301–330). Sycamore, IL: Sycamore.

Jackson, D. A., & Wallace, R. F. (1974). The modification and generalization of voice loudness in a 15-year-old retarded girl. *Journal of Applied Behavior Analysis, 7,* 461–471.

Jacobs, G. D., Benson, H., & Friedman, R. (1993). Home-based central nervous system assessment of a multifactor behavioral intervention for chronic sleep-onset insomnia. *Behavior Therapy, 24,* 159–174.

Jacobs, H. E., Fairbanks, D., Poche, C. E., & Bailey, J. S. (1982). Multiple incentives in encouraging car pool information on a university campus. *Journal of Applied Behavior Analysis, 15,* 141–149.

Jacobson, N. S., & Revenstorf, D. (1988). Statistics for assessing the clinical significance of psychotherapy techniques: Issues, problems, and new developments. *Behavioral Assessment, 10,* 133–145.

James, J. E. (1981). Behavioral self-control of stuttering using time out from speaking. *Journal of Applied Behavior Analysis, 14,* 25–37.

James, S. D., & Egel, A. L. (1986). A direct prompting strategy for increasing reciprocal interactions between handicapped and nonhandicapped siblings. *Journal of Applied Behavior Analysis, 19,* 173–186.

Jason, L. A., & Liotta, R. (1982). Pedestrian jaywalking under facilitating and nonfacilitating conditions. *Journal of Applied Behavior Analysis, 15,* 469–473.

Jason, L. A., Neal, A. M., & Marinakis, G. (1985). Altering contingencies to facilitate compliance with traffic light systems. *Journal of Applied Behavior Analysis, 18,* 95–100.

Jay, S. M., Elliot, C. H., Katz, E., & Siegel, S. E. (1987). Cognitive-behavioral and pharmacologic interventions for children's distress during painful medical procedures. *Journal of Consulting and Clinical Psychology, 55,* 860–865.

Jessor, R., Donovan, J. E., & Costa, F. M. (1991). *Beyond adolescence: Problem behavior and young adult development.* Cambridge, England: Cambridge University Press.

Johnson, M. S., & Bailey, J. S. (1977). The modification of leisure behavior in a halfway house for retarded women. *Journal of Applied Behavior Analysis, 10,* 273–282.

Jones, M. C. (1924). A laboratory study of fear: The case of Peter. *Pedagogical Seminary, 31,* 308–315.

Jones, R. R., Weinrott, M. R., & Howard, J. R. (1981, June). *The national evaluation of the teaching family model.* Final report to the National Institute of Mental Health, Center for Studies in Crime and Delinquency. Washington, D. C.

Jones, R. T., Kazdin, A. E., & Haney, J. I. (1981). Social validation and training of emergency fire safety skills for potential injury prevention and life-saving. *Journal of Applied Behavior Analysis, 14,* 249–260.

Jones, R. T., Nelson, R. E., & Kazdin, A. E. (1977). The role of external variables in self-reinforcement: A review. *Behavior Modification, 1,* 147–178.

Jones, R. T., Sisson, L. A., & Van Hasselt, V. B. (1984). Emergency fire-safety skills for blind children and adolescents: Group training and generalization. *Behavior Modification, 8,* 267–286.

Kallman, W. H., Hersen, M., & O'Toole, D. H. (1975). The use of social reinforcement in a case of conversion reaction. *Behavior Therapy, 6,* 411–413.

Kanfer, F. H. (1977). The many faces of self-control, or behavior modification changes its focus. In R. B. Stuart (Ed.), *Behavioral self-management: Strategies, techniques, and outcomes* (pp. 1–48). New York: Brunner/Mazel.

Kanfer, F. H., Karoly, P., & Newman, A. (1975). Reduction of children's fear of the dark by competence-related and situational threat-related verbal cues. *Journal of Consulting and Clinical Psychology, 43,* 251–258.

Karasu, T. B. (1985, March 1). Personal communication.

Karoly, P., & Kanfer, F. H. (Eds.). (1982). *Self-management and behavior change: From theory to practice.* Elmsford, NY: Pergamon Press.

Kazdin, A. E. (1971). The effect of response cost in suppressing behavior in a pre-psychotic retardate. *Journal of Behavior Therapy and Experimental Psychiatry, 2,* 137–140.

Kazdin, A. E. (1972). Response cost: The removal of conditioned reinforcers for therapeutic change. *Behavior Therapy, 3,* 533–546.

Kazdin, A. E. (1973a). Role of instructions and reinforcement in behavior changes in token reinforcement programs. *Journal of Educational Psychology, 64,* 63–71.

Kazdin, A. E. (1973b). The effect of vicarious reinforcement on attentive behavior in the classroom. *Journal of Applied Behavior Analysis, 6,* 71–78.

Kazdin, A. E. (1974). Self-monitoring and behavior change. In M. J. Mahoney & C. E. Thoresen (Eds.), *Self-control: Power to the person* (pp. 218–246). Pacific Grove, CA: Brooks/Cole.

Kazdin, A. E. (1977a). *The token economy: A review and evaluation.* New York: Plenum.

Kazdin, A. E. (1977b). Artifact, bias, and complexity of assessment: The ABC's of reliability. *Journal of Applied Behavior Analysis, 10,* 141–150.

Kazdin, A. E. (1977c). Assessing the clinical or applied importance of behavior change through social validation. *Behavior Modification, 1,* 427–452.

Kazdin, A. E. (1977d). Vicarious reinforcement and direction of behavior change in the classroom. *Behavior Therapy, 8,* 57–63.

Kazdin, A. E. (1978). *History of behavior modification: Experimental foundations of contemporary research.* Baltimore: University Park Press.

Kazdin, A. E. (1979a). Vicarious reinforcement and punishment in operant programs for children. *Child Behavior Therapy, 1,* 13–36.

Kazdin, A. E. (1979b). Unobtrusive measures in behavioral assessment. *Journal of Applied Behavior Analysis, 12,* 713–724.

Kazdin, A. E. (1980a). Acceptability of time out from reinforcement procedures for disruptive child behavior. *Behavior Therapy, 11,* 329–344.

Kazdin, A. E. (1980b). Acceptability of alternative treatments for deviant child behavior. *Journal of Applied Behavior Analysis, 13,* 259–273.

Kazdin, A. E. (1981a). Behavior modification in education: Contributions and limitations. *Developmental Review, 1,* 34–57.

Kazdin, A. E. (1981b). Acceptability of child treatment techniques: The influence of treatment efficacy and adverse side effects. *Behavior Therapy, 12,* 493–506.

Kazdin, A. E. (1982a). Symptom substitution, generalization, and response covariation: Implications for psychotherapy outcome. *Psychological Bulletin, 91,* 349–365.

Kazdin, A. E. (1982b). Observer effects: Reactivity of direct observation. *New Directions for Methodology of Social and Behavioral Science, 14,* 5–19.

Kazdin, A. E. (1982c). *Single-case research designs: Methods for clinical and applied settings.* New York: Oxford University Press.

Kazdin, A. E. (1982d). The token economy: A decade later. *Journal of Applied Behavior Analysis, 15,* 431–445.

Kazdin, A. E. (1983). Failure of persons to respond to the token economy. In E. B. Foa & P. M. G. Emmelkamp (Eds.), *Failures in behavior therapy* (pp. 335–354). New York: Wiley.

Kazdin, A. E. (1984). Covert modeling. In P. C. Kendall (Ed.), *Advances in cognitive-behavioral research and therapy* (Vol. 3, pp. 103–129). New York: Academic Press.

Kazdin, A. E. (1985a). *Treatment of antisocial behavior in children and adolescents.* Pacific Grove, CA: Brooks/Cole.

Kazdin, A. E. (1985b). Selection of target behaviors: The relationship of the treatment focus to clinical dysfunction. *Behavioral Assessment, 7,* 33–47.

Kazdin, A. E. (1987a). *Conduct disorder in childhood and adolescence.* Newbury Park, CA: Sage.

Kazdin, A. E. (1987b). Treatment of antisocial behavior in children: Current status and future directions. *Psychological Bulletin, 102,* 187–203.

Kazdin, A. E. (1988). *Child psychotherapy: Developing and identifying effective treatments.* New York: Pergamon Press.

Kazdin, A. E. (1992). *Research design in clinical psychology* (2nd ed.). Needham Heights, MA: Allyn & Bacon.

Kazdin, A. E. (1993a). Evaluation in clinical practice: Clinically sensitive and systematic methods of treatment delivery. *Behavior Therapy, 24,* 11–45.

Kazdin, A. E. (1993b). Treatment of conduct disorder: Progress and directions in psychotherapy research. *Development and Psychopathology, 5,* 277–310.

Kazdin, A. E. (in press). Informant variability in assessment. In W. M. Reynolds & H. Johnston (Eds.), *Handbook of depression of children and adolescents.* New York: Plenum.

Kazdin, A. E., Bass, D., Ayers, W. A., & Rodgers, A. (1990). Empirical and clinical focus of child and adolescent psychotherapy research. *Journal of Consulting and Clinical Psychology, 58,* 729–740.

Kazdin, A. E., Bass, D., Siegel, T., & Thomas, C. (1989). Cognitive-behavioral therapy and relationship therapy in the treatment of children referred for antisocial behavior. *Journal of Consulting and Clinical Psychology, 57,* 522–535.

Kazdin, A. E., & Cole, P. M. (1981). Attitudes and labeling biases toward behavior modification: The effects of labels, content, and jargon. *Behavior Therapy, 12,* 56–68.

Kazdin, A. E., Esveldt-Dawson, K., French, N. H., & Unis, A. S. (1987). Problem-solving skills training and relationship therapy in the treatment of antisocial child behavior. *Journal of Consulting and Clinical Psychology, 55,* 76–85.

Kazdin, A. E., French, N. H., & Sherick, R. B. (1981). Acceptability of alternative treatments for children: Evaluations by inpatient children, parents, and staff. *Journal of Consulting and Clinical Psychology, 49,* 900–907.

Kazdin, A. E., French, N. H., Unis, A. S., Esveldt-Dawson, K., & Sherick, R. B. (1983). Hopelessness, depression, and suicidal intent among psychiatrically disturbed inpatient children. *Journal of Consulting and Clinical Psychology, 51,* 504–510.

Kazdin, A. E., & Geesey, S. (1977). Simultaneous-treatment design comparisons of the effects of earning reinforcers for one's peers versus for oneself. *Behavior Therapy, 8,* 682–693.

Kazdin, A. E., & Klock, J. (1973). The effect of nonverbal teacher approval on student attentive behavior. *Journal of Applied Behavior Analysis, 6,* 643–654.

Kazdin, A. E., & Mascitelli, S. (1980). The opportunity to earn oneself off a token system as a reinforcer for attentive behavior. *Behavior Therapy, 11,* 68–78.

Kazdin, A. E., & Moyer, W. (1976). Training teachers to use behavior modification. In S. Yen & R. W. McIntire (Eds.), *Training behavior modification* (pp. 171–200). Kalamazoo: Behaviordelia.

Kazdin, A. E., & Polster, R. (1973). Intermittent token reinforcement and response maintenance in extinction. *Behavior Therapy, 4,* 386–391.

Kazdin, A. E., Siegel, T., & Bass, D. (1992). Cognitive problem-solving skills training and parent management training in the treatment of antisocial behavior in children. *Journal of Consulting and Clinical Psychology, 60,* 733–747.

Kazdin, A. E., Silverman, N. A., & Sittler, J. L. (1975). The use of prompts to enhance vicarious effects of nonverbal approval. *Journal of Applied Behavior Analysis, 8,* 279–286.

Kelly, J. A., & Drabman, R. S. (1977). Overcorrection: An effective procedure that failed. *Journal of Clinical Child Psychology, 6,* 38–40.

Kelly, J. A., & Murphy, D. A. (1992). Psychological interventions with AIDS and HIV: Prevention and treatment. *Journal of Consulting and Clinical Psychology, 60,* 576–585.

Kelly, J. A., St. Lawrence, J. S., Hood, H. V., & Brasfield, T. L. (1989). Behavioral intervention to reduce AIDS risk activities. *Journal of Consulting and Clinical Psychology, 57,* 60–67.

Kendall, P. C. (Ed.). (1991). *Child and adolescent therapy: Cognitive-behavioral procedures.* New York: Guilford.

Kendall, P. C., & Braswell, L. (1993). *Cognitive behavioral therapy for impulsive children* (2nd ed.). New York: Guilford.

Kettlewell, P. S., Mizes, J. S., & Wasylyshyn, N. A. (1992). A cognitive-behavioral group treatment of bulimia. *Behavior Therapy, 23,* 657–670.

Kiecolt-Glaser, J. K., & Glaser, R. (1992). Psychoneuroimmunology: Can psychological interventions modulate immunity? *Journal of Consulting and Clinical Psychology, 60,* 569–575.

King, G. F., Armitage, S. G., & Tilton, J. R. (1960). A therapeutic approach to schizophrenics of extreme pathology: An operant-interpersonal method. *Journal of Abnormal and Social Psychology, 61,* 276–286.

Kinkade, K. (1973). *A Walden Two experiment: The first five years of Twin Oaks Community.* New York: Morrow.

Kirby, F. D., & Shields, F. (1972). Modification of arithmetic response rate and attending behavior in a seventh-grade student. *Journal of Applied Behavior Analysis, 5,* 79–84.

Kirigin, K. A., Braukmann, C. J., Atwater, J. D., & Wolf, M. M. (1982). An evaluation of teaching-family (Achievement Place) group homes for juvenile offenders. *Journal of Applied Behavior Analysis, 15,* 1–16.

Kirigin, K. A., Wolf, M. M., Braukmann, C. J., Fixsen, D. L., & Phillips, E. L. (1979). Achievement Place: A preliminary outcome evaluation. In J. S. Stumphauzer (Ed.), *Progress in behavior therapy with delinquents.* Springfield, IL: Charles C Thomas.

Koegel, R. L., O'Dell, M. C., & Koegel, L. K. (1987). A natural language teaching paradigm for nonverbal autistic children. *Journal of Autism and Developmental Disorders, 17,* 187–200.

Koegel, R. L., & Rincover, A. (1974). Treatment of psychotic children in a classroom environment: 1. Learning in a large group. *Journal of Applied Behavior Analysis, 7,* 45–59.

Kohlberg, L., Yaeger, H., & Hjerthuim, E. (1968). Private speech: Four studies and a review of theories. *Child Development, 39,* 691–736.

Kohler, F. W., & Greenwood, C. R. (1990). Effects of collateral peer supportive behaviors within the classwide peer tutoring program. *Journal of Applied Behavior Analysis, 23,* 307–322.

Kohler, F. W., & Strain, P. S. (1990). Peer-assisted interventions: Early promises, notable achievements, and future aspirations. *Clinical Psychology Review, 10,* 441–452.

Konarski, E. A., Johnson, M. R., Crowell, C. R., & Whitman, T. L. (1981). An alternative approach to reinforcement for applied researchers: Response deprivation. *Behavior Therapy, 12,* 653–666.

Krantz, P. J., & Risley, T. R. (1977). Behavioral ecology in the classroom. In K. D. O'Leary & S. G. O'Leary (Eds.), *Classroom management: The successful use of behavior modification* (pp. 349–366). New York: Pergamon Press.

Kunkel, J. H. (1987). The future of JABA: A comment. *Journal of Applied Behavior Analysis, 20,* 329–334.

Lancioni, G. E. (1982). Normal children as tutors to teach social responses to withdrawn mentally retarded schoolmates: Training, maintenance, and generalization. *Journal of Applied Behavior Analysis, 15,* 17–40.

Landrum, T. J., & Lloyd, J. W. (1992). Generalization in social behavior research with children and youth who have emotional or behavioral problems. *Behavior Modification, 16,* 593–616.

Lattal, K. A. (1969). Contingency management of toothbrushing behavior in a summer camp for children. *Journal of Applied Behavior Analysis, 2,* 195–198.

Lattal, K. A. (Guest Ed.). (1992). Special issue: Reflections on B. F. Skinner and psychology. *American Psychologist, 47,* 1269–1533.

LaVigna, G. W., & Donnellan, A. M. (1986). *Alternatives to punishment: Solving behavior problems with non-aversive strategies.* New York: Irvington.

LeBlanc, J. M., Busby, K. H., & Thomson, C. L. (1974). The functions of time out for changing the aggressive behaviors of a preschool child: A multiple-baseline analysis. In R. Ulrich, T. Stachnik, & J. Mabry (Eds.), *Control of human behavior* (Vol. 3). Glenview, IL: Scott, Foresman.

Lennox, D. B., Miltenberger, R. G., & Donnelly, D. R. (1987). Response interruption and DRL for the reduction of rapid eating. *Journal of Applied Behavior Analysis, 20,* 279–284.

Lennox, D. B., Miltenberger, R. G., Spengler, P., & Erfanian, N. (1988). Decelerative treatment practices with persons who have mental retardation: A review of five years of the literature. *American Journal on Mental Retardation, 92,* 492–501.

Liberman, R. P., Teigen, J., Patterson, R., & Baker, V. (1973). Reducing delusional speech in chronic, paranoid schizophrenics. *Journal of Applied Behavior Analysis, 6,* 57–64.

Lichstein, K. L. (1988). *Clinical relaxation strategies.* New York: Wiley.

Lindsley, O. R. (1956). Operant conditioning methods applied to research in chronic schizophrenia. *Psychiatric Research Reports, 24,* 289–291.

Lindsley, O. R. (1960). Characteristics of the behavior of chronic psychotics as revealed by free-operant conditioning methods. *Diseases of the Nervous System* (Monograph Supplement), *21*, 66–78.

Linscheid, T. R., & Cunningham, C. E. (1977). A controlled demonstration of the effectiveness of electric shock in the elimination of chronic infant rumination. *Journal of Applied Behavior Analysis, 10*, 500.

Linscheid, T. R., Iwata, B. A., Ricketts, R. W., Williams, D. E., & Griffin, J. C. (1990). Clinical evaluation of the self-injurious behavior inhibiting system (SIBIS). *Journal of Applied Behavior Analysis, 23*, 53–78.

Linscheid, T. R., & Meinhold, P. (1990). The controversy over aversives: Basic operant research and the side effects of punishment. In A. C. Repp & N. N. Singh (Eds.), *Perspectives on the use of nonaversive and aversive interventions for persons with developmental disabilities* (pp. 435–450). Sycamore, IL: Sycamore.

Lombard, D., Neubauer, T. E., Canfield, D., & Winett, R. A. (1991). Behavioral community intervention to reduce the risk of skin cancer. *Journal of Applied Behavior Analysis, 24*, 677–686.

Lovaas, O. I. (1987). Behavioral treatment and normal educational/intellectual functioning in young autistic children. *Journal of Consulting and Clinical Psychology, 55*, 3–9.

Lovaas, O. I., Koegel, R. L., Simmons, J. Q., & Long, J. S. (1973). Some generalization and follow-up measures on autistic children in behavior therapy. *Journal of Applied Behavior Analysis, 6*, 131–166.

Lovaas, O. I., & Simmons, J. Q. (1969). Manipulation of self-destruction in three retarded children. *Journal of Applied Behavior Analysis, 2*, 143–157.

Lowe, C. F., & Chadwick, P. D. J. (1990). Verbal control of delusions. *Behavior Therapy, 21*, 461–479.

Lowe, K., & Lutzker, J. R. (1979). Increasing compliance to a medical regimen with a juvenile diabetic. *Behavior Therapy, 10*, 57–64.

Luce, S. C., Delquadri, J., & Hall, R. V. (1980). Contingent exercise: A mild but powerful procedure for suppressing inappropriate verbal and aggressive behavior. *Journal of Applied Behavior Analysis, 13*, 583–594.

Luce, S. C., & Hall, R. V. (1981). Contingent exercise: A procedure used with differential reinforcement to reduce bizarre verbal behavior. *Education and Treatment of Children, 4*, 309–327.

Ludwig, T. D., & Geller, E. S. (1991). Improving the driving practices of pizza deliverers: Response generalization and moderating effects of driving history. *Journal of Applied Behavior Analysis, 24*, 32–44.

Lyons, L. C., & Woods, P. J. (1991). The efficacy of rational-emotive therapy: A quantitative review of the outcome research. *Clinical Psychology Review, 11*, 357–369.

MacPherson, E. M., Candee, B. L., & Hohman, R. J. (1974). A comparison of three methods for eliminating disruptive lunchroom behavior. *Journal of Applied Behavior Analysis, 7*, 287–297.

Madsen, C. H., Becker, W. C., & Thomas, D. R. (1968). Rules, praise, and ignoring: Elements of elementary classroom control. *Journal of Applied Behavior Analysis, 1*, 139–150.

Madsen, C. H., Becker, W. C., Thomas, D. R., Koser, L., & Plager, E. (1970). An analysis of the reinforcing function of "sit down" commands. In R. K. Parker (Ed.), *Readings in educational psychology* (pp. 265–278). Boston: Allyn & Bacon.

Mahoney, K., Van Wagenen, R. K., & Meyerson, L. (1971). Toilet training of normal and retarded children. *Journal of Applied Behavior Analysis, 4*, 173–181.

Maloney, K. B., & Hopkins, B. L. (1973). The modification of sentence structure and its relationship to subjective judgments of creativity in writing. *Journal of Applied Behavior Analysis, 6,* 425–433.

Mank, D. M., & Horner, R. H. (1987). Self-recruited feedback: A cost-effective procedure for maintaining behavior. *Research in Developmental Disabilities, 8,* 91–112.

Manne, S. L., Redd, W. H., Jacobsen, P. B., Gorfinkle, K., Schorr, O., & Rapkin, B. (1990). Behavioral intervention to reduce child and parent distress during venipuncture. *Journal of Consulting and Clinical Psychology, 58,* 565–572.

Mansdorf, I. J. (1977). Reinforcer isolation: An alternative to subject isolation in time out from positive reinforcement. *Journal of Behavior Therapy and Experimental Psychiatry, 8,* 391–393.

Marchand-Martella, N. E., Martella, R. C., Agran, M., Salzberg, C. L., Young, K. R., & Morgan, D. (1992). Generalized effects of a peer-delivered first aid program for students with moderate intellectual disabilities. *Journal of Applied Behavior Analysis, 25,* 841–851.

Marholin, D., II, & Gray, D. (1976). Effects of group response cost procedures on cash shortages in a small business. *Journal of Applied Behavior Analysis, 9,* 25–30.

Marholin, D., II, & Townsend, N. M. (1978). An experimental analysis of side effects and response maintenance of a modified overcorrection procedure: The case of a persistent twiddler. *Behavior Therapy, 9,* 383–390.

Marks, I. M. (1987). *Fears, phobias, and rituals.* New York: Oxford University Press.

Marshall, W. L., Presse, L., & Andrews, W. R. (1976). A self-administered program for public speaking anxiety. *Behaviour Research and Therapy, 14,* 33–40.

Mathews, R. M., & Dix, M. (1992). Behavior change in the funny papers: Feedback to cartoonists on safety belt use. *Journal of Applied Behavior Analysis, 25,* 769–775.

Matson, J. L. (1983). Exploration of phobic behavior in a small child. *Journal of Behavior Therapy and Experimental Psychiatry, 14,* 257–259.

Matson, J. L., & Ollendick, T. H. (1977). Issues in toilet training normal children. *Behavior Therapy, 8,* 549–553.

Matson, J. L., & Taras, M. E. (1989). A 20-year review of punishment and alternative methods to treat problem behaviors in developmentally disabled persons. *Research in Developmental Disabilities, 10,* 85–104.

Mayhew, G. L., & Harris, F. C. (1978). Some negative side effects of a punishment procedure for stereotyped behavior. *Journal of Behavior Therapy and Experimental Psychiatry, 9,* 245–251.

McClannahan, L. E., McGee, G. G., MacDuff, G. S., & Krantz, P. J. (1990). Assessing and improving child care: A personal appearance index for children with autism. *Journal of Applied Behavior Analysis, 23,* 469–482.

McClannahan, L. E., & Risley, T. R. (1975). Design of living environments for nursing-home residents: Increasing participation in recreation activities. *Journal of Applied Behavior Analysis, 8,* 261–268.

McConaghy, N. (1990). Sexual deviation. In A. S. Bellack, M. Hersen, & A. E. Kazdin (Eds.), *International handbook of behavior modification and therapy* (2nd ed., pp. 565–580). New York: Plenum.

McEachin, J. J., Smith, T., & Lovaas, O. I. (1993). Outcome in adolescence of autistic children receiving early intensive behavior treatment. *American Journal of Mental Retardation.*

McGee, G. G., Almeida, M. C., Sulzer-Azaroff, & Feldman, R. S. (1992). Prompting reciprocal interactions via peer incidental teaching. *Journal of Applied Behavior Analysis, 25,* 117–126.

McGrady, A., & Gerstenmaier, L. (1990). Effect of biofeedback assisted relaxation training on blood glucose levels in a Type I insulin dependent diabetic: A case report. *Journal of Behavior Therapy and Experimental Psychiatry, 21,* 69–75.

McMahon, R. J., & Forehand, R. (1978). Nonprescription behavior therapy: Effectiveness of a brochure in teaching mothers to correct their children's inappropriate mealtime behaviors. *Behavior Therapy, 9,* 814–820.

McNees, M. P., Egli, D. S., Marshall, D. S., Schnelle, R. S., Schnelle, J. F., & Risley, T. R. (1976). Shoplifting prevention: Providing information through signs. *Journal of Applied Behavior Analysis, 9,* 399–405.

McNeil, C. B., Eyberg, S., Eisenstadt, T. H., Newcomb, K., & Funderburk, B. (1991). Parent-child interaction therapy with behavior problem children: Generalization of treatment effects to the school setting. *Journal of Clinical Child Psychology, 20,* 140–151.

McReynolds, W. T., & Church, A. (1973). Self-control study skills development and counseling approaches to the improvement of study behavior. *Behaviour Research and Therapy, 11,* 233–235.

Meichenbaum, D. H. (1985). *Stress inoculation training.* Elmsford, NY: Pergamon Press.

Meichenbaum, D. H., & Goodman, J. (1971). Training impulsive children to talk to themselves: A means of developing self-control. *Journal of Abnormal Psychology, 77,* 115–126.

Meyers, A. (Ed.). (1991). Mini-series on: Cognitive behavioral contributions to sport psychology. *Behavior Therapy, 22,* 305–392.

Miller, G. E., & Prinz, R. J. (1990). Enhancement of social learning family interventions for child conduct disorder. *Psychological Bulletin, 108,* 291–307.

Miller, P. M. (1972). The use of behavioral contracting in the treatment of alcoholism: A case report. *Behavior Therapy, 3,* 593–596.

Miller, W. R. (1977). Behavioral self-control training in the treatment of problem drinkers. In R. B. Stuart (Ed.), *Behavioral self-management: Strategies, techniques, and outcomes* (pp. 154–175). New York: Brunner/Mazel.

Mirman, R. (1982). Performance management in sales organizations. In L. W. Frederiksen (Ed.), *Handbook of organizational behavior management.* New York: Wiley.

Mitchell, W. S., & Stoffelmayr, B. E. (1973). Application of the Premack principle to the behavioral control of extremely inactive schizophrenics. *Journal of Applied Behavior Analysis, 6,* 419–423.

Morin, C., Ladouceur, R., & Cloutier, R. (1982). Reinforcement procedure in the treatment of reluctant speech. *Journal of Behavior Therapy and Experimental Psychiatry, 13,* 145–147.

Morris, E. K., & Redd, W. H. (1975). Children's performance and social preference for positive, negative, and mixed adult-child interactions. *Child Development, 46,* 525–531.

Mowrer, O. H., & Mowrer, W. M. (1938). Enuresis: A method for its study and treatment. *American Journal of Orthopsychiatry, 8,* 436–459.

Murphy, H. A., Hutchison, J. M., & Bailey, J. S. (1983). Behavioral school psychology goes outdoors: The effect of organized games on playground aggression. *Journal of Applied Behavior Analysis, 16,* 29–36.

Nakano, K. (1990). Operant self-control procedure in modifying Type A behavior. *Journal of Behavior Therapy and Experimental Psychiatry, 21,* 249–255.

Neef, N. A., Iwata, B. A., & Page, T. J. (1978). Public transportation training: In vivo versus classroom instruction. *Journal of Applied Behavior Analysis, 11,* 331–344.

Neef, N. A., Lensbower, J., Hockersmith, I., DePalma, V., & Gray, K. (1990). In vivo versus simulation training: An interactional analysis of range and type of training exemplars. *Journal of Applied Behavior Analysis, 23,* 447–458.

Neef, N. A., Mace, F. C., Shea, M. C., & Shade, D. (1992). Effects of reinforcer rate and reinforcer quality on time allocation: Extensions of matching theory to educational settings. *Journal of Applied Behavior Analysis, 25,* 691–699.

Neisworth, J. T., & Moore, F. (1972). Operant treatment of asthmatic responding with the parent as therapist. *Behavior Therapy, 3,* 95–99.

Nelson, G., & Carson, P. (1988). Evaluation of a social problem-solving skills program for third- and fourth-grade students. *American Journal of Community Psychology, 16,* 79–99.

Nelson, R. O., & Hayes, S. C. (1981). Theoretical explanations for reactivity in self-monitoring. *Behavior Modification, 5,* 3–14.

Nelson, R. O., & Hayes, S. C. (Eds.). (1986). *Conceptual foundations of behavioral assessment.* New York: Guilford.

Nelton, S. (1988, March). Motivating for success. *Nation's Business, 76,* 18–26.

New Tool: "Reinforcement" for good work. (1971, December 18). *Business Week,* pp. 76–77.

Nezu, A. M., & Nezu, C. M. (Eds.). (1989). *Clinical decision making in behavior therapy: A problem-solving perspective.* Champaign, IL: Research Press.

Nezu, A. M., & Perri, M. G. (1989). Social problem-solving therapy for unipolar depresssion: An initial dismantling investigation. *Journal of Consulting and Clinical Psychology, 57,* 408–413.

Ninness, H. A. C., Fuerst, J., Rutherford, R. D., & Glenn, S. S. (1991). Effects of self-management training and reinforcement on the transfer of improved conduct in the absence of supervision. *Journal of Applied Behavior Analysis, 24,* 499–508.

Nordyke, N. S., Baer, D. M., Etzel, B. C., & LeBlanc, J. M. (1977). Implications of the stereotyping and modification of sex role. *Journal of Applied Behavior Analysis, 10,* 553–557.

Novaco, R. W. (1979). The cognitive regulation of anger and stress. In P. C. Kendall & S. D. Hollon (Eds.), *Cognitive-behavioral interventions: Theory, research, and procedures* (pp. 241–285). New York: Academic Press.

Nunes, D. L., Murphy, R. J., & Ruprecht, M. L. (1977). Reducing self-injurious behavior of severely retarded individuals through withdrawal-of-reinforcement procedures. *Behavior Modification, 1,* 499–516.

O'Banion, D. R., & Whaley, D. L. (1981). *Behavior contracting: Arranging contingencies of reinforcement.* New York: Springer.

O'Brien, F., Azrin, N. H., & Bugle, C. (1972). Training profoundly retarded children to stop crawling. *Journal of Applied Behavior Analysis, 5,* 131–137.

O'Brien, F., Bugle, C., & Azrin, N. H. (1972). Training and maintaining a retarded child's proper eating. *Journal of Applied Behavior Analysis, 5,* 67–72.

O'Brien, S., & Karsh, K. G. (1990). Treatment acceptability: Consumer, therapist, and society. In A. C. Repp & N. N. Singh (Eds.), *Perspectives on the use of nonaversive and aversive interventions for persons with developmental disabilities* (pp. 503–516). Sycamore, IL: Sycamore.

O'Brien, S., & Repp, A. C. (in press). A review of 30 years of research on the use of differential reinforcement to reduce inappropriate responding. *Behavior Modification.*

O'Brien, T. P., Riner, L. S., & Budd, K. S. (1983). The effects of a child's self-evaluation program on compliance with parental instructions in the home. *Journal of Applied Behavior Analysis, 16,* 69–79.

O'Leary, K. D., & Wilson, G. T. (1987). *Behavior therapy: Application and outcome* (2nd ed.). Englewood Cliffs, NJ: Prentice-Hall.

Ollendick, T. H., Hagopian, L. P., & Huntzinger, R. M. (1991). Cognitive-behavior therapy with nighttime fearful children. *Journal of Behavior Therapy and Experimental Psychiatry, 22,* 113–121.

Ollendick, T. H., Shapiro, E. S., & Barrett, R. P. (1981). Reducing stereotypic behaviors: An analysis of treatment procedures using an alternating-treatments design. *Behavior Therapy, 12,* 570–577.

O'Neill, R. E., Horner, R. H., Albin, R. W., Storey, K., & Sprague, J. R. (1990). *Functional analysis of problem behavior: A practical assessment guide.* Sycamore, IL: Sycamore.

O'Reilly, M. F., Green, G., & Braunling-McMorrow, D. (1990). Self-administered written prompts to teach home accident prevention skills to adults with brain injuries. *Journal of Applied Behavior Analysis, 23,* 431–446.

Pace, G. M., Iwata, B. A., Edwards, G. L., & McCosh, K. C. (1986). Stimulus fading and transfer in the treatment of self-restraint and self-injurious behavior. *Journal of Applied Behavior Analysis, 19,* 381–389.

Page, T. J., Iwata, B. A., & Neef, N. A. (1976). Teaching pedestrian skills to retarded persons: Generalization from the classroom to the natural environment. *Journal of Applied Behavior Analysis, 9,* 433–444.

Paine, S. C., Hops, H., Walker, H. M., Greenwood, C. R., Fleischman, D. H., & Guild, J. J. (1982). Repeated treatment effects: A study of maintaining behavior change in socially withdrawn children. *Behavior Modification, 6,* 171–199.

Parrish, J. M., Cataldo, M. F., Kolko, D. J., Neef, N. A., & Egel, A. L. (1986). Experimental analysis of response covariation among compliant and inappropriate behaviors. *Journal of Applied Behavior Analysis, 19,* 241–254.

Parsons, M. B., Schepis, M. M., Reid, D. H., McCarn, J. E., & Green, C. W. (1987). Expanding the impact of behavioral staff management: A large-scale, long-term application in schools serving severely handicapped persons. *Journal of Applied Behavior Analysis, 20,* 139–150.

Patterson, G. R. (1982). *Coercive family process.* Eugene, OR: Castalia.

Patterson, G. R., Reid, J. B., & Dishion, T. J. (1992). *Antisocial boys.* Eugene, OR: Castalia.

Paul, G. L., & Lentz, R. J. (1977). *Psychosocial treatment of chronic mental patients: Milieu versus social learning program.* Cambridge: Harvard University Press.

Peacock, R., Lyman, R. D., & Rickard, H. C. (1978). Correspondence between self-report and observer-report as a function of task difficulty. *Behavior Therapy, 9,* 578–583.

Peck, C. A., Apolloni, T., Cooke, T. P., Raver, S. A. (1978). Teaching retarded preschoolers to initiate the free-play behavior of nonretarded classmates: Trained and generalized effects. *Journal of Special Education, 12,* 195–207.

Peck, C. A., Cooke, T. P., & Apolloni, T. (1981). Utilization of peer imitation in therapeutic and instructional contexts. In P. S. Strain (Ed.), *The utilization of classroom peers as behavior change agents* (pp. 69–99). New York: Plenum.

Pedalino, E., & Gamboa, V. U. (1974). Behavior modification and absenteeism:

Intervention in one industrial setting. *Journal of Applied Psychology, 59,* 694–698.

Peniston, E. G., (1988). Evaluation of long-term therapeutic efficacy of behavior modification program with chronic male psychiatric patients. *Journal of Behavior Therapy and Experimental Psychiatry, 19,* 95–101.

Pertschuk, M. J., Edwards, N., & Pomerleau, O. F. (1978). A multiple-baseline approach to behavioral intervention in anorexia nervosa. *Behavior Therapy, 9,* 368–376.

Peterson, L. (1984). Teaching home safety and survival skills to latch-key children: A comparison of two manuals and methods. *Journal of Applied Behavior Analysis, 17,* 279–294.

Pfiffner, L. J., & O'Leary, S. G. (1987). The efficacy of all-positive management as a function of the prior use of negative consequences. *Journal of Applied Behavior Analysis, 20,* 265–271.

Phillips, E. L., Phillips, E. A., Fixsen, D. L., & Wolf, M. M. (1971). Achievement Place: Modification of the behaviors of predelinquent boys within a token economy. *Journal of Applied Behavior Analysis, 4,* 45–59.

Phillips, E. L., Phillips, E. A., Wolf, M. M., & Fixsen, D. L. (1973). Achievement Place: Development of the elected-manager system. *Journal of Applied Behavior Analysis, 6,* 541–561.

Piaget, J. (1928). *Judgment and reasoning of the child.* New York: Harcourt.

Pigott, H. E., Fantuzzo, J. W., & Clement, P. W. (1986). The effects of reciprocal peer tutoring and group contingencies on the academic performance of elementary school children. *Journal of Applied Behavior Analysis, 19,* 93–98.

Pinkston, E. M., Reese, N. M., LeBlanc, J. M., & Baer, D. M. (1973). Independent control of a preschool child's aggression and peer interaction by contingent teacher attention. *Journal of Applied Behavior Analysis, 6,* 115–124.

Plummer, S., Baer, D. M., & LeBlanc, J. M. (1977). Functional considerations in the use of procedural time out and an effective alternative. *Journal of Applied Behavior Analysis, 10,* 689–705.

Poche, C., Brouwer, R., & Swearingen, M. (1981). Teaching self-protection to young children. *Journal of Applied Behavior Analysis, 14,* 169–176.

Poche, C., Yoder, P., & Miltenberger, R. (1988). Teaching self-protection to children using television techniques. *Journal of Applied Behavior Analysis, 21,* 253–261.

Poling, A., & Ryan, C. (1982). Differential-reinforcement-of-other-behavior schedules. *Behavior Modification, 6,* 3–21.

Porterfield, J. K., Herbert-Jackson, E., & Risley, T. R. (1976). Contingent observation: An effective and acceptable procedure for reducing disruptive behavior of young children in a group setting. *Journal of Applied Behavior Analysis, 9,* 55–64.

Praderas, K., & MacDonald, M. L. (1986). Telephone conversational skills training with socially isolated, impaired nursing home residents. *Journal of Applied Behavior Analysis, 19,* 337–348.

Premack, D. (1965). Reinforcement theory. In D. Levine (Ed.), *Nebraska symposium on motivation* (pp. 123–180). Lincoln: University of Nebraska Press.

Puder, R., Lacks, P., Bertelson, A. D., & Storandt, M. (1983). Short-term stimulus control treatment of insomnia in older adults. *Behavior Therapy, 14,* 424–429.

Pyles, D. A. M., & Bailey, J. S. (1990). Diagnosing severe behavior problems. In A. C.

Repp & N. N. Singh (Eds.), *Perspectives on the use of nonaversive interventions for persons with developmental disabilities* (pp. 381–401). Sycamore, IL: Sycamore.

Ragnarsson, R. S., & Björgvinsson, T. (1991). Effects of public posting on driving speed in Icelandic traffic. *Journal of Applied Behavior Analysis, 24,* 53–58.

Rapport, M. D., Murphy, H. A., & Bailey, J. S. (1982). Ritalin versus response cost in the control of hyperactive children: A within-subject comparison. *Journal of Applied Behavior Analysis, 15,* 205–216.

Rasing, E. J., & Duker, P. C. (1992). Effects of a multifaceted training procedure on acquisition and generalization of social behaviors in language-disabled deaf children. *Journal of Applied Behavior Analysis, 25,* 723–734.

Redd, W. H., & Birnbrauer, J. S. (1969). Adults as discriminative stimuli for different reinforcement contingencies with retarded children. *Journal of Experimental Child Psychology, 7,* 440–447.

Redd, W. H., Morris, E. K., & Martin, J. A. (1975). Effects of positive and negative adult-child interactions on children's social preference. *Journal of Experimental Child Psychology, 19,* 153–164.

Reid, D. H., Luyben, P. L., Rawers, F. A., & Bailey, J. S. (1976). The effects of prompting and proximity of containers on newspaper recycling behavior. *Environment and Behavior, 8,* 471–482.

Reisinger, J. J. (1972). Treatment of "anxiety depression" via positive reinforcement and response cost. *Journal of Applied Behavior Analysis, 5,* 125–130.

Reiss, S. (Ed.). (1991). Special issue: Applied learning theory: Research issues for the 1990s. *Clinical Psychology Review, 11,* 123–203.

Rekers, G. A. (1977). Atypical gender development and psychosocial adjustment. *Journal of Applied Behavior Analysis, 10,* 559–571.

Rekers, G. A., & Lovaas, O. I. (1974). Behavioral treatment of deviant sex role behaviors in a male child. *Journal of Applied Behavior Analysis, 7,* 173–190.

Repp, A. C., Felce, D., & Barton, L. E. (1988). Basing the treatment of stereotypic and self-injurious behaviors on hypotheses of their causes. *Journal of Applied Behavior Analysis, 21,* 281–289.

Repp, A. C., & Karsh, K. G. (1990). A taxonomic approach to the nonaversive treatment of maladaptive behavior of persons with developmental disabilities. In A. C. Repp & N. N. Singh (Eds.), *Perspectives on the use of nonaversive and aversive interventions for persons with developmental disabilities.* (pp. 331–347). Sycamore, IL: Sycamore.

Repp, A. C., & Karsh, K. G. (1992). An analysis of a group teaching procedure for persons with developmental disabilities. *Journal of Applied Behavior Analysis, 25,* 701–712.

Repp, A. C., & Singh, N. N. (Eds.). (1990). *Perspectives on the use of nonaversive and aversive interventions for persons with developmental disabilities.* Sycamore, IL: Sycamore.

Rescorla, R. A. (1988). Pavlovian conditioning: It's not what you think it is. *American Psychologist, 43,* 151–160.

Resick, P. A., Forehand, R., & McWhorter, A. Q. (1976). The effect of parental treatment with one child on an untreated sibling. *Behavior Therapy, 7,* 544–548.

Resick, P. A., Forehand, R., & Peed, S. (1974). Prestatement of contingencies: The effects on acquisition maintenance of behavior. *Behavior Therapy, 5,* 642–647.

Rilling, M. (1977). Stimulus control and inhibitory processes. In W. K. Honig &

J. E. R. Staddon (Eds.), *Handbook of operant behavior* (pp. 432–480). Englewood Cliffs, NJ: Prentice-Hall.

Riordan, M. M., Iwata, B. A., Finney, J. W., Wohl, M. K., & Stanley, A. E. (1984). Behavioral assessment and treatment of chronic food refusal in handicapped children. *Journal of Applied Behavior Analysis, 17*, 327–342.

Roberts, M. C., & Fanurik, D. (1986). Rewarding elementary school children for their use of safety belts. *Health Psychology, 5*, 185–196.

Roberts, M. W., Hatzenbuehler, L. C., & Bean, A. W. (1981). The effects of differential attention and time out on child noncompliance. *Behavior Therapy, 12*, 93–99.

Roberts, R. M., Nelson, R. O., & Olson, T. W. (1987). Self-instruction: An analysis of the differential effects of instruction and reinforcement. *Journal of Applied Behavior Analysis, 20*, 235–242.

Robertson, S. J., DeReus, D. M., & Drabman, R. S. (1976). Peer and college-student tutoring as reinforcement in a token economy. *Journal of Applied Behavior Analysis, 9*, 169–177.

Robertson, S. J., Simon, S. J., Pachman, J. S., & Drabman, R. S. (1979). Self-control and generalization procedures in a classroom of disruptive retarded children. *Child Behavior Therapy, 1*, 347–362.

Rolider, A., Cummings, A., & Van Houten, R. (1991). Side effects of therapeutic punishment on academic performance and eye contact. *Journal of Applied Behavior Analysis, 24*, 763–773.

Rollings, J. P., Baumeister, A. A., & Baumeister, A. A. (1977). The use of overcorrection procedures to eliminate the stereotyped behaviors of retarded individuals: An analysis of collateral behaviors and generalization of suppressive effects. *Behavior Modification, 1*, 29–46.

Rollins, H. A., McCandless, B. R., Thompson, M., & Brassell, W. R. (1974). Project Success Environment: An extended application of contingency management in inner-city schools. *Journal of Education Psychology, 66*, 167–178.

Ronen, T. (1991). Intervention package for treating sleep disorders in a four-year-old girl. *Journal of Behavior Therapy and Experimental Psychiatry, 22*, 141–148.

Roqué, F. M., & Roberts, M. C. (1989). A replication of the use of public posting in traffic speed control. *Journal of Applied Behavior Analysis, 22*, 325–330.

Rosen, G. M. (1987). Self-help treatment books and the commercialization of psychotherapy. *American Psychologist, 42*, 46–51.

Rosen, G. M., Glasgow, R. E., & Barrera, M., Jr. (1976). A controlled study to assess the clinical efficacy of totally self-administered systematic desensitization. *Journal of Consulting and Clinical Psychology, 44*, 208–217.

Rosen, G. M., Glasgow, R. E., & Barrera, M., Jr. (1977). A two-year follow-up on systematic desensitization with data pertaining to the external validity of laboratory fear assessment. *Journal of Consulting and Clinical Psychology, 45*, 1188–1189.

Rosen, H. S., & Rosen, L. A. (1983). Eliminating stealing: Use of stimulus control with an elementary student. *Behavior Modification, 7*, 56–63.

Ruggles, T. R., & LeBlanc, J. M. (1982). Behavior analysis procedures in classroom teaching. In A. S. Bellack, M. Hersen, & A. E. Kazdin (Eds.), *International handbook of behavior modification and therapy* (pp. 959–996). New York: Plenum.

Russo, D. C., & Koegel, R. L. (1977). A method for integrating an autistic child into a normal public school classroom. *Journal of Applied Behavior Analysis, 10,* 579–590.

Russo, D. C., & Varni, J. W. (Eds.). (1982). *Behavior pediatrics: Research and practice.* New York: Plenum.

Safer, D. J., Heaton, R. C., & Parker, F. C. (1981). A behavioral program for disruptive junior high school students: Results and follow-up. *Journal of Abnormal Child Psychology, 9,* 483–494.

Saigh, P. A. (1986). In vitro flooding in the treatment of a 6-year-old boy's post-traumatic stress disorder. *Behaviour Research and Therapy, 24,* 685–688.

Sajwaj, T., Libert, J., & Agras, W. S. (1974). Lemon juice therapy: The control of life-threatening rumination in a six-month-old infant. *Journal of Applied Behavior Analysis, 7,* 557–563.

Sajwaj, T. E., Twardosz, S., & Burke, M. (1972). Side effects of extinction procedures in a remedial preschool. *Journal of Applied Behavior Analysis, 5,* 163–175.

Salter, A. (1952). *The case against psychoanalysis.* New York: Holt.

Sanders, M. R., & Glynn, T. L. (1977). Functional analysis of a program for training high- and low-preference peers to modify disruptive classroom behavior. *Journal of Applied Behavior Analysis, 10,* 503.

Sanders, M. R., & Glynn, T. L. (1981). Training parents in behavioral self-management: An analysis of generalization and maintenance. *Journal of Applied Behavior Analysis, 14,* 223–237.

Sanders, M. R., Regbetz, M., Morrison, M., Bor, W., Gordon, A., Dadds, M., & Shepherd, R. (1989). Cognitive-behavioral treatment of recurrent nonspecific abdominal pain in children: An analysis of generalization, maintenance, and side effects. *Journal of Consulting and Clinical Psychology, 57,* 294–300.

Sasso, G. M., Reimers, T. M., Cooper, L. J., Wacker, D. P., Berg, W. K., Steege, M., Kelly, L., & Allaire, A. (1992). Use of descriptive and experimental analyses to identify the functional properties of aberrant behavior in school settings. *Journal of Applied Behavior Analysis, 25,* 809–821.

Schepis, M. M., Reid, D. H., & Fitzgerald, J. R. (1987). Group instruction with profoundly retarded persons: Acquisition, generalization, and maintenance of a remunerative work skill. *Journal of Applied Behavior Analysis, 20,* 97–108.

Schloss, P. J., Santoro, C., Wood, C. E., Bedner, M. J. (1988). A comparison of peer-directed and teacher-directed employment interview training for mentally retarded adults. *Journal of Applied Behavioral Analysis, 21,* 97–102.

Schnelle, J. F. (1974). A brief report on invalidity of parent evaluations of behavior change. *Journal of Applied Behavior Analysis, 7,* 341–343.

Schnelle, J. F., Kirchner, R. E., Macrae, J. W., McNees, M. P., Eck, R. H., Snodgrass, S., Casey, J. D., & Uselton, P. H. (1978). Police evaluation research: An experimental and cost-benefit analysis of a helicopter patrol in a high-crime area. *Journal of Applied Behavior Analysis, 11,* 11–21.

Schreibman, L. (1988). *Autism.* Newbury Park, CA: Sage.

Schwartz, I. S., & Baer, D. M. (1991). Social validity assessments: Is current practice state of the art? *Journal of Applied Behavior Analysis, 24,* 189–204.

Seaman, J. E., Greene, B. F., & Watson-Perczel, M. (1986). A behavioral system for assessing and training cardiopulmonary resuscitation skills among emergency medical technicians. *Journal of Applied Behavior Analysis, 19,* 125–136.

Seaver, W. B., & Patterson, A. H. (1976). Decreasing fuel oil consumption through feedback and social commendation. *Journal of Applied Behavior Analysis, 10,* 147–152.

Selinske, J. E., Greer, R. D., & Lodhi, S. (1991). A functional analysis of the comprehensive application of behavior analysis to schooling. *Journal of Applied Behavior Analysis, 24,* 107–117.

Serna, L. A., Schumaker, J. B., Sherman, J. A., & Sheldon, J. B. (1991). *Journal of Applied Behavior Analysis, 24,* 733–746.

Shaffer, D., Vieland, V., Garland, A., Rojas, M., Underwood, M., & Busner, C. (1990). Adolescent suicide attempters: Response to suicide prevention program. *Journal of the American Medical Association, 264,* 3151–3155.

Shapiro, E. S., & Shapiro, S. (1985). Behavioral coaching in the development of skills in track. *Behavior Modification, 9,* 211–224.

Shure, M. B., & Spivack, G. (1982). Interpersonal problem solving in young children: A cognitive approach to prevention. *American Journal of Community Psychology, 10,* 341–356.

Singh, N. N., Dawson, M. J., & Manning, P. (1981). Effects of spaced responding DRL on the stereotyped behavior of profoundly retarded persons. *Journal of Applied Behavior Analysis, 14,* 521–526.

Singh, N. N., Lloyd, J. W., & Kendall, K. A. (1990). Nonaversive and aversive interventions: Issues. In A. C. Repp & N. N. Singh (Eds.), *Perspectives on the use of nonaversive and aversive interventions for persons with developmental disabilities* (pp. 3–16). Sycamore, IL: Sycamore.

Singh, N. N., Watson, J. E., & Winton, A. S. W. (1986). Treating self-injury: Water mist spray versus facial screening or forced arm exercise. *Journal of Applied Behavior Analysis, 19,* 403–410.

Skinner, B. F. (1938). *The behavior of organisms: An experimental analysis.* New York: Appleton-Century.

Skinner, B. F. (1948). *Walden Two.* New York: Macmillan.

Skinner, B. F. (1953). *Science and human behavior.* New York: Free Press.

Skinner, B. F. (1974). *About behaviorism.* New York: Knopf.

Smith, B. M., Schumaker, J. B., Schaeffer, J., & Sherman, J. A. (1982). Increasing participation and improving the quality of discussions in seventh-grade social studies classes. *Journal of Applied Behavior Analysis, 15,* 97–110.

Smith, L. K. C., & Fowler, S. A. (1984). Positive peer pressure: The effects of peer monitoring on children's disruptive behavior. *Journal of Applied Behavior Analysis, 17,* 213–227.

Solnick, J. V., Rincover, A., & Peterson, C. R. (1977). Some determinants of the reinforcing and punishing effects of time out. *Journal of Applied Behavior Analysis, 10,* 415–424.

Solomon, R. L., Kamin, L. J., & Wynne, L. C. (1953). Traumatic avoidance learning: The outcomes of several extinction procedures with dogs. *Journal of Abnormal and Social Psychology, 48,* 291–302.

Sowers-Hoag, K. M., Thyer, B. A., & Bailey, J. S. (1987). Promoting automobile safety belt use by young children. *Journal of Applied Behavioral Analysis, 20,* 133–138.

Spivack, G., Platt, J. J., & Shure, M. B. (1976). *The problem-solving approach to adjustment.* San Francisco: Jossey-Bass.

Spivack, G., & Shure, M. B. (1982). The cognition of social adjustment: Interpersonal cognitive problem-solving thinking. In B. B. Lahey & A. E. Kazdin (Eds.), *Advances in clinical child psychology* (Vol. 5, pp. 323–372). New York: Plenum.

Stahl, J. R., Thomson, L. E., Leitenberg, H., & Hasazi, J. E. (1974). Establishment of praise as a conditioned reinforcer in socially unresponsive psychiatric patients. *Journal of Abnormal Psychology, 83,* 488–496.

Steege, M. W., Wacker, D. P., Cigrand, K. C., Berg, W. K., Novak, C. G., Reimers, T. M., Sasso, G. M., & DeRaad, A. (1990). Use of negative reinforcement in the treatment of self-injurious behavior. *Journal of Applied Behavior Analysis, 23,* 459–467.

Stein, D. J., & Young, J. E. (Eds.). (1992). *Cognitive science and clinical disorders.* San Diego: Academic Press.

Stern, G. W., Fowler, S. A., & Kohler, F. W. (1988). A comparison of two intervention roles: Peer monitor and point earner. *Journal of Applied Behavior Analysis, 21,* 103–109.

Stokes, T. F., & Baer, D. M. (1976). Preschool peers as mutual generalization-facilitating agents. *Behavior Therapy, 7,* 549–556.

Stokes, T. F., & Baer, D. M. (1977). An implicit technology of generalization. *Journal of Applied Behavior Analysis, 10,* 349–367.

Stokes, T. F., Baer, D. M., & Jackson, R. L. (1974). Programming the generalization of a greeting response in four retarded children. *Journal of Applied Behavior Analysis, 7,* 599–610.

Stokes, T. F., & Osnes, P. G. (1989). An operant pursuit of generalization. *Behavior Therapy, 20,* 337–355.

Strain, P. S. (Ed.). (1981). *The utilization of classroom peers as behavior change agents.* New York: Plenum.

Strain, P. S., Shores, R. E., & Kerr, M. M. (1976). An experimental analysis of "spillover" effects on the social interaction of behaviorally handicapped pre-school children. *Journal of Applied Behavior Analysis, 9,* 31–40.

Strain, P. S., Shores, R. E., & Timm, M. A. (1977). Effects of peer social initiations on the behavior of withdrawn preschool children. *Journal of Applied Behavior Analysis, 10,* 289–298.

Stuart, R. B. (1970). *Trick or treatment: How and when psychotherapy fails.* Champaign, IL: Research Press.

Stuart, R. B. (1971). Behavioral contracting with the families of delinquents. *Journal of Behavior Therapy and Experimental Psychiatry, 2,* 1–11.

Stuart, R. B. (Ed.). (1982). *Adherence, compliance, and generalization in behavioral medicine.* New York: Brunner/Mazel.

Sullivan, M. A., & O'Leary, S. G. (1990). Maintenance following reward and cost token programs. *Behavior Therapy, 21,* 139–149.

Sulzer-Azaroff, B., & de Santamaria, C. (1980). Industrial safety hazard reduction through performance feedback. *Journal of Applied Behavior Analysis, 13,* 287–295.

Sulzer-Azaroff, B., Drabman, R. M., Greer, R. D., Hall, R. V., Iwata, B. A., & O'Leary, S. G. (Eds.). (1988). *Behavior analysis in education.* Lawrence, KS: Society for the Experimental Analysis of Behavior.

Sulzer-Azaroff, B., & Mayer, G. R. (1991). *Behavior analysis for lasting change.* Fort Worth: Holt, Rinehart & Winston.

Surwit, R. S., & Keefe, F. J. (1978). Frontalis EMG feedback training: An electronic panacea? *Behavior Therapy, 9,* 779–792.

Swain, J. J., Allard, G. B., & Holborn, S. W. (1982). The good toothbrushing game: A school-based dental hygiene program for increasing the toothbrushing effectiveness of children. *Journal of Applied Behavior Analysis, 15,* 171–176.

Switzer, E. B., Deal, T. E., & Bailey, J. S. (1977). The reduction of stealing in second graders using a group contingency. *Journal of Applied Behavior Analysis, 10,* 267–272.

Tertinger, D. A., Greene, B. F., & Lutzker, J. R. (1984). Home safety: Development and validation of one component of an ecobehavioral treatment program for abused and neglected children. *Journal of Applied Behavior Analysis, 17,* 159–174.

Tharp, R. G. (1991). Cultural diversity and treatment of children. *Journal of Consulting and Clinical Psychology, 59,* 799–812.

Thomas, J. D., Presland, I. E., Grant, M. D., & Glynn, T. L. (1978). Natural rates of teacher approval and disapproval in grade-seven classrooms. *Journal of Applied Behavior Analysis, 11,* 91–94.

Thompson, M., Brassell, W. R., Persons, S., Tucker, R., & Rollins, H. A. (1974). Contingency management in the schools: How often and how well does it work? *American Educational Research Journal, 11,* 19–28.

Timberlake, E. M. (1981). Child abuse and externalized aggression: Preventing a delinquent lifestyle. In R. J. Hunner & Y. E. Walker (Eds.), *Exploring the relationship between child abuse and delinquency.* Montclair, NJ: Allanheld, Osmun.

Timberlake, W., & Allison, J. (1974). Response deprivation: An empirical approach to instrumental performance. *Psychological Review, 81,* 146–164.

Turk, D. C., Meichenbaum, D. H., & Genest, M. (1983). *Pain and behavioral medicine: A cognitive behavioral perspective.* New York: Guilford.

Upper, D. (1973). A "ticket" system for reducing ward rule violations on a token-economy program. *Journal of Behavior Therapy and Experimental Psychiatry, 4,* 137–140.

Van Houten, R. (1988). The effects of advance stop lines and sign prompts on pedestrian safety in a crosswalk on a multilane highway. *Journal of Applied Behavior Analysis, 21,* 245–251.

Van Houten, R., Malenfant, L., & Rolider, A. (1985). Increasing driver yielding and pedestrian signaling with prompting, feedback, and enforcement. *Journal of Applied Behavior Analysis, 18,* 103–110.

Van Houten, R., Nau, P. A., MacKenzie-Keating, S. E., Sameoto, D., & Colavecchia, B. (1982). An analysis of some variables influencing the effectiveness of reprimands. *Journal of Applied Behavior Analysis, 15,* 65–83.

Van Houten, R., Nau, P. A., & Marini, Z. (1980). An analysis of public posting in reducing speeding behavior on an urban highway. *Journal of Applied Behavior Analysis, 13,* 383–395.

Van Houten, R., & Rolider, A. (1989, May). *The side effects of punishment: Does it matter how well punishment is applied? You bet it does!* Paper presented at the 15th annual convention of the Association for Behavior Analysis, Milwaukee.

Van Houten, R., Rolider, A., Nau, P. A., Friedman, R., Becker, M., Chalodovsky, I., & Scherer, M. (1985). Large-scale reductions in speeding and accidents in Canada and Israel: A behavioral ecological perspective. *Journal of Applied Behavior Analysis, 18,* 87–93.

Varni, J. W. (1981). Self-regulation techniques in the management of chronic arthritic pain in hemophilia. *Behavior Therapy, 12,* 185–194.

Vollmer, T. R., & Iwata, B. A. (1991). Establishing operations and reinforcement. *Journal of Applied Behavior Analysis, 24,* 279–291.

Wacker, D. P., McMahon, C., Steege, M., Berg, W. K., Sasso, G., & Melloy, K. (1990). Applications of a sequential alternating treatments design. *Journal of Applied Behavior Analysis, 23,* 333–339.

Wagner, J. L., & Winett, R. A. (1988). Prompting one low-fat, high-fiber selection in a fast-food restaurant. *Journal of Applied Behavior Analysis, 21,* 179–185.

Wahler, R. G. (1975). Some structural aspects of deviant child behavior. *Journal of Applied Behavior Analysis, 8,* 27–42.

Wahler, R. G. (1980). The insular mother: Her problems in a parent-child treatment. *Journal of Applied Behavior Analysis, 13,* 207–219.

Wahler, R. G., & Fox, J. J. (1980). Solitary toy play and time out: A family treatment package for children with aggressive and oppositional behavior. *Journal of Applied Behavior Analysis, 13,* 23–29.

Wahler, R. G., & Fox, J. J. (1981). Setting events in applied behavior analysis: Toward a conceptual and methodological expansion. *Journal of Applied Behavior Analysis, 14,* 327–338.

Walker, H. M., Hops, H., & Fiegenbaum, E. (1976). Deviant classroom behavior as a function of combination of social and token reinforcement and cost contingency. *Behavior Therapy, 7,* 76–88.

Walker, H. M., Hops, H., & Greenwood, C. R. (1981). RECESS: Research and development of a behavior management package for remediating social aggression in the school setting. In P. S. Strain (Ed.), *The utilization of classroom peers as behavior change agents* (pp. 261–303). New York: Plenum.

Walker, H. M., Hops, H., & Johnson, S. M. (1975). Generalization and maintenance of classroom treatment effects. *Behavior Therapy, 6,* 188–200.

Warr, P. (1987). *Work, unemployment, and mental health.* New York: Oxford University Press.

Watson, D. L., & Tharp, R. G. (1992). *Self-directed behavior: Self-modification for personal adjustment* (6th ed.). Pacific Grove, CA: Brooks/Cole.

Watson, J. B., & Rayner, R. (1920). Conditioned emotional reactions. *Journal of Experimental Psychology, 3,* 1–14.

Webster-Stratton, C. (1992). Individually administered videotape parent training: "Who benefits?" *Cognitive Therapy and Research, 16,* 31–52.

Weissberg, R. P., Caplan, M., & Harwood, R. L. (1991). Promoting competent young people in competence-enhancing environments: A systems-based perspective on primary prevention. *Journal of Consulting and Clinical Psychology, 59,* 830–841.

Weissberg, R. P., & Gesten, E. L. (1982). Considerations for developing effective school-based social problem-solving (SPS) training programs. *School Psychology Review, 11,* 56–63.

Weissberg, R. P., Gesten, E. L., Carnike, C. L., Toro, P. A., Rapkin, B. D., Davidson, E., & Cowen, E. L. (1981). Social problem-solving skills training: A competence-building intervention with second- to fourth-grade children. *American Journal of Community Psychology, 9,* 411–423.

Wells, J. K., Howard, G. S., Nowlin, W. F., & Vargas, M. J. (1986). Presurgical anxiety and postsurgical pain and adjustment: Effects of a stress inoculation procedure. *Journal of Consulting and Clinical Psychology, 54,* 831–835.

White, L., & Tursky, D. (Eds.). (1982). *Clinical biofeedback: Efficacy and mechanisms.* New York: Guilford.

White, M. A. (1975). Natural rates of teacher approval and disapproval in the classroom. *Journal of Applied Behavior Analysis, 8,* 367–372.

Whitman, T. L., Mercurio, J. R., & Caponigri, V. (1970). Development of social responses in two severely retarded children. *Journal of Applied Behavior Analysis, 3,* 133–138.

Williams, C. D. (1959). The elimination of tantrum behaviors by extinction procedures. *Journal of Abnormal and Social Psychology, 59,* 269.

Williamson, D. A., Williamson, S. A., Watkins, P. C., & Hughes, H. H. (1992). Increasing cooperation among children using dependent group-oriented reinforcement contingencies. *Behavior Modification, 16,* 414–425.

Wilson, D. D., Robertson, S. J., Herlong, L. H., & Haynes, S. N. (1979). Vicarious effects of time out in the modification of aggression in the classroom. *Behavior Modification, 3,* 97–111.

Wilson, G. T., Leaf, R. C., & Nathan, P. E. (1975). The aversive control of excessive alcohol consumption by chronic alcoholics in the laboratory setting. *Journal of Applied Behavior Analysis, 8,* 13–26.

Winett, R. A., Moore, J. F., Wagner, J. L., Hite, L. A., Leahy, M., Neubauer, T. E., Walberg, J. L., Walker, W. B., Lombard, D., Geller, E. S., & Mundy, L. L. (1991). Altering shoppers' supermarket purchases to fit nutritional guidelines: An interactive information system. *Journal of Applied Behavior Analysis, 24,* 95–105.

Winett, R. A., & Winkler, R. C. (1972). Current behavior modification in the classroom: Be still, be quiet, be docile. *Journal of Applied Behavior Analysis, 5,* 499–504.

Winkler, R. C. (1977). What types of sex role behavior should behavior modifiers promote? *Journal of Applied Behavior Analysis, 10,* 549–552.

Wolf, M. M. (1978). Social validity: The case for subjective measurement, or how applied behavior analysis is finding its heart. *Journal of Applied Behavior Analysis, 11,* 203–214.

Wolf, M. M., Braukmann, C. J., & Ramp, K. A. (1987). Serious delinquent behavior as part of a significantly handicapping condition: Cures and supportive environments. *Journal of Applied Behavior Analysis, 20,* 347–359.

Wolfe, D. A. (1987). *Child abuse.* Newbury Park, CA: Sage.

Wolfe, D. A., Mendes, M. G., & Factor, D. (1984). A parent-administered program to reduce children's television viewing. *Journal of Applied Behavior Analysis, 17,* 267–272.

Wolpe, J. (1958). *Psychotherapy by reciprocal inhibition.* Stanford: Stanford University Press.

Wong, S. E., Terranova, M. D., Bowen, L., Zarate, R., Massel, H. K., & Liberman, R. P. (1987). Providing independent recreational activities to reduce stereotypic vocalizations in chronic schizophrenics. *Journal of Applied Behavior Analysis, 20,* 77–82.

Woolfolk, A. E., Woolfolk, R. L., & Wilson, G. T. (1977). A rose by another name . . . : Labeling bias and attitudes toward behavior modification. *Journal of Consulting and Clinical Psychology, 45,* 184–191.

Wright, D. G., Brown, R. A., & Andrews, M. E. (1978). Remission of chronic ruminative vomiting through a reversal of social contingencies. *Behaviour Research and Therapy, 16,* 134–136.

Wright, K. M., & Miltenberger, R. G. (1987). Awareness training in the treatment of head and facial tics. *Journal of Behavior Therapy and Experimental Psychiatry, 18,* 269–274.

Wyatt v. *Stickney,* 344 F. Supp. 373, 344 F. Supp. 387 (M.D. Ala. 1972); affirmed sub nom. *Wyatt* v. *Aderholt,* 503 F.2d 1305 (5th Cir. 1974).

Yeaton, W. H., & Bailey, J. S. (1978). Teaching pedestrian skills to young children using an instructional package: An analysis and one-year follow-up. *Journal of Applied Behavior Analysis, 11,* 315–329.

Zeiss, R. A. (1978). Self-directed treatment for premature ejaculation. *Journal of Consulting and Clinical Psychology, 46,* 1234–1241.

Zivin, G. (Ed.) (1979). *The development of self-regulation through private speech.* New York: Wiley.

AUTHOR INDEX

Subject Index

CREDITS

TO THE OWNER OF THIS BOOK:

I hope you found *Behavior Modification in Applied Settings, Fifth Edition,* useful. So this book can be improved in a future edition, would you take the time to complete this sheet and return it? Thank you.

School and address: _____

Department: _____

Instructor's name: _____

1. What I like most about this book is: _____

_____

2. What I like least about this book is: _____

_____

3. My general reaction to this book is: _____

_____

4. The name of the course in which I used this book is: _____

_____

5. Were all of the chapters of the book assigned for you to read? _____

   If not, which ones weren't? _____

_____

6. In the space below, or on a separate sheet of paper, please write specific suggestions for improving this book and anything else you'd like to share about your experience in using the book.

_____

_____

_____

_____

_____

_____

Optional:

Your name: _____ Date: _____

May Brooks/Cole quote you either in promotion for *Behavior Modification in Applied Settings, Fifth Edition*, or in future publishing ventures?

Yes: _____ No: _____

Sincerely,

Alan E. Kazdin

Brooks/Cole is dedicated to publishing quality publications for education in the human services fields. If you are interested in learning more about our publications, please fill in your name and address and request our latest catalogue.

Name _____

Street Address _____

City, State, and Zip _____

FOLD HERE

FOLD HERE